African American Life in South Carolina's Upper Piedmont
1780–1900

*African American Life in
South Carolina's Upper Piedmont*
1780–1900

W. J. MEGGINSON

University of South Carolina Press

© 2006 University of South Carolina

Published by the University of South Carolina Press
Columbia, South Carolina 29208

www.sc.edu/uscpress

Manufactured in the United States of America

15 14 13 12 11 10 09 08 07 06   10 9 8 7 6 5 4 3 2 1

Library of Congress Cataloging-in-Publication Data

Megginson, W. J.
   African American life in South Carolina's Upper Piedmont, 1780–1900 / W. J. Megginson.
      p. cm.
   Includes bibliographical references and index.
   ISBN-13: 978-1-57003-626-2 (cloth : alk. paper)
   ISBN-10: 1-57003-626-8 (cloth : alk. paper)
   1. African Americans—South Carolina—History. 2. African Americans—South Carolina—Social conditions. 3. Slaves—South Carolina—History. 4. Slaves—South Carolina—Social conditions. 5. South Carolina—Race relations—History. 6. South Carolina—Social conditions.   I. Title.
   E185.93.S7M43 2006
   305.896'07307573—dc22
                                                                        2006001974

*To the African Americans of Anderson, Oconee, and Pickens counties,
who persisted and persevered; to those whose names and stories are included here;
to those omitted for lack of space; and to others whose existence has been forgotten*

Contents

List of Illustrations   *ix*
List of Tables   *xi*
Acknowledgments   *xiii*
Editorial Note   *xvii*

Prologue: Milly Dupree   *1*
Introduction: A Piedmont Setting   *4*

PART 1   *The Setting, the Peoples, and Their Work*

   Introduction to Part 1   *17*
   1   The Early Years, 1784–1810   *19*
   2   Piedmont Peoples, Their Environment, and Their Work   *30*
   3   The Puzzling Free Persons of Color   *51*
   4   Those Who Were Free Persons of Color   *60*

PART 2   *Interactions between Black and White*

   Introduction to Part 2   *73*
   5   Laws, Courts, and Resistance   *75*
   6   Churches, a Shared Setting   *96*
   7   Ambivalent Interactions   *113*

PART 3   *African American Subculture and Life on the Plantation*

   Introduction to Part 3   *123*
   8   Carving out a Niche   *125*
   9   Families, Mortality, and Names   *140*
   10   Material and Emotional Conditions   *157*

PART 4   *Transitions*

   Introduction to Part 4   *179*
   11   War Years, the Home Front, and African Americans   *181*
   12   Reconstruction's First Months, 1865   *196*

13 Reconstruction Evolves, 1866–68   *213*
14 Panorama of Black Families in Freedom   *230*

PART 5 ∽ *Community Building: Organizations, Concepts, and Opportunities*

Introduction to Part 5   *251*
15 Black Political Activity, 1867–75   *253*
16 Black Politics Curtailed, 1876–90   *274*
17 Community Building: Churches and Schools   *286*
18 Black Communities, Town and Rural   *311*
19 Anderson's Urban Community   *335*
20 Divergent Views of Blacks   *354*

PART 6 ∽ *Changing Conditions, for Better, for Worse*

Introduction to Part 6   *371*
21 Societal Attitudes and Oppression   *373*
22 Political and Economic Subjugation   *391*
23 1900: One Year in the Life of a Community   *405*

List of Abbreviations   *421*
Notes   *423*
Selected Bibliography: An Essay   *509*
Index of People   *519*
Index of Subjects   *533*
About the Author   *547*

Illustrations

Figures

Milly Dupree   *2*
Frances Dupree   *3*
Greenville laundress, 1899   *32*
Thompson family tools   *33*
Reuben and Martha Thompson and seven children   *38*
Charcoal drawing of Patsy, a cook   *49*
Runaway advertisement   *79*
Pass forged by Gilbert, a slave, 1842   *83*
Pass issued for Henry in 1830   *126*
Easter Reid   *143*
Nancy Legree   *148*
Ledger of John C. Calhoun's slaves, 1854   *152*
Keowee plantation ledger (typescript), 1857   *152*
Batting tools for making quilts   *159*
Stone cabins on John C. Calhoun plantation   *162*
Lucinda's cemetery marker   *169*
Aunt Becky Reed   *175*
Harrison Wiggins's 1924 pension application   *194*
Dr. William Pickens   *232*
Jane Hunter   *232*
"Grandpa (George) Scott"   *238*
Thomas and Frances Fruster   *243*
"Ku Klucks" warning, 1868   *256*
Petition for a governor's pardon, 1870   *268*
Silver Spring Baptist Church   *291*
Kings Chapel African Methodist Episcopal Church, Pendleton   *295*
Kings Chapel AME stewardesses   *298*
1870 "Teacher's Reports"   *302*
Vineland school, Pickens County   *307*
Railroad workers: Prince Nash   *315*
Gassaway bedroom suite   *318*
Middle-class family furnishings   *318*
Cotton hauled to the Greenville market, 1899   *321*
Sidney Burt's blacksmith shop artifacts   *322*

P. S. Little's advertisements for school and shoe work   *322*
Masonic regalia, early 1900s   *325*
Von Hasseln 1897 map of Anderson County   *325*
Addison's family cabin, 1899   *327*
Addison cabin interior view   *327*
Susie Haywood   *333*
Workers building a road near Anderson   *335*
Sanborn Fire Insurance Company 1901 map of Anderson   *348*
Anderson street scene, early 1900s   *349*
Racist stereotypes   *364*
Seneca Institute trustees   *364*
Chain gang of prisoners building a public road   *377*
"Next to last legal hanging in Pickens Co., ca. 1910–20"   *377*
Harrison Haywood home   *384*
Jack Carter's 1881 mortgage of cotton   *396*
J. S. Fowler's stables, Anderson   *401*
Sidney Burt's family, Pendleton, 1902   *405*
Terrel Wright's 1906 mortgage of his cow   *406*
Hunter General Store charge account   *407*
Convict labor at Clemson Agricultural College   *411*
Ruthie Guyton   *418*

Maps

Pendleton District's location within the state   *5*
Pendleton District area, 1784–1850   *22*
Anderson, Oconee, and Pickens counties, 1868–1900   *313*

TABLES

I.1 Density and Average Sizes of Slave Holdings by Region, 1860   7
1.1 Pendleton District Slave Holdings, 1790–1820   28
2.1 Population and Holdings: Pendleton, Anderson, and Pickens Districts   34
2.2 Taliaferro-Simpson Families and Slaves   36
2.3 Thompson Family Genealogy   39
2.4 Samuel Earle's Slaves and Their Occupations   42
5.1 Capital Offenses: Anderson, Oconee, and Pickens, 1784–1865   90
6.1 Slave and FPC Church Members, ca. 1860   106
6.2 Church Minutes Consulted   111
9.1 Calhoun and Colhoun Family Genealogies (Selective), 1750–1865   149
9.2 Changes (Selected Years) on the Keowee Plantation   154
14.1 Comparison of AOP Population in Four Censuses   230
14.2 Black People Living in AOP, 1870, and Born beyond South Carolina   234
14.3 Distribution of Black People by Household Types, 1870   241
14.4 Skilled Crafts and Professions, 1870   244
16.1 Eligible Voters and Votes Cast by Race and by Party, 1876   280
17.1 Estimates of Black Church Members, 1900   299
17.2 Official State Superintendent of Education Reports   308
18.1 Town Populations and Occupations, 1880   315
19.1 Anderson City, 1880: Distribution of Black Occupations   337
19.2 Distribution of Black Occupations, 1880 and 1900   343
19.3 Analysis of Black Households and Population, 1870–1900   350
21.1 Lynchings in Anderson, Oconee, and Pickens: A Tentative List   385
21.2 Alleged Lynchings in Anderson, Oconee, and Pickens   387

Acknowledgments

This work emerges in part from ongoing conversations with several people. They include Rik Booream, Vennie Deas-Moore, Elsie Goins, Will Goins, Stefan Goodwin, Fred C. Holder Jr., Anne McCuen, John Middleton, John Hammond Moore, Anna Reid, Peggy Rich, Anne Sheriff, and Dot and Bruce Yandle. All of these have also read portions of the manuscript and offered helpful suggestions and insights, as has been true of our dialog over fifteen years as well. Among these, Baker, Deas-Moore, Goodwin, Holder, and Moore have read extensive portions, as has Kenneth Whitney. Deas-Moore, Goodwin, and Holder have been involved, helpful, and supportive since I began this work in 1989 and have endured many inquiries, pleadings, and belabored stories of the latest findings. Bruce Baker, also reading much of the manuscript, has shared his insights, wide-ranging knowledge, and literary skills. These all deserve enormous thanks and credit for having read chapters in draft form, asking probing questions, and helping get it more coherently presented.

I am especially indebted to Fred Holder, John Middleton, Peggy Rich, and Anne Sheriff for supplying me with compiled data in electronic format: 1790 census; 1850 and 1860 slave censuses; 1850 Oconee County census; 1867 tax records; Pickens County teachers' certifications; and black Baptist memberships, clergy, and baptisms. Without this assistance, I would never have used those materials as extensively.

Others who have read portions and shared comments include Emma G. Anderson, Allen Ballard, William Brice, Philip Chancellor, Chris Elam, Willard Gatewood, Carl Gilmore, Gloria Hipple, J. B. Howell, Joy King, Charles Martin, Patrick McCawley, Jo McConnell, Don McKale, Joann Mickens, Elizabeth Sharpe Overman, Annie Patrick, Jesse Pennington, Heather Pritchard, Donna Roper, Ann Russell, Allen Stokes, Dean Wagner, Royce Walters, Anne Webster, and Jerry West. All have been gracious, helpful, and supportive as they found errors and gaps and provided compliments and support. Collectively they taught me much about writing and editing.

Among those who were especially helpful in the 1989–90 Black Heritage in the Upper Piedmont project and on later occasions are Sid Durham, Yolanda Harrell, Susan Hiott, Laurel Horton, Al Norris, and Dennis Taylor. Two colleagues from other projects, Pat Pritchard with his Tenus Maxwell Cemetery endeavor and Wendy Marshall, former director of Piedmont Harmony, have been friends and fountains of much insight and knowledge. Steve West supplied helpful materials from his research, and discussions with him sharpened some of my insights.

Many other people over a period of time have discussed this work with me, answered letters, helped find answers, or otherwise assisted. And many friends, relatives, and colleagues—including those mentioned by name here—have listened, usually patiently, as I talked repeatedly about the project over many years. My entire perspective has been shaped, less immediately, by friends, acquaintances, and strangers who have sensitized me over many years to a variety of minority problems, including class, disabilities, ethnicity, gender, poverty, religion, and sexual orientation.

Working with the University of South Carolina Press has been cordial and pleasurable. Acquisitions editor Alexander Moore has been invaluable in bringing this project to fruition through prodding, incisive, and constructive guidance. He believed in the project before almost anyone else and helped make this a much better book than it was a manuscript. Readers may thank him for its being one-third smaller. Managing editor Bill Adams has patiently and skillfully transformed the manuscript, photographs, and tables into a handsome book. Marketing namager Jonathan Haupt has then capably publicized the book's existence and significance.

African American families in Anderson, Oconee, and Pickens counties have shared generously their time, memories, and photographs. Many discussions and visits with them have enriched my work and understanding. Through those contacts and membership in the Pendleton Foundation for Black History and Culture (PFBHC), I have learned much from them, and especially, as PFBHC board members as well as resource persons and interesting people, Albert Gantt, Annie Webb Morse, Robert and Elsie Thompson, and Lenora Vance-Robinson. Other families with ancestors from the area have corresponded with me, sharing information and insights.

Research and background study have taken me to over fifty libraries, archives, universities, courthouses, and museums; their staffs have often have been helpful and shared resources and knowledge gladly. Special recognition and thanks go to three institutions where I have spent the most time: Clemson University Library and its Special Collections; the South Carolina Department of Archives and History, with special thanks to Steve Tuttle, reference room supervisor, and his staff; and the University of South Carolina's libraries, especially the South Caroliniana Library, headed then by Allen Stokes. Staff members at each of these have often shared relevant materials they found and assisted with special arrangements to view materials or photograph documents.

Several institutions have provided local support. The Pendleton District Historical, Recreational, and Tourism Commission (now Pendleton District Commission) sponsored an early phase, "Black Heritage in the Upper Piedmont," and contributed substantially to its fulfillment. My thanks go to its then director, Hurley Badders, Donna Roper (especially for continuing interest, information, and other assistance), and Jo McConnell. The South Carolina Humanities Council awarded some financial support for that project in 1989–90 and provided encouragement. And the

Clemson University History Department earlier supplied a courtesy appointment and access to library facilities; several department members have shared interest and encouragement in the research.

The University of South Carolina's Institute for Southern Studies appointed me as a summer research fellow in 1994–96. Thanks are due there to Walter Edgar and to Nancy Vance Ashmore Cooper, Tom Brown, and Tibby Dozier. The Seneca River Missionary Baptist Association served as cosponsor for the Black Heritage Project and encouraged support from its member churches; J. D. Rutledge, its president, shared his time, knowledge, and insight.

Clemson University, Historic Columbia, the Institute for Southern Studies, the Pendleton Foundation for Black History and Culture, Pickens County Library, Richland County Library, and Tri-County Technical College sponsored talks involving earlier stages of this work. The South Carolina State Museum sponsored a traveling exhibit that similarly portrayed an early version of this study. Both the *South Carolina Historical Magazine* and the Oconee County Historical Society published my related writings on black soldiers in World War I.

Military reference and other reference staff at the National Archives in Washington and its regional branch in Atlanta have been kind and helpful. Documents of the federal army and the Freedmen's Bureau are so voluminous that a novice could hardly begin to find relevant materials without skilled guidance.

Several libraries, including those of Clemson University, Drexel University, La Salle University, and the University of South Carolina, have provided interlibrary loan assistance.

Additional thanks are due to the persons and institutions that supplied illustrations, to Clemson University photographer Patrick Humphrey, and to Nathan Robertson for his maps.

Family members taught me much about the area during my childhood. Reputations of two—Louie S. Cochran and Charlie C. Bennett—in the local community have smoothed access to many people.

Interviewees and Participants

Sadly most of the people interviewed in 1989–91 then in their eighties and nineties are not alive to see what they helped accomplish. Fortunately some memories of all those formally interviewed have been preserved in taped interviews, and hundreds of their photographs have been duplicated for Clemson University's Special Collections.

Cornelia Alexander	Ida Mae Clinkscales	Leah Greer
James and Alberta	Allen Code	Douglas Hagood
Mattison Benson	Tom Dupree	Douglas Harbin
Clotell Brown	Alice Gassaway	Rhuney Hawthorne
Irwin Brown	David Green	Montana Haynes
Velma Childers	Agnes Greenlee	Elsie Henderson

Stacy Hicks
Harold Hill
Doris Hillerbrand
Emma Howard
Laura Keasler
Brenda Knox
Alice Lee
Lou Ida Maddox
Donnie Massey
Floy McDonald
Ida McDowell
Mr. and Mrs. Willie
  Mickler

Annie Webb Morse
Arminius Perry
Hiawatha Pettigrew
Runette Ponder
Anna Reed
Bessie Reese
Mattie Ross
J. D. and Mildred B.
  Rutledge
Grace Shaw
Cato Spencer
Bessie Stevens
Bertha Strickland
Dora Tidmore

Elsie and Robert
  Thompson
Lucille Vance
Lenora Vance-Robinson
Minnie and T. C. Walker
George Washington
Ernest Watkins
Eldora White
E. W. Whittenberg
Lucille Williams
Maxie Williams
Mrs. Red Williams
Viola Williams

Editorial Note

People familiar with the political history of Anderson, Oconee, and Pickens counties may find strange my simplified and sometimes idiosyncratic use of terminology, adapted to help readers unfamiliar with changing details; see chapter 1 and its notes.

Spelling in the nineteenth century was not yet standardized and so varied enormously. Even John C. Calhoun, vice president of the United States and a Yale graduate, used erratic spelling and sometimes faulty grammar. Readers should assume that odd spelling in a quotation appeared in the original version. I found at least thirteen variant spellings of "colored" in nineteenth-century materials, most written by white men.

I have reproduced names of slaves, other African Americans, and whites as they appear in original sources, except when there is a reasonably definitive means of spelling that name for a specific individual. I have standardized one spelling, that of Frances for females and Francis for males, to avoid confusion.

I have put aside gender-neutral language when referring to runaways and for slave owners, instead using the masculine "he" or "his." With rare exceptions, known runaways were male, and few women had absolute ownership of slaves.

White people, and sometimes those of African derivations also, used "colored," "negro" (but rarely "Negro"), and "black" somewhat interchangeably. All three sometimes appeared on the same page of a "white" newspaper or in the minutes of a "white-identified" church; all appear at various times in black Baptist minutes.

Anyone familiar with census records knows that ages, far from accurate, often vary significantly (see chapter 8). Birth years or ages in this book are dependent on census or other records.

A parenthetical name appearing after a slave's name refers to the owner, for example, Wiley (James Anderson). A name in brackets following a slave's name indicates the slave's known postbellum surname.

Reference notes are omitted for most resources, cited in the text, that are organized in chronological order: newspapers (which had only four pages prior to 1900), church and association minutes, petitions to the general assembly, as well as most other South Carolina Department of Archives and History series of documents (including governors' papers), and most private collections. Deeds, wills, and similar documents are indexed at the relevant courthouse or at the SCDAH. Reference notes in chapters 5, 6, 7, and 17 supply details on locations of magistrates and freeholders trial accounts, church minutes (1790–1870), wills and estate proceedings, and postbellum black church records.

African American Life in South Carolina's Upper Piedmont
1780–1900

Prologue ॐ Milly Dupree

ROCKING BY HER FIREPLACE in January 1900, Milly Dupree reflected on changes during the past century and major transformations in her own life. Nearly eighty years earlier she had been born ten miles away on Keowee plantation, owned by John Ewing Colhoun (Jr.), brother-in-law of Vice President John C. Calhoun. At Milly's birth her family had already served the Colhouns and their in-laws for several decades. Brought from the lowcountry to the upper piedmont, Milly's family enjoyed its healthier climate, which may have helped her survive so long. Utilizing Dr. William L. Jenkins's services from Pendleton, Colhoun provided medical care for Milly and other Keowee people; that surely helped also.

Milly, a cook for the Colhouns for twenty-five years, married a man ten years her elder from the same plantation. They had thirteen children. Like many other women of her era, Milly lost several of them to childhood diseases and to fevers. After the war's end brought freedom, Milly's family continued to work the same land. Then, however, they had formal written labor agreements approved by the Freedmen's Bureau. Within a few years she and her sons and daughters, mostly adults, began moving a few miles farther away. Two of her sons and other people from the plantation helped launch nearby Mount Nebo Baptist Church, which stood along the recently laid railroad. The plantation itself was sold, as almost all of the owner's family died and his survivors were bankrupt.

Milly's family not only held church offices but also had educational accomplishments and brushes with the law. Her grandson, Aleck Dupree—along with others from the same plantation—was among the area's earliest students to attend Benedict College, a Baptist school in Columbia for freed people. Having graduated, Aleck taught at ungraded schools in Seneca—a town that was home also of Seneca Institute, supported by local black Baptists—and in the Abel community near the Calhoun plantation. Another of Milly's descendants was charged with and cleared of killing her own baby. Two of Milly's granddaughters moved into a new town, Calhoun, and worked as laundresses for townspeople and Clemson College faculty. They did their washing in a creek along former slave cabins at Cold Spring, previously another Colhoun plantation. Now they had new houses in town, in contrast to those who still lived in dilapidated antebellum cabins.

Milly Dupree, born ca. 1822 as a slave on John Ewing Colhoun Jr.'s Keowee plantation; photographed circa 1890s. Black Heritage in the Upper Piedmont

Political circumstances had fluctuated often since 1865. The protective federal army left after only a few months. Several from her plantation were present in 1867 when a white boy was murdered; six black men were soon sentenced for that crime. Reconstruction ended when Wade Hampton, a Civil War military hero, became the first Democratic governor following Reconstruction. The 1890s brought more dire circumstances with a new "Jim Crow" constitution and laws. While her family could get more education and job choices, they faced more legally enforced segregation and deprivation of voting rights. Five of Milly's sons who registered to vote in 1867, and now their sons, could no longer exercise that right.

Milly, photographed wearing distinctive clothing and jewelry, reflected a serenity and dignity won by her many years. Her life, encompassing three-quarters of a century, spanned bondage as a slave, emancipation, an era of lively black political activity, and renewed repression. She and others had been called slaves and servants before 1865, freed people in the 1860s and 1870s, and—throughout her life—blacks, Negroes, servants (now legally free), and colored people. Before 1865 her family lived together on the plantation; now the younger generations spread over a wider area, concentrated primarily in or near new towns that offered better and more affordable housing and more employment opportunities. Most of them, however, still lived within fifteen miles of Milly's birthplace.

This vignette of Milly Dupree's life is something of a docudrama. There is no direct evidence that her parents or grandparents came from the lowcountry, the primary source of Colhoun's slaves; nor is there specific information that she was born at Keowee, although that is highly likely. In the late 1790s Colhoun noted that forty-three slaves were at Keowee. Milly may be the daughter of Fanny and the granddaughter of Harriott, both among those forty-three, as were Cato and Sue, evidently other relatives.[1] The number of her children and the name of Milly's husband also are not certain. In a Keowee plantation ledger she seems to be identified with Moses, who may have died before 1870, when she is shown without a spouse present. I have tentatively described him as her husband.[2]

A photograph of what evidently is Milly may have been taken in the late 1890s, but she has not been found in the 1900 census. Photographic and textile specialists place the photograph's date as likely late 1890s. So I have set her in January 1900 for a convenient retrospective of the past century.[3]

Frances Dupree, Milly's granddaughter, 106 years old, ca. 1960. Black Heritage in the Upper Piedmont

Introduction ~ A Piedmont Setting

THIS STORY FOLLOWS Milly's African American community in one locale for over one hundred years. Tracing perseverance, persistence, and accomplishments there has proved to be a daunting task. But it has yielded illuminating discoveries and abundant materials, far more than ever imagined; "each piece . . . both told and withheld stories." The richly textured fabric of African American life in South Carolina's old Pendleton District—now a three-county area—unfolds from these resources. And they help explore big issues in a small place, as a noted South Carolina folklorist advocates.[1] Facing many conditions beyond their control, African Americans, a subordinated minority, persevered through the strengths of their subculture and their families.

Examining three northwestern South Carolina counties—Anderson, Oconee, and Pickens—for nearly 120 years takes place within a rich localized context. It also adds new dimensions—in both location and time-span—to the state's historical scholarship about African Americans. This account, studying African Americans in a small, white-dominated area and its black-white relationships, weaves together various aspects of black life during antebellum and postbellum eras, in rural areas and towns.[2]

Milly Dupree's family itself blends together various settings and time periods. Her great-grandson Tom Dupree, whom I visited a few years ago, was living within a few miles of the Colhoun plantation where she had been enslaved. The Duprees are typical of other families who remained in the area not only throughout the nineteenth century but in many cases have done so until the present. "Persistence" is a technical term applied to people staying in one place over a period of time. Evidently 80 to 90 percent of the area's African Americans in 1900 had ancestors who were there nearly a century earlier, perhaps longer in some instances. Persistence also means to endure to the end, or to persevere. Together both terms in this account mean hard work, both as slaves and as freed people; oppression through enslavement, impoverishment in freedom; and deprivation of most fruits of their labor.

Their story, however, is neither uniform nor unilinear. Although relatively small, this area still had many internal variations. Even on a narrow issue during a brief period, nearby churches dealing with freed African Americans shortly after 1865 adopted quite different dispositions. Throughout the 1800s a very mixed bag of white attitudes mingled paternalism, arrogance, oppression, kindness, and—whites probably thought—friendship in some cases. Some slaves fared better than others, and freed people prior to 1895 had more opportunities than often assumed. Generalizing about that period, many people have imposed onto it their views of a later, more racially polarized era. And accomplishments often occurred even during repression.

Persistence and perseverance took place amid a culture that African Americans did not make. Contrasted to the much-studied and celebrated Sea Islands and lowcountry Gullah culture, upstate black people were never a majority. They typically constituted less than 30 percent of northwestern South Carolina's population, depending on time and location. Moreover, with small numbers dispersed over a large rural area, especially in the early 1800s, they had limited opportunity to preserve African traditions. Lowcountry African American culture began development in the late 1600s, but Pendleton District was first settled by black and white over one hundred years later.

Relatively few African-born men and women, then, could help mold a culture. Blacks were largely subsumed within the dominant culture, that of whites who shaped the politico-socio-economic-religious order. Nevertheless, within, or perhaps underneath, the prevailing culture, enslaved peoples shaped a subcultural community that included an extended communications network and a microeconomy. With freedom in 1865, newly emancipated people built on their slave subculture by establishing schools, churches, and—later on—beneficent, economic, and professional organizations.

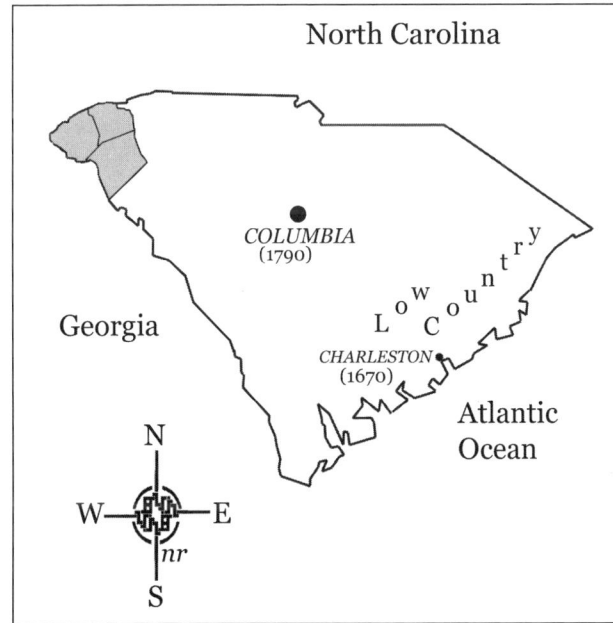

Pendleton District's location within the state

Although this is not an anthropological study, neither trained observers nor I detect many African continuities there today. At least during part of the nineteenth century, naming practices, some skills, and a black adaptation of Christianity perpetuated some African heritage. As late as 1880 a few elderly, African-born people were still living in the area, and about sixty others whose parents were born in Africa. New linkages were formed as a few people moved to Liberia and Sierra Leone, some returned, and black churches contributed to African missions.

This study traces the development of an African American subculture during slavery and its postbellum flowering. Set in one specific white-majority locale, this saga moves from frontier through slavery, Civil War and Reconstruction, to late nineteenth-century racism. In contrast to this account, many earlier studies of slavery by John Hope Franklin, Winthrop Jordan, Eugene Genovese, John W. Blassingame, and others—originally ground-breaking, now standards—dealt with the entire South, as have many postbellum studies. Other writers have turned to broad regions, such as western North Carolina in *Mountain Masters* and coastal South Carolina in *Black Majority* among others, or individual cities such as Baltimore or Charleston.[3]

Most scholars in African American studies have neglected or totally ignored northwestern South Carolina and rural areas like it, which constituted large parts of southern states. This has happened partly because cities and rich plantation areas seem more interesting and also because upstate, rural sources are more scattered and elusive.

Among the state's better antebellum studies, Charles Joyner chose to focus on Georgetown County for *Down by the Riverside*, and Margaret Creel limited her study of slave religion to the Gullah culture. Joel Williamson, Francis Simkins, and George Tindall largely omit northwestern South Carolina—except for brief references—from their studies of Reconstruction and the latter 1800s. Considering limited cataloging and indexing at the time of their research, they acted very sensibly. This is, in fact, one of the few studies that deal with South Carolina blacks beyond the lowcountry. Vernon Burton stands virtually alone among those who have systematically examined African Americans in the state's interior.[4]

Locations with huge plantations have been more dramatized and more studied than Anderson, Oconee, and Pickens, an area that resembles in many ways regions of the South. The former really were an exception, compared to a large swath including Appalachian counties, where slaveholdings were relatively small, no major cash crop was produced, and, presumably, white and black lived and worked in close proximity. A glance at the *Atlas of Antebellum Southern Agriculture* and maps of slaveholding areas shows that northwestern South Carolina fits more neatly within those patterns than it matches lower parts of its own state.[5]

South Carolina's upper piedmont is dramatically different from the lowcountry, even in respective terms "low" and "up," referring to altitude, terrain, and, by implication, crops. Societal patterns and ethnic mixes vary also. African Americans,

Table I.1 **Density and Average Sizes of Slave Holdings by Region, 1860**

	Density of Pop./ Sq. Mile	Density of Slaves/ Sq. Mile	Slaves as % of Pop.	Average Holding/ Owner	% of Families Owning Slaves
Upper Piedmont					
Anderson	31.8	11.7	37 %	7.6	40 %
Greenville	28.7	9.3	32	8.6	14
Lancaster	25.5	12.2	48	10.7	43
Pickens-Oconee	16.6	3.6	21	7.9	12
Spartanburg	29.3	9.0	31	8.3	30
York	33.1	13.5	41	9.1	47
U.P. average	26.7	9.1	34	8.6	25
Lower Piedmont					
Abbeville	33.4	21.1	63 %	14.0	65 %
Chester	32.4	19.4	60	12.0	57
Edgefield	26.4	15.9	60	14.3	56
Fairfield	29.6	20.8	70	18.9	57
Laurens	34.1	18.8	55	12.1	50
Newberry	35.5	23.3	66	14.6	63
Union	31.0	17.2	55	16.0	37
L.P. average	31.0	20.9	72	15.7	55
Lowcountry district or parish					
Beaufort			80 %	30.4	82 %
St. Helena		60.1	86		
Colleton			77	33.4	45
St. John's,		58.1	94		
Georgetown			62	27.3	62
All Saints		18.5	82		
Lowcountry (selected)		39.0	75	30.9	60

Sources: U.S. Census Bureau, *Population of the United States in 1860*, 452, and *Agriculture . . . 1860*, 237; "Census of South Carolina from 1809 to 1859, Inclusive," *Reports and Resolutions*, 1860: 522–23; "Exhibit of the General Taxes of the Upper Division for the year ending 30th September, 1860" and "Exhibit of the General Taxes of the Lower Division for the year ending 30th September, 1860," part of the report of the Comptroller General, *Reports and Resolutions*, 1860: 134–37; and manuscript 1860 Population Schedules. These two "Exhibits" give the number of taxed acres, which fall short of the total area of the respective districts and parishes. That figure (converted to square miles), used to calculate density, does indicate the claimed and mostly settled area. It also allows comparisons with three parishes, which represent coastal rice areas; I omitted the three with the largest number of slaves. Most of the Lower Division is reported by parish; white population for the three parishes comes from the 1859 state census, slave population and acreage from the 1860 tax schedules. The figure for Union acreage (substituted from an earlier year) is missing in the 1859/60 report.

a coastal majority, were a minority in Anderson, Oconee, and Pickens counties and had few African retentions, partly because they represented more diverse parts of Africa than did lowcountry counterparts. Both upcountry plantations and their holdings were smaller, and no single crop dominated life there, as did rice for coastal residents. Variations among the upper piedmont, lower piedmont, and coastal rice parishes appear clearly in the table. It shows wide differences in percentages of whites who held slaves, sizes of their holdings, and density of black population. A sharp contrast appears in holdings: 15 wealthy planters in All Saints Parish, studied by Joyner, owned 4383 slaves in 1860; all 500 owners in Pickens and Oconee had among them only 4195 slaves there.[6]

Writers have chosen various terms to describe that area. In the later 1700s and early 1800s people living near the Atlantic Ocean in All Saints, Georgetown, Charleston, Savannah and the surrounding area referred to the "backcountry," which then applied to most of the state. "Upcountry" came into use to describe portions of the state north of the new capital, Columbia. Scholars such as Lacy Ford have more recently used the terms "upper piedmont" and "lower piedmont" to distinguish two cultural, geographic, and agricultural zones north of Columbia. Ford groups a northern tier of counties as "upper piedmont." His area includes Anderson, Oconee, and Pickens, the primary focus of this study, plus Greenville, Lancaster, Spartanburg, and York.[6]

Perhaps called accurately the "far northwestern corner of South Carolina," Anderson, Oconee, and Pickens have formed an historically distinct unit of sorts. From the area's first white and black settlement, it was known as Pendleton District. Various organizational forms still use that term, such as Pendleton District Historical, Recreational, and Tourism Commission (currently shortened to Pendleton District Commission), and the Old Pendleton District Genealogical Society. There is also a Tri-County Technical College, and the state's Heritage Corridor designates Anderson, Oconee, and Pickens as a separate region.

Contrasted to extensive lowcountry or Mississippi River plantations, the upstate's scale of operation was quite different: relatively small slaveholdings; few overseers, let alone black "drivers"; daily contacts with owners in most cases; slaves who were known individually by their owners; lack of bachelors' quarters or chapels (praise houses); many families divided among plantations; and more complicated naming practices on a single plantation.

These characteristics, hardly resembling fictional stereotypes, are much more complex than indicated by studies of slavery that treat the subject in broad terms. Those in turn have thrived during several decades of social and comparative history. The latter has spawned cross-cultural studies of New World slavery—a growing industry—that show varied patterns of slavery in Brazil, the Caribbean, and North America's mainland. Less comparison, however, has been done *within* mainland North American colonies and among states. This is surprising since social history stresses *variations*.[7]

Looking at a black-minority, inland society, this book focuses on a variant form of African American life during the entire nineteenth century. This is the first effort to deal continuously and analytically with any specific group of South Carolina's African Americans for over one hundred years.[8] Doing so, it demonstrates continuities between antebellum and postbellum eras—not polarized opposites. Burton and Bernard Powers rank among those who bridge the supposed Civil War divide. Rapid change during the 1850s, 1860s, and 1870s was not all generated by war. Most black people in 1800, virtually all slaves, tilled white-owned land; most did so in 1900. A statement in the introduction to part 4 applies to the whole century: "much changed, much stayed the same."[9]

This exploration attempts to embrace the range of black life and draws upon all types of known, deposited documents, a "sifting of every kind of available [written] record."[10] Its major themes that run throughout the 1800s and interpretations emerge from this research. It was not designed to prove a predetermined argument, nor does it have the focus and slant produced by limitation to one particular subject—for example, religion, family, economics—or type of source material, such as 1930s WPA interviews or Freedmen's Bureau records. Intending to encompass rather than to exclude, it results in a more rounded understanding of an African American community. Consequently it raises numerous "big issues" in one location, a "full social context."

Working in most cases directly with owners who lived on the plantation, upstate African Americans had more interaction with whites, which may have softened some hardships. It also meant that slaves seemed far less of a threat to whites than in heavily black majority coastal and island areas. No Denmark Vesey– or Nat Turner–type revolt disrupted the upper piedmont. Those same whites feared rebellion less and operated in a more relaxed atmosphere than did lowcountry owners. Thus upper-piedmont African Americans had some latitude in their daily lives, including local travel and contacts.

Despite its title, this book is not confined to African Americans. It often turns to interactions with whites, who controlled most of the economic, political, and societal environments. Because blacks lived within a white-dominated area, understanding these interactions becomes all the more important. A focus on blacks alone would miss much of the story. Setting the African American account within its local white context sheds light on white fears, economic and other societal pressures, and repressions of slaves; it also shows linkages among these factors. Frequent cross-racial interpersonal contacts, which took place within an unequal equation, are highlighted. That is part of the "full social context."[11]

Almost all known sources come from whites, which affects the perspective.[12] I have tried to avoid that distortion as much as possible, or at least to make explicit that most information derives from white sources. On the other hand, virtually all of them were contemporaneous. Without more information directly from African Americans, it is hard to know what they *thought*. What they *did*, however—especially in terms of a subcultural communications network, involvement in churches, and Reconstruction political activity—sheds light on each of these subjects.

Much resource material may exist that has not yet been found or explored; much has perished; and most harshness—especially whippings, brutality, and sexual exploitation—was rarely recorded. Every sentence should be read with an implied "evidently," "as far as is known," or "based on known, surviving sources."

Slavery was wrong, inhumane, and oppressive. Starting from that fundamental truth, this account is not a diatribe against slavery, which many writers have already done well. Vivid examples and statements by masters certainly reinforce those truths.[13] Research and writing in recent decades, following a critique of slavery itself, have moved further to a focus on slave life and its nuances. As Mechal Sobel wrote, "For over a generation we have been witness to a major reevaluation of American slave life . . . in which family, religion and community have been seen anew." Development of social history, quantitative analysis, and relatively new archaeological excavations of African American sites have laid the basis for these studies.[14]

This account builds on these insights, as it does on recent decades of increased attention to black-white relations and shared experiences. Burton described his dissertation as a step toward a unified black-white history of Edgefield County, a process elaborated further in his book *In My Father's House*. John Boles and his students stress felicitous biracial experiences. Symposium volumes such as Ted Ownby's *Black and White Cultural Interaction in the Antebellum South* have extended this emphasis on interactions and cultural exchanges. Elizabeth Fox-Genovese's *Within the Plantation Household* provides a valuable dimension of space and relationships, as has Joyner's *Shared Traditions: Southern History and Folk Traditions*.[15]

Some of these, especially authors in Ownby's book, emphasize happy interactions and relationships while mostly omitting unpleasant ones. A focus on only one or the other produces a partial, misleading image and ignores both complications and contradictions. Inherent convolutions occurred as whites conceived of slaves simultaneously as humans and as chattel. While examining ways in which blacks and whites interacted, I have kept a constant emphasis on their unequal standings, harsh interactions, and convoluted white thoughts. But the story is primarily an assessment of constraints, latitude, and accomplishments during both slavery and freedom throughout 120 years. It stresses especially an expanding and richer African American subculture as it developed during slavery and in freedom.

Focusing throughout on the Anderson, Oconee, and Pickens tricounty area, this story does not assert grander generalizations. Any reference or statement should be construed to apply specifically to that area, unless otherwise stated. Issues raised, findings, and broader implications need testing by more studies for similar white-majority areas. Then, a much more complete understanding will emerge about variations of southern slavery.

Seven broad themes, characterizing the entire 1780–1900 span in the three counties, run through virtually every chapter. Significant variations, however, occur within the way each theme is played out. Several subjects are directly treated in specific chapters for both antebellum and postbellum periods: types of work, families, black subculture, churches, literacy and education, and laws constraining African Americans. The seven major themes follow.

Most African Americans remained in the three counties by 1810 and became a continuous, cohesive community. Although population was transitory during early decades of frontier settlement, it became much more stabilized by 1810, perhaps earlier. Similarly only a small percentage, probably less than 5 percent, of freed people left Anderson, Oconee, and Pickens counties after emancipation, and fewer moved in. The word "community" is used here without precise definition and in more than one sense: either all African Americans within three counties, ones on a particular plantation, or those in a post-1865 town or rural grouping.[16] Because of extensive contacts among blacks, considering these counties together as a community fits with available evidence.

Families over generations formed a strong core of the African American community in the counties. Despite many complications and obstacles, African Americans maintained a core institution: their families. Sometimes separated by owners during slavery and afterward by economic necessities, slave and free families nevertheless often maintained close contacts. When families were divided, they mostly lived within a few miles, and often their white owners were related, which increased opportunities for slave visits. Even without such occasions, families otherwise kept up contacts through a communications system. They passed family names, skills, and sometimes prized possessions to successive generations. Men who lived on a different plantation from their wives and children still played an important role in African American family life and headed most black households in 1870.

Many conditions impacting African Americans' lives and their community depended on circumstances beyond their control. Matters beyond African Americans' control began with slavery itself and consequences that flowed from it. A central factor of enslavement was their status as property that could be relocated at their owners' whim. Slaves had no choice about where they lived, limited selection—sometimes none— of spouses, and little control over their families, especially when separated between two or more plantations. Immediately after emancipation, freed people's lives were framed in part by federal laws, programs, and failure to support economic policies that would enable independence. "Forty acres and a mule" may have been mentioned in Sherman's Special Field Orders, No. 15, on January 16, 1865, but they were not forthcoming. Soon, freed people again faced more repression as southern whites lashed out at them. Late-1800s racism, which accelerated worldwide, thrived in South Carolina. Conversely technological change led to benefits as it spurred growth of towns, communities, and new job opportunities.

African Americans constituted a minority population; their status was complicated further by living in a rural, piedmont region. Whether during enslavement or under the 1895 "Jim Crow" constitution, African Americans were legally subjugated. However, because slaves were a sparse minority in Anderson, Oconee, and Pickens counties, whites there tended to be less fearful than those in black-majority areas. Rural people, then, had more opportunity for travel on weekends and in various facets of their daily lives. Living among a dominant white population, peoples of African descent were partly subsumed by white culture, including the English language—in contrast to lowcountry Gullah—and Christianity. So, there was little cohesion based on shared African culture. Rather, they had more in common because of their status: as slaves, as a racial minority, and as a subordinated class. The latter two factors persisted after emancipation.

Although a minority, slaves often were not passive. Some objected to owners' treatment, occasionally by accusing masters in church, more often by grumbling or slowing their work pace. Other forms of resistance involved running away, though often only for a few days, stealing, and standing up for themselves or for relatives against whites. Repeatedly they tested and challenged some constraints of their enslaved status. Testing boundaries, African Americans slowly reshaped them.[17] After enjoying political opportunities during Reconstruction, African Americans faced a major obstacle again, their minority status. It remained an enduring constraint on political, social, and economic advancement.

Interpersonal relations and paternalism affected whites and blacks in unequal, complex, and contradictory ways. Because of their sparse, minority population, blacks lived among whites and interacted often with them, although on unequal terms. White owners acted in inconsistent and unpredictable ways. Given their contradictory concepts, that is not surprising. Individual owners and South Carolina's laws dealing with slaves considered them simultaneously as both chattel and human beings. Whether during or after slavery, blacks worked mostly for whites and were, in most cases, supervised directly by them. They lived near one another, went to the same churches prior to 1865, and often were buried in the same cemeteries. Throughout the entire 1800s whites and blacks periodically shared social occasions: circuses, fairs, antebellum musters, camp meetings, executions, and parades.

Plantations, as conglomerations of black and white folk, encompassed complicated emotional and sometimes sexual relationships. All those on a plantation, both black and white, were considered by some as a family, but they certainly were not equal. Interpersonal relationships did not always follow predictable lines. White kindness could quickly disappear, to be replaced by hostility and harsh racist attitudes. Complex relationships between blacks and whites involved many complications: paternalism, black economic dependency for work and housing, a white presumption of superiority, and a symbiosis created by long-term interactions.

A black subculture developed and thrived. A subculture emerged early in Pendleton District and developed further throughout the nineteenth century. Some slaves could travel for their work, church services, social events, and trading. Travel and weekend family reunions forged an extensive communications system—building on a strong African tradition of oral culture—complemented by a microeconomy of goods and money. African Americans also had ritual and occasional celebrations during slavery—especially year-end, weeklong holidays—and after emancipation. Although few African continuities are readily apparent there today, naming practices, skills, and a black adaptation of Christianity perpetuated some African traits during the nineteenth century.[18]

This subculture depended more on its status as a minority, subjugated group than it did on African traditions. Churches provided important occasions for socializing during slavery and formed a core of the black community after emancipation. Most postbellum leaders emerged from people previously enslaved there. Virtually none came from the North or from the lowcountry. In contrast to Charleston, upper-piedmont antebellum free people were never a dominating factor.

By the 1880s African Americans increasingly articulated their views in racial terms and talked of race improvement, including education. They made progress, aided by individual ambitions of improving their own status through education, economic betterment, and, occasionally, ownership of land. Simultaneously there was community development in rural areas, towns, and cities. As numbers of churches, schools, and property owners increased, the African American subculture grew stronger.

African Americans, occupying a subordinate status, suffered structural oppression: slavery, racism, and dependency. From 1780 through 1900 and beyond, most blacks lacked political, economic, or legal clout and thus suffered disproportionately. Whites had legal controls over blacks during slavery, and also under a later racist constitution. Sexual exploitation of women occurred during slavery and in later decades. After 1865 blacks faced economic subservience through sharecropping and the crop lien system, which created a dependency relationship. Most brutality was not recorded in contemporaneous documents, and there are few African American sources in the three counties prior to the twentieth century.[19] A larger percentage of white families had blacks working for them in the late 1800s than did so during slavery.

As a minority blacks in Anderson, Oconee, and Pickens counties did not successfully organize any sustained, meaningful political or economic challenge to the dominant white population. This should not suggest, however, that they—both as slaves and later as freed people—were constantly passive or did not develop means of asserting their views and displeasure. Their complaints, resistance, and sometimes voices of freedom resonate throughout the text. A century later one funeral there resounded with "Lift Every Voice."

Slave owners, and later all whites, collectively controlled the law, courts, churches, and economic system. Except for a minority who achieved land ownership, had independent, skilled craft work, or migrated elsewhere, most African Americans lived under white societal control. That African Americans as individuals, families, and communities persevered and developed an effective subculture is striking proof of their persistence. Their story, explored for more than a century, is a rich account of this perseverance.

PART I ⁂ *The Setting, the Peoples, and Their Work*

Introduction to Part 1

As MILLY'S ANCESTORS and many others arrived at South Carolina's far northwestern corner, becoming its first permanent black residents, they did not do so willingly. During their first century, and later, most African Americans lived, worked, suffered, and endured under conditions not of their own choosing. Black and white had to clear land, erect living quarters, and cultivate crops. The hilly terrain, subject to flooding, dictated much of their labor and lives. During their early decades, many slaves either were the solitary one on their farm, or shared it with only one or two others and surely had few, if any, choices about spouses.

The upper piedmont's hilly, red-dirt land did not yield a dominant cash crop during antebellum years. Washed by rains, it also demanded much human labor to prevent deterioration. Lives did not revolve around a single crop as in some other areas. Corn was a major foodstuff for humans and animals, but tobacco and cotton provided income for hundreds of landowners.

Other factors shaped slaves' lives. These included the human environment, especially the average size of holdings and African Americans' minority status. Sparse population, small slaveholdings, and low percentages of African Americans meant much personal interaction with whites in work, living space, and worship. Although on grossly unequal planes, lives of black and white people were closely linked and intertwined. These factors hindered development of a slave culture based largely on African derivations.

Small percentage of slaves, however, made them less of a threat than did a "black majority" in the lowcountry, tidewater Virginia, or Caribbean islands. Upper-piedmont African Americans, then, had more latitude in daily lives. By the early 1800s white and black population became stabilized, and most families remained there. While white residents created political, religious, and societal institutions, blacks participated in communal religious life and, in some cases, resisted their status as slaves.

Describing peoples as slaves and owners oversimplifies. Depending on period, hardly more than one-fourth of white families there owned slaves, and only 2 percent ever owned twenty or more. Whites formed an ethnically and religiously, if not economically, cohesive society. Their origins were predominantly British—primarily Scots-Irish and English—and low Protestant. African Americans came from more diversified areas, and some of their ancestors were taken from Africa before their owners' families left Britain. They became acculturated to white society while creating their own subculture and distinctive niche.

While all whites did not own slaves, not all blacks were enslaved. A small proportion, approximately 2 percent, were free people of color. Even they were not a homogenous group, as they included various components of African, European, and Native American ancestries—sometimes all of these in one family. Free people of color were anomalous, not fitting neatly into a world divided between free whites and enslaved blacks. Whites harassed and prosecuted free persons of color disproportionately, partly to control them, partly to warn slaves against straying.

African American experiences in Pendleton District depended on these physical and human environments, constraints derived substantially from enslaved conditions. Physical, human, and societal circumstances there created forms of enslavement, work, and relationships to whites and their culture substantially different from those in South Carolina's lowcountry. Many conditions, however, would be shared among other southern piedmont areas.

All of this happened within a very small southern locale. Pendleton District is about the size of Delaware, double that of Rhode Island. Even the most placid painting of antebellum piedmont life has many nuances underlying it.

ONE

The Early Years, 1784–1810

MILLY DUPREE'S LIFE, which began in the 1820s, can be documented considerably better than the earliest decades of her plantation and its surroundings. When her ancestors traveled over two hundred miles to reach South Carolina's far northwestern corner, they moved steadily uphill, a significant change from the lowcountry land they knew. A northward trek from Charleston to Pendleton—then, or today by Interstates 26 and 385—ascends through rolling hills into the piedmont and finally low mountains near North Carolina. Cultivating red-dirt hills, washed soil, and gullies involved much labor—often by slaves—to make the land productive.

Most slaves came not from the lowcountry but along the eastern Appalachians. Those who traveled this migration route left a piedmont topography, climate, and slaveholding patterns similar to those of upper South Carolina. Its hilly piedmont had small farms and small slaveholdings; almost all owners in 1790 had fewer than ten, and probably few recent arrivals from Africa. Life for most African Americans in their new area would be both hard and bleak.[1]

That their enslaved status was permanent was not a foregone conclusion, however. As northwestern South Carolina was first being settled by whites and blacks, 1784–87, the nation simultaneously was undergoing a fierce challenge to the existence of slavery.[2] But these issues hardly benefited enslaved African Americans just arrived in South Carolina's far northwestern corner. There, they faced new challenges, as they had since arriving on the North American continent. Eager for fresh opportunities, white settlers—usually migrating as whole families—moved into this region quickly and willingly. Their slaves had no choice and in most cases, moreover, were taken from their own families. Finding themselves in a relatively untamed area, they knew they would have to do much of the work making the land livable for white and black alike. As a sparse population scattered over almost two thousand square miles, they faced a difficult existence.

Major ingredients of the area's subsequent nature developed quite early. African Americans constituted a small percentage of the population; their numerical minority, race, and enslaved status all made them a subordinated class. Black involvement in Christian churches emerged very early, but so did slave resistance. Their minority standing, the climate and terrain, and, most of all, enslavement were beyond their control. Yet they fashioned for themselves a distinctive subculture at the same time they absorbed much of European-derived culture. Black and white who moved through the Virginia–North Carolina–South Carolina piedmont into this area probably experienced similar societal conditions where they previously lived. Because newly arriving African Americans lived and worked in an environment dominated and shaped by whites, the nature and structure of that area must be understood.

Settlement and Frontier Life

Although available lands drew settlers to South Carolina's newly opened frontier, white and black expansion did not follow immediately when the state of South Carolina concluded a treaty in 1777 at DeWitts Corner (Abbeville County). There, the Cherokee ceded land that would become Greenville, Anderson, Pickens, and Oconee counties. Although most Native Americans were expelled from these regions, white people displacing them preserved many names—Seneca, Eastatoe, and Generostee. A few Native Americans remained; some intermarried with whites or blacks; some families included all three origins. Juxtapositions survive today. At least one cemetery, established before 1800 and still in use, includes Native, African, and European American burials.[3]

Urgent concerns related to the Revolutionary War intervened immediately following the 1777 cession. After the war, a United States treaty, signed November 18, 1785, at General Andrew Pickens's Hopewell plantation on the Seneca River, confirmed this earlier cession. Symbolic of area development, the treaty signing's assemblage included Native Americans as abdicators, peoples of European descent as conquerors, and African Americans as servants.

Postwar movement into this area occurred at the same time that many political authorities elsewhere wanted a stronger system of government, which resulted in the 1787 federal Constitution. Ratifying that document was a hard-fought battle, as most frontier districts throughout the country, including much of upper South Carolina, voted against a government with more powers.

This relatively late opening of a large section of land—extending nearly to South Carolina's later, permanent boundaries with Georgia and North Carolina—immediately attracted settlers and speculators. The state in effect opened a land office in 1784, and peoples of European and African origins—almost sixteen thousand within six years—poured in. Anticipating new opportunities for both political influence and economic growth, many lowcountry investors bought land for speculation, very few for settlement. Many men who came to stay were Revolutionary War veterans. As late as the 1840s Pendleton's newspaper was still publishing Revolutionary soldiers' obituaries.[4]

This land that soon became Pendleton and Greenville Districts was South Carolina's last frontier. In many ways it fulfilled characteristics of a frontier, however defined, until 1800 and beyond. It had five persons per square mile in 1790, with small farming operations and limited societal institutions—judicial, political, social, educational, or religious. Adjacent Greenville District, linked politically with

Pendleton for a few years, experienced similar patterns of settlement and development although it was not as populous.

People living in Pendleton District considered themselves on a frontier. Writing to John Ewing Colhoun, his agent John Green observed in August 1793: "We are all peaceable at present unless it is when a horse is stolen from the frontier," a few miles away. Colhoun should advise his wife "not to be afraid to visit the back country once more[,] tell her I have got 5 Guns all sure fir and when dangr is approaching[,] myself and you will Each of us shoulder a few of them and march up the hill as a Reinforcement." Like Green, people from coastal Carolina considered the area a "backcountry," their usage in writing about it or addressing mail.[5]

This frontier did not have many solitary individuals. Transported by wagon, many white families traveled together. Nearly three-fourths of all 1790 heads of households were related to others there. Many extended families—parents and their adult sons and daughters, and several adult brothers—and unrelated neighbors often arrived either at the same time or within a few years of one another. "Households" often included distant relatives, unrelated workers, and bound white apprentices as well as a white nuclear family and slaves.[6]

Typical of a transitory society, many people were moving into and out of the area, some after only a few years; others just passed through. As many families moved from Maryland, Virginia, North Carolina, and other parts of upper South Carolina, they brought slaves with them. Quite a few migrants who arrived by 1790, in fact, spent only a few years there before moving, in many cases either across the river to Georgia or through the mountains into Tennessee. Much of this area's early settlement, then, was temporary, reflecting its frontier status. But most families with several slaves stayed, tilled the land, established churches, and shaped a settled society. Even after ceasing to be a frontier, it retained some maverick characteristics.[7] Yet it also would have a significant role in state politics as the home of John C. Calhoun, senator and vice president, and other prominent officials.

Pendleton District's Political Structure

The word *area*, used so far to describe this region, hints at two frontier characteristics: geographic boundaries not clearly distinguished, and periodic changes in political organization, as well as name, that occurred between 1785 and 1800. The legislature would make further alterations in the nineteenth century. As people moved inland from the coast, they challenged Charleston's dominating role. Several backcountry men first won legislative seats in 1768, and a year later secured four new judicial districts, the first not bordering the Atlantic Ocean. Since people in South Carolina, as elsewhere in America, had for decades been moving farther inland, legislators in 1790 created a new capital, Columbia, nearly the state's geographic center.

Flux and rapid change affected northwestern South Carolina's political structure between 1777 and 1800.[8] Pendleton District—centered at Pendleton village, which

22 / *The Setting, the Peoples, and Their Work*

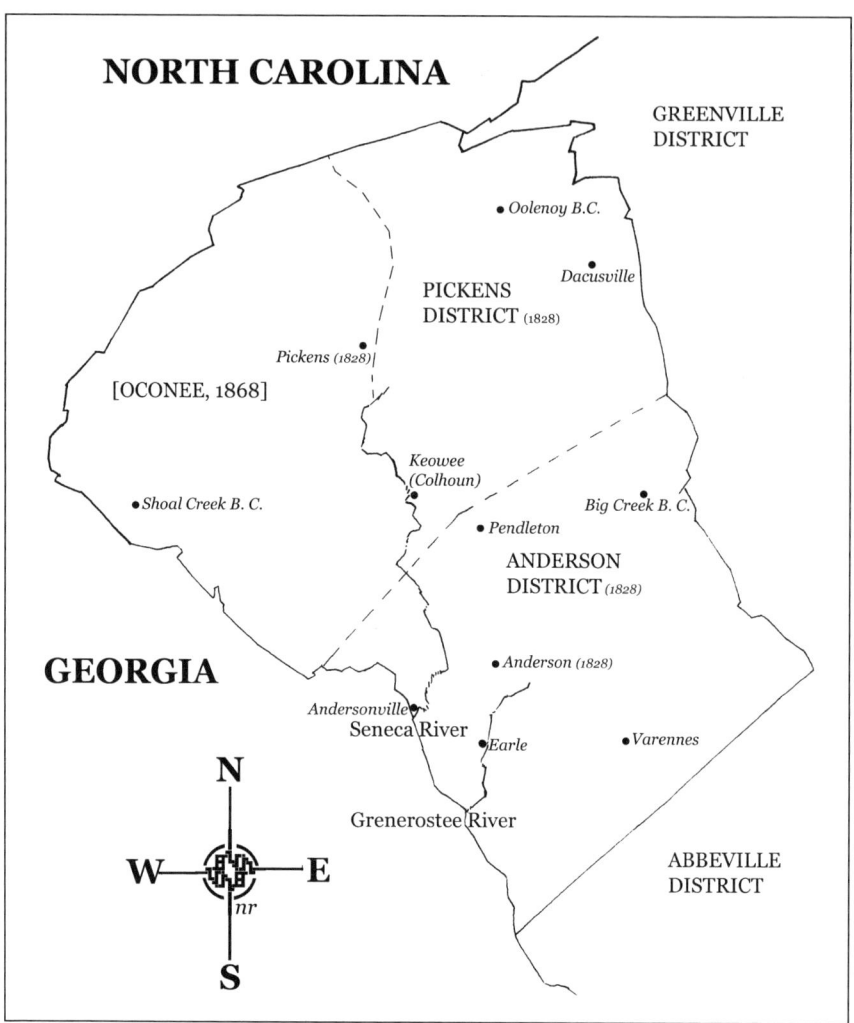

Pendleton District area, 1784–1850

had at most only a few dozen white inhabitants plus their slaves—would survive as the major local unit from 1790 through 1828. This is the "area" that in changing political forms constitutes the geographic focus of this study. Pendleton District disappeared in 1828, when it was split into the new Pickens and Anderson Districts. Pickens District itself in 1868 would be divided into Pickens and Oconee counties.

For simplicity, this text uses two sets of terms: Pendleton District for the 1784–1828 period, and Anderson, Oconee, and Pickens counties (AOP) after 1828. Although technically inaccurate, these simplified terms will help readers unfamiliar with the area's changing terminology.[9] Boundaries of this frontier area—nebulous at times, changing at others—involved disputes with Georgia, North Carolina, and the Cherokee. The sense of a frontier lingered with frequent references to abandoned forts whose earthworks survived. Additionally there were several outposts; the closing in 1799 of the last of these, Oconee Station, was a symbolic closing of the frontier. Frontier characteristics would persevere for years to come, however.[10] By contrast, authorities quickly established political and judicial apparatus once Pendleton District was created.

Interactions among Peoples of European and African Origins

Enslaved African Americans arrived along with early white settlers. Families able to afford slaves surely brought them along. Some owners may well have bought young, able-bodied men and women specifically for the move or selected them from their parents' holdings. Those slaves would have been employed for the earliest work of clearing land to plant crops and erecting a cabin and perhaps a barn. They would have been even more desired for large plantations where buildings were made from brick and sawed timber. No regularly operating slave market existed in Pendleton District, although individual owners sold slaves. For a large market, potential buyers would likely have gone to Augusta or to Charleston, commonly a journey of ten to twelve days each way.[11]

Just as on the trek to northwestern South Carolina, patterns of everyday life in early decades there meant continuous interaction between blacks and whites. In many cases they shared a dwelling, often a substantial distance from their nearest neighbors. Black and white shared farming and household work. They came together for church services. Contacts in work, in church, and in complicated human relationships would characterize the area for many decades.

Interaction, frequent and pervasive, resembled descriptions of the lowcountry when it was first settled a hundred years earlier. It was not unusual for "all the male members to participate . . . [in clearing and planting, and white men often] worked many days with a Negro man at the Whip saw." Frontier conditions, then, in early years characterized both areas: sparse population, small percentage of slaves, and shared endeavors to clear land and to feed household members. Other types of black-white interaction emerge from Pendleton District criminal records. As "Negro-stealing" occurred periodically, slaves were in danger of being forcibly removed. Some whites then, as throughout antebellum years, traded goods illegally with slaves. And two men were charged in 1797 with "suffering them [slaves] to assemble in an unlawful manner, and permitting 'Negroe' dances in their house."[12]

Contrasted to a "Black Majority" that gradually emerged in the lowcountry, Pendleton District remained predominantly white. African Americans in 1790 constituted only 9 percent of its population, smaller than in any later period. Slightly more than half of all slaves lived among holdings of five to thirty-three. But another quarter lived in households with only one or two slaves. Their lives must have been very lonely. This small proportion of African Americans was an omen that the area would be characterized by a dominating white presence, not only in numbers, ownership, control, and politics, but also in culture. A slave subculture would, and did, indeed have difficulty retaining significant African features in such an environment. "White households" is an especially appropriate term as 1790's census recorded only three free persons of color, all living with white families. A substantial percentage of whites were nonlandowning throughout the nineteenth century.

Only one-fifth of 1790 households owned slaves, a lower percentage than in subsequent decades. Holdings for all 253 owners averaged 3.3 slaves; slightly more than half of these owners possessed only one or two. At the other end of the spectrum, however, 17 men—7 percent of all owners—had 10 or more slaves, who equaled over one-fourth of the black population. Veteran Revolutionary officers accounted for several of the largest holders, notably Brigadier General Andrew Pickens (33 slaves), Colonel Robert Anderson (28), and Colonel Benjamin Cleveland (17). Together these men owned almost 10 percent of the district's slaves in 1790. All but one of the 17 families remained prosperous and influential for decades and would have some of the largest holdings in 1860 as well.[13]

Land, Agriculture, and Other Work

Although people then, and later, referred to their land elegantly as "plantations," these were often no more than two hundred acres, if that, with only a small portion being tilled. Most farms had just a few acres in cultivation along with many more —perhaps ten to twenty times as much acreage—of "unimproved" land. Usually farmers, or their slaves, would have had to start from scratch, cutting trees and clearing fields. Many families would have had hogs and chickens; fewer could afford milk cows; and even fewer owned horses, mules, or oxen for work. Basic crops included corn, other grains, and vegetables for the family; tobacco and upland rice provided cash. Cotton had yet to become a significant piedmont crop.[14]

A rare list of crops grown on a single wealthy plantation, where Milly would live, comes from John E. Colhoun, a state representative and soon-to-be U.S. senator. His instructions, "delivered to Mr. Jno Wadle at 12 Mile River Plantation 3 Jany 1797," were: "12 Mile Memorandum to plant in yr 1797: 80 acres of Corn of [which]—30 acres yellow, 3 of flint, 4 acres with Beans, 6 with Peas, Pumpkins in all the Rest [in between rows of corn to help enrich the soil]; 23 Do. [ditto] of Indigo; 40 Do. of Rye; 3 Do. of Wheat; 2 Do. of Barley; 15 Do. of Oats; 4 Do. of Rice; 2 Do. of Potatoes; 2 Do. of Cotton; 2 Do. of Flax for self; 1 Do. of Do. for Mrs. Kerr [Colhoun's sister]; 1/2 Do. of Hemp."[15] Colhoun inventoried "48 head of cattle, 19 head of sheep, 9 sows with 40 pigs, 4 sows yet to have pigs, 4 shoals well grown, 8 Do. smaller, 3 barrows, near 2 year old, 6, year-old, 4 sows of Bratcher's."

His nearly 175 cultivated acres put Colhoun far ahead of other planters in the area. He supervised his thousand-plus-acre holding where the Seneca River forks into the Keowee and Twelve Mile rivers from a distance, spending time mostly on his Cooper River plantations northeast of Charleston. Although dramatically beyond the local scale of operation, Colhoun's list indicates crops that could be, and were being, grown there. He advised his overseer that a slave man "Philip knows how & when to plant." A much more typical inventory totaling 14 acres appears in James Gilliland's June 1795 sale of "4 acres of corn standing in the field where I now live, 4 acres of tobacco and 6 acres of wheat standing."[16]

Over 80 percent of white families, having no slaves, would have worked the land they occupied, as would most owners who had fewer than ten slaves. Shared work and space continued into the house. Most white women in slave-owning families would have undertaken housework—cooking, cleaning, laundry, weaving—along with black females; very few families were prosperous enough to relieve the wife from laboring also. Surely most of 146 families with only one or two slaves allocated space for them in their houses; a similar situation probably existed for many of 81 owners with three or four slaves. An area settled for only a few years offered few comforts for whites, let alone blacks; most whites would have lived in small, probably chinked, log cabins. Three of the best houses in 1805 had only four rooms, two upstairs and two downstairs. Houses as well as cabins often had sleeping lofts for white children and slaves of all ages.[17]

Interactions in Churches

Churches brought together whites, slaves, and free people of color. Some African Americans, then, participated in Christian worship from Pendleton District's earliest years. Although churches were among Pendleton's first institutions, very few early congregational records survive. Some churches with tentative dates were: Shoal Creek Baptist Church, organized in the late 1780s near the Tugalo River; Carmel Presbyterian (1787) in upper Anderson County; Secona Baptist (1789) near the current town of Pickens; Hopewell Presbyterian (Old Stone Church; ca. 1790) near Pendleton; some Methodist congregations served by circuit riders, including Francis Asbury; and Big Creek Baptist (eastern Anderson County) near the Saluda River, organized in 1798. Baptists predominated, followed by Methodists and Presbyterians. There were no other denominations prior to 1816, when St. Paul's Episcopal Church began services in Pendleton village. These churches, most of which still survive, are now identified as white, but in the 1790s—as throughout antebellum years—they served all peoples.[18]

Despite small congregations often having between twenty-five and one hundred worshipers, churches were determined to enforce religious standards and to expel unrepentant, erring members. Shoal Creek excluded at least thirty-eight of its first three hundred members for varied offenses, including drinking, fighting, slander, and adultery. Exclusion from church—slaves as well as whites—brought not only religious but also social disdain and perhaps economic hardship.

African Americans joined several early churches as charter members. Shoal Creek included "harises tom" among its first twelve members; Secona Baptist Church "Rcvd. br[other] Toney by experience Dec. 1797"; and Big Creek had seven blacks in 1801. African American membership approximated at times their proportion of the population. About 7 percent of Shoal Creek's members prior to 1805 were blacks, roughly their percentage in Pendleton District. Two of the earliest free people of color found as members were "free Jinney" at Shoal Creek, circa 1803, and Salem Baptist's Samuel Bugg in 1805. That year Salem had eight blacks—seven slave, one free—out of sixty-two members, about 13 percent. In contrast to proverbial accounts of slaves relegated to balconies, hardly any early church had one—probably only Hopewell Presbyterian.[19]

The earliest record of racial conflict within a church, however, concerned Shoal Creek's seating arrangements. There, "the Church is informed that the black brethren is not satisfied with the appointment of the shed for them . . . [as] they ar[e] deprived of their privldge in the meeting house." White leaders responded that "wee gave them all the priveledge that any of the Rest of the members have. . . . Either in dealing or hearing Experiences or to Receive the Sacraments." But during public worship—by whites—blacks are "all to go into the Shed without being intrarupted while they keep good order." Immediately afterward, the church received as a new member a "Sister," a "Servant" who was not deterred by the church's ruling.

Resistance

Slaves asserted themselves in other dissident ways beyond the church. These activities fall within a broad spectrum termed slave resistance, which may have been as intense from 1784 to 1799 as at any later period. With sparse population, heavily wooded areas, and nearby Cherokee lands, slaves would have had a better chance of escaping than in subsequent years. Slaves fled into Native American territory. Despite treaty provisions (1777) that the Cherokee would return, for a bounty, any runaway, no cases of their doing so are known. Located near the Georgia boundary, Shoal Creek Baptist Church charged Mr. Hardin's slave James in September 1797 with "Knowing of Negroes Runing away and giving No notis in time." He was cleared of the charge, but the runaways evidently escaped. As late as 1819, an Abbeville man advertised for his escaped slave who was heading for the Cherokee nation, then centered in Georgia.[20]

The area's first recorded resistance happened in 1787, barely three years into white and black settlement. Barnett—Andrew Kennedy's slave convicted of crimes against the property of Sheriff Robert Maxwell—was hanged, probably just across the river in Greenville District. Because of that, Barnett is one of the first African Americans there whose name has survived.[21]

Lowcountry slaves brought to John Ewing Colhoun's plantation in the early 1790s tried to murder Colhoun and flee the state, an instance of especially serious early resistance. According to testimony in their August 12, 1798, trial, Suky and Hazzard attempted "to seduce other negroes out of the state." To escape, they intended to poison Colhoun. Tried and convicted, they were punished with, respectively, one hundred and twenty-five lashes and were branded in the forehead and chopped in both ears. Sue and Jack, also found guilty, received the same disfigurement and fifty and twenty-five lashes, respectively. Will, who obtained the poison—its source unrecorded—was hanged at the forks of the road near Glenn's weaving house. Although only five slaves were involved, they constituted about half of those Colhoun initially brought from the lowcountry.

Their punishments conformed with South Carolina's slave laws, mostly dating from 1720 and 1740. When rumors spread that Colhoun mistreated his slaves, he promptly refuted those charges. Nearly three years earlier a runaway died in December shortly after returning and being beaten. Colhoun circulated an account in which his overseer took full responsibility and claimed that the man perished from exposure, not his "moderate" punishment.[22]

Changing Population and Slaveholdings, 1800–1810

Sparsely settled, Pendleton District still had several major concentrations of population. They included southern Anderson County with Varennes as a commercial and religious center; plantations along the Rocky and Generostee rivers in lower Anderson County; Seneca and Keowee River plantations with Pendleton village as their hub; the Chauga and Tugaloo River land holdings; and the Big Creek area in southeastern Anderson County. By contrast the Oolenoy Valley community in northern Pickens County, established by people migrating from North Carolina, was more mountainous, lacked river connections to the lower part of the state, and had small slaveholdings. A new Andersonville settlement on the Savannah, sanctioned by the legislature in 1801, became Pendleton District's major commercial center for four decades. Owned by Elias Earle and related Harrison families who moved there from Centerville, its small-scale factories hired dozens of white men and probably utilized slave labor also. Also operating gun factories in Georgia, the Earles held government contracts during the War of 1812.[23]

Amid Pendleton District's fluid political and demographic nature, population grew rapidly between 1784 and 1800. Numbers of both people and households more than doubled during the 1790s despite departures of many moving westward. New arrivals, evidently coming mostly from the same locations as their predecessors, included more owners with a higher total number—but not percentage—of slaves than in the 1780s.

Slave population increased more rapidly than did the white population. Although black numbers grew over two and a half times between 1790 and 1800, average holdings in 1800 were only one-fifth of a slave larger than in 1790. Owners in 1800 consisted of three major groups: (1) Of the 590 owners in 1800, only 113 of them had owned slaves in Pendleton District in 1790. Earlier owners still possessing slaves in 1800 almost doubled their holdings. (2) Over 100 heads of households, present in 1790 without slaves, became owners by 1800, then averaging 2.4 slaves each, often acquired from family by inheritance, sale, or gift.[24] (3) Most of the increase came from nearly 400 newly arrived slaveholding families, mostly with small numbers.

Patterns of slaveholding also changed within that decade. More large holdings emerged. Forty-one families in 1800 owned 10 or more slaves, a significant increase. Five of the eight families owning 20 or more slaves in 1800 were among 1790's larger owners; only one was a recent arrival. These changes directly grouped African Americans in larger numbers. By 1800 nearly one-third in Pendleton District lived among ten or more slaves. Many, however, still lived with few others nearby in more remote areas: 230 slaves were each the only one in their households, while 182 resided where there were only two. Separation of families was inevitable in small holdings.

Mortality was an even more critical factor for African Americans than for European Americans. Green wrote Colhoun in March 1792 "one [negro] has had a few fits of the fevour and agaue tho lightly."[25] By 1800 death may well have eliminated

Table 1.1 **Pendleton District Slave Holdings, 1790–1820**

	1790	1800	1810	1820
population:	9,568.0	20,052.0	22,897.0	27,022.0
white	8,731.0	17,760.0	19,364.0	22,140.0
slave	834.0	2,224.0	3,485.0	4,715.0
free people of color	3.0	68.0	48.0	167.0
# households	1,433.0	3,013.0	3,084.0	3,574.0
# average whites/household	6.1	5.9	6.3	6.8
% slaves	8.7	11.1	15.2	17.4
# slaveholders	253.0	588.0	733.0	861.0
% slave holders/white families	17.7	19.5	23.8	24.1
% owners with 10–19 slaves	6.7	5.6	8.8	12.0
% owners with 20+ slaves	0.4	1.2	3.5	3.8
# average slave holding	3.3	3.8	4.8	5.5
persons/sq mile	4.9	10.3	11.7	13.8
median holding for African Am.	4.0	6.0	>10.0	10.0
% 1 or 2/holding	22.9	18.6	9.4	10.6
% 10 or more/holding	31.1	30.8	44.6	50.8
% 20 or more/holding	7.3	12.0	20.9	22.2

Sources: calculated from the respective census microfilm and/or published versions. Households for 1820 estimated, based on a typical page. Stewart, *1800 Census*; and G. Anne Sheriff and Lavina Moore, compil., *Pendleton District South Carolina: 1810 Census* (Central: privately printed, 1994); cited as Sheriff, *Pendleton 1810 Census*. Figures for 1800 are skewed by John Ewing Colhoun's 103 slaves, most of whom remained in the lowcountry.

large numbers of the 1790 Pendleton District slaves, based on devastating epidemics in the 1790s and on mid-nineteenth-century data. Reproduction apparently more than replaced numbers lost by death.

A new feature of African American life in the area was a significantly larger number of free people of color (FPC), increased from only three in 1790 to sixty-eight by 1800, likely resulting from an influx from outside. Only one documented manumission occurred there within that decade, when Henry Wakefield's will freed his slave Bob. Typically there was one free person of color with a white family; only four households had more than two. Amos Ladd and Joel Terrell each had 4 FPC living with them in eastern Pickens County. Terrell families, who freed some slaves in Albemarle County, Virginia, housed FPC through 1830, and Ladds would have continuing associations with FPC for decades. Five free people of color lived with Benjamin Cleveland and 3 with John Shannon, both in Oconee County. Fifteen of the forty-three white households with FPC also owned slaves.

Over two-thirds of Pendleton District's FPC in 1800 lived in the southern section that would become Anderson County. They included all ten free men of color who had their own independent households, nine of them alone and one who shared his house with a free woman. Most Anderson FPC lived near others. Most of Anderson's free people of color and white families housing them left before 1810. By contrast few, if any, departed from Dacusville (Pickens) and Shoal Creek (Oconee) concentrations. There, the Baptist church had eight free members of color.[26]

From its initial black and white settlement in 1784, Pendleton District's population grew rapidly. It would not duplicate this 1790–1800 proportionate growth again. Between 1790 and 1810, most antislavery sentiments among whites waned throughout the country, and only a tiny number of slaves were emancipated locally. Throughout antebellum years percentages of slaves would grow, as would proportions of slave owners and their average holding. Consequently larger holdings strengthened the African American community. White and black were locked together within slavery's expansion in Pendleton District.

TWO

Piedmont Peoples, Their Environment, and Their Work

BLACK AND WHITE PEOPLE, having traveled together from their previous homes, arrived in Pendleton District knowing much about each other and interacting in diverse ways. They shared common space for work, sometimes for living, and for church; mostly they consumed only food grown on their premises.

Much they did not share. Slaves occupied a subordinate status for multiple reasons: as slaves, as a small percentage of the population sparsely dispersed over the district initially, and as a distinct but ethnically diverse group. Although Pendleton District's white settlers derived almost exclusively from the British Isles with shared culture and language, African Americans descended from many African regions, cultures, languages, and traditions. Their status as slaves gave people of African descent in piedmont Carolina more in common than did their African culture.

The Peoples and Their Origins

Most African Americans brought to Pendleton District had been born in America, often with several generations of American-born ancestors, sometimes more than their owners had. If not moving into Pendleton volitionally, some did have decades of acclimation and perhaps even acculturation; they hardly resembled Africans arriving in Charleston literally straight off the boat. Some, maybe all, free people of color came by choice, though perhaps impelled by restrictions and harassment elsewhere. The few free blacks—sixty-eight in 1800—were even more acculturated than most slaves.

Virtually all white families moving into Pendleton District were Scots-Irish, along with a sprinkling of English, Scottish, and Welsh. Names such as McAllister, McCaleb, McMahan, Armstrong, Miller, Thompson, Montgomery, Kilpatrick, Morgan, and Perkins clearly indicate British Isles ancestry. Many followed the wagon road through the Virginia Valley. Another distinct, much smaller, ethnicity was the Huguenots, Protestants who fled from France in the late 1600s because of religious persecution. Some lowcountry Huguenots intermarried with Scots-Irish and English—among them the Floride Bonneau–John Ewing Colhoun family who came to Pendleton in the 1790s. The area's European-derived ethnic mix would remain unchanged until the 1850s. By 1820, probably as early as 1810, both Pendleton District's white and black populations became stabilized, local historians believe, with relatively few families moving into or out of the area. Many who moved westward, like the Halberts, had other relatives who stayed behind. Movements of black people still depended mainly on whites.[1]

Following their owners, then, Pendleton's African Americans in 1790 or 1800 mostly would have come from Virginia, North Carolina, or elsewhere in South Carolina. A few white families in 1790 moved from the Charleston area; that number would increase during following decades. All families known to have come from Charleston owned slaves, usually in sizable numbers. Frequent lowcountry influxes brought both whites and blacks throughout antebellum and war years.[2]

Although few Pendleton District slaves seem to have been direct arrivals from Africa or from Caribbean islands, there were some notables. One couple—Monemi and Polydore—on John C. Calhoun's plantation had been born in Africa ca. 1740, and lived until the mid-1800s: "The negroes on this place pay as much respect to the old negress [Monemi] as if she was a queen"; she had sixty-three living descendants. Three area slaves born in Africa during the late 1700s died in late antebellum years.[3]

Other African-born people survived until late in the century. Nine residents reported in 1870 that they were born in Africa. Typical ages indicate births between 1770 and 1800: Lindsey and Data (?) Smart, a couple in Honea Path (Anderson County), born 1790 and 1795; and Charity Bozeman (Anderson), born about 1782. Anderson County's 1880 census lists seven men and women who stated African birth places with dates between 1770 and 1810. Thirteen others reported both parents as Africa-born, and an additional fifty-five had one parent born there.[4] Determining African origins of Pendleton District slaves is a near-impossible undertaking. They are even harder to trace because many thousands of slaves spent years on Caribbean islands before reaching North America's mainland. Research concerning slave arrivals at Charleston and at Virginia ports provides some pointers to specific African locations.

Daniel Littlefield demonstrates that slaves imported into the lowcountry came from many parts of Africa extending from the western coast (e.g., Gambia, of Alex Haley's *Roots* fame), the Gold and Grain Coasts, the Congo, and Angola, to the eastern coast including Mozambique and Madagascar. Elizabeth Donnan and more recent researchers examining Virginia importation find similarly diversified origins. Littlefield and others—including scholars from Sierra Leone—have traced linkages of Africans with rice-growing skills being deliberately captured and brought to produce rice in South Carolina. Coastal rice areas and sea islands off the Georgia and South Carolina mainland had holdings that came almost exclusively from a single African region. Much literature on lowcountry African Americans relates how these homogenous groups with little white interaction were able to continue over centuries their African skills, customs, language, and beliefs—many incorporated into Gullah.[5]

By about 1800, it seems, Pendleton's slaves had lost much of their African languages and some African customs. Presumably some beliefs, words, stories, and customs remained, not readily visible within the white context then and virtually impossible to detect today. One Pendleton slave around 1800 was called Joseph Africanus. At least one slave, Celia, was sent to Liberia in 1832.[6]

This book, based primarily on documents, finds little written evidence of African retentions. An African American folklorist, an anthropologist, and an archaeologist, observing but not extensively studying the area in the 1990s, similarly found few African traits. Some aspects, however, continued throughout the nineteenth century: crafts, such as basket weaving, blacksmithing, carpentry, and quilting. As late as 1900 some Greenville laundresses carried burdens African-style on their heads. Naming practices kept alive some African names and values, and other words lingered, including one sexual term. Studies elsewhere have emphasized also herb medicines, musical styles, foods, and adaptations of Christianity. Derivations, such as use of okra in cooking, were often forgotten as whites co-opted

Greenville laundress, carrying her burden African style, 1899; by C. L. Baley, a U.S Army photographer at Camp Wetherill, Greenville, S.C. Courtesy Schomberg Center for Research in Black Culture, New York Public Library

Thompson family tools; the earliest, a tongue-in groove, was owned ca. 1850s by Reuben Thompson; others were acquired by succeeding generations. Black Heritage in the Upper Piedmont

African contributions.[7] These interactions and diverse African origins—sometimes several generations past—shaped a culture dramatically different from that of the lowcountry and severely limited African retentions, while some were, so to speak, smuggled into white culture.

Slaveholdings, 1790–1860

Slaveholding patterns differed over time from 1790 to 1860. These also varied depending on whether the owners' or the slaves' perspectives are considered, as both should be. Pendleton's earliest decades probably were the most unsettled for slaves due to a transitory frontier society. All of the 101 families in 1790 with one slave (40 percent of slave owners), many of the 57 (another 20 percent) with two slaves, and some others with fewer than five slaves (nearly 30 percent) would have mated males and females from different plantations. Few slaves in these early years would have had much choice of spouses.

Slaves in low numbers and percentages constituted only 9 percent of the population at the first census, 1790, several years after settlement was under way. Since owners migrating to Pendleton District likely brought slaves of working age whenever they could, rather than infants and the elderly, it is possible that a higher percentage of the 1790 slaves were in their reproductive years than those of a later period.

White population in 1800 was 221 percent that of 1790, while slaves were 268 percent. Much of this larger number of slaves, like that for whites, seems to have come from new arrivals, whose rate outstripped the numbers of those who moved away or died. As both white and black population continued to grow in the early nineteenth century, patterns of slaveholding changed for owners and those they owned. African Americans as a percentage of overall population increased dramatically from their 1790 level to Anderson's 37 percent in 1860, Pickens-Oconee's 22 percent. During these same years Anderson owners almost doubled in proportion to all white households, with smaller increases in Oconee and Pickens.

Average sizes of holdings more than doubled in all three counties. Although in 1790 half of all African Americans lived in holdings of 4 or less, by 1850 nearly 40 percent lived on plantations with 20 or more slaves in Pickens and Oconee and over 30 percent in Anderson. Most bigger holdings in 1860 belonged to the same families who had large numbers in earlier decades. Relatively few larger owners left the area; rather, they stayed, managed well, and intermarried with other slave-owning families, further increasing their holdings. Several families held slaves in more than

Table 2.1 **Population and Holdings: Pendleton, Anderson, and Pickens Districts**

	1790 Pton	1810 Pton	1830 And	1830 Pkns	1850 And	1850 Pkns
% slaves	8.7	15.2	25.8	19.8	35.0	21.8
% HOH slave holders	17.7	23.8	32.7	21.9	38.9	18.8
% owners 20+	0.4	3.5	5.9	6.6	8.1	9.9
av. holding	3.3	4.8	6.3	6.7	7.4	8.2
persons/sq mile	4.9	11.7	22.0	12.3	27.5	14.4
median holding for African-Am:	4.0	>10.0	11.0	12.0	13.0	15.0
% of A-A in holdings of:						
1 or 2	22.9	9.4	7.8	8.4	5.9	4.9
10 & up	31.9	44.6	57.8	55.7	62.9	68.9
20+	7.3	20.9	28.7	34.7	30.9	30.9

HOH = head of household. Calculated from census microfilm and/or published versions including these for 1810 and 1830: Sheriff, *Pendleton 1810 Census;* Anne Sheriff, Tom Wilkinson, Lavina Moore, and Jay Young, compil., *Pickens District, S.C. 1830 Census* (Central: Faith Clayton Family Research Center, Central Wesleyan College, 1988). Anderson households for 1830 estimated, based on a typical page. Pickens District (including the later Pickens and Oconee counties) reported together. Figures for Anderson slaves in 1850 are murky and difficult to calculate. I have used my adjusted figures for Anderson: 7,230 slaves, compared to 5,683 in 1840 and 8,425 in 1860.

one county or state, as did J. W. Harrison with holdings in Florida as well as Anderson County or the Townes families, owning slaves in Abbeville and Greenville counties plus Alabama, frequently moving some from one site to another.

Owners typically acquired their holdings piecemeal, from their parents, from in-laws, through purchases, and by natural reproduction. No surviving records cover the full lifetime of any owner in Anderson, Oconee, and Pickens counties. Some men gained slaves only through marriage, but others married women who did not come from slaveholding families. Many owners never bought any slaves. Other variables included bequests from adult siblings, grandparents, or other relatives. The actual number owned probably fluctuated, not only year by year, but also throughout a year.[8]

Slaves who lived among a plantation holding of 25 or 30 had several advantages over those whose master owned only a few, perhaps under 5 or 10. A holding of 25 would increase the likelihood of marrying a spouse on the same premises. Also, there were perhaps enough slaves to divide them by whole families among their owner's respective heirs when he died. Larger holdings usually had a few slaves who sometimes could earn money by their skills. And, most writers assume, house servants probably received better treatment than field hands. A small holding of 10, perhaps, like David Golightly Harris's (Spartanburg) or J. D. Ashmore's (Anderson), did not allow a distinct separation between house and field. In one period in 1857 Ashmore's Amritta washed on April 9, ironed the next day, worked in the garden on April 16, and five days later cleaned out the fence-side ditches. On other occasions she plowed.[9]

Discussing an individual holding misses the broader context. Many owners were related to others; children of wealthy families tended to extend marriage linkages with spouses of similar background, as did Zacharias Taliaferro and his daughters. Born ca. 1759 in Amherst County, Virginia, Taliaferro came to Pendleton District in the 1790s when he was approximately thirty-five years old. A lawyer and Revolutionary war veteran, he had 19 slaves in 1800, the same number as in Virginia in the 1780s. Shortly afterward he married Margaret Carter, a descendant of Virginia's wealthy Chew and Carter families. In 1802 he petitioned the legislature to bring into South Carolina 5 Virginia slaves acquired by marriage. About twenty years later his four daughters (no sons) married into locally prominent families.

Zacharias's 51 slaves in 1830 constituted Anderson County's second-largest holding; he died a year later. His four sons-in-law in 1850 had 140 slaves among them. These husbands had siblings who married other owners. Slaveholding families very much, then, constituted a class, or at least a series of overlapping cliques, rather than discrete individuals. African Americans belonging to these families probably had interlocking relationships also.[10]

Among all Pendleton District families, the Maxwells increased their holdings most dramatically. Robert Maxwell was one of Greenville's earliest settlers, just opposite Pendleton District's Saluda River boundary. Married to Robert Anderson's daughter,

36 / *The Setting, the Peoples, and Their Work*

Table 2.2 **Taliaferro-Simpson Families and Slaves**

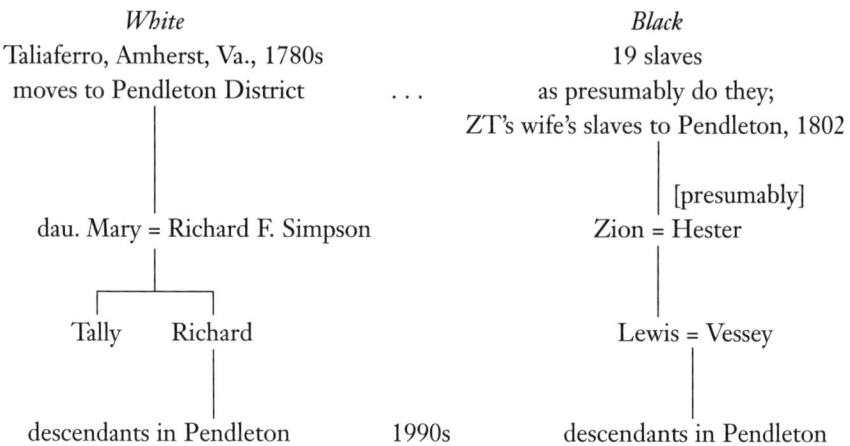

he likely acquired some slaves through her. Two sons, John and Robert, married daughters of Samuel Earle, part of another major slave-owning family. By 1860 John's son Samuel E. Maxwell had 130 slaves. Maxwell families owned several Anderson and Oconee plantations, totaling 305 slaves among them in 1860.[11]

Southerners periodically examined, at least superficially, the economic benefits or detriments of owning slaves, sometimes reacting against abolitionist literature. John C. Calhoun in 1820 wrote enthusiastically about a Pennsylvania man whose land had high yields without slave labor. Many people may not have considered their reasons for owning slaves beyond having inherited some and presuming it a natural aspect of their status in society. Slaves furnished something of a status symbol and ostensible measure of wealth, although many owners went into debt buying them, then maintaining both land and labor force. Prosperous owners lived a leisured, affluent life because of their slaves' labor: "slavery helped make possible an extremely cultured group in Edgefield. Time was available for leisure, politics, and travel." Slaves also provided pleasant comforts such as lighting fires so owners could wake up to a warmed house or relieving the white family from nuisance chores such as emptying chamber pots. For elderly owners and single or widowed women, slaves often helped them survive when they could not easily have managed the work alone, especially in the fields. All of these chores, nuisances, and burdens got shifted to those in bondage: "servants waited on the family as long as they were up—making fires—taking the table into the piazza and carrying it back, and shutting up the houses."[12]

Black and white, linked together on one plantation, had complicated interpersonal relations. Given short life expectancies for both slaves and owners, average ages on a plantation typically would have been around twenty. Going beyond white-propagated stereotypes of an elderly faithful servant and an aged owner sharing emotional bonds, that surely must have happened. People—white or black—in their sixties, seventies, or eighties would have had a limited number of peers. Especially a white and a black person who grew up together shared many memories, including playing together as children. Robert Anderson refused to allow "old Rose" to be sold for she "was always a faithful servant to her old Mistress, they were raised together and were of an age." Black and white who came together from Virginia would have a particular frame of reference that all younger people could not understand, although the owner hardly shared the slaves' other, painful experiences.

For whatever it meant, many owners spoke of all people on their plantation as "my family white or black," as Charles M. Lay wrote in 1863. Similarly Robert Guyton's 1841 will directed that his "family be kept together, both black and white." As written by white Tally Simpson for a slave accompanying him to Virginia Civil War battlefields, "Zion is well again and sends his love to [his wife] Hester and his family and begs to be remembered to the white family."[13]

Sizable numbers of mulattos attest to more intimate plantation relationships. Numerous instances of slave mistresses and casual sexual exploitation may well have existed. Personal recorded accounts by whites were rare, those by blacks in the three counties were not much more frequent and were always provided in later years. Many African American families, however, retain an oral tradition acknowledging among themselves their white ancestors. Louisa Gassaway reported in the 1880 census that her father was born in Scotland, while Eliza Rice indicated a mother born in France. Descendants of Anderson County Thompsons have written about their ancestor from Ireland.[14] Other European-born parents are noted in the 1880 and 1900 censuses. Speaking from a lower part of the state, Mary Chesnut said that "every lady tells you who is the father of all the mulatto children in everybody's household, but those in her own she seems to think drop down from the clouds, or pretends so to think," even though "the mulattoes one sees in every family exactly resemble the white children."[15]

Upper-piedmont whites liked to say in both the nineteenth and twentieth centuries that mulattos were fathered by lowcountry planters. Although mulattos in 1850 constituted only about 5 percent of slaves in Anderson, Oconee, and Pickens counties, they could be found on one-fourth of all plantations. Certain areas had more mulattos than did other regions.

Mulattos seemed to get better treatment than did black slaves. Some writers suggest that they were more likely to be house servants, who typically had better housing, nicer clothing, and more furnishings. House servants also had more contact with owners, for better or worse, and more opportunities to travel with, or without, owners and to learn more about the world beyond. Mulattos had a slightly longer average life span than did "black" slaves. Proportionately more mulattos could read and write than could blacks. About half of free people of color were mulattos, very high compared to the overall African American population. Some mulattos may have been emancipated because they were children of the owner or other family members.

Reuben and Martha Thompson's seven children: Stewart (seated, second from right), Florence (left), and Lizzie (right); the other four are presumed to be, although not necessarily in sequence, James, John, Henry, and Eddie; ca. 1880. Black Heritage in the Upper Piedmont

Owners certainly had favored slaves. Whether they were mulattos and perhaps their offspring is evidently beyond proof for the tricountry area except in rare instances. Elizabeth Mills (Anderson) provided well for Amy, willing her to executors in 1837 and directing that they should "build a cabin on land purchased from Steel and 3 acres cleared and fenced and Amy be allowed to live there for her lifetime." Amy, who should have use of a cow and calf, sow and pigs, and their increase, could dispose of them as she pleased. Some owners valued specific slaves as plantation managers more highly than their own relatives. Robert Guyton specified in his will "that my man Isaac be allowed a reasonable share of direction and management of my farm for raising of my children so long as he shall conduct as well as he has done heretofore."[16]

Large numbers of slaves in 1820 remained in the three counties, along with their descendants, for many decades. But contrasted to slaves taken away by owners moving westward, documented cases of individuals being sold from their owners and families for punishment are rare, less than one per year. Such happened occasionally by court order for slaves found guilty of heinous crimes; that was also the fate for others labeled unruly or dangerous on the plantation, sometimes in conflict with other slaves, a decision entirely the owner's. Calhoun in 1830 directed his Charleston agent to sell Peggy and in 1832 elaborated on one fellow "now in Abbeville jail on charge of being connected with . . . stealing a watch. As I am adverse to having

Table 2.3 **Thompson Family Genealogy**

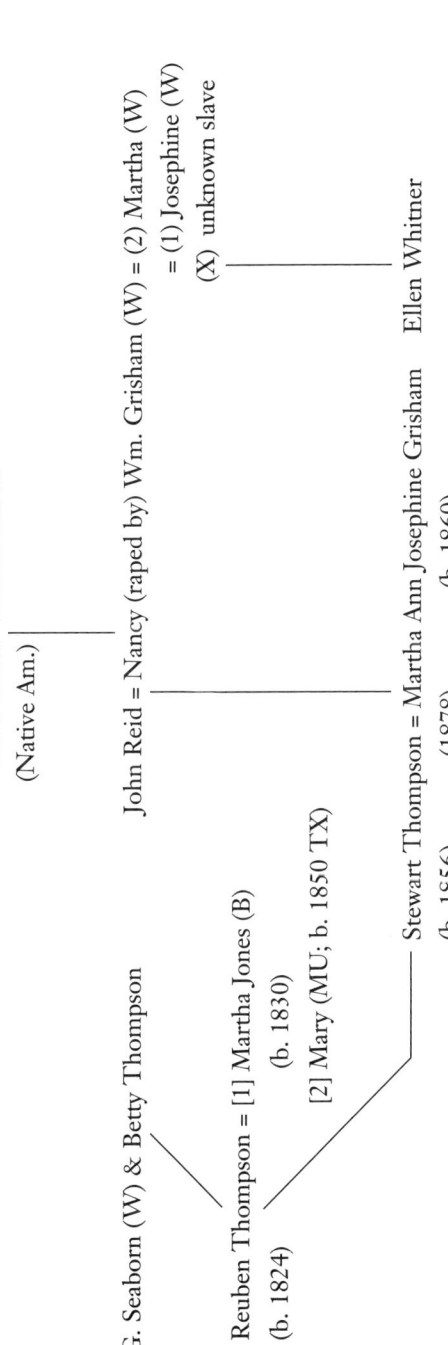

Sources: Josephine Sherard Davis, "Facts from the Family Tree of the Thompsons of Pendleton South Carolina," July 1977, and "The Thompson Family Reunion, Pendleton, S.C., July 1–14 1985" (compiler not stated); both SCL. The 1870 census lists Reuben as a carpenter, and descendants still have some of his tools; Edinburg (b. ca. 1818) indicated his ancestor's foreign birth in the 1880 census and probably was Reuben's brother; there was also a Moses (b. ca. 1805). The 1880 census shows Mary, wife of Reuben Thompson, as born in Texas ca. 1850.

a negro of his character in my gang, I would be glad to sell him, but not at a sacrifice."[17] Most slaves remained, however, and continuity of the specific population would strengthen both the community and families.

Agriculture Prevails

As African Americans well knew, the area of Pendleton District was agricultural well into the twentieth century. Virtually all antebellum families undertook agricultural work, full- or part-time, and everybody talked about it. Correspondence from local writers often mentioned weather and crops, as letters from rural and farming families still do. Ezekiel Noble, writing just a few lines in 1820, included: "The present appearance of Crops in this Neighborhood are flattering. . . . Waiting for a Rain, which is Somewhat wanted."[18]

This preoccupation reflected an outlook of people, black and white, who tended the land and produced crops. Their lives were determined substantially by climate, terrain, and crops that grew there. Enslavement dictated their condition, but agriculture shaped their day-to-day work; it would continue to do so long after emancipation. Producing primarily food for plantation consumption, upper-piedmont slaves had a more direct stake in their work than did those who cultivated cash crops. And mostly small-scale farming operations brought slaves into direct daily contact with owners: "Labor was all-pervasive in slave life. The sheer range of work blacks undertook in the Old South was remarkable, and remarkably expanding . . . agricultural production, plantation artisanship, and domestic service."[19]

In a region where farming dominated, most work consisted of labor in the fields and elsewhere on plantations. A predominantly agricultural area with primarily wagon, stagecoach, and river transportation required few established towns. Rather, some people lived in small settlements around crossroads, general stores, or churches. Most families resided on small plantations that hardly lent themselves to concentrated population. There were only three incorporated towns—Pendleton, Anderson, and Pickens. Transportation routes were limited: a major road to Columbia and Charleston, auxiliary roads, and rivers serviceable for transport, but no railroad lines prior to the 1850s. As late as 1848, Andersonian J. P. Reed could describe his area as a "(comparatively) vast unoccupied Country."

With such restricted means for shipping, agricultural production served primarily local consumption. No single product dominated black labor as did, elsewhere, lowcountry rice, tobacco in the Chesapeake, or "King Cotton" throughout South Carolina later in the century. Only a few well-to-do planters could ship cotton or other goods down the Savannah River—beginning on its Seneca, Generostee, or other tributaries—to Augusta (Georgia) and Hamburg (South Carolina).[20] Like much else in their lives, slaves' work depended on natural and economic forces beyond their control.

Nearly 95 percent of early-1800s households derived their income exclusively from agriculture, a figure that would drop to nearer 80 percent by 1860. The earliest data on kinds of work come from the 1820 census when 94 percent of Pendleton households reported agriculture as their employment compared to 5 percent in manufacturing—small-scale, water-powered—and 1 percent in commerce, mostly general stores and ferry operations. Most households involved in commerce and manufacturing also farmed. Not until the arrival of textile mills in the late 1800s was there any large-scale alternative employment, available for whites only.

The area was only slightly less agricultural by 1850, when the census first listed specific occupations for free people. For Oconee and Pickens counties, 82 percent of white heads of households reported their work as "farmer" or "farming." Blacksmiths, millers, carpenters, shoemakers, teachers, and the clergy accounted for most others, with a sprinkling of cabinetmakers, wheelwrights, merchants, and public officials plus three doctors and a dentist. Many craftsmen, professionals, and public officials operated farm land as well.

Somewhat more diversified, Anderson still had over 70 percent of household heads reporting agriculture as their occupation. Encompassing Pendleton and Anderson villages and a population otherwise more densely settled than Oconee and Pickens, the county had more professionals and more skilled craftsmen; 664 white men listed their work as other than agriculture. Anderson with small-scale industry had more carriage and coach makers than millers. Lawyers, physicians, the clergy, and merchants dominated among nonagricultural work.

Only 125 of those 664 men owned slaves. Joseph N. Whitner, a lawyer with 78, and Daniel Brown, a merchant with 49, would have used them mostly on their land; Brown, in fact, had three plantations. Both Clerk of Court Elijah Webb with 21 slaves and Congressman James L. Orr with 14 also owned plantations. Virtually all men described as professionals with 13 or more slaves, although needing several of them as agricultural workers, would have utilized a staff of domestic servants—cooks, ladies' maids, butlers, and coach drivers. Holdings varied significantly among white occupations. Craftsmen probably trained one or two slaves to assist in their craft but used others in the house, and perhaps one or more in some agricultural work.[21]

Many free families of color also farmed as their primary livelihood but some had other skills. For Oconee and Pickens free black heads of households listing an occupation in 1850, 71 percent described themselves as farmers. As with white families, Anderson free persons of color had a wider array of occupations that year. Free black heads of households included three laborers (both town and country), a carpenter, a tailor, and a shoemaker. Dependents or those living in white households, had additional skills. Only two free wives had occupations listed.[22]

Conditions of agricultural work varied enormously according to scale and utilization of slaves. Only about forty farmers in Oconee and Pickens counties—about 2 percent—qualified as "planters" having sizable holdings of land and slaves. An apparent similarity among 82 percent of Oconee and Pickens white household heads engaged primarily in agriculture masks significant differences. The term encompassed nearly 35 percent of all households with no real property value shown; even most landowning farmers tilled it without slaves.[23] Less is known about tenant farmers as a class than about slaves. Clearly the broad label "farmer" covers diverse groups.

Upper-piedmont counties with their heavy agricultural emphasis were largely self-sufficient. They could provide all the pork and poultry, grains, molasses, and vegetables that local folk needed. When drovers brought livestock from the mountains, additional meat could be bought locally. Massive quantities of corn, smaller amounts of wheat, and even less of rye, oats, and barley furnished food for people and livestock, and sizable amounts of corn wound up as whiskey. Although vegetables, grains, meat, and liquor were locally abundant, families had to acquire some staples from elsewhere. Coffee, tea, sugar, and salt came from Charleston or Augusta, either by direct purchase there or through local general stores. Area farms supplied virtually all other items.[24]

Corn, "as basic to southern history as were Thomas Jefferson and John C. Calhoun," was the primary grain consumed by white and black alike. Of households in the 1850 agricultural schedules, 95 percent produced corn. It grew well on hilly land, not suitable for rice, and its growing cycle complemented cotton especially well. Anderson in 1860 harvested one and a half, and Pickens and Oconee nearly

Table 2.4 **Samuel Earle's Slaves and Their Occupations**

Name	Description	Appraised Value	Name	Description	Appraised Value
Field Hands (24; 51% of all slaves except those labeled "child"):					
Lydia	girl	500	Henry Jr.	boy	600
Austin	boy	475	Terry	?	boy 550
Armstead	boy	600	Sam	boy	550
Milly	woman	150	Smith	boy	400
Sally and child	woman	500	John	boy	400
Frances	girl	250	Edward	boy	350
Thomas	boy	375	Phoebe	woman	500
Fielding	boy	375	Minerva	girl	500
Bob	man	350	Clarissa and child	girl	600
Dick	boy	650	Charity & child	girl	600
Ransom	boy	650	Flora	woman	350
Tom Jr.	boy	400	Hagar & child	woman	450
no occupation listed (under 10?)			Rosetta	girl	250
Louisa	girl	325	Daphne	girl	200
Jane	girl	275	Louisa	girl	250
Grace	girl	350	Judy	girl	225

double, the state's per capita corn production. Rations allocated to slaves centered on corn meal for bread; they received much less wheat, and some likely got none.[25]

Distillers kept imbibers amply supplied with corn whiskey. Pendleton in 1810 led the state (for districts reporting) by distilling 77,340 gallons, about six for each adult, white and black; thirty years later Pickens and Oconee produced a record 33,455 gallons—about 5 for each adult. Anderson followed distantly with 15,515— only 1.5 per adult. Along with whiskey, local farmers turned some fruit, especially apples and peaches, into brandy. Distilling ranked among slaves' nonagricultural work, and several slave inventories mentioned stilling hands. Revenue officials in postbellum years found stills operated jointly by black and white men.[26]

Usually self-sustaining, plantations produced a variety of crops; that meant work throughout the year. Washington Taylor's diary from Greenville County recorded his agricultural cycle, as did Spartanburg County's David Golightly Harris's diary. Samples of varied work performed on Taylor's plantation, mostly by slave labor, for three months illustrate the calendar of crops being grown simultaneously:

Table 2.4 (*continued*)

Name	Descriptions; Work		Appraised Value
Charles	man,	runaway (supposed)	200
Charles Sr.	(blind) man,	blind	0
other occupations (34% of all slaves except those labeled "child"):			
Nancy & child	woman	house servant	450
Lucretia	girl	house servant	550
Julia	girl	house servant	450
Rebecca	woman	house servant, etc.	200
Nancy	woman	house servant, etc.	550
Sarah	girl	house servant	350
Dennis	boy	tailor	800
Thomas Sr.	man	carpenter, etc.	350
Allen	man	blacksmith	600
Henry	man	blacksmith	900
Peter	boy	blacksmith apprentice	600
Taber	man	coachman, shoemaker, etc.	400
Sophia & child	woman	seamstress	700
Violet [elderly?]	woman	cook, etc.	200
Tabby [elderly?]	woman	cook	150
Jacob [elderly?]	man	miller	200
Total appraised value:			20,650

Source: Estate appraisal, 1833, Anderson County, Clerk of Court. Taber [Warren], see note in "Schools, 1865–1900," ch. 17.

April milled the crop of winter wheat
    planted corn, potatoes
    hauled manure and planted corn
    bedded cotton ground, hauled manure
May put up fences, rolled logs, fired new ground
    put up a horse stable
    put out yams
    planted second crop of corn; set out cabbage
June sheared sheep [in May some years]
    harvested rye
    harvested wheat [threshed about three weeks later]

A given day might include diverse tasks. Harris recorded on June 16, 1858, that "the boys are still cutting wheat. . . . Yesterday & to day the hands are planting cotton." Six weeks earlier the work on April 29 was even more varied: "Finished plowing at home (corn) then plowed the potatoe land and the irish potatoes a[t] Meadows. Pepairing to go to the Mountain to plow the corn there. To day I have been making some bee-stands. . . . Washing & suning wheat to take to mill. . . . Four hands plowing at the Mountain. Edom & York are burning off of the new ground."[27]

Crops were only one part of plantation work, as Harris's and Taylor's accounts make vividly clear. Many hands—black and white, residents and hired laborers—were needed for diverse work on a large plantation. The land itself required careful attention. Machinery did not help much, and slaves had to till, manually, steep hills to increase productive land, as they did on S. E. Maxwell's Toxaway plantation. Fencing took a substantial amount of time between planting and harvesting, and before next spring's planting. Livestock generally roamed free, foraging for themselves, and farmers fenced crops rather than pasture land.

A hilly terrain both dictated the crops that could be profitably grown and demanded hard work by black and white. Eroding hillsides were the biggest problem facing piedmont farmers and their slaves. Esli Hunt (Pickens) reported his efforts in 1839 "to keep the ditches from filling up with sand so that the bottom lands of said plantation may not over flow with water." Preventing washing away, Calhoun said, "is after all the most indispensable work on the place, next to that immediately connected with making the crop.[28] Frequent references to a "gully-washer" rain were reminders of the damage that could occur.

Rainy weather and short winter days called off the intense work of plowing, planting, and harvesting. However, chores were always waiting for such occasions —repairing tools, cutting timber in the barns, and tending to fences and ditches. Even winter work included sowing rye in November or early December and harvesting winter wheat in January. In January and February, Taylor and his slaves also cut rails, then split and hauled them; repaired fences; cut logs for new outbuildings; chopped logs and brush; milled wheat; plowed; broke up ground in the corn field; and planted the first crop of Irish potatoes. The cycle was relentless.

Limited Innovations and Machinery

Agriculture in Anderson, Oconee, and Pickens counties—largely self-sufficient and diversified—was relatively primitive. Innovations there lagged far behind Britain and New England. James W. Crawford, living on the Seneca River above Pendleton, wrote an 1850 newspaper article about his productivity from fertilizers, obviously a technique new to local farmers although used elsewhere for decades—reprinted over fifteen years later as not many were yet acting on his advice. Neighbor John C. Calhoun observed in 1845 that few overseers knew much about manuring.

Because of relatively poor agricultural practice in the early 1800s, several plantation owners sought better methods. Pendleton boasted one of the state's first local agricultural societies, the Pendleton Farmers' Society organized in 1815, and much later a separate Pickens Agricultural Society. The Pendleton society's membership, judged by land ownership, slaveholdings, and social and political prominence, drew primarily from the upper crust of plantation owners. Donna Roper, studying four South Carolina agricultural societies including that in Pendleton, demonstrates that they constituted primarily an elite group, especially as reflected by their officers.

Pendleton Farmers' Society held annual exhibitions and awarded prizes for best livestock, crop specimens, productivity, and domestic industries. It also presented occasional lectures on agricultural management, which seldom went much beyond advice to take care of the land and to plant wisely. George Seaborn, a "negro trader," launched in the 1850s *Farmer and Planter*, published in Pendleton and loosely connected with the farmers' society. Pendleton lectures and awards seem to have had little effect on the vast majority of area farmers.[29]

One new gadget, however, produced far-reaching effects in Pendleton District, as it did throughout the South. Eli Whitney's cotton gin, invented for a South Carolina plantation, has been celebrated and lamented for its decisive role in cotton production, the nineteenth-century economy, and slavery. Other inventions improved processes of packing cotton into bales and wrapping them for transportation. Although local farmers were slow to adopt other innovations, some took quickly to "cotton machines." Barely a decade after Whitney's first gin, they began to appear in estate inventories.[30]

Early nineteenth-century gins, small enough to be portable, could be leased and hauled from one plantation to another. Relatively few farmers, except more prosperous ones like the Calhouns, bought other newly developed farm machinery. Although the cotton gin mechanized one process, others—plowing, planting, hoeing, and picking—had to be done manually, often by slaves. Technological developments produced factors that shaped slave lives beyond their control.

Cotton, Not Yet King

Whether a farmer owned slaves made little difference in which crops he raised, even in the case of cotton, although it significantly affected the scale of operation.

Cotton evidently took years to become a major crop in Pendleton District, even with readily available ginning machines. John E. Colhoun's 175 cultivated acres included in 1797 only two of cotton. After 1800, cotton appears in estate appraisals and other records with increasing frequency but in small quantities. Some slaves in the 1820s, as well as later, were growing and selling their own cotton.[31]

For many antebellum farmers, cotton served more as a locally used product than as a cash crop. Observers such as Robert Mills in 1823 and J. S. Buckingham in 1842 reported that virtually every home had a spinning wheel for household production.[32] Many plantation wives and slave women made cotton and woolen clothes for their own use. Factories in Andersonville, on the Colhoun plantation, and near Pendleton village evidently produced a substantial amount of cotton.

As a bulky product cotton was cumbersome to ship by wagons or boat. Anderson cultivated cotton earlier than did Oconee and Pickens because of richer soil, warmer temperatures, and rivers with unimpeded flow down-river to Augusta. Anderson in 1840 was ninth among 29 counties in the state, but—eclipsed in part by counties that had railroad freight service—fell to twenty-second in 1850. Pickens and Oconee, twenty-fifth in pounds of cotton gathered that year, dropped to twenty-seventh in 1850. Over 25 percent of Oconee and Pickens farmers grew cotton in 1850, but their average of four bales each indicates a small-scale operation. More than three-quarters of Anderson's farmers raised cotton, but they also just exceeded four bales each.[33]

Too little is known about local agriculture to attribute larger late-antebellum slaveholdings to the need for cotton hands. But sizes of slaveholdings and growth of cotton both expanded during the same period. Virtually all farmers who produced at least ten bales of cotton in 1850 owned slaves and included almost all owners with thirty or more slaves. With variations these farmers had about one bale of cotton per slave, indicating, for them at least, a close correlation. Smaller-scale production centered on farmers who owned few or no slaves.

Although cotton grew in varied conditions—terrain, climate, and soil—sizable areas of Oconee and Pickens had virtually no cotton. Sheep raising often occurred in these areas—presumably both cooler and more hilly—of little cotton. Anderson's 1568 cotton producers that same year totaled 80 percent of farmers, but only 147 had ten or more bales. Again, there was an approximate match between slaveholdings and bales; for example, Joseph Taylor with 56 slaves produced 50 bales, while John B. Sloan had 25 slaves and 25 bales. Many nonowners grew cotton, using their own labor and perhaps that of hired hands or tenants. Cotton was a demanding crop that required much backbreaking labor, requiring constant attention to "the preparation, the culture, and the gathering of it."[34]

Shipping cotton to Columbia, Augusta, or Charleston was an endeavor feasible only for merchants or wealthier planters. Transportation clearly was a key factor. Since fertile land typically lay along navigable rivers with their own landings, larger slaveholdings often converged with river access, advantages in transportation as well as scale of operation. Typically slaves helped transport cotton down the river. They would have spent some time at Hamburg or Augusta before their return. Buying whiskey in Augusta, slaves Lige and Jerry likely accompanied their owners there.[35]

Like other crops, cotton fared better in some years, worse during drought or flood. Calhoun in 1830 reported having made 60 bales of cotton, 300 pounds each, from 92 acres including 15 acres "inferior & of a bad stand." He also had a surplus beyond plantation needs of 500–1000 bushels of corn, which he could sell. But a year later Calhoun suffered major losses at both his Abbeville plantation and Fort Hill, "which is literally every thing, except about 50 acres of cotton, [which] renders it a calamitous year for me." Yearly fluctuations occurred in weather and the resulting yield: in 1837 Calhoun produced 65,000 pounds of cotton, 75,000 in 1842, but 53,000 in 1844. Families such as the Calhouns who owned lands in several areas—Pickens, Abbeville and Alabama—might have a successful crop on one plantation when another suffered from unfavorable weather. Few farmers had this advantage.[36]

Cotton, rice, and tobacco mostly were mutually exclusive as major crops for any given plantation. Tobacco, an early Pendleton District cash crop, did not dominate the area's economy. Some slaves with earlier experience growing tobacco in Virginia or parts of North Carolina may have contributed to the crop's success. Buyers during the 1790s occasionally paid for land or slaves with tobacco. Upcountry cotton, which would replace tobacco as the primary export to the coast and abroad, was late taking hold in Pendleton District. Tobacco continued to be important until the Civil War, although it appears in few contemporary area records or correspondence. Oconee and Pickens produced 40 percent of the state's total crop in 1850.[37]

Anderson produced more rice in 1850 than did any other county beyond four coastal ones. Sixty-eight farmers—or probably their slaves—raised 956,940 pounds.[38] Like tobacco, only the largest producers relied primarily on slaves for rice; more than half of all Pickens farmers growing rice had no slaves, and another ten percent had fewer than five. Some slaves raised their own, as J. D. Ashmore noted in his journal "one hand Hoeing negro Rice" on May 18, 1856. Local production virtually disappeared by 1870.

Overseers, Planters, and Working Owners

Many types of people—slave men, women, and children; hired white and black laborers; overseers; and, on most plantations, the white family as well—undertook plantation chores. Averaging eight slaves in 1850, most owners would have had no more than two or three adult hands; even a holding of twenty might include only five males over the age of sixteen. A glance at total ownership obscures large numbers of children and elderly who did limited work. Rather, all but wealthier owners and full-time professionals would have been working in the fields and supervising overall work. Small-scale owners, such as Taylor and Harris, periodically hired white laborers to help during planting or harvesting seasons. If not employing an overseer, owners of middle-sized holdings, perhaps twenty to forty slaves, sometimes used slaves as managers: "Thomas R. Brackenridge says that he gave Willis authority to make the negroes work and to whip the small ones if they did not work," similar to Robert Guyton's "my man Isaac be allowed a reasonable share of direction and management of my farm."[39]

Given the generally accepted definition of a planter as someone with twenty or more slaves, only 8 percent to 10 percent of the area's 1850 owners qualified. Even then some of them would have participated in farming work themselves. Although employing an overseer, Calhoun thrived on personal involvement.[40] Scanty information available suggests that only holdings of roughly thirty or more slaves would regularly have had overseers, as also did smaller holdings belonging to widows and professional men whose daily work was removed from their farms.

Overseers are a virtually invisible component of the area's history. There are hardly any plantation accounts, and only a few overseers are specifically named in the census, which does not state employers' names. Other records supply information for a few men, including those employed by John C. Calhoun, nephew H. D. Colhoun, and the Kilpatrick estate. Each of their overseers lasted only a few years at most, soon to be replaced by another one. No will in any of the three counties mentioned a faithful overseer.

Failing to manage slaves properly—that is, efficiently and humanely, a tricky combination—often caused an overseer's dismissal. John E. Colhoun (Sr.) frequently changed his lowcountry managers, and son-in-law John C. Calhoun followed that pattern, but his correspondence chronicled further overseer malfeasance. Overseers typically got an annual salary, use of a house, and specific quantities of meat, grain, and often sugar and coffee. Careful owners inventoried all tools, livestock, slaves, and stocks of foodstuffs, as Colhoun did in 1797, to prevent plundering by overseers.[41]

Other Slave Labor on Plantations and in Towns

Plantation work required not only field hands. Larger holdings included a blacksmith, several carpenters, perhaps a miller, and a stone mason or bricklayer, who often would have done field work also, along with men and boys assigned to tend the livestock (herders) and horses (ostlers). Samuel Maverick's 1853 estate sale bill listed thirty-seven slaves, of whom half were fifteen years of age or younger. His adult males included one blacksmith, one bricklayer, three carpenters, and four field hands. Owners loaned their slaves' labor. Adult brothers, sons and fathers, or neighbors undertook harvesting or other farm work together, helping one another during busy seasons and sharing both machinery and slaves. The Kilpatricks and the Colhouns periodically hired hands for a few days during busy harvesting seasons. Sharing or hiring occurred especially when slaves had specialized skills. Although grain had to be milled, relatively few plantations could afford their own facilities. Rather, they took grain to commercial mills, about fifteen each in Anderson, Oconee, and Pickens. Some mills on plantations, such as Kilpatrick's or J. P. Bearden's,

Charcoal drawing of Patsy, a cook, commissioned by her owners. Black Heritage in the Upper Piedmont

would have utilized skilled slave labor. Other occupations included a carriage driver and, inside the house, a valet and butler, found only on larger plantations or in towns.[42]

Household positions included most importantly a cook, the only female listed by occupation in Maverick's appraisal. Another Pendleton village family so highly regarded their cook that they had a charcoal drawing made of her, which the white family kept for more than a hundred years and then gave to the cook's descendants. Other girls and women served as laundresses, one or more housemaids, and a lady's maid. Wealthier plantations had a real specialist, a pastry cook. Because most antebellum sources come from men, agricultural labor is recorded in more detail than is household work. Chapter 10 explores provision of clothing and medical care, tasks typically undertaken by women and shared by black and white.

Women worked in the fields, too. An 1819 advertisement seeking a buyer for a slave couple with three children specified that the man was a good field hand and his wife "an excellent cook and has been accustomed to washing and working in the field." J. D. Ashmore noted on January 1, 1857, "Amritta & Bella attending to hog guts and offal," while on March 24 Amritta was "dropping corn."[43]

Enslaved people worked at skilled crafts beyond the plantation. Four blacksmiths in Pickens County had collectively thirty-three slaves, including children and house servants; some must, however, have worked in shops. White blacksmiths probably took on apprentices from owners who wanted their slaves trained. Towns such as Anderson and Pendleton had blacksmith shops, among them J. J. Acker's, where his slave Perry worked, and Perry's father-in-law Charles was a blacksmith for A. M. Smith. The presence of three free men of color as shoemakers in 1850 Anderson households along with white shoemakers illustrates cross-racial skilled work, which likely applied to blacksmiths also. Slave labor for railroads included blacksmithing. Slaves helped build Greenville's Episcopal church; bricks in its steeple show handprints of small children who pressed the bricks into molds.[44]

Slaves and occasionally free persons of color worked at small-scale factories. Both a gun factory and a powder mill were among early manufacturing enterprises, and the Lawrences utilized slave labor in their timber business, just north of the Colhoun plantation. Quarrying, done in Pickens County, likely involved slave labor also. Pickens and Oconee in 1840 ranked fifth in tanneries and fourth in sides of leather tanned; and the two counties milled lumber worth $16,175. John B. Sitton, using slave labor, produced fancy carriages in Pendleton, as did others elsewhere in Anderson County.

Textiles probably absorbed black and white labor. John Ewing Colhoun (Jr.) opened a textile mill for woolens and cottons in 1829, and soon added a tailoring shop. The *Pendleton Messenger* editorialized that "if slaves can be made to perform the labour of a manufactory"—implying that Colhoun was attempting to do that—"there can be no doubt whatever that they may be employed to more advantage in this way than in the culture of cotton."[45] In 1840 Pickens and Oconee had the state's most expensive woolen manufacturing plant, supplied by heavy sheep production, and Anderson's one cotton manufacturer—Pendleton Manufacturing Company established at Autun in 1838—produced enough to rank fifteenth in the state.

Despite small numbers of whites and slaves in specialized crafts and skills, agriculture clearly dominated the area, their work, and their lives. A typical plantation schedule usually included a break for black and white alike, with Saturday afternoons and Sundays off—though presumably not during peak harvesting or before expected heavy rains or other adverse weather. Generally slaves got off the week between Christmas and New Year's; even federal military officials in December 1865 commented on the forthcoming traditional holiday week. Postbellum freed people, tied almost as much to the soil as slaves had been, continued this pattern of year-end holidays. Celebrations and other areas of plantation life including food, medical care, and housing appear in chapter 10.

THREE

The Puzzling Free Persons of Color

AFRICAN AMERICANS free before the Civil War have been a puzzle in many ways, first to that era's white population and more recently to descendants and researchers.[1] Calling them "a World of Shadow," Marina Wikramanayake characterized their ambiguous status, neither slave, as were most African Americans in the South, nor completely free, as were whites. At times their legal standing—which was imposed on them—resembled that of enslaved blacks, at others that of free whites. They did not fit neatly into a simply described "white and slave" society. Their status and accomplishments threatened whites while also demonstrating to slaves the advantages of freedom. Holding such an ambivalent position, especially as a minority within a minority, these free people were often harassed. Ability to move between white and slave "worlds" made them particularly vulnerable.

Free people of color are shadowy also in documentary records.[2] Censuses prior to 1850 listed by name only those few who headed households. Of Pendleton District's sixty-eight FPC in 1800, that year's census named only ten. Other legal papers provide few additional names since many FPC did not own land or have probate records. Even the legal term "free person of color" might refer to a very black emancipated African American, a mulatto born of a white woman and a black man, people of Native American ancestry, and other combinations as well. People designated as free persons of color not only held an important if anomalous role in antebellum society but also shed light on its complicated relationships and pressures. Repression of FPC often reflected white fears and signaled tighter controls on slaves.

The Puzzle

Their origins are the most puzzling aspect about Pendleton's free people of color. Four issues lack easy answers: their earlier geographic locations, dates of their arrival, reasons for their free status, and their later life. There is a glaring disconnect between FPC named in the 1800 census, as well as white families housing them, and those by 1830. None of the ten free men in 1800 is found by name in Pendleton's 1810 census. Similarly no white household that included FPC in 1800 had any there ten years later. Many seem to have moved westward. By 1820 or 1830 most FPC evidently stayed in Pendleton District or nearby.

Information about origins, available for only a few individuals, indicates that free people of color followed the same migration pattern as white families, that is Virginia, North Carolina, and other piedmont South Carolina areas. Several Pendleton FPC originated in Virginia. Anthony Coats, first appearing in Pendleton records in 1813, and Betty Oglesby, the oldest of a large free family, were both born around 1780 in Virginia. The mother of the Paytons, a sizable free mulatto family in Anderson County, may also have come from Virginia, as both the Payton name and that of son Richmond have Virginia connotations.[3]

Fewer Pendleton FPC had North Caolina birthplaces. They include Caesar, emancipated by Thomas Winslow of Randolph County, N.C. (probably late 1700s); Henrietta Williams, born 1805; and Warren Wilson, 1835. Others came from Georgia. Ezekiel Hudnal established in an 1806 Pendleton deed that he previously freed "Negro woman Bridget Waters and her five children," by act of Georgia's assembly, and then deeded them land in Pendleton District, where they were living with Hudnal in 1810. Polly Allen, born 1794, and Mary Allen, born 1800, are listed as born in Georgia; Hill O'Neal was born around 1825 in either Georgia or North Carolina.[4]

All of these data raise as many questions as they answer. No information shows when the free persons of color arrived, previous owners, or dates of emancipation. Several people, notably Warren Wilson from North Carolina and Hill O'Neal from Georgia, came into South Carolina after 1820 when it was illegal for FPC to do so. Names of only two previous owners, Winslow and Hudnal, appear in these materials. But Caesar's surname is missing, and Hudnal's freed Waters family returned to Franklin County, Georgia. So those two named emancipators do not help us understand broader issues. Records are murky indeed.

Murkiness continues when examining known emancipations in Pendleton District. Between 1795 and 1819 fourteen owners freed fifteen slaves, for whom there is later information on only three. Several of these manumissions involved elderly people who probably did not live many years of freedom or produce any free children, and eleven were men, whose children would be free only if their mother was also free. Today we might assume that a recently emancipated person would wish to move far away. However, friendly whites plus the freed person's relatives may have been in the area and provided reasons to stay. Justice John Belton O'Neall later wrote about free families well accepted in South Carolina communities where they lived for many years. In some cases individuals were so fair complected that determining their status was difficult. O'Neall said that depended in part on long-standing social perceptions and "previous reception into society." In later decades numbers fluctuated substantially among counties as FPC, evidently leaving harassment in some locations, moved to less hostile ones.[5]

Reasons for Emancipations

It may be helpful to consider theoretical reasons for freedom and attempt matches with known cases. The simplest reason for "people of color" to be free was to be born of a "free white woman"—the legal term—or any other free woman, including also those "of color" and of Native American ancestry. These white women included Priscilla Timbers, mother of free mulatto Burdines; Polly Peyden, mother of mulatto Fanny Payton; Levina Sizemore, mother of Fanny Sizemore, both white, although Fanny's children were not; and Mary Jeffries, mother of white Holly Agusta, evidently a similar case. Other white women present at the births swore affidavits, entered as official papers, concerning these mothers. Being born of a free woman guaranteed freedom, which followed the mother's legal condition. Free persons of color were, however, considered "colored." Nothing is known about the black fathers in these families.[6]

Most documented emancipations, proclaimed by the owner's will, would take effect after not only his death but also that of his wife. Three owners who died between 1800 and 1805 each freed only one slave by will, although one man owned ten, the others three each. Robert Dowdle, freeing only Morris by his 1820 will, owned twelve slaves. As with Thomas Jefferson and Sally Hemings's family, Pendleton emancipations by will usually specified one or a few out of a larger holding.

Pendleton deeds and wills include few emancipations or affidavits about white mothers, even though free persons of color had to be able to prove their free status or risk being sold into slavery. A slave in 1856 stole Wade Dennis's free pass, not known to have been issued in Pendleton. Others in Pendleton may have been freed elsewhere, as were Hudnal's six, and have carried papers from those jurisdictions.[7] Freeing slaves by one's will provided no absolute guarantee that heirs would comply. In most Pendleton District cases there is no subsequent proof that emancipation did occur.

William Hallum, who owned ten slaves, provided by his 1803 will freedom only for Peter, inherited from Hallum's father a decade earlier. Having a strong affinity for Peter, Hallum bequeathed him land and money as well as freedom. Hallum may have feared for Peter, giving him a gun also. Although this will, like several others, specified that Peter would not be freed until the widow's death, she emancipated him in 1804 and described him as having been "a good slave and . . . behaved as well as any of his colour." Hallum's apprehensions were fulfilled, as other heirs, contesting the will, said that a black man could not own land, which Pendleton Judge John Harris confirmed in 1827. White heirs then successfully seized that land for themselves. Nothing further is known about Peter.[8]

Emancipation by will may have benefited those who were the owner's children by a female slave; the man who freed "Sall of yellow complexion" may well fall into this category. Or it may have rewarded "long honest and faithful service," as the state legislature periodically did, and as Thomas Farrar did in 1819 for Harry Farrar, then sixty or sixty-five years old.[9]

Owners who had no other motivation for emancipating slaves might sell them freedom in exchange for money. Although his reasons are unknown, Ellis Harlin did that in 1804 for James (one of three slaves), who paid three hundred dollars, probably the going rate. Around 1813 Ruth Oglesby, a free woman, bought her husband Peter Johnson from William Morris. She left a clear legal account that Johnson provided his own money, and she deposited both her bill of sale and proof of Johnson's money with another white man for safekeeping. Although there is extensive information on the Oglesbys, nothing further is known about Peter Johnson—yet another puzzling episode.[10]

Still further motivation for manumission derived from religious or moral opposition to slavery. Antislavery sentiments, flourishing during the late eighteenth century, were expressed forcefully by Methodists, Quakers, and northern delegates to the constitutional convention. No widespread antislavery religious attitudes have been discovered in Pendleton District. Quakers were then in Greenville and elsewhere in the state, and their views may have had some impact. But the Methodist Church retreated on its antislavery posture. One Pendleton Presbyterian minister publicly expressed antislavery views in 1795, for which he was nearly not ordained.[11]

Antislavery religious sentiments especially affected Virginia. Freeing many slaves who fought in the Revolutionary War, Virginia in 1790 had over twelve thousand free persons of color, the largest number in the country, more than even Pennsylvania, which abolished slavery. Virginia, later unhappy about their growing free black population, passed laws restricting them, which spurred many FPC departures—likely many of Pendleton District's sixty-eight free people in 1800 were part of this out-migration.[12]

Short of expressed religious conditions, some owners may have freed slaves for humane reasons or as gratitude. Both General Andrew Pickens and Colonel Robert Anderson—two of Pendleton District's largest slave owners, Revolutionary War heroes, and founders of Hopewell Presbyterian Church—made special provisions for their slaves. Pickens wrote that because my "negroes . . . have been a means under Providence to procure many of the comforts of life which myself and others have enjoyed, I request that they might be used with justice and humanity." Should Pickens's son not survive to adulthood, his executors should free nine specified slaves among his 35 and provide them with 150 acres, work horses, plows, tools, livestock, and a spinning wheel. As it happened the occasion did not arise; even if they were not freed, Pickens still urged "that comfortable warm clothing may be had at all times for the negroes."[13]

Legal Standing

The legal status of free persons of color, like the rest of their lives, was complicated, and they were neither completely free nor slaves. FPC could legally learn to read and write. Evidently no law prohibited them from owning guns, as William Hallum left one to Peter and in 1867 Cato Hallum owned one. FPC could own land, could—and sometimes did—own slaves, have wills and direct disposition of their property, and initiate law suits. And they paid taxes. South Carolina beginning in

1756 levied a special annual capitation tax that amounted to two dollars per year in the 1800s on each FPC between the ages of fifteen and fifty.[14]

FPC were free to travel throughout the state, although they had to be able to prove their free status. So far, then, their legal standing, although substantially inferior to that of white people, was significantly better than that of slaves. On the other hand, free people of color were subject to many of the same laws and punishments as slaves and were tried before the same magistrate and freeholder courts, which provided fewer legal safeguards than did those for whites. Moreover, free people of color were hauled before these courts disproportionately often as a means of harassment and control, and they had no owner to protect them.

Legal restrictions on FPC changed over time and often reflected what whites perceived as threats to their "public order." In 1820 a law forbade both future emancipations except those specifically approved by the legislature and permitted no further FPC immigration into the state. Soon, Denmark Vesey's 1822 revolt in Charleston had repercussions for free people of color. Because he was free, the legislature clamped down on other FPC. "An Act for the Better Regulation and Government of Free Negroes and Persons of Color" in 1822 required adult FPC males to have as sponsors respectable freeholders of the district. Although they were called guardians and helped to protect their free wards legally and practically, these men also served the public order.[15]

Long-standing connections existed between some whites and FPC. Several white families—among them Ackers, Kirkseys, and Terrells—served as guardians for many years, sometimes over two or three generations. Some FPC and nearby white families shared a surname. Three of ten FPC households in 1800 had the same surnames as nearby white families with other free people of color in their households. Moreover, extended white families, sometimes in several counties, maintained long associations with FPC. These could be found in Greenville, Laurens, and Abbeville, and also adjacent Elbert, Franklin, and Hart counties in Georgia. Abbeville and Pickens FPC lived with white Cannons, and white Douthets were associated with Anderson and Greenville FPC. Several ministers in Greenville, Abbeville, and Anderson, Oconee, and Pickens counties housed FPC in their residences.

Free people of color, occupying a legal status between free whites and slaves, served as intermediaries between those two worlds. At least five extended FPC families—Sizemores, Hallums, Arters, Burdines, and Paytons—had relatives who were slaves and others who were whites, sometimes on the same plantation. Other than 1820 census listings, FPC Burdines' first appearance in Pendleton records comes from their being charged in 1825 for "trading with a Negro slave for stolen property."[16] Magistrates and freeholders courts cited Arters and Burdines for entertaining slaves who shared or bought liquor. There were many opportunities to pass information, even letters, and gifts. And free people of color may have taught some slaves to read and write.

Jackson Arter, four other free Arters, two other FPC (otherwise unknown), and four slaves got into trouble in 1845. J. J. Hunt and S. A. Major on patrol at FPC Simon Cannon's house were "correcting"—whipping, probably—free Clint Arter for what they called his threats and impudence; an unnamed slave stopped them and said they would not mistreat his brother Clint. Their charges were "unlawful assemblage rioting drinking quarrelling & fighting"—and, for two of them, intent to kill—on the Sabbath among "free negroes & slaves." Twenty or more people present included FPC, slaves, and one or more white men. Lemuel Arter and Wesley Arter, the only two convicted, each received twenty lashes. A year later the state charged both patrollers with three counts each of assault and battery; they were found guilty on one count. This is the only case found in the three counties in which white men were convicted of assaulting FPC or slaves.[17]

Two free women of color living in the same area, Polly Burdine and Eleanor Waters, faced similar charges for selling liquor on the Sabbath to FPC, slaves, and whites—fifteen to twenty people were present—at that "riotous assembly." Polly Burdine pleaded guilty and received 12 lashes; Eleanor Waters was acquitted due to lack of evidence. The Arters managed to stay out of the courts for over a decade until 1857, when trouble occurred with patrol officers.

More peacefully, FPC could legally own property, borrow money, as some did, and make loans. Most FPC families managed to accumulate some property. The majority of FPC farmers in 1850 reported land worth one hundred to six hundred dollars, while Jesse Oglesby in 1860 listed mining property worth eighteen hundred dollars. Transactions by FPC appear in several white estate accounts, and FPC were sometimes sued for defaults on debts or taxes.[18] The Pickens Court of Commons Pleas in 1850 and 1851 alone received suits against free Gabriel Shumate, Peter Reid, and Olly Burden. But FPC could also sue whites, as Betsey Burdine did in 1855 against Alvin Jenkins for fourteen dollars, and Polly Allen against John S. Dickson for trespass.

The Paytons reached a sufficiently prosperous standing, thanks to their role in the brick industry, for Amaziah to claim payments due from dozens of white families. In unusual legal proceedings instituted by a free man of color, he sued in 1860 to recover substantial loans—hundreds of dollars—from two Anderson County white men who defaulted. Payton himself owed $415 in three separate notes to J. B. Benson, while his brothers Zachariah and Richmond owed smaller amounts totaling under $100.

A few free people of color owned slaves. Evidently only one, Daniel Burdine, did so before 1850, with one young female slave in 1820. FPC masters in 1850 included Lydia Holly with two; Lucinda Holly, one; and Anthony Coats with a 30-year-old female. Anderson mulatto town barber Benjamin Roberts in 1860 owned twenty-five hundred dollars' worth of personal property, including two slaves. Some or all of these slaves may have been relatives. Strangely Caesar bought his own brother and held him as a slave while he was himself still legally Robert Maxwell's slave but de facto free.[19]

Occupations and Color

Occupations for free people of color varied depending on gender and location, whether rural or town. Outside of a few small towns or villages virtually all free families pursued agricultural work. Twenty-nine free families for 1850 or 1860 stated "farming" or "farmer" as their occupation, and four others, "farm laborer." Additionally, younger members of these households and three free men living with whites were farm laborers. Both men and women were "farmers," and some older women who reported no occupation had farmer sons living with them.

Skilled craftsmen held an important niche not only among FPC but also in town life. Often they practiced skills critical to town endeavors, especially since area towns were small and each supported only a few craftsmen. Four towns and rural areas together had five shoemakers, four bricklayers, three carpenters, and two mechanics. For some skills there was only one each: barber, blacksmith, cooper, currier, miner, tailor, and tanner.[20]

These twenty-one men were not all heads of households. Fanny Payton's family accounted for four bricklayers and one carpenter. Although this list is broader than farming roles, adjacent Abbeville and Greenville counties offered further options for FPC, and even more were available in Charleston, Columbia, and cities such as Alexandria, Richmond, and Baltimore. Alfred (Forch) Allen (Oconee) was the only FPC railroad worker in Anderson, Oconee, Pickens, Abbeville, or Greenville. Charleston's three thousand free people had a wide range of occupations and dominated some of them.[21] Labor brought FPC into some white households. In several rural households a single free man of color worked as farm laborer for the white family. Urban work linked skilled craftspeople, such as FPC Henry Holdman, a twenty-one-year-old shoemaker in Anderson living with S. T. Horn, a white shoemaker.

The few free women of color who varied from agricultural work had traditional, gender-defined skills. They were two mantua makers in one household, evidently sisters; one servant, probably for the white family with whom she resided; and another servant in a Walhalla hotel. A ninety-five-year-old woman lived in Anderson's county poor house. The only additional occupations for free FPC women found in Abbeville and Greenville were also gender-stereotyped: laundresses, seamstresses, and a tailoress.

Free families with no stated work are more intriguing than these occupations. Five Oglesby households with twelve people and a neighboring, allied Allen household with six people had no stated occupations in 1850. One Oglesby household's blacksmith and four male farmers (aged nineteen to twenty-five) could hardly have supported all of the others. The census ignores, however, Jesse Oglesby's mining property, which may have yielded income. Four related, adjacent Anderson households, Strothers and Gwinns, had among their seventeen people only two, farmers, indicating income-producing work.

Many households, as listed in the census, were headed by females, lacked a resident husband, but often included other people without any clear source of income. Only 29 percent of FPC lived in 1850 Pickens and Oconee households where both parents were present, while 40 percent in Anderson did so. There are only a few local documented cases of FPC's slave relatives, but others likely existed. Since a substantial percentage of free people of color were mulattos, they clearly had white relatives also. Specific numbers of mulattos appear for the first time in the 1850 and 1860 census, when each free individual is named and described by age, gender, and color.

Distinctions between free mulattos and blacks, as designated in the census, seem to have had little significance regarding occupations in the area, although they did in Charleston. But color did matter concerning their place in the overall population. Mulattos constituted only 5 percent of Pickens's and Oconee's slaves but 57 percent of FPC there; similar figures also applied to Anderson. Mulattos were even more likely than that to be free, as 21 percent of all Oconee and Pickens mulattos in 1850 were free, compared to only 1.5 percent of blacks. Mulattos and blacks varied by age distribution also.[22]

Very light FPC could pass as whites, especially when they traveled to other towns. Some FPC missing from local censuses in specific years may have done exactly that. A Sizemore relative said: "The whites can't tell. They are the biggest fools in the world when it comes down to color of negroes. There've been a lots of light negroes they thought were white. I knew the difference and they didn't." Some whites, mulattos, and blacks believed that "the mulattos wouldn't even marry the blacks," and the son of white William Sizemore, who married a mulatto, "didn't care too much about dark complexioned people." A scandal occurred in that family when "the middle girl ran away and married my uncle, . . . dark complexioned." Further, the Sizemores "with all that blood mix up there . . . they only wanted certain people marrying into their family. . . . Each one of my aunties, like my mother, was real light. All her sisters, each one married a man as black as soot. . . . It actually made a difference between the light children and the dark ones."[23] Color—whether mulatto or black—sometimes had important implications.

Changing Locations and Surnames

Tracking FPC is complicated not only by sparse information but also by their moving from one county to another. Charting free African Americans by county since 1790 shows significant population fluctuations. Local repression seems to have led to widespread departure from some counties into more favorable ones.[24]

Relocations into Anderson and Pickens counties sprang from other motivations. Many families lived near county boundaries, as did Arters and Burdines in both Greenville and Pickens, and moved back and forth. Five of 1860 Abbeville's free families of color lived in Anderson County ten years later. They included Valentines, probably part of an extended family that lived in Abbeville, Oconee, Anderson, and Greenville. Not only did locations change, but so did some surnames.

Greenville FPC listed as Lovelands in 1850 appeared as Arters in 1860. And a Pickens family, entered as Borin in 1850 and 1860, have the Hallum surname in the 1870 census, as do descendants today.

African Americans connected with the white Hallum family provide a final mystery. Peter's abortive emancipation by owner William Hallum's 1803 will anticipated subsequent curiosities. Much later a Freedmen's Bureau officer in 1866 described Cato Hallum as an elderly man who was born free, but in another context said he bought his freedom. Cato Hallum is not in the 1850 or 1860 censuses, however. And there is no reference to his emancipation.[25]

Hallums included in their households FPC for whom there is no prior evidence of freedom. Four FPC lived with white Richard Hallum in 1830, and eight with white Benjamin Hallum in 1840. These households may have included Cato, his wife, and most likely Mary Ann Borin's family. Mary Ann's daughter Mary married Cary Pickens, Jemima's grandson. Their descendants acknowledge physical traits derived from their white ancestry. Despite these visible inheritances, they have not yet retrieved the names of their specific white ancestors from the shadows.[26]

The Puzzle Continues

For a researcher or for Sizemore and Hallum descendants, free people of color fulfill their "world in shadow" description. It is hard to shed sufficient light into these corners to understand FPC collectively as fully as desired, let alone compile accurate genealogies and family histories. For some FPC many, if not enough, details are available; for others even their names are unknown. On some bases FPC should not be nearly so elusive. They occupied a highly conspicuous, if anomalous, role in society. Disproportionately more skilled than the overall white population, they were excluded from professions. Perhaps to emphasize their status, they had personal names drawn mostly from those commonly used by whites rather than African-based choices or classical names imposed on slaves. To paraphrase a title, there were no Cuffees, Neros, Minervas, or Napoleons among area free persons of color.

They occupied an odd niche in the antebellum world, one which at times seemed threatening to whites. Details as rich as those that *No Chariot Let Down* provides for the Charleston area are lacking for the upstate. Clearly, however, many FPC lived near and interacted with slaves, which alarmed whites all the more. FPC moved freely among whites, other FPC, Native Americans, and slaves, while power-holders wanted to demarcate these groups into separated spheres. Some FPC included all of those elements in their own families. Several Sizemores and related families had cross-racial marriages, including "all . . . three bloods. White, Indian, and black blood. . . . My grandmother wore her hair in Indian style and on the grandfather's side, the Griffins, he had red hair and blue eyes." Some free people of color lived in an eastern Pickens County area where racial lines became blurred on various occasions. Perhaps fifteen "white" families, some of them prominent, in that section may have had black offspring, mostly unacknowledged publicly.[27]

FOUR

Those Who Were Free Persons of Color

LOOKING AT SEVERAL specific individuals and three families may help to better understand complex roles of free people of color, especially their relationships with whites, sometimes Native Americans, and slaves.

Early Free Persons of Color

Anthony Coats is the earliest free person of color for whom there is any substantial information. Born ca. 1780 in Virginia, he probably was the one FPC living there with John Coats in Chesterfield County in 1810. Both of Anthony's parents may have been African American as the 1850 and 1860 censuses describe him as black, not always a reliable guide. By 1813 he began to acquire land in Pendleton District, making two purchases that year of adjacent tracts totaling 140 acres for $270, and in 1819 another 52 acres for $150, thus spending $420 in seven years. Coats headed an 1820 household with two other FPC, perhaps relatives. He joined Mount Pisgah Baptist Church in the early 1820s; there he and FPC Toney were cited in 1825 for reasons not stated in the minutes.

Coats appears in varied legal records during the next forty years. Although he bought another 48 acres adjoining his land in 1829, he is not named in the 1830 census, but listed regularly among free blacks paying taxes in Anderson County. Charged before the Pickens magistrates and freeholders court in 1836 for stealing, he was found not guilty. Six years later he filed a civil suit against W. Roberson for $183.79.

Coats, described as a farmer, lived alone in 1840, but two free men of color, laborers Robert Wadsworth (age thirty) and Levi Wadsworth (twenty-four), shared his 1850 household. Polly Coats, fifty years old and residing with him in 1860, corresponds to the age of his slave in 1840. Although she could not have been legally freed, censuses included a number of people who seem to have been free de facto, if not de jure, on no consistent basis. Polly may have died or moved in the 1860s. When Coats died in early 1869, he willed his land to Mary Smith, saying she tended to him in his failing years.[1]

Jack Baskin's much shorter story has an interesting twist. First appearing by name in the 1820 census, he was a free man between twenty-six and forty-five years old; his own household had two other FPC, a young boy and a woman over forty-five.

At some point Baskin acquired 230 acres; when he died in 1833, he bequeathed 180 to his former master, Robert McKinley Baskin. He also left 50 acres and his other possessions—"one horse, cows, hogs, & other household and kitchen furniture"—to his son Davy, daughter Ginney, and "bound boy Hamilton." His "good friend," J. H. Baskin, evidently white, was executor.[2] Nothing further is known about Davy, Ginney, or Hamilton; they may not have been free. Baskin, as both a personal and a family name, reappeared among African Americans in the 1870 census.

Emancipated by Robert Dowdle's 1820 will after the wife's death in 1825, Morris Dawdle—the name had varied spellings—left a brief account that further illustrates gaps in records. Morris's first census entry, 1840 as Dawdy, shows his own household (Anderson) with three other FPC, perhaps the same ones with him in 1850: Hannah, evidently his wife—although, thirty-seven years younger, she could have been a daughter or granddaughter—and children Harriet, then twelve, and William, ten. J. Vandiver's estate papers mention "Free Morris" buying items in 1847; two years later, a slave robbed Morris's house; and in 1850 he reappears in the census as a farmer with Hannah and the two children. Morris, mentioned as a sexual partner with a white woman in 1856, was not prosecuted. When Morris became ill in 1858, Grief Tate (white) helped tend him until Morris, nearly eighty, soon died from "dropsy of the heart," the coroner ruled. But in 1861 "Free Morris" was a witness for another slave trial in Williamston. Evidently there were two men called Free Morris, usually so mentioned without surname. This account, then, may combine references to both.[3]

All three men—Coats, Baskin, and Dawdle—have abbreviated stories with few relatives identified by name, let alone developed as characters in their own right. They were all connected with white men bearing the same surname. Even these brief accounts are more complete than could be told for most early area FPC. Although their records, naming both Baskin and Dawdle's previous owners, are unusual, they are typical in leaving an incomplete and perplexing documentary trail.

Three families, one for each county, provide deeper understanding of FPC lives. Several generations and collateral branches can be identified for each, and some members were harassed with magistrates and freeholders courts charges or lawsuits. All three had varied combinations of African American (labeled both black and mulatto in the census), European American, and, in two cases, Native American (Cherokee) members. Contrasted to the three men just explored, women headed early generations of these three families: the Oglesbys (Oconee), Sizemores (Pickens), and Paytons (Anderson). All three had descendants who became teachers or ministers in black schools and churches after the Civil War.[4]

The Oglesby Families

The local Oglesby story begins after their arrival in South Carolina. Earlier stages include their free status and arrival in Pendleton District, whose records lack critical and interesting details. Although their surname first appears there in 1813, they evidently arrived during the 1790s. Betty, the oldest of Pendleton District's free Oglesbys, was born in Virginia around 1780; six Oglesbys, all women, were born in South Carolina between 1790 and 1805.

By family tradition "they were always free and of Scotch Irish ancestry." The Oglesby name, that of a Scottish clan, was found in various areas of Virginia. Although Oconee descendants do not link their family specifically to Virginia's Amherst County, Oglesbys and Terrells lived there, as did several other families who moved to Pendleton District. The Oglesbys reportedly passed through the Appalachian region; some came to Pendleton District, others went into Tennessee. While journeying, they came "in regular contact with Native American peoples in this area heavily populated by Cherokee. Some Oglesby offspring were of mixed Native American and Scottish-Irish ancestry which resulted in their later classification as 'Free People of Color'" according to family researchers.[5]

Consistently identified as free people of color in Oconee records, the Oglesbys were described as black or mulatto in 1850 and 1860. One daughter, born circa 1833, was listed as mulatto in 1850, black in 1860, and white in 1870, as was her husband of Cherokee ancestry, a most unusual transition within censuses. Regardless of their background, the white establishment, viewing the Oglesbys as troublesome, charged them with various offenses before magistrates and freeholders courts. Censuses give supplementary details on households and hint at relationships. Citing an earlier birth year for Betty, descendants believe her to be mother of the other Oglesby women. By whatever combination, they formed an extended matriarchal family living near one another. None of the older generation had spouses shown in the census, but Ruth's (b. 1791) husband is documented. She bought Peter Johnson with his own money, then freed him—after which he unfortunately disappears.

The name Oglesby appears rarely prior to the 1830s but frequently thereafter. Old Westminster Baptist rolls include the Oglesbee surname for Prissy, Elizabeth, and Jesse. Sophia, Richard, and Betsey Oglesby—making their surname's first appearance in surviving records for over twenty years—were cited in 1834 for failure to pay taxes. Family connections of these three, not in the 1850 census, are uncertain. The next reference in legal papers, much more unhappily, occurred in 1837. Thomas, Ruth Oglesby's eleven-year-old son, was abducted to Georgia to be sold as a slave. The governor offered a two-hundred-dollar reward for Thomas's return, along with two hundred dollars for the thief's conviction; the boy was restored, the culprit (John Calhoun) was fined one thousand dollars and jailed, and the governor paid the reward.

Oglesby families evidently did not have their own houses prior to 1840. Oconee families who had FPC living with them during those years include the Terrells and Shannons, Shoal Creek Baptists like the Oglesbys; no specific connection is known. The most likely candidate in 1820, based only on geography and number of people, is FPC "Doctor Tom," whose household included thirteen FPC.[6]

Households of four Oglesby women continue the female-focused story in 1840. Together they had a total of twenty-five people, nine of them in agriculture. Several Oglesbys could read or write. Only one of the six Oglesby households in 1850 has any occupation or source of income indicated. The 1860 listings include five households headed by Oglesby women, three by the older generation, Ruth (sixty), Margaret (fifty-five), and Milly (fifty-four), and two by younger women. Jesse Oglesby headed the only other family household, which included three siblings. Two of them farmed while he mined, presumably near Tunnel Hill. Collectively the six households had thirty-seven members.

Legal processes demanded family attention, starting with efforts to recover Tom in 1837–39, followed by other problems and obligations. William C. Lee became guardian in 1844 for Dennis and Joberry Oglesby, and a few years later for Andrew and Tom. P. L. Howard, William Dickson, and Asa Leathers also served as guardians.[7]

The 1850s began and ended for the Oglesbys with trials and pain. In January 1850 an argument began between slave Parris (Thomas Alexander's) and Rachel Oglesby. Parris, who lost fifteen dollars at J. W. L. Cary's house, claimed that Rachel Oglesby and slave Tom (W. L. Keith's) stole his money. Parris began choking Rachel, whose yells scared her mother, Milly. Rachel ran into a white neighbor's house for help. Parris followed her, despite his owner's efforts to restrain him; Parris then hit Milly. Tried, he was found guilty and sentenced to twenty-five lashes. A countersuit—filed the next day and instigated by Cary against Betty (evidently the grandmother), Margaret, and Rachel Oglesby—charged them with larceny. A magistrates and freeholders court found Rachel guilty of theft, evidenced by her surrendering some money to Parris in the meantime. The other two women were judged not guilty. Muddled and abbreviated testimony suggests that both Cary and Alexander were involved in the fracas and were partly at fault. W. K. Easley, a young attorney, represented the Oglesbys, but Rachel lost nevertheless.[8]

Both trials seem to be reasonable efforts to solve legally a quarrel that involved physical violence and theft by several parties. But ten Pickens and Oconee FPC trials during the 1850s far exceeded only two in the 1840s; Anderson likewise had ten in the 1850s. Like slaves, the Oglesbys were buffeted during the 1850s due to conditions beyond their control. Increasing tensions characterized the decade throughout the country.

More trouble followed. Westminster Baptists excluded James Oglesby in 1854 for retailing spirits. Sam Oglesby was accused in 1856 of breaking into Ebenezer Verner's store and stealing fifteen dollars. Found guilty, Sam was fined fifteen dollars and sentenced to 110 lashes, excessive compared to other magistrates and freeholders cases. Still more suits brought Oglesbys before the courts in 1859; five of the twenty-nine cases against FPC over a twenty-five-year span occurred in that one year. Peg, Tom, and Sarah Oglesby allegedly stole Samuel J. Verner's wheat in December 1858 with a slave's help; but Verner only produced his complaint on April 25, 1859, months after the incident. Disposition of this case is unknown.

Verner probably coordinated his action with S. H. Johns, who that same day complained that Sam Oglesby and others broke into his store, stole seventy to eighty dollars, and burned Johns's building.[9] The magistrates and freeholders court found Sam guilty and ordered that he be hanged at the Cross Roads near Bachelor's Retreat, his Oconee community, as whites had a great, long-standing fear of arson. He was the only FPC sentenced to execution in Anderson, Oconee, or Pickens counties, in nearby Spartanburg (for which good records survive), or perhaps, since 1822, in the state. Like most punishments, Oglesby's was clearly intended as a warning to other FPC and slaves to conform to rigid, white-defined standards.

The story, however, is more convoluted. Sam Oglesby, who is not in the 1850 or 1860 censuses for any of the three counties, escaped from jail, then was captured. The judge offered him an alternative to execution—being sold into slavery. Sam managed to escape again, according to the *Keowee Courier*. He, one Samuel Oglesby paying taxes in 1866 and registering to vote in 1867, and a thirty-year-old Sam Oglesby in Oconee's Tugaloo Township in 1870 may all be the same man. What happened to him in the meantime is unknown. The episode reflects intense local tensions and conflicts. The Oglesbys' status must have been a major irritant.[10]

The 1850s were difficult, as Oglesbys were involved in three trials and Sam was sentenced to hang. Elizabeth died in 1852, Priscilla in 1853, and Rachel—under mysterious circumstances—in 1855.[11] Seven Oglesby males listed in the 1850 census are missing in 1860, when they would have been ages fifteen to thirty-seven; they may have sensibly fled the area after Sam's sentence. Oglesbys were victims of their conspicuousness, local conflicts, growing sectional difficulties, and increased white alarm over slaves and their FPC neighbors.

Allens, another free family of color, lived nearby. By family tradition, they descended from early white Allens, one of whom evidently married a Cherokee woman, whose name is unknown. Like the Oglesbys, these Allens were classified as free people of color.

Someone who emerges in shadows from early Pendleton District records is called variously Alphin, Alphane, Alphon, Alphon Ferch, Olphin Ferch, Alphon Force (b. 1785, Ga.), and Olphin—assuming they are all the same man—between 1812 and 1856.[12] He may have actually been called Forch Allen, as an younger man by that name—perhaps a son—later married one of the Oglesbys. Betsy Allen, heading a household with three other FPC in 1820 and six others in 1830, is the first free person to appear clearly as "Allen" in Pendleton records. Family tradition describes Mary (1802), a Georgia-born Allen woman who lived near the Oglesbys, as Betsy Allen's daughter.[13] The marriage, ca. 1848, of Margaret Oglesby's daughter Martha, then about sixteen, to Polly Allen's son Alfred Forch Allen formally linked two families closely associated for decades.

Descendants emphasize Native American ancestry for both Martha Oglesby and Forch Allen. They are the couple who in 1870 would be described as white in the census, as Martha's daughter and grandchildren certainly appeared in early twentieth-century photographs. Forch Allen and some Oglesby men were founding members of Cross Roads Baptist Church, used a hundred years later for family reunions. Forch Allen, according to a great-granddaughter, "lived a typical Indian lifestyle of the time, hunting, fishing, farming, using herbal and Native American medical plants for healing, the knowledge of which he passed down to his son, . . . [who] consequently was called Doc by virtue of his education in the Native American healing and herbal medicine."[14]

Native American ancestry characterized both the Oglesby-Allen families and the Sizemores, who lived about fifty miles away in eastern Pickens County. They shared many common factors, as did the Paytons: numerous and long-standing free people of color; pursuit by magistrates and freeholders courts for Oglesbys and for Sizemore relatives; periodic contacts with slaves; white and Cherokee components of the extended family; and relations with nearby free families. Sizemores, like the Oglesbys/Allens, would have changing racial designations among the censuses.

The Sizemore Families

Trying to understand their ancestry, later Sizemore generations found it puzzling. Several complained to each other of their elders' failure to pass along family history accurately; rather, older relatives tried to hide part of it. When some people, obviously related, would come to visit, "they kept everyone in the dark about how they fit in the family."[15] Sizemores intermarried over time with other free families of color. Each of these families had white, black, and mulatto members, as described in the census and by descendants trying to understand their relationships.

They first enter official records in 1830 when Elisha Sizemore, a free man of color, headed an eastern Pickens County household with six other FPC. Four years later his mother Frances Sizemore swore before a Pickens official that she—a free white woman as the daughter of Levina, also a free white woman—was the mother of Elisha, Richard, Sarah, and others. By 1850 this Sizemore family apparently disappears from the record and another, with no clear relationship, emerges. Another Frances Sisemore (spellings varied) in 1850 was a thirty-seven-year-old white woman in the household headed by Rhoda Duke, then seventy-five.

Dukes, Arters, and other families connect with Sizemores in both censuses and family history. Duke descendants described complexities within their family and further Sizemore connections. Julia Ann Sizemore's mother (Melinda Sizemore in the 1870 census), white, married William Duke, a Native American.[16]

Another man cannot be satisfactorily connected, if in fact he was, with Frances Sizemore's children. White, born around 1822, William Sizemore fought in the Civil War "for whites to keep slaves and he had a house full of black kids," a great-grandson said. Actually Sizemore seems to have fought in the Union army. His wife Martha Arter was a Native; "you could see it from the eyes" of her children according to the family, who called William variously white or a "Black Indian." Their explanation was: "The only people they [FPC] could associate with was plantation owners or another Indian. . . . they would tie up with some plantation owner to better their family, and you see the results now. . . . This places them on the same level as free whites and they didn't mix with slaves. . . . The Arters, Cannons, Arthurs, and Sizemores married offspring from Indians, whites and free born blacks. They were called mulattos."[17] Sizemore's oldest child, born in 1847, along with younger siblings avoided involvement with magistrates and freeholders courts. The entire family, not found in the 1860 census, was listed as mulatto in 1870 and 1880.

Relationships among various Sizemores are confusing not only to someone attempting to deduce them from the census but also to family members trying to disentangle them. "The Sizemore family has always been a mystery to me. I never could figure them out," said one in 1978. "It gets kind of touchy whenever you start to meddling in families' affairs."

Clues to Sizemore family complexities may be found among three adjacent households (nos. 661–663) in the 1850 Pickens census. Simon Sizemore (no. 663) was a thirty-five-year-old white shoemaker with white wife and children and no slaves; he lived next to Sarah Sizemore (no. 662), described as a fifty-two-year-old free black woman (daughter of free white Frances), with Martha, twenty years old and black, and Joberry, three-year-old mulatto—William Sizemore's wife and son; he is missing from the census. Although descendants call Martha an Arter, she is the right age to be Sarah Sizemore's daughter, which would only complicate family relationships further. Possibly Sarah Sizemore and an Arter man, name unknown, were her parents.[18]

They lived next to Simon Cannon, a seventy-five-year-old free man, black, with his wife Mary, a forty-year-old white woman—a Sizemore, according to family history. Simon Cannon owned seven hundred dollars worth of land, and apparently could read, as could his wife. The household included five children: age nineteen, white; seventeen, black; eleven, mulatto; eight, black; and one, black. Nearby was Elijah Cannon (no. 757), white, with twenty-three slaves. The FPC Sizemores lived near and, based on family accounts, intermarried with five other free families of color: the Arters, Cannons, Dukes, Kirkseys, and Ladds. White and FPC Ladds and Arters all resided within the same area.[19]

The Pickens Sizemores are not in church records (scanty for their geographic area) or magistrates and freeholders trials, and only one, Elias, had guardianship papers (1863). Arters showed up in courts periodically, as did Sizemores in Anderson County. While most of the Pickens Sizemores were black or mulatto and a few were white, the opposite situation applied in Anderson County. There in April 1841 whites Henry Sizemore, wife Temperance, and Isaac Sizemore—over seventy years old and perhaps Henry's father—were hauled before a magistrates and freeholders court for vagrancy, as was Thomas Sizemore in 1852. Years later an Anderson court accused an otherwise unknown Sarah Sizemore of trading with Negroes.[20]

Many of the white, black, and mulatto Sizemores—some of them with Native American ancestry as well—in Pickens and Anderson cannot be linked together genealogically and perhaps should not be. Color designations and ages are notoriously inaccurate and inconsistent in the census. Their descendants' perplexity readily becomes apparent. These relationships, which seem ambiguous today, mirror their status in Pickens County. William Sizemore's family and its ties illustrate a complicated world in which they lived and intermarried. Other families of that area, with varied ethnic mixtures, evidently had cross-racial involvements also. There must have been more tolerance there than elsewhere in the area.[21]

The Payton Families

The Paytons, an Anderson County family, had as many opportunities to come before magistrates and freeholders courts as did the Oglesbys and Arters. The Paytons' crimes similarly involved their interaction with slaves. One Payton son, convicted in 1839, was judged responsible, along with a slave, for organizing a "frolic" for slaves from at least twelve plantations. The Paytons' first record as free mulattos was unfortunately as the accused in several 1838, 1839, and 1840 trials.[22]

Frances Payton, called Fanny, was matriarch of this Anderson free family. Born in South Carolina around 1795, she was the daughter of a white woman, Polly Peyden, and a black man, perhaps a slave. Fanny's husband Richmond was a slave, called "a beloved man" of Fenton Hall (Jr.) in First Creek Baptist's November 1834 minutes when he joined. Hall acquired Richmond, then "a young fellow," for seven hundred dollars from his father's estate in 1829. Fanny and Richmond had at least six free children: Joseph, called Joberry (b. ca. 1820; dates vary), Zachariah (1822), Amaziah (1824), Richmond (1826), Narcissa (1835), and Eliza Jane (1839). Several bore names of Hall slaves, who may have been older relatives, perhaps father Richmond's siblings. Rebecca (1828), with whom Fanny was living in 1870, probably was another daughter. Fanny's husband Richmond, not listed in Anderson's 1870 census, may have died in recent years.[23]

Fanny's slave husband, named and recorded over a period of time, sets her apart from all other area free women of color. Frances Payton in the 1840 census headed her own household with six children. Where she lived between 1795 and 1840 is unknown. Fanny and son Richmond, accused in 1838 of assault and battery, then got twenty and ten lashes, respectively, even though the white complainant evidently started the fracas. Two charges levied against Fanny's son Joberry in 1839 resulted in forty lashes for one, the other being dropped. Fanny and husband Richmond got into a fuss, also in 1839, with R. H. Hall (related to Richmond's owner). Variously described in census records as "black" or "mulatto," she was taunted about "Fanny's yellow hide" when she called a woman a "nasty Black bitch" in 1840. This again brought her, husband Richmond, and two sons, charged with various offenses, before a magistrates and freeholders court. Fanny received thirty lashes; the others escaped punishment this time.[24]

Evidently the Paytons bowed to the system. All five cases occurred between 1838 and 1840; afterward they faced no more legal accusations until 1860. During intervening decades they appear primarily as stable and skilled people in the town of Anderson who regularly paid taxes and applied for guardians. Sons Richmond and Amaziah learned to read and write. Amaziah, Joberry, and Richmond became bricklayers; Zachariah was a carpenter. Their wives must have been free women of color whose maiden names and circumstances are unknown. Amaziah apparently was unmarried. Owning a site near the Benson Hotel, the Paytons in 1860 collectively had two thousand dollars of real and thirteen hundred dollars of personal property, some of it tools and a kiln. That same year Amaziah Payton filed suit against two white men who refused court orders to pay him more than six hundred dollars in loans. Found guilty in his absence of selling spiritous liquors, Payton, rather than suffer prescribed whippings, fled to New York. While there, he joined the black Prince Hall Masonic order and likely plied his trade as a brick mason. Returning to Anderson after the Civil War, Payton brought a variety of tools, books, and psalm books.[25]

Postwar years would bring changed circumstances to the Paytons, as well as to other free families of color. Two Paytons died within four years—Amaziah, who was murdered, and Fanny; several attended Freedmen's schools; some taught; and Richmond was a assistant marshal for the 1870 federal census. Some Oglesbys became ministers and deacons; others had problems with the law. The Sizemores acquired more property, then lost it in the twentieth century, and moved three counties to the east.[26]

Collectively these three families show the varied and complex lives of free peoples. Some went to church, most developed trades, acquired prosperity and land, paid taxes, maintained contacts with slaves, and answered varied magistrates and freeholders charges with verdicts ranging from acquittal to many lashes to execution. They lived near and married with other free families. An enslaved relative is clearly stated for both Clint Arter and Fanny Payton; probably other FPC families also had slave relations. Since early 1800s emancipations often favored only one slave, other relatives would have remained locked in slavery. Oglesbys, Sizemores, and Paytons all had whites among their ancestry.

These families, buffeted with pressures and harassment, endured well with stable households and middle-class accomplishments of property, possessions, and skilled crafts. Surely they also shared their values and perhaps the Paytons' literacy skills with some neighboring slaves. They served as beacons of freedom because of white fears about runaways, uprisings, and abolition.

Glimpses

These family accounts dramatize much about lives of free people of color. A few additional, brief sketches, shed more light, or prove darkness. This brevity derives from momentary appearances in documentary records.

Free Hannah made simultaneously her debut and exit in the historical record when Ben (Thomas K. Edwards) murdered her. Hannah, probably one of two unnamed free people in John B. Earle's 1820 household, was discovered to be missing on a December 1825 morning when Jim, another Earle's slave and evidently Hannah's husband, reported her absence. After Major J. T. Earle ordered a search, she was found the next morning drowned in a swamp. Following an inquest and warrant for Ben's arrest, Coroner John T. Lewis called it a "most atrocious murder." Ben was seen in that vicinity with a flask of spirits, found near her body, and his shoes had swamp mud stuck to them. A magistrates and freeholders jury found Ben guilty and ordered him to be hanged—the three counties' only slave executed for killing another African American.[27]

Joseph Clarke paid his 1844 FPC tax in Anderson; this constitutes his solitary appearance. In adjacent Greenville County, James Fordin, who had a guardian appointed in 1853, bought his wife and children, then sold them into slavery for protection—from what, is not known. "Free Dinah" in still another brief story belonged to Hopewell Presbyterian Church as early as 1846; she died still a member there, reportedly one hundred years old, in early 1870. But she does not appear in free listings for 1850 and 1860. Wash's story in Pendleton is equally puzzling. Tried in 1856, he was described as "claiming to be free" from Samuel Maverick, his former owner. When Wash died, aged thirty in 1857, he was buried at St. Paul's Episcopal Church, whose vestry records labeled him a "free man" connected to Maverick.[28]

Emily Elliott (b. 1820), also in Pendleton village, definitely was free, having paid her FPC tax in 1847. She inherited property from white Mary Elliott (1774), grateful to Emily for assistance during Mary's latter years and illnesses. Emily was a "washer woman" who had $600 of real and $200 of personal property in 1860. Emily's daughter Mary Jane (1839) and FPC Daniel Grier (1827) married at St. Paul's in 1855. Daniel was a Williamston bricklayer with $150 of real and $500 of personal property. Her name also is found on an 1864 scrap of tax lists used to record a magistrates and freeholders trial, an especially clear lesson of the fragmentary documentary trail.[29]

The only information about many FPC is a single census listing as heading their own households. Some, among others, include, in 1800, Hugh Brouster, David Barnhill, James White, and Moses Whitley and, in 1810, Moses Redman and Daniel Means. The list could easily continue through later censuses where many more FPC are found only once. Redmans, not among FPC in the 1850 or 1860 census, reappear in 1870 Anderson, Oconee, and Pickens counties.

Families with their own households in 1840 included some now familiar names such as Oglesbys, Burdines, Arters, and Paytons, primarily the reason why we know more about them. Of 1840's free people of color, 43 percent in Anderson and 62 percent in Pickens and Oconee lived in their own households, while the remainder resided with whites. This 1840 configuration contrasts sharply with 1800 when only 16 percent lived independently. For whatever reason, by 1850 most FPC had their own households. Those with exclusively FPC in 1850 accounted for 85 percent (Anderson) to 97 percent (Pickens-Oconee) of total FPC population. Fourteen of twenty-four FPC living with white families were mulatto children. Two adult FPC without a stated occupation each lived with a white family who had long included freed people in their households.

Ten years later fourteen free children of color—all but three mulatto—lived among white families. For both 1850 and 1860 most of these children—typically one per household, though occasionally more—did not share the white surname. That raises more complicated questions about their relationships, if any; they may have been offspring of either white people in those households or of their relatives. Three nearby white Simms households (Anderson) had five FPC with them, four children and one woman of color. And a Methodist clergyman housed a twenty-year-old free mulatto woman and her infant. None of these fourteen mulatto children in 1850 or fourteen black and mulatto children in 1860 living with white families has been located in any other source. Pursuing some FPC in the census is almost literally a game of "Now you see them, now you don't." Out-migration may explain some absences.

PART 2 ↷ *Interactions between Black and White*

Introduction to Part 2

BLACKS, MOST OF WHOM had daily plantation contacts with owners, also encountered white society in other arenas. These included, notably, the legal system that defined slave transgressions and punished them; worship and sanctions at churches; and legal and moral relationships between masters and their human property.

Laws concerning slaves and courts that tried African Americans constituted institutionalized, legalistic controls. Although South Carolina's legal system was far beyond influence by slaves, they tested and sometimes flouted its constraints. Because whites dominated lawmaking, it, as well as slavery itself, constituted structural oppression. An upper tier of wealthy slave owners controlled the law, courts, churches, and the economic system. Each strand of this elaborate linkage reinforced the others.

Churches provided a quite different setting. Many slaves attended along with masters, other whites, and free people of color. In theory, at least, they were all equals before God. There, white and black met on a less unequal footing than at other times. African Americans often exercised their own judgment in joining churches, sometimes one the owner did not belong to. Along with religious and social fellowship came additional control mechanisms. Churches taught obedience to masters and "excluded" (expulsed) those who disobeyed or strayed from religious and moral standards.

Churches—especially as they furnished opportunities for slaves and free people of color to meet, as well as to travel there, often in groups—aided substantially, if unintentionally, in fostering a slave subculture. And the Christianity that slaves absorbed, as experienced within black churches after 1865, became a major cornerstone of postbellum African American culture and community. Antebellum churches also, as it happened, provided some training in discourse, literacy, and leadership for those who would later guide their churches in freedom.

An increase in church exclusions frequently converged with more trials of slaves before civil courts. Both often reflected depressed economic conditions, mostly poor cotton sales, and other societal pressures, as slaves frequently found themselves victims of external circumstances. Church and civil proceedings against slaves frequently paralleled intensified strictures against free persons of color. Various components of antebellum controls converged, with African Americans as their target.

Both legal and religious structures subordinated slaves as did, more fundamentally, their classification as property. Black and white interacted within human and legal dimensions of slaves as chattel. Their treatment as property on the one hand and as human beings on the other further illustrates this society's convoluted and compartmentalized thoughts. In the midst of these interactions African Americans shaped a subculture of their own, as elaborated more fully in part 3.

FIVE

Laws, Courts, and Resistance

WHITES EXCLUSIVELY CONTROLLED South Carolina's antebellum legal apparatus. It totally subordinated slaves to laws and courts, just as they were to their status as property. But personal interactions and humane considerations sometimes modified compliance with laws and even court decisions. Resistance, however, challenged laws and the societal order that whites ordained.

Relations between owners and slaves regarding laws derived from diverse factors. They included, on one side, white fears and resulting oppression; on another, slaves evading the system. Beyond either side, external factors, such as cotton prices and revolts elsewhere, also affected relations. Laws, courts, and their operations reflected varied circumstances that produced fluctuating periods of repression. South Carolina's political leaders and wealthy landowners believed that slaves were necessary to work plantations while fearing their increased numbers. The elite, then, sought more and more legal restrictions to control them. Resistance, demonstrating limitations of existing laws, impelled legislators to pass even more.

Prosecutions and laws mirrored broader societal concerns. Neither new regulations nor frequency of charged offenses followed a constant path. Both flourished when white fears flared over threats to their societal order, notably a 1739 Stono rebellion, Denmark Vesey's revolt in 1822, and Nat Turner's 1831 uprising in Virginia. Economic problems, closely linked to the cotton market, as well as political conflict with the North often found a parallel in many repressive measures against slaves.

South Carolina's earliest legislation about slaves, two decades after the colony's founding, dealt with immediate issues. These included escalating numbers of slaves and, as perceived by the colonial assembly, unruliness—concerns both well treated in Peter Wood's *Black Majority*. White fears about slave opposition, including prospects of revolts and murder, rose along with growing proportions of African Americans, soon a "black majority." Increasingly, officials passed laws to control slaves and to limit their numbers. These controls, honed over decades, shaped the lives of Pendleton District residents.

Unruliness, from a perspective quite different from the legislature's, would be called resistance, a mainstay of scholarly literature during recent decades. Cumulatively, these writings portray slaves not as passive but as people seizing initiatives to oppose slavery through immediate, personal, and local acts such as deliberately breaking a hoe, escaping, or plotting and executing revolts. On a minor level, some resistance involved grumbling. Much later in a vivid, large-scale demonstration, lowcountry enslaved people fled to federal armies and freedom during the Civil War.

A specialized mechanism, magistrates and freeholders courts, handled cases involving African Americans. Although their primary purpose was to deal with crime, as local courts they frequently were involved with conflicts among whites. While local, they still reflected larger societal tensions.[1]

Laws Constraining Slaves, 1690–1820

Anyone without prior knowledge about slavery or South Carolina's legal provisions could reach several conclusions. They seem to be not abstract principles but responses to immediate problems that grew more serious over time and required more complicated approaches to resolve them. Legal provisions also show curious mixtures of preventive and punitive measures, as well as harshness and professed humaneness. These laws, fears underlying them, and convoluted logic would all become part of the means of dealing with slaves.[2] Early laws were modified and broadened over 150 years as new problems and crises required measures to forestall similar acts or revolts in the future. Except for occasional additions, the state's slave code was already well established when Pendleton was founded.

South Carolina's first Act for the Better Ordering of Slaves in 1690 dealt with a wide range of controls. These included requiring passes, establishing a patrol system, searching cabins for weapons and stolen goods, trying and punishing slaves for crimes, and capturing runaways. These provisions had inconsistent application throughout the antebellum era. Ten revisions, additions, and renewals occurred between 1714 and 1751. Already, both 1712 and 1722 acts proclaimed that slaves had "barbarous, wild and savage natures . . . wholly unqualified to be governed by the laws, customs and practices."

Early eighteenth-century laws described the conditions they were meant to correct. Large numbers of slaves not living in Charleston spent Sundays there drinking, quarreling, and fighting, the law said; constables should search for and whip them. These provisions not only forbade certain slave activities but also made owners and public officials responsible for preventing violations. Masters were not to let slaves "do what and go whither they will and work where they please" and were to supervise hired slaves. Both owners and law officials were to search more diligently for weapons and restrict access—complicated since slaves were needed to hunt game and kill vermin. Many slaves had wide latitude in traveling, especially on Sundays, and ready means of transportation, often the use of boats and even horses.

Latitude was a problem; if it led to revolt, that endangered the white establishment. A revolt in 1739, discovered accidentally, sharply escalated white panic. Dozens of slaves west of Charleston, arming themselves with weapons, intended to massacre owners and escape to Spanish settlements in Florida. Named for a nearby river, this

Stono rebellion led quickly to new repressive legislation and shaped white perceptions and fears for generations.

South Carolina's 1740 post-Stono law further forbade slaves from using "mischievous and dangerous weapons, or using or keeping of drums, [or] horns . . . which may call together or give sign or notice." Any owner allowing "public meetings or feastings of strange negroes" could be fined £ 10. Any white person could apprehend and whip slaves presumed to be violating these prohibitions—still applicable in Pendleton District.

These various enactments were clearly meant to restrict slave activities. Yet the legislature also had to contend with their human nature, for both ethical reasons and public safety, a continuing and inherent contradiction. A 1735 act sought to prevent slaves from running away due to inadequate food. Justices could inquire whether they were sufficiently provided for, and, if not, could penalize owners. Five years later a measure fined masters requiring work on Sunday for each violation, excepting "absolute necessity and the necessary occasions of the family." It also proclaimed that "cruelty . . . is odious."

Owners were increasingly called to a higher standard of accountability. "To restrain and prevent barbarity being exercised towards slaves," a master who deliberately murdered one of his own would be fined far more than the slave's value. Slaves were not to be overworked: fifteen hours a day the maximum in summer, fourteen in winter. They must have time for natural rest, this 1740 law said; offending owners would be fined. Laws dealt with varied levels: humane treatment of slaves, activities forbidden to them, punishments for violations, masters' obligations to prevent misdeeds, control mechanisms, and penalties for white negligence. Owners as well as offending slaves were sanctioned. This mixture symbolized the state's complex relationship with slavery.

South Carolina, like other southern states, prevented in 1787 a federal constitutional prohibition against importing slaves. But state officials also worried about high proportions of blacks. Only five years later the state legislature passed its first law to halt importation temporarily, compared to an earlier law making it more expensive. No one could bring a slave from Africa or the West Indies for two years, nor from another state for sale. The only persons who could relocate them into the state were whites settling in South Carolina for at least five years or marrying someone from another state who had slaves. These prohibitions continued through 1803, when a new act allowed most importations, but not males over fifteen years old from other states unless magistrates certified their good character. Excepting legal loopholes and smuggling, the only slaves brought from Africa into South Carolina after 1792 came between 1804 and 1808, as happened in large numbers. However, many others fleeing Haiti reached Charleston in the 1790s.

Wanting new white settlers from other states, South Carolina modified these proscriptions. An 1800 law allowed new residents who owned slaves for at least two years to bring as many as twenty with them, called "importation." Some Pendleton

District owners petitioned the legislature to bring in slaves inherited from Virginia, North Carolina, or Georgia relatives.[3] Suddenly in 1818 the legislature repealed restrictions against arrivals from other states. Birth dates, as reflected in the 1870 census, demonstrate that sizable numbers did arrive throughout remaining antebellum years. Although these laws constituted most of South Carolina's slave code between 1800 and 1865, additional laws virtually eliminated emancipations and forbade teaching slaves to read.

Resistance and Runaways, 1784–1820

White fears, slave behavior regarded as lax, insolent, or dangerous, and revolts affected development of South Carolina's laws. Slaves periodically took matters into their own hands by running away, thus challenging a master's fundamental authority, even if briefly, and by undertaking other acts of resistance. Just as slaves in early years of lowcountry settlement, when the region was still a sparsely populated frontier, attempted flight and murder of owners, so did some counterparts newly arrived in the backcountry. Judged by several standards, resistance during Pendleton's early decades rivaled that of later years. A slave named Barnett was executed in 1787 for "crimes against the property"—likely arson—of Sheriff Robert Maxwell. Slaves that Colhoun brought from the lowcountry attempted in 1798 to poison him so they could escape from the state.[4] Will, who had acquired the poison, was executed; the others were branded and whipped.

At least three more death sentences followed in the next twenty years. Lew (John B. Earle) was executed in 1808 for raping a white woman. Afterward, his head was severed and "stuck on a pole as a terror to other evildoers." Two years later Wiley (James Anderson) hanged himself while in jail for sodomy, and in 1818 Dot (Thomas Adams) was hanged for murdering her own child. The 1820s were an intense decade for slave dissidence, repression, and brutal executions.

Escaping from owners constituted another form of resistance, one considerably safer than attempting murder. Running away was not a capital crime nor even a chargeable offense. Thus it hardly ever entered public enforcement, judicial proceedings, or official records. An owner, however, could punish his runaway, as could any white man apprehending him. Calculating numbers of runaways, then, becomes very difficult; complications of intent and purposes make it even more so.

Advertisements placed by owners seeking their runaway slaves and by local officers about captured runaways provide some details. Newspapers used stock woodcut illustrations to announce rewards. Shortly after Pendleton village in 1807 acquired a newspaper, *Miller's Weekly Messenger* contained a notice about Highter (Billy Thompson), lodged as a runaway in Pendleton's jail. Typical advertisements during the newspaper's first year include "Five Negroes; three of them Africans . . . speak tolerable good English," and two "country-born," fled from Abbeville owner George Brownlee, who offered a reward. Runaways from Abbeville and from Oconee's Shoal Creek area may have been trying to flee the state.[5] When an unknown

Laws, Courts, and Resistance / 79

Runaway advertisement from the *Pendleton Messenger*; note also J. E. Colhoun's "Good Land for Sale." Black Heritage in the Upper Piedmont

runaway was captured, local officers jailed him and placed a newspaper notice. An owner would have to pay costs for the newspaper, of jailing his slave, and of any travel required of a constable or captor.

Few Pendleton District owners placed notices—and if so, usually waited several weeks—expecting to find their slave or for him to be recognized in his home neighborhood. Advertisements and promised rewards incurred cost, which owners would have wished to avoid; published information, then, documents only a small proportion of runaways. Because of strong family ties, very few slaves tried to escape from Pendleton District to another state or even to freedom.

The Tense and Brutal 1820s

The 1820s brought a convergence of Vesey's revolt in Charleston, new laws, a depressed cotton market, and slave dissidence in Pendleton and Greenville Districts, resulting in executions. That decade followed an 1816 insurrection in Camden. There several slaves planned "to raise an army [and seize arms from the magazine] and fight the white people." That created "a state of alarm" statewide. Four years later an appellate court declared that "the Patrol Law . . . ought to be considered as one of the safe guards of the people of South-Carolina, for the protection of their dwellings . . . and as a security against insurrection; a danger of such a nature, that it never can or ought to be lost sight of in the southern states."[6]

Denmark Vesey, a free man of color, plotted along with free and enslaved African Americans an 1822 revolt in Charleston. It aborted when a slave warned officials. Many of the accused were promptly executed. At least one Pendletonian was acutely aware of the uprising, as Secretary of War John C. Calhoun ordered reinforcements to Charleston's garrison. News quickly reached other upper-piedmont whites. Because Vesey was a literate, free man who reputedly laid his plot in Charleston's African Methodist Episcopal (AME) church, the legislature severely restricted future emancipations, and lowcountry officials soon extinguished AME churches there.[7] Vesey's attempted "insurrection," although thwarted, spread fear among whites throughout the state. Numbers of slaves accused of various church offenses soared in 1824, 1825, and 1826; in 1825 churches expelled an unusually large number of free people of color. Four times as many slaves were hauled before magistrates and freeholders courts in the 1825–28 period as in the previous five years.[8]

These societal stresses abounded during a period of sectional strife and economic pressures, a nearly decade-long slump of cotton prices since 1817. Slave owning increased sectional economic conflicts, derived from divergent experiences in agriculture and industry. Calhoun, objecting in 1824 when President John Quincy Adams boasted about national prosperity, complained that the South "was in a state of great depression—never greater." Four years later, Calhoun again described southern plight: "Never was there such universal, and severe pressure on the whole South excepting the portion, which plants sugar. Our staples hardly return the expense of cultivation, and land and Negroes have fallen to the lowest price, and can scarcely be sold at the present depressed prices." For society and especially for African Americans, this combination of economic distress, other societal pressures, and repression against slaves was dangerous, even deadly.[9]

Whether occasioned by increased dissidence, heightened white fears, or both, Pendleton's authorities executed more of its slaves during the 1820s than in any other decade. Executions also seemed to abound in neighboring Greenville and Abbeville. Bob (Alexander Colhoun) was hanged in 1822 in Abbeville for administering poison, and a year later Dave (John Burress) was hanged in Pendleton District. Two December 1825 crimes brought convictions and hangings, Tildy (Archibald Bowman) for murdering Bowman's daughter, and Ben (Thomas Edwards) for murdering Free Hannah.

Executions were staged for maximum display and deterrence—Ben at the forks of a road, Tildy at Brown's muster field. Also in 1825, one of Jeremiah Forester's slaves was convicted and hanged in Greenville for breaking and entering and for stealing from a storehouse. A gruesome story follows.

Greenville's major event in 1825 was its execution of William (Mr. Cokergee), a runaway from Georgia. While hiding in a Greenville barn, William heard someone he thought was about to capture him and murdered that man, Peter Garrison.

Fleeing, William evaded detection for about a month, during which the governor offered a reward for his capture. After authorities seized William he was tried and then executed by burning. Thousands—young and old, white and slave—witnessed the event, newspapers reported. A lowcountry family visiting Pickensville, about fifteen miles away, noted, "Early this morning we were awoke by the bustling noises of the neighborhood people who were getting ready to go to Greenville" to watch the event, followed three days later by July 4 festivities and a ball. This burning evidently delighted some white spectators but appalled James Edward Calhoun and others. Calhoun called it an "unhuman mode of punishment [that] . . . will soon of itself become obsolete." Its barbarity deeply disturbed a young white man who wrote movingly about it sixty years later. News of the event reached a Philadelphia newspaper and perhaps others in the North.[10]

This 1825 barbarity had an impact on African Americans that can hardly be imagined. Greenville historian A. V. Huff observes that, if a white man writing more than half a century afterward still remembered its cruelty so intensely, it surely had incredible reverberations immediately among African Americans for miles around. As if to reinforce this message, white citizens in Abbeville three years later sentenced slave Jerry, convicted of rape, to be burned. Public clamor finally induced the legislature in 1833 to ban burning as a form of execution; in the 1890s some lynch mobs revived that practice on an extralegal basis.

Charles Ball, who escaped from South Carolina enslavement, described a huge crowd attending an execution in the state's midlands. A slave and a mulatto woman killed a white man with whom she was living. Many people gathered days in advance, entertained by "music, dancing, trading in horses, gambling, drinking, fighting, and every other species of amusement and excess to which the southern people are addicted." Slaves forced to witness the hanging made up half of the crowd of fifteen thousand.[11]

Following 1825 executions in both Greenville and Pendleton districts, Abbeville hanged two "old men" in 1826 and burned Jerry in 1828. Lew (Nathan Boon), convicted in 1828 of rape, became on January 17, 1829, the first person hanged at newly established Pickens Court House.[12] The 1830s were considerably less tense, and fewer African Americans appeared before both church and magistrates and freeholders hearings than in the mid-1820s. No more slave executions took place in Anderson, Oconee, or Pickens counties until the 1850s, another stressful decade, when slaves again would suffer for conditions elsewhere.

Runaways, 1820s–1865

Running away was much more frequent and widespread than relatively rare offenses leading to executions; runaways were noted in newspapers and in church and court records beginning in the 1820s. Approximately two-thirds of 1820s runaways recorded in Pendleton District involved those from there and another third from Georgia and Abbeville. David Sloan's March 21, 1821, advertisement reflected a harsher attitude than in earlier notices. Sloan offered a fifty dollar reward for information about anyone harboring his slave Major, or ten dollars for Major dead or alive. Resulting from an increased belief that sympathetic whites sheltered runaways, the legislature that fall passed an Act . . . against the Offence of Harbouring Negro or Other Slaves.[13]

Varied resources existed to detect runaways. Since the 1690s the militia, and later a more specialized patrol, were responsible for searching for slaves absent from their own plantations and for seizing those who lacked passes. Although patrollers, constables, and sheriffs were subject to fines if they neglected this duty, no records in Anderson, Oconee, or Pickens counties have been found of any person so fined. Any white person finding an escaped slave could legally capture him, take him to jail, and even injure him if he resisted. Many men were apprehended less than twenty miles from their plantations and within a few days, although Nelson (John S. Allen, Abbeville) was not found for almost eight months.[14]

Once caught, a runaway could be whipped by any person who captured him, perhaps on patrol, and then by his owner. And he likely would be expelled if he belonged to a church. Slaves harboring a runaway similarly could be excluded, as was Dave (Jolly) from Shoal Creek in August 1824, and were subject also to the magistrates and freeholders courts. When Prince ran away from Olly Mattison (Anderson County) in spring 1829, Mattison accused five slaves—all on different plantations and all found innocent—of harboring Prince, and another of slanderous talk against Mattison.[15]

Running away continued until after the Civil War. Many slaves were not seeking ultimate escape. Rather, some fled temporarily to avoid immediate punishment for an infraction, many simply wanted a few days of temporary respite, and others wanted to visit their wives. Often advertisements noted that an escapee might likely be found near either his wife's or his former owner's plantation. Julius N. Ross from Florence advertised in 1861 for Barry, whose wife lived on Dr. H. C. Miller's plantation near Pendleton. Jane Hunter said that "the Negro of those days used to betake himself to the woods, when his overwrought soul felt the need of more than usually fervent prayer. . . . It was their intuitive knowledge of the healing strength that comes from growing things, and of the quiet of the woods where they could hear the 'still small voice.'"[16]

The two most fascinating runaways involve Stephen's forged pass and a folksy legend, recorded decades later, of Jack, who periodically wandered away, then back again. In the first case, Stephen escaped from his owner Thomas Williams (Anderson) in October 1842. Staying in a field three nights, Stephen got provisions from Buck and Jim (both Leah Moore's). When later found a hundred miles farther south near Edgefield Court House and jailed there, Stephen had a pass forged by Gilbert (Elizabeth Thomson), who lived near him. Presumably Williams punished Stephen, but strangely the magistrates and freeholders court did not convict Jim and Buck for assisting him. Nor did it charge or punish Gilbert with forging the pass.[17] The

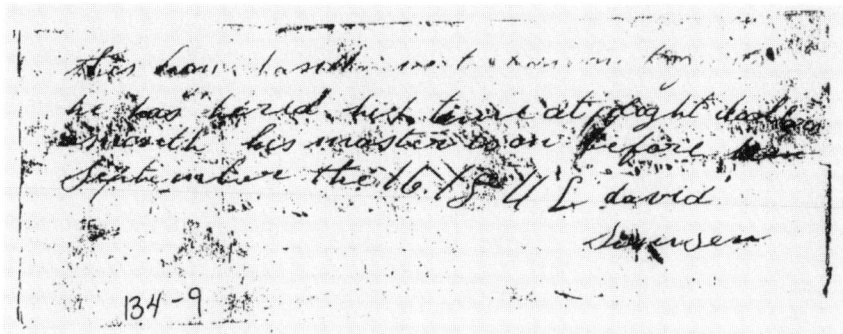

Pass forged by Gilbert, a slave, 1842. Black Heritage in the Upper Piedmont, S.C Department of Archives and History

following year Stephen provided a rare instance in which an owner clearly expected flight to a free state. Williams advertised in the September 1843 *Pendleton Messenger* that Stephen—his only slave—escaped in July, had lots of money (evidently Stephen's own), announced intentions of going to a free state, and was last seen in Greenville.

The second account is of "'Goober Jack,' The Runaway Slave, The Story of One of the Piedmont's Most Picturesque and Notorious Slave-Time Characters." This article, published in the Charleston *News and Courier* in 1908, recounted Jack's "reputation among those of his own race." Written by local native Colonel J. C. Stribling sixty or seventy years after Jack's activities, this article probably details a legend rather than fact.[18] His owner, Pendletonian John T. Sloan, grew accustomed to Jack's periodic wanderings until finally Jack became "so unruly and unreliable as a hand on the plantation," Stribling wrote, that Sloan decided to sell the man. Chained at Pendleton's hotel the night before a slave trader would carry Jack away, he picked his locks and drank the hotel's liquor, the story went. But Jack walked willingly behind the trader's wagon to Mississippi, where he was sold. However, Jack escaped again, then walked back to Pendleton, where he apparently stayed while Sloan "felt a degree of pride in . . . [owning the] most noted slave character in the Piedmont section of the state."

Stribling's remarkable story celebrated a slave who "simply followed the bent of inclination" and frequently absented himself. However exaggerated this account may be, several aspects of it raise to legendary status the experiences of other slaves. Having escaped, Goober Jack stayed near home, finding food and getting help. He helped himself also to potatoes and corn from the field, apples from the orchard, and milk directly from unpenned cows. At other times Goober Jack "would sometimes loiter among the shadows round the old time kitchens in the back yards of plantation homes, biding his time" until the cook left and then would "make a sudden raid," grabbing a ham or a corn pone.

Jack constructed a hideout shelter complete with shutters pierced with augur holes, a ventilator shaft, and vines to cover its existence. His structure was near a river—perhaps the Seneca—so Jack could jump in, befuddling the dogs' efforts to find his scent, at other times "floating down the river on a log or leaping upon the back of a work ox or an unbridled horse," somewhat reminiscent of the exploits of Paul Bunyan, also called a trickster.

But elements of Jack's story find contemporary documentation for other slaves. Sylvia (Martha Williams) hid eleven weeks in a barn until she accidentally left some clothing in nearby Pendleton and other pieces under the floor of "Harry's house." Clearly, she could move around while hiding. The court imposed on Harry (Joseph Taylor) 57 lashes for harboring her, but other slaves also helping were not identified. During that same time Simon (John E. Norris) lived in the woods for three months beginning in November 1842 and got food and whiskey from Mary Ann (Dr. O. R. Broyles). And three slaves, all belonging to James Keith, Sr., were charged in another case with harboring a runaway, concealing him, and buying him a pass; the one found guilty endured fifty lashes.[19]

Food, clothing, and hiding places seemed readily available from other slaves, especially ones known and trusted by a runaway. Runaway Lewis (Dr. Addison Thompson) at various times in 1822 got food from other slaves, even at Sandy Springs Camp Meeting, and sometimes lodging. Ten slaves, all from different plantations in a several-mile radius, were charged with aiding Lewis; only two were convicted. Federal soldiers who escaped during the Civil War were amazed at the abundant food, even in winter, that slaves provided them. At one stop "the boys on this place were good foragers, for while with them we lived on the fat of the land," and another got "five nice fat fowl."[20]

Essex, who lived on a Clinkscales plantation just across the county line in Abbeville, also had his adventures narrated, although somewhat less vividly than did Goober Jack. Writing in 1916, the owner's son John George Clinkscales related this account.[21] Essex hid three years, often, like Goober Jack, jumping into a river to evade "the best-trained hounds on either side of the river." Advertisements, a reward for his capture, and hunt parties failed to locate him.

He successfully "lived in the swamps and forests on both [the Carolina and Georgia] sides of the Savannah River, not many miles from the City of Augusta, Georgia." Essex managed to find food in the woods and fields, and "a copper-colored woman on a Georgia plantation baked a 'pone of bread' for him occasionally and regularly washed and mended his scanty supply of clothing." Essex ultimately tired of this existence, returned home on his own, and promised—faithfully, it proved—never to cause trouble again. He married a young woman on the plantation shortly afterward.

This Georgia woman's care for Essex and Harriet's assistance to Alfred, an 1854 runaway, may typify support by many other women. Alfred, escaping from George Mattison of Alabama, returned to his previous Anderson County neighborhood. Initially he stayed with Bob (Hugh Gantt) in Gantt's cellars, got aid from other Gantt slaves, and wore women's dresses when he went outside. When hunters got close,

Alfred asked to stay with Harriet (Ira Arnold). When Alfred and Harriet were apprehended, she received ten lashes.

Although constituting fewer than a dozen of the three counties' documented runaways between 1820 and 1865, women periodically supplied food, clothing, and other aid to men who fled. Sarah (Ira G. Gambrell), one of these few known women runaways, received help from John and Hannah (both Mrs. Elizabeth Stribling's) in August 1849. On a more personal level, Phillis was excluded by First Creek Baptists for hiding her sister during the 1830–31 winter.[22]

Sparse evidence makes it difficult to form a complete picture of how pervasive running away was or how frequently slaves resorted to it.[23] Clearly, however, it happened more than rarely, and courts used phrases such as "notorious" or "habitual runaway." Runaways managed to hide for days, weeks, and even months not far from home without being found by owners or by the patrol. The only known antebellum documentation of discovery by patrollers was of an accidental discovery. When Captain A. N. McFall in April 1839 stopped several of Mrs. Mary Mattison's slaves (Varennes) headed for a frolic, one was found to be Col. J. W. Norris's runaway.[24]

Another instance shows a fierce determination to escape permanently from the master and reach a free state. Mattison and Stephen (both John Brown Jr.'s) fled from Anderson County into nearby Georgia, where they periodically hid in a cave for several winter months (1851–52). Mattison, "frequently in the habit of running away," would rather die than return to his master, he said, and found a white man who sold him a pistol. Three months later a party pursued them, and Mattison "swore he would be damned if he would" surrender and "would kill or be killed" before being taken. Shot, he continued running and finally collapsed. The magistrates and freeholders court ordered 425 lashes, given at least 100 at a time, and several months in jail.[25]

Defying the law, the lash, and their masters, numerous slaves absented themselves each year. They survived partly by help from others, drawing on an extended African American community with many contacts. Even though these slaves conspicuously rejected their prescribed status, owners seemed to accept short-term absences as likely occurrences. People in bondage, asserting themselves while risking punishment, gained some quiet time from enslavement and created small corners of resistance within a system largely beyond their control. That such resistance resulted in relatively mild punishment sheds more light about complex relationships between owners and slaves.

Other Resistance

Other types of resistance, much harder to trace than running away, left little evidence. Various studies report deliberately broken farm implements, especially hoes. Scholars have also debated the likelihood and frequency of mothers' smothering their own babies to prevent their becoming slaves and increasing an owner's wealth. The absence of trials in Anderson, Oconee, and Pickens counties for mothers' intentionally smothering babies suggests either that it did not happen or that they were successful in disguising it.[26] Lesser types of resistance, from scorching a mistress's dress to damaging a plow, could have occurred without any surviving record.

Standing up for themselves against white people constituted significant acts of resistance beyond arson and rare attempts to murder one's owner. Slaves on documented occasions defended themselves against physical assaults and verbal taunts from whites. Only cases involving people other than their owners would ordinarily have entered public records, as owners could quickly discipline their own offenders. One example appears within J. D. Ashmore's 1856 diary:

2/5 Difficulty with Pompey—who used violence upon me.
2/6 Pompey in Jail.
2/18 Pompey still in Jail. Whipped him.
2/19 Took Pompey out of jail this morning. & put him to work. Seemed very humble & obedient.

Like Ashmore, owners could pay privately to have their slaves jailed as punishment and also whipped by an official.

Apparently minor incidents escalated when African Americans refused to accept offensive treatment. Bailus Hester, objecting to Tom's (Mary Keith) facial expression, attacked him with a stick. Yelling "damn you" and "go to hell," Tom grabbed the stick. Although Tom did not attempt any harm, he still was found guilty of assault and battery and punished with ten stripes. Two instances involved FPC Paytons, and FPC Peter Keith was found guilty of an 1856 assault and battery on Margaret Gunter when he seized her arm. She complained that "he just Kept jawing me as impudent as he possibly could." Keith countered that her boy not only cursed him but said he would do so whenever he chose, imitating his mother, who called Keith "nigger."[27]

Several slaves wound up in court after making vague threats about what they would do if they were white. Trial papers, specifically mentioning taunts about "white" status, indicate that they compounded a slave's physical actions. Angry that R. Hall called Fanny Payton names, her husband slave Richmond said that, if "he was half white, there would be bloodshed," Hall's. And Tom (Henry Adams), being pursued by Johnson Hall, struck him with a stick and cut a gash in Hall's head; Tom, who said he would not be whipped by any white man, had to endure sixty lashes, however.[28]

Stealing was another form of resistance, although it is hard to separate deliberate sabotage from personal greed or hunger. Moreover, many considered it their right to take food and other items from the owner, as their own labor produced these goods. Numerous cases of theft follow in chapters 8 through 10.[29]

Music disguised still other dissidence. Spirituals with words such as "steal away to Jesus" and "swing low, sweet chariot, coming for to carry me home" cradled messages of hope and perhaps physical escape as well as religious refuge. So, probably, did "I Am Bound for de Promise Land." Another song, "Follow the Drinking Gourd," conveyed directions: follow the Big Dipper, or Gourd, northward to freedom.[30] White children for decades blithely sang "Gimme cracked corn, I don't care, the Master's gone away" without perceiving its implications.

Slaves adopted means of resistance ranging from subtle, such as their songs, to blatant—running away, standing up for themselves, or, rarely, committing murder or arson.[31] Resisting, they challenged the very system that enslaved them.

Convergences

Offenses, real or perceived, official charges and punishments, and church sanctions varied dramatically over time. Often they converged with external problems. Some explanations for unusually high numbers of thefts and of running away at certain times may lie in the same depressed conditions that caused the white community's stresses. If white people were disturbed during years of low cotton production due to bad weather, slaves must have suffered from diminished harvests of foodstuffs, which gave them strategic occasions to intensify their assertiveness. On numerous occasions slaves stole food or staged other forms of resistance when they were hungry. Surely agricultural and other distress, affecting African Americans too, filtered among black and white plantation moods.

Because running away and other noncriminal forms of resistance did not ordinarily enter church and magistrates and freeholders court records, these occurrences are hard to chart by years or time periods. Offenses before courts and churches, however, show clear patterns. Fluctuations in numbers of civil and church accusations, convictions, and severity of punishments reflect broader concerns. A variety of economic problems (including depressed cotton prices and droughts), congressional wrangles over tariffs, and abolitionist issues created societal stresses. Pendleton and its successor counties produced five hundred cases from 1820 to 1865, and nearby Spartanburg's set of almost three hundred (1831–65) allows comparisons with Anderson, Oconee, and Pickens counties.

Following the tense 1820s, the 1830s had both a lull in magistrates and freeholders court charges against African Americans and good cotton production most years. Near the decade's end, things changed. Spartanburg's magistrates and freeholders courts in 1838 had their largest number of trials to date, while more slaves were also accused in the three counties than ever before. Anderson's court charged forty-one, a record number, in 1839, but remarkably found none guilty—evidently paranoia ran ahead of legal realities. Whether by coincidence or not, 1838–39 was South Carolina's and the nation's worst cotton yield in nearly forty years. It was followed shortly by a worldwide glut, rapidly plunging prices, and acute distress.

After the relatively calm 1830s, numbers of slaves tried from 1838 through 1865 increased when calculated by five-year brackets.[32] Surprisingly, pressures that induced more church and magistrates and freeholders cases did not automatically lead to a comparable rise in convictions. Many conditions created problems for planters:

a serious drought in 1845 and another in 1848; agricultural problems in Europe curtailed sales there; the price of cotton dropped; and strained Anglo-American relations due partly to the British abolitionist movement. Within each bracket peak years mostly came to the three counties and Spartanburg simultaneously, with slight variations in timing, being responsive partly to local moods and issues that have not yet been discovered. Clear convergences emerge by charting church offenses and exclusions with magistrates and freeholders court cases and guilty verdicts.[33]

The 1850s generally were the most tense decade yet in American history with the Bleeding Kansas episode and the founding in Anderson of a Southern Rights Association at its beginning. There were also the deaths of U.S. Senators John C. Calhoun, Henry Clay, and Daniel Webster. Two additional factors applied more heat to the cauldron: British criticism of American slaveholding, and the U.S. Supreme Court's 1857 decision that Dred Scott, an African American suing to retain his free status, was not legally a "person."

Numbers of slaves residing in Anderson, Oconee, and Pickens counties who were charged rose from 56 in 1830–34 to 262 in 1850–54, much more rapidly than did population, and reached their record high of 314 in 1860–64. The 1855–59 period showed, overall, a temporary respite in Anderson, Oconee, and Pickens counties and Spartanburg. County officials, who last had a slave execution in 1829, ordered four during the 1850s plus a hanging for a free man of color. John Brown's slave Ned was executed in 1852 for attempting both murder and insurrection, and Jerry (Wm. N. Martin) was hanged for rape that same year. Three executions punished unsuccessful attempts: Ned's; Sam's (Silas Massey) assault and battery with intent to kill in 1851; and Solomon's (Ira G. Campbell) attempted rape in 1857. Two years later Sam Oglesby became the only free person of color sentenced to execution—although it aborted—most likely in the upper piedmont and perhaps anywhere in the state since Vesey's revolt. In a nearby county during July 1855 "2 negroes of old Holeman Smith's hung to day for the murder of their master."[34]

A surprising calm in 1861 briefly reduced church trials of slaves, numbers of runaways, and cases of slaves tried and convicted in Anderson, Oconee, and Pickens counties plus Spartanburg. Some pending magistrates and freeholders court cases were evidently canceled in early 1861. Tightened wartime measures along with other factors may have accounted for the respite, badly needed before greater tensions in the following years.

Magistrates and Freeholders Courts and Slave Trials: Procedures

Magistrates and Freeholders trials, convictions, and punishments—just as they fluctuated with broad societal concerns—also reflect wide variations that stemmed in part from local conflicts among whites. African Americans faced official criminal complaints only before the court, specializing in their cases. Sometimes court-imposed whippings followed those already inflicted by patrollers, owners, or both. Punishments varied enormously, ranging from a few lashes to execution, often with no obvious correspondence to either offense or surviving testimony. About one-third of all those charged were found innocent. Free people of color, subject to the same courts, proceedings, and penalties as slaves, were disproportionately tried and punished, as occurred with the Arters, Oglesbys, and Paytons (see chapter 4).

Designated specifically to try nonwhites and established with different procedural standards, magistrates and freeholders courts were in many ways typical judicial bodies following standard legal processes.[35] They judged many defendants guilty and acquitted others, sometimes convicted on lesser charges, and nol-prossed other cases. Further, they selected juries and occasionally experienced jury nullification.

Although replicating many judicial procedures, in practice these magistrates and freeholders courts hardly resembled the formality of the court of general sessions where whites were tried. Each magistrates and freeholders court was convened on an ad hoc basis with no permanent judge or fixed seat. Defendants were tried by a jury, not of their peers but of white men, often slaveholders. Magistrates or justices of the peace presided; numbers of neighbors and justices varied according to severity of the crime and to changing laws. Trials could be arranged very quickly. Occasionally the offense, complaint, trial, verdict, and punishment all transpired during one or two days.

Crimes tried by these courts were committed usually against white people although occasionally against other African Americans, slave or free. As already noted, other offenses—stealing from an owner, being impudent, even running away—were handled privately on the plantation and did not go to court. Courts dealt primarily with crimes beyond an owner's plantation. A slave's arson or murder of an owner or any white person was considered a grave public danger and a capital offense under magistrates and freeholders court jurisdiction.

Offenses before the magistrates and freeholders courts fall into four broad categories:

(1) crimes against people: assault and battery, rape, intent to kill, and murder, all with varied degrees;
(2) crimes against property: theft (burglary and larceny), house breaking, destruction, and arson;
(3) violations of the moral or social order: drinking or gambling on the Sabbath, disrupting religious services, slander, and lying; and
(4) political offenses: unlawful assembly, riot, insurrection, and harboring runaways.

Punishments for slaves did not follow a prescribed standard and varied widely among cases with much court discretion and inconsistency. Highly decentralized in the hands of a local magistrate or justice of the peace and of a jury, magistrates and freeholders trials were largely removed from the county's elected officials or state judiciary. And results varied significantly across small distances within the area.

Capital Crimes: Executions, Reduced Charges, and Acquittals

The most serious charges concerned capital offenses. These included rape, murder, arson, and burglary. Surprisingly few—one or two per year—of these cases arose, and often juries convicted on lesser charges that did not carry death penalties. Sixteen known slave executions occurred between 1784 and 1865 plus one Civil War–era lynching; four of them between 1787 and 1818 were for arson, murdering one's child, attempt to poison master, and rape.

Reflecting white fears following Denmark Vesey's 1822 revolt, the three counties executed four slaves between 1823 and 1829, two for murder, two for rape. Greenville executed two slaves in 1825, one especially brutally—William, burned alive, as was Jerry in Abbeville in 1828. Lew's 1829 execution was the last in Anderson, Oconee, and Pickens counties for over twenty years. Spartanburg County hanged only five slaves between 1824 and 1865, all for murder, arson, or both. But the times—1824, 1849, and 1860–65—coincided both with periods of societal stress and approximately with executions in the three counties.[36]

Table 5.1 **Capital Offenses: Anderson, Oconee, and Pickens, 1784–1865**

Initial Charge	#	Years of Executions	NG	NP	Lesser	T
arson	2	1859 (escaped), 1863	11	13		
buggery	1	1810 (hanged himself)	1			
rape	4	1808, 1823, 1829, 1852	3	6	8	21
murder of own child	1	1818	1			
murder of whites	1	1825	5	6		
murder of FPC	1	1825	1			
attempt to poison	1	1798	1			
A&B, intent to kill	2	1851, 1852	1	3		
A&B, intent, house burglary	1	1861 (evid. canceled)	1			
burglary, threat to kill	1	1864	1			
larceny, breaking into house	1	1862	1			
attempted rape	1	1857	1			
larceny	2	1864 (joint execution)	2			
totals	19	sentenced to death	20	6	8	53
	16	executed; 34 not sentenced to death				

Abbreviations: A&B = assault and battery; NG = not guilty; NP = nol-prossed or otherwise dropped from records; lesser = punishment short of execution; T = total.

The counties next hanged three slaves in 1851 and 1852, two of them for lesser offenses than previously resulted in death sentences. Silas Massey's Sam was hanged for assault and battery with intent to kill, Ned for attempted murder and insurrection, and Jerry for rape. Two more sentences of hanging in 1857 and 1859 made the 1850s the area's second-deadliest decade for convicted slaves and free persons of color. In 1857 runaway Solomon (Ira Gambrell) tried to rape Melinda Russell but managed only to beat her. Still, he was hanged. The most fascinating and puzzling sentence of hanging was the tricounty's only one pronounced on a free person of color: Sam Oglesby, convicted of breaking into a store in 1859, stealing seventy-five to eighty dollars, and committing arson. Tried almost immediately, he was convicted and sentenced, like slaves, to two months in jail awaiting execution. Oglesby, however, escaped. Three or four legal executions plus a lynching all occurred during the Civil War.[37]

Among capital offenses, charges of sexual assault by slaves surprisingly were seldom lodged or upheld. Accused of Pendleton District's earliest known rape by a slave, Lew was executed in 1808. During the next fifty-five years, however, only three others were executed for raping a white woman. Dave (John Burress) was hanged in 1823; Ben got fifty lashes in 1825; Pickens executed another Lew (N. Boon) in 1829; and, following a twenty-six-year gap, Jerry was hanged in 1852 for assault and rape. These four constituted a quarter of the area's slave executions.

In eight other convictions, a slave man failed to complete the act, not having gotten beyond exposure, sexual solicitation, or intrusion into the woman's bedroom. But Martha Day conceived a "Black child" in 1853 after Charles (Martha Bowen) drugged her and took her to bed. He was sentenced to 150 lashes in two installments, then was to be sold and removed from South Carolina. By contrast another woman who had a bastard child in 1858 by Anthony (Isaac Clement) never alleged rape; the official charge against him was "depredation and slander upon a white woman." The court inflicted on him 100 lashes immediately, two weeks in jail, and 100 more, the largest yet in the three counties. During the Civil War Phil (R. B. Hutchison), who solicited a white woman and touched her, got 500 lashes and was banished from Anderson County.[38]

Compared to eleven cases with guilty verdicts for rape, attempted or accomplished, the accused was found not guilty in three others, and three more were evidently dropped. Some white women who filed complaints had their characters dissected in court. Witnesses testified that one woman charging assault had sex with her own slave and with other "colored men." Offended neighbors called out names of frequent male visitors or customers at that woman's house and complained more directly: "Her livelihood [is] principally by having conversation with the opposite sex rather than by any manual labor. . . . she is altogether too common in her embraces both with black and white. . . . She does not discriminate between colors." Greenville and Spartanburg cases referred to white women offering sex to slaves or free people of color. One Greenville slave received only five lashes after white witnesses said that "negroes . . . [were] there frequently. . . . seamed [sic] to act like they were at home." Similarly, Spartanburg's town council lamented activity in back alleys where free men of color drank and shared women with whites.[39]

Like rape, surprising numbers of arson, murder, and burglary charges did not result in executions. Ellen (William Nevitt Jr.), tried in 1846 for burning James Todd's log house, escaped that capital charge but was found guilty of stealing gold coins. Seven arson trials between 1828 and 1861 either resulted in a not-guilty verdict or were not pursued. Three took place in 1855, 1860, and 1861, years of many charges against slaves. A strange 1855 case concerned John (Susan Lewis) allegedly burning a carriage shop, other buildings, and part of the house of John B. Sitton, a prominent Pendleton resident. Lengthy testimony indicated that slave John was out and about the town but could not link him directly to the fire. Jurors found suspicious circumstances, but not enough to convict. Although Lewis was an influential owner, it is unlikely that Sitton would not have demanded compensation. If she provided that privately, she must have held John in high esteem. Even stranger, six slaves were accused on November 15, 1860, of burning a house; after they were charged and fourteen witnesses called for a trial, the case disappeared from court records.[40]

At least seven defendants escaped punishment for charges that they killed their owner, someone in that family, or other whites. Among them, magistrates and freeholders juries ruled Caleb (Jacob Gueren?) not guilty in 1830 of choking his master to death. When slave William was accused of strangling a little white boy in 1854, Dr. Johnson may have used personal influence, as the case was "discharged by order of the prosecutor" without further explanation. In most of these cases, bare facts and legal procedures are all that are known. On only two occasions has explicit evidence survived about the slaves' purposes. Three Abbeville slaves who killed their owner were hanged in 1848: "impenitent to the last hour they were taken from the jail, & said they had done right & expected to be forgiven for it & get to Heaven! They regard themselves as martyrs in the cause of liberty & say they cheerfully die to better the condition of the other [one hundred plus] blacks on their plantation." During the Civil War two Pickens slaves, about to be executed, said they would rather die than return to their master.[41]

Noncapital Crimes and Punishments

Capital crimes encompassed only a small number of those that might be committed. Slaves convicted for noncapital crimes were charged with a wide variety of offenses and received diverse punishments. It was not unusual for juries to reduce these charges or to find defendants not guilty. Aside from judicial processes, these cases reveal much about slave interactions. They also indicate critical roles of wealthy and influential owners who sometimes protected their slaves by hiding crimes or by hiring attorneys to defend them. And white fears, feuds, and conflicts underlie these stories.

That dozens of cases—these and other accusations of various assaults—resulted in not-guilty judgments, reduced punishments, or interrupted proceedings may say something about fairness of courts that would not convict slaves without proof. Other cases seem to argue the reverse. Influential owners evidently could intervene successfully, but most executed slaves lacked such support. It hardly was accidental that the slave burned in 1825 came from a Georgia owner, evidently lacking influence in Greenville and not entitled to compensation. At times slaves of prosperous and influential owners did receive heavy punishments, and there is no clear explanation of those variations.

Corporal punishments usually ranged from 5 lashes to a typical high of 39 (though some went much higher) until the 1840s, when numbers rose dramatically. The lightest sentences were 2 and 5 lashes imposed on two Pickens women who hid and fed an 1841 runaway. Exceptions exceeding 39 notably included Isaac's (Amy Borough) 100 lashes in 1831 for stealing corn, a felony, and Cain's (John Robinson) 175 in 1838 also for a felony. Slave woman May (Dr. James Stuart) in 1832 was the first to receive exactly 40 lashes, evidently a symbolic increase beyond the traditional 39. Increased corporal punishments affected Andrew (Thomas Duckworth), convicted of housebreaking and assault with intent to kill and punished with 200 lashes in 1842. Such heavy punishments were not meted out all at once; most parties received, like Andrew, a portion of the lashes—50 at once in his case—followed by time in jail, then repetitions of both until the sentence was completed. That these heavier punishments began at a time of societal stress hardly seems coincidental.[42]

Juries clearly evaluated, sometimes with malice or occasionally with mercy, the impact of lashes they imposed. One slave did not have to remove his shirt due to a boil on his arm. Rachel (J. P. ODell), who in 1830 insulted a white woman, was sentenced to 10 lashes, lightly applied; and Willis (Martha Lawrence), convicted of manslaughter against another slave, got 50 lashes on his bare back. Each one would hurt still more with "the lash hissing through the air like cold water on a red-hot iron."[43]

Implements for administering lashings ranged from a hickory to cow hides. James, convicted of accusing a white man of stealing fruit from his owner, was to be struck with 10 lashes, "well laid on in a way not to cut the flesh," then whipped with a switch, "not . . . more than one inch round the but." In 1852 another Pickens slave, Kin (Jeremiah Looper), attempted to kill Harry (R. T. C. Foster), whose son quarreled with Kin. Kin was struck while tied to a tree with 39 stripes laid on so that "red" showed. With more precise instructions in 1856, Bailas's (Esli Hunt) 20 lashes should "cut Blod every Fith Lick." But if the proverbial cat-of-nine-tails was used, it did not survive in court records.

Punishments often differed among those convicted together. Four who assaulted another slave got punishments in 1826 ranging from 5 to 20 lashes. Four others jointly convicted of larceny in 1864 received 15, 30, 60, and 75. Numbers varied among counties. Pickens and Oconee typically imposed lighter punishments than did Anderson, while Spartanburg excelled in excess, with one defendant being sentenced to 1,029 lashes. Although men usually received heavier punishments than did women, there were exceptions.[44]

Other than death the heaviest corporal punishment for a slave assaulting a white person short of murder went to Mariah (James C. Williams), who in 1854 got 176 lashes, inflicted 44 at a time each week. She hit a white woman, Lucinda McCollum, with a fire shovel—judged intent to kill by the court—after McCollum told her slave Louisa uncomplimentary things about Mariah. Although expected to die, McCollum survived, or Mariah almost certainly would have been executed.[45]

Banishment sometimes served as further preventive against more crime, at least in Anderson, Oconee, and Pickens counties. Convicted of stealing bacon in 1853, Jim and Green (both Thomas Murphy's) were "ordered to leave the neighborhood of Walhalla" after their 39 lashes each. Free black Jefferson Potts from Greenville County murdered Pickens FPC James Arter with an ax in 1852. Jailed, Potts got 150 lashes and had to leave the state.

Variations are easier to find among magistrates and freeholders verdicts and punishments than are coherent explanations. The word "neighboring" is a significant clue.

Influences, Neighboring and Farther Afield

Neighborhood aspects of trials affected African Americans in many ways. Defendants could call white and slave witnesses on their behalf, and many trials included testimony about the accused's character, good or bad. Sometimes there were local conflicts between a defendant and a white person. Testimony at least twice indicated that a white complainant hated the accused for years and wanted that slave killed. More often, a defendant was merely a pawn between local white arguments and factions. Several families in Anderson's Varennes area, for example, had running feuds and several times accused each other's slaves of crimes. This had distinct advantages for whites, who, if they wrongly accused another, could be sued for slander or false suit. If they falsely charged an enemy's slave, however, there was no legal recourse. Such trials resounded with retorts that one witness would never believe a certain white person's testimony, or that, more bluntly, that person was lying. Although Olly Mattison accused five owners' slaves of harboring his runaway, all were found not guilty in an episode evidently involving complicated local white conflicts.

An accused's owner faced at minimum some embarrassment and lost his own and his slave's labor on the trial date, and perhaps that of slave witnesses as well. Just as owners had to pay when their runaways were captured, jailed, and fed, they also had to pay fees and fines for their slaves who were whipped or imprisoned.[46]

Powerful and prosperous owners could exercise their influence to protect slaves accused of crimes, or to keep them from being charged. That no slaves of John C. Calhoun ever faced an accusation does not mean they were innocent. His wife, Floride, closely guarded a family secret that one night Izzy, a house servant, let an ember catch fire in the room where she should have been watching a Calhoun child, endangering the child's life, her own, perhaps others in the house, and the house itself. Floride Calhoun did not want to have to sell the girl but did send her to son Andrew's Alabama plantation, there "not being a prospect of her coming where I shall ever see her again." Two years later she wanted, and got, Izzy returned. Nor did Floride Calhoun report Old Sawney, who carried a knife around the plantation for months. Even earlier, although Floride's mother was "in great distress" when "her driver William has threatened her life and insulted her grossly &c," Floride did not report him to the magistrates and freeholders court. Hundreds of other families, like the Calhouns, owned many slaves over several decades without one of them ever brought before the court.[47]

Slaves of some well-to-do owners, however, did wind up in court. A few owners, like Dr. O. R. Broyles and Daniel Brown, succeeded in stopping proceedings. Brown in 1860 evidently got his slave's offense reduced from burglary—stealing goods worth $188, including gold and silver—to larceny, which prevented Marshall's being subject to execution. Sometimes owners hired attorneys to defend their slaves, as Jesse McGee did in 1861. W. K. Easley unsuccessfully represented the Oglesbys.[48]

Buttressed with many legal protections and procedures, trials before the magistrates and freeholders courts still were affected by neighborhood influences and status of owners. Widely varying verdicts and sentences that seem, in both directions, to defy evidence, must have arisen out of local cliques, rivalries, and power. Trials, however, also served as a control mechanism beyond general enforcement of law. Some severe punishments, unjustified by court testimony, must have targeted slaves whom whites considered unruly or dangerous. Delayed complaints—more often in the 1850s and 1860s than before—are another indicator both of local conflicts and of general societal pressure.[49]

Counting only total numbers of slaves tried—as done so far—can be somewhat misleading because those figures obscure types of separate incidents and numbers involved in a specific episode. From 1835 through 1865 thirty-five cases in Anderson County involved groups, usually from several plantations. They totaled 226, nearly 33 percent of all those accused during those years. These cases, each averaging about 6.5 slaves, ranged from 4 to over 20. In almost all cases accused slaves came from several owners, thus revealing slave interactions and travels. Half of these cases occurred between 1860 and 1865. With more charges of resisting the patrol, harboring a runaway (Alfred), and riotous conduct, these groups violated a social order in crisis during the Civil War.

Trials of slaves, then, like much else in the area, had a complicated and intricately varied pattern. They wove together elements of crime control, punishment, and deterrence; their impact varied according to owners' wealth and use of influential attorneys; and they reflected local feuds and conflicts while mirroring broader concerns about slave "unrest" and eventually the Civil War. These contradictory factors undermine simplistic interpretations of slavery and black-white interactions.

SIX

Churches, a Shared Setting

CHURCHGOING BROUGHT TOGETHER owners, slaves, and free people of color in a setting more nearly equal than at any other occasion. There they all took part in a shared activity at the same time. Indeed, according to their theology, they sat before God as brothers and sisters in Christ. Especially in Baptist churches, and probably Methodist as well, white members referred to slaves as Sister Mary or Brother Tom, or in minutes as "black sister Priscilla." Equality hardly worked in practice, however; even though white women were a majority in many churches, white men held all positions of formal authority.

Slave presence at churches involved multiple levels of motivations and perceptions. Churches had vested interests in adding numbers, gaining converts, and enforcing obedience—a mutually advantageous alliance with owners, who used churches and religion as another tool for control. And slaves may have been currying favor with owners by attendance, exercising their own religious experiences, enjoying associations with other African Americans, or perhaps all of these. As they traveled to services and met together, slave and free, especially at night and during weeklong revivals, interactions played a central role in their own network. And slaves who became exhorters, elders, and preachers had a leadership role formally sanctioned by white society; this was almost the only local arena where that was possible. African Americans found in churches their widest range for personal expressions within a white-controlled environment.[1]

Minutes from thirty-five churches, providing a broad perspective of the three counties, are the basis for this chapter.[2] Although other studies emphasize slave beliefs, especially as linked to African values and practices, the focus here is what slaves *did* as church members, how many were involved, and what they got out of it.

Early Slave Involvement

Pendleton District's earliest churches, organized only shortly after the district itself, included whites, slaves, and free members. Baptists predominated then as in later years, followed by Methodists. All American denominations were recently created following revolutionary breaks not only from England but also from its churches.

Just as constitutional convention delegates debated whether to allow slavery to continue, new religious groups, notably Methodists, dealt with the issue.

Even before formal organization as a church, Methodism attracted many black people, an early emphasis that laid the groundwork for slaves from Anderson, Oconee, and Pickens counties to be members. Francis Asbury, prominent American "circuit rider" in the late eighteenth and early nineteenth centuries, preached to black and white, as had his predecessor, John Wesley, Methodist founder and a leader of the Great Awakening. A 1787 Methodist General Conference required preachers "to leave nothing undone . . . [among slaves for] their spiritual benefit and salvation," and Asbury developed a "catechism for colored children."[3]

Asbury and others by 1800 helped convert 1,535 South Carolina slaves, constituting about 11 percent of the nation's black Methodists. By 1828 the figure was 18,475, constituting 34 percent of America's black Methodists. Traveling through Pendleton several times, Asbury held services in homes there. There is no evidence either about his impact among slaves or views expressed on slavery while there. Nor is anything known about early black Methodist members. The earliest report available (1825) shows 486 "Whites" and 42 "Coldrd.," who were 8 percent of the Keowee Circuit (Holstein Conference).[4]

Methodists, who appealed to slaves primarily through religious instruction at Sunday schools and through camp meetings, soon drew the area's second-largest number of black worshipers. State mission work, begun on the coast, evidently did not reach much farther north than Columbia, but circuit preacher John Mote organized a Sunday school in 1824 at Ebenezer Methodist Church (lower Pendleton District); others may have existed in the area also. Pendleton Circuit in 1840 sponsored fifty-three Sunday schools with 373 children (racial composition unknown); whites attended similar schools.

Baptist attitudes toward slavery and black members are difficult to determine due to lack of coordinated action and to limited accounts. Baptists hold firmly to principles of congregational autonomy—there is no higher authority above the local church. Given this strong conviction, Baptists—black or white, in 1800 or 2000—sometimes refuse to affiliate on a regional, state, or national level.

This autonomy contrasts with hierarchical denominations, which must sanction both establishment of new congregations and choices of their ministers. Any group of Baptists, acting by themselves, could create a church. That relatively impromptu nature assisted rapid Baptist growth in frontier areas, including Pendleton District; so did lack of formal requirements for trained ministers. The vast majority of church members, white and black, were Baptists. The South Carolina Baptist Convention (SCBC) was not begun until 1821, and many groups would not join even then. These included Saluda Baptist Association, based largely in Anderson County. The SCBC dealt periodically with issues of slavery, beginning with its 1822 meeting, shortly after Denmark Vesey's revolt. Baptists defended "the lawfulness of holding slaves" in an *Exposition of the Views of Baptists Relative to the Colored Population*, submitted to the governor.[5]

As Methodists were already doing, South Carolina Baptists launched Sunday schools and created in 1822 an Educational and Missionary Association to direct that work. Anderson Baptists established their own Educational and Missionary Association of Saluda, not connected with the SCBC; W. B. Johnson directed that effort. Sunday schools filled a void in both religious and scholastic education, combining literacy with religious content.

Urging further instruction for slaves, the SCBC in 1828 offered guidance to accomplish that. Member churches should "assemble the colored people together, and engage in the business of reading and explaining the Scriptures to them in a manner suited to their capacities; and encouraging them to repeat and commit to memory such parts of them as may be suited to their case." They should be taught to obey the Ten Commandments and to fulfill "their duty as servants, as neighbours, and members of the church." Further, "some discreet coloured member of the church [should] be placed as leader, who shall watch over their conduct." A year later Anderson Baptists adopted the same principle.

Hopewell Presbyterian (Pendleton) was already holding Sunday schools specifically for slaves around 1820. Its Sunday School Society appointed "a Teacher to be at and constantly attend every sabbath to the School which is, to, and does consist of, coloured learners."[6] Baptists, Methodists, and Presbyterians, then, all conducted Sunday schools for Pendleton District slaves. Teaching them to read was not yet illegal; some learned to read the Bible in these schools.

Like national political arguments over slavery, controversies of the 1790s subsided for several decades among the upstate's three major denominations: Baptists, Methodists, and Presbyterians. Their national bodies later suffered prolonged conflicts over slavery, followed by ruptures between northern and southern groups beginning in the 1840s for Methodists and Baptists, later for Presbyterians. Methodists split in 1845 after years of discussion and argument. The church's requirement that leaders could not hold slaves was an immediate spark to long-smoldering Methodist tensions that produced the Methodist Episcopal Church, South. Although Baptists also divided over slaveholding in 1845, Presbyterians held their denomination together until 1860, when their rupture occurred.

All three faiths then had separate southern denominations identified with slavery, while northerners opposed it. Southern clergymen of all denominations increasingly defended slavery in the 1840s and 1850s, sometimes virulently. Religious splinterings mirrored larger political controversies over slavery that led to the Civil War.

Types of Slave Participation

If black and white stood equally before God as brothers and sisters in Christ, that raised serious questions about African American roles in churches. Just as enforcement by magistrates and freeholders varied, treatment of slaves differed among churches. Baptist congregational decision making and autonomy of individual churches imply equal voting rights. In some recorded instances slaves could vote. Significant pressure, however, likely caused them to support the majority among whites.

Slaves occasionally protested their subordinate status. In 1806 they did so about having to sit in a shed at Shoal Creek, which faced another instance of dissension twenty-five years later. In 1831 "Brother Benjamin black man bein dissatisfyed with the Church for not allowing him to become a witness against white members, he declared nonfellowship and was excluded." By contrast, "our Black Bro[ther] Mulbery" testified at First Creek on March 7, 1829, along with several whites, against a white man accused of drinking. Some churches tried to improve worship conditions for blacks. At Anderson Presbyterian Church, Elder Norris in May 1850 recommended "a change in the mode of conducting the singing . . . that for the benefit of Negroes in attendance it was adviseable to parcel the lines out either by the officiating minister or by one of the Elders."[7]

Churches of any denomination have rituals including membership, baptism, communion, and the collection plate. New Baptist church members are baptized by immersion. Whites and blacks joining a church at the same time would be baptized in the same water—unlikely a hundred years later. And they shared fully in communion. Information on slave contributions is rare. Holly Springs Baptist Church (Oconee) in August 1834 received five cents from "Negro Jane" in its collection, and Saluda Baptists in 1849 reported $2.24 "by colored people" for African missions.

Slaves, just as whites and free persons of color, could join a church by profession of faith and baptism or by transfer from another church. Declaring one's faith was sometimes more than just a brief statement, as with an unnamed "black woman of Mrs. Barton's by relation of the work of grace with her" at Secona Baptist (Pickens) in April 1822. Several slaves moved membership from Charleston, Columbia, Alabama, Florida, and local churches.[8]

African Americans, like all members, left their church rolls by transfer, expulsion, or death. Some slaves remained members for decades; occasionally their deaths are mentioned in minutes. Slaves sometimes belonged to churches or transferred membership independently of their owners. Although exclusions typically occurred for grosser offenses, departing from one's denominational community also was a sufficient cause. On the same day in June 1863, First Creek Baptists dismissed both Andy (J. B. Haddon) for joining the Methodist church at Shiloh and Sarah (James Harkness) for having united with Varennes Presbyterian Church (Anderson).

Slave participation in a wider range of religious activities varied by churches, by denominations, and over time. In an unusual example, around 1829 slaves endorsed a temperance pledge along with whites at an independent society, evidently loosely affiliated with Carmel Presbyterian Church.[9] Some denominations administered baptism to infants, another form of participation. Hopewell Presbyterian in 1835 recorded "3 Coulered children Baptised servants of Genl Whitners," the first local reference to the baptism of black children. That issue arose relatively late at Roberts Presbyterian Church. Member Eli wanted his infants baptized in 1863; the church, although this was the first such request from black parents, concurred, baptizing Eli and Mary's four children. Baptizing slave children was never an issue at St. Paul's Episcopal Church (Pendleton), which baptized approximately 150 black infants and children and about 75 adults (1842–65).

African Americans had access approximately equal with whites into churches and in rituals. Resulting from black presence, other, divergent issues arose, including acceptance of some in formal roles but also controls over church members.

Exhorters and Preachers

Some African Americans wished to lead more active religious lives by exhorting and preaching. Pendleton District's earliest-known slave speaking publicly, presumably to other slaves, was "Black Peter," whose "gift [was] called into question" in September 1806 by Big Creek Baptists (Anderson), who prohibited him from preaching but allowed him to continue exhorting. Methodists appointed Lot (Asbury Taylor) as a licensed preacher in 1836. Three years later he was "reported to have been guilty of imprudent conduct with a [named white] woman." When he was proved guilty by witnesses, the church reprimanded him and suspended his license to preach.[10]

Some black preachers became popular and were well liked by whites also. Abbeville County had a Methodist clergyman who was a free person of color, Cyrus Patterson, eighty years old in the 1850 census. Two noted slaves, Caesar in Anderson and Jim in Greenville counties, often preached to predominantly white congregations and sometimes traveled substantial distances for these services. Jim did not learn to read while a slave; Caesar, however, evidently could read. Caesar began his preaching career in 1811, probably then twenty to thirty years old. He led his first recorded public worship in October 1823 and periodically thereafter preached at Big Creek. The church granted him permission to go into Georgia "to exercise his gift," extending blanket approval in May 1826 for him "to go wherever, . . . by his Master's leave." Often in demand, Caesar occasionally led services at his own and at other churches over two decades.

His path was not always smooth, however. Domestic conflict with his wife led to censure. He was expelled in May 1832 for "knocking . . . down his fellow servant with an axe," but, having repented, he was restored to full fellowship in September and soon won approval to preach at other churches. He led Big Creek worship in 1844 but encountered troubles that same year when his church, split into factions, banished him. Within a year, however, it again restored him as a full member. As late as 1846 there were incidental references to his preaching. According to Robert Maxwell's petition to the general assembly, Caesar owned land, bought his own freedom and later purchased his brother, who could not be freed. He was buried around 1848 in a field behind Williamston Female Academy.[11]

By contrast Jim, known as Greenville's "slave preacher," was then just beginning his career, a story told in *Christ in Black*. Often traveling to various churches like Caesar, Jim appeared before antebellum Methodist congregations of both white and black. Around 1857 "the white people [at Pickensville] invited him to preach a sermon during their campmeeting." The following year he began preaching for Sharon Methodists (Anderson), so moved that they offered to buy him from his master, but the Civil War intervened.[12] After 1865 the Reverend James Rosemond, as he was then known, founded dozens of Methodist churches and eventually became senior minister of the South Carolina Conference. Both Caesar and Jim were remarkable men with exceptional accomplishments. Unfortunately there is no record of how African Americans responded to their preaching.

Several churches also had slave exhorters and elders. Hopewell Presbyterian appointed two elders in December 1832: "The Session taking into consideration the number of coloured communicants . . . [decided to choose] two individuals who should superintend the Spiritual walk and conversation [of other slaves]. . . . Richard, Servant of Dr. Dart and Sam, Servant of Mr. Charles Story, were duly elected."[13] Former Charlestonians Dart and Story were among Hopewell's larger owners. Richard's and Sam's role included monitoring slave members and perhaps admonishing them.

Varennes Presbyterian Church, using much more explicit language about its expectations, in 1860 appointed Willis (J. W. Norris), "(being experienced and Sustaining a good Character for Consistant [behaviour; page torn]) as a Monitor over the Coloured Members of this Church to look after their Spiritual interests and also to act as Squire, being authorized to perform Marriages among the Colored Congregation." His function coincided with 1828 Baptist language: "some discreet coloured member of the church [should] be placed as leader, who shall watch over their conduct."[14] Churches occasionally sent one or two black members to approach another one about alleged offenses.

Presumably elders and exhorters were involved in some worship services that took place on plantations; although nothing is known to have been written about them, there likely was singing. Upper-piedmont plantations were too small to have praise houses, separate buildings for slave services often anchoring a row of low-country cabins. The only specific surviving local example that has survived involves Dr. Adger's slaves, whose "wife continually assembled both children and grown people on Sunday afternoons on our wide piazzas, reading and explaining the Scriptures to them, and teaching them to commit to memory verses of the Bible, and many of our best hymns, and to sing them to such tunes as best suited their musical taste."[15]

Men known as preachers shortly after emancipation likely were antebellum exhorters or unlicensed ministers. Within three years of freedom, dozens filled Baptist and Methodist pulpits, while others served as deacons and elders. Antebellum experience proved critical. Five men involved in an 1867 Union League meeting were described as preachers.[16] Among them, "Old Simon" probably had been, informally, a Calhoun plantation preacher.

Church Controls

Churches not only appointed black deacons and elders but also established committees of white men to "manage" black members. These monitors formed only one prong of a broader effort to control slaves, a goal that appealed to owners. Hopewell throughout 1832, 1833, and 1834 set special times "to instruct the colored communicants" and called meetings for them as late as 1860. First Creek Baptist created a similar committee. When Lucinda was cited in January 1855 for acting impetuously, her case was referred to First Creek's "committee on collerd members." Evidently a long-standing body, its role was reaffirmed in 1847 in a section following one on white offenders, noting that it would be conducted by a committee and that the "church shall proceed as she has heretofore in receiving Colored Members by a permit from their owners and in dealing with them as offenders."

Slaves could not join churches freely. Being examined on their faith was not enough; they also needed an owner's "permit," like First Creek's "tickets." At Hopewell in May 1834 "16 coulered people were examined on their faith in Christ & fitness for membership[.] 8 were received on condition they obtain Certificates of good Character from their masters & 8 are to wait for further instructions."[17]

Another form of control, as at Shoal Creek, involved segregated seating. The stereotypical arrangement is slaves in a gallery, with whites occupying the main pews. Certainly that happened in many places, especially cities, but few churches in northwestern South Carolina were large enough to have balconies. The area's most historic church structure with a gallery, the Old Stone Church (originally Hopewell Presbyterian), can seat few people upstairs. In many churches, then, slaves sat on the same level with whites and, perhaps, in at least one case, side by side. At Shady Grove Baptist, a slave arrived late, sat beside a white man, and went to sleep, lying down on the pew. His nap and especially the drunkenness that caused it got him into trouble, but evidently nobody objected to his being in the pew with whites.[18]

Some churches held separate or additional services. Periodically Hopewell offered segregated religious instruction and examination. Anderson Presbyterian Church also had additional services: in May 1843 "the Colored people assembled in the afternoon by appointment and were addressed from the Pulpit by Rev. Mr. davis and an appointment made for service for them especially every other Sabbath afternoon." These sessions seem to have been more instruction in obedience than worship.

Owners' Attitudes

Many church practices regarding slaves furnished owners with additional controls. Salem Baptists (Anderson) cited Harry in February 1811 as he needed to be shown "his duty towards his mistress, as well as his Creator." When churches had separate sermons, ministers presumably stressed obedience to masters, as do surviving printed sermons and catechisms. Since most ministers owned slaves, as often did elders and deacons, that likelihood is even greater. Only twelve Pendleton District men owned more slaves in 1800 than did Presbyterian minister James McElhenney. Joseph L. Grisham (Oconee), clergyman and prosperous landowner, and Anthony Ross (Anderson), a later Hopewell cleric, were among the larger owners in 1840.

Charles C. Pinckney, a Pendleton resident from one of South Carolina's prominent families, linked instruction for slaves with obedience and greater agricultural productivity. Using an 1829 address to the Agricultural Society of South Carolina, he urged religious instruction for slaves. He believed that with education "a sense of duty would counteract their reluctance to labour . . . [and] would augment their numerical force and consequent production."[19]

Even after South Carolina in 1834 forbade teaching slaves to read and write, some clergy believed they should be taught the scriptures, as did Abbeville layman Robert A. Fair, who spoke on why *Our Slaves Should Have the Bible*. *Religious Instructions for Slaves* was among John D. Ashmore's extensive library. For quite different reasons Justice O'Neall regarded the 1834 act as unwise, having grown "out of a feverish state of excitement produced by the *impudent* meddling of persons out of the slave States." Moreover, "when we reflect *as Christians, how can we justify it, that a slave is not to be permitted to read the Bible?* . . . The best slaves in the State, are those who can and do read the Scriptures."[20]

Presbyterian Dr. John B. Adger became a lightning rod for debates on church-slave relationships. Although coming from one of Charleston's most prestigious and affluent families, Adger spent several years in Turkey as a missionary. After health problems forced his family to return home, he launched a church building for Charleston slaves. Adger's inaugural sermon in 1847 was printed as *The Religious Instruction of the Colored Population*. Although his slave congregation began and continued as an auxiliary to Second Presbyterian with full sanction, it quickly ran into problems. Adger later moved to Pendleton, joining relatives who already lived there, served Hopewell Presbyterian Church, which was 39 percent black, and, along with his daughters, taught his slaves to read, illegally. He owned five slaves, and his brothers in the Pendleton area, with fifty-three, were among Anderson's upper 5 percent of slave-owning families in 1860.[21]

Owners, who on some plantations had services for slaves, may well have used those occasions to reiterate obedience to masters. Presbyterians published suitable materials, such as Orangeburg County's Presbyterian minister Andrew Flynn Dickson's two volumes of *Plantation Sermons*. Since joining a church required a master's permission, that emphasized owners' control while it also erased any sense of equality of believers within the church.[22]

Church Discipline

Just as religious instruction for slaves emphasized obeying owners, church membership involved communal supervision. Churches pronounced what they considered right behavior, occasionally answering queries about disputed principles. Church minutes reviewed are predominantly Baptist, so references to exclusion are skewed heavily toward Baptist concerns. Presbyterians excluded members far less often than did Baptists. Because faith and conversion were only initial steps, there were many occasions to err during "a pilgrim's progress."

Churches expected—and in those years could enforce—attendance and obedience to their strictures. They frequently called both white and black members to task for quarrels or alleged infractions. African Americans were excluded, as were whites, for stealing, drinking, cursing, dancing, and lying. Overall, charges fell disproportionately to blacks, however, and were often phrased ambiguously; by contrast white members usually faced specific accusations. Minutes frequently omit exact charges against a slave or use more general terms such as "misbehavior" or "disorderly" conduct. That may have meant relationship to the church itself, or, as with two Barker's Creek slaves in May 1848, "unchristian Conduct," which may cover a multitude of sins.

Congregations sanctioned those, white or black, who spoke against their own church, created dissension, or refused to answer charges. Churches settled disputes among members, including quarrels among slaves and, more rarely, between slaves and owners, and occasionally served as mediators at other churches. Periodically a dispute or offense linked people from two churches, as happened twice with First Creek slaves in 1834–35 and 1839.

Religious advocates then, as at other times, established and monitored standards for morality, marriage, and sexual behavior. Toney, Secona's first black member, was expelled six months later in May 1798 for "whoredom[,] swearing and other evil things." A few slave men were excluded for bigamy, adultery, or fornication. Old Liberty on a busy October 1813 day expelled Dick and Cynthia (both Clark's), who presumably was the "other woman," for adultery, and also dealt with a domestic quarrel, excluding a couple—Cato (Dobson) and Leah (J. Smith)—for fighting. In April 1814 and June 1815 the church censured two more women, Venus and Dinah, for adultery with unnamed men.

Although Baptists pursued these matters more fervently than did other denominations, Hopewell Presbyterian in October 1842 accused Mary of "forming a connection without a formal marriage." She repented and was counseled. Hopewell in November 1857 excommunicated three women belonging to Mrs. Pickens—Bina, Sally, and Sarah—for "immoral conduct," leaving specifics to a reader's imagination, as also occurred with Billy (Col. Pickens), suspended in December 1864 for "gross immorality."

Charges of sexual irregularity, including conceiving a child out of wedlock, fell more often on women, slave or white, than on men. Salem Baptists expelled Katy (Brooks) in August 1831 because she "had been in a pregnant state . . . [and] has neither a name nor a place amongst us." When Big Creek censured one male and two female slaves in November 1839, it may have been for joint sexual misconduct, for "as soon as the case was understood they were excluded for sin." And one 1844 incident produced expulsions from two churches.[23] Cases of unmarried slave women having children were considered especially serious when a child was of mixed race. Censuring Patsy (Joseph Rogers) in 1835 for her "white child," Big Creek Baptists specifically condemned "mixing of her increase out of color." Similarly, Salem in 1844 ousted Hannah (Thornton Coleman; he brought the complaint) for "having a child without any husband & it a mulatto."

While whites were censured at approximately the same rate for varied offenses charged against African Americans, churches also exercised controls specific to slavery. Slaves periodically were called before their church for disobedience to masters, telling lies about their master, and running away. First Creek expelled Meser in May 1843 "for Abusing of his Master Bro Gantt" and Mack (Taylor) on Christmas 1847 "for Bad Conduct to his Master."

Conversely, a few white people were cited or excluded for mistreating their own, or other people's, slaves. One bizarre case involved a slave woman, Judy, and her owner, Johnson, both Big Creek members. They had a running feud for years that the church tried, unsuccessfully, to settle. Johnson acknowledged "whipping his servant." Despite efforts of a committee that met with Johnson and Judy, their dispute recurred in 1833, when the help of intermediaries from four other churches was necessary. Shoal Creek heard in April 1813 that John Cleveland was "too intimate with his own negro woman," a charge dropped due to insufficient evidence, but Salem Baptists expelled Elias Watson on similar charges in November 1844.[24]

Stealing was a crime practiced by white and black, slave and free. Slaves were frequently hauled before magistrates and freeholders courts for stealing, as was Lewis (Betsey Burris), found guilty in 1836 and given twelve lashes. Mountain Creek then excluded him, and in 1837 excommunicated Sophy (Sister McGregor) for concealing stolen property and sent her to a magistrates and freeholders court, which had her whipped.[25] Exclusions of slaves for theft reached an all-time high in the 1830s, when there occurred more than half of all such cases between 1790 and 1865. Charges before the magistrates and freeholders of theft were similarly high in the 1830s, although that decade was more prosperous than the 1820s.

Sanctions against slaves and exhortations to be obedient did not occur on either a random or a consistent pattern. Over a seventy-year period, exclusions happened much more frequently during times of societal stress and generally at the same times as more magistrates and freeholders trials, as "Convergences" demonstrated in the previous chapter. Similarly, special church instruction for slaves often coincided with white concerns about "slave unrest." The largest numbers of slaves excluded for disobedience or disrespect to masters and overseers occurred in the 1810s and 1840s.

Because exclusions affected many slaves, their membership averaged only two years.[26] Old Liberty Baptist, which received twenty new black members in 1812, excluded six of them the following year. Like white counterparts, an ousted slave could later express repentance, ask forgiveness, and be restored as a member, as happened to as many as one-third of expelled blacks.

How Many?

Issues of adequate seating for slaves, owners' attitudes, and controls raise a bigger question: how many slaves were church members? The answer for Anderson, Oconee, and Pickens counties is about one-third of those fifteen or older, approximately the age of accountability for religious decisions. The figures in the accompanying table come from the late antebellum period. Membership—like population—was considerably higher in Anderson than in Oconee and Pickens.[27]

Denominational proportions of blacks varied in these three counties as well as throughout the state. Churches usually reported slave and free people of color as one "colored" total. Baptists and Methodists both had about 30 percent "colored" members, approximating their proportion of the population. These denominations statewide had 45 percent and 55 percent respectively, with Methodists very close to the state's percentage of blacks. Presbyterians had 37 percent statewide but only 12 percent in the three counties, concentrated mostly in Anderson; Oconee and Pickens had few Presbyterian churches.

Slaves, who constituted about 33 percent of Anderson's population, made up 32 percent of Baptists in that county in 1850. Individual Baptist churches in the county ranged that year from 2 percent black in both Williamston and Andersonville, to 62 percent in Lebanon. Pickens and Oconee had smaller percentages of black population than did Anderson, but disproportionately even fewer slave members. The Methodist Pickens Circuit, including Oconee, was only 8 percent black, the same figure as in 1825, although slaves were 22 percent of the population of Oconee and Pickens. Located mostly in those counties, Twelve Mile River Baptist Association churches similarly had few black members. Baptist and Methodist churches in mountainous sections of Oconee and Pickens had few, if any, blacks, while churches in areas with more slaves often reached 35 percent or 40 percent.

Local situations produced a wide range of figures. These fluctuations also occurred over time as some churches declined, then had an influx of new mem-

Table 6.1 **Slave and FPC Church Members, ca. 1860**

Denomination	State	Region	AOP	Comments/Regions (Not Identical Areas)
Baptists	45%	31%		
Methodists	55	53	29	circuits (4)
Presbyterians	37	23	12	presbytery (1)
black % of population:	57	34	30	Pickens-Oconee, 22% Anderson, 37%

Sources: state and regional denominational reports (see table 6.2).

bers.[28] Although African Americans constituted about 11 percent of Presbyterians in Anderson, Oconee, and Pickens counties in 1859, individual congregations varied enormously. Four small Presbyterian churches reported no blacks; Hopewell's 39 percent in Pendleton village was the highest Presbyterian percentage. Anderson County had only two Episcopal churches, St. Paul's with an estimated 25 percent black membership by 1860, and Anderson village, which had only a handful of members. Slaves, a majority of the population within Pendleton, were 55 percent of the town's Baptists (1850). About 33 percent of the membership of the four Methodist circuits were black, and 47 percent for the Pendleton Circuit, higher than that of the town's Presbyterian and Episcopal churches.

These figures, only approximating total religious impact, do not reveal information about involvement, if any, in Sunday schools after 1830. Other slaves, not church members, probably attended camp meetings and protracted services, revival-type events typically held at churches and lasting several nights, sometimes a month or longer.

Analyzing individual church membership lists, it quickly becomes apparent that typically only some slaves of individual owners belonged to a church. Among Hopewell owners, only 8 percent of their slaves in 1852 were members there, or about 15 percent of those over fifteen years old. Although John E. Colhoun (Jr.) evidently had none of his slaves baptized or married at St. Paul's, his son had twelve baptized, married, or buried by the minister in the 1850s while dispensing with services for others. Counting baptism, confirmation, marriage, and burial, the percentage of owners' slaves at St. Paul's was significantly higher than for most other churches, primarily due to marriages there and to infant baptism. The number of full-fledged black communicants, though not clear, was much smaller. Only two or three attended most services.

Slave membership depended substantially on owners' attitudes. Perhaps house servants, with closer contact with the white family, and perhaps required to accompany them, were more likely to attend and become members than were others. Generally, members from a single plantation who belonged to a specific church joined over a period of years, which suggests substantial individual volition. During protracted meetings several from one plantation joined on different nights. Owners at St. Paul's, however, exercised more prerogative in having slave children baptized, although not at uniform ages. In 1842 alone the church baptized sixty-five slaves—ages of many unknown—belonging to owners mostly from Charleston.[29]

A closer examination of church rolls shows many slaves were members of churches where their owners were not. One possible explanation may be slave husbands joining churches attended by their wives or other relatives. However, as with whites, late antebellum black members were disproportionately female. Sarah, transferring from First Creek Baptist to Varennes Presbyterian, about five miles away, seems to have done so while her owner did not. Whatever the explanation, slaves as a group clearly had some autonomy in joining and attending churches.

This expanded their own interactions and aided in maintaining an African American subculture.

Many churches—about half of those examined—also included one or more free members of color. Rolls frequently stressed "free," especially as "colored" rosters had columns for owners' names. Smaller percentages of free people of color than of slaves belonged to churches. Churches with free members incidentally provided contacts with them by slaves who attended. Like slave counterparts, free people of color frequently found themselves sanctioned or excluded from their churches, evidently more often, in part because they had more opportunities to stray.

Why Join?

Why would slaves join churches, knowing they would come under congregational scrutiny and discipline and might remain members for only a few months? Some would have done so because of their beliefs, often intensified by religious services, especially during protracted meetings. Although frequent references appear elsewhere in the South to frenzied emotions that drove blacks and whites to "mourners' benches," only scanty local instances survive. At a September 1833 camp meeting at Bethel, sponsored primarily by Carmel and Hopewell Presbyterian churches, "the occasion was one of awful solemnity & deep interest[.] A great many filled the anxious seats during the meeting. Four persons were admitted for the first time," without specific reference to African Americans.[30]

Church membership sometimes involved favor from peers and family, as it did for whites, and from owners. Beyond the faithful, others—and perhaps some devout believers too—joined, knowing that such an act might encourage indulgence from owners who were members. Peer or family pressure may have induced still others to join. Besides religious atmosphere of church membership and attendance, slaves, like their owners, participated in churches because they were also social settings. These benefits began for African Americans on the walk, often several miles, to church. Walking, and joining those from other plantations, was itself a social occasion, and even more so after evening services. A number of magistrates and freeholders cases concerned alleged events between home and church. Some African Americans saw relatives only at church; and services sometimes became part of weekend visits by husbands to their wives. Membership rosters seldom identified slave couples, but occasionally some were noted who belonged to different owners.

A network of contacts likely extended to other churches also. That was all the more probable because white, and presumably black, people went to services outside their own churches. Most antebellum churches held services only once a month. It was not unusual, then, for people to visit other churches and denominations. Washington Taylor (Greenville County), pursuing his normal activities and visits, attended eight churches in one year. African Americans likely experienced some variety as well.

Much social activity took place outside the walls of the church; some people never made it inside. Cases dot antebellum records of slaves drinking, playing cards, and gambling nearby during church services. They could be punished by courts for these activities as well as for disturbing the Sabbath, all civil offenses. Other socializing, sanctioned by churches, occurred outdoors. Once-a-month services could become quite lengthy. Coupled with long trips to rural churches, churchgoers periodically held "dinner on the grounds." Contemporary local references are rare, but twentieth-century people harked back to them as traditional occasions. Prolonged postbellum services and church dinners likely were a continuity of these earlier experiences. Similarly, current African American church homecomings may recapture social elements of earlier protracted and camp meetings.[31]

Athough they were held for religious purposes, such meetings also provided many social opportunities, as often a thousand or more people encamped for several days, perhaps a week. Camps were usually held at dedicated sites during slack agricultural periods, especially in August. Originally interdenominational, they became primarily Methodist sponsored. There are frequent references around the South to slave participation and white enjoyment of black music and preaching. It is not known how many slaves attended camp meetings; certainly some did. Four joined Salem Baptist in 1832 as "Sardis Camp Meeting converts." In a more secular capacity, vendors sold food while others hawked various items for sale. One runaway lurking around Sandy Springs camp ground obtained ample food. Oral tradition refers to a predominantly black antebellum camp ground in Pickens County.[32]

Sunday and special services did not reach the entire population, black or white. If one-third of slaves fifteen years or older belonged to churches, that raises questions about the other two-thirds. To what degree were they exposed to, and affected by, Christianity? No reliable evidence exists for Anderson, Oconee, or Pickens counties. Over 40 percent of area whites fifteen and older were not church members either. Yet Christianity was part of the general culture, at least for whites. Black members likely talked about their religious views and sang spirituals and hymns around others. Services were held on some plantations, and exhorters probably spoke often and informally outside of organized services. Many people who never attended church would have nevertheless learned something about Christianity.

Virtually nothing is known about local religious views of African, Caribbean, or Islamic derivation. Lowcountry slave burials employed many African traditions, both in beliefs and in accouterments (plants, shells, etc.), but slave burials in the three counties, as elsewhere in the piedmont, seem to have followed the same configurations and grave decorations as those for whites.

Works Progress Administration (WPA) interviewers in the 1930s asked many questions about "root doctors." One practitioner, Berry (Lemuel Hall), was tried in 1833 for "giving roots to slaves for unknown purposes." One slave witness against him said that Berry had "offered to give her Little girl roots[.] she understood the object was to make her mistress good to her[.] she saw the roots. he told her it was sampson snake root and hart leaves roots that he gave to her for the cholic." Berry advised that, by following him, Gilbert "would find him a second saviour[.] he would take his right foot and kiss it[.] he repeated it over several times." Berry supposedly told other slaves "to join him or do as he would tell them and he would Bring them out." Whether he was establishing himself as a religious leader, planning an escape, or doing both is not clear.[33]

African Americans seemed to join churches at specific times, suggesting that their motivation derived partly from societal factors beyond their own faith. They often joined in large numbers at protracted meetings when typically many white people also responded. These waves of new members frequently coincided with broader religious movements or societal stresses in the South or the whole nation. Anderson Baptists more than doubled their memberships in 1832, a year "noted for numerous and extensive revivals of religion, extending from Maine to Mexico" according to their history.[34]

Typical of successful revivals, First Creek, holding one September 25 through October 23, 1841, brought in seven blacks among ninety-six new members. Barker's Creek's September 1859 protracted meetings "at night" resulted in fourteen new white and ten slave members, followed a month later by Mountain Creek, where thirty-six joined including fourteen "black" members. Churches experienced similar influxes during the Civil War.

Besides social functions, churches offered other advantages for slaves. Studies of religions describe them as providing comfort. Certainly belief offered some solace from slavery's daily grind, epitomized in the spirituals "Nobody Knows the Trouble I've Seen" and "Deep River," which states, "going over to camp ground." Spirituals emphasized "King Jesus," which elevated him all the more above earthly masters. African Americans particularly identified with ancient Hebrews enslaved in Egypt and lyrics that included the phrase "let my people go." Names of brothers Moses and Aaron, who led the Hebrews from Egypt, were popular among slaves; and references to the Promised Land, Canaan, appeared frequently in spirituals and in names of postbellum churches. Although both white and black shared many Old Testament names, blacks had a virtual monopoly on Hagar, the name of Abraham's servant who was driven into the desert. Even when white and black used the same names, such as Esther and Moses, slaves likely saw different symbolism in their choices.

Churches also provided, both deliberately and unintentionally, rudimentary literacy for some. Before it became illegal in 1834 to teach slaves to read or write, Hopewell Presbyterians, as well as others, had Sabbath schools for them, using books donated by a white elder. Listening to hymns and sermons provided an opportunity to learn both content and grammar of standard white expression. It is difficult to prove or disprove that some slaves learned to read by memorizing scriptures heard in church and then comparing those memories with texts they saw illegally. The SCBC urged constituent churches to have slaves memorize scripture.

Table 6.2 **Church Minutes Consulted**

Church	County	Date Org.	Date of Minutes (Earliest Surviving)
Shoal Creek Baptist	Oconee	1790s	1796
Secona Baptist	Pickens	1790s	1795
Mountain Creek Baptist (aka Bethesda, 1812+)	Anderson	1789	1798
Big Creek Baptist	Anderson	1798	1801
Salem Baptist	Anderson	1802	1805
Old Liberty Baptist	Oconee	1804	1815
Barker's Creek Baptist	Anderson	1821	1821
Mount Pisgah Baptist	Anderson	1791	ca. 1824
Peter's Creek Baptist	Pickens	1826	1825
First Creek Baptist	Anderson	1824	1827?
Holly Springs Baptist	Oconee	1828	1828
Bethel Baptist	Oconee	ca. 1832	1832
Oolenoy Baptist	Pickens	ca. 1795	1832
Carmel Presbyterian	Pickens	1787	1832
Hopewell Presbyterian	Anderson	ca. 1790	1832
Coneross Baptist	Oconee	1812	1833
Mount Carmel Baptist	Pickens	1837	1836
Westminster First Baptist	Oconee	1836	1836
Cross Roads Baptist	Pickens	1797	1838
Anderson Presbyterian	Anderson	1837	1839
Holly Springs Baptist	Pickens	1839	1839
Roberts Presbyterian	Anderson	1831?	1839
St. Pauls Episcopal	Anderson	1816	1842 *
Salem, First Baptist	Oconee	1844	1844
West Union Baptist	Oconee	1848?	1848
Belton Presbyterian	Anderson	ca. 1770	1851
Midway Presbyterian	Anderson	ca. 1833	1856
Retreat Presbyterian	Oconee	1851	1856
Griffin Baptist	Pickens	1857	1857
Richland Presbyterian	Oconee	1833?	1857
George's Creek Baptist	Pickens	1856	1859
Pleasant Hill Baptist	Pickens	1848	1860
Honea Path Presbyterian	Anderson	1860	1860
Varennes Presbyterian	Anderson	1813	1860
Hopewell Baptist	Anderson	1803	1868

Also: South Carolina Baptist Convention (printed); Holstein Conference and South Carolina Conference (Methodist; printed); South Carolina Synod

Table 6.2 *(continued)*

(Presbyterian; printed statistics and ministers); Baptist associations: Bethel, Edgefield, Fork, Fork Shoals, Reedy River, Saluda, Twelve Mile River, Tugalo.

Source: All minutes used are deposited in denominational historical collections at Furman University (microfilm) for Baptists; Wofford College for Methodists; or Montreat, N.C. (some microfilm, some original) for Presbyterians; or are published (St. Paul's; * not minutes but lists of baptisms, confirmations, marriages, deaths, and burials).

Finally, as enslaved peoples were exposed to the teachings of Christianity, became familiar with the Bible, and sat through procedural meetings, they acquired a foundation for their major post–Civil War institution, black churches. Without this decades-long acquaintance with Christianity, that core institution of African Americans in freedom would have been absent. Despite intense scholarly interest in African religious views, these did not have the same organizing structure or constancy as Sunday church services. Many early postbellum religious and educational leaders came from church elders and slave preachers. Other than families and agricultural work, no other factor of enslaved life was as continuous after 1865 as was religion.

SEVEN

Ambivalent Interactions

JUST AS FREE PERSONS OF COLOR occupied an odd niche in antebellum life and laws, slaves too held a unique position. Although taxed and treated legally as property, their humanity set them apart from livestock or furniture. On the one hand, they could run away. On the other, their families could be disrupted, they could express themselves when disgruntled, and their status as humans provided some legal, religious, and moral protections. And they shared intricate emotions with owners and one another.

Interactions by masters with their human chattel were far more complicated than those in church and court settings. Multiple issues of legalities, contracts, control, economics, and human factors were so complex that hundreds of South Carolina cases reached appellate courts during the 1800s.[1] Owners regarded their slaves both as property and as humans—additional layers of antebellum complexity—and treated them accordingly. Edgefield's James Henry Hammond insisted that owners should act justly if they wished to be obeyed, given slaves' "keen sense of justice," but also argued that it was "necessary that the negro must fear."[2]

Slaves Considered as Property

Slaves were technically classified as "personal property" along with household possessions, clothing, professional tools, livestock, and agricultural implements, in contrast to "real property," or land. One man wrote in 1843 that "negroes, hogs, and sheep all arrived safely." Periodically when an owner died, heirs drew for slaves divided into lots.[3] This legal status angered antebellum abolitionists and African Americans for centuries.

Analyzing slaves as property, as they legally were, however, does furnish a useful vehicle for describing many conditions of their status and their lives. No other issue so dramatically demonstrates conditions beyond their own control. Like other chattel, slaves could be bought, sold, leased, rented, bequeathed, loaned, and moved from one place to another. During their lives and at their deaths, owners could dispose of slaves as they pleased. Moving to Alabama, Florida, or elsewhere, masters were entitled to take their human subjects with them. Whether buildings, land, vehicles, or other machinery, property has to be maintained, as did slaves, who required food, housing, clothing, and medical care.

As property, slaves might be owned not by individuals but instead by firms or jointly by heirs, usually minor children or unmarried adult siblings. Anderson County sisters Leah Williams and Rachel Moore together controlled their inherited holding. While the 1860 census listed four slaves for Pendleton village firm W. H. D. Gaillard & Co., Gaillard possessed thirteen personally.

Owners could make money by hiring out their slaves, by no means permanently located on their owner's premises. An early 1808 *Miller's Weekly Messenger* issue advertised "Negroes for Hire." That matched a need by other whites, usually nonowners. William Robertson wanted to hire "a Good Young Negro Woman suitable for the Business of the House." Also, labor by slaves could offset either a white man's obligation for road work or, as done for Dr. T. J. Pickens in 1861, a portion of his taxes. Owners occasionally traded slaves, perhaps to dispose of an unruly one or to acquire another with special skills.[4]

Like other property, slaves when sold came with receipts of purchase. Although Pendleton's deed books include transfers of nearly a thousand slaves, relatively few transactions appear after 1828. Slaves could also be insured and certainly were taxed; during most antebellum years their rate was 60 cents each, although occasionally higher. And items of property may be branded or marked indelibly, but the only slaves in Anderson, Oconee, or Pickens counties known to have been so marked were done as punishment, such as Colhoun's, chopped in both ears.[5]

Buyers had safeguards, as slaves could not be legally sold with hidden defects. Lucy and her child, bought for $830 in 1851, were returned as "unsound" and "severely afflicted with fits." Her value, even with a child, went down to $300. Occasionally sellers specifically warranted slaves as sound, or otherwise described defects and let a buyer accept those terms. John Chapman bought Rachel in 1825 with full warning that she is "blind in one eye and she is subject to a swelling in her legs and feet when she is with child."[6]

Typically investors of any property prefer a diversified portfolio, just as owners needed field hands, skilled carpenters and blacksmiths, fertile young women, house servants, and cooks. Major Aaron Broyles's executors in 1845 advertised a sale including "the whole of his Real and Personal Estate, consisting of thirty-eight Likely Negroes[.] Among the men are various mechanics. Two young Blacksmiths, and a distiller of uncommon skill and experience. And among the females are good Cookes, Weavers, Washers, and Seamstresses. It is a singular fact that in the whole number, there are not more than four older than thirty years." Samuel Maverick's 1853 estate appraisal listed one blacksmith, three carpenters, one bricklayer, four field hands, and one cook. With no local heirs, a holding of thirty-seven went to seventeen buyers.[7]

Owners at times had to decide relative investment advantages of buying more land or additional slaves, or, when hard pressed, disposing of one or the other. Thomas Clemson for years worried about such decisions, delayed for lack of a buyer. By contrast, his grandmother-in-law quickly and firmly rejected a suggestion that she buy additional ones.⁸ Slaves, however, were not predictable investments. Some died young, while others survived for decades. Like compound interest, natural reproduction often increased size and value of holdings. But ratios of field hands might change with too few or too many, leading to purchases or sales. When those with specific skills died, they usually had to be replaced at a premium.

The Townes family, based in Abbeville and Greenville counties, talked bluntly about slaves as investments. H. H. Townes observed that "good young negro fellows sell in this district now for upward of $800," and Samuel Townes in 1836 hired out all of his slaves for $960, better than the income from working them. A year later H. H. Townes advised, "Don't sell negroes—they are the best stock a man can own. . . . The truth is there is no investment so safe and so profitable as land and negroes." Like their Calhoun relations, the Townes families relocated slaves among their various holdings.⁹

Upstate owners seldom sold slaves. Sales occurred for three primary reasons: an owner needed additional cash; he fell into debt and creditors had his slaves sold to repay themselves; or he died. Mortgaged at times against borrowed money, slaves could be seized, whether obligated or not, and sold to satisfy debts. Sheriffs' records and advertisements are replete with such notices, followed by sales if debts remained unpaid. A randomly selected *Pendleton Messenger* issue, May 19, 1843, ran advertisements for ten Anderson sheriff's sales. Approximately 150–200 slaves were advertised for sheriff's sales a year. Owners who raised money to repay creditors avoided the sale. One owner in 1842 had to sell a forty-three-year-old carpenter, already mortgaged, as did another in 1845, two boys eleven and nineteen years old. Often only one or a few of an owners' holding were mortgaged and then sold for debt. S. R. McFall's estate in 1862 had eleven slaves, eight of them being sold to satisfy his debt to J. N. Whitner. An owner selling slaves for debts had to be in dire straits. Most white men of property owed money to several others, while at the same time holding notes due to themselves. Estate accounts with lengthy schedules of obligations suggest a complex financial world with much indebtedness.¹⁰

"Sale days," a fixed time such as the first Monday in each month, were big antebellum events as hundreds of people also conducted their legal business or shopping at the county seat. Offerings almost always included land, slaves, agricultural implements, and household furnishings. These sales ritually followed an owner's death unless each slave was individually willed to heirs. Often white family members bought most or all slaves themselves, the sale serving as a mechanism to divide equally the value of slaves and of other possessions. Rarely did an owner's widow and children not buy some family slaves.

African Americans had their own families, and anything involving one member affected others. Since their families often transcended a single plantation, actions by other masters impacted slaves elsewhere. And they could and did run away, sometimes after being sold to a new owner and separated from their family.

Changes in Slave Lives When Owners Died

Fluctuations in owners' circumstances, including marriage of sons or daughters, directly affected African Americans. Pendleton did not have, or evidently need, a regularly operating slave market. Rather, most exchanges occurred when an owner died either by will, by estate auction, or by sales for indebtedness. But parents also frequently gave, or transferred on semipermanent loan, slaves to their adult daughters and sons. Thomas Dean confirmed for each of his children "the deed of gift heretofore made by me." Language applied to humans considered property varied enormously. Most owners preferred the word "negroes" in wills, although some used "servant" or a phrase such as "my woman." Although "slave" appears frequently in estate appraisals, it occurs only sporadically in wills.[11]

An owner's death almost certainly brought major changes for his slaves. Only rarely was that not the case; for example, the Kilpatrick estate remained mostly intact for almost twenty years.[12] Since slaves often represented owners' most valuable property, those who wrote wills—only about half did—took special care in their provisions. Limited only by emotional reactions of heirs and legal protections for widows and minor children, owners could make dispositions as they chose. Masters varied enormously in bequeathing holdings, thus affecting slaves in quite different ways that they could not themselves predict, let alone control. Some wills, like Thomas W. Harbin's (Pickens) in 1853, itemized each slave for a specific recipient, often with various contingencies. At the opposite extreme, some men simply said that "negroes," themselves or their value after being sold, should be divided among heirs.

More often, owners specified some bequests and then directed that those remaining be divided by lots or sold. Pendleton Isbell in 1846, after devising certain slaves to his children, provided that "the increase of negro Harriet" be sold, along with other property, and that income be shared among his children. White deaths thus often seriously disrupted African American families.

Estate records almost always itemized slaves, a major asset, by name in either a will, inventory, or sale account. Appraisers usually specified a value, sometimes ages, and occasionally occupations such as carpenter, coachman, or seamstress. Advertisements for estate sales listed skills, which should command higher prices. Some families, including that of Old Jack, wife Kate, and children Esther and Lancaster, had their relationships spelled out in Samuel Taylor's 1798 estate; and Joshua Mansell in 1854 named Matilda and her three children, ranking them in birth order.[13]

Elderly servants sometimes received special attention. Robert Anderson—among all owners demonstrating in his will the most concern for slave welfare—provided for Old Rose and also listed other "old and decrepit negroes, which are of little or no value, but which must be supported while they live viz: Monday, Solomon, old Cato and young Cato, Old Dede and old Nancy. It is my wish that these old and infirm negroes should be supported, and made comfortable on the plantation while they live." One appellate case in 1812 earned this judicial statement: "Many cases of beneficent provision for slaves, are allowed to take effect *sub silentio* by the humanity of those interested."[14]

Decades after the legislature in 1820 forbade emancipations, a few owners found other ways to provide for favored slaves. Robert McCann wanted "Byna to live with any of my children she may choose, not as a slave for if the law would allow her emancipation I would do it, for she has been a trusty, honest, faithful servant to me and I give her one cow and one calf to be her own." Abbeville's Williamson Norwood could not legally free two women and their four children. Instead, he willed them in trust to his son, directing in 1847 that if an opportunity arose, he should educate them or get them to a free state. The legislature in 1839 outlawed covert emancipations, such as Byna's, but some favored, especially elderly, slaves lived as de facto free.[15]

Some owners paid careful attention to retaining slave families together. Methodist minister James Douthet (1848) directed that his oldest slaves keep their youngest children; Joseph Whitner in 1821 wanted "Negroes possessing families to be divided without separating mothers from younger children as far as possible"; and others directed that slaves should be kept in proximity to one another.[16]

Sometimes wills allowed slaves to select their own masters among heirs. Douthet prescribed "that the two oldest ones with their youngest child have the privilege of disposing of themselves to any person in or out of the family that they may choose to live with that will take them at their evaluation," and "those my wife chooses shall have the same privileges at her death of choosing their future homes." James Hembree (1849) directed that "my Black woman Peggy & her son Grief Presly have the liberty to chose their master" with a pass for five days "to look out for a person of their Choice."[17]

Several people stipulated that slaves should not be separated from their owner's family. Robert Anderson provided, as did a few others, that slaves were "not to be sold out of the family" and "none [were] to be sold unless they turn out to be thieves and unless they cannot be restrained by good treatment, friendly cautions, admonitions and a merciful use of the rod of correction"—similar to Thomas Caradine (1820), Joseph Reid (1828), and Elizabeth Reeder (1851).

Owners' primary concerns, of course, were not slaves' welfare but care of their own families, especially the surviving wife, minor children, and other needy relatives. Peter Greenlee in 1798 named six slaves who would support his wife and minor children; when all his children reached adulthood, the slaves were to be divided. Since estates stayed open until the youngest child reached twenty-one, owners would be particularly concerned to arrange their affairs to benefit minor children. Andrew Reeder (1856) provided generally that "if any of my negroes become unmanageable in any way[,] they are to be sold." Sometimes a slave was not objectionable, but income was required to sustain heirs, especially children.

White women had few rights regarding slaves, as in other things. A husband assumed legal control of his bride's slaves as well as those she inherited later during their marriage. A man could direct that, on his death, slaves be allocated to his widow to support her, while also specifying who received them after his wife's death. Only rarely did a husband's will give the widow absolute control. Almost always a widow lost her right to any slaves when she remarried. The practical reality was that widows had slaves on loan only, not by outright ownership, unless there were no children of that marriage or of her husband's previous marriage. Some owners, not wanting sons-in-law to control inherited slaves, resorted to deeds of trust. Women could protect their own property, including slaves, by prenuptial agreements.[18]

Wills sometimes dealt as much with family disputes as they did with slaves and other assets. Quarrels plagued many families. Heirs squabbled among themselves and in courts over ownership of slaves, very much pawns in these family arguments. Some heirs removed slaves from South Carolina without legal title, which usually led to lengthy, disputed estate settlements.[19]

African Americans at their owner's death, then, found themselves at the mercies of any provisions that he made. But protections for keeping slave families together or for choosing their own masters came rarely. Frequently at an owner's death they were sold to settle his estate and pay debts. However, they often were bought by the deceased's family or by neighbors.[20] Despite perilous conditions of being sold, African Americans often found themselves living not much farther away. Their families, then, usually remained in contact and were less permanently disrupted, even if separated, than might be imagined.

Legal, Religious, and Moral Standards for Treating Slaves

Legal standing as property often placed slaves in precarious situations more than once in their lives. But they were not only property. Legal title did not give owners a right to treat, or mistreat, African Americans at whim. Although enslaved, they were human beings for whom some legal, moral, and religious sanctions demanded proper treatment. Other mechanisms, including social disdain for cruel owners, protected slaves on certain levels. Some masters treated their slaves more kindly than did others and took particular care to protect some, if not all.

Both white neighbors and slaves' descendants were well aware of who were especially cruel masters. A relatively sparse, rural population did not mean anonymity. Thus an Anderson County chronicler could write seventy years after the fact about Silas Massey's starving his slaves. Stories about slave preacher Caesar and fabled runaway Goober Jack lingered into the twentieth century, and the black Sherard family's late twentieth-century account told of good treatment by white Sherard owners. But Viola Williams was able in 1990 to describe cruel treatment that her grandmother suffered under a named Abbeville County owner.[21]

Early-eighteenth-century laws voiced more clearly slaves' humanity than did later enactments. Colonial texts combined both ethical considerations and public safety, as badly treated slaves might rebel or run away. A 1735 Act for the Better Ordering and Governing . . . of Slaves allowed justices to inquire whether masters supplied adequate provisions. Five years later a supplementary regulation punished both owners who compelled Sunday work other than "absolute necessity" and those who overworked slaves, who must have "sufficient time for natural rest," the law said.

Adequate food was necessary both for humane purposes and also for slaves to continue work. When Big Creek Baptists in 1823 censured Judy for telling lies against her owner, she claimed she did so because "she had not enough to eat." Slaves James and Toney justified their stealing hogs because they were not provided with sufficient food by their owners.[22]

National debates about abolishing slavery, coupled with antislavery preaching, especially Methodist, led to more concerns about standards of treatment. Allegations of mistreating or abusing slaves sometimes brought vigorous denials, as with Colhoun's 1798 vindication of his own actions. When accused in 1790 of beating to death a child he had borne by a "negro woman," a Henderson man not only denied it but compelled his accuser to retract with a sworn affidavit.

Baptists pondered proper treatment of slaves, especially fellow members. Replying to a 1793 query whether a master was justified in applying "stripes for disobedience," the Bethesda Association ruled that, like parents, masters "have a right to govern their household, and to use the rod, if need be, yet are subject to the discipline of the church, for cruelty or oppression."

Criminal trials for mistreatment were rare. A few instances emerge, as do some instances of severe whippings. Several slaves, when cross-examined by suspicious jurors, admitted they had confessed to committing crimes only "under the lash," as Cresia did in 1851 while tied and whipped. To punish Nero in 1838, Dr. William Anderson chained Nero's neck to a pole, and Whitner then whipped him. The account made no reference to this being ill-treatment; that threshold must have been very high. The worst documented ill-treatment occurred during the Civil War when a coroner's jury charged a Baptist minister with causing his slave's death by neglect; yet the minister evidently suffered no punishment. Neither did an overseer, who shot and killed a slave for disobedience during the Civil War.

A few additional protections for slaves were added in the 1800s. Judge O'Neall praised 1821 laws that made murdering a slave a felony and that forbade unlawful whipping or beating of a slave: "They protect slaves, who dare not raise their own hands in defence, against brutal violence." Not until 1858 did the legislature forbid "any cruel or unusual punishment," while emphasizing an owner's right "of inflicting on such slave such punishment as may be necessary for the good government of the same."[23]

Some slave deaths raised questions of suspicious circumstances. An 1834 Anderson inquest on Sam's body yielded a verdict that he "came to his death by an unmerciful beating supposed to be inflicted by his master sd. [said] John W. Beson." If Beson was tried for it, no documents have been found. And a long-running local quarrel erupted when Benjamin Hagood accused Alfred Hester of beating a slave to death.[24]

Owners seldom recorded whippings inflicted on slaves, so there is little documentation of what may have been a frequent occurrence. WPA interviews with elderly former slaves elsewhere in the state elicited many comments on frequent whippings experienced by either themselves or other slaves on the same plantation. Dozens of interviewees, however, said they witnessed no whippings. Using language similar to Harris's "genteel flogging" to one of his father's slaves, Margaret Castleberry in 1823 acknowledged that she "moderately corrected a negro for a willful disobedience of his." A rare account of whipping comes from Georgetown's Davison McDowell in 1839: "Found John trenching and pretending to do nothing from old age[,] told him to do his task[,] was very impertinent—I gave him a whipping (Intended giving him a few cuts) but he would not deign to beg untill I gave him 32 lashes. [And the next day] . . . he took himself off [and] returned in a day or two."

Similarly, a Spartanburg slave testified that "his master will sometimes when excited fly into a passion and act with a great deal of violence, draws his gun and threatens to shoot his negroes." This was all confirmed by the owner's son. Although the law affirmed an owner's right to correct slaves by whipping and set other provisions as barriers against brutality, slaves had to cope with drunkenness and bad tempers taken out upon themselves. Elsewhere, "Miss Annie was her own whuppin' boss."[25]

Robert Anderson's will implicitly recognized his slaves' humanity as it safeguarded them from being sold or separated from their own families and provided for elderly slaves. Samuel Blair (Abbeville) in 1813 prescribed that slave Jack should be treated "in a human Christian like manner." But only Douthet, among local ministers, spoke explicitly about slaves' humanity: "They are human beings and have high claims upon the humanity of those in whose hands they are and I wish [them] . . . to have all the privileges of suiting themselves that their situation and the laws of the country will justify."[26]

African Americans found themselves in a strange dichotomy, considered property while called part of the plantation family. Their servile condition was enshrined by the same laws that required humane treatment, just as some wills bequeathed them as property but demanded kindness from heirs. Other contradictions occurred both at churches and in trials of slaves before magistrates and freeholders courts, which often found them innocent. Societal attitudes, complacency by whites about enslavement, religious beliefs, human psychology, and laws all encompassed convoluted dichotomies.

PART 3 ∾ *African American Subculture and Life on the Plantation*

Introduction to Part 3

THE LAST THREE CHAPTERS focus on white-controlled environments where slaves and whites interacted. Attention now shifts to daily life, families, and an African American subculture. In these areas African Americans had more influence over their own lives than in churches, magistrates and freeholders courts, and their legal standing as property.

No longer a tiny percentage of a sparse rural population, blacks increased in both numbers and concentrations by 1820. This enhanced their ability to sustain an effective network for exchanging goods and information while maintaining family contacts, even if separated among diverse plantations. African Americans in 1850 constituted almost 30 percent of the population of Anderson, Oconee, and Pickens counties. That same year nearly 40 percent of them lived in holdings with 20 or more slaves, and just barely 5 percent where there were only one or two. By 1820 most whites and blacks remained in Pendleton District with few families leaving in subsequent years. African Americans, clustered in larger numbers, both persisted and persevered.

Although whites dominated churches and entirely controlled both legal and political structures, African Americans developed a significant and effective culture. Ironically, this culture was fostered by socializing at churches and by weekend visits among divided family members. Slave life and slavery itself were not monolithic but institutions shaped, and reshaped, piecemeal over time by human factors. They were also susceptible to slaves testing boundaries and extending them outward.

Although part 2 shows multiple layers of interaction, the following three chapters demonstrate even more complexity within plantation life and an African American subculture. The subculture thrived because many slaves were able to travel—for work, on weekend visits to family, and for religious services. This facilitated an extensive communications system, reinforced by a microeconomy of goods and money. Not always a cohesive group, slaves had rivalries and conflicts among themselves and multifaceted, sometimes friendly, associations with their owners.

The plantation itself was a mostly self-contained economic unit. Owners sometimes referred to its inhabitants as a "family, white and black." Myopic, paternalistic, and sentimental in expressing these views, those using this phrase clearly understood that all peoples on a single estate were linked together in many ways. Blacks and whites jointly provided medical care, food, clothing, and shelter for one another, acting from dramatically unequal positions of power and resources. They shared not only material things but emotions also. Life among black and white on the same plantation was richly textured as well as multicolored.

African Americans, constrained by slavery, successfully maintained strong family relationships in many cases. They also managed to accumulate distinctive personal possessions and to pass them, their skills, and family names through generations. Families, both nuclear and extended, were key to a subculture and its communications network.

Analysis of both black-white interrelationships and the African American subculture must start from five basic points: (1) Much of slaves' condition, which was beyond their control, was determined by owners. (2) African Americans comprised 25–30 percent of a rural population—too limited in both numbers and percentage to have cultural cohesion such as that achieved in black-majority areas. On the other hand, both their numbers and ratio were too small to constitute a major threat to whites. So, upper-piedmont African Americans had, in some ways, more latitude than did their lowcountry counterparts.

Further, (3) most slaves had frequent and significant interaction with white people, producing, for good or ill, personal relationships. They would not have experienced a virtually all-black existence as happened on the state's Sea Islands. Few slaves in northwestern South Carolina toiled under black supervisors, like those called drivers in the lowcountry, and few even under white overseers. White families with small holdings labored along with slaves in fields and kitchens. (4) By the 1820s, most Pendleton District slaves were some generations removed from Africa —perhaps by as many as fifty or a hundred years—with diminishing African retentions. (5) Few slaves were sold or removed out of the area after 1820; most, then, lived within thirty miles (often much less) of their parents, spouse, and children. Many had close family ties and, by 1820, there was a strong continuity of the overall African American population.

Examining the Colhoun family and their slaves provides a case study of one plantation with its changes and relocations brought about by white family marriages, deaths, and indebtedness. And it further illustrates slaves' ambivalent status as property and as people. Despite disruptions in slaves' lives, continuity of slave families and of names also appears.

An intricate web involved owners living from their slaves' labor, giving them gifts, sometimes buying produce from them, and hunting or quilting together, but at other times whipping and even assaulting them. Given multiple tensions and complicated layering, emotions and relationships were complex, often bizarre. They all derived, however, from enslavement, the fundamental starting point.

As African Americans in the upper piedmont led their lives within the confines of bondage, they reshaped the boundaries that constrained them. Through resistance, strong families, and their communications network, they formed an effective, cohesive subculture despite internal frictions, conflicts, and frequent interactions with whites.

EIGHT

Carving out a Niche

ALONGSIDE MAINSTREAM CULTURE of European Americans and their societal structure emphasized in earlier chapters, African Americans developed an alternative culture.[1] Generally, it seems, African culture was subsumed within this white context through acculturation. But closely examining interactions among African Americans unveils a distinctive subculture with extensive connections. Presumably not as richly African as found in heavily black-majority areas such as coastal Carolina and the Sea Islands, the upstate's black community had its own effective network. It was basically a parallel culture, but, belonging to a minority and not always visible on the surface, it is more appropriately called a subculture.

This network, predicated on many overlapping personal contacts among slaves, consisted of communications that included information as well as trading and selling. It involved much travel for some slaves throughout the three-county area, sometimes to Abbeville and Greenville counties, and even to Charleston, located over two hundred miles away, at least a ten-day trip by carriage. Some of John C. Calhoun's slaves could quote current cotton prices not only for Charleston but also for Philadelphia, New York, and Liverpool. Reporting this, a New York newspaper correspondent visiting Calhoun's plantation was amazed at the information they possessed and implicitly recognized the subcultural network. Ability of some slaves and free people of color to read or write gained for them exposure to a wider world. Small numbers learned to read, often in secret. This chapter explores how the slaves' economic system, network of personal contacts, and literacy shaped their subculture, gradually pushing its boundaries wider.

An African American Subculture and Microeconomy

Any subculture depends on contacts and communications among its members. It thrives only by developing and continuing its own traditions, customs, and celebrations. African Americans managed to do these things while living within and interacting with a white dominance and having daily contacts with owners. This subculture was limited by the fundamental conditions of enslavement and by the laws. However, patterns of slaveholdings and interactions with whites often led to some laws being overlooked and also facilitated, unintentionally, this subculture's functioning.

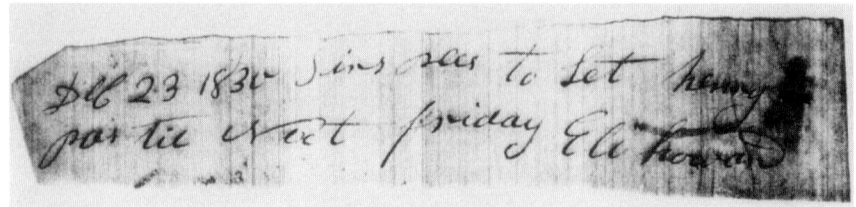

Pass, issued for Henry in 1830, for year-end holidays; found in his pocket when he froze to death. Black Heritage in the Upper Piedmont, S.C Department of Archives and History

Contacts among slaves, especially exchanges viewed as potentially subversive, preoccupied South Carolina's legislature as early as 1690. Although it sought to curtail such contacts, repeated legislation, often more restrictive, over 170 years attests to the legislature's failure to accomplish its goal. A 1740 law, passed shortly after the Stono rebellion, forbade "using or keeping of drums, [or] horns . . . which may call together or give sign or notice," as was thought to have been done during the rebellion of 1739. Later restrictions required a white person in attendance for any meeting at night and prohibited locked doors on such occasions.

Controls included passes for absences from one's plantation, permits for any goods a slave might sell, and patrols to search for runaways and stolen items. A slave warning about patrollers was reported in virtually every state's WPA interviews: "Run, nigger, run, de pader-roller'll git yuh! Won't git me, git dat nigger'hin' that tree." But the local patrol was seldom effective in finding runaways or stolen items. Despite varied legal restraints, African Americans achieved an incredible ability to travel throughout the region, to visit, and to establish connections for information and goods.[2]

Daily life often strayed from this strict legal code. While absent from their own plantation, slaves had to carry a pass stating their destination and the length of time they were permitted to be away. When a slave named Henry died in 1830 in Anderson County, a small paper found on his body read, "Sirs pleas Let henry pas til Next Friday," dated December 23, 1830. Yet periodic announcements reminding owners to furnish such permits indicate large-scale lapses, at least during certain periods. The July 16, 1834, *Pendleton Messenger* warned owners that passes were required, but "perhaps it is not generally known, or is forgotten."[3]

Such legalities certainly were not always observed. Two decades later the *Keowee Courier* printed a similar reminder. Because of white-black interaction, increased by attending church together, individual slaves were recognizable throughout a wide area, and owners were often casual about passes, it seems. This laxity facilitated extralegal slave travel and suggests a highly relaxed attitude, if not disregard, by whites for some laws. In fact it is hard to imagine owners writing a pass for each slave going to church on Sunday or for each errand to neighboring plantations or to the general store. Moreover, some owners could not write. Some slaves dropped in at each other's houses to visit or to sleep overnight. With frequent opportunities to meet each other and to exchange both information and goods, African Americans maneuvered their way through, around, and underneath a dominant white structure.

Some slaves led lives more varied in personal activities, possessions, and even money than traditional stereotypes allowed. Surely a far greater number had tedious lives with few variations or pleasantries, and some at times were destitute of food and clothing. But the rarer stories stand out conspicuously. Devoid of any firsthand local slave testimony, we have to rely on incidental comments, each telling and withholding stories. No owner wrote systematically about his or her slaves' lives, let alone the slaves' possessions or entertainments. A dearth of significant coverage makes it hard to distinguish a rare instance from that typical for other African Americans.[4] This discussion focuses on money, goods, and transactions involving them. But the underlying theme is that of a substantial latitude to travel, occasionally long distances.

The richest source for such information comes from records of approximately 550 slave trials. These magistrates and freeholders trials compensate for a major gap in information. Hardly any among thousands of "ex-slave" interviews conducted by the Writers Project of the WPA dealt with Anderson, Oconee, and Pickens counties.[5] Although not as lengthy, magistrates and freeholders summaries were contemporaneous, written at least seventy years before WPA interviewing. The court files illuminate much of slave life otherwise inaccessible. But their focus on criminality must be viewed cautiously, as only an infinitesimal percentage of slaves was accused and found guilty of crimes. Those, however, are the ones whose actions made the news. By contrast, Spartanburg's David Harris reported dull evenings on patrol, which sought to halt slave misdoings. On December 1, 1860, he recorded, "Went pateroling in the early part of the night, but made no discoveries," and on December 3, "last night went to father's plantation and examined the negro-houses, and found all right."[6] Even during the Civil War, on March 23, 1862, "I went patrolling in company of Mr. Hawkins. We caught no negroes, and my ride otherwise was rather uninteresting." Patrollers' efforts often found no wrongdoing.

Widespread and frequent contacts—both personal and economic—among some African Americans emerge from these records. Clearly slaves had an extensive, multidimensional microeconomy. Legal components include earnings, authorized sales to white customers, and legitimate selling and trading within the black community. By contrast illegal aspects encompass stolen money or goods, improper trading with whites, and gambling. These activities occurred at plantations, stores, hotels, railroads, secret rendezvous points, and even camp meetings. They also extended to adjacent Greenville and Abbeville counties and occasionally to Charleston or Augusta. Through these varied means slaves managed to accumulate money, sometimes a sizable amount.[7]

Numbers of slaves throughout the South possessed enough cash to buy their freedom, as did Peter Johnson, husband of free Ruth Oglesby. Although still himself a slave, Caesar had sufficient money to buy freedom and property for his brother. Others bought freedom, and a few purchased land through white men, who held the title.[8]

Such examples, along with freed people's ownership of livestock and other possessions in 1870, further suggest that some already had money and farm animals when emancipation came in 1865. The subsequent five years were an unlikely time to accumulate such resources. Sylvia Cannon, a WPA interviewee from outside the upper-piedmont region, claimed that some slaves got rich from selling produce from their patches and had "big rolls of money" when freedom came. Perhaps exaggerated, her statement indicates both sizable quantities of money held by some slaves and memories of that surviving decades later.[9]

Legal Sources of Money and Goods, and Sales

Although not an absolute requirement, possession of money and goods substantially benefited the subculture, just as a slave network made acquisitions possible. Though enslaved, African Americans still had opportunities to make money, acquire goods, sell them, and trade; some methods were legal, others were not. Means for legitimately obtaining funds, usually small, began with the plantation and one's owner. Occasionally masters elsewhere in the state, and perhaps in Anderson, Oconee, and Pickens counties, gave slaves small gifts of money, usually coins, or paid small amounts for extra chores. Slaves typically had patches of land on which they could grow crops or raise small livestock for their own consumption to supplement plantation allocations. The few references to these products include primarily grain and molasses, along with chickens and free-roaming pigs.

Slaves also could legally raise produce beyond their family's needs and generally were allowed to sell the excess. The word "patches" implies a row or two of assorted vegetables, but some plots may have been larger. In 1852 two men worked a patch together, surely more than kitchen vegetables. A July 1865 labor agreement provided that "freedmen are to retain the products of their patches of corn, gardens, chickenyards, etc. as heretofore."[10] One freedman got rights in his labor contract to an acre, called a "patch." That size may have had antebellum precedents. Since many acres went untilled on a typical upstate plantation, owners could easily afford such land for slaves' own produce.

Some slaves raised and sold their own cotton and other cash crops as well as livestock and game. Growing any sizable quantity of cotton as early as the mid-1820s suggests that several people on a plantation may have pooled their patches. On May 29, 1863, Harris noted that "the negroes have been nearly all day planting tobacco for themselves & for me," and J. D. Ashmore recorded on May 18, 1856, "one hand Hoeing negro Rice." One astute observer noted that most rice grown locally was "confined to negroes" who achieved "an abundant yield." Another report indicated that some Calhoun slaves earned as much as forty dollars each year from selling their own cotton and other produce.

Other African Americans raised and sold hogs and poultry. Henry D. Colhoun in the 1850s periodically bought hogs from his own slaves, and Thornton (Silas Massey) had a permit to sell rabbits. Apparently other men sold game they hunted and killed. Some had weapons available for that purpose, as well as dogs to help with the hunt.[11]

Besides selling crops, animals, and game, slaves could also market their own handicrafts. Brummer (Col. John McFall), like others, sold baskets. George Seaborn's slave won the Pendleton Farmers' Society agricultural implements prize—worth one dollar—in 1853 for his oxen yoke. Some women developed reputations for their fine lace or other handwork and may have been able to sell some of their products. Katy (W. J. Jones) won the society's 1859 cash prize for best pantalets, and Candas (Andrew Oliver) bought materials and made a quilt, in this case for herself. She paid a white woman to weave for her.[12]

Slaves sometimes were hired to people other than their owners, especially in Charleston and in smaller cities and towns but also in the upper-piedmont countryside. Workers sometimes got to keep a portion of fees paid for their services. And slaves could earn additional income by part-time jobs on the side, as several did serving as sexton for St. Paul's Episcopal Church, and as did Henry (Dr. Gibbes), cleaning and locking up the Farmers' Society building.[13]

Hiring could be either a short-term or annual arrangement. The Kilpatrick estate (Oconee), leasing out several excess slaves on a yearly basis, received $394.55 —wages received for several hands—which amounted to more than 10 percent of its total cash revenues in 1855.[14] Only the most prosperous owners could afford to keep their own blacksmiths, tanners, and carpenters. Other masters periodically hired these specialists for a short-term job. The Kilpatricks in 1856 received $12.50 from J. B. Earle for their blacksmith's skills, while paying $30.00 for work by Mrs. Lorton's carpenter. Some women served as midwives, and Dr. F. W. Symmes's Pendleton practice had its own slave midwife. She and others were likely to keep part of their fees, as were blacksmiths and carpenters.[15]

Construction in the 1850s of the Greenville and Columbia Railroad through Anderson County and the Blue Ridge Railroad branch line, serving Anderson and Oconee, utilized hired slaves. A railroad officer in Pendleton advertised in 1854 for one hundred railroad hands, evidently either white or black. Squire (John Donald Jr.) and Austin (James Bigby) worked that year for the Greenville and Columbia line, and Cyrus, a Blue Ridge brakeman, died from an 1860 accident when his head hit a bridge. These railroad workers went to somewhat more distant locations and came into contact with wider segments of the African American community. And they developed skills useful for sizable numbers of postbellum men who worked for railroads.[16]

Towns afforded even more opportunities for slaves' labor to be passed from owner to leasee and perhaps to make some money for themselves. Various white merchants and skilled craftsmen in Anderson, Belton, and other towns periodically needed help and hired black labor to supplement other employees. Hotels in new towns along the Blue Ridge Railroad route and at mineral springs resorts, such as Williamston or Greenville County's Chick Springs, required many workers. Hotel managers, almost none of whom owned slaves, may well have leased those serving as porters, livery staff, maids, and cooks from area owners. Mary (Williams) was hired to the Williamston hotel, while in 1860 free Mary Oglesby was a servant at D. Biemann's Walhalla hotel.[17]

Whether acquired legally or otherwise, this money still entered the legitimate economy. Since many African Americans had some cash through their hired labor or legal sales, its possession or expenditure alone did not suggest criminality. Slaves, then, could buy clothing, jewelry, watches, and perhaps small animals to raise. They often legally sold or bartered these items to each other. When slave Jim reported that he had left his wet, soaked "great coat" in Abbeville, John C. Calhoun suspected "that the whole [story] is a fabrication of his, and that he sold, or gambled away the coat." Unsettled debts among slaves led to problems that were resolved often by barter but occasionally by quarrels and fights. Berry (Lemuel Hall) in 1844 owed Samuel $1.75 for a wool hat, but successfully bartered factory cotton and a bonnet instead.[18]

Several examples illustrate some slaves' possession of money. Parris (Thomas Alexander) swore that the Oglesbys stole his coins amounting to almost twenty dollars, including twenty eagle half dollars and two gold pieces; and George (Daniel Mattison) and Manuel (Alex. Ramsey) were convicted of stealing thirty-nine dollars from Isaac's (Mattison) cabin. One woman changed lowcountry bills for quarters with slaves.

Slaves saved money for festive occasions, especially year-end holidays. A white Simpson man recorded, "The more industrious and thrifty hire out their services, for which they are well paid by their employers, and not infrequently this class can sport more ready change than their improvident masters. . . . For months before the holliday arrive they are planning out their field of operations. Chickens eggs baskets and all their little earnings are carefully hoarded away to be lavishly expended [in celebrating]."[19] As numerous opportunities arose to earn and keep money, slaves laid the basis for an African American microeconomy. By legitimately earning money and selling goods, they worked within the system. Some, however, went beyond its boundaries, pushing them farther.

Thefts, Illegal Sales, and Bartering Stolen Goods

Although several aboveboard sources existed for money, some slaves resorted to ilegal means, especially theft. Often whites were active or complicit partners. Examples of stolen items, sometimes from slaves, reveal as much about slave interaction and their network as about pilfering. In at least twenty-three cases over a forty-year span, slaves were convicted of stealing money from stores, houses, and hotels. Amounting to barely more than one incident every two years, these examples involved those arrested before trying to spend the money. Their takings, surely seized from them, ranged from a few dollars to an extraordinary $1,170.50.

Certainly slaves taking these coins and bills thought they could spend them without inducing a challenge. Since criminal cases dealt with apprehended, alleged felons, these specific individuals thought wrong. Yet enough other slaves must have been spending money legitimately to make it likely that they could do the same without being caught. One man tried to get a hundred-dollar bill changed, presumably expecting to manage his transaction safely.[20]

Other thefts involved a variety of goods, including watches, stolen from whites. When Daniel H. Cochran, an Anderson town peddler, saw his silver watch in Harbert's (James C. Keys) possession at muster, Cochran charged him with its theft. But the story as it unfolded was not so simple. Lewis (Joseph Whitefield), having stolen the watch, sold it to Harbert, who later offered it to Bob (John Fretwell) for seven dollars. Lewis also stole, then sold, whiskey, a pig, and tobacco. Simon (Dr. O. R. Broyles), who supposedly stole a watch at an Anderson hotel, and other slaves were arrested not for having watches, but only because these specific ones were reported stolen.[21]

It was dangerous to steal and try to sell distinctive goods. Many products made by hand, from homespun cloth to tanned leather and shoes, had such unique characteristics that they could be readily identified. Dozens of slaves who stole hides or tanned leather were caught because owners recognized their purloined property. Although patrollers could search cabins at will for stolen property, in only a few cases did the patrol find stolen goods through random searches. On the other hand, as is true today, we know only about the criminals who were caught, not about those who succeeded in escaping notice. Slaves had only a small role in theft compared to many white culprits tried before criminal courts.[22]

The legislature repeatedly enacted laws to prevent slaves from stealing goods, especially grain, poultry, or cotton. Any slave offering these items for sale was required to have a "ticket" or permit from his owner verifying that a transaction was legitimate. Joe (Archibald Simpson) had tickets to sell grain in 1842, but Peter (Noah Richardson) and Bob (Martin H. Smith), offering stolen chickens and corn without a permit in 1851, quickly got caught.[23]

In buying stolen items from slaves, whites also acted illegally. Actively encouraging theft, numerous people acquired a reputation—all bad, as far as other whites were concerned—of buying from slaves without required tickets. A former Marion County slave told a WPA interviewer that some whites, poorer than slaves, would "take anything you carry dem." Hundreds of cases came before the court of general sessions in which white men, along with some women, were charged with such illegal trade, sometimes as repeat offenders—a practice that must have been both widespread and lucrative enough for more than a few people to indulge in it. Churches throughout antebellum years cited and expelled white members for "trading with negroes."[24]

White collaboration sometimes went beyond receiving stolen goods. According to 1838 testimony, Alfred Moore helped Nero (Dr. William Anderson) to steal by providing him with "false keys." Clearly many white people dealing with slaves operated on the fringes of, or beyond, the law. J. R. Casey and R. T. Casey, both accused in Pendleton of trading with slaves for whiskey and bacon, fled. The *Keowee Courier* reported, "The citizens of Pendleton village have recently found it necessary to rid that community of certain persons of this character."[25]

Despite the temperance movement, liquor was in demand by white and black alike. Although several slaves were convicted of stealing liquor, usually whiskey, only one guilty verdict occurred after 1843. Some slaves and free blacks operated a thriving liquor trade. Lige, whose owner Micajah Carter lived in Franklin County, Georgia, and Jerry, whose owner John Brown (Anderson) operated a ferry across the Savannah River, bought liquor to sell. Traveling to Augusta in December 1845, they purchased four gallons, using chickens as payment. They then sold whiskey to various Anderson County whites. One white woman in 1846 referred to slaves keeping a tavern, evidently an ongoing operation.[26]

Although much slave trading or stealing involved whites as willing if illegal buyers and thefts often left other whites as victims, sometimes blacks stole from one another, further demonstrating slave possession of desired goods and money. Joe (James Burriss), who had a permit to sell turkeys, sold them to other slaves. But Nero (Dr. William Anderson) in 1842 traded a coat for a double-wool counterpane to Ephraim (Sherrill), who gave it to Nancy (Duckworth). The gift turned out to have been stolen from G. W. Masters, thus involving four plantations, as did an 1850 incident.[27]

African American Communications Network

African Americans' possession of money, liquor, and goods, and their ability to earn or to trade these items, indicate widespread economic activities constituting a microeconomy, itself only a small part of slave contacts. This also suggests, in many instances, capacity of some to travel widely on their personal time, including visits to each other and even to the jeweler's shop or to hotels. The preponderance of magistrates and freeholders trials concerned offenses on weekends, especially on Saturday nights, and year-end holidays. But numerous alleged crimes occurred on midweek nights, sometimes miles from the slaves' plantation.

Using opportunities for travel and for meeting, African Americans extended their activities and contacts. Both extensive and effective, this network provided a quick means of circulating news, gossip, and ideas as well as goods. Estimates of its reach show a spiraling potential. Families, especially those divided between two or more plantations, formed a key link as they maintained contact. African Americans expanded this network on their own. Owners who often hindered it unintentionally provided other opportunities for its success.

A possible scenario describes the network's functioning. A man from the fictitious Thomas holding of fifty slaves, who visited his wife on another plantation with fifty—where there would be other visiting husbands, attended a church with slaves from twenty other plantations, and ran errands to his owner's relatives, might well have contacts directly or indirectly with hundreds of slaves in a given week.

Even within a single plantation's confines, the majority of slaves would hardly have been isolated. Nearly half of all slaves by 1810 lived on plantations with ten or more slaves, and by 1830 one-third lived in holdings of thirty or larger. For those African Americans, even their plantation itself afforded more people on a daily basis to chit-chat with or share thoughts, moods, problems, or uplifting words than had all the whites on the same plantation.

Opportunities for conversing often extended beyond one's own plantation even on workdays. House servants got sent on errands to the general store, post office, or other plantations. Someone undertaking these tasks might encounter, if only briefly, slaves from several other plantations as well as from the town itself. When owners sold wheat, corn, timber, or livestock, slaves of either seller or buyer handled the delivery. Extended white families had slaves deliver notes, gifts, and items on loan. When owners traveled, they often had drivers and perhaps other servants in attendance, affording them yet more opportunities to cultivate further contacts although under confined conditions of enslavement.[28]

An ever-expanding array of contacts ranged from similar opportunistic meetings for a large plantation with many comings and goings to constant visitings back and forth in towns like Pendleton, Walhalla, Anderson, or Honea Path. But potential encounters dropped dramatically for anyone living in the more isolated Oolenoy Valley with relatively few other African Americans within miles. Even there, however, Sunday contacts would have broadened horizons.

While engaged in a week's typical activities, a slave man could come into direct if brief contact with one hundred slaves from thirty plantations, which together would have had nearly 800 slaves. That would have included a surprising percentage of eleven thousand slaves in 1850, collectively an extended network. News of any kind could travel quickly. Encounters may additionally have included several free persons of color. That many contacts would have been available only to slaves on larger plantations who also left their premises on errands.[29]

Weekends were often a special and lively break in a continuous round of labor. Released from work on Saturday afternoon, slaves had a day and a half for their own activities, for salving the previous week's aches prior to acquiring new ones in the week ahead, and for socializing with African Americans beyond their own plantation. In a gender-stereotyped world, it was almost always husbands who traveled to visit their wives, seldom the reverse. Women sometimes were granted permission to visit siblings, parents, or children and thus occasionally traveled, too. Former slave William Ballard recalled that "slaves carried news from one plantation to another by riding mules or horses. . . . I remember my mother rode side-saddle one Saturday night. I reckon she had a pass to go; she come back without being bothered."[30]

Numerous instances suggest that many people were coming and going, even throughout the night, at plantations during this break and at other times. A holding of fifty to seventy-five slaves might have husbands visiting from five or ten plantations. David G. Harris in fall 1860 went to his father's "negro-house" to inquire about a stolen turkey; there he "dismised one of Esthers visitors." On another occasion "last night I went to father's negro-quarter. I had a lively chase after two negroes. Came home late." And an appellate case noted that "the strictest watching could not, at times, prevent them from visiting their acquaintances in a neighboring plantation or yard." Beech Island Farmers' Society's concern (Edgefield) had a core truth: patrols were needed to stop slaves' "rambling around at night."[31]

Large numbers of slaves and sometimes free people of color could meet informally on Sundays at church and with their families. A typical church membership might include African Americans from ten to twenty different plantations. "We got most of our outside news Sunday at church," a former slave reported. Since churches were often several miles away, walking there afforded opportunities for socializing and relatively unmonitored contacts, as we saw earlier. Homes of free families of color were sometimes popular as Sunday meeting places. Whites joined in these festivities at times, presumably both for their own enjoyment and for token compliance with laws about monitoring black "assemblies."[32]

Examples in magistrates and freeholders trials illustrate groups of slaves gathered in varied places; many wound up as innocent witnesses. Witnesses and defendants in a given case sometimes came from plantations many miles apart, even from throughout the county. In 1859 a thief, his victim, and nine witnesses all had different owners. And a group who heard runaway Alfred in 1862 included at least twenty slaves belonging to eleven owners.[33]

Towns especially provided daily opportunities for casual meetings while slaves did their owners' shopping, took cows to a common pasture, ran errands to the store, or just "loafed," a common term then for white and black. Testimony concerning an 1855 fire in Pendleton village demonstrated that sixteen slaves of five owners, and probably others, were out and about that evening.[34]

Other larger but less frequent occasions brought together many people, both black and white, from across a wide geographic area. Musters, for example, required white men to attend and drill; some of them took a slave. Yearly militia inspections were major social occasions attended by many people, some bringing slaves as servants and drivers as well as cooks and serving staff for festive meals. Some African Americans, attracted by crowds and excitement, went voluntarily. Sale days took many white men, some slaves typically accompanying them, to the county seat, attending sales or conducting business there; wives occasionally joined them to shop and visit.

Some events attracted reportedly large numbers of both races, as often did parades and circuses. Revivals and camp meetings, much larger than Sunday church services, drew hundreds and sometimes thousands of people for nights and days on end. Thousands of whites and blacks also attended executions of slaves, as in Greenville's 1825 brutality. In Charles Ball's account, prolonged partying at a hanging site lasted several days.[35]

A small number of slaves went long distances while doing their duties. They accompanied and served owners traveling to Columbia for business, shopping, or visiting; women going to Charleston for similar activities or for months of schooling; men taking goods to Hamburg and Augusta for markets; and others visiting their relatives elsewhere in the state. While Pendleton's elite frequently visited Charleston, lowcountry planters summering in Pendleton brought household and personal servants for stays typically as long as nine months, creating a special Charleston connection. Networks involving slaves provided opportunities to know about larger cities and their happenings.[36]

Extended families, such as the Calhouns, frequently employed slaves on errands among their three contiguous Pickens plantations, to neighbors, and to farther destinations. In 1843 Calhoun, having just received a letter from his Charleston agent, gave "directions to my servant to leave it [at Mrs. Placidia Adams's home] as he goes & return for it when he comes from the Village [Pendleton] with the mail." The Pickens and Abbeville Calhouns periodically sent a man, unaccompanied, between plantations fifty miles apart. At least one overnight stop, perhaps two, along the way would be necessary. When John C. Calhoun's runaway was captured in Abbeville County, another slave, Lewis, went to fetch him; this required nearly a week's round trip. Other Pendleton-area families sent a slave by himself to their own Abbeville, Laurens, or Greenville relations.[37]

Others occasionally traveled alone on long journeys. Illegal runaway Goober Jack was able to find his way home from Mississippi to Pendleton, a trip lasting perhaps a month by foot. Longer, authorized Civil War travel occurred for several slaves in Anderson, Oconee, and Pickens counties who went back and forth between Pendleton village and Simpson sons encamped in Virginia. Another young fellow returned his master's body by train; that cost "$197.50 fare for transporting corpse from Richmond VA & fare for negro boy."[38]

During frequent contacts in field, kitchen, and church, African Americans often overheard white people discussing various matters. A man who drove the carriage or ran errands to the general store would have heard other news in passing. A former Chester County slave told a WPA interviewer, "How did we get news? Many plantations were strict about this, but the greater the precaution the alerter became the slaves, the wider they opened their ears and the more eager they became for outside information. The sources were: Girls that waited on the tables, the ladies' maids and the drivers; they would pick up everything they heard and pass it as to the other slaves."[39]

Information that flowed among African Americans constituted an oral culture. African languages, mostly unwritten, fostered oral communication and transmission of knowledge, skills that survived the Middle Passage and well served descendants in Anderson, Oconee, and Pickens counties. This network would have been efficient for transmitting information and rumors, as well as for extending the informal trading system. It would also have been most helpful for keeping in contact with family members who lived elsewhere in the region. It may well have facilitated some reading and writing skills during enslavement. Surely it quickly passed along disturbing news of brutalities, executions, and slave resistance elsewhere. Many white people may have talked about slaves punished for crimes and running away as warnings with the full expectation that the tales would be repeated.

The best evidence of the network's potential value was white efforts to curtail circulation of political news among slaves, especially during late antebellum and war years. Legislators often passed various laws as they understood that trouble in one part of the state might soon appear elsewhere. Erroneous news in 1865 that all emancipated slaves were promised "forty acres and a mule" traveled rapidly throughout the South, as reported then by federal officials. That December both state and federal authorities foresaw major disturbances if freed people around South Carolina had a simultaneous protest or uprising against their government's failure to distribute land to them. These officials clearly recognized that a far-reaching slave communications system operated throughout the state. Further indications come from the quick registration of black voters, exceeding 90 percent of eligible men, in 1867, and of large numbers of black men in Anderson County who joined petitions to Reconstruction governors.[40]

Broader Horizons: Charleston Connections and Literacy

Communications reached even farther among both whites and blacks because of Pendleton's Charleston connections. These contacts linked Pendletonians with South Carolina's largest city and most-developed African American urban life. Owners directly facilitated these exchanges, which enriched slave subculture and extended its linkages.[41]

Affluent lowcountry planters and Charleston merchants in the late 1700s speculated in newly available backcountry lands.[42] Relocations began slowly in the 1780s, and the Pendleton village area gradually attracted families of similar wealth and sophistication. John Ewing Colhoun in the mid-1790s established Pendleton District as legal residence for his state legislative seat.

Post-1800 arrivals included the Reverend James McElhenney and his well-to-do second wife Susannah, a widow with twenty-five slaves. Other prominent lowcountry families—including Mavericks, Gaillards, Duprees, and Norths—also settled in Pendleton. Together eight such families in 1810 owned nearly 5 percent of Pendleton District slaves and a much higher percentage in the immediate village area. By 1820 former Charleston-area slaves totaled at least 350. Mostly concentrated within a six-mile radius from Pendleton village, relocated African Americans likely were a majority of that vicinity's black population. Lowcountry families with their slaves attended Pendleton's Hopewell Presbyterian and St. Paul's Episcopal churches.

More important than their numbers, surely these urbanized slaves from the country's fourth-largest city in 1800 brought with them knowledge of Charleston's almost two thousand free people of color, including recent émigrés from Haiti. Charleston was then the South's primary metropolis. African Americans coming to Pendleton in the mid-1820s would have stories to tell of Denmark Vesey's 1822 revolt and of the creation, then suppression, of African Methodist Episcopal (AME) churches between 1817 and 1822. Influences from Charleston were diffused throughout the Pendleton area society as more and more slaves accompanied their masters there.[43]

Pendleton's black population increasingly represented a sophisticated level. Robert Mills, famed architect and publisher of South Carolina's first atlas in 1825, observed that "a very select society is found here, and in the neighborhood, where some gentlemen of fortune and high respectability from the low-country have located themselves and their families," accompanied also by slaves. This "select society" soon expanded as Colonel Francis K. Huger and John C. Calhoun followed. One Peedee planter moved ca. 1839 to Pendleton, along with seventy slaves including African-born Tombo. African American contacts expanded. Later trains brought war-time refugees, an influx of several hundred lowcountry blacks and whites during 1862–65. Some Pendleton-area African Americans moved to Charleston after emancipation seeking job opportunities or reuniting with family there.[44]

Many freed people in Anderson, Oconee, and Pickens counties in the latter 1860s adopted lowcountry Huguenot surnames such as Drayton, Dupree, Gaillard, Manigault, Mazyck, Middleton, and Pinckney. And Pendleton blacks established the upper piedmont's first African Methodist Episcopal churches, based partly on their knowledge of Charleston's AME church fifty years earlier. Charleston connections enriched Pendleton's African American community while broadening their perspectives and their network.

For a much smaller number, their ability to read multiplied opportunities significantly. In *No Chariot Let Down*, Charleston-area free blacks conveyed family information and gifts among some slaves and read letters to them. Similar contacts may also have occurred in the upcountry. Free people of color likely transmitted literacy skills to some slaves, especially their own relatives. In the 1850s a few slaves and one-fourth of free persons of color in Anderson, Oconee, and Pickens counties were able to read and write.[45]

Access to written materials expanded horizons. Following an Abbeville protest against "Negroes . . . Instructed to read . . . in Several Sunday Schools," the state legislature in 1834 enacted prohibitions against teaching slaves to read or write, even specifically forbidding slaves from holding schools. By that time some already had learned to read, at least on a rudimentary level. Around 1820 Hopewell Presbyterians sponsored Sunday school classes for slaves. Its superintendent Elam Sharpe, an elder originally from Charleston, said that the "negroes [were] . . . generally very attentive to their Books." Some of these were provided by Joseph Grisham, but in some cases they were bought: "Cash of a negro for a spell book," 25 cents. Several evidently acquired reading ability there.[46]

Slaves and free people of color listened to scriptures read aloud at church. If they memorized what they heard and could locate that same passage in a Bible, they could teach themselves to read. South Carolina Baptists in 1828 urged churches to read scriptures to "the colored people . . . encouraging them to repeat and commit to memory such parts of them as may be suited to their case." Religious materials designed for masters to use with slaves stressed memorization. One slave near Belton began learning to read and write while driving his owners' children in a carriage to and from school.[47]

Evidence survives of some free people of color and slaves who could read or write and of masters who taught slaves to read. Free Columbus and Salathail K. Graham signed their 1862 request for a guardian, while he could not do so. Also, preacher Caesar, a slave, complained once about contents of a letter shown him by another slave, and Stephen (T. Williams) had a pass and accompanying letter that slave Gilbert forged for him. Occasionally owners taught slaves to read and write, as did John B. Adger's family on their Pendleton-area plantation.[48]

Surprising stories of African American literacy involve three school settings. Free Columbus Graham in fact taught white Pickens County children during the Civil War. Ellison Williams, a freedman organizing a school near Seneca, was described in June 1866 as a teacher who "can read quite well and writes a good hand." His first students included two who could read and spell, plus six others who spelled. A white teacher at a nearby freedmen's school reported that many pupils already had books at home or could borrow them from other relatives or friends.[49]

The 1870 census furnishes significant clues to slave literacy. Several hundred adults in Anderson, Oconee, and Pickens counties are reported as able to read, write, or both. It is highly doubtful that many of them acquired these skills in just five years of freedom, years marked by turmoil and limited educational opportunities. Lists of students attending freedmen's schools include some adults, but only a small fraction of those claiming literacy in the 1870 census. Many of these 1870 literates evidently came from a few plantations that had some tradition of literacy, over several generations in a few cases, and provided core leadership during Reconstruction.

When freedom came in 1865, African Americans already had a wide network of contacts and communications and included perhaps a few hundred literate people. Many traveled throughout their immediate area, a fifteen-mile radius or more. Even most divided families managed to unite their households shortly after 1865. Church attendance, weekend visits to spouses or relatives, errands for owners, and trading brought enslaved African Americans a substantial knowledge of the surrounding world. South Carolina whites during the 1850s were increasingly alarmed at abolitionist activities and the potential for "unrest," that is, slave assertiveness or insurrection by African Americans. Evidently these fearful whites understood that an effective and extensive black network flourished.

NINE

Families, Mortality, and Names

DETERMINING WHAT AFRICAN AMERICAN daily routine and family life were like in northwestern South Carolina is a formidable task. Hardly any contemporary account commented directly on these issues. Fortunately, many pieces of evidence together provide significant insights. Despite conditions of enslavement, families achieved a remarkable degree of contacts and continuity. Even geographic separations within the area often were not an insurmountable obstacle. Rather, they aided a subcultural communications network. Parameters, outlined in the introduction to part 3, shaped much of the slaves' world, which they adapted for their advantage.

Families, the core of African American subculture, demonstrate perseverance more forcefully than do any other aspects of enslaved life. Both high mortality rates and divisions among different plantations presented obstacles. Still, families often maintained close contacts, as revealed especially in naming practices and in the 1870 census. "Families" in a variety of forms, persisting into postbellum years, became the strongest continuity between the two periods.

Mortality was the most devastating attack on black families. Conversely, naming practices demonstrated a strong sense of family as reflected by passing names from one generation to another. Names derived from both African and European cultures further indicate the usage of both traditions. A case study of the best-documented plantation, that of the white Colhoun family, links black families, naming, and deaths along with the impact on slaves by owners' debts and deaths—more connections between black and white. Analyzing that plantation will help to personalize these issues as they affected African Americans who lived there.

Families

Slaves in Anderson, Oconee, and Pickens counties often had well-established, functioning, nuclear families despite separations inflicted on them. Substantial numbers of estate appraisals show husband, wife, and several children living together on one plantation. However, another frequent pattern has a husband living elsewhere, often nearby, and spending weekends with his wife and children. Still other variations appear as well: relations widely separated, orphans with no immediate relatives, and ad hoc, "fictive" families of unrelated persons living together as a household. Plantations sometimes had a number of slaves unrelated to anyone else there. They either occupied a cabin together or each was attached to a family. Some postbellum households shared by apparently unrelated people may have resulted from plantation associations formed outside of biological relationships. No evidence suggests that local owners wanted to separate husband and wife, although various people have charged that masters throughout the South did that as an additional means of control.[1]

Illustrations of wrenching family separations elsewhere serve as reminders of what could happen. They emerge from otherwise dry data on Freedmen's Savings Banks depositors' forms around 1870. Frank Watkins told the Atlanta staff that he "was brought away from S.C. when he was small and does not know anything about his relation." Having been "sold so often," Elizabeth Edy remembered her parents' names but did "not know where [she was] born." Six of William Redman's children were, he said, "scattered about somewhere."[2]

Rather than by deliberate division, separations of spouses and/or children locally occurred primarily for other reasons (see in chapter 7): (1) Many owners of fewer than ten slaves—virtually all of them in Pendleton District's early decades and still 75 percent in 1850—could not afford to own all members of a family. (2) When white adult daughters and sons married, their parents often gave them slaves as wedding gifts. William Keaton wrote in 1799 that his four married daughters each had two slaves already in their possession. Surely that meant breaking up slave families. (3) When an owner died, slaves were often divided first by his heirs and further among buyers at an estate sale. This resulted in separating dozens of families each year. Elisha Bennett's 1833 will directed that a couple, Sam and Lucy, likely to go to different Bennetts, should "not be separated at a distance from each other." Often when slaves were sold at an estate auction, nearby neighbors of the deceased bought those not claimed by his relatives.[3]

Both the slaves' search for a desired spouse and their own deaths brought about further separations. (4) With only a few holdings exceeding fifty slaves, a young person of marriageable age might not find a suitable spouse on the same plantation of ten, twenty, or even thirty slaves.[4] (5) Death frequently divided spouses and robbed children of one or both parents, leaving children to be raised by other people. High mortality rates and a short average life span ended more marriages and separated more children from mothers than did any other cause. Enduring all of these problems, many African Americans managed to maintain close family ties, even when living on different plantations.

Couples typically lost several children due to many infant deaths. It was not unusual for white contemporaries to lose 25 percent or more of their children, and slave mortality was somewhat higher. Contradicting stereotypes of slaves having large numbers of children, analysis by Elizabeth Fox-Genovese and others shows that slave and white women may have borne comparable numbers and suffered similar losses. Some black women, in contrast to persistent stereotypes, had only a few or no children during slavery.[5]

Children who survived may well have lost one or both parents, then been raised by grandparents, aunts, or nonrelatives. Due to a short average life expectancy, about eighteen, and also to women's deaths in childbirth, men often had, sequentially, two or more wives. Many couples during and after slavery involved a man with a wife ten to thirty or more years younger than himself as they both undertook a second or third marriage following deaths of their spouses.[6]

Orphans were often found among African Americans. Slave inventories sometimes specifically mentioned them, Freedmen's Bureau agents dealt with orphans, and many children in the 1870 census seem to be orphaned. Frequently, parentless children would be absorbed into a deceased mother's extended family. Several young women on the Colhoun plantation died during the 1850s; relatives then took care of most of these children. If there were no relatives, that child would likely be assigned to another female to raise. Fostering, which already had a long history in Africa, continued on southern plantations and in postbellum years, as reflected in 1880 and 1900 censuses, describing dozens of children as "adopted," probably without legal processes.[7]

Having survived early childhood diseases, many slaves lived to advanced ages. Elderly people seem to have been honored, even revered, not only within the community but also by whites as well. However, black ages in nineteenth-century sources, before or after emancipation, have to be treated cautiously, as stated ages for older slaves, often rounded off or estimated, are very imprecise. Ages for many specific individuals varied widely among censuses. Those for 1850 and 1860 show many more slaves 70, 80, or 90 years old than for 69, 79, or 89. The few records that allow comparison of a slave's age over an extended period suggest that sometimes that age was artificially inflated as she or he got older, even after 1865.[8]

Both slave inventories and 1870 family groupings show a significant number of older African Americans living with their adult sons or daughters and grandchildren; occasionally a fourth generation was also present. It was not unusual for older people to be raising their grandchildren if both parents had died, or if the mother died and the father married again or lived on a different plantation.[9]

Even when living apart, spouses often lived within a few miles or a few hours' walk from the rest of their family. Because owners constituted overlapping networks of white families and their in-laws, their visits also provided opportunities for some slaves, divided among these white relatives, to keep in touch. Instances exist where both husband and wife are named in church or legal documents along with respective owners. Alfred and Caroline, identified as a couple who belonged to different owners, joined Anderson Presbyterian Church together in February 1844.[10]

Weekend visits, often an integral part of slave family life, involved husbands who would "get a note from your bossman to let you go over to see your wife and be back in so much time Monday morning before day," or Sunday night, depending on distance and their masters' permission. Anybody returning late could be subjected to serious punishment. Gutman recounts that "the roads were, in consequence, filled

Easter Reid, formerly a slave in Pickens District, practiced as a midwife after emancipation. Black Heritage in the Upper Piedmont

with men on their way to the 'wife house,' each pedestrian or horseman bearing in his bag his soiled clothes and all the good things he could collect during the week for the delectation of the household." Easter [Reid]'s story, recounted in 1988, told of her husband walking long distances—once on a frozen river—to see his wife. Clearly these memories lingered in African American families.[11]

As a general rule, owners and churches tried to regularize marriages among slaves. Only one set of area slave marriage records survives, that by the rector of St. Paul's Episcopal Church (Pendleton). All but six of those twenty-four marriages wedded a bride and groom of two owners. Other references to couples and to marriage throughout this chapter refer broadly to any continuing relationship regardless of ritual or formality involved.[12]

Details on other marriages—the great bulk of them—are lacking. But antebellum churches, concerned for marriage sanctity, censured and expelled numerous slaves for adultery, fornication, or having babies out of wedlock. A typical complaint was a slave "taking up" another spouse while having one still living, especially when a spouse was removed elsewhere.[13]

Some owners made special efforts in their wills, and presumably during their lives as well, to maintain families intact. A Greenville man, Zerah Davis, knowing that his heirs would need to hire out his slaves, directed in 1838 that his slave family be kept together. Occasionally owners tried during their lives to unite families by buying a spouse or child at the urgent request of his or her own slave, and by selling in 1845 a "prime fellow, a good farmer, [who has] been in the district and [is] adverse to removing" with his owner to Texas.[14]

Significant insights into African American families can be gleaned from the post-emancipation 1870 census. Hundreds of area families then consisted of both parents and several sons and daughters, often ranging into their teens or twenties. Even if living on separate plantations, these families clearly maintained close enough contact—both communication and sentiment—that they got together after freedom. Strong family households derived from decades of close family ties during slavery.

Mortality

Proverbial inevitabilities, death and taxes, were beyond the influence of African Americans in bondage yet deeply affected them. Obviously deaths of immediate family members impacted them directly. The owner's death, somewhat more distant, still was portentous, as enslaved people faced prospects of being sold to settle his estate. Certainly a new owner, whether from the deceased's family or not, would assume control. That person might be more or less kindly disposed, a kinder or harsher taskmaster with a wife more thoughtful or more bitterly critical. Whatever happened, changes resulted. Another inevitability, taxes, confronted slaves less often. If an owner failed to meet his annual tax obligations, slaves as property might be attached to satisfy the state's demand, another potential disruption to African American life. Sales for taxes or owners' debts happened to dozens of slaves each year. If only one or two canceled a debt, families were further divided.

Death, however, shaped more of African American circumstances than did anything except slavery itself. Often it resulted from various nineteenth-century diseases that ran rampant on either a local, regional, or national level. Illness, perhaps malaria, struck the Pendleton area in 1812, when six of the seven Cannon plantation slaves died. Such diseases devastated both white and black, but with more cramped living quarters, harder work, and often less food, black people suffered more heavily. Of the Keowee plantation's forty-eight slaves ten years or older in 1850, seventeen (35 percent) died during the decade, as did about half of sixty-five children born during the 1850s.[15]

Slave infants faced a high risk of dying within their first year, roughly 10 percent for Anderson, Oconee, and Pickens counties in 1850, with higher figures for 1860. Even in 1870, chances of an infant dying were serious enough that many were not named until they were one or two years old. A physician in 1880 noted that a black Clinkscales baby, deceased, had "no name, to[o] young."[16] A proposed law in 1848 to register all births and deaths stated that, among slave babies, information recorded should include "its name, if one has been given to it."

Slave mortality, a matter of natural course, still involved emotional pain. Robert Anderson in his 1806 will directed that the baby of pregnant Moll, "and She is very big," should go to his granddaughter if Moll "should live to have it, and the Child should live." And Floride Calhoun lamented little Nelly's infant son who died at the age of only one month. For a plantation of twenty or more slaves, births, marriages, and deaths within a year would make it a frequently changing combination of white and black—not static as much written about slavery implies. Table 9.2 summarizes yearly changes on Keowee plantation.

South Carolina's 1859 mortality report shows the average age of Pickens and Oconee slave deaths that year to be 14.2 years, slightly below the state's average. By contrast, all slaves *living* in Pickens County in 1850 averaged 18.2.[17] Compared to 87 1-year-old children that year, there were only 50 who were 9 years old, a sharp decline. "Mulattos" in 1850 were on the whole older than "blacks," partly due to a skewing that year among mulattos toward the 50–69 age bracket. All free people of color in 1850 and 1860 listed in Abbeville, Greenville, and Anderson, Oconee, and Pickens counties censuses averaged 21.2 years, a three-year advantage over slaves.

White mortality, while also high, did not reach the same level as that for slaves. All whites who died in Oconee and Pickens in 1850 averaged 23.7, about 6 years older than that for slaves; 27 percent of white deaths consisted of infants under 1 year. Based on readily available 1850 data about living population, a sample of whites averaged 20.3 years, compared to 18.2 for all Pickens County slaves. These statistics for both local whites and slaves parallel national figures. The first federal report, 1850, showed early 20s to be both median and modal ages for all free Americans.[18]

Names of Slaves

Names assigned to African Americans during antebellum years reflect values from both European and African cultures. With few exceptions names that prevailed among local slaves did so throughout the South. They show African choices blending with a predominately European-based culture, while also demonstrating family continuities.

These names—nearly 1700 different ones in 13,588 upper-piedmont citations, mostly for Anderson, Oconee, and Pickens counties—provide a fascinating insight into both black and white cultures, as well as influences that shaped them. European-derived names dominated; however, African values and words sometimes lay behind a name apparently European in origin. Results of the *Black Names in America* survey of 14,142 citations throughout the South parallel closely South Carolina's upper-piedmont group despite different geographic coverage.[19]

Surviving stereotypes based on *Uncle Tom's Cabin,* Uncle Remus stories, and *Gone with the Wind* stress names such as Jemima and Sambo.[20] To reflect those most often used in the period, couples might more aptly be called Mary and John, George and Sarah, Hannah and Jack, or Sam and Jane. Together, these eight names comprise 13 percent of all citations in Anderson, Oconee, and Pickens counties. In that survey there are, by contrast, only fourteen Sambos and thirteen Jemimas (0.1 percent each). Prevailing names, in fact, were those standard for England in the same period; most, such as those above, are still widely used today throughout the United States by both black and white. Most names of slaves could also be found among whites except for distinctive African derivations and a few others, especially classical ones such as Nero.

European-derived values include Christian religion, literature, the classics, and family surnames. Old Testament names were popular in the early nineteenth century for whites and blacks. Typical ones for both included Isaac, Rachel, Daniel, Esther, Abram/Abraham, Elias, Solomon, and Leah, while Hagar was used almost exclusively by blacks. Frequently used New Testament names such as John, Mary, Elizabeth, and Paul were in widespread white usage too.

During the eighteenth-century Enlightenment and early nineteenth-century Romantic period, classical themes captivated Europeans, at home or relocated to America. So slaves were named Caesar, Minerva, Scipio, Venus, Polydore, Sophia, Augustus, and Cornelia. Patriotic sources included America, Washington, Columbus, Jefferson, and Lafayette.

Many cultures favor adopting a mother's or grandmother's surname as a personal name. Dozens of prominent South Carolina families were popular as personal slave names, such as Hammond, Hampton, Middleton, Pinckney, and Poinsett, or, of more local renown, Cherry, Reese, Simpson, and Sloan. A few recalled Virginia heritage of white settlers and slaves who moved to upper South Carolina. Cultures merged.

Styles and tastes in naming change over time. Old Testament choices such as Zachariah and Shadrach mostly disappeared for children by midcentury, especially among whites. Similarly, specifically African-based names such as Cudjo, Quash, and Cuffee were found more often in the early 1800s than by 1850.[21] It is possible that some slaves with African-derived names were first- or second-generation from Africa via Charleston, Virginia, or Maryland. On some plantations, for example, the Colhouns' and Calhouns,' many names continued among family holdings from the 1790s into the 1850s.

This discussion of names associated with or preferred by whites should not suggest that slaves had no role in these choices. Local evidence is too slender to ascertain who assigned them. It is worth noting, however, that most arguments about naming practices assume a stable, closed plantation setting. But a single plantation's twenty or fifty slaves may have come from several sources—an owner's father, his father-in-law, and estate sales—with distinct naming patterns.

It seems equally unlikely that owners controlled all selections or that slaves picked every name without considering their owners' wishes. Slaves who could choose might well select from the area's dominant culture, that of whites. In *Down by the Riverside* Charles Joyner points out, however, that slaves often had hidden or "basket" names used among themselves, distinct from those employed by owners. These hidden names may well have strengthened the subculture.

Some African influences are obvious, including specifically African words and values. Some such as Cudjo, Mingo, Binky, Affy, and Cinda came directly from

African usage. Others such as Cuffy were often found in the West Indies. Even English names such as Billy or Lizzie shadowed the African Bilah and Liceta, Joyner demonstrates. Slaves may well have pronounced a name differently when speaking to owners than when talking to each other. Washington or Wash for short, a popular choice, resembled the African Quash. It is important to remember that most slave names recorded in the nineteenth century were written by white men, some of them barely literate.[22] What was written may not always be what was spoken or meant.

Names sometimes followed African traditions based on day of the week or month when born; other choices included natural phenomena. Once again, diverse cultural traditions blended, being seen, heard, and understood differently by owners and by slaves. A few names referred to season, especially Easter, or natural conditions at birth, notably Jane Hurricane. S. E. Maxwell's Oconee plantation had, at emancipation, more African-derived names than did most others.[23]

Some double names, such as Joe Dart or Bob Hampton, evidently applied to slaves bearing the same personal name who came from a different plantation, perhaps that of the owner's father-in-law. Other usages to distinguish slaves with identical names involved adjectives such as Yellow Sall, Black Harriet, or Town Jim. Numerous people bore prefixes Big, Old, or Young.

Scholars have debated slave-naming practices and their perpetuation within families. Generally, these debates have ignored the possibility that owners themselves liked and continued such names. Two distinct groups shed some additional light: (1) Forty percent of personal names found among Senator John Ewing Colhoun's slaves in 1793 were still used by younger generations belonging to families of his son J. E. Colhoun (Jr.) and son-in-law John C. Calhoun sixty years later. (2) Names for free persons of color show a different style than those for slaves.[24] Their choices indicate a greater trend toward mainstream English names.

Naming clearly shows an intermingling of African- and European-based traditions and interactions between them. Wills and estate appraisals, coupled with 1870 census listings and a study of Calhoun/Colhoun plantation slaves, demonstrate that many African American families, despite separations and other problems, managed to perpetuate their own personal names in many cases as they passed names from one generation to the next. Often a younger male or female is denoted as "Jr.," sharing the same name as a parent. Due to high mortality rates, African Americans sometimes deferred naming a "Junior" until later in the birth order. More African usages and family traditions emerge from naming than in any other surviving source.[25]

African Americans on the Colhoun and Calhoun Plantations, 1790–1865

Focusing on one specific plantation—Keowee, its slaves, and changes within a decade—illustrates family, mortality and naming patterns. Only the Calhouns and Colhouns among hundreds of area families have extant papers that allow analysis of

Nancy Legree, former slave of John C. Calhoun, at 106 years old. Black Heritage in the Upper Piedmont

their slaves over time. These records, however, come from two widely separated periods, the 1790s and the 1850s. Life cycles of the white families—births, marriages, and deaths—as well as diverse locations of their plantations and their changing fortunes, sometimes downward, all directly affected African Americans. Transfers among plantations and sales created numerous separations of Keowee plantation families and also reflect critical influences of both mortality and an owner's indebtedness, each shattering some slave families. Colhoun marriages, deaths, and financial straits over three generations repeatedly dispersed some of the family's slaves. Nevertheless over two-thirds of Keowee plantation's African Americans can be grouped into families and matched with postbellum surnames, a rarity for upstate South Carolina.[26]

Slaves likely accompanied Ezekiel Calhoun's family from Virginia into South Carolina, then in the 1750s to Upper Long Cane Creek, a Scots-Irish settlement in Abbeville District. Ezekiel's sons included Patrick, who was John C. Calhoun's father, and John Ewing. Both Patrick Calhoun and John Ewing Colhoun, who adopted a variant spelling, held several official positions and won election as early backcountry legislators.[27] John Ewing Colhoun in 1786 married Floride, descended from the Bonneaus and deLonguemares, wealthy Huguenot families who bequeathed Cooper River rice plantations and many slaves to her.

Because Colhoun not only assumed his wife's property but also acquired early grants along the Keowee River and owned lands elsewhere in the state, he operated a thriving and complex array of plantations and slaves. In addition to slaves acquired from his wife's and his own families, Colhoun bought additional ones in Charleston, including 1793 purchases—Hazzard, Rose, and Cella. His holding, typical of many

Table 9.1 **Calhoun and Colhoun Family Genealogies (selective), 1750–1865**

(Huguenots)

```
                                    Ezekiel Calhoun
                                          |
        ┌─────────────────────────────────┴──────────────────────┐
Floride Bonneau = John Ewing Colhoun [Sr]              Patrick Calhoun
[inherited land,   [Bonneau's Ferry,                   [Abbeville]
slaves]; d. 1836    Keowee] d. 1802                           |
        |                                                     |
  ┌─────┼──────────────────────────┬───────────────┐     3 brothers
  |     |                          |               |    [shared Abbeville
John Ewing   James Edward      Floride Colhoun  = John C. Calhoun  plantation]
Colhoun [Jr.]  Colhoun         [Cold Spring]      [Fort Hill]           |
[Keowee]     [Millwood Plantation,                d. 1850         descendants
[gold, Ga.]   Abbeville]               |
d. 1846                                |
  |                          ┌─────────┴──────────┐
W. R. Colhoun   Thomas G. Clemson = Anna Maria Calhoun   Andrew P. Calhoun
[Affleck Ledger]  [Edgefield]                            [Cane Brake Ala.]
                  bought JEC slaves, ca. 1843;           d. 1865
                  sold 51 slaves in 1851;
                  moved to Md. with slaves
                           |
                      Floride Clemson
                    (A Rebel Came Home)
```

Sources: Only family members with a direct bearing on this text are included; most dates omitted except for deaths. No one chart satisfactorily portrays both John C. Calhoun's and John Ewing Colhoun Jr.'s lines. The best for JCC appears on the flyleaf of Lander, *Calhoun Family*; there is a variant chart (xi) in Floride Clemson, *A Rebel Came Home: The Diary and Letters of Floride Clemson, 1863–66* (Columbia: Univ. of South Carolina Press, 1961), which he edited; cited as *Rebel*. A. S. Salley, Jr., *The Calhoun Family of South Carolina* [Columbia?: n.p., 1906?] is still the most extensive Calhoun genealogy. See Calhoun and Colhoun in *Biographical Directory of the American Congress* and in volumes for the S.C. House and Senate.

others, brought together unrelated African Americans from different sources and assembled a new plantation "family."[28]

Colhoun owned Pendleton District's largest holding along with recalcitrant slaves, including Hazard, who tried to poison him. Relocated to Keowee, they were among Pendleton's first lowcountry African Americans. Colhoun represented Pendleton in the South Carolina House of Representatives for three terms. While a U.S. senator, Colhoun died in 1802 at Keowee and was buried there. His will recommended that his trustees "keep my negroes together."

Information on family holdings, management, and transfers of slaves during the next fifty years is sketchy. Colhoun's children were all very young, and his estate was not finally settled for decades. When daughter Floride married her cousin John C. Calhoun, some slaves from the estate were given to her, and thus to her husband; their number and names are not known. More issues arose in 1836 when widow Floride Colhoun died; details during those years evidently have perished.

Colhoun slaves and lands in Pendleton District were shared but not legally divided until 1836, among son John E. Colhoun (Jr.) at Keowee; widow Floride Colhoun, who lived at Cold Spring, an adjacent plantation to the south; and John C. and Floride Calhoun. Their home was on still another contiguous tract, Fort Hill—now Clemson University campus. Several families descended from Calhoun and Colhoun slaves still live in that vicinity.[29]

Like many prosperous owners, Calhoun acquired slaves from several sources and deployed them in diverse locations. Inheriting many from father Patrick's Abbeville estate, John C. and his brothers worked them in common for several decades. Calhoun bought additional slaves for Fort Hill. Resulting Calhoun holdings, then, included those from his father, from his wife's parents—both when he married and when his mother-in-law died, and by purchases. Calhoun utilized them at Fort Hill, in Abbeville, at his Georgia gold mines, and in Alabama. The extended Calhoun family's operations and problems certainly disrupted slave families with periodic relocations, almost a chess game as owners, to suit their own purposes, moved slaves around, including some to Alabama, others to Maryland.[30]

Financial acumen varied enormously. John Ewing Colhoun (Sr.) evidently was very successful and prosperous. Widowed, Mrs. Colhoun seems to have remained solvent despite extravagant pleasures, and her youngest child, James Edward Calhoun, operated a thriving Abbeville plantation. But son John Ewing Colhoun (Jr.) became deeply submerged in debt, and son-in-law John C. Calhoun owed such huge loans that supporters began a campaign to salvage his financial position, by chance not long before he died. Had they not done so, his estate would have been bankrupt and his slaves sold, breaking up more families.[31]

Meanwhile John E. Colhoun (Jr.) became a state representative, Pendleton Farmers' Society president, investor in his own woolen factory, and a big spender.[32] Because lavish expenditures exceeded his income, debts in the 1830s and 1840s brought him frequently to the courthouse to answer numerous suits. John C. Calhoun in 1834 bought several of his brother-in-law's male slaves, evidently Georgia gold-mine workers, for son Andrew. Throughout the 1840s Colhoun, or the sheriff, placed many of his slaves for sale. Thomas Clemson, buying one lot of five males advertised in 1842, relocated them and their families to Edgefield. Two years later the sheriff advertised sixteen more; Colhoun did not deliver them by the due date. Angered, the sheriff seized all he could, but others fled to the woods.[33] Eighty slaves could not produce enough to keep up with Colhoun's spending.

He found funds—selling the woolen factory and eight hundred acres—to repay his creditors, and those slaves were still on the plantation a decade later. Their threat of being sold, however, illustrates African American fates being held hostage to their owners' spendthrift habits. After an illness killed Colhoun in 1846, commissioners who handled the estate commented on its "Negroes . . . growth and increase of which is beyond doubt in this country more profitable than any other property." Adult Colhoun sons managed to operate Keowee jointly until after the Civil War, by which time two of them died and the plantation was nearly bankrupt again. Meanwhile Clemson, who bought Colhoun slaves but was not receiving annual repayments on funds he loaned Calhoun and son Andrew, had to sell his own Edgefield plantation and slaves. They included those bought from Colhoun.[34] Still more disruptions shook African American lives and families.

Colhoun slaves are fairly well documented for the 1850s due to son W. R. Colhoun's *Plantation Ledger*. Printed by the Affleck Company with blank forms for inventories and advice on managing overseers, it is the only-known surviving ledger for Anderson, Oconee, and Pickens counties. Although not systematically maintained, it contains sufficient information, when complemented with census and church records, to follow many African American births, marriages, and deaths during the 1850s. It begins in 1853—after widow Margaret Colhoun's death—with a listing of seventy-six slaves, separated by gender and organized by descending age. Assigned individual appraisals that averaged $425, slave values ranged from $50 for an eighty-year-old man to $1,100 for males seventeen to nineteen years old. Similar figures applied to Calhoun slaves that son Andrew bought in 1854 and Pendleton slaves in John North's 1858 estate appraisal.

Attempting to describe changes within slave families and Keowee's overall holding depends on many interpretations of data difficult to reconcile and on numerous interpolations. The following account for 1850–60 is an approximation rather than a complete, accurate, contemporaneous record.[35] Colhoun holdings, as entered in the 1850 census, consisted of 75 slaves, disproportionately divided, 30 males and 45 females. They included only two men between the ages of twenty and forty-nine, as Colhoun had to sell valuable field hands to deal with heavy indebtedness. Over half of the total were 27 children under ten and 12 adults fifty-five or older. The Colhouns appraised older slaves as of minimal or no value.

The 1850 plantation included eight men and two women born before 1800, some likely his parents' slaves in the lowcountry. Three—Robin, Vulcan, and Simon—

Ledger of John C. Calhoun's slaves, 1854, sold to his son Andrew Pickens Calhoun; grouped by families, starting with "Old Sawney." S.C. Department of Archives and History

Extracts from Keowee Plantation Ledger; location of the original ledger is unknown.

4 [May] Tuesday [1854]

Sphy died this morning — Several of the negroes quite sick Milly, Binah, Billy, ...

5 [May]

Milly quite sick still

Quarterly Inventory . . . 3rd day of October 1857

Simon	200
Cretia	200
Giney 3	1500
Phoebe	1000
Bess	900
Matilda	[no value listed]
Ned	400
Jack	200
Peter	1000

Meat in pounds

Peter & Rose	5	
Tye & Lavinia	5	
Billy & Cumba	3 1/2	
Toney & Matilda	5 1/2	
Robin & family	7 1/2	
Simon, family, & Hank		15

List of Negroes January 1 1856

. . .

$10,750

Keowee plantation ledger (typescript), showing family groupings and food allocations, October 3, 1857. Black Heritage in the Upper Piedmont, South Caroliniana Library, University of South Carolina evidently survived from Colhoun's 1816 purchases, and elderly Rose may have been the one Colhoun Sr. bought in 1793. Although there were sixteen females of childbearing age for future benefit, any children they bore would be years away from productive labor. As inventoried in 1853, seven fifteen- to eighteen-year-old females rated seven hundred dollars each. There were also eight males between ten and nineteen years of age, just becoming hardy field-workers; the most valuable were the four males, seventeen to nineteen years old. Together they constituted almost 15 percent of the total net worth. Ordinarily the blacksmith might have had the highest value, but, at age sixty, Peter was set at four hundred dollars.

Workers—listed in 1857 as fifteen males and seventeen females, about 40 percent of the total—functioned both as field hands and in other plantation roles. Simon [Calhoun] (then 59) tended the livestock; Moses [Calhoun] (44) handled the horses and their equipment and probably drove the carriage; and brothers Turner (17) and Harrison (16) were house boys. Their mother Betty [Wiggins] (31) along with Margaret (20) coped with the housework, and Milly [Dupree] (40) was the cook. Days when the family had a butler, chambermaid, and pastry cook had already "gone with the wind." Two of Milly's sons married Betty's daughters, thus forming linkages among house servants.

Six couples can be identified, five (among them Betty and Milly) with their children; those families collectively included thirty-eight of seventy-five slaves on the 1853 plantation.[36] Relationships among most other people cannot be determined. Some may have been single or had spouses on other plantations, and some of the eight adults over the age of fifty-five may not have had surviving spouses. In many cases postemancipation surnames and geographic locations have been determined.

Detailed yearly changes (table 9.2) demonstrate constant fluctuations in African American families. Their own deaths and Colhoun sales to settle further debts disrupted the plantation. These factors, summarized for the decade, follow:

> The Colhouns, who had 75 slaves in 1850, had 80 in 1860, similar figures that mask enormous changes.
> Nine adults over the age of 50 died during the decade.
> Eight people aged 15–50 also died, mostly females, since Keowee had few males of that age range.
> Sixty-five children were born to 14 females, several in their teens.
> Thirty-four children aged 15 or younger died; most, born during the 1850s, were under two years, many of them only a few days or months old.
> Evidently there were five sets of twins on the plantation; twins appeared more often in some African cultures than elsewhere, which was continued among some African Americans.
> Contagion may have caused the four deaths in November 1855 and perhaps the October one as well.
> Marriages: three females from the plantation were married by the Episcopal rector, two husbands from Keowee, the third from a nearby plantation; Annie and

Table 9.2 **Changes (Selected Years) on the Keowee Plantation**

1850 July– 1852 Dec.	10 girls, born 1843–50, died; about 5 infants born and died 14 girls and 2 boys born and survived
1853	Vulcan (80) and Billy (70) died Milly (36) had Delia; Elizabeth's Dinah (19) born in July
1855	Hannah (72) died February 6; Matilda's four-month-old child also died in February; Simon (15) was buried October 15; Serenah (25), Minerva (14), Catherine (13), & Rebecca (4) all died in November, probably of a contagious disease Phebe (18), daughter of (old) Simon, was baptized on October 14, and Polly (16) was baptized on December 2 Clarissa (20) and Peter (19) were married on April 14 by the Episcopal rector—both husband and wife from the plantation, parents not listed (probably dead); Clarissa died in October, perhaps of complications from pregnancy children born: Becky (18) had twins Perry and Lindy on January 2; Margaret's (18) son Henderson born November 18, anniversary of her 1855 marriage; Ginny (23) had Lenah in December; Sarah's mother and birth month unknown
1856:	Jack (83) died October; Marilla, infant of Annie (16) and Billy (21), was buried June 1 children born: Betty's (30) Sophy, February 12, and Matilda's (18) Paul, March 19 sales: evidently to raise funds, the Colhouns sold Jack (53) and Lenah (46), their daughter Becky (19) and her boy Grandisson (5); Frank (16); Peggy (15); Susan (5); and Lucy (5); John Flander (18), also listed, was withheld until harder times; four young girls (3 to 5) along with Polly (16) either died or were sold
1858	Toney (27) and Matilda (20), a couple since about 1853, had a child born in 1854 who died in 1855, Paul born in 1856, and Toney (Junior) born in 1858, perhaps posthumously; father Toney (27) died February 14 and was buried the next day; Matilda and children then lived with her step-mother Lucretia and father Simon [Matilda remarried, ca. 1860–61, Wilson, from another plantation] Rose (75) died; perhaps the Rose bought in 1793 Billy (23; Simon and Lucretia's) and Binky (17; Milly and Moses's) were married April 24 by Episcopal rector sales: harder times evidently had come; John Flander was sold; Robin (65), Amy (27), and Ginny (26) died or were sold; other women were raising Amy's and Ginny's children

Billy, as well as Matilda and Toney, all from Keowee, became couples without Episcopalian marriage; Matilda was widowed five years later and moved back into her parents' cabin; spouses of other females aged 14–20 are not known, and given small numbers of Keowee males, probably came from other plantations.

Sold: nine people, all evidently an extended family of three generations, in 1856; one, John Flander, was deferred from sale until harder times forced his disposition a year later.

The decade's impact on one family may help dramatize personal changes. George (1823) and Betty (1826) [Wiggins] likely were both born on the Colhoun plantation. One of only two males aged twenty to forty-nine in 1850, George was probably retained because Betty was a housemaid. When Betty was fourteen, they had their first child, Turner (1840), soon followed by Harrison (1841). By 1853 Betty had no surviving children born between 1842 and 1847; probably two or three young girls who died were hers.[37] Later babies were Ephraim (1848) and, evidently twins, Maria (1849) and Thomas (1849). During the 1850s Betty had six more girls, all but one living at the decade's end, as were the four sons.

As a younger woman Betty did not share some circumstances of neighbors Lucretia and Milly, who had adult sons and daughters or their spouses die during the decade and who then took in their grandchildren. Betty's family remained intact despite Colhoun's financial straits and compulsory sales. Known as Wiggins after emancipation, adult siblings lived near each other, mostly within ten miles of Keowee, and took active roles in politics and in church.

Women formed the key to Keowee's family life. Most prime males had been sold, leaving families behind. Many young females, as they matured, had to find spouses elsewhere. Through these marriages, Keowee women linked their own plantation with slaves on perhaps half a dozen others in the vicinity, thus extending their own communications network. They suffered from heavy mortality—their children's and their own. Other women gathered in motherless children, sometimes their own grandchildren or nieces and nephews.

Clearly mortality as well as an owner's indebtedness heavily affected African American life. Five people died in October and November 1855, probably through contagion. Research into the Colhoun plantation's family graveyard suggests that slaves, perhaps only house servants, were buried in the area outside a walled space for the owners.[38] Nearly half of all children born during the decade died before it was over. Most older adults, those with strongest links to the lowcountry and perhaps through parents to Africa, perished.

Still, Keowee's seventy-five slaves constituted a large enough group for some to choose spouses on the plantation. The one known marriage between a woman, Amy, from Keowee with a man, Isaac [Butler], evidently from Fort Hill, probably understates long-term family relationships between the two plantations. Keowee's African Americans and their relatives on other nearby plantations came from divergent sources—some descended from Ezekiel Calhoun's Virginia slaves, others from Floride Bonneau Colhoun's lowcountry holdings, perhaps some from Colhoun's father-in-law, some from local families, and a few by purchases. This combination multiplied family patterns, African origins, cultural traits, and naming practices found on a single plantation.

Usage of personal names in the 1850s strongly suggests a close linkage with the elder Colhoun's lowcountry slaves of the 1790s. Many names persisted throughout the antebellum era: Alick, Becky, Billy, Binah, Clarinda, Cumba, Dinah, George, Isaac, Kitty, Lucy, Nancy, Ned, Peggy, Peter, Philis, Polydore, Rose, Thomas, and Toney. Although most of these appeared often among area slaves, several were not otherwise used in Keowee's vicinity, and only eight were among the area's twenty-six found most frequently. Most of these were perpetuated at Fort Hill also. On some other plantations, slave and white personal names coincided. The Calhouns and Colhouns, however, did not have Annas, Florides, Cornelias, Henrys, or several other white family names among slaves, which suggests owner veto.

Continuity of Keowee's extended families transcended emancipation. Forty freed African Americans, including John Flander, were working at Keowee in 1866; small children would have raised black presence there to approximately 1860 figures. Large numbers of former Colhoun slaves in 1870 lived within ten miles of Keowee, many within a mile or two, or still there as hired laborers. More than a century later, by 2000, several families remained within a few miles of these Calhoun and Colhoun plantations where their ancestors labored. Several Keowee African Americans, especially families of Betty and George Wiggins and of Milly Dupree, appear later in postbellum contexts.[39]

Many families from the Calhoun and Colhoun holdings persevered. Even personal names for those born both before and after 1865 show a strong continuity. Not all families were so fortunate. Despite problems and sufferings, slaves on large plantations often had advantages that those in small holdings did not. With their intermarriages to those on other large plantations, residents of a large plantation were key to the communications system; and these bigger holdings produced much of the postbellum leadership. But whether in large or small holdings, all were subject to factors beyond their control, particularly high mortality and enforced relocations due to owners' debts. Often surmounting these difficulties, families formed a cohesive core of the African American community in slavery and in freedom.

TEN

Material and Emotional Conditions

AN EXAMINATION OF MATERIAL and emotional conditions reveals intricate textures of daily life for slaves. These matters involved both interpersonal relations with owners and slaves supplying some of their own food, clothing, and health care. Living on the same land in quite different circumstances—especially quality of housing and food—white and black shared complex plantation moods and quarrels as well as work and diseases.

Issues in this chapter pose as formidable a task as those in the previous one. Critical starting points, stated in the introduction to this part, apply here as in exploring slave families. Small patches of evidence, stitched together, show the pattern of slaves' material conditions. These include clothing, housing, food, and medical care. Owners provided some of each, but slaves relied on themselves and perhaps on some African traditions for supplements.

As a semiclosed environment, a plantation constituted something of a family, as some owners called all the peoples, white and black, on their land. Complicated emotional relationships must have existed between owners and owned; only a few are examined here. But strong tensions also developed among slaves, some of them typical human interactions, much intensified by their enslaved condition. Sexual complications involved both owners' exploitation of enslaved women and conflicts among slaves due to jealousies and extramarital affairs, especially when couples lived on different plantations.

Slaves also had occasions for celebrations. Black and white shared some festivities, further evidence of an interwoven plantation web. Both material and emotional conditions meant constant black-white interactions, which form an important subtext, as they constantly did for lives of both enslaved and owners. Together, matters spanning clothing, conflict and jealousies among slaves, and miscegenation help reveal strands of a complicated plantation fabric.

Clothing

Clothing, especially for a plantation with thirty to a hundred residents, required much planning and diversified activities. Providing necessary supplies might well be a joint undertaking by the plantation owner, his wife, and slave women. Beyond stereotypes of work garb, some slaves accumulated a wider array of clothing than that provided by masters. Slaves who had money sometimes used part of it for clothing beyond their standard issue. Even wearing plantation clothes, African Americans managed to fashion variations and individual styling. Some advertisements for runaways, especially in the early 1800s, described distinctive clothing.[1]

Generally they got new work clothes and shoes each year, and every second year a winter blanket and jacket as well. South Carolina's first slave law, in 1690, required owners to provide a set of clothing each year, a standard that survived. Much later, James H. Hammond's "Plantation Manual" for his Beech Island plantation (Edgefield) itemized these allocations for adults: "Each *man* gets in the fall 1 cotton shirt and 1 pr. woolen pants and 1 woolen jacket. In the spring they get 1 shirt and 2 pair of cotton pants. Each woman gets 6 yards of woolen cloth and 3 yards of cotton shirting in the fall, with a needle, shein of thread and dozen buttons. In the spring they get 6 yards of cotton drillings, 3 yards of shirting with needle thread and buttons. A stout pair of shoes is given to each in the fall and blanket every third year."[2] Children got specified clothing also. Clearly these women were expected to sew their own clothes, which allowed individual styling.

Murray Hill plantation's "Recapitulation from Book of 1857" listed "1 Nov. To every man 1 jacket & pants except Adam; Joby—Jacket, have had no Jacket; Titus has had 2 breeches—2 jackets; Boys have had jacket & pants except Sandy, Ishmael, Jem have no Jacket; 12 Blankets somewhat Moth eaten given out" to five women and two men; "the worse were given to infants."[3] On this plantation there was not a standard allotment but a review of individual shortages.

Clothing, blankets, and shoes might come either from a general store or from the plantation itself. Much consisted of "Negro cloth" and "Negro shoes," with the word describing not only the recipients but also a cruder, rougher variety than used in the white household. A plantation frequently supplied its own cloth. Colhoun's factory could turn out enough woolen fabric for everyone on the plantation plus more to sell. The Kilpatrick estate in 1846 bought "1 pair [weaving] cards (for Peggy)," who evidently was assigned the task of making clothing. Northern manufacturers also produced Negro cloth and shoes, which could be bought in Charleston or at general stores. As at Murray Hill, white women may have planned for needed supplies, then supervised sewing and perhaps distribution.[4]

Women, both white and black, did the plantation's weaving and sewing. Thomas Clemson wrote that some of his slave women were good weavers, while his mother-in-law evidently contributed to weaving and knitting for her hands. In an odd exchange of differentiated abilities, Huger women would sit by the fire in the evenings and "knit coarse socks & stockings for the Negroes . . . but we were not taught to sew well, as there were two or three Negro women who had nothing else to do" and created fancy lace work for the white family. Sarah Ann Broyles Williams, who lived in Pendleton, recalled, "Southern ladies understood housekeeping and . . . did direct and teach servants how to spin and weave cotton and woolen cloth for their own use."[5]

Batting tools for making quilts that belonged to Rosie Lee Rutledge (Oconee) and probably to her mother. Black Heritage in the Upper Piedmont

Plantation-woven cloth was distinctive enough that people, black or white, could recognize that made on their plantation. Henry, accused in 1828 of stealing a homespun coat, was clearly guilty because of its unique weave. And a small mistake led to Buck's conviction in 1840 when a torn piece of his cloak was traced to him.[6] Large plantations had their own tanning processes and made shoes; the originating plantation could be identified for both leather and shoes.

Clothing varied beyond simple, standard issue. Some owners bought extra clothing for specific slaves, probably house servants. White ladies attending St. Paul's Episcopal Church apparently were not content with their accompanying servants to be seen in ordinary work garb. Andrew P. Calhoun's purchases were highly individualized, ranging from handkerchiefs for two women and cloth (two to ten yards) for them to make family clothes; all of the direct recipients were men. The Kilpatricks made large purchases of "negro shoes (50 pairs stout, @$1.30 in 1856)."[7]

Some slaves bought additional items and sometimes traded clothes. Large-scale trading occurred, as Toby (Mrs. Stone) found a ready market for a stolen overcoat in Greenville. Andrew (Thos. Duckworth) and his wife Candas (Andrew Oliver), who lived on different plantations, got into a fuss. Andrew broke into her locked house and took clothing and a counterpane, claiming to have bought it for her. She insisted that she bought the materials and made the quilt herself and that Miss Owens had woven one of the sheets for her.[8]

There was enough clothing and bed coverings to entice some slaves to steal from others. Stephen (John Brown), although he claimed to have bought coarse shoes (worth one dollar) from slave woman Betty Poll during the Sandy Springs Camp Meeting, was found guilty of stealing them in 1845. But stealing, as portrayed by magistrates and freeholders trials, reached more often into plantation houses than into slave cabins.

Some stolen goods entered the slave market economy, both nearby and farther away. Bob was acquitted of stealing gloves and handkerchiefs found on Jane, however, when her owner Martin Smith reluctantly acknowledged having bought them for her. Smith's grudging statement of buying these accessories for Jane hints at sexual conduct. When missing items turned up at slave Mary Ann's residence, she was accused as an accessory. Mary Ann (Micajah Williams) testified that she did not know these stolen clothes were in her house, as they were under a dress that had been "hanging there six months." Jurors, evidently believing that explanation, acquitted her. Despite these cases, most slaves who acquired additional clothing did so by gifts, honest purchases, or home weaving.

Cleaning clothes occupied considerable time on a plantation. Several men were convicted of stealing slabs of pork when their clothing was found to be greasy. A white woman, defending them, said that Jake's (Samuel Johnston) clothes "were dirty but not greasier than common negroes clothes gets in a two weeks wear."[9] Some postbellum laundresses may have earlier been in charge of plantation washing.

Clothing and other possessions needed protection against theft, and a number of slaves had locked trunks or boxes, which sometimes concealed stolen property. The fine clothing Cain stole in 1838 was found in his "box," and Candas (Andrew Oliver) had a padlock on her cabin. A far from inexpensive item, the lock was given by her owner; it may have indicated an intimate relationship. One man, Edmund (Ezekiel Murphy), had a locked chest containing stolen items and a pistol.[10]

A product of both white and black efforts, slave clothing at times was more varied than its stereotypical illustrations. It could be readily distinguished by owners and was clearly individualized, as were slave cabins.

Houses and Household Items

There are no known local slave houses surviving, perhaps not for many decades, few contemporary descriptions, and no known photographs. Hardly any deeds, plats, or advertisements for plantations referred to cabins. In 1860 these cabins averaged only two persons, with wide fluctuations, skewed because many owners had only one or two slaves. White contemporaries usually called them "houses." They were cheap to build—land, timber, and labor were all free of additional costs to owners. That did not, however, inspire lavishness. The caliber of cabins can be judged by Andrew P. Calhoun's report that after only two days, he had "half of my negro quarter finished."[11]

Harris's Spartanburg diary includes several references to cabins. Better landscaped than Calhoun's, they had sycamore trees planted around them. He built a house for "Old Judy" in January 1856—cutting logs, erecting the structure, and attaching a chimney a month later. That took two days, evidently including making the brick. Harris added an extension the following year. Judy did some plantation weaving and spinning, which may have been based there.[12]

Houses probably varied in size, as they each held from one to eight persons, and occasionally more. Use of lofts, especially for children, helped maximize available space. Typical houses surviving elsewhere have rooms from sixteen by sixteen feet, the maximum efficiency for heating from a fireplace, to sixteen by twenty-four. Cabins at Appomattox (Va.), Walnut Grove in Spartanburg County, and Lexington (S.C.) fall within that range. Some houses consisted of two or more rooms either for extended families or for two or more families, just as the MacLeod plantation's surviving James Island (S.C.) cabins differ in size. Ben [Guyton] and his wife Eliza (J. P. Reed) occupied a double kitchen in Anderson town.[13] It was probably a two-room building, a kitchen and separate living quarters, such as is found at Walnut Grove and at Williamsburg (Va.). Elsewhere there were often "double cabins," in essence duplexes utilizing the same chimney with separate fireplaces.

Certainly one hopes that cabins varied in size since in 1860 they housed from one or two slaves each, with six as a typical high occupancy. Larger slave owners were more likely to have lower averages, as did Samuel E. Maxwell with 5 slaves per house for 114 slaves. Just as a plantation's number of slaves varied on a frequent basis with births and deaths, so would a particular house's occupants. A specific cabin might house three generations of one family, or it might include one or more persons unrelated to the family living there. A newly acquired slave would have to be absorbed by an existing household. Sometimes none of the people in a given cabin would be related. Along with permanent residents there might be husbands visiting on weekends, other relatives at times, or friends dropping by. Nearly a hundred black men at an 1867 meeting crowded into a house that must have been a slave home, surely among the larger ones.[14]

Virtually no information survives about local slave houses or their contents, nor has any archaeological work explored such sites. On larger plantations elsewhere, such as Mount Vernon, Monticello, the Chesapeake, or Charleston-area's Drayton Hall and Boone Hall, excavations have shown a surprising array of slave furnishings. This archaeological work has focused largely on house servants or craftsmen of wealthy owners, which likely skews resulting interpretations, as with excavations in Annapolis and Williamsburg dealing with house servants in towns. At his Edgefield plantation James Hammond gave, "as an encouragement to Marriage[,] the first time any two get married a bounty of $4.00 to be invested in house hold goods or an equivalent of articles shall be given." With the likelihood of spouses dying, Hammond provided $2.50 at a second marriage but nothing for a third.

A list of furnishings for John C. Calhoun's house-servant quarters is the area's only specific contemporary evidence. It includes a stove, coal shuttle, and stokers plus a brush for the stove. Minor comforts such as an entry carpet, three doormats,

Stone cabins (bottom left) on John C. Calhoun plantation, artistic rendering. Black Heritage in the Upper Piedmont, Clemson University

a scraper, and a bootjack probably were not found in many slave cabins, nor was a pewter chamber pot. A ladder's presence strongly suggests use of a loft. Occupants had various cleaning implements such as a straw broom, spider broom, and duster brush. Kitchen items included six aprons, two square tin boxes, and two tea canisters. A corkscrew and a "coat holder" are the most fascinating items. Since house servants must appear neat, they also had blacking brushes for shoes plus a hair broom and soap dish for grooming. Furniture is not mentioned.[15]

That document lists only the Calhouns' own property in the "House servants Apartment," a separate dwelling beyond the outdoor kitchen. It tells nothing about what those servants themselves owned. G. W. Featherstonhaugh described Calhoun's outbuildings: "the apartments for servants, the coachhouse, stables, and outhouses were a little detached from the family mansion." In late 1865 former slaves of Crawford Keys (Anderson County) lived in quarters near his barn and other outbuildings, part of a compound including the Keys house.[16]

Other people itemized cabin contents. The Reverend James Hembree in 1847 provided specifically for forty-seven-year-old Peggy and her twelve-year-old son Grief Presley and made in his will "no claim to anything in Peggy's house except the coton wheel and cards and old table." When Andrew broke into his wife Candas's locked cabin in 1841, he damaged two quilts, two sheets, a pillow, a small cotton frock, a pitcher, and a sideboard.[17]

Many slaves would have lived in cabins somewhat removed from the "big house." Among the 521 Oconee and Pickens owners, only eight plantations—most within a few miles of Pendleton—had ten or more cabins in 1860. Maxwell's Toxaway plantation with twenty-three represented the most, Andrew P. Calhoun's fourteen a distant second. Sixteen families with only one or two slaves had no separate dwelling for them in 1860; they must have had a room in their owners' houses or other buildings.

Mary F. Huger, describing her plantation near Pendleton as it appeared circa 1827, referred both to quarters and to work space for craftsmen and cooks. There was a detached kitchen with a sitting room for the cook and a separate pastry room. Behind the blacksmiths' and carpenters' shops, "to the right, scattered throughout the woods, surrounding a large spring of pure water, were the Negro houses. Each family had their own establishment, usually a two-roomed log house, with a little garden fenced in, chicken coop & pig pens. The carpenters and shoemaker had their work sheds near the houses." One nearby plantation had a servants' hall with a living room for eight or ten people, which kept them out of the kitchen, Mary Huger wrote.[18]

In virtually all these cases cabins may have been grouped together—probably not in a neat row, like many in the lowcountry, because of land contours. Cabins would likely have been erected on poor land. Mrs. Colhoun's plantation, which adjoined the Calhouns, had approximately six cabins along Cold Spring creek's sloping banks. Even on the Calhoun plantation, there were "washed hillsides before the negroe houses." Still, Calhoun's stone cabins, connected in a row, won Pendleton Farmers' Society recognition for what it considered their model quality.

Snippets of testimony from slaves indicate that they regarded residences as their own space, individualized with varied internal arrangements and prized personal possessions. John Michael Vlach describes the slaves "personal space and property" and "slave quarters together with the adjacent fields and forests" as "an alternative territorial system."[19] Some family items, like quilts and tools, may have been passed from one generation to another. After a few decades a family could accumulate quilts, dresses, coats, money, furnishings, and livestock through inheritance. Hundreds of freed families had personal property in 1870 worth one hundred dollars or more.

Health: Food and Medical Care

The absence in the three-country area of plantation ledgers complicates research about its slaves. These ledgers would have included names, ages, births, deaths, perhaps family groupings, food allocations, and medical care. They would tell much that can otherwise only be assembled from scanty, piecemeal comments. Like many other components of plantation life, food was a combination of supplies dispensed by owners and those furnished by slaves themselves, blending European and African traditions. The Colhoun plantation ledger, which was not kept systematically, and Harris's Spartanburg diary supply some clues. WPA interviewees from other South Carolina areas reported rations, with some variations, of about three pounds of meat per week—less for children and older people, a quart of molasses, a cup or two of flour, and a peck of cornmeal. Hammond allowed a peck of cornmeal and three pounds of pork, bacon, or beef per person each week plus extra rations for "ditchers." They and everyone "in cotton picking time, when sickness is prevalent" got a dram of whiskey daily.[20]

Colhoun's figures for pork and corn suggest similar quantities of these items, adjusted for ages in each slave family, but do not mention molasses or flour. J. D. Ashmore noted on December 7, 1857, "Killed 805 *lbs* Pork for next years Bacon." Pork was the prevalent meat throughout the South for both white and black, supplemented occasionally by beef for whites, rarely for blacks. Of nearly four thousand farmers in the 1850 agricultural schedule, 95 percent had swine. Harris paid careful attention to quantities of pork slaughtered and cured for each coming year. For 1859 he planned on 3,500 pounds, which equaled about 161 pounds each (three pounds per week).

Neither Colhoun, Harris, nor WPA interviewees referred to owners' providing vegetables on a regular basis; slaves evidently had to raise their own vegetables on patches. Clarissa Adger Bowen wrote in July 1865 that "the freedmen are to retain the products of their patches of corn, gardens, chickenyards, etc. as heretofore."[21]

South Carolina's upper piedmont still remains lush with summer vegetables and fruit, which would have supplied variety and nutrition in a diet often austere and boring. Except in preserved or dried form, most vegetables and fruits would not have been available between November and May. Sorghum molasses would have been the primary sweetener for slaves, as it could be easily produced on the plantation, but sugar from Charleston was expensive.

Slaves could keep their own chickens for additional meat, and some slaves raised hogs for themselves. Sporadic references also mention hunting rabbits, raccoons, possums, turkeys, or other game. Although rabbits could be trapped, most game had to be shot, and some slaves did have guns, either their own or those borrowed from owners for hunting. Harris and his father's slave Julius went hunting together for raccoons and presumably shared their catch. People living near a river or creek, which included most area plantations, could fish.[22]

Cooking processes and rituals of eating probably varied enormously among plantations and perhaps on different days. On some larger plantations one or two women may have cooked some foods for all slaves. Many slave households may have typically prepared their own foods, independent of others, and even within a household unrelated people at times evidently cooked separately for themselves. Fieldworkers likely took their noon meals with them, or had them delivered by women or children.

Ordinarily slaves would have had virtually no access to items not produced locally, especially tea and coffee, as well as sugar and perhaps salt. That meant a greater use of onions and peppers for seasoning, and certainly the pervasive southern fatback. Stews and barbecue continued African and Afro-Caribbean traditions. In theory slaves were not allowed to drink liquor, but some produced their own, probably peach or apple brandy, wine, bourbon, and beer. At harvestings and other occasions, some owners supplied whiskey; the Kilpatricks bought a gallon for hands during the 1850 harvest.[23]

Despite occasional festivities, slave life ordinarily consisted of a limited diet, hard work, and cramped living quarters. Slave mortality was consequently high, as we have seen, especially for infants and women in childbirth. Once past early childhood, some slaves lived to an advanced age. As a significant investment, the health of slaves was an important concern of owners, for economic if no other reasons. Some owners, evidently nearer towns, had regular medical attention for those who were seriously ill. The Kilpatricks paid physician John C. Cherry in 1848 one dollar for "Extracting for Negro." Accounts of Dr. W. L. Jenkins show that an important part—nearly a thousand dollars in a few years—of his income was derived from tending slaves.[24]

A combination of medical care and "granny midwives" supported slave and white women through childbirth if they had assistance at all. The Harris family initially called a white midwife for slave Manerva but decided that a doctor was also needed. Her midwife, who stayed longer, was paid two dollars, the doctor three dollars. After the birth, slave "Aunt" Niry nursed Manerva during the following week.[25] Easter Reid (born ca. 1840), who served as a midwife in postbellum years, probably did so as a slave as well.

Disease killed many white and black with little successful treatment by doctors. Just as yellow fever raged in 1793, Saluda Baptists in 1832 referred to cholera, along with the federal tariff, as "awful visitations of Divine Providence." Thomas Clemson wrote in 1843 that "there has been a good deal of Scarlet fever & putrid sore throat & a good number of deaths[;] 8 in three families died of it." Mortality censuses indicate many cases of white and black dying from a shared disease. Nonfatal diseases ravaged plantations.[26]

Plantation mistresses handled minor ailments. When Edom, a young man, got critically ill, Emily Harris successfully treated him with whiskey and red pepper. Floride Calhoun anxiously watched over, and perhaps nursed, favorite slaves who were ill, including Nelly and her son Andy, for whom she hired a nurse. In 1845 and other years the Kilpatricks treated with "sugar & coffee (for sick negro)" at a cost of twenty-five cents for each case.[27]

Numbers of both blacks and whites believed in, knew, and used herbal remedies. Some also employed other methods, as when a Georgia man traveled to Pendleton in October 1802, where he was treated by an "old African" using "some kind of spell or charm." Traditional or herbal medicine, based in part on African practices with adaptations to plants locally available, served as one part of African American treatments. Free "Doctor Tom" evidently was such a practitioner—called a "negro quack" by the *Pendleton Messenger*—as probably was Dick Walker. Forch Allen's descendants celebrate his skill as an Indian herb doctor. As late as the 1970s, a Sizemore relative was "living under the care of a root doctor . . . that type of medicine, herb medicine." But some practitioners supposedly used magic roots to exercise control over other slaves.[28]

Celebrations and Life Cycles

Celebrations, holidays, and special occasions—some shared, some specifically African American—provided interludes between the drudgeries of work. Weekends, harvests, and year-end breaks occasioned festivities, often with black and white people from several plantations. They afforded more and better food than did a daily diet. More important, they also constituted a valuable component of the African American subculture.

Some activities centered around churchgoing and other religious events. Attending church was an occasion not only for preaching but also for social contacts with many slaves from different plantations. Socializing took place along the road to and from church and on the premises; they sometimes shared a meal there. The same opportunities, repeated for several nights, came from attending protracted services. Camp meetings, however, were grander social occasions. Events drew up to two thousand people and occasionally more; although intended primarily for whites, they also had a sizable black attendance. Some blacks attended services during these meetings. Others spent time enjoying food, social contacts, and bartering. Slaves at times traded clothes or other goods at camp meetings, which combined religion, drinking, sex, merchandising, and violence for blacks as they did for whites.

Secular entertainments and special events drew both black and white crowds. Musters, formally a militia activity, attracted many people to observe and socialize. Executions had large numbers of attendees, some compelled to be there. Slaves could enjoy at reduced rates small-scale circuses, open to all, such as an 1845 one in Pendleton.[29] African Americans may have participated in Fourth of July public celebrations and perhaps stood around the fringes of mass political rallies, popular in antebellum years.

African Americans lived for weekends when, for most, there was no work from Saturday afternoon until Monday morning. Exceptions included house servants and everyone during intense harvesting times, as we have seen. For this short break they had opportunities to rest, to visit relatives, to attend church—for worship, socializing, or both—and especially for husbands to travel to their wives' plantations. Crimes occurred disproportionately often on weekends, a further suggestion of latitude afforded then. Part of this break might be spent working on garden patches or hunting and fishing.

Slaves organized festive occasions for themselves on weekends and at other times. Numerous WPA interviewees spoke about weekend festivities. A woman from Whitmire said that her plantation's sixty-four slaves had fun each Saturday night away from the white folks' hearing. Often they stole and barbecued a hog in a gully where they would not be observed, she said. Parties, called "negro frolics" both before and after emancipation, frequently involved the consumption of liquor. All of these festivities presuppose ability to afford the cost; Austin (Mrs. Mattison) catered an 1839 frolic at twenty-five cents a head.

Occasionally, there were shared celebratory events with barbecue or other feasts held by owners, often attracting people from several plantations. These typically involved music, eating, and dancing. Slave fiddlers were popular, and at times both black and white danced simultaneously on a raised platform. Other rural events included quiltings either by white or by slave women, sometimes jointly.[30]

Typical harvest festivities, as described in adjacent Greenwood County, included shuckings, which combined work on one plantation by many white and black people —including neighbors—shucking corn. "They had neighborhood parties for cornshuckings, cotton pickings, quiltings and other things." The host family provided good suppers at these parties, with whiskey, and sometimes had square dancing or cakewalks, with fiddlers, one interviewee said.[31]

Year-end holidays were African Americans' biggest festivities. Nothing suggests that religious activities had a role in these late-December celebrations. Rather, this week consisted of rest, family gatherings, festivities, and extra food and drink. Financing special meals and balls required some personal expenditures and donations from the master. As a postbellum continuity, tenants and sharecroppers often remained on their former premises, making any change only after the holidays were over.[32]

As noted in chapter 2, between Christmas and New Year many slaves had a week's release from work with opportunities to enjoy life communally. By contrast, white families paid little attention to the Christmas season other than as a religious event. African American celebrations evidently began a few days before Christmas and lasted until year's end. At that time of year only minimal agricultural work had to be done; it was also the cold season when hogs were slaughtered, and fresh meat was more abundant than at any other time. Larger plantations saw special festivities, such as those when the Calhouns allowed slaves to use the detached kitchen for Christmas celebrations. Also, "Wednesday night before Christmas [1841] . . . there was a frolick (negro)" at the Widow Duckworth's. While her slave Sam "played the fiddle nearly all night . . . they danced until an hour before day."[33]

Liquor held an important place during year-end festivities for some. One man went away for the holidays, perhaps to relatives, got drunk, and froze to death by exposure on his way home. Jerry and Lige's liquor-importing business from Augusta came to light with arrests just before 1845 holidays, as happened also with Lewis in 1854 and free Wade Dennis in 1857. Sometimes festivities degenerated into violence, as in 1856 when Edmund was found guilty of carrying firearms on a public highway on December 25 and threatening to shoot another slave, George, reputedly sleeping with Edmund's wife. Slave consumption and sale of liquor, however, could hardly rival white drunkenness on muster and election days or widespread illegal distilling.[34]

Other cases involved more violent activity, such as fourteen slaves charged with fighting, rioting, and unlawful assembly at William Anderson's, along with stabbing one with a knife, on December 16, 1846, shortly before holidays. Those fourteen men came from ten different plantations; only three were found guilty. Several involved stealing. Like whiskey dealing, offenses before Christmas suggest that African Americans were trying to find extra goods and money to use for celebrations. Patrol and magistrates and freeholders court intrusion into holidays became a form of control and punishment. Solomon (Violet Bowman) was sentenced to stay home during the 1853 season. Two years later, Tom (Wm. Sutherland) was punished with two installments of twenty-five stripes and a month in jail in between; the second twenty-five lashes were scheduled for the holidays.[35]

Year-end and weekend socializing and festivities strengthened the slave communications network and subculture. Besides holidays, other notable dates in human experience include marriages, births, and deaths. No examples indicate any celebration connected with a baby's birth, perhaps because many would likely die before they were a year old. The fact that some people later in the century could not give the specific date, or even the month and day, of their birth suggests that such events had little place in antebellum life.[36]

Weddings, however, were more festive. St. Paul's rector performed ceremonies in a variety of settings: the plantation of either bride or groom; the church itself after evening service; the rector's home; and a white home in Pendleton. One Anderson County Presbyterian church authorized a member to perform marriages among other slaves, a practice probably more widespread than this solitary example. No contemporary account of Anderson, Oconee, or Pickens counties mentions practices such as jumping over the broomstick, and hardly any describe any celebrations surrounding marital commitments. A visiting journalist described a Fort Hill wedding: "A very intelligent house servant of Mr. Calhoun was married . . . to a female slave on an adjoining plantation. The marriage ceremony was performed in the evening, and in the mansion of the proprietor of the plantation. I listened to the fiddles and the happy songs of the negroes. . . . The ceremony was performed by the oldest negro, who was a sort of authorized, or rather recognised parson . . . Methodist."[37]

Slightly more information survives about burials and funeral observances. Ashmore's diary noted starkly, "Jim helping Mr. Morse bury negro woman." Slave burials occurred in church cemeteries and on plantations, either by the white family's graves or in separate areas. Calhoun and Colhoun family slaves were buried a few yards from the white family according to oral tradition in both white and black communities. Given large numbers of slaves involved, perhaps only house servants were buried near the white family, a practice better documented for Amherst County, Virginia.[38]

Other accounts refer to slave burials. Harris recorded that "Elifus has gone to see his wife, Lucy [belonging to Harris's father], buried." When a slave child died late one October 1860 evening, Harris helped build a coffin the following morning, Sunday. That couple had three children buried on the plantation and one in the

Material and Emotional Conditions / 169

Lucinda's cemetery marker at King's Chapel AME cemetery (Pendleton) is the only known marked grave for a named slave in this area: "In Memory of LUCINDA, A faithful Servant, Died July 1854, Aged 65 Years." Black Heritage in the Upper Piedmont

village, evidently at a church cemetery. As with Morse and Harris, whites at times shared in black burials. Jane Hunter recorded much later about coffins "made from the wood of this tree [poplar], Negroes believing that since the fibers of the poplar disintegrated rapidly, the bodies of the dead would soon return to dust."[39]

Some church cemeteries had areas specifically for slaves. Their Oolenoy Baptist Church (upper Pickens County) burials are designated by one marker of recent vintage for all, without names. A wide central area now missing its fieldstones at Old Stone Church (near Pendleton), resembling Oolenoy's section, evidently served as a burying site for slaves, as did a similar, large unmarked circular space occupying Bethlehem Methodist (near Liberty) cemetery's middle area.[40]

Only one tombstone has been found that was erected during slavery; it is now in King's Chapel AME cemetery, Pendleton. Reading "In Memory of LUCINDA, A faithful Servant, Died July 1854, Aged 65 Years," it was made by Charleston's W. T. White, one of the state's premier marble cutters, shipping monuments throughout North and South Carolina. Clearly the family highly prized Lucinda. At least two other monuments exist for individual slaves, a postbellum one for former slave Jemima, who belonged to the Pickens family and died in 1868, and a twentieth-century marker at Old Pickens.[41]

Burials, both black and white, typically occurred within twenty-four hours in an era before embalming. Prompt burials also made sense as cabins afforded little space for a coffin or mourners, and slaves had little time for ceremony. Oral interviews about the Tenus Maxwell cemetery told of early postbellum practices, likely resembling those during slavery: a slow procession up a steep hill with religious music and probably a preacher.

These observances and especially happier celebrations were important events in slave life. They constituted a distinctive aspect of African American subculture and reinforced it. A central ingredient was ability to travel beyond their own premises and socialize with slaves from other plantations. Some socializing occurred when slaves had their own activities around "white" events, such as religious settings or parades; others, such as weekend and year-end festivities, were uniquely their own. Involvement of both white and black in harvest and other celebrations reveals more layers of plantation life.

The Plantation as a Family

As a complicated assemblage of people living on the same premises, a plantation encompassed emotions that must have been very complex. Its residents included a white household, sometimes with three generations plus some unrelated persons sharing their house, and African Americans, who consisted of some nuclear and some extended families and perhaps unrelated individuals. Some may have had spouses living on other plantations. Yet on some levels, these people were all connected with one another.

Some whites referred, loosely, to the whole plantation as a "family," but understanding what owners meant by this is difficult. As we saw in chapter 2, Robert Guyton's 1841 will directed that his "family be kept together, both black and white," and Calhoun consoled a Maryland friend (Virgil Maxcy) about the death of a servant, "the loss of a faithful domestick raised in the family . . . that of a friend, humble indeed, but still a friend." Most white owners would have had more frequent contact with their slaves than with white neighbors, and knew these slaves much better than they did the unlanded white population. Twenty-six white families in Anderson, Oconee, and Pickens counties owned exactly ten slaves in 1860; there was an average of 5.4 whites for these households (almost identical to David Golightly Harris's); human relationships among slaves and whites must have been frequent, familiar, and complicated.[42]

Numerous southern accounts relate whites' sentimental memories from childhood of favored house servants. Decades later elderly Louisa McCord, formerly of Pendleton, wrote, "Maum Di was our stay and comfort in trouble, our companion and sympathiser in happiness. All the same we had an immense respect for her." Another woman wrote of her joy as a girl when the carriage driver "Old Sam would help us out & see each of us holding on to a strap" to ride on the rear board.[43]

David Golightly Harris made periodic observations that included all people on his plantation. These dealt especially with health. Harris noted in 1860, "White & black family all well," and later in the year, "nearly all the family both white and black are much anoyed with distressing colds." On other occasions he specifically referred to his "white family," but when a slave "Old Will" got into trouble, Harris lamented, "I am sorry to have a rougher in my family."[44]

As suggested by Harris, illnesses, especially when serious, affected collective moods. Shared ailments would have depressed the whole plantation. He specifically addressed results of various black and white people getting on each other's nerves: "To day has been uncomfortable to me, wife is mad, the children cross, the negroes sick, and every thing is wrong." Exactly a year later he reported a similar situation: "Of course had a row with the negroes, before I could get them off. . . . All cross & mad this week."[45]

Owners like the Calhouns evidently treated their slaves comparatively well, were sensitive to grumblings, and tried to prevent any eruption of trouble, as when son-in-law Thomas Clemson told Calhoun that "the negroes are unruly." John E. Colhoun (Jr.) learned that family "Negroes had rebelled but that prompt measures had been taken to restore peace." He advised the overseer that "the only method is to be decisive and punish on the spot all attempts at insubordination," advice evidently similar to that Calhoun gave a few years later. In 1827 "the Negroes . . . have been in some instances disorderly. . . . I hope they have been brought into entire subjection; but . . . if not, the most decided measures [must] be adopted to bring them to a sense of duty."[46] How "the negroes" were "unruly" and how they could be "brought into entire subjection" can only be imagined, unpleasantly.

On a more harmonious note, two young Simpson men who served in Virginia during the Civil War frequently sent greetings both to their own relatives and to slaves. Tally Simpson a few months after leaving Pendleton wrote, "My respects to the Pickens [white family] and howdy to all the negros." And slaves Zion, Lewis, and Jim, who attended the brothers in Virginia, often sent salutations to others at home: "Zion is doing finely and wishes to be remembered to all at home, white and black."[47]

Clearly neither Simpsons nor slaves had any illusions about their status. But on some plantations, at least, the people felt some type of connection. Shared bonds likely existed between aged black and white who lived on the same plantation all of their lives. But white sources do not document the pain, sufferings, deprivations, resentment, and anger felt by slaves.

Interracial Sex and Exploitation

If owners believed that black and white constituted a family, then some white men practiced incest within that extended family. The image of white men forcing slave women to submit their bodies runs throughout popular literature and cinema with antebellum settings. Human nature would certainly involve some such exploitation; it would also avoid leaving written documentation. Expressed in other ways, the presence of mulattos on a quarter of local plantations indicates its occurrence without telling its frequency. William Pickens, a Pendleton-area native, wrote about a stranger viewing "resemblances" of a white and a black person, who although not "legally akin . . . very much resembled" each other with "little boys . . . so indistinguishably alike" that they could easily be confused. One WPA interview recorded a similar situation in which the plantation mistress treated black children kindly but not so those who were "yellow."[48]

Various African American family histories refer to white ancestors, and several people reported in 1870 and 1880 censuses that their fathers came from Ireland, France, Spain, or other European countries. Both the Pickens and Anderson newspapers in 1886 wrote about local "red-headed colored" people and made snide comments that "there are whole families of them in this country." Local communities, white and black, separately have their own legends about which white men fathered various black children in the vicinity.[49]

Several owners in these antebellum chapters evidently had a continuing involvement with slave women. It is virtually impossible to imagine another explanation why one man bought a padlock for his slave's cabin, a lock which even her husband had to break—even more so as the husband attacked and threatened to kill his wife's owner. Churches censured both owners and slaves for their mutual sexual involvements. And a Greenville owner, tried in 1856 for murder of his wife, was accused during the trial of being in love with a slave woman, Liza, and having fathered a mulatto child by her.[50]

Some owners who emancipated slaves or provided kindly for them in their wills likely had familial reasons for doing so, but knowing the circumstances of each case is impossible. Although census designations of "black" and "mulatto" are not reliable, an occasional mulatto among a black mother's black children may, in some cases, be attributable to her owner's assaults.

Slaves often knew which white men were taking sexual advantage of black women. Several magistrates' and freeholders' charges of "slander" and "telling falsehoods" allude to these affairs. Mack and Adeline reportedly spread stories about Jesse Ingram and slave girl Louisa; after several witnesses testified that they saw Ingram with Louisa, the magistrates and freeholders court found Mack not guilty. And a white wife, jealous of her husband's temptations, accused her slave of pulling "her clothes too high."[51]

Another stereotype of antebellum miscegenation portrays African American males as predators of white women. Yet numerous slave men were found not guilty of rape or sexual assaults. Julius, however, was convicted of going to A. Partain's house, winking at daughter Maria, showing her money, and trying to entice her into the woods. Other convictions involved exposure and solicitations.[52]

Some white women had sexual relations with slave men, and at least sometimes the woman consented. The white woman who bore a black child but did not charge the slave with rape has already been noted in chapter 5. So have mulatto children living in white households in 1850 and 1860; they could have been legally free only if their mothers—most likely white women—were also. On the other hand, some white women repudiated allegations. One woman sued Alfred Hester for repeating slave Seab's bragging that he had sexual intercourse and "could do what he pleased" with her. Renowned attorney Benjamin Perry extracted one thousand dollars from Hester in a successful suit. But other white women, evidently prostitutes, offered sex for pay to slave and free men. Anderson's Town Council complained (chapter 11) about one white woman trading with slaves, selling them liquor, and keeping a house of ill fame.[53]

Easter Reid's granddaughter Lucinda said that as a slave Easter bore her owner's children but would not tell them who their father was. Other African American families identify their white slave-owning ancestor and in some cases attribute gifts of land or other resources to him. By contrast African American Hallums have yet to learn their full ancestry. It is nevertheless clear that there were in many cases, as explored by Edward Ball, "slaves in the family" in more ways than one. Occasionally slave women could repulse unwanted advances. Haner in 1835, who claimed that a patrol captain felt her private parts, was charged with insulting him but found not guilty. Evidently the man's reputation was well known by "neighboring freeholders."[54]

More often an owner was successful. Many consider any sexual encounter between a slave and her owner to be rape by definition, because of the owner's power over her. Based on that premise, hundreds, perhaps thousands, of slave women residing in Anderson, Oconee, and Pickens counties were raped between 1784 and 1865. "Interpersonal relations," a continuing theme, took on other connotations when slave women were violated. These attacks added a sinister, painful element to plantation life.

Conflicts among Slaves

Typical disagreements and irritations that might arise among any group of people living in proximity also occurred behind the big house. Enslaved conditions produced further complications and fostered causes for disputes and fights. Slaves took a great risk in venting their frustrations against owners or overseers, but they faced little danger in transferring their anger to one another. They lived in conditions far more cramped than did owners, with some cabins shared by people unrelated to each other. Husbands who lived on different plantations from their wives frequently developed jealousies of any attention paid their wives by other men.[55]

Arguments based on marital conflict and jealousies evidently abounded given constrictions imposed by slave life, but few incidents were recorded. Tom (Lemuel Hall) beat Mariah (John McPhail) so violently in 1824 that she lost a week's work. Tom said that she had the clap, evidently complaining that she passed it on to him. Issues concerning loans and theft also led to violence.[56]

Controversies sometimes involved slaves defending or allying with their relatives. Edmund complained in 1856 about George C. Irby): the "damned rascal [George] is bed[ding] my wife every night." Edmond then threatened to "blow out his damned brains." Several free people of color, especially Fanny Payton, got into disputes and retaliated physically while defending some of their relatives.

Sometimes slaves on one plantation developed rivalries and feuds with neighbors. When three of Mrs. Mary Mattison's slaves assaulted J. W. Norris's slave "in a Riotous manner," they claimed to be retaliating for Norris slaves having stolen bacon. And a December 26, 1846, episode involved fourteen slaves (ten owners, three of them Duckworths), charged with fighting, rioting, unlawful assembly, and inflicting knife wounds.[57] Many magistrates and freeholders cases involved slave testimony against a black defendant. Surely at times owners coerced this damaging evidence. At others, however, intense dislike seems to have motivated blacks to testify, almost eagerly.

Numerous slave conflicts were recorded without any explanation or causation. Several cases in Anderson, Oconee, and Pickens counties and in neighboring counties involved slaves killing other slaves and some free people of color.[58] Shared enslavement did not necessarily produce harmony among those on a single plantation, let alone throughout the area. Quarrels among slaves, sometimes erupting into violence, further illustrate multilayered plantation relationships.

Shared Experiences

Although slaves did not always get along together, at times white and black formed bonds between themselves. Many of these would have been based on gender and age. Children sometimes related to each other because of their age and gender, regardless of being white and slave. Abundant stories throughout the South tell of such children playing together. At times a slave woman would nurse both a white and black baby simultaneously. Children of both races, especially boys, would have gone swimming and exploring the woods together. Slave and white boys lurked under Anderson's depot platform, eavesdropping and "looking up . . . under the dresses of Ladies" and went "under the platform to make water." S. E. Maxwell and his slave Tenus evidently had a lifelong relationship, as did "Old Rose" and Robert Anderson's wife, who "were raised together and were of an age."[59]

Similarly, minister J. B. Adger in May 1847 wrote, "Their children are, to some extent the playmates of our childhood . . . sometimes pass through all the changes of life with us, and then, either they stand weeping by our bedside, or we . . . by theirs, when death comes to close the long connection and to separate the good master and his good servant."[60]

Adults, black and white, in slavery and afterward, shared some same-gender relationships. Certainly that often included work, but extended beyond that. Men likely hunted and fished together and may well have shared sexual jokes. Black and white men gambling or drinking together, a criminal offense, produced some trials of whites as well as slaves. Seab (above) evidently shared stories of his sexual conquests with Hester. In a poignant 1813 episode, two men—one a slave, the other white—tried to rescue four young white girls from drowning; another slave, a "young

Aunt Becky Reed, probably a former servant of the J. P. Reed family and likely the wife of McDuffie Singleton. Pendleton District Commission

fellow," died in the accident.⁶¹ Women at times supported each other in childbirth, in mourning deaths of their children, and on other occasions. They may have discussed their husbands together and likely talked about their daughters' maturation. Collaborating in health care, white women served as nurses, and black nannies and midwives with herbal medicines treated others on the plantation. Many plantation mistresses shared discarded clothing with slave women.

"Preacher Jim" Rosemond received in 1894 a letter from his former master, a man two years younger, who wrote, "I used to think that he was the sweetest singer I ever heard, and I think so now, and I have as much proper respect for him as I have for any one in the State, and hope I shall ever have." Rosemond's biographer added, "These were the words of a true white friend in commendation of a true colored friend. In fact, there seems to be a tie of love that cannot be broken, existing between the ex-master and the ex-slave up this way [Greenville]. They often attend the funerals of each other, and shed tears as if it were some kindred that had gone to rest." Although postbellum whites often made such comments, this is the only contemporary one found from a black perspective.⁶²

As a human community, a plantation was more than work, which consumed much of their lives. It also encompassed rituals of marriage, birth, and death as well as festive celebrations. Just as among whites, the slaves' world was afflicted by conflicts among people. But their personal difficulties were intensified due to the inhumanity of slavery, as some people acted out brutality that was inflicted on them. Complex socio-psychological dimensions of a plantation involved complicated bonds between owners and slaves. In a different context, Mechal Sobel refers to a "deep symbiotic relatedness that must be explored if we are to understand either of them."[63]

Despite textbook descriptions and easy stereotypes, the antebellum world was not simple. There were variations even in burial sites for slaves, as well as differing attitudes and temperaments of owners. Some slaves accumulated money, others absorbed religion and leadership training in churches, and a few led quarrelsome lives. The forthcoming war, described by some as "a world turned upside down," would result in freeing enslaved African Americans, but it would not totally transform society. Complicated relationships, social and economic inequality between races, and contorted white views continued despite the war and emancipation.

PART 4 ❧ *Transitions*

Introduction to Part 4

SLAVERY DID NOT REMAIN STATIC from Pendleton District's first white and black settlement in 1784 throughout the next seventy-five years. Enslavement, the central factor, was a constant. But denser population and larger holdings sustained a more extensive and better-developed African American subculture.

Changes occurred more rapidly between 1850 and 1870, with the Civil War playing a major role. Yet heightened tensions of the 1850s indicate that the war did not suddenly intrude into American life; rather, it was a cataclysmic eruption of many regional and societal fissures wedged apart over decades. Perhaps no events were so totally beyond the area's African American control or influence as the Civil War or Reconstruction. Certainly, however, they had their own reactions, responses, and opportunities.

The war and surrender did not transform southern society immediately. Fought initially to preserve the Union, the war changed through Abraham Lincoln's prodding into a cause also to emancipate slaves. But neither his program nor that of those called "Radical Republicans" planned, let alone provided, for enabling freed peoples to have a place in society. "Forty acres and a mule" might have done so, but they were not forthcoming. Rather, those forty acres in 1870 still belonged to a white landlord—probably a former slave owner—supplying them to a laborer, who in most cases would be no better off than the year before. More often, sharecroppers would sink deeper in debt.

"Reconstruction," as far as the federal government was concerned, meant little more than readmitting rebel states to the Union after they promised political equality to former slaves and protection during a decade of Republican state government. Both an occupation army and the Freedmen's Bureau tried to enforce these measures and to prevent brutality and bloodshed during the years 1865–68. Afterward, black people were left on their own, most lacking any "means of production" and thus often exploited. Whites remained in control.

A 1998 panel, discussing historical interpretation since Eric Foner's definitive *Reconstruction: America's Unfinished Revolution*, pointed out three significantly different scholarly approaches to the era. (1) The traditional treatment has centered on Reconstruction, which implies, and usually stresses, federal policies and politics. (2) Dealing with the period as emancipation shifts the emphasis somewhat, but still treats African Americans partly as objects. By contrast, (3) a liberation approach both recognizes freed people as actors on their own behalf and allows comparisons to, and links with, similar movements in other societies.

This work combines elements of each approach. It is virtually impossible to conceive of emancipation, political and legal equality, and black voting in Anderson, Oconee, and Pickens counties without strong federal pressure. Local presence of both the army and the Freedmen's Bureau were critical in 1865 and 1867. In many ways emancipation there was a different and narrower process than Reconstruction. Turning to freed peoples' initiatives to shape their own lives, the next four chapters emphasize development of churches, schools, and political activity, which included forming Union Leagues and registering to vote. Blacks' reactions over the October 1867 Hunnicutt murder crisis made it a transforming event, despite their minority status.

America's first comprehensive view of its black population comes from the 1870 census. It records for the three counties a strong cohesiveness of families, almost certainly perpetuating their ties during slavery. It shows not only strides in literacy achieved at freedmen's schools beginning in 1866 but also accomplishments before 1861. And it portrays a landless agricultural caste.

During these decades, transitions were exactly that, not sudden events. Even emancipation changed little except abolishing slavery's legal status; most area freed people lived and worked on the same land in December 1865 as in December 1860. Dispersals occurred gradually, often breaking up clusters of slave quarters and forcing new forms of communities. Yet many people in 1870 or 1900 still lived within five or fifteen miles of their former plantations, and many bore their former owner's surname. Much changed, much stayed the same.

ELEVEN

War Years, the Home Front, and African Americans

CIVIL WAR CONDITIONS of life for slaves in Anderson, Oconee, and Pickens counties varied from those in other parts of the state. Except for Charleston and the Port Royal area, there are no sustained local accounts of black life during the war for comparison. The area remained isolated from fighting and from many other factors of the war. Unlike Charleston and the Port Royal area, federal forces did not occupy or bombard AOP, nor emancipate any slaves there. And the area missed the high tension and political hubbub of Columbia, as well as that city's movement of troops by train; even Spartanburg experienced more of the latter than did AOP. Slaves there probably had less white male supervision than those elsewhere in the state.[1] For both prewar and wartime years, the fears, hopes, and responses of whites are easier to decipher than are those among African Americans. Whites, with fewer men still at home, tried to control slave offenses and gatherings. As a result of both increased opportunities and wartime shortages, slaves seem to have resorted to stealing food more often. And some African Americans, having ample sources of news despite the area's relative isolation, believed—even before the Emancipation Proclamation—that the war would bring their freedom.

The Civil War was beyond control or influence of slaves in Anderson, Oconee, and Pickens counties. Many were pressed into service either laboring on defensive coastal balustrades or tending their masters at the front. Hundreds of slaves were relocated, disrupting lives of African American families. At home they had to work harder and eat less due to military demands on crops and even on themselves. But the war's promise of freedom would not find ready fulfillment. As the home front changed, slaves came under more pressures and controls. Others experienced extended travel to Virginia. There, at home, and in labor on coastal defenses, they interacted with a wider array of free people of color, slaves, and escaping blacks. Voices of freedom occasionally emerged as some slaves spoke about their future when the North won the war.

The Tense 1850s

Events and emotions of the 1850s made war increasingly likely, if not inevitable. Tensions were building in South Carolina, as around the country. Slavery often was the key issue, but other conflicts also produced strong emotions. Whether Kansas should be a free or a slave state led to bitter controversy, two competing governments, and fraudulent voting by both sides. "Bleeding Kansas"—the victim both of John Brown's fervent message and raids and of proslavery forces—in many ways symbolized national attitudes. Abolitionists like Brown seemed determined to crush slavery, which made southerners increasingly anxious to protect "our way of life" against outsiders. Perceived northern threats led to fearful southern reactions.

Efforts at compromise that steadied national policies for over three decades disappeared with deaths of U.S. Senators John C. Calhoun, Henry Clay, and Daniel Webster as the decade began. Elsewhere, northern laborers clashed with, and often beat up, recently arrived immigrants from Ireland and Germany, while Chinese encountered similar problems amid California's gold rush. Temperance societies also escalated their activities. People became more agitated on many issues.

As abolitionists sent more agents to the South, and as locals reacted more strongly against their efforts, problems and emotions reached a higher level—throughout the South and certainly in the upper piedmont. South Carolinians again established local Vigilance Committees, as they had in the 1830s, to ferret out suspected abolitionist activity. The Pickens *Keowee Courier* on May 30, 1857, editorialized against those "trafficking with Negroes" and argued that when men did so, "other measures [than the law] must be resorted to." Elsewhere in the state, a Williamsburg grand jury urged that free people of color be banished or sold into slavery, and in 1859 an Oconee judge imposed such a sentence on free Sam Oglesby. These actions followed a long tradition of local, extralegal pressure on people believed to have committed offenses against society, but vigilantism became more intensified in the late 1850s.[2] In 1859 a white man, "detected in trading with negroes, selling them whiskey &c," was roughed up near Pendleton; seditious language occasioned similar treatment for another man near Anderson in early 1860; and South Carolina owners beat their slaves more often in 1859 than earlier according to Judge O'Neall.[3]

John Brown's November 1859 abortive raid at Harpers Ferry—another vigilante action—raised emotions even higher throughout the South. Following Brown's raid more vigilance committees appeared and involved direct intervention. Pickens whites ordered a self-described book dealer from Massachusetts, being from a "hotbed of abolition," to leave town within two days, but he "left instanter." General F. N. Garvin helped organize vigilance committees, three men from each Pickens and Oconee militia beat company agreeing "to look after and watch the movements of the abolition emissaries . . . scattering the seeds of dissension among our slaves." The Anderson Committee of Twenty-three had a similar mandate, and Pendleton's young men volunteered to become Minutemen.[4]

Apparently contradictory movements marked the late 1850s: more slaves were hauled before magistrates and freeholders courts and into church trials than earlier, and more church exclusions of slaves similarly occurred. Whites were alarmed by a reported fall 1860 slave gathering in upper Anderson County. Religious fervor also characterized immediate antebellum years with larger church membership, both white and black. But during these same years, it seems, more young white females conceived children out of wedlock, in rare cases by a slave, than in prior years—or at least churches censured more. Although the war often has been the pivotal focus of southern and national historical analysis, many societal changes began before the war and would transcend it. Both at that time and in later histories, however, the war was more conspicuous and has attracted more attention.[5]

Secession talk, which bubbled up periodically during the nineteenth century, became more prolific following John Brown's raid and Lincoln's nomination in 1860. Following his election, a state convention quickly passed a secession ordinance, and rallies fueled enthusiasm, as did Pendleton's November 23 barbecue and torchlight militia parade. Floride Calhoun, a special guest, observed ironically "that the governor's Negro band played most delightfully between the speakers." Despite wild enthusiasm for secession—repeated over Fort Sumter's bombardment in 1861—Harris had portentous thoughts: "It is a source of rejoyceing to many, and grevious to a few. Who can tell what the consequence will be?" Not all South Carolinians rejoiced; some opposed the war. The *Keowee Courier* noted throughout most of 1860 that its entire area was opposed to secession. Greenville and Spartanburg Unionists were ready to rally their troops, as they did against nullification thirty years earlier. Later, some Unionists aided escaping federal prisoners during the war, and a Unionist meeting occurred in Anderson during January 1864.[6] Others refused to serve or deserted. Later called "the solid South," it was not completely united in the 1860s.

No War in Anderson, Oconee, or Pickens Counties

The area's Civil War years surprisingly are among the most difficult to document for either whites or African Americans. Local newspapers did not publish during much of the war, copies are missing for many months when they did, and few diaries or letters exist for these war years. David and Emily Harris's Spartanburg diary probably reflects conditions similar to those in Anderson, Oconee, and Pickens counties. Emily's entries are especially useful as a woman's insight into wartime conditions and fears. Stresses filled daily wartime life, as did shortages, disruptions, and changing social mores. Slaves would have shared all of these changes, and perhaps many more.

As the war's front came no closer than a hundred miles away in South Carolina plus some raids in North Carolina, the region falls outside of most Civil War accounts.[7] Although federal forces occupied coastal Port Royal in late 1861 and Union ships bombarded Charleston's harbor throughout the war, enemy soldiers did not venture beyond the coast until General W. T. Sherman's 1865 march.

Major disruptions experienced in many other areas did not touch AOP. No houses were burned, no lands seized by the federal army, no slaves liberated by conquering forces, no fields ravaged by either battle or troops tromping through them —in many ways a boring story. Some schools continued to function, though many were interrupted when teachers were conscripted.[8] Wartime intrusions on local whites resulted primarily from the absence of many fighting men, deaths of some of them, war taxes, and occasional food shortages. Many months passed in 1863 and 1864 without the Harrises recording any battle news even from elsewhere. The war's progress seems to have had limited impact on upstate African Americans.

The easiest place to begin discussing the war is with soldiers, themselves better documented than civilians. Approximately two thousand men and boys in Anderson, Oconee, and Pickens counties—representing about 26 percent of draft-age white males—served in the Confederate army. One South Carolina historian estimates the statewide figure at 33 percent. The area lost about six hundred men, representing 31 percent of those who served, and 8 percent of all white males who were ten to forty years old in 1860. That loss, nearly 10 percent of adult white males under the age of forty-five, marked the most significant impact of the war itself. Orr's Regiment—officially, South Carolina 1st Infantry Regiment, Rifles, organized in May 1861—contained many volunteers from the three counties. That unit spent the war mostly in Virginia campaigns, and the 4th South Carolina Infantry Regiment, drawing heavily from Anderson County, reached Virginia by July 1861. Consequently local men died mostly in Virginia; few lost their lives in South Carolina.[9]

Sufferings and deaths run throughout surviving newspapers, family letters, and church memorial pages. Even John Long's will, written in July 1862, began, "At the call of my country, [I] have volunteered for its defence." He died the following June. Wartime deaths swelled church and family cemeteries and would occasion frequent memorials in postwar years.

Agricultural production suffered from absences of a quarter of working-age white males and hundreds of the most able-bodied slaves. "So many soldiers have gone to the war & so few are left at home to work the farms," Harris recorded. "Provisions are very high [in cost], & I much fear they will be higher." Yet shortages were more spotty than consistent throughout the entire upstate. Anything that had to be shipped from Charleston, such as coffee and salt, was a problem. Locally produced grains, meat, and vegetables evidently were not. During the war, however, farmers had to turn over 10 percent of their crops for the army. Periodic campaigns also raised voluntary contributions of food and other supplies for soldiers. Shortages are not mentioned even among May and June 1865 diary entries that noted other local sufferings.[10]

Those who stayed behind maintained production, if at reduced levels. Several families whose white men were in the army and who owned only a few slaves had to hire slave labor, as did the Striblings. Overseers on large plantations were exempt from the draft, which drew complaints by men who had to serve. Both large plantations and others where the owner was too old to fight, yet able to work hard, evidently yielded harvests comparable to antebellum levels. J. E. Hagood managed to distill ample liquor to sell to the army. Andrew Calhoun, now owning his father's land, grew abundant wheat and corn that he sold throughout the area and had delivered by slaves. Even in January 1865 his niece Floride Clemson, newly arrived in

Pendleton, reported "plenty corn, flour, salt, sorghum, & even poultry," although "luxuries are almost unobtainable, sugar & meat dear."[11]

As in other wars, special hardships fell on women, who had to assume additional burdens. Emily Harris often lamented her hard life, managing crops, supervising slaves, and handling finances amid shortages and rapidly escalating prices and taxes. She knitted clothes for her husband, worried about him as he fulfilled his military obligations, and complained on October 1, 1864, "There is no one on the place that has the welfare and prosperity of the family at heart but me. No one helps me to care and to think. . . . Losses, crosses and disappointments assail me on every hand."[12]

Severed communications were another frequent reminder of war. Newspapers frequently did not publish, fewer trains ran, and letters bearing precious news from army camps took much longer to arrive. Short supplies of paper stopped some newspapers. Some legal documents from magistrates and freeholders courts and other official bodies appear on odd scraps of paper, often torn from courthouse ledgers. Paper, salt, and coffee shortages resulted from federal blockade and later occupation of Charleston as well as transportation irregularities. More communication interruptions came in February 1865, near the war's end, as heavy rains and flooding destroyed upstate roads and bridges, including railroad trestles. These damaged systems would create continued problems for months after the war's end.

Local disruption came as bands of outlaws swept down from the mountains on periodic raids for foodstuffs. These mountains harbored many white men who either never reported for enlistment or deserted afterward. Conscription officer J. D. Ashmore in August 1863 arrested 502 deserters, plus many others who never reported to the army. Hiding in almost every intermediate pass and valley, these men had "taken refuge in the mountain fastnesses and passes of the districts of Greenville, Pickens [including Oconee], and Spartanburg . . . spread over a large frontier border of over 150 miles, every foot of which is a mountain country and much of it almost inaccessible . . . banded together in tens, twenties, and thirties, are bold, defiant, and even threatening . . . [with] spies and signals . . . [and armed] with weapons such as fowling pieces, revolvers, &c." During the winter of 1864 "an organized gang of bushwhackers" raided far and wide.[13]

Wartime pressures led to religious intensity while also disrupting church functions. Anderson Presbyterian minutes observed in 1862, as many could have done, that "nearly all the [white] male portion of our Congregation are in the Army." There was still a good attendance due to "strangers from the invaded portion of our state, who have sought a Temporary refuge among us."

Church attendance boomed, as often happens during wars, and protracted meetings produced many new members, both white and black. These additions consisted disproportionately of slaves, which suggests owner pressure to bring them into the fold and thus under controls of church membership and discipline. Saluda Baptists' white membership increased 10 percent between 1860 and 1865, despite wartime deaths, battle and otherwise, but that of blacks grew 45 percent. This boom resumed late-antebellum growth after few 1860–62 additions. Noticeable spurts took place in 1863, with even larger ones in 1864.

Southern Anderson County churches experienced the area's biggest gains, both numerically and proportionally—further indication that owners with a higher percentage of slaves and nearer the federal presence often pressured them to join churches. However, African Americans may have reacted as much to intense wartime emotions, both generalized and religious, as large numbers of whites were joining also. St. Paul's Episcopal Church rolls in Pendleton swelled with both whites and blacks relocated from the lowcountry.

While attending church, slaves listened to commemorations of brave soldiers, sometimes their owners, who had died in battle. Slaves endured many sermons exhorting greater sacrifice and commitment to the Confederacy. Periodically Confederate President Jefferson Davis proclaimed specific days of fasting and prayer for victory. African Americans heard, moreover, fervent convictions that God endorsed the Confederate cause.[14]

Changing social controls within the white community during the war and the absence of many white men evidently fostered sexual relations between some white women and slave men. Perhaps the only unanimous sentiment ever among Barker's Creek Baptist whites occurred in March 1865 when "there was a charge preferred against Clarissa Adams for having a Bastard child [conceived presumably in spring 1864] and it a mulatto. She was unanimously excluded from the church." Mixed white-black households in the 1870 census suggest other cases of interracial relationships during the war.[15]

Slaves' Lives, Dissidence, Magistrates and Freeholders Trials, and Perceptions of War

Slave reactions to the war, their emotions about it, and perceptions about the war's course and purpose are harder to trace than are those of whites. Like Mary Chesnut, living then in Columbia, and Spartanburg's David and Emily Harris, many whites sometimes became discouraged. Long periods of collective war weariness occurred, which surely affected slaves. Chesnut and Harris reported that slaves were less willing to work and more inclined to absent themselves temporarily.[16]

Just as many upper-piedmont whites led a relatively normal existence, life seems to have continued mostly as usual for many African Americans. Certainly they were keenly aware of the war and the resulting absence of many white men and ultimately hundreds of slaves. Blacks received war news both from the lowcountry about battles and blockades there and from some slaves who accompanied masters to Virginia battlefields.

Sparse wartime diaries and letters hardly mention slave unrest or changed dispositions. More often, writers spoke of their slaves' loyalty. Most slaves evidently stayed at home, appeared to follow orders, and waited. Harris's December 8, 1860, entry reflects complicated strands of life during this period: "I sometimes go patrolling. And sometimes go coon-hunting with [father's slave] Julius." A few weeks later

Floride Calhoun "was much struck at [her slave] Jackson's running into the house saying good news, good news, another state has seceded." Both Harris and Calhoun seemed to continue the same relations with slaves as they had for decades.[17]

Other masters were apprehensive. A Laurens man, concerned about slave obedience during the war, wrote his wife in fall 1861: "I want you to tell my negroes that if they will push ahead & try to tend the crops & do their work as they ought to do it—... I'll reward them for it—but that if they become careless & lazy & give you trouble & don't mind Jonathon—and are disposed to be insubordinate that I will sell the last one of them to the first Speculator that will buy them." Harris recorded low-key slave resistance at his Spartanburg County plantation on March 4, 1862: "Early this morning I gave York a genteel flogging for leaving home without orders. He is becoming a little wild and needs close watching." Later, Harris noted in September, "My hands have been pretending to sprout the fence corners & the stuble-land. They are not doing much of anything." But numerous tributes testified to dutiful slaves, as did the *Pickens Sentinel* thirty years later upon Chesley Boggs's death: "In war times Ches was a faithful servant" on the farm owned by the editor's father.[18]

Trials and punishments tell a different story, however. They document that slaves knew much of the war's events and fluctuations and that whites sought to suppress both information and dissidence. One slave was hanged in Greenville in early 1861 for "insurrection." Reportedly he said "that the negrose would be free and that there would be bloody times about Christmas [1860].... [They will] get fifteen Dollars to Join the pledge to kill the white folks ... to join an insurrection in Laurens.... Other negroes tried to pursuade him into it (Insurrection) ... and that each negro was to kill his Master with an axe or Something." A similar story emerged in Spartanburg in September 1860. It included the prospect of being free by Christmas, leadership from elsewhere—Union District in that case—and reports "that the woods are full of armed Negroes, and runaways hiding in caves."[19] Controls were strongest in 1860 and 1862–64.

Few 1861 magistrates and freeholders trials or church exclusions occurred; but Confederate losses and increased demands for soldiers, for slaves, for money, and for crops soon changed the milieu. Slave knowledge about the war's purposes and vicissitudes led to several trials. John L. Briant complained on April 9, 1862, that a slave tried to arouse insurrection at Cross Roads Baptist Church (Anderson). Evidently while drinking, Aleck (John Warnock) said that Yankees were gaining after their last two battles and that, when all white men had left for the army, he would do as he pleased. The court inflicted fifty lashes. And Elvey Smith wrote her soldier husband from Pickens on June 1, 1862, that "there is great talk of the negors [sic] risen."[20]

An unusual messenger, less than two weeks later, brought news of the war's potential impact on slaves: their emancipation. Alfred, a slave escaped from Georgia, arrived in Anderson preaching a unique gospel, a "millennium" to be brought about by Lincoln's armies. They would, he said, lift the "yoke of bondage" and set slaves free, a prediction of the 1863 Emancipation Proclamation. Caught as a runaway, Alfred was imprisoned in Williamston; white men seized him from jail and lynched him. He was "found next morning, hanging from a neighboring tree *dead*," a constable reported, "hung by the citizens of Williamston for incendiary conduct in an attempt to Raise insurection."[21]

With such potentially demoralizing effects on slaves, intimidation and control intensified. Trials, convictions, and executions of slaves reached their highest levels, rivaled by only a few tense antebellum years. Between 1860 and 1864 Anderson prosecuted 20 percent and Spartanburg 25 percent of their 1828–65 cases. Fifteen percent of all Anderson's magistrates and freeholders trials occurred in just three years, 1862–64. Anderson courts convicted nearly three-fourths of slaves charged during 1860–64; only occasionally before had the rate of convictions reached that level. By contrast, Pickens and Oconee, farther removed from the enemy—and also having fewer slaves and less fear of them, as in antebellum years, had only six wartime trials in surviving, incomplete magistrates and freeholders accounts, actually fewer than for any other five-year period since 1840.[22]

Increasingly during 1860 and 1862–64, groups of slaves, ranging from four to more than twenty, were tried for collective offenses, which appeared more dangerous during the war than in earlier years. Over twenty slaves were convicted in 1862 for encounters with runaway Alfred. Owners seemed primarily concerned about his proclaimed millennium of freedom, but harboring was the legal charge. In fact, slaves were punished merely for listening to him, as only one provided any food or lodging. In 1864 three slaves of Ezekiel Murphy (Anderson) were convicted of harboring an Abbeville runaway. Most other magistrates and freeholders cases dealt with typical prewar crimes of theft, attempted arson, assault and battery, and attempted assaults on white women. These crimes, though not new, took on more serious connotations during the war and often resulted in heavier punishments.[23]

More trials for what might have been minor, overlooked infractions before the war and tougher church discipline were only two prongs of tightened wartime controls. Some owners periodically placed slaves in Walhalla's jail. Although one assumes that patrols increased, the number of men to serve shrank considerably; frequent duty would have placed a heavy burden on those who took part. Anderson's town council, creating its own "extraordinary patrol" in late 1862, ordered all slaves to be home after dark. More slaves complained about patrollers during the war. When these men visited Martha Rankin's slave cabins, Esther accused them of stealing a pocketbook from an old man; they countercharged that, by doing so, Esther slandered a white man. A few days later another slave was tried for "insulting language," saying patrollers stole. Evidently they too were suffering shortages.[24]

Slaves either stole more often for foodstuffs—grain and hams or whole hogs— than before the war, got caught more frequently, or were handled more seriously by the courts. On the night of January 1, 1861, Anderson County patrollers discovered twenty bushels of wheat in Sye's possession and filed a formal complaint before the magistrates and freeholders court. On December 25, 1862, patroller Samuel Williford said that Peter (James Clinkscales) confessed to stealing six hogs. And the patrol charged two slaves with stealing wheat belonging to Amanda Teat. Testifying that she bought three bushels from Perry (Major Joseph Thomson), who "often some time previous [used] to bring her wheat," her admission surely helped neither Perry's case nor her own prospects. Emily Harris noted, "Several negroes belonging to our neighbors have been stealing on [a] small scale to the great annoyance of their owners and others. Times are getting more desperate everyday." But Harris's white neighbors also stole often, and in spring 1864 deserters seized livestock near Pendleton and Walhalla and again in April 1865.[25]

Along with more patrols, prosecutions, and convictions came a higher percentage of executions. More than 60 percent of Anderson's 1820–65 slave executions occurred during the war. They resulted from larceny, burglary, arson, assault, and attempt to kill one's owner. Anderson County hanged three of its own slaves from 1862 through 1864 and had its first lynching, that of Alfred, "incendiary" runaway from Georgia. Several executions occurred in adjacent Abbeville, Greenville, and Spartanburg counties. With no slave executions in Anderson, Oconee, and Pickens counties in the 1830s or 1840s, these Civil War figures are more compelling. None of the recorded evidence justifies hanging Dick (William Harrison) for larceny and housebreaking in 1862. Like many cases in the 1850s, the June 19 complaint, with trial almost three weeks later, came months after an alleged March incident. The most striking Anderson case, dealing more with public concerns than with the accused crime, occurred in 1864 when a presiding magistrate overrode legal procedures for what he called "public safety." Ultimately Willis (A. W. Ramsay) was hanged for threatening his owner's life.[26]

Pickens on January 1, 1864, hanged three people, one of them John Cotrell, a white man, for a joint crime. The other two were a slave man and woman, names unknown and both belonging to Elihu Griffin. The slaves were hanged for larceny and Cotrell for assault and battery. The three robbed Griffin, whom Cotrell struck. Narcissa Clayton, visiting nearby, wrote that two "negroes . . . were hung yesterday at the P.C.H., 2 only. They said they had rather be hung than to go back to live with Griffin." White-black collaboration may well have contributed to their being executed, a joint hanging unprecedented in the tricounty area and perhaps in the state. Similarly, both courts and churches charged larger numbers of whites with illegally "trading with negroes."[27]

Although tried in record numbers during the 1850s, surprisingly few free people of color—a total of four—came before the law, and were all found not guilty. Pickens had only one trial involving free blacks, evidently recent arrivals. Henry Hortman accused Washington Graham and Columbus Graham of stealing his firewood, a larceny. White neighbors testified that a misunderstanding occurred as the Grahams did not realize that wood found by the road belonged to Hortman and that, when so informed, they stopped taking it. Locally important men testified to the Grahams' good character. Moreover, Washington Graham "taught a school & some of the neighbors sent [their children] to him," an incredibly unusual situation. Both men were acquitted. Free persons of color encountered harsher treatment in nearby counties.[28]

Churches excluded slave members between 1860 and 1865 in numbers similar to those of the 1850s, already the highest in half a century. Churches ousted as many slaves in 1864 as in the past three years combined. Slaves were expelled for the usual reasons we have already seen, primarily for fornication, adultery, and conceiving children out of wedlock; so were white women in evidently larger numbers than before. Big Creek in November 1862 excommunicated one white man in February 1865 for joining the Yankee army. As if that were not bad enough, he also ran off with a woman and they had illegitimate children; she too was expelled.

Slaves might be influenced, owners feared, by Unionists or escaping federal prisoners as they fled through the area. Three months after South Carolina's secession, Crawford Keys (to achieve fame or notoriety in fall 1865), acting on behalf of a public meeting, whipped John J. Horn, found to be in communication with Republicans outside the state and "endeavoring to organize the Negro slaves of Anderson County and incite them to rebellion against their masters." White Andersonians were so riled that "it required considerable effort . . . to prevent a summary execution," and he and his family were placed on a train headed north. Keys was "notorious as a member of the Vigilance Committee during the War," federal sources reported. A month later one man "had the lash well applied to his back last week, on account of his Lincoln proclivities and tampering with slaves. Notice was given him to leave the District," which he did.[29]

Some Union soldiers found safe harbor with Unionists and slaves and later recorded their experiences. These escapees then moved through mountainous passages into North Carolina or Tennessee, often with slave help. Many who aided them were white yeoman "who had no sympathy with the war cause" but may have deserted as much from economic hardship as from a political stance. Freedmen's Bureau Officer William DeForest later reported seeing many certificates by escaped Union soldiers testifying to this help. Walhalla resident Mary Lathem, who supported the Union, reported that "arrests were made in my house of union officers in disguise." Her sixteen-year-old son was taken for the Confederate army in retaliation. "I was persecuted, tormented, & threatened."[30]

Several Yankee officers reminisced about slave assistance. In lower Anderson County, two Unionist sympathizers helped the Yankees, turning them over to slave Andrew, "who hid us in the woods for the balance of the night," followed by a "nice breakfast of chicken, wheat bread, and preserves. At dark after taking a warm supper, [slave] Ned took us six miles." Helped in succession by a white Unionist, a slave, another white Unionist, and another slave, the escapees found friends who "hid us for the day in a negro cabin, at night some negroes came six miles through the storm to bring us food."

Similarly, Emily Harris on December 16, 1864, "learned through negroes that three Yankee prisoners have been living for several days in our gin house and been fed by our negroes. The neighbors are now watching for them with their guns." Whites, then, may have known or suspected black help for some escaped prisoners but were not always able to pinpoint it and could do virtually nothing to stop it. Contrasted to these instances, however, slaves reportedly captured Yankee officers near Pendleton and delivered them to local authorities.[31]

Few slaves in Anderson, Oconee, and Pickens counties escaped during the war. No increase in runaways is mentioned in correspondence between white families and soldiers, church minutes, postbellum letters and diaries, or federal reports immediately after the war. It seems unlikely that departures of whole families or significantly more individuals would have escaped some comment. Surely white reportage of slaves loyally serving owners during the war must be evaluated with caution, but there is no counter evidence of extensive slave flight.[32]

African Americans suffered from wartime shortages and from disruptions of their families. A few glimpses show that some, at least, looked forward to a northern victory and their own liberation. Emily Harris noted on March 6, 1865, that "the negroes are all expecting to be set free very soon and it causes them to be troublesome." Instead, many had to contribute to the Confederate war effort.

Enforced Slave Contributions to the War Effort

While most slaves stayed at home and worked, many were being moved around, some of them relocated to safety and others pushed into harm's way. Without any choice on their part, they were forced to serve Confederate masters and defensive operations. By January 1862, fear of advancing federal troops along South Carolina's coast led the government to remove people and property farther inland. Authorities ordered evacuation of nonessential slaves, and thousands of white civilians also fled. Dozens of white families with hundreds of slaves came to the tricountry area, undoubtedly bringing much news of the war and of suffering in the Charleston area. Lowcountry slaves surely reported that federal troops, controlling St. Helena and other coastal regions, emancipated slaves there. Once again white actions accidentally expanded subcultural communications.

The nearly five hundred slaves who came to the area, plus many to adjacent Greenville and Laurens, must have had a significant impact on those already living there. W. H. Trescot, a wealthy Beaufort planter who earlier served as U.S. assistant secretary of state and who owned a home in Pendleton, brought ninety slaves, plus seven hundred bushels of corn. Coming from Charleston, Colleton, Georgetown, and Santee, others took refuge in Pendleton, Williamston, Greenville, Pickens, and Walhalla. Those removed from the lowcountry brought news to upstate African Americans.[33]

Other slaves were drafted, practically if not technically, to serve the armies. Some went with their own masters, others became labor conscripts. In both cases many suffered injuries or death, while they and their own families keenly felt their absence. No lists exist of all slaves who accompanied masters to army camps and fronts. Presumably many owners—perhaps three hundred—took a slave with them. These served mostly as cooks and attendants, but Dick [Lewis] was a drummer "and was held in high esteem by members of both races." L. K. Knight, wrote a Confederate soldier's daughter, "was one of my father's old family servants. He went all through the Civil War with my father, Dr. James Perry Knight. . . . [L. K. Knight] was wounded in the fight around Petersburg, is now blind at 86 yrs. of age. . . . Any favor you can show this faithful old servant will be much appreciated by [me]."[34] Surely many died without being noted in official records.

Pendleton brothers Dick and Tally Simpson, serving in Virginia, recorded prolifically and kindly the help they got from family servants. Dick wrote his father in August 1861, "About sending Mose. We must have a boy whether he takes the measles or not. . . . Give him a suit of clothes just like our uniform for it is of great importance (we now have a frock coat), a couple of blankets, and an oil cloth. He must have everything comfortable." Fearing a measles epidemic in Virginia, Mose refused to go; a few weeks later Zion went instead. "Zion stands it very well and says he likes the camp life very much indeed. Tell [his wife] Hester, as long as we are able, he shall not suffer."[35] Tally often wrote about Zion foraging for food, baking biscuits, and preparing meals.

When Zion returned to Pendleton, his son Lewis replaced him. Later, a cousin's slave James helped when Tally was wounded: "So soon as James heard that I had gone into the fight, he packed up my blanket and started to where I was. But Sam Sammons told him he had better wait for he might get killed. . . . He says he was going to me anyhow. He knew if I was wounded I would need my blanket and his assistance. I mentioned this to show how faithful a servant Jim is." Often when Tally wrote his family in Pendleton, he enclosed greetings from slaves Zion, Lewis, or James. Tally frequently wrote "howdy to the negros." Similarly, "Lewis is doing well and sends love to his family and howdy to all the white folks." Tally enclosed Lewis's message to wife Vessy: "Lewis wished to write his wife a few lines," actually dictated to Tally.[36]

African Americans attending the troops held an ambivalent position. Serving with the regiments, they initially did not get army rations, but that changed in October 1862. They wore uniforms with greatcoats similar to the soldiers' own. Evidently they also drew compensation. Tally in July 1862 sent Zion's money to his family: "Enclosed you will find from Zion $20.00 dollars for Hester—$5.00 for Emma, Clara, and Lucy, and $15.00 for Hester. Tell Hester if [?] needs a pair of shoes, buy her a pair out of the 15.00, and for her to take the balance for her own use. Buy a hog with part of it. Be careful and get it as cheap as possible. Tell her to be as careful as she can with the rest of it, for he says he may not be able to send her any more. He means that she must buy what she wishes, but not be too extravagant." Zion and white Warren Stribling both gave directions for their families at home.[37] Although leaving no evidence behind, Vessy, Hester, and other wives had to shoulder additional burdens and endure concerns about husbands serving at the front or on the coast. Their families were disrupted, deprived of game and other additional food ordinarily secured by their husbands, and worried in ways that can only be imagined.

Some slaves died or were injured. Sam Black lost his leg in 1862 while a servant with Orr's regiment. What happened to those whose masters perished in Virginia is not clear. Some may have tried to flee to freedom. In September 1861 Dick Simpson reported, "A few nights ago five negros belonging to different men in our reg[imen]t slipped off and have not been heard from since. We have good reason to know they have gone to Yankee land," as may have been the case with Sam Rosemon, found in Pittsburgh in 1867.

But some accounts tell of others faithfully tending their dead masters and accompanying the body on its return home. John W. Philpot's estate in 1863 paid $197.50 train fare for transporting the corpse and a "negro boy" from Richmond. Jackson Wright went to Virginia as a "body servant" to Captain Kilpatrick, who was killed there in 1863. Jackson, like these others, returned to his owner's family. When Tally Simpson died near Chickamauga in September 1863, "James coming up shortly afterwards, his body was turned over to him for burial, which he attended to immediately.... James has, I think, all of Tally's papers, watch, [ring], &c. [and] ... will turn them over to Harry ... or send them" to Tally's father. Even after Confederate surrender at Appomattox Court House, Reed family servant Manuel who was there "wouldn't go to the Yanks—after all inducements."[38]

Other African Americans were placed more dangerously as conscripts for coastal defenses at Charleston. They worked under state conscription laws and suffered more than slaves who accompanied masters. Captain Jacob Griffin wrote about his family slave there: "I am not able at this late date to say when Ben's master giv Ben [Griffin] to the Confederate government but will say he searved allmost the entire 4 years ... [Ben] was sent by my Father.... Mr. Bob Bowen['s] father sent 1 of His [slaves] who you no with Ben ... they Both don good servis and awght to Hav something in thear old days."

Masters often resisted sending their slaves. In 1863 at least 48 Oconee and Pickens families failing to do so paid a fine of $22.50 for each one they did not deliver. Mary Chesnut observed that men "gave their sons to their country cheerfully. But when the council calls for ... sacred property in the shape of negroes for coast defenses—a howl." Owners whose slaves were killed were entitled to, demanded, and received compensation, but it was paid out in devalued Confederate currency. J. E. Hagood was among 261 throughout the state who claimed compensation for a slave who died laboring on the balustrades. Deaths of eighteen area slaves who died between 1862 and 1864 resulted in claims for nearly fifty thousand dollars.[39]

Slave labor during the Civil War did not qualify for pensions from either the federal government or the state, which paid for Confederate soldiers only. But blacks would belatedly receive official State of South Carolina recognition and

State of South Carolina,
County of Oconee

TO THE COUNTY PENSION BOARD:

The undersigned applies for enrollment under the Act of 1923. I served the State of South Carolina in the War between the States, as __Servant__ under __Rauson Calhoun Teddy Calho__ who was in Company __A__ __Lucas Batallion__ Regiment _____ Captain __Teddy Calhoun__ I went in the service __April__ 186_1_, and served continuously until _____ 18_64_ remaining faithful to the Confederacy throughout the said war, and my conduct since the war has been such that I am entitled to a pension under the above Act. I reside at __Seneca__ in __Oconee__ County, S. C.

Sworn to and Subscribed before me this _19_ day of __May__ 192_3_

__Harrison Wiggins__
Give name in full.

STATE OF SOUTH CAROLINA,
County of __Oconee__

Personally appeared before me __A W Elrod__ and _____ and being duly sworn, each of them deposes and says that they know __Harrison Wiggins__ who is an applicant for a pension, and they have read the said application; that they know of their own knowledge that the applicant served the State of South Carolina for more than six (6) months during the War between the States under __Capt Cochran__ and remained faithful to the Confederacy during the said war and that his conduct since then has been such that will entitle him to a pension under the Act of 1923; that the applicant is a resident of the State and resides in __Seneca__ County, S. C.

Sworn to before me this _19_ day of __May__, 192_3_.

__A. W. Elrod__

Approved by __W J Magill__, Chairman Board of Honor, __of Oconee__ County, this _20_ day of __May__, 1923.

Harrison Wiggins's 1924 application for a state pension for his service during the Civil War. Black Heritage in the Upper Piedmont, S.C. Department of Archives and History compensation. Eleven from Anderson, Oconee, and Pickens applied for pensions. Their wartime duties ranged from valet and cook to labor on fortifications, especially at Charleston, such as Ben P. Griffin.[40]

By contrast to what upstate African Americans experienced, conditions were dramatically different in the lowcountry. The federal army occupied portions of it during much of the war and freed slaves there. Some of these freed men, joining their liberators, constituted part of the United States Colored Troops (USCT), similar to the Massachusetts 54th Regiment portrayed in the 1989 movie *Glory*. The 33rd USCT included Richard Green, a forty-two-year-old waiter from Pendleton.[41]

The year 1864 was marked by further decline of white morale, more magistrates and freeholders trials, and fiercer punishments. Prices continued high during persistent shortages, while war taxes, compulsory 10 percent contribution of crops, and government demands for more slave labor led to a widespread despondency among whites. Emily Harris recorded on January 1, "Many are willing to unite again with the hated Yankees rather than continue the hard and seemingly hopeless struggle." After Sherman captured Savannah in December 1864, his troops occupied a burning Columbia, and federal forces marched into Charleston, whites felt nearly beaten, as they were.[42]

Liberation Deferred

As the Union army occupied Charleston in February 1865, it deliberately marched black troops through the city to reward them and to humiliate its white populace, while a meeting of "colored citizens of Charleston So. Ca." formally expressed thanks for their timely arrival. From a different perspective, Floride Clemson recorded in her Pendleton diary several weeks afterward, "The suffering in the lower part of the state is very great they say, negroes unmanageable, & the Yankees barbarous."[43] Five days later Robert E. Lee would surrender at Appomattox Court House. Although "God's truth goes marching on," neither it nor federal troops had yet come to northwestern Carolina, and freedom took even longer to arrive. Four weeks after Lee's surrender "Yankees barbarous" would venture near Floride Clemson's Pendleton home. Freedom, still beyond local slaves' reach, did not come immediately with the war's end.

TWELVE

Reconstruction's First Months, 1865

MONTHS FOLLOWING THE WAR'S END could be described as the great unknown. Not knowing what the future held for them, white feared massive changes. Not yet freed, slaves remained cautious from May until late summer, when they finally became free. For most in Anderson, Oconee, and Pickens counties, their unanswered question was "free to do what?" Excepting small numbers, they had nowhere else to go; most in December 1865 would still be in their same places. Federal troops, the only possible agent to change their conditions, had virtually no presence in the area prior to mid-July 1865. Even then, knowing that it faced unprecedented tasks and not knowing what lay ahead but fearing social upheaval, the army often supported the status quo.

Except in its most technical sense, little emancipation, or Reconstruction, or liberation occurred during 1865. Rather, African Americans remained in a subordinated position, slightly redefined. Whites, despite fears that plagued them, suffered little deprivation in 1865 other than altered relations with African Americans, but not loss of control, authority, or resources.

A potentially tumultuous, but mostly just unsettled, time for both blacks and whites followed the Civil War. Slaves gained freedom, but that meant deciding where to live and work and, hopefully, managing to earn a living. By 1866 and 1867, families declared surnames and sought to establish their own households. Collectively, freed people began organizing their own churches and schools and in 1867 would venture into political activity. Deprived of land, African Americans improved those areas of their lives that they could.

Former owners and other whites in general hardly liked these changes any more than they welcomed either federal occupation or the Freedmen's Bureau. Together those forces tried to preserve peace, guarantee emancipation, supervise these processes, and manage specific facets, such as written labor agreements. Successful efforts by local whites, the army, and the bureau to ensure stability—in essence the status quo—were further conditions beyond African American control.

Lincoln's January 1, 1863, Emancipation Proclamation did nothing to end slavery in upper South Carolina; it affected only areas under federal control. Only on May 1, 1865, did the state's northwestern corner first see federal troops. The army's arrival dramatically changed the milieu but not underlying conditions. Freedom came more slowly than did soldiers. Some freed people left their former owners within a few hours, days, or weeks. Most stayed on the same plantation in 1865, many during 1866 or later, as in fact federal officers ordered them to do, unless they had firm arrangements with an employer elsewhere. That these newly freed people constituted 57 percent of the state's population makes the army's strategy more understandable.

Largely because of the federal presence and bureaucracy, 1865–70 are the best documented years for upstate African Americans.[1] Hardly any of these multitudinous sources, however, come from African Americans, whose views and actions have to be disentangled from the focus of whites, both southern and northern. Despite abundant documents, most accounts covering May and June 1865 are from local whites—diaries by young women, correspondence, and newspapers. Their dominant theme, then, is one of fears among whites, plunder by federal soldiers, and insolence from former slaves. This pervasive sense of white fright and humiliation, thriving primarily in the first weeks, soon declined markedly in diaries and letters, perhaps because they became old news. For these early months no firsthand reactions have been found from the federal army or from blacks.[2]

First Army Presence—Very Temporary

After Robert E. Lee's surrender, upstate whites—who had yet to see enemy troops in their area—began to fear what might lie ahead. Floride Clemson, twenty-five years old, recorded rumors on April 16 that "a large force of Yankees, Tories, & deserters had come down from the mountains & were marching either on this place or Greenville . . . 1500, to 25000! This afternoon however we hear that the report arose from a raid of a couple of hundreds of deserters, &c who went back to the mountains after having taken some cattle &c."

Two weeks later federal soldiers, evidently all white, did arrive, causing near panic among whites. Rather than a continuing occupation force, these units had a single official purpose—to find fleeing Jefferson Davis, his cabinet, and the Confederate treasury's gold. Major-General George Stoneman dispatched these troops from western North Carolina in a two-pronged maneuver.[3] The first soldiers passed near Pendleton, then marched into the town of Anderson; another unit arrived in Greenville the following day.

On May 1 Clarissa Adger Bowen, residing at Ashtabula, about a mile north of Pendleton, described the changing scene of soldiers. First came "paroled men from General Lee's army." A few hours later Yankees (Stoneman's) arrived at our house, she said, "pillage began—jewelry, firearms and specie . . . flannel shirts, shoes, wine, coffee, tea, loaf sugar, etc. . . . even . . . the strawberries, bread, etc. out of the storeroom. . . . It was all as sudden as a clap of thunder—all over in three hours time."

Federal soldiers, including Captain Williamson—convinced that Clarissa's father Robert Adger entertained Davis and then hid the gold—went to nearby Rivoli asking for firearms and the Confederate treasury. Soldiers thoroughly searched lard cans, chests, and a trunk of flannel petticoats. By contrast, a federal soldier who "seemed so humble and looked so badly" went to the Lortons' back door several days later begging for food.[4]

Hearing that numerous Confederate troops were in Pendleton—actually there were only a few dozen armed young men—Union soldiers bypassed that town and headed for Anderson. En route, "the Yankees also went to Boscobel, taking all they wanted" when they visited another family member, Dr. John B. Adger. A small group demanded watches, gold, pistols, and horses, which Adger successfully hid. When a soldier accidentally shot himself, watches and jewelry stolen from other homes poured from his pockets. Raiders, harassing other neighbors, took their horses.

Then a twenty-four-hour occupation of Anderson left a bitter legacy for decades. Union troops disrupted a large May Day children's picnic and, in the eyes of whites, terrorized the community. Caroline Ravenel wrote that Yankees, waving swords and firing pistols, came to their house, taking gold and watches. J. P. Reed's family fled and hid in nearby swamps; one family slave brought them food there and another buried the family's jewels. Although white emotions may have exaggerated Yankee despoliation, army officials in private communiqué confirmed widespread looting despite explicit orders not to do so. The armies helped themselves not only to plunder, such as the oft-recited watches and gold, but also to food for ill-fed men and to horses for transportation. Unpleasant recollections of this Yankee invasion lingered long. They boiled to the surface a year later when Anderson's newspaper reviewed the incident at length and had a featured role in Louise Vandiver's county history half a century afterward.[5]

Soldiers departed almost as quickly as they swept in. General Simeon B. Brown on May 2 ordered them to march southwest from Anderson toward Abbeville, then into Georgia, still pursuing Jefferson Davis. A smaller detachment went northwest to Walhalla. Various military troops would remain there during the next two years.[6] Clarissa Bowen wrote as initial contingents left the area, "The negroes are all much demoralized. Many have gone with their friends L., T., and July from here. The Yankees talked much to them, advising them to go with them, promising to hang Mr. Rochester and other overseers and drivers . . . and to burn all houses where the owners were cruel." Very few slaves seem to have left, however. On May 7, Roberts Presbyterian Church lamented that "this day had been appointed for Communion but the Enemy having taken possession of the country on the 1st rendered the meeting impracticable."

Evidently no soldiers came to the area for another two and a half months except for a brief and calm May 21 return passage of Brown's men, ordered to Tennessee via South Carolina after other troops captured Davis in Georgia. Floride Clemson observed, "Last Sunday about a thousand Yankees under Gen. Brown passed through. . . . they did little or no harm to private property. They took all government meat & corn, & destroyed all public arms but never even took private guns. . . . Some few negroes went with them. . . . [Yankees] say this is the worst secession hole they have seen, as they were not only treated with contempt but abuse, & swear vengeance against the whole community for they were bush whacked near here."[7]

With no federal authority remaining in the region, conditions changed only slowly for whites or blacks. Troops had come and gone, but slaves were not yet free. Despite Major General Q. A. Gillmore's May 14 proclamation affirming that South Carolina slaves were now free, Spartanburg's David Golightly Harris noted, accurately, "I do not much think it will have much effect." Certainly it did not in the immediate future. One Pendleton slave rapidly changed his expectations. Toney, accompanying his master to Columbia in late June, saw both federal troops there and emancipation actually effected. Then he "got somewhat excited and talked of making a 'bargain' when he returned to Pendleton." For many people—local whites and the army—potential starvation and dislocation of the labor force posed immediate problems.[8]

Other arenas of life continued normally. Churches resumed worship services, and several held protracted meetings during August and September. When Saluda Baptists met August 18–20 at Calhoun Falls, there were six hundred "colored people [among twenty-five hundred to three thousand attending] conducting religious exercise peculiar and suitable to themselves in a very decent, becoming and interesting manner."[9]

Protecting the harvest and preventing mass idleness headed the military's agenda when forces returned in July. This time they established a continuing presence. Officers ordered owners to free slaves and offer written contracts guaranteeing wages for 1865. Ostensibly, social relations and conditions changed dramatically for white and black. Occasionally, soldiers got shot for their troubles.

Occupation Forces

The military role following Confederate surrender was ill defined and not enthusiastically supported, as the U.S. army had no experience in peacetime occupation. Volunteers, whose terms would soon expire, wanted to return home. Certainly as "Yankees" and as forces that just fought a rebellion, the army was mostly unsympathetic to the South. Ideologically, the army believed that African Americans should be emancipated and should have equal judicial treatment. But the military often viewed freed slaves as potentially lazy. Officers greatly feared chaos if freed people demanded food from the army but refused to help harvest crops. Sherman wrote U.S. Chief Justice S. P. Chase on May 6, "I am not yet prepared to receive the negro on terms of political equality. . . . Our own armed soldiers have prejudices that, right or wrong, should be consulted." Sometimes racial and class identification led officers to enjoy southern hospitality with white landowners and perhaps swayed their attitudes as well.[10]

President Andrew Johnson's reconstruction plan called for only limited and— by implication—short-term military functions in the South. Initially the army had to forestall further southern resistance, seize Confederate property, and administer loyalty oaths. The military also took control of judicial processes involving freed people and supervised, at least in theory, all other judicial cases. County and town officials, as well as magistrates, were not sure whether they could assert their authority, and terms often expired without a replacement.[11]

Any military program faced logistical obstacles. Communications, transportation, and administration were all chaotic. Many railroads were inoperable and bridges impassable due to damage by war and bad weather, including heavy rains in early 1865. These conditions interrupted transportation of food, consumer goods, newsprint, and troops. Reconstruction had to proceed in a most literal as well as its political sense.

Few post offices reopened before late 1865, others not until subsequent years, and many newspapers had yet to resume publishing. Editors faced problems of obtaining adequate newsprint and of actually shipping the papers. Federal authorities also exercised de facto censorship. Throughout 1865 and, to lesser degrees, 1866 and 1867, the *Anderson Intelligencer* and *Keowee Courier* printed very limited local news or commentary on conditions. Generally bland coverage during 1865 consisted mostly of official military orders, candidates' announcements for office, notices of court-ordered sales, and a surprising array of local merchants' advertisements. Editorial sentiment generally favored cooperation with federal authorities and condemned lawlessness, including armed attacks on federal troops and on freed people. Newspapers would change this cautious tone dramatically by 1868. *Intelligencer* editor James Hoyt headed Anderson's home police, organized at the war's end; then, cooperating with military authorities at Anderson, he served on the summer 1865 superior provost court and the 1866 board that approved labor contracts.[12]

New federal structures to manage occupied South Carolina emerged slowly. Reorganizing the army, President Andrew Johnson created on June 27 the Department of South Carolina, commanded by Maj. Gen. Gillmore, who retained his headquarters at Hilton Head. He then established four military districts. The District of Western South Carolina occupied thirteen upstate counties, roughly Orangeburg northward. Its Anderson subdistrict, which served as a post for eighteen months, initially included five counties—Anderson, Pickens, Oconee, Greenville, and Abbeville—but territorial responsibilities changed periodically.[13]

Specific troops occupying Anderson rotated frequently, sometimes as often as within two weeks. A "gaping crowd" that included freedmen observed the town's first occupation soldiers arriving on July 24. These men, the 56th New York Volunteers, left only three weeks later. Beginning on August 14, Lieutenant Colonel C. T. Trowbridge assumed command at Anderson, from which he detached one company to Walhalla and another to Greenville. That these men were part of the U.S. Colored Troops infuriated many Anderson whites, even though their officers there were white.

Increasingly, individual USCT excesses throughout the state, as reported by military officers, led to white objections and USCT relocation to the coast. Gillmore's inspector general charged on September 7 that the USCT were "unsoldierly" and "lax" in discipline, and that there were "very frequent... conflicts and deeds of lawless violation" by the 56th USCT. Local black interaction with USCT intensified white objections. After USCT departure, all forces in Anderson, Oconee, and Pickens counties were white, mostly volunteers from Maine. White Andersonians in mid-September welcomed these newly arrived soldiers, commanded by twenty-eight-year-old Lieutenant Colonel Calvin S. Brown. Brown's adjutant, First Lieutenant H. A. Johnson, had escaped through the area in late 1864. While serving at Anderson, he encountered several men who as slaves helped during his flight. As slaves were emancipated and began to assert themselves, accounts of whites harassing freed people increased.

Conditions in the District of Western South Carolina seemed serious enough that Gillmore made a personal tour in August, evidently his first excursion beyond the coast. Gillmore's inspector general charged on September 7 that widespread abuses were occurring. Despite harsh judgments of USCT by Carolina whites and by army officers, other assessments rank much of the USCT service as meritorious.[14]

Clearly, however, an "occupation" settled in and was especially visible in towns. Troops frequently drilled and marched, exercises that emphasized their armed presence. The Freedmen's Bureau, more formally the Bureau of Refugees, Freedmen and Abandoned Lands, was created on May 12, 1865, a month after Lee's surrender. Other army officers handled Freedmen's Bureau tasks until its own appointees could assume them—spring 1866—and also served at later times when no bureau staff was available. Bureau men were, in fact, army officers but had a command separate from that of occupation forces.[15]

Cooperation between military and provisional civilian authorities often was difficult. The army arrested and imprisoned Civil War–era governor A. G. Magrath. As it happened, Anderson and Greenville had a large role among subsequent 1865–68 civilian leadership. B. F. Perry was appointed provisional governor on June 13 by President Johnson, who once worked briefly in Greenville and met Perry then. An antebellum Unionist, Perry urged support of the Confederacy once war broke out. He served six months in 1865 until an election, by white men only, chose Anderson-native James Orr as governor. Both men had national reputations, Orr having served as U.S. House of Representatives speaker.[16]

Perry, who had no particular sympathy for freed people, cooperated cordially with Gillmore and his successor Major General Daniel E. Sickles, as would Orr. Both Gillmore and Sickles sought to restore many functions to civilian authority as quickly as possible, a goal Perry and Orr shared. The generals' intent was based on both principle and practicality, as the army was stretched impossibly thin with many problems facing it. One of the army's first duties in restoring political order was to collect oaths of allegiance to the federal government, as required by Johnson's proclamation, from white South Carolinians, including women. USCT officers assigned to Anderson began taking these oaths at both Walhalla and Anderson during August. By September 1865 civil courts resumed functioning, unhindered, except in cases involving freed people.[17]

Delayed Emancipation and First Labor Agreements

Freedom, promised for southern slaves, came belatedly in many parts of the South. Neither Confederate surrender nor arrival of the first troops brought emancipation. Until late July 1865 the U.S. Army did nothing to enforce emancipation in upstate South Carolina. There were a few pending magistrates and freeholders trials after the war's end, which seems to have put a stop to them, although a Spartanburg magistrates and freeholders court on May 5 sentenced an accused man to solitary confinement for several days. Anderson's town council, issuing an ordinance on May 22 that referred to "all persons, free and slave," clearly did not recognize emancipation. Even later, Mount Pisgah Baptists in July excluded "Simeon Smith's boy Will for absconding from his master."

Similarly, in mid-June Harris wrote, "There is much talk about the negroes being free. . . . I have heard mine say nothing on the subject." A month later he could still note "much talk about freeing the negroes. Some are said already to have freed them." But not in the three-county area, where freedom came for most African Americans only after the July 24 arrival of troops, welcomed by blacks. Shortly thereafter officers visited area plantations to announce freedom and freed people's right to written agreements for 1865 wages, both of which would have been revolutionary changes had they been fulfilled.

Once they were freed, people still had to work. It was difficult to convince African Americans to remain working on plantations where they had been enslaved while guaranteeing them wages in cash or in kind and freedom from oppression. An army officer in southwestern Georgia reported on June 27 finding "the old system of slavery working with even more vigor than formerly at a few miles distant from any point where U.S. troops are stationed," comments equally valid for AOP.

The Freedmen's Bureau required landowners to complete a written labor agreement, read to freed people, that spelled out all terms of labor and its compensation. During the summer months many former owners were busily making agreements. In mid-July Ashtabula's former slaves were still among the earliest to get a labor proposal from their former owner, O. A. Bowen. His wife Clarissa noted that "at first only two house servants (Rex and Anna Whitner) availed themselves of the offer but afterwards all the field hands but four. Poor creatures! What is to become of them? *Truly the future looks dark for us but it is blacker for them.*"

As military officers visited plantations to ensure that black people understood they were free and must be offered the opportunity to leave or to have a written contract, they earned Clarissa Bowen's comment on August 10: "A Yankee Lieutenant and ten men were here today, lecturing the [freed] people. They came by invitation and were very civil and obliging." Hundreds of similar dramas transpired within the next few weeks. During the summer and fall additional contracts were concluded. Unfortunately there are no firsthand accounts by African Americans as they heard these tidings of emancipation and wages. Decades later a WPA interviewee recalled that one woman was so excited "de day dey told us de war was over and us was free" that she "started shouting: 'Thank God-a-Moughty I'se free at last!'" But, hearing this, her owner knocked her down.[18]

It is difficult to imagine the range of emotions felt by newly freed people. Indeed it is hard to comprehend exactly what freedom meant to those who previously did not have it. Certainly the social order did not change immediately or quickly in 1865, especially in a white-majority area. Throughout the remainder of 1865 and 1866, and beyond, army officers would report that white people were not ready to accept a new socioeconomic structure. The change presented many challenges to African Americans also.

White Reactions: Harassment and Violence

Numerous instances reveal unreconstructed white attitudes. Floride Clemson expressed widespread sentiments: "The negroes being freed, almost everyone is turning them away by hundreds to starve, plunder, & do worse. The times ahead are fearful." Emancipation, perceptions that freed people were unwilling to work, the prospect of poor harvests, and white fears were closely intertwined. On August 24 Clarissa Bowen rued black insolence and white humiliation: "Mr.   's old servant has been very impudent . . . Dave T. went to Anderson to complain[,] the negro was there first and they were shown into the officer's room together. Col. Parker's negro [USCT] threatened Mrs. P. with an ax. . . . We began to realize that we are a conquered people and to expect humiliations and insults."[19]

Harassment and occasional shootings by whites started immediately after the troops' arrival. On May 1, as Union soldiers marched near Pendleton, there was a volley of gunfire from local defenders, although they inflicted no damage. Later that summer black soldiers' horses were stolen by three white men; one may have been Manse Jolly. As Trowbridge's troops left Anderson white men fired on their train along its Anderson-Belton route. And in late August someone murdered white Lieutenant Furman, USCT officer in Walhalla.[20] His death caused little furor compared to further murders in October.

Manse Jolly, celebrated bushwhacker of federal troops, attacked soldiers in Anderson. A Confederate veteran whose brother was killed in the war, Jolly "avenged his [brother's] death by taking a hand in the death of some straggling Union soldiers." Sickles testified in January 1867 that Jolly undoubtedly was "one of the worst" of the men who fired on soldiers in an October 1865 incident (see below); other sources also implicated Sargent. Otherwise, he hardly appears in Anderson post reports. He escaped to Texas in 1866. One officer later described Jolly and Sargent as living on area farms, "sometimes remaining several weeks in one lurking place, sometimes changing their den every night. The inhabitants gave them shelter, partly from admiration of their defiance of the Yankees and partly from fear of their vindictiveness."[21]

Following the army's visits, Clarissa Bowen's diary complained in late August and early September: "Many of our neighbors are having trouble with their servants. . . . This makes six of them we have gotten clear of. . . . Our days are marked by annoyances with the 'freedmen.'" One elderly Pendleton woman who died a year later "would not believe that the Yankees had conquered us and that the negroes were free and in her will she disposed of all of the slaves."[22] As a brutal episode soon demonstrated, attitudes, they were not "a'changing."

The most serious attack against federal troops in Anderson, Oconee, and Pickens counties indirectly led to the 1867 Reconstruction Acts. It occurred during the night of October 7, when several white men killed three Maine soldiers. Stationed at William P. Brown's Savannah River ferry landing, they were guarding a large quantity of cotton, seized from Crawford Keys, which U.S. Treasury agents deemed Confederate property. Reported missing, the soldiers were soon found in the river. Keys, immediately suspected, was arrested along with two sons (a third escaped), a nephew, a neighbor, and Francis Stowers, who owned a nearby Georgia plantation. Much vocal public opinion—including Anderson and Pickens newspapers plus local officials and professionals—condemned violent acts. Although those attending an October 13 public meeting deplored these murders and pledged cooperation, army authorities were not convinced.[23]

Contrasted to these public sentiments, General Gillmore's staff advised that Anderson people "are disposed to shield the criminals" and that persons testifying against them are likely to be murdered. Believing that whites there "can prove any thing they may wish to prove" about the murders, or other incidents, Gillmore recommended that a military commission hear the Keys trial, which was done.[24] As that case dragged on for almost a year, there were periodic resurgences of strong white sentiments in Anderson.

Freedom: Food and Work, but No Land

Far more immediate matters concerned most people in later 1865. While blacks might wish to test their freedom, there was a fundamental need to get crops harvested, top priority for both landowners and the army. Officers issued an August 14 order forbidding freedmen from plantations to stroll on Anderson streets and instructing planters to stress to "freedmen on their plantations . . . that it is necessary for their own sustenance during the coming winter that they should labor diligently and faithfully to gather the crops which are now ready to harvest." Passing instructions through plantation owners reinforced their continued control over "free" people.

Conceiving of African American attitudes toward newfound freedom and work is virtually impossible, despite many accounts by whites attributing various emotions and motives to them. They faced enormous logistical obstacles. Wherever freed people chose to live, it would be on land owned by whites, requiring their permission. The war years were not a likely time for construction; most housing, then, was existing slave cabins. The white attitude, as well as that of army officers, was that freed people should stay where they lived as slaves: "A Yankee Collonel made them some speeches about here, telling them they would not uphold them, & advising them to be peacable & quiet," reported Floride Clemson.[25]

Contracts issued during summer 1865 would all expire in December. Throughout the summer many freed people hoped for land of their own, the "forty acres and a mule" they mistakenly believed were promised them. Sherman's Field Order No. 15 actually applied only to certain islands between Savannah and Charleston. However, word obviously spread among blacks throughout the South as the phrase became almost a litany. It later appeared often in WPA interviews and continued among those demanding reparations into the 2000s.

To counter such hopes in 1865, Robert Scott, directing South Carolina's Freedmen's Bureau, issued an October 19 proclamation that expectation of getting forty acres was a misconception and that new contracts for 1866 should be signed. A month later the bureau further directed that unless freed people had specific work elsewhere, "in order not to break up their homes for the present[,] freedmen be employed & make contracts with their former masters."[26]

Freed people still may have anticipated or hoped for distribution of land at Christmas time; at least whites feared that. Floride Clemson wrote on December 17 that "every one expects trouble about Xmas. with the negroes, who expect land. Matters are pretty quiet now except casual disturbances thefts & murders." Similar views came from high-ranking officers. Army staff warned Major General Daniel E. Sickles, who recently replaced Gillmore, of a potentially insurrectionary movement by "colored people" to get "White" lands and livestock during Christmas week, a traditional holiday. Orr, far more skeptical that an uprising would occur, persuaded Sickles to reject his own staff advice. Sickles ordered local officers to persuade "negroes . . . that the expectation of a division of lands among them is a mere delusion." No trouble occurred.[27]

Hopes for land slowed the process of completing labor contracts, many of them signed only in late December and early January 1866, and some not until March or even April. Military officials in northwestern South Carolina, however, continued to fear that freedmen were refusing to sign 1866 agreements based on the "erroneous impression" that on January 1, 1866, the government "will give them each a farm." General Adelbert Ames, commanding the army's District of Western South Carolina, dreaded a prospect after January 1 of having hundreds of freed people, "old, infirm, destitute, and homeless and no one to care for them."[28]

Concern for elderly freed people—by the people themselves and by their families—must have been a major problem. Owners had been legally and morally obligated to care for elderly slaves; nobody now had these responsibilities. Many of the aged came to depend on army-distributed rations, which were in short supply. Judging from 1870 census returns and from white oral tradition, some former owners did care for elderly former slaves. However, many in their sixties, seventies, and eighties had to work as cooks, servants, or farm laborers.[29]

Freedom: Departures, Taxes, Black Codes, and Churches

Factors other than freedom initially shaped freed people's lives. The legislature sought to impose controls through newly passed Black Codes, and blacks as free people now had to pay taxes. Both South Carolina's 1865 constitutional convention and the legislature quickly interpreted freedom within their own restrictions. A convention whose membership included nearly thirty former Confederate officers reinstated the previous constitution except for references to slavery. Chosen in October elections, legislators created a new set of Black Codes that imposed terms "master" and "servant" onto all labor contracts. Sickles promptly suspended these codes.[30]

Some freed people chose to leave in order to join their families elsewhere, to escape enslaved surroundings, or to find work in cities such as Charleston or Atlanta. Some moved locally, such as "Old Kate Maum," who ran away from one Calhoun plantation to stay with Floride Calhoun in Pendleton. Newspaper advertisements clearly indicated needs for labor and at least local relocations, as did a November 2 notice for a "colored woman without children" to become a nurse, "consent of former owner required." At least a few freed people made much longer journeys, as did long-time Kilpatrick slave Sally, who left Pendleton in December 1865 and headed for Virginia in hopes of finding her mother, whom she had not seen in decades.[31]

More people probably made short moves, without comparable employment opportunities, to join families in nearby counties. Similarly, freed people from elsewhere likely returned to their families in Anderson, Oconee, and Pickens counties. Adger's former slave family, "most valued servant, Alfred, and [his mother] old Nina, the wife of Charles," reached divergent decisions. Alfred, other relatives, and his mother moved to Memphis. That valued servants offered the most resistance shocked the Adgers.[32] But Charles "was not willing to go with them, nor yet dared to remain in Pendleton . . . [as] he had made many enemies to himself" on Adger's behalf. Adger "agreed, therefore, with Charles to let him have my four mules, and a big wagon, that he might go down [to Columbia], do some of this hauling [of the city's charred buildings], and make something for himself and for me too."[33] Whatever hardships and difficulties may have been encountered on such endeavors, freed people now had the choice to undertake them.

Along with freedom, adults gained virtually no other legal rights in 1865 except formal labor contracts, regularization of their marriages, and legitimization of their children born during slavery. Men did, however, get a significant liability, a two-dollar annual tax per adult male, which few blacks could afford to pay. Within a year or two many families fell into debt just for these assessments alone. A quarter of Oconee and Pickens black men failed to pay their 1866–67 per capita taxes, then only one dollar.[34]

Some recently freed families had taxable farm animals. Stories of white families magnanimously sharing livestock with their former slaves have to be taken cautiously. However, livestock owned by freed people within five years after emancipation, a period of poor compensation, often paid only in crops, suggests that some former owners did, in fact, supply pigs, chickens, cows, sheep, and a few mules or horses. Freedmen also acquired dogs, valuable because their barks warned of approaching strangers, but expensive because of taxes.[35]

Although freedom brought tax burdens and continued "servant" status, it did not initially mean a mass departure from churches shared with former masters. Initially, most white-identified churches showed no inclination by freed people to leave. One Anderson Baptist church history cites an 1865 founding: First Freedmen's, later St. Paul (Anderson city), claiming to have been the county's first black church. Most freed people still attended the same churches as during slavery. Some, however, left and worshiped in brush arbors before organizing churches.

Mixed messages occurred elsewhere, often from the same person. Sickles, while corresponding cordially with the new governor, Andersonian James L. Orr, wrote privately that northwestern counties consisted of a "hostile and turbulent" white population. Ames believed that, as upstate areas were not in the military theater during the war, people there exhibited a "defiant and aggressive temper of the population."[36]

Local whites indeed displayed diverse and strange reactions to their freed people. Clarissa Adger Bowen's "Poor creatures! What is to become of them?" of July 15 turned six weeks later to "Many of our neighbors are having trouble with their servants. . . . This makes six of them we have gotten clear of. . . . Our days are marked by annoyances with the 'freedmen.'" And David Harris wrote on December 19 that "I do wish the negroes would all go to the Yankeys and stay with them until they all got their satisfaction," which would also leave him with fewer hands to feed. Attitudes surely were calmer by the year's end as whites found the Freedmen's Bureau continuing much of the status quo and most freed people still on the same plantations as in 1860.

Other whites expressed contradictory views. Sarah Ann Atkins Cromer recorded that "Our Bet goes free today. Thank God, for I believe it was wrong to hold slaves." The date—November 8, 1865—was strangely late. Writing decades later, and perhaps influenced by more intense racism of that era, Dr. Adger spoke of "my deliverance from a very serious and weighty responsibility" as "the negroes were brought to us as naked savages; many of them, perhaps most of them, had been slaves in their own country; of the rest, some had been cannibals." This was the same man whose family taught slaves to read and who launched a church for slaves in Charleston.[37]

African Americans, observing year-end holidays in 1865, must have been subdued. Disappointed, they saw little change in their circumstances and still lacked land of their own. They were still "servants," mostly for the same people as a year earlier. Exhilarating promises when troops visited plantations to announce freedom had yet to reach meaningful fulfillment.

On the last day of 1865, a Pickens farm manager wrote about freed people on his land. "I . . . cannot find out what they are aiming to Do," whether staying on the premises another year or "trying to get homes" elsewhere. Whites grappled with the realization that they did not know what their slaves had thought or what they would now do as freed people. There is no evidence that whites bothered to wonder about or reflect on previous decades. At least one planter, J. J. Norton, pondered, "If the Yanks can make a living without the negro, why cant we."[38] The year ended as the past eight months began, with many unknowns.

Analysis of Labor Agreements, 1865–67

Concerns that freedmen were reluctant to work—such as those expressed above, reflected purposes underlying labor agreements under the supervision of the Freedmen's Bureau. Procedurally, agreements were to be read verbally to freed people, who were to sign or, usually, make an "X" with witnesses. Although intended to guarantee a fair return to freed workers, contracts also ensured that, working, they not become a burden to the bureau or source of social disorder and violence, as perceived by the army and the bureau.[39]

Labor contracts involved a geographic determination of where to live; they affected whether family members could be either brought or kept together; and they specified working arrangements with the employer, almost certainly white and likely a former master, perhaps one's own. Freed people had to find a place to live, food to sustain themselves, and some means of affording all this. How these relationships and decisions worked out in practice—complicated for freed people then—is hard to ascertain now.[40]

Starting from an impoverished position, freed people experienced Karl Marx's contemporaneous theory that exploitation derived from ownership of the means of production. Lacking these resources—land, tools, or work animals—freed people were at a serious disadvantage. However, the Freedmen's Bureau provided some protection. Also, some advantages accrued to labor from depressed agricultural production and a shortage of workers, more serious in 1866 than during the previous year.

Some freed people in summer 1865, reveling in their newfound freedom, opted to leave. Most remained on their own plantations, having no other place to go. Several labor contracts specifically mention that laborers were the employers' former slaves; George Seaborn used the phrase my "late servants." For several large plantations, such as the Colhoun one, a very high percentage of slaves whose names are known appear in 1865 labor contracts. The Freedmen's Bureau in November 1865 directed that "in order not to break up their homes for the present[,] freedmen be employed & make [1866] contracts with their former masters." But the standard form also specified that laborers were "to be treated in a manner consistent with their freedom." According to some federal officers, freed people were apprehensive about the "whipping post," a dreaded symbol of slavery. Major General Sickles, early in 1866, forbade physical punishment of freed people.[41]

Work contracts for 1865 and 1866, unless otherwise specified, provided for food, lodging, clothing, and medical care, some of which could be charged to laborers. By 1866 more landlords increasingly demanded reimbursement for provisions, lodging, and medical expenses. The most frequent compensation was a portion of the crop. Laborers in 1865 usually got a fixed quantity of corn, molasses, and sometimes other products. By 1866 typical allotments were a percentage of the crop, generally one-quarter to one-half, depending in part on other "benefits." Periodically landowners offered a higher figure, sometimes 100 percent, for crops that workers grew on previously uncleared land. Percentage distributions usually varied by crop and often excluded wheat, shucks, fodder, and cotton seed, reserved for landowners.

Some freed people were paid a stated sum of money for their work. More often agreements in 1866 and 1867 included a mix of money, specified quantities of corn, and percentages of other crops. Often workers or families party to the same document got different types and percentages of crops, varied wages, or other benefits. Frequently, though not always, laborers also had their own gardens or "patches," and continued to keep their own hogs and poultry. Some laborers were allowed the use of a milk cow. And a few employers offered wages for additional work not included in the contract. On the Colhoun plantation, 1866 work beyond the contract was to be paid "as it is usually done by the best white laborers."[42]

Several issues deserve thought but have no documented answers. Could the freed people bargain with landowners and negotiate terms, or did the landowner dictate them? If freed people could bargain, likely one of their number would do the negotiating—so how was that person chosen? Presumably natural leaders from slavery continued to be influential, with a special bonus now for the most assertive: "At the head of the [Dr. John Adger] offenders stands his most valued servant, Alfred, and [his mother] old Nina, the wife of Charles." It is not clear whether potential workers could successfully hold out while seeking a better deal, or whether they became more desperate and landowners could drive a harder bargain.[43]

Since freed people could theoretically decide who they would work for, family members previously held as slaves on different plantations now might reunite. That did not always happen, however. Sometimes parents were unable to provide for their children and thus had to contract them to other white employers. Moreover, many contracts involved two, three, or more families, perhaps unrelated. Some agreements listed several young single men who, for whatever reason, would join forces and work the land together. Some documents specified mass removals at the landowners' expense, one returning thirteen freed people to their former Florida location and another taking ten workers to Monroe County, Arkansas.[44]

Plantations were not simply functioning as they did before the Civil War except for contracts with the labor force. Rather, many plantations were divided into separate tracts, each independently contracted. It might take several agreements, with widely varied terms, to cover all workers on a single landlord's holding, as happened with Spartanburg's David Golightly Harris. J. W. Livingston made three separate contracts in January and March 1866 with thirty-nine people for his plantation. Some former owners undertook to support orphaned, aged, and infirm people, presumably from among their former slaves. Many freed people endeavored to keep older relatives with them; a number of agreements refer to aged mothers and infirm relatives. Jack Harrison, working in J. B. Sitton's carriage shop, was to "have the House next the Depot with the rooms and the privledge of letting his Father & sister live in the Kitchen room," paying rent for them.[45]

Agrarian dominance and the linkages between the contract system and sharecropping usually meant that contracts were agricultural. However, some dealt with other duties, especially for many freed women who had household chores—often in addition to their farm work, as in slavery. Single women with small children often had to accept work that provided virtually no compensation beyond food, clothing, lodging, and perhaps medical expenses. Although one contract included payment for a wife's confinement, others penalized women for time lost in pregnancy and childbirth. Some women agreed to be house servants and cooks in towns. Occasionally young children were signed up as servants—with or without their parents' presence—in effect apprenticed for a number of years.

Several agreements for men specified work as blacksmith, tinsmith, or shoemaker in a shop, in some instances for half of their net proceeds. One contract dealt with distilling, and another leased a saw and grist mill. J. P. Reed contracted in January 1866 with Abram Jenkins as a tinker and Benjamin Guyton for his son Elbert's services in a blacksmith shop; B. Guyton and family had to serve Reed in his home, while Guyton got use of a "house in which he now lives."[46]

This system provided for continued white control of most African Americans. Either in freelance style or on standard printed Freedmen's Bureau agreements, laborers were obligated to obey reasonable orders and treat the white family civilly and respectfully. Two 1865 contracts specified that freed people "will be respectful and cortious, sober & honest, and that they will give no insolence to anyone" and will be "orderly in deportment, obedient to Instructions, punctual," while the standard form specified that "they will yield prompt obedience to all orders." Some could not have firearms or liquor, receive company, or use "profane language." Nor could they leave the plantation without permission. Some scholars, who emphasize contracts' "control" language, have overlooked derivations from Freedmen's Bureau forms.[47]

Contracts imposed many additional restrictions and penalties on workers. Wages, if paid in cash, were usually held until after harvest. Contracted people could buy, at market prices, provisions from landlords, which would be deducted from their year-end wages or share of the crop. Absenteeism could be penalized, up to two dollars a day of wages less than one hundred dollars a year, as could sick days, and most required permission to leave the plantation. A few documents specified that people could attend church or that small children could go to school.[48] Penalties for sick days and damaged tools and restrictions on weekend family visitation made for a harsher law than practices during slavery. Control clauses expressed, more often in 1866 and 1867, white fears of armed former slaves, such as "pollicing," political activity, or disruptive gatherings. Laborers were "not to allow Negroes or Whites to congregate . . . in any disorderly manner."

Although contracts usually contained a variety of prohibitions and penalties, some were basic, hardly a hundred words without such clauses. A few referred to treating laborers humanely. J. P. Reed, among others, wrote provisions for his servant in 1866, outlining work and promised to "treat him kindly and humanely, Just as he has heretofore." Similarly, Ella Lorton in August 1865 promised to furnish food for "them as she has hitherto done." These phrases seem, in part, an effort to justify their own behavior as masters.[49]

Before the year 1865 was out, the largest former owners signed labor agreements whose coverage probably exceeded 90 percent of their former holdings. Increasingly by late 1865 the Bureau exerted pressure on landowners to offer contracts by levying penalties plus awarding higher wages for uncontracted workers. A sample of 1865, 1866, and 1867 contracts—about 325—shows that most contractors, 64 percent, were former owners; another 27 percent probably were widows, other heirs, or relatives of owners; and only 9 percent had not held slaves. Former owners contracted for 80 percent of people covered—not surprising, since former owners generally had the largest land holdings. Their agreements averaged fifteen people each, but nonowners only four. Additionally, free Jackson Arter offered a contract to a laborer.

Enforcing contracts occupied a significant amount of bureau time. Anderson Freedmen's Bureau officers charged, impartially it seems, both landowners and laborers who failed to live up to their contractual terms. Laborers especially suffered if they abandoned their work, as clauses required forfeiture of their entire share in the fall crop. Often the bureau intervened to insist that wages be provided for months worked to date. Freedmen's Bureau Officer William Stone reported in September 1866 that Anderson disputes generally were settled quickly, and when he had to adjudicate, freed men had not objected in any case.

Several changes occurred by 1867 and 1868. The bureau ceased to require contracts, and in late 1867 local army posts were abolished. Without both bureau requirements and local army supervision, white landowners were far less likely to use written contracts; official files of agreements ended in 1867. After that it is harder to document subsequent changes. It appears, however, that more freed people then moved away from plantations where they had been enslaved. Some Anderson County landowners in 1868 ejected laborers for political activity; many more expulsions probably were not recorded.[50]

Agreements provided a system for housing freed people in 1865–67 and for ensuring labor to produce food but minimized overall societal change. They also avoided what the army feared, either massive upheaval or long lines of freed people demanding support. Labor agreements were the most formal evidence of the changed status between white landowners and black laborers, now emancipated in law if not in practice. Yet many remained on the same land where they were formerly enslaved and attended the same churches. While complying with contracts as required by federal authorities, white landlords remained essentially in control. The first months since emancipation altered little. More drastic changes would occur in the next three years.

THIRTEEN

Reconstruction Evolves, 1866–68

STILL OPERATING UNDER presidential Reconstruction, federal officials in Washington and in South Carolina pursued limited goals in 1866, as they had since the war's end. The army, serving primarily to keep peace, took no major role in changing society. It dealt with white reactions, violence, and, through military courts, white-black disputes. The Freedmen's Bureau, continuing to require and enforce labor agreements, also helped in 1866 to launch freedmen's schools. Troops remained in Anderson, Oconee, and Pickens counties throughout the year, a constant reminder of federal force, although substantially diminished. Improving conditions for blacks only superficially, the army did provide limited protection.

Changes in 1867 brought by "congressional Reconstruction," as studies of the era typically portray it, had less effect in the three counties than did withdrawal of local military and the Freedmen's Bureau in late 1867. Still protected by federal presence in summer 1867, blacks flocked to South Carolina's newly organized Republican party. Registering to vote in large numbers, they also formed Union Leagues, secret societies otherwise resembling political action groups. Leagues helped mobilize political participation but in so doing attracted white antagonism. Major conflict following a League meeting in October 1867 helped transform blacks politically. Soon, however, the army left. Still, blacks voted in large numbers. As more people left their white-identified churches, blacks directed their energy simultaneously to exercising political rights and to establishing their own churches—primarily between July 1867 and April 1868. As societal changes accelerated in 1867, African Americans claimed a larger role, expanding and enriching their community.

Early 1866
Unwelcome New Year's surprises began 1866 for some freed people, who had few positive gains in 1865. Now a combination of Freedmen's Bureau rules left them little choice other than to remain working on plantations where previously enslaved, unless they had written contracts elsewhere. Military and bureau concerns about stability meant a strong inclination toward maintaining the status quo. On January 1 Major General Sickles ordered that freedmen refusing to work on their plantations could be removed by landowners. To encourage work and to reduce "idleness and vagrancy," any who left contracted labor would be arrested. Bureau

rations would be issued only to those too infirm or destitute to work, and landowners were forbidden to expel such people. The *Keowee Courier* editorialized on January 6, 1866, that the new South Carolina constitution needed an amendment "to make the niggers work." By March greater bureau concern focused on unwillingness not of freed people to work but of owners to provide contracts.[1]

Divergent views came from Lieutenant Colonel Brown's subordinate and superior officers in early March. In contrast to Anderson whites undermining contracts, Captain Bray, handling Freedmen's Bureau matters in Pickens and Oconee, reported on March 7 that planters there "have shown a willingness to give the freed people of this District employment and the freed people have entered into contracts willingly"; and as "far as I can ascertain, everything . . . is going on well." But General Adelbert Ames, commanding the District of Western South Carolina, found that freedmen—still located mostly on or near the plantations where they had been slaves—were working more earnestly than in 1865 and likely to live up to their contracts. Demand for labor was high, Ames believed, perhaps a third more than was available, as some workers, promised higher wages, left for the Mississippi Valley. Landowners mistreated workers primarily "to keep them in the same state of subordination as when slaves," and any black resistance was seen by whites as insurrection, Ames said.[2]

Supervising labor contracts increasingly occupied much bureau time. Shortly after spring 1866 arrivals at Anderson and Greenville, full-time Freedmen's Bureau officers began pursuing landowners who refused to pay contract wages, forced work from elderly freed people, or failed to pay or to support children. The bureau, however, evenhandedly arrested freedmen for trespass, theft, or violations of contract.[3] Technical emancipation, contracted labor, and limited protection constituted the total change, so far, for African Americans.

A surprising episode involving blacks and some whites together occurred in Pendleton in May 1866. Ella Lorton recorded, "The freedmen were marching by a band of music to 'Dixie,' arm in arm, and in the centre of the procession a Maypole with wreath suspended—The Yankees from Anderson, two in number, came up to see they were not molested; in the evening was a ball, and humiliating to narrate, our white boys attended, danced with the Afric maidens, and was devoted in their attentions generally." Emphasis below on violence, much better recorded than such events as this dance, should not obscure more positive contacts that still occurred, such as the October 1866 circus in Anderson.[4]

1866: Violence, Limited Military Force, and White Preoccupations

Local white people, newspapers, and officials in 1866 became increasingly concerned about crime, by which they usually meant black offenses. But attorney J. J. Norton, writing Governor Orr on February 1, reported that "Our District [Pickens and Oconee] is very much infected with the idea that there is no law to punish [white] crime." And some violent acts targeted African Americans, as happened to the Paytons. According to testimony taken by the Freedman's Bureau, John Watson burst into free Lucinda Payton's home on January 4, ordered her and four children into the woods, had them all strip, then beat them.[5]

Bureau officials assisted the military in investigating alleged crimes against freedmen as well as those they committed against whites. Three Pickens County white men—Allen Durham (aged forty-five), his son Perry A. Durham (twenty-two), and relative J. Perry Looper (nineteen)—were convicted in April 1866 for murdering a freed man and sentenced to be hanged. Looper and Durham convictions aroused an enormous amount of local protest. Governor Orr, as he often did, commuted their terms. The Durham case marked a new stage in black-white relations: white men convicted and sentenced for crimes against blacks.[6]

The military itself was attacked. In early 1866 Captain Bray and an army squad sought to arrest men who beat black Cato Allums. "Sargent"—a Manse Jolly cohort—fired twenty shots at Bray's men and escaped, leaving behind a mare with the "US" brand, obviously stolen from the army.[7] General Sickles, reacting to several reports of upcountry assaults on troops, directed that such attackers be treated as guerrillas under wartime orders, which still applied. Orr supported such action. Having local papers publish those orders, Sickles warned that lawless men firing on soldiers would be tried before military courts and that anyone concealing them would be arrested. He also renewed a prohibition against carrying concealed weapons. Additional attacks occurred, however.[8]

Whites in Anderson—their emotions aroused by military trials of Crawford and Robert Keys, Elisha Bynum, and Francis Stowers—viewed the army with even more hostility. Found guilty on April 11, partly because of testimony against them by "Negroes who were recently his slaves," the four were sentenced to be hanged. When Keys's attorney tried to claim bias by freed people, prosecutors responded that defendants "do not yet realize the vast change that has been wrought in the condition of the former slaves, and in their relations to the white[s]," echoing Ames's comments.[9]

Summing up that case, the judge advocate damned Anderson County for "armed bands; and murders, thefts, and crimes"—language ironically paralleling that of Floride Clemson several months earlier. In the three weeks preceding the verdict, one corporal was shot "wantonly" and unprovoked at Hodges Station (Abbeville County). A few days later three whites shot at soldiers on a train leaving Belton, but nobody was injured. Lieutenant Colonel Brown aptly reported that "there is a good deal of lawlessness in the district."[10]

Governor Orr, who frequently visited his native Anderson, reacted more energetically to the Keys verdicts than to other incidents. That issue became entangled with Washington conflicts among President Andrew Johnson, Secretary of War Edwin Stanton—who kept from Johnson significant decisions on the case—and Congress. Orr and William Trescot, his representative in Washington, protested the death sentences to the president; other challenges came from attorneys Burt and

Conner; petitions, such as one from Charleston bearing 1545 names; and a U.S. Supreme Court ruling. After the court's opinion on April 3 that President Lincoln unconstitutionally suspended habeas corpus by substituting a military court—the precedent used for Keys's military trial—Johnson ordered their sentences suspended. That decision would frame a successful legal challenge to the Keys verdicts, an argument that ultimately would persuade the circuit court to order prisoners released in November 1866.

The army encountered not only white opposition but also internal problems. The acting inspector general found that internal matters and logistical problems did not help the army cope with attacks on freed people or on its own men. Anderson's post during 1866 never exceeded 270 men, who attempted to monitor several counties. Hardly exercising significant control, they resembled a peacekeeping mission rather than an oppressive occupation. Since troops arrived in July 1865, their announced tasks were limited and remained so: to administer oaths, supervise labor contracts, settle disputes, and preserve order.

This all became increasingly difficult in 1866. Numbers assigned to the post dwindled below a hundred and shrank further after deducting deserters, sometimes several a month, those sick, and men on furlough. Often due to mustering out of units completing service terms, military companies posted at Anderson changed frequently. Moreover, Freedmen's Bureau and army administrative boundaries often did not match. Pickens and Oconee were under Anderson's military post but assigned to Greenville's bureau officer.[11] Forces, small and ineffectively assigned, faced major obstacles. Given these many problems, it is remarkable that more abuse of freedmen did not occur.

Violence was rampant regardless of race. Federal soldiers in Anderson were among the culprits, sometimes plundering the local area and at least once killing one of their own comrades. Freed people killed one another and whites; and whites killed one another, a federal soldier, and freed people. July and August, months of the most serious food shortages, also were the most crime ridden. Army personnel at times perpetrated crimes. Soldiers in Anderson were arrested for breaking into an occupied house on three occasions in two weeks. Then on August 13 Private Charles Kelley was discovered in a well with his throat slit; the bloody razor was found in the hands of Private Thomas Berry.[12]

Also during August two white men turned up dead in retaliation for their crimes. Bones of a notorious Abbeville horse thief, evidently headed for Walhalla, were found two miles from Anderson Court House; and a Pickens man was "hung up without ceremony for horse stealing." Another white man from Pickens got one hundred lashes for theft and obeyed warnings to leave the area within twenty-four hours. Similar cases occurred in Anderson County.[13]

White vengeance turned against freed people and federal soldiers more readily than against horse thieves. Federal authorities frequently reported that most white people obeyed the law and only a small element caused disorder. Reuben Golding, a "notorious and desperate character," shot and killed Amaziah Payton. Moving to New York before the war, Payton returned in 1866. Anderson's commanding officer praised local authorities' efforts to apprehend Golding, who fled to Georgia; the governor then offered a two-hundred-dollar reward for his capture. Payton may well have intended to establish a black Masonic lodge in Anderson as he carried regalia with him.[14]

The litany continues. In October five whites tried to break into Cato Hallum's house. Unfortunately for Hallum, he shot and killed one of the invaders, Joseph Williams, and was convicted of murder. But "the Solicitor promises that they shall be arrested or driven from the country, and 'nothing will afford him more pleasure than to prosecute them,'" relayed Freedmen's Bureau officer William DeForest.[15]

Freed people also committed theft and murder. During June, bureau officer William Stone reported incidents of Anderson town freed people stealing vegetables and fruit from gardens at night. And in the fall freedmen Henry Cheatham and Daniel Johnson faced trial for their January 1866 murder of white Samuel A. Geer. Cheatham, convicted, was ordered "to be hung" on November 23, but Johnson escaped, was captured, and escaped again. In December his body, evidently killed in retaliation, was found near Johnson City, Tennessee, at the plantation of Dr. O. R. Broyles, formerly of Anderson. Other Anderson and Greenville freed people were convicted of miscellaneous crimes.[16]

Lieutenant Charles G. Niles reported that, as Greenville's army garrison was reduced, white people became more insolent toward both federal authorities and freedmen. The last soldiers mustered out left Greenville on June 18, 1866. That same month Stone—deeply concerned about what would happen to blacks and those loyal to the Union during the war if all forces were withdrawn—warned that "there is a class in the community which can only be held in check by military power." A week later Anderson's troops, there only a few weeks, were also mustered out. New units arrived, but these changes and temporary absence of any force added to summer disorders. Further, both Stone and Niles, who headed Anderson and Greenville bureau offices, were soon replaced by G. P. McDougall and DeForest. The army and the Freedmen's Bureau seemed to excel in disarray.[17]

An August 1866 letter from Greenville County "Union Men" to Secretary of State William Seward echoed Niles's apprehension about more violence. The writers—many sharing the tricounty's surnames—left their homes during the war; some hid in the mountains, as Ashmore described. Recently, "the Rebels have now banded themselves together, have all the officers, we cannot get redress, these officers refuse to grant warrants to Union Men . . . [and] intend to drive every Union Man from this section."[18] The summer's violence demonstrated both lawlessness and military inability to curb it. Collectively, these incidents portray a marked degree of lawlessness and violence, which sprang, at least in part, from agricultural distress, reduction of military forces in Greenville and Anderson, and intensified white organizing.

Several societal circumstances changed during the fall. There were better autumn harvests and more fulfillment of contracts than predicted. As civil and judicial authorities—county and state—regained most of their functions and more local white groups began to develop during these same months, whites clearly maintained power; blacks had gained none. Religious and Masonic meetings were the only large white assemblings since April 1865 besides courthouse sale days. Now new political and veterans' groups began as did women's endeavors to decorate graves. Whites periodically held other public meetings, such as one on October 8 in Anderson.[19] Although many such occasions served their stated purpose, they also provided opportunities to gather and voice pent-up sentiments.

The number of upstate white Masonic lodges increased substantially throughout 1866 and 1867. *Anderson Intelligencer* editor James Hoyt held high offices in both local and state lodges, while Governor Orr was the state grand master–designate. Hoyt, a wounded Confederate veteran, also served as secretary of the Anderson Soldiers' Aid Association. No evidence suggests that Masons institutionally took a political stance, but their meetings surely provided opportunities to exchange views before evening gatherings and afterward.[20]

Even former Confederate soldiers began to organize. They established Soldiers Associations, styled as relief agencies and often addressed by General Wade Hampton, a Civil War hero, who also spoke in the North. His frequent appearances, unrepentant language, and evidently disloyal comments attracted official military attention and increasingly appeared as a problem, someone potentially liable to arrest for incendiary language. Alarmed, the War Department ordered an officer to report on Hampton's Walhalla speech; he flagged comments perceived as dangerous. Sickles, calling Hampton's "manner well calculated to incite discontent and hostility against the authorities of the United States," ordered him to obey his parole terms.[21]

White anger toward federal presence and toward freed people often lay just beneath the surface, as did strong black sentiments. Effectively expressing antifederal anger, a Greenville resident, Campbell Williams, without direct provocation, yelled at DeForest, "God damn your Yankee soul to hell." Even freedmen might challenge the army. On one occasion the solicitor feared that blacks might try to rescue prisoner Henry Cheatham and murder the sheriff.[22]

Not all societal changes or daily life revolved around the war and emancipation. Sexual mores and practices seem to have been changing since the late 1850s. A white woman in March 1865 was expelled from her church "for bearing a child out of wedlock, and it a mulatto." Two months later Old Westminster Baptists excluded a freed woman for having an illegitimate child. In the best-known case, white Mrs. Sarah Calhoun and black Floyd Craig faced infanticide charges in October 1866. The presiding judge, pronouncing it his most revolting case in forty years, ordered that Calhoun be hanged, a sentence commuted to life imprisonment by Governor Orr; Craig was found not guilty.[23] Calhoun's imprisonment would become a critical factor in the Hunnicutt murder case.

Religious observances continued to attract large attendance. Mount Carmel Baptists in July held their annual protracted meeting. Most churches still included both black and white members. Hardly any black churches were established, and most white-controlled churches were not pushing blacks to leave. Between May and December, however, white attitudes toward freed members began to harden. Mount Pisgah Baptists, who in June granted freed people permission to hold a Sabbath school on church premises, revoked that approval in August. Growing tensions occurred at other churches during the next two years.

Generally, late 1866 saw fewer conflicts than in summer months, due to continued troop presence, a general white acquiescence to what seemed inevitable, and a decent harvest. On August 20, William Trescot addressed fifteen hundred freed people holding a picnic in Pendleton. Stone reported that freed people were working well and "giving general satisfaction" to their employers, who "willingly" provided contracts. Similarly, Greenville's military commander observed in September that freedmen "are generally well disposed," and neither they nor planters were trying to violate contracts. Moreover, "there is perhaps better feeling existing between the Whites and the Colored people of this District, than in any other portion of the State," he said—opinions shared by Freedmen's Bureau officer McDougall (Anderson). Further encouraging news resulted from both good weather and fulfilled labor contracts. In contrast to earlier expectations, Commissioner of Agriculture Isaac Newton predicted that the 1866 wheat crop would exceed that of the most recent peak year, 1859.[24]

Both the Freedmen's Bureau and military command increasingly shifted responsibility to civil authorities and tried to sustain a good relationship with them, that is, within the status quo. Anderson commander Smith recommended in August that town council members in Anderson, Pendleton, and Greenville be continued in office and that Sickles approve a Pendleton petition to retain James Hunter as mayor. Only rarely did the military remove elected officials and virtually never in northwestern counties, further preserving the existing white structure. By November the bureau turned over to white civilian authorities the chore of dispensing relief rations.[25]

Sickles, continually pressed by Orr to yield full jurisdiction over all persons to civil officials and state courts, transferred that authority in October, following newly passed federal legislation that applied justice equally to black and white. Sickles told Orr that new prohibitions against whipping, closely associated with slavery, would ease freed people's concerns. Sickles, however, ordered all sheriffs and chiefs of police to submit monthly accountings of crimes committed, prisoners confined, and escapes. Officials and other whites would be less enthusiastic a year later, when equal status under the law meant large numbers of freedmen would vote in elections, choose black legislators, and endorse a new state constitution.[26]

By the end of 1866 federal troops had occupied the upper piedmont for eighteen months. Despite negative white reactions and black hopes, relatively little changed.

Emancipation occurred, technically, but many former slaves still worked the same land as before and under worse economic terms. Positive accomplishments included freed people getting control of their families and beginning freedmen's schools. Late 1866 saw dramatic changes elsewhere in the country based on Congressional elections. Victories of ardent Republicans then would shape Reconstruction politics during the next decade.

1866: Freedmen's Schools, Social Welfare, and Protection of Freedmen

As the first full-time Freedmen's Bureau officers in Anderson and Greenville towns opened their offices in spring 1866, they found many pressing matters, some involving personal distress but others more uplifting. The first formal educational opportunities for freed people in Anderson, Oconee, and Pickens counties also marked early spring 1866. Soon after Lieutenant William Stone arrived in Anderson, he advertised in the newspaper that the bureau would enforce these agreements and treat freed people equally, then quickly began pursuing employers who were not honoring their contracts.[27]

Blacks' efforts to improve their lives emerged most clearly in pursuit of education. During his first days in Anderson, Stone learned of freedmen's strong desires to educate their children. Two freedmen on their own initiative secured Town Council permission to use the Male Academy for a school and asked Private Lewis Phillips (Maine Volunteers) to teach. When Phillips was transferred after only a few weeks, freedman Samuel Crawford succeeded him. White churches also offered Sunday schools for freed people.[28]

Other freedmen's schools opened elsewhere. Stone sought books for freed people starting a school at Belton, taught by white P. L. Walker. With Stone's approval Ellison Williams, a freed man who "can read quite well and writes a good hand," started a Sabbath school "near Seneca" with thirty-five students, half over the age of sixteen. Anderson's Presbyterian minister got Bibles supplied through the Freedmen's Bureau for those who could read and write, and several sabbath schools offered additional training.[29]

A late-July freedmen's school picnic in Anderson honored its two hundred scholars, gave them a chance to display their accomplishments, and offered the governor a speaking occasion. A guard protected attendees to prevent an incident like a recent black melee. Governor Orr spoke to over a thousand freed people attending —more than 20 percent of the county's black population—telling them of rights ensured by forthcoming state laws. But *Intelligencer* editor Hoyt told the Freedmen's Bureau that blacks' desire "to educate their children meets with very little sympathy from their white neighbors." Schools attempted in Oconee and Pickens during 1868 did not fare well, largely because whites opposed the use of northern teachers in local schools. Evidently the first freedmen's schools to survive in Oconee or Pickens began only in 1869, a clear contrast to Anderson schools, which had local white and black teachers.[30]

The Freedmen's Bureau itself did not supply teachers, books, or buildings. Rather, its agents negotiated rental for schools and solicited northern financial aid. At least two northern groups provided funds: the Methodist Episcopal Church's Freedmen's Aid Society, supporting Fannie A. Tudor (1869–70) at Walhalla; and the Freedmen's Aid Society, Salem, Massachusetts, which assisted only one school in the state, P. L. Walker's at Belton. Bureau aid dwindled in 1867. As hundreds of freed people eagerly attended bureau schools, many learned to read and write and acquired a basic education.[31]

Bureau efforts extended also to social welfare. Partly for humanitarian reasons, partly to reduce financial support for the destitute, officers ordered freedmen to support aged parents and abandoned wives. The Freedmen's Bureau pursued freed men to return to wives they deserted or to support them. The bureau also endeavored to reunite separated families. In May, for example, Anderson's officer sought to bring back Lucretia, taken to Texas years earlier, to husband John and their children. Stone requested transportation for numerous others and sought missing relatives in Abbeville, Savannah, and other locations. Generally, however, most bureau contacts involved men.[32]

Agents turned impartially to ensuring that freedmen did not abandon their contractual work, to demanding that all able-bodied people find jobs, and to investigating mistreatment of them. Stone instructed Mayor James Hunter to deal with several Pendleton freedmen who were not working: unless they got jobs, they should be considered vagrants, then hired out, and their wages given to the bureau to support orphans and children. In June, Hunter's own contracted worker, Charles Wright, failed to return as agreed after a permitted trip to Columbia. Stone had the army arrest Wright. Greenville bureau officer Niles in late July warned freed people who quit after crops were planted that they must work their whole year's contract or suffer reduced wages. That same month Stone wrote several landowners complaining that they mistreated freed people through abuse, expelling them from the plantation, and depriving them of food. Stone allowed most of these freed people to break their contracts.[33]

Officers monitored not only treatment of freed people but also weather conditions. Crops ran very short as summer 1866 rains failed to appear. Niles requested 50,415 rations for Pickens and Oconee in July but smaller quantities in August. Niles went to Walhalla himself to distribute food. Fortunately, with the harvest coming in, September requests declined substantially. County officers and militia beat companies designated personnel to locate and verify common black and white suffering, then to help distribute rations. New private relief efforts such as the Anderson Soldiers' Aid Association aided Confederate veterans, their widows, and orphans.[34]

The June–December 1866 period presents a muddled story with no dominant theme or emotion. Freed people continued educational efforts and generally fulfilled contract responsibilities, as did landowners, the Freedmen's Bureau said.

Although violence increased, garrisons were reduced while white organizations expanded—not a fortuitous combination.

1867: Reconstruction Politics, National and Local

Reconstruction politics continued to blaze in Washington. Congress in December 1865 refused to seat South Carolina's legislative delegation because of the state's Black Codes. That placed Congress at odds with President Johnson, who, already declaring insurrection ended, restored the right of habeas corpus that Lincoln suspended in 1863. Both Johnson and the federal courts further curtailed military authority.

Larger Reconstruction politics had little bearing on day-to-day lives in Anderson, Oconee, and Pickens counties. There, a more critical factor was the army's daily presence in the area, and Freedmen's Bureau officers' periodic visits to verify or challenge landowners' compliance with their contracts. Generally, 1867 seemed to be a quieter year than 1866, with fewer conflicts reported. A major exception occurred in October when a black man killed a fifteen-year-old white boy, Miles Hunnicutt. Most issues in late 1866 and throughout 1867 centered on federal judicial and legislative actions affecting Reconstruction and their consequent impact on South Carolina. Increasingly, conflicts among President Johnson, his cabinet, Congress, and federal courts shaped the year's broader story. At the same time the bureau continued its efforts to extend welfare and to obtain food supplies from civilian authorities for the poor.[35]

Once again controversies about Keys, Stowers, and others became enmeshed in national feuds over Reconstruction. In November 1866, U.S. District Judge Willard Hall (Delaware) ordered prisoners released. On their return home the town was drunk with joy, according to one federal account. Three weeks later an angry Congress created a House Select Committee on the Murder of Union Soldiers in South Carolina. Sickles testified in January 1867 that Jolly, "one of the worst" bushwhackers, undoubtedly fired on federal soldiers. The U.S. House report insisted that only the military, not state courts, could reliably provide justice and protect freedmen.[36] Soon military districts would oversee southern states.

Conflict between President Johnson and Congress became sharper in 1867 as they wrangled over Reconstruction. November 1866 national elections produced an overwhelming congressional majority of Republicans who in many cases were leading abolitionists eager to do battle with Johnson. Outnumbered, Democrats no longer had any effective role in Reconstruction legislation.

Congress, wanting more punitive action against southern states, passed two Reconstruction Acts on March 2 and 23, 1867, over presidential vetoes. Together, these acts declared southern states still to be in rebellion and created military districts to supervise them. These laws also provided that states where voters irrespective of race elected constitutional conventions and ratified new constitutions could qualify for congressional representation. A second act required military-supervised registration, constitutional elections, and revised, simpler oaths. Establishment in March 1867 of the Second Military District, supervising both Carolinas, carried with it greater powers legally defined by this legislation. Sickles remained in Charleston as head of federal forces. Logistical changes were few but added responsibilities many.[37]

Much has been made in studies of national politics and of southern reactions about sterner congressional Reconstruction compared to a milder presidential version (1865–66). Viewed from national and legal perspectives, those distinctions appear sharp indeed. In daily life, however, there was little difference to the white community until fall elections. Rather, a more critical factor was the dwindling numbers of troops stationed there. By late 1867 troops were removed from local stations throughout the state and concentrated in a few strategic sites, Laurens being the nearest. That distance allowed more white harassment of freed people. So did the Freedmen's Bureau's end to enforcing labor contracts. A local historian wrote, "The war was over, the Yankees were gone, and the negroes had settled back into their position of subservience to their former masters." Locally, a sharply reduced federal presence overshadowed harsher congressional Reconstruction.[38]

The military exercised in 1867 critical functions that the Reconstruction Acts required. It supervised registration and elections for a constitutional convention and ensured that freed men, once registered, were included in jury pools. Increasingly in 1867 many white leaders evidently decided to play a politic game by bowing to inevitable changes, hopefully temporary, and making public statements acceptable to the military. At an April all-white public meeting in Pickens, the publicly expressed consensus supported the Bill of Reconstruction. Pickens Clerk of Court J. E. Hagood wrote Orr that "a very large majority of our people go for Reconstruction under the military Bill, while there are others, who say they will have nothing to do with [it]." He had a ready audience, as Orr believed that Carolinians must "accept the situation," or even harsher penalties might result.[39]

Forthcoming registration and elections, as ordered by Congress, set in motion several processes. Republicans needed to organize in South Carolina, whites opposed had to decide whether to participate in the election and if so under what party label. Further, freed people should be informed and energized to register and vote Republican. Avoiding a racially defined Republican party, state organizers included a former Confederate officer in the executive committee, along with a white federal officer, Gilbert Pillsbury. Several Charleston African Americans also won seats. Anderson's freed people celebrated emancipation on July 4; there were black and white speakers and a large attendance. Black organizers held a large, mixed meeting in Anderson in mid-July to boost the Republican Party and the Union League.[40]

South Carolina's Republican convention in July was led primarily by northerners, according to historian Francis Simkins, and was headed by a mulatto, J. R. Greaves. Its seventy delegates came from nineteen counties, not including Pickens or Oconee. Anderson County was represented by two black men: forty-year-old carpenter Samuel Johnson, who would be elected in November as constitutional convention delegate, and twenty-eight-year-old blacksmith Henry Kennedy. Johnson soon became a member of the state executive committee.[41]

After adopting a platform, delegates went home to establish local organizations. Created during the war to support Republicans in the North, Union Leagues now became a major vehicle to recruit local leadership in the South and to get freed people registered to vote. Several Leagues soon emerged in Walhalla and Anderson. Evidently their top recruits came from the better informed, perhaps literate, and assertive men during slavery. Several lay ministers from slavery years took an active role in the Republican party and in Union Leagues. One was Andrew Cherry, appointed Hopewell Presbyterian elder in 1832. No records indicate numbers of leagues in Anderson, Oconee, and Pickens counties nor their membership. Locations included the towns of Williamston and Belton plus Pleasant Grove and Diamond Hill rural chapters, among others.

Prospects of registering, voting, and serving on juries for the first time proved to be a heady mix. Organization of Union Leagues accompanied and fostered these flourishing opportunities. Leagues accumulated weapons for both display and protection, and armed groups occasionally drilled and marched. Freed people were soon "parading in a political procession with arms," which led to arrests. DeForest advised the Pickens sheriff that, as "carrying arms being contrary to law . . . the prosecution is just," but cautioned him to consider also the "ignorance" and "the fear with which they regard the dominant white race."[42]

Black organizing took place far more rapidly than local newspapers willingly acknowledged. Two weeks later Samuel Johnson, recently returned from the state Republican meeting, urged in an *Intelligencer* letter that all blacks should register. White scalawag John R. Cochran (twenty-seven years old), free Richmond Payton (forty-four), and freedman Napoleon Gaillard (forty-five)—important Republicans in Anderson for at least another decade—placed notices of several Union League meetings in the *Intelligencer*.[43]

Various white public meetings occurred between August and November to decide how to respond to scheduled elections. Some white leaders and newspapers recommended a complicated maneuver: not to vote either way concerning the constitutional convention, which might prevent it by a vote too small to meet the prescribed minimum percentage, but to vote for white delegates should the convention occur. Initially, some precincts had a black majority, which precipitated a surge of white registration.[44]

Establishing procedures for registration, selecting registrars, registering, and supervising elections preoccupied the military in 1867. Sickles worked closely with Orr about processes and choices of registrars. Legal and procedural matters delayed registration until August 19; elections occurred on November 19 and 20, 1867. In between, Sickles was dismissed and replaced by General E. R. S. Canby, and of course other problems and controversies intervened.[45]

The Hunnicutt Murder Crisis

Attention paid to impending elections paled compared with an Oconee fracas when a black man killed a fifteen-year-old white boy, followed by massive emotional and legal repercussions. Two groups, separated by a hundred yards, met the night of October 12. While Union Leaguers gathered at Fred Garrett's house, dozens of white men and boys held a "debating society," perhaps for the first time, at nearby Oak Grove Academy. A melee occurred, after which the body of young Miles M. Hunnicutt lay in the school yard. Nobody thought that he was killed intentionally; rather, he was shot in the midst of a crowd. Both black and white people were incensed for different reasons.[46]

League supporters believed that Robert Smith, white, spied upon their meeting and fired at the building. When armed guards chased Smith and shot at him, a bullet accidentally hit Miles Hunnicutt, who fell wounded and died within minutes. League guards then hunted Smith that evening and the following day, unsuccessfully. Alarmed by these men exercising what seemed to be "vigilante authority," many whites reacted fearfully and soon retaliated.

Their first vehicle for retaliation was the coroner's inquest, held at Hunnicutt's house. This inquest, which began about thirty-six hours after the shooting, elicited a general account but failed to determine who fired the fatal bullet. At the first day's adjournment, several jurors, all white, told black witnesses—in some cases working the jurors' land—to report more fully the following day. After more testimony then, the coroner suspended proceedings for a week. A series of criminal indictments, prepared over several days, accused nearly seventy men—present the night of the killing—of varied offenses that ranged from murder, riot, and assault and battery with intent to kill, to simple assault—and combinations of these. The "vigilante" group faced additional counts of false imprisonment.

Resuming deliberations, inquest jurors issued their verdict that Miles Hunnicutt died from a pistol shot in the back of his neck, "inflicted by a certain Black Man unknown to the Jurors by name." Nine blacks aided, abetted, and therefore, killed Hunnicutt: December Gadsden, Green Cleveland Jr., John Keith, Jackson Henderson, Nat Frazier, Jack Walker, Captain Dean, Bob Brackenridge, and Mark Adams, plus white Alexander Bryce Jr. Excluding Bryce (thirty-four), they ranged from eighteen to twenty-eight years of age and averaged twenty-three. Elias Kennedy, found guilty of assault and battery and false imprisonment, was a Baptist minister and father of Henry Kennedy, a constitutional convention candidate.[47]

This matter quickly attracted military attention. A day after the killing, Captain Alfred T. Smith, commanding at Anderson, began his own investigation, then arrested and charged Bryce with stationing armed guards without authorization and serving as a Union League officer. Concluding that neither was accurate, Smith released Bryce, but Pickens-Oconee officials arrested him for murder. The only prisoner released on bail, he later was one of four acquitted of murder.

Well-oiled legal processes moved quickly. The court of general sessions, by chance then meeting on its regular schedule, issued indictments even before the coroner's verdict. Five days later, with a grand jury quickly assembled, and concluded, a two-day trial began. Two weeks after Hunnicutt's death it found six men guilty of murder and sentenced them to be hanged. In separate cases for other offenses, jurors convicted an additional nineteen men on at least one other count; sentences ranged from twelve to fourteen months. Twelve more were found not guilty or their cases were nol-prossed.[48]

In reading the inquest testimony it becomes obvious that officials carefully used this process to elicit an enormous amount of information. Besides narrower issues of criminality, they extracted from witnesses details on weapons and their owners, and names of both Union League officers and ministers involved. Gradually, jurors compiled a list of nearly a hundred men who attended the league meeting and an additional sixty who were in the immediate vicinity. For a small crossroads setting, that was a surprising number; it equaled roughly 20 percent of Oconee and Pickens black voter registration. Attendees included league officers from Walhalla and Anderson, fifteen to twenty miles from the meeting site. Clearly, white officials were anxious to retaliate massively not just for the "murder" but also for voter registration; they also meant to discourage further political activity.

At any time the case would have caused a major disturbance, but with elections scheduled within a month, Captain Smith deployed soldiers to ensure that neither blacks nor whites disturbed the peace. Smith, who had fewer than fifty soldiers available for three counties, also alerted General Canby to the possibility of a flare-up. In late October Governor Orr ordered that prisoners be transferred to the penitentiary. But they were not moved; their continued presence in the Pickens jail must have intensified local feelings.[49]

Simultaneously, Orr, Canby, and others became disturbed at news that several hundred Abbeville County freedmen, allegedly "preparing to fight for land," drilled with weapons on Saturdays. So, reportedly, did hundreds of armed Union Leaguers in Anderson near the Abbeville line. "Many [white] citizens" complained in a petition that they felt "threatened with an Insurrection among the Negroes." After investigating both situations, Canby determined that those men were acting peacefully, and the only danger was an accidental clash with whites—as just happened in Oconee. Increasingly, then, Orr and Canby paid closer attention to these reports and to the aftermath of the Hunnicutt trials. Meanwhile, elections followed peacefully in Anderson, Oconee, and Pickens.[50]

Documents focus almost exclusively on white attitudes, but African American emotions can still be deduced. Freedmen in Oconee and Pickens, excited about forthcoming elections, registered to vote in large numbers, while several sought to become convention delegates. Moreover, freed people now had Union Leagues in Walhalla and Anderson and another one being organized within a few miles of John C. Calhoun's home.[51] Acquiring a few weapons, they began to have some sense of military power as well.

More immediate emotions boiled up on the night of the Hunnicutt fracas and after arrests. There clearly was much anger at the white man trying to overhear their plans and to shoot into the building. There was more generalized resentment over other harassment. Both massive arrests and intimidation through the coroner's inquest antagonized them further. Upset at five innocent men having been sentenced to die, the black community petitioned Orr and used their suasion with local, influential whites.

Several convicted men had substantial white support, as many whites urged the governor to commute sentences, and prominent whites on a first-name basis with Orr submitted certificates of character for several prisoners. Some arrested men were former slaves of the Kilpatricks, Maxwells, Calhouns, Colhouns, and other prestigious families. Paternalism thrived as John C. Calhoun's sons sought clemency for Aleck Robinson, raised by them as a house servant who "has never left us since emancipation . . . *honest, faithful, diligent*" and who must help support his mother and grandmother.

Similarly, J. W. Livingston wrote to support Stafford Grant, a "favorite servant of his Master Col. F. W. Kilpatrick. . . . uniformly industrious, sober, and respectful . . . he is a timid person and I think that the Old men . . . are wholly responsible" for his being in the riot. Afraid, "he slept in the room with me a few nights after the riot, and manifested no disposition to conceal anything that he saw or heard at the Meeting." Strongly supportive, if briefer, endorsements pled for other convicted men. If taken at his word, Livingston must have believed older former slaves to be causing disturbances, implications not fully spelled out. The prisoners had superb white legal representation; who paid their fees is unknown, but surely it was not their black clients.[52]

A petition from fifty-seven "Colored Citizens of Pickens District" asked Orr to pardon or commute those sentenced to be hanged, and one by seventeen convicted men pled their own cause. These petitions themselves signal a new level of participation by local freed people. Orr's and Canby's fears of a major disruption also show greater potential black activism than appears elsewhere. Surviving local accounts, primarily press reports, do not convey the deep level of concern that Orr and Canby shared, as Anderson and Pickens newspapers evidently tried to play down the crisis.[53] Several leading citizens, communicating directly with Orr, convinced him that the situation was volatile.

Throughout the next three weeks a flurry of letters and telegrams flew among Pickens's white leaders, Orr, and Canby. Orr, visiting at his Anderson County home, went to Pickens to pursue the matter personally. The governor and Canby desperately wanted to ascertain which of the six men fired the fatal shot. That would defuse wider black anger, they thought. The uproar that would likely follow hangings of five innocent freed men horrified Orr and Canby. Even the prospect of interference when the six would be transferred to the penitentiary led Orr to issue an order: "in view of the excitement existing in that District on the part of both the white and colored population, I think it expedient that some U. S. Soldiers should accompany the civil guard," which would prevent either an escape of prisoners or an assault on them en route.

If the prisoners would name the guilty man, that would absolve the others. Still hoping to pinpoint the killer, Canby sent a detective to investigate. But the convicted prisoners stuck together and refused to reveal who fired the fatal shot; one prisoner "admitted that the League oath bound them to stand by one another." In mid-November attorney J. J. Norton, representing some of them, suggested to Orr that fathers of two men condemned to be hanged might divulge the guilty man's name.

High-level involvement indicates how seriously Orr and Canby feared a spark that would ignite the explosive situation. Orr not only went to Pickens in early November but also personally transmitted the bulk of Elias Kennedy's three-hundred-dollar fine, paid by his son Henry, relied on him to pay the fifty-dollar balance, and ordered the sheriff to release Kennedy. Afterward Orr traveled in midmonth to Charleston, where he and Canby discussed the crisis, then returned to Pickens again in late November. There he directly examined the prisoners.[54]

Conversing in the Pickens jail, these six men were overheard by a fellow prisoner—white Sarah Calhoun, convicted earlier of infanticide. Her information proved a boon for Canby and Orr. Earlier believing that Gadsden was guilty, they changed their minds due to her evidence that Nat Frazier was the murderer. Receiving that news four days before scheduled hangings, Orr instructed the Pickens sheriff, using a posse of thirty men as a guard, to proceed with Frazier's execution. As ordered, the sheriff had Frazier hanged on December 6. There is no hint about black reaction then, but no outbursts occurred; relief that others were spared must have been a dominant mood.

Later, sentences were reduced further. Some released prisoners subsequently became deacons in their churches. After Frazier's execution, other prisoners were transferred to the penitentiary. He commuted sentences of the other five men to two to five years' hard labor. A year later Governor Scott pardoned most of them.[55] Sarah Calhoun, rewarded for her assistance, got a full pardon in April 1868. That same month Canby filed charges against Robert Smith, finally captured, for inciting the incident. This entire affair showed a striking willingness of local white and black leaders, the local military, Canby, and Orr to work together. The *Keowee Courier* praised Captain Smith for his cooperation. Anderson, Oconee, and Pickens counties benefited from the governor's local ties; otherwise he would not likely have been closely involved. A potentially explosive crisis was satisfactorily resolved.

Elections, Constitutional Convention, and Adoption of the Constitution

Registration and then elections that occurred during the Hunnicutt case passed, despite some tensions, with barely a ripple in Anderson, Oconee, or Pickens—in sharp contrast to 1868. A bountiful fall harvest—"abundant corn, venison, hams"— may have led to a calm mood. During registration many white people, alarmed at numbers of black voters, urged other white men to register and prevent a black victory. Registered black men both in the three counties and throughout the state participated in very high proportions. Turnout by white men protesting against the convention was substantially lighter.[56]

The November 19–20 ballot had two parts: a vote to approve, or not, holding a constitutional convention and then election of delegates to the convention, should it be held. Winning enough votes, mostly black, the convention had a black majority, 76 of 124 seats, perhaps all Republicans, plus 48 whites. Only Pickens-Oconee and Lexington sent all-white delegations. Several black men who ran in Pickens-Oconee reportedly gathered few votes. Black Samuel Johnson and two white Republicans won in Anderson, and three white Republicans from Pickens-Oconee.[57]

By military orders South Carolinians voted in April 1868 whether to approve the constitution and elected new state officials, all Republicans. Black men again voted, overwhelmingly, for the new constitution, statewide executive officers, and the state legislature. Robert K. Scott, who directed Freedmen's Bureau operations in South Carolina, won as governor and would serve two terms through 1872.

The constitution, passed almost entirely by African Americans, dramatically changed South Carolina's government, or more precisely its political base, now all adult males whether black or white. The provision for free public education would have immediate repercussions, which extended throughout the rest of the century and still forms the basis of the state's schools. Opening of juries and public office to both races likewise had critical consequences. It also provided that nobody would be disqualified from voting for failure to pay taxes. In a different item of business, the convention divided Pickens District into Oconee and Pickens counties. Approval of this constitution also qualified South Carolina, now meeting congressional standards, for readmission to full statehood and representation in Congress, which was effected July 1. Military control of South Carolina officially ceased, although a presence continued for a while. Occasionally troops would return to the state in larger numbers, especially at election times.[58]

Mobilization of the electorate proved effective. About 90 percent of Anderson's black males over twenty-one voted, and nearly 100 percent in Pickens-Oconee. Credit belongs to black aspirations to achieve political influence and real substance of freedom and to skillful organizing by community leaders and Union Leagues. Before 1868 was out, however, whites would intensify not only their own voter participation but also intimidation, harassment, and physical brutality to deter black voting.[59] Slavery, although officially ended, still affected blacks, whites, and their interactions.

FOURTEEN

Panorama of Black Families in Freedom

RECONSTRUCTION'S PHILOSOPHICAL ISSUES, personal battles, and unsettling social change continued at local, state, and national levels. Meanwhile, freed people dealt with their more immediate need for work, housing, and food. Personal accomplishments can be identified for some families, but a wider lens—the whole three counties—captures these changes much better. The 1870 federal census provides the nation's first comprehensive listing of African Americans and offers a good frame for this panoramic view. In addition to names the census also includes ages, occupations, state of birth, literacy, and value of real and personal property, as well as details of agricultural and industrial production. Compared to later censuses, the most glaring omissions are marital status and relationships among people in a household, which, at best, have to be deduced.[1]

Researchers have criticized the 1870 census, especially in the South, for undercounting people. That seems not to be a major problem locally, as the total population compares closely with the 1869 state census—varying by only eighteen people—and shows 6 percent increase since 1860 (table 14.1). As a federal project, it seems unlikely that Republican-appointed officials would have wanted to undercount blacks. The 1870 census employed some black staff, but Richmond Payton was the only one in Anderson, Oconee, and Pickens counties. Researchers studying

Table 14.1 **Comparison of AOP Population in Four Censuses**

Year	Total Pop.	White	Black	% Black
1859	41,531	29,439	12,092	29 [incl. ca. 271 FPC]
1860	42,512	29,621	12,891	30
1869	44,871	30,768	14,103	31
1870	44,853	30,300	14,553	32
gain, 1860–70	6%	1%	13%	

Estimated deaths of white soldiers: 600

Sources: 1859 figure is a combination of the 1859 state census, which included only whites, and the 1859 Comptroller General's report on "General Taxes of the Upper Division" for 1859 (*Reports and Resolutions, 1860*, 522–23, 197). The "Free Negros" figures (84 for AOP) are not a total count, but only those taxed (ages 21–50 years).

white families believe specific households were omitted. Also, some black men who registered to vote in 1867–68 and who appeared later in 1880 are missing from 1870's census. Clearly there are problems concerning some families and individuals, but total figures, at least for Anderson, Oconee, and Pickens counties, are probably not far off the mark.[2] Assessing the tricounty area's census listings yields two critical conclusions, both helping to illuminate conditions under slavery: the large percentage of nuclear families (husband, wife, and children), and approximately 10 percent literacy for those over ten years old. Other distinctions include skilled crafts and ownership of personal property.

1870 Overview

Using an aggregate portrait helps overcome absence of specific families. This broader view shows that, overwhelmingly, freed people worked as agricultural or domestic laborers. A predominantly rural area offered few alternatives, especially to the 98 percent of those free only since the Civil War. Oconee and Pickens had just two incorporated towns: county seats Walhalla, approximately 100 households and 789 people, and, much smaller, "New Pickens," which replaced the older Pickens Court House only two years earlier. Anderson, the largest town in its county, had 1,432 people; Pendleton fewer; and—considerably smaller—1850s railroad towns Williamston, Belton, and Honea Path. Town population hardly exceeded 5 percent of the total; about 10 percent of black people, together perhaps 1,500, lived in these seven towns. Locally, there was very limited opportunity to improve one's conditions by moving into towns, which would change by 1880.

South Carolinians were not only predominantly rural but also insular. Although peoples arrived in earlier centuries from several countries and states, mid-nineteenth century South Carolina increasingly was housing its own people. With variations, that statement applies to black and white as well as to the state and to Anderson, Oconee, and Pickens counties. Only 6 percent of whites were born elsewhere, mostly Georgia, compared to 2 percent for blacks. Few people, foreign or domestic, came to the three-county area in recent decades. Exceptions included Germans who moved to Walhalla around 1850 and additional German and Irish laborers working on the Blue Ridge Railroad near Walhalla.

Most African Americans, mostly sharecroppers in 1870, worked the soil, as they had been doing there, collectively, for almost a century. Just as slaves were known by whites as "Mr. Smith's Betty" or "Tom," freed people were often identified as "living on Mr. Jones's land," sometimes with the phrase "this year" added, suggesting frequent relocations. Black men testifying in 1869 legislative hearings detailed their own changes, and similar results appear in a Honea Path Township case study.[3] Two Pendleton-area natives, William Pickens and Jane Harris Hunter, later referred to their moving sometimes more than once a year. Evidently typical of many others, her father Ed Harris moved at least eight times, all within a four-mile radius, before she was sixteen.

Left: Dr. William Pickens, native of Pendleton area, dean of Morgan State College, and author of *Bursting Bonds*. Black Heritage in the Upper Piedmont

Jane Hunter, native of Pendleton area, founder of the Phillis Wheatley Association, and author of *A Nickel and a Prayer*. Black Heritage in the Upper Piedmont

Nearly two years older than Jane Hunter (b. 1882), William Pickens was born, like her, near Pendleton. "My parents were farmers of the tenant or day-labor class and were ever on the move from cabin to cabin," he wrote. "Till I reached the age of eighteen I can count no less than twenty removals of our family," exceeding the Harrises' experience. A typical, early move was just "'over the river' to 'Price's place,' . . . [to] our one-room cabin on a small hill facing the larger hill on which stood the 'great house' of the landowner."

Pickens further described this geographical context of laborers and their white employers. The white landlord resided in the "'Big House' . . . near the center of his estates, while the Negroes lived in cabins of one or two rooms, all over the great plantations, each cabin being situated on or near the little farm that was assigned or allotted to its occupants." Tenants got foodstuffs "once each month," for which they were charged. "This system kept them tied close to their master and periodically reminded of their dependence upon him." Although Pickens was describing a slightly later era, the latter 1860s and the 1870s must have been similar. Antebellum groups of slave cabins gave way to separated plots and houses for agricultural workers. Some cabins, in fact, may have been slave dwellings dragged from their original sites to these dispersed settings.[4]

While families may have been brought together, antebellum clusters of blacks were fragmented. David Golightly Harris provided details for his 1868 and 1869 arrangements in Spartanburg County. He divided one of his farms among four freedmen for 1868, and rented other land to another freedman—none of them his former slaves. Harris charged fixed rent rather than shares of crops, but the tenants also were "all to make considerable improvements besides paying the rent. Miller has built a house, Stable & lot. Prince Moore has built a house, garden," and another tenant "cleared & fenced ten acres of newground." Similar arrangements seem to have applied in Anderson, Oconee, and Pickens counties.[5]

Census listings record in a different format this pattern that Pickens described. Hardly any page of forty names and typically eight to ten households contains only black or only white people. Usually, a white landowner is listed with several black families before and after him, a pattern that matches Pickens's prose. About 8 percent of all black people in seven sample townships were living with whites—some were the whites' former slaves or contracted postbellum laborers, or both.[6]

As many plantations were now being divided into tracts for individual sharecroppers' families, average farm sizes shrank. White and black laborers had to work harder to maintain production, and many owners offered somewhat better lease deals on uncleared land just to get it cultivated. Afterward, of course, it would be worth more and the owner could drive a harder bargain for newly improved acreage. Tilled area shrank by a third compared to 1860. Black people listed in the agricultural census accounted for only 8 percent of planted acreage, but many worked other land as sharecroppers or as farm laborers. Both typical sizes and values for black farms were smaller than for whites. Making a living was difficult for many "farmers" and especially "farm laborers." Many such families had unrelated people living with them to help with the farming, and some farmers may have had their sons working as sharecroppers on other land so the family could make ends meet.[7]

Aside from changing agricultural patterns, bad weather meant that most local people, white and black, were eating less in 1870 than in 1860. Crop production in 1869 was only 55 percent of that in 1859 for wheat, 52 percent for corn. These figures are misleading, however, as the 1859 crop—reported in the 1860 census—was the largest since the early 1800s, while that of 1869 suffered from the worst weather conditions in decades. Several recent bad harvests meant that there would have been virtually no surplus on hand in 1870, compounding distress. Compared to 1859, the value of slaughtered animals dropped by 20 percent in Anderson, 40 percent in Oconee and Pickens.

Mobility

Where freed people moved, or whether they did at all, after the Civil War remains both a puzzle and a contentious scholarly issue. That few families left records complicates any prospect of an accurate answer. Some freed persons stayed on the plantations where they had been slaves, in some cases for decades or generations. Late nineteenth-century newspaper articles refer to such instances, evidently very much exceptions rather than a general rule. Until her death in December 1891, "Aunt Lizette Edwards" was still living with Elijah Webb's family: "in her old age she has been kindly cared by them." Also in the 1890s white G. R. Cherry was housing and caring for an elderly former slave, Andy Cherry. It was still possible in 2000 to find descendants of some of Colhoun's freed people living not far from his land. Freedman Tenus Maxwell in 1874 acquired part of his former owner's land; dozens of those once slaves on the same plantation continued to live there.[8]

What is fairly certain is that only a few thousand freed people left South Carolina between 1865 and 1870. Of approximately 100,000 black people born in South Carolina but living elsewhere in 1870, almost 90 percent could be found to the west in Georgia, Mississippi, Alabama, Texas, Louisiana, Arkansas, and Tennessee (in descending order), or southward in Florida. Many were taken to those states during slavery; additionally, some South Carolina relatives joined them after 1865. A few thousand also sought better work opportunities in these states. DeForest wrote that "during the fall of 1866 probably a thousand freedpeople left . . . Pickens[-Oconee] and Greenville to settle in Florida, Louisiana, Arkansas, and Tennessee."[9] Only 2,107 South Carolina–born blacks were living in New York, Ohio, Missouri, Kentucky, Illinois, and Indiana (descending order) in 1870. Clearly there was not yet sizable out-migration to northern states. Maryland and the District of Columbia, with 275 South Carolina–born blacks, may have gained many of them since 1865, as freed people returned to families there.

Similarly, there was not much migration into the state. Among African Americans living in South Carolina in 1870, 98 percent were born there. An identical figure applied to Anderson, Oconee, and Pickens counties also, and all but 72 of those born elsewhere came from Virginia, North Carolina, and Georgia. There was especially much moving back and forth between Anderson and Georgia, just across the river, for job, family, and other reasons. Virtually all Virginia natives came to South Carolina as slaves. Among those from other states, one woman, born in New York in the late eighteenth century, evidently lived in South Carolina since at least 1825.[10] Forty-four people from the three-county area were born in westward states: Tennessee, Alabama, Texas, Mississippi, Kentucky, and Missouri (descending order) —a mixture of those were brought to South Carolina before or during the war and others returning after freedom.[11]

Table 14.2 **Black People Living in AOP, 1870, and Born beyond South Carolina**

Born in

VA	NC	GA	AL	MS	TX	FL
210	48	146	12	5	6	5

MD	DC	TN	KY	MO	NY	AFRICA
10	3	16	4	1	1	9

Some blacks from Anderson, Oconee, and Pickens counties moved to Charleston, Atlanta, and Virginia following emancipation; their numbers probably barely exceeded a few hundred. Despite its Civil War burning, Atlanta became a postbellum boom town that attracted thousands of freed people. Among them, Emma Rebecca Fields (b. 1835) left Pendleton around 1867, evidently with her father and half siblings, and worked as a "washerwoman" while her son James Richard (1853) became an "office boy." Other departures include James (1850), Charles (1852), and their father Sampson McNeil, who moved from Greenville to Charleston, where James worked for his father and Charles attended school, while Allen B. Alston (1850), accompanying parents and siblings from Walhalla, sold milk in Charleston.[12] Presumably dozens or hundreds of others likewise gradually relocated to these cities. Others worked temporarily in Georgia, laying a new Atlanta–Charlotte railroad.

Deducing the numbers of who went elsewhere in South Carolina or moved from other counties into the area is more difficult. Anecdotal material suggests many freed people moved often after the war, partly to find satisfactory working arrangements, but mostly within a small geographic area. Vernon Burton found rather much that pattern in Edgefield County. Some from Anderson, Oconee, and Pickens counties likely went to adjacent Greenville, partly for family reasons, partly for work, as did barbers Sam Black and Benjamin Roberts (who was free in antebellum years).

South Carolina's 1870 black population, as measured by the federal census, only marginally exceeded 1860's figure. Although it grew by only 3,500 people (half of them in Anderson, Oconee, and Pickens counties), less than 1 percent, major changes occurred in locations. Black population dropped in some counties like Abbeville, reputedly due to especially severe racism during slavery and early Reconstruction years. But in Pickens and Oconee it rose 15 percent. Anderson's 12 percent gain, resulting in a total of 9,593, may include much of adjacent Abbeville's 656 loss.[13]

Two primary motivations for coming to the upper piedmont presumably would have been uniting families or escaping harsher conditions—economic and racial—elsewhere in the state. Locally, there was no work available other than farm labor except for those with skills. Carpenter Samuel Johnson, blacksmith Joseph Dooley, and Reconstruction politician, teacher, and preacher W. R. Parker were born in Georgia; their children's ages and birth places indicate that these men came to South Carolina as slaves rather than being postbellum arrivals. Later, a small number would relocate to Anderson, Oconee, and Pickens counties to teach or preach.

Many people moved locally after 1865. They may have gone no more than ten or fifteen miles based on comparing census records with former slaveholdings and 1865–68 documents. Analysis of 1865, 1866, and 1867 tax rolls and 1867–68 voter registration for all three counties indicates shifting locations of some workers from one year to another. For two large plantations, those of Colhoun (Pickens County) and Kilpatrick (Oconee), most former slaves who can be identified in the 1870 census were living within a ten- to fifteen-mile radius from their antebellum plantations. Oral tradition also refers to freed people moving from a church they attended as slaves to another that they established nearby.[14]

A critical, seldom-considered factor affecting any opportunity to move elsewhere was housing. Almost certainly there would have been a shortage of new housing during the 1865–70 period. Many freed people, then, would have been living in what had been slave cabins and often tied to sites where these existed. But some freed people may, by 1866, have been able to obtain new houses of their own. William Van Wyck (Pendleton) erected a log cabin for aged, infirm Benjamin Small, formerly owned by Van Wyck's wife. Also W. C. Hillhouse promised to build a house for a family of ten, probably his former slaves.[15]

The paucity of land ownership among freed people made them very dependent on white owners. Any disgruntled employer could force them to leave his land. One man, testifying in 1869, reported that he—like others—was told during 1868 elections that if he did not vote Democratic, "that I should be turned out of the County and have no home." Barely over fifty black families owned property; its total value of $17,310 averaged $310/family. Individually holdings ranged from $40 to $1,500. Almost a third belonged to antebellum free people of color.[16]

Several other characteristics distinguished many landowners. Some property, especially that held by blacksmiths and carpenters, was in Blue Ridge Railroad towns. Mulattos constituted a disproportionate number of owners, 18 out of 54, including some antebellum freed families. Owners were also more likely to be literate and to have been born outside of South Carolina (nearly one-third) than other blacks. On the other hand, one descendant said that "a lots of those negroes was the children of those slave and plantation owners who had a heart and gave them [land] . . . and set them up with this property." Some freed people who bought land between 1865 and 1875 might fit that description.[17]

People living in Anderson, Oconee, and Pickens counties moved often after emancipation, frequently in search of work, like Pickens's family. Some people who maintained good relationships with former owners stayed nearby. Anyone offending a white landlord would soon be forced to move. But personal reasons surely factored into the equation. Gradually the area's black community developed major segments: those more permanently located in the same farming area over many years; others who moved often; and people who settled in towns.

Those Who Had Been Free Persons of Color

Contrasted to most freed slaves, for free antebellum African Americans there is reasonably clear information about their earlier lives to compare with their 1870 situations. Nearly 65 percent of free people of color in the 1860 census for Anderson, Oconee, and Pickens counties can be identified there in 1870. Larger families —including the Paytons, Sizemores, Oglesbys, Allens, Burdines, and Arters—are amply represented among 1870 listings and are found primarily in locations similar to those in 1860. Almost all mulatto children living with white families in 1860 evidently are absent from the 1870 census or have been absorbed into African American households. Other missing families are mostly those for whom little information was available before the war also. All but one shown with property in 1860 stayed in the three-county area; Benjamin Roberts moved to Greenville and would run in 1872 as state superintendent of education. Bricklayer Joseph Payton evidently died, as his wife and children were still in Anderson. Relocations from the upper piedmont affected especially those involved in the crafts. Two shoemakers, a carpenter, two mechanics, and two mantua makers are missing in 1870. Only three craftsmen still there are listed by their trades; three others appear in 1870 as farmers or farm laborers. Silas Jefferson (then presiding elder in Abbeville) lamented "the neglect of our people in letting the trades slip out of their hands."[18]

Other FPC families had varied experiences. All of the older Oglesbys died before 1870, and mine owner Jesse Oglesby moved to Leavenworth, Kansas. Four Oglesby households had twenty-two people; all four heads—three of them males— were between the ages of twenty-three and thirty-three. William Sizemore's family of ten appears more clearly in 1870 than in earlier censuses. Related Arters, Ladds, Cannons, and other families—almost all farming—lived nearby. Stephen Ladd, a thirty-one-year-old tanner not found in the 1860 census, owned one thousand dollars' worth of property. And the Hallums appear under that surname for the first time. Although Richmond Payton thrived personally as a bricklayer who was politically active during Reconstruction and served as assistant marshal for the 1870 census, postbellum years were not happy for the rest of the family. Several were beaten on January 4, 1866, by white John Watson; just returned from New York, Amaziah Payton was slain in mid-July 1866; and Fanny died in June 1870.[19]

Contrasted with Charleston, antebellum free persons of color did not dominate upper-piedmont African American politics, society, churches, and schools after the Civil War. There were too few of them to do so, and they lacked an urban concentration; but people from all the larger antebellum freed families played some type of leadership role.

Surnames

Besides finding places to live and work, choosing surnames was yet another post-emancipation endeavor, one that seems to have transpired over several years. Surnames appear for only about 15 percent of freed people in 325 labor contracts sampled for 1865–67. One of the earliest agreements, July 17, 1865, for Ashtabula's former slaves, has surnames for all, while other contracts as late as 1867 have none. Only 8 percent of Pickens and Oconee black men filing their capitation taxes in 1866 are listed by surnames, and most of these were either antebellum free people of color or came from the Colhoun plantation. A year later that number was 55 percent.

Use of surnames evidently occurred earlier in Anderson. There, only a handful—less than 1 percent—of black tax entries in 1866 did not list surnames. But postbellum marriages recorded in St. Paul's Episcopal register often lacked surnames, as did most reports of blacks joining white-identified churches in 1865–67. Some freed people filing for Anderson's 1866 taxes may have had ascribed to them, temporarily, their former owners' surnames, later discarded. Many Oconee and Pickens people still did not have surnames in late 1866 and early 1867 documents. But all black men registering to vote in the three-county area in 1867–68, families individually listed in the 1869 state census, and families in the 1870 federal census used surnames. Their absence in some earlier official records may have been due to white compilers.[20]

How to choose surnames raised additional problems. When family members were spread over an extended area, coordinating a choice among parents, their siblings, and their adult sons and daughters may have been difficult. In a few verified cases brothers who worked on different plantations chose different surnames, as also happened with some adult sons whose choices varied from their fathers' names.[21]

Writers have expressed opposite opinions about whether freed people would want to take a former owner's family name or not. In Ashtabula's 1865 contract, nobody did so. Ten percent of freed people using surnames in 1865–67 contracts had the same as the landowners, perhaps imposed in some cases, whether the freed people used them or not. In two other samples—one hundred each—about half matched their former owner's name, half did not.[22]

Many diverse experiences occurred while choosing names. Isaac Benson (b. 1851) took his Spartanburg owner's name. Similarly, "the man [who] bought my parent was named Cannon. And they stayed in that name," a descendant said. By contrast Oconee man George said he would rather be called by his dog's name than by his former master's, so he became Scott from his Scottish terrier. Several Georges and

"Grandpa (George) Scott," who preferred to be called by his dog's name than that of his slave master. Black Heritage in the Upper Piedmont

Thomases added Washington and Jefferson to parallel the presidents, while some Bens and one Doc became Franklins. Names Arter and Sizemore, borne by long-free families, became popular, perhaps for previously enslaved relatives. That dozens of freed families used Scots-Irish surnames such as McCury, McDow, and McKinney indicates a high level of acculturation.[23]

African Americans in Pendleton Township used lowcountry surnames but had fewer matches with local whites than did other areas in the upper piedmont. Prestigious family names such as Butler, Drayton, DuPree, Gaillard, Hamilton, Manigault, Mazyck, Middleton, and Rutledge were adopted in the area. In some cases there may have been a connection to those families in decades past. Although only 2 percent of Pendleton precinct's black registered voters had surnames matching those of whites registered there, more typically half of Seneca Township's 1870 black family surnames matched whites there.[24]

Throughout the area many black and white families living near each other shared a surname, as did Fork Township Hollands (Anderson). Black Isac Holland lived next to white William Holland's and Jeremiah Holland's families. Elsewhere, white W. T. Holland and black Simeon Holland had adjacent houses, and W. T.'s household itself included four black Hollands. A few houses away black George Holland's family of eight lived in white William W. Holland's household; George worked as a farm laborer, his wife as cook. Benjamin Holland, white, provided land and building for the area's black school.

Some owners' surnames were very popular. More African Americans chose the names Alexander, Anderson, Blassingame, Bowen, Hagood, Reed/Reid, and Williams than were ever connected with those plantations. Some people from the Kilpatrick, Maxwell, and Pickens plantations used those names; others did not. Throughout the South some people, but not all, who took a former owner's surname may have been expressing biological connections. Names of certain harsh or detested masters were seldom used.[25]

Joyful over freedom, some former slaves chose new first names, and others changed surnames more than once during the next few years. Joel Williamson's *After Slavery* cites several families elsewhere in the state who did so. Numerous surnames found in 1865–68 AOP records are missing from the 1870 federal census. Other people seem to have adopted new personal names; quite a few old-fashioned classical or calendar names used during slavery do not appear as often in 1870 as they did in slave inventories or in the 1865–67 labor agreements. "Yankee" was the personal name given to a boy born at the Civil War's end. These changes complicate tracing one's family during those years, but also display exuberance over emancipation.[26]

Families and Households

The most impressive characteristic of African Americans in the 1870 census is that they successfully brought together families sometimes separated under slavery. Over 90 percent of all blacks in Anderson, Oconee, and Pickens counties lived in families related by blood or by marriage. Among them, nuclear families—typically five or six people per household—were the predominant pattern. They included over 45 percent of the area's black population.

An additional 4.3 percent lived in nuclear families plus at least one older person, sometimes sharing the husband's surname. It is assumed that these were one or two parents—typically sixty to ninety-five years old—of either spouse. These three-generational families testify powerfully to their ability to stay together, or keep in close touch, during slavery and in early years of freedom. Further, 10 percent of the population included both a nuclear family and additional people who appear to be aunts, uncles, cousins, or adult siblings. Nuclear families, alone or with other relatives, accounted for over 75 percent of African Americans.[27]

Historians, sociologists, and anthropologists have long debated definitions of families and households and their classifications, without reaching uniformly accepted conclusions. I am following classifications used by Vernon Burton, who studied South Carolina's Edgefield County, and Herbert Gutman. My analysis differs from theirs, however, by dealing primarily with percentages of people rather than of households. "Household" in this discussion applies to all people living in one "dwelling," the term used in the 1870 census.

Compiling a sample of seven townships out of thirty-two, I have surveyed all black people and calculated percentages of individuals in varied family and household configurations.[28] Unless otherwise stated, further references apply specifically to AOP blacks. This emphasis on people shows that almost 8 percent of them lived within households headed by whites; it also notes the 4 percent living in three-generational families and nearly 21 percent living in family units headed by women. About 9 percent lived alone or with no one else of the same surname.[29]

Because the 1870 census did not state relationships among household members, these have to be deduced. Nuclear families present the least problem of classification: adult male and female, and people young enough to be their children, all sharing a surname in one dwelling. Other combinations of people are more difficult to ascertain and classify, although even what appear to be nuclear families may actually be more diverse relationships.[30] Other variations, over 13 percent of the population, encompassed people living in households that included two or more families—perhaps related households with different surnames, or sometimes two unrelated families.

My dominant conclusion, which Gutman and Burton share, regardless of definitional details, is that a very high percentage of African Americans lived in family groupings. These were primarily a large nuclear family, often with older parents or grandparents added. A striking feature of many nuclear families is the number of unmarried adult sons and daughters living at home. Seneca Township's Edward (forty-eight) and Kate (forty-six) Evans family—a not-unusual one—included seven unmarried sons and daughters ranging from fifteen to twenty-six. And in Pickens Court House Township, both twenty-seven-year-old Dilsey Hagood with a child

Table 14.3 **Distribution of Black People by Household Types, 1870**

Percentage of black households by classification (following Burton)

Classification/ townships (average size)	Anderson			Oconee		Pickens		Total
	C	P	S	C	S	G/C	PCH	
Nuclear* (4.9)	54.8	67.2	66.9	71.0	60.7	60.7	47.3	61.5
Extended (4.9)	14.3	9.7	15.8	8.8	16.8	15.7	20.0	14.2
Augmented (5.9)	19.0	9.6	8.8	9.0	12.8	13.7	20.3	13.2
Irregular** (1.7)	11.6	13.5	8.4	11.3	9.7	9.9	12.5	11.1

Each total is approximately 100 due to rounding.

Percentage of black population in selected subcategories

"Full Nuclear"	42.2	45.6	52.6	49.8	46.9	50.5	37.4	46.2
Nuclear + Older Generation	9.0	0.1	6.3	0.0	3.3	4.6	9.4	4.3
Blacks Who Lived with Whites	7.5	9.0	12.9	10.5	10.9	9.1	11.7	7.8
Female-headed Family Units	21.8	28.2	16.1	30.3	16.4	18.2	13.2	20.9
Singles***								9.1

Township abbreviations and black population

Anderson County		Population	Notes
C	Centerville	786	(includes part of Anderson city)
P	Pendleton	979	(includes Pendleton town)
S	Savannah	441	
			23.0% of county's total black population
Oconee County			
C	Center	400	(includes site of Old Pickens)
S	Seneca	919	
			54.5% of county's total black population
Pickens County			
G/C	Garvin/Central	547	(called Garvin, 1870; Central, 1880+)
PCH	Pickens Court House	385	(includes New Pickens village, 1868)
			40.7% of county's total black population

Notes: * "Nuclear" in this sense includes households with spouse absent and couples without children present, plus the following: my term "Full Nuclear" applies only to families that contain both parents plus children living in their own households without others present. Other "full nuclear" families are also found within extended, augmented, and white households.

** "Irregular" includes people living alone; blacks (sometimes as the only one) in white households; and a few people in the poor house (including one family unit of 4).

*** "Singles" (who may be married but living apart from their spouse) in this case include people living alone as well as singles within extended, augmented, and white households; since the classification is based on census listings and surnames only, some of these likely were living with related family units that bore a different surname.

and twenty-five-year-old Amanda Hagood with two children lived in nearby white households. Togetherness, not neatly represented in statistics, often transcended individual households.[31]

Family patterns in the 1870 census cannot address significant omissions. Household listings represent only people residing together and do not tell how many other family members lived elsewhere due to forced relocations during slavery, economic necessity to find work, or varied other reasons. In most cases African Americans with white parents or other relatives did not live with them; even when they did, that relationship is virtually never clear from the census. Although slave offspring of owners often would have lived on the same premises as their white fathers prior to 1865, many were now separated geographically. Racial complexities of families such as the Sizemores continued. One Pickens County family reported that their mulatto "grandfather [evidently in the late 1800s and early 1900s] had a white brother there in Greenville, South Carolina, and he'd always dress and go over and spend a week or two with him, but he never would tell anyone his brother's name."[32]

Some children lived apart from their parents, often in white households. In Varennes Township Jack Dean (sixteen) and William Dean (eighteen), working as farm laborers, each stayed with nearby white families. They may have been orphaned or may have left home to make their own living. Dozens of similar cases exist where children, evidently siblings, have been taken in, one each, by either white or black households. A small but surprising number of white people included in their households very young black children, too young in most cases to work or to have been family slaves—though perhaps their offspring. Apparently these situations derived either from genuine concern about black orphans' plight or from continued sentiment for former slaves' families.

Large numbers of orphaned children existed (i.e., both parents deceased); not all of them were absorbed into extended families. Ella Lorton's agreement with fifty-four freed people in August 1865 described six as orphans. Occasionally some black households had young white children living with them, perhaps orphans of the former owner's family. Long-term fostering among black families of related or unrelated children does not emerge clearly from the census, which does not state family relationships. DeForest observed in 1867 that "the negroes, from affection, pride & perhaps other motives, are extremely adverse to parting with children who are related to them even remotely."[33]

Surnames provide additional clues to family proximity. In Brushy Creek Township (Anderson) six Gambrell men heading households probably were several brothers and cousins, with the eldest perhaps being father of some younger ones. Further, two Broadway Township (Anderson) households had three Hiram Greenlees, aged sixty-seven, thirty, and fifteen, thus continuing the personal name over three generations. All three Hirams could read and write. About 4 percent of all black people lived in households that appear to be composed of unrelated individuals, often groups of young men or women with separate surnames. They may, in part, have

Thomas and Frances Fruster worked for Thomas G. Clemson; evidently once enslaved on that plantation, the Frusters owned nearby land before 1900. Black Heritage in the Upper Piedmont, Clemson University

perpetuated fictive families from antebellum years. Others, like groups of railroad laborers, were clearly work related.

Some 1870 households contained one or more people apparently unrelated to the head of household; they perhaps were boarders. Sometimes two families, apparently unrelated, shared a house.[34] Households of relatives, especially with nuclear families, clearly predominated in 1870. Families, now frequently united, remained core of the community.

Occupations: The Same Old Story

Occupations for freed people in 1870 fell almost entirely into three traditional categories, largely the same labor as during slavery. They were (1) agriculture—farmers or farm laborers, for over 95 percent of adult men and a much smaller percentage of women; (2) day laborers; and (3) domestic service—cooks, servants, or nurses for children, about two-thirds of employed women. Twenty-two men, aged seventeen to forty-four, found work, laborers mostly, with the railroad, as some of them may have done earlier as hired slaves. Warren Benson, although blind, worked as pumper for the railroad. One man reported his occupation as fisherman, and two as gardeners. Three women were seamstresses.

A few people evidently enjoyed declaring their status as retired, as did 72-year-old Charlotte Wilson, a former domestic servant, and 80-year-old Hall Hammond, retired miller. William Wilson, 98, listed his skill as "cooper by trade." But 94-year-old

Jackson Brown was a farmer; 82-year-old Spencer Adams and Rachel Simpson, 75, still worked as farm laborers; and Judy Young at 86 was a domestic servant.

Sizable numbers of women evidently did not have to work outside the home. It seemed a matter of pride for many husbands not to have to send their wives to the fields. Families living on separate tracts of land, as William Pickens described, no longer had collective plantation child care or cooking, so more domestic duties fell to wives and mothers. When wives had jobs listed, the eldest daughter often took charge of "keeping house," an official census description.[35]

Beyond agriculture, labor, and domestic service, a small percentage of men worked in various skilled crafts—blacksmiths, carpenters, and tailors—or professions—teachers, ministers, and a doctor (traditional). They amounted to only 154 among more than 3,000 adult men. Most skilled blacksmiths, carpenters, and brick masons came from larger plantations, where they likely acquired their skills during slavery. Only a very small number of craftsmen, including the Paytons, were antebellum free persons of color. While men held all of those positions and women had most domestic service jobs (some boys, called "nurses," cared for still younger white children), both farm laborers and day laborers were gender-neutral occupations.

Although a small group, these 154 men constituted something of an elite with several overlapping characteristics. Not surprisingly, professionals and craftspeople were more likely to own land than other blacks; they included ten of the fifty-three

Table 14.4 **Skilled Crafts and Professions, 1870**

26	blacksmiths	4	mechanics
1	blacksmith apprentice	1	engine builder
16	work in blacksmith shop	2	tailors
42	carpenters (incl. 14 house carp.)	2	gardeners
1	apprentice carpenter	1	wheelwright
13	shoe/boot makers,	1	coachman
2	work in shoe/boot shops	3	ostlers
6	brick makers, brick masons	2	painters
4	millers	1	sawyer
2	ministers	1	painter
5	teachers	1	violinist
1	tinner	1	cooper
1	works in tin shop	1	factory hand
3	tanners	1	doctor
1	works in tanning	1	fisherman
2	harness makers		
2	carriage/coach painters	154	men
2	work in carriage shop		
1	apprentice, carriage	3	seamstresses

landowners, almost 20 percent. Nearly a third could read, write, or both. They were also more likely to have been born outside of South Carolina, 9 percent—mostly from Virginia, North Carolina, and Georgia—and to be mulatto, 18 percent. One, James Harrison, a seventy-five-year-old shoemaker, was born in Africa in 1795.[36]

Nearly 325 black households in 1870 (about 11 percent) reported some personal property, a figure consistent with 1871 tax returns. Their holdings evidently were a blend of possessions, including some livestock, held during slavery, some gifts from former owners, and purchases made between 1865 and 1870. Estate sales during those years attracted freed people who had cash, including that earned by selling produce or services after 1865. The Charles Haynie estate in 1868 paid Jack Humphreys five dollars for fodder and Alfred Haynie ten dollars for "labor 1867."

Occupational choices would expand slightly during succeeding years, especially in towns. But most people would still be working the soil in 1900 and in 1950. Even when it paid no dividends in their work, however, many endeavored to learn to read and write.

Literacy

After family groupings, literacy is the most striking insight from 1870's census. Although difficult to interpret, figure still represent a surprising percentage of people who, slaves five years earlier, could by 1870 read or write, or both. About 630 adults and 366 people ten to nineteen years old, reported as able to read and/or write, are lumped together in this discussion. Forty-four adults sixty or over could read or write, which included three in their eighties; all could have learned before the 1834 law prohibiting teaching slaves to read. Relatively few adults and perhaps not all children could have acquired these skills since 1865. Presumably, then, many of these adults learned to read while enslaved.[37]

Several specific groups were more likely to be literate than the general population, including mulattos; people born in Virginia; persons living in white households or working with whites in the same skilled trade; and townspeople, partly because of freedmen's schools located in Anderson, Belton, Pendleton, and Walhalla. Most families of Anderson town students had books available even in 1866 according to Freedmen's Bureau correspondence. Mulattos attended schools in disproportionately higher numbers than blacks, so these categories overlap.

More men than women could read or write and more likely had illiterate spouses. Among literate husbands, 229 had wives who did not read, but only 67 wives who were literate had husbands who were not. Couples with both spouses literate accounted for 16 percent of literate blacks. Literate parents had children who read disproportionately more often than those of illiterate ones. Many people, themselves unable to read or write, were determined that their offspring would, as 163 children who read—nearly half the total—came from such families.

Literate people lived more often in households of skilled black craftspeople and professionals, themselves more likely to live in towns, than in other families. About

12 percent of all literate persons were in these households, although skilled or professional people constituted barely 2 percent of adults. Often, however, it was the spouse or children who could read, not the craftsman. Only 9 of 44 blacksmiths, apprentices, or shop workers could read, compared to a somewhat higher figure, 12 of 43, for carpenters and apprentices. However, in an overwhelmingly agricultural area over half of all literate people were farm laborers or farm hands; at least 60 were farmers.

Not surprisingly, households with real or personal property were more likely to have literate members than those destitute of resources. They represent almost 25 percent of literate blacks. These include a disproportionately high number of people from households of blacksmiths, carpenters, and professionals.

Literacy rates varied among age groups, but not along predictable lines. Surprisingly, children ten to fourteen in 1870 were no more likely to be literate than were people over twenty. Twelve percent of Anderson County's black population twenty-one years or older could read, a striking figure since many of that number must have acquired some literacy skills during slavery. At least 53 students in Anderson County Freedmen's Bureau schools in 1866 would have been twenty-one years or older by 1870. Figures were more heavily skewed in favor of men for those over twenty-one than in any other age group. The average age for all literate blacks in Anderson was 27.3, and half of all literate adults were over 35.

The highest rate, 14 percent, was that for fifteen to twenty-year-olds, less skewed against females. The figure drops to 12 percent of those aged ten to fourteen, favoring females. Literacy was evidently available to more females after emancipation than during slavery. Anderson had both higher numbers and percentages of literacy than did Pickens or Oconee.[38] Pickens's most literate group, though only 9 percent, was over twenty.

Census data for Seneca Township is so difficult to interpret that overall Oconee figures would be misleading. Oconee, however, did have a large freedmen's school in Walhalla during 1869–70. At least 10 percent of blacks aged ten to twenty in Oconee could read or write; Seneca figures would raise the figure somewhat. For all three counties the fifteen-to-twenty-one age group likely benefited most from freedmen's schools.

Comparing census data on literacy with freedmen's school rosters presents complexities. The most that freedmen's schools in Anderson, Oconee, and Pickens counties together had on their peak days in 1866 was 348; others who attended at different occasions may have raised the total to 500 or 600. Students, listed by names, in 1869–70 total 993; they include nearly 50 individuals for Anderson County schools, 117 for Walhalla, 27 for a rural Oconee school, and 139 for Pickens. How many of these 1869–70 students overlap with those attending in 1866 is unknown. Anywhere from 1,000 to perhaps 2,000 freed people may have attended some school between 1865 and 1870.

Since only those who stayed in school for many weeks could have succeeded in reading or writing, while most schools lacked slates, literacy rates even for those who attended were low. The census reported many children attending school as unable to read or write, not surprising since some were actually in school only a few days—at least thirty students in 1869–70 for fewer than twenty days. Testimony shows that many diligent attendees at bureau schools learned rapidly. Over fifty students were above the age of sixteen. With more than a thousand freed people ten years and older reported able to read or write, they represent a strong desire to gain education, a driving force in future decades.[39]

Each component of the 1870 census shows significant advances by people free only five years. Despite hardships of making arrangements with landowners for work and housing, most African Americans successfully kept or brought together their families. For men, having charge of their families—no longer subject to sale as property—was a major accomplishment. Hundreds of freed people acquired an ability to read or write. A small number practiced a skill or craft, and an even smaller number owned land.

Yet transitions were not complete. "Much stayed the same." Emancipated in its most technical, legal sense, people enjoyed no economic liberation. Most blacks—and virtually all adult men—tilled someone else's soil. Although many families no longer lived on their former owner's plantation or were known by his surname, hundreds of others remained on the premises and often shared his surname.

However, patterns of emancipated community life had emerged. Blacks by 1870 mostly left white-dominated churches and established dozens of their own with perhaps two thousand members. In other arenas men voted in large percentages in 1867, 1868, and 1870, and many took an active role in Oconee and Anderson county Republican organizations. Despite harassment over voting in 1867 and 1868 and increased terror by the Ku Klux Klan, mostly elsewhere in South Carolina, the future must have looked bright.

PART 5 ❧ *Community Building*
Organizations, Concepts, and Opportunities

Introduction to Part 5

FOLLOWING THE TRANSITIONS of the 1850s and 1860s, the next three decades, by contrast, would be marked by community building. Freed, African Americans began structuring their world, individually and collectively, as best they could. Early priorities naturally included their own arrangements for family, work, and lodging. Other issues affected the wider community: political activity, churches, and schools. In each of these areas freed people found new opportunities, enjoyed newly available freedoms, and encountered various problems. Denied political success after 1876, other aspects of community building—more directly under their own control—became even more important.

Many accomplishments after emancipation depended on their own efforts. Blacks in Anderson, Oconee, and Pickens counties as in other areas devoted much energy and resources to churches and schools. Later, they established self-help, benevolent, and fraternal organizations. And as more families combined skills and meager resources, some began to own property and to create their own businesses. That produced opportunities to buy goods within their community, to build a middle class, and to provide some jobs not controlled by whites. Such possibilities were found mostly in towns rather than in the countryside, where 95 percent of freed people lived in 1870 and an even larger percentage relied on farming for their livelihood, almost always on land owned by whites.

Although black people took full responsibility for their churches and for sending their children to school, other advancements depended in part on overall societal changes. Rapid growth of population and transportation facilities in the area's few towns led to new opportunities. And a railroad from Atlanta to Richmond, passing through lower Oconee and Pickens counties, helped spawn six new towns. In each one, black churches and distinctive communities quickly emerged.

Far outpacing others, the town of Anderson swelled dramatically from 625 people in 1870. By 1900, its 5,498 residents made it South Carolina's sixth-largest city. Successful schools, churches, other community organizations, and businesses thrived there. A new Savannah Valley Railroad not only connected the city with Augusta but also spurred emergence of towns in lower Anderson County. Textile factories spread throughout the upstate, based often at railroad towns as well as at two new centers, Piedmont and Pelzer, along Anderson's Saluda River boundary.

Although shut out from most factory and mill jobs except as laborers, black people benefited from other nearby work at mill towns that emerged due to technological changes.

A black press was conspicuously missing, at least partly due to small numbers of African Americans in the area. Rather, specifically black thought had to be developed through political activity, church contacts, state conferences, and connections to the larger world. As racism by whites became increasingly forceful in the 1880s, African Americans themselves more clearly articulated "race consciousness." Blacks were well aware of national issues and thought on these topics.

The six chapters in this part often take a different tone than did earlier ones. Firsthand statements emerge and offer insight into black thought. Blacks sent petitions to Reconstruction governors and testified before a legislative committee on voting harassment. Records of black Baptists reveal much about "race" and other issues. And several people with connections in the three-county area left autobiographies: Jane Hunter and William Pickens, both born near Pendleton and both nationally famed, as well as ministers and teachers J. J. Starks and D. M. Minus; or in one case, former slave preacher James Rosemond, a short biography. These are all richer sources from the black perspective than is available for antebellum years.

Freed, African Americans concentrated energy and skills on building their lives and communities. Deprived of land, they focused on arenas where they could and did create their own accomplishments.

FIFTEEN

Black Political Activity, 1867–75

Excluded previously from politics, many emancipated men readily participated during Reconstruction. Their first opportunities came in summer 1867. By that time liberated peoples were already uniting separated families, finding places for them to live and work, and declaring surnames. Freed from legal prohibitions against learning to read and write, hundreds attended freedmen's schools beginning in spring 1866, while some communities were organizing their own churches. These personal activities were highly political as they, on a grand scale, changed fundamental societal roles.[1]

Within more traditionally defined politics, freed men now could vote, run for and hold office, serve on juries, testify, sue in courts, and own land. Reconstruction Acts required legal equality regardless of race. Energized by 1867 and early 1868 elections and by the Hunnicutt murder crisis (see chapter 13), African Americans, asserting their own roles, took an active part in parties, primarily Republican; and more than twelve hundred men petitioned Reconstruction governors on various matters. The black community flourished in the midst of new opportunities but individually and collectively also suffered white retaliation.

Enthusiastic political activity occurred between federal support on one hand and local white opposition on the other. Beneficent outside influences could do little to provide local protection. Once both troops and federal interest disappeared from South Carolina, political roles dropped sharply and then faded slowly away. Minority status in Anderson, Oconee, and Pickens counties severely limited what could be achieved. Moreover, local black Republicans, who could not accomplish much in their counties, carried little weight in the statewide party. By contrast, representing white-majority counties, tricounty whites held important positions in state political organizations.

A controlling majority, whites used paternalism, harassment, and intimidation—physical, emotional, and economic—to curb activism, especially in 1868 and 1876. Examining South Carolina's Reconstruction from a local perspective, this account emphasizes individual activity, widespread black involvement, and white opposition.[2] It shows that most leadership developed locally, and it also provides a measurement of how many men were involved in various political roles.

Opportunities fell into three broad phases from 1865 through 1895, when a new, restrictive state constitution signaled a halt to most of them. National Reconstruction policies, statewide issues and conflicts, black participation, and white political maneuvering all characterized each period:

1. May 1865–spring 1868: being emancipated, organizing Union Leagues, voting, serving on juries, and being involved in the new state constitutional process;
2. Spring 1868–spring 1877: Republican-dominated state government, increased clout of substantially black Republican county organizations, some candidates and a few local officeholders, black militia units, and petitions to the governors; and white Democrats' "redemption" of the state;
3. Summer 1877–1895: curtailed influence as Democrats controlled state politics; reduced impact of black voting through intimidation and use of Democratic primaries; and, nevertheless, continued Republican party activity and blacks exercising their right to vote, although less successfully.

Political participation involved deliberate organizing efforts, which built on the subcultural network of antebellum years. But it was only a part of community development as African Americans, often acting for individual advancement, collectively forged vital community institutions and resources.

Spring to Fall 1868: Republican Triumphs and White Intimidation

Political activity, infused by a spirit of freedom, blossomed in 1867. Concluding both with popular ratification of a new constitution that included and empowered blacks and also with election of state officers, it launched another stage (1868–77). That began with South Carolina's readmission to the Union in July 1868 and consequently to Congress. Military rule in South Carolina ended.

Intense white opposition grew as spring 1867 statements by moderate white leaders gave way in early 1868 to blunter talk. James Hoyt told an Anderson public meeting on March 4 that "we are unalterably opposed to political and social equality with the black race." The *Keowee Courier*'s new, short-lived editor proclaimed that "THIS IS A WHITE MAN'S GOVERNMENT" and that whites are "opposed to Negrodom in toto. . . . We shall not crawl on our belly and eat Radical dirt."[3]

Statewide, 70,758 voters, mostly black, approved the Constitution in April 1868; 27,288 voted against it, mostly whites, as were the 35,551 who did not vote. Governor Robert Scott headed a slate of eight Republicans elected to state offices; they included two of his successors, Franklin J. Moses Jr. and Daniel H. Chamberlain, as well as Niles G. Parker, USCT officer in Walhalla three years earlier. Together, the state house and senate contained 135 Republicans and 20 Democrats. Six counties only—Anderson, Oconee, Pickens, Spartanburg, Lancaster, and Horry—sent exclusively white Democrats. The house was 63 percent black, the senate 52 percent.[4]

Once the new Constitution was ratified in April 1868, almost entirely by black voters, prospects of blacks continuing their newfound political clout and winning county offices in June alarmed whites even more. To prevent that, "a reign of terror is being inaugurated" according to the Freedmen's Bureau officer for Pickens, Oconee, and Greenville, and "secret organizations of a diabolical character exist throughout the Country pledged to the very worst measures to suppress the loyal and oppress and subjugate the Freedmen."[5]

The white majority in Anderson, Oconee, and Pickens counties employed harassment and intimidation against potential black voters, efforts that ensured white domination of the voting processes. Newspapers increasingly emphasized the exhortative slogan, "organize," strongly encouraging whites to unite effectively rather than to split into factions. Local Democratic clubs sprouted like mushrooms. In some cases, for example, Anderson town, "colored people" were invited to enroll and cooperate, and there was a "colored Democratic meeting" in Walhalla. Clearly showing linkage between memberships, the white Anderson Farmers' Association, organized early in the morning of on July 18, was followed by a mass meeting of county Democratic clubs that afternoon. *Anderson Intelligencer* editor Hoyt served as Anderson County Democratic president and as Farmers' Association secretary; former Governor Orr was its president.[6]

Compared to incidents of the two previous years, more freedmen during March through May 1868 suffered attacks for political views. Two freedmen assaulted and beat Burris Hallum in Pickens, and armed young whites beat Andrew Walker and threatened his life to force him to divulge league secrets. Although in several cases the Freedmen's Bureau secured warrants, local white officials would not make the necessary arrests.[7]

County elections followed in early June amid strong editorial language in the May 29 *Keowee Courier*, using phrases such as "Reign of Terror," "Jacobin," or "Radicals" to label Republicans and "Congo Convention" for the constitutional assembly. These local elections provided both a test of black voting and a challenge for whites to prevent as many black votes as possible. A federal cavalry detachment from Laurens stayed in Anderson just for election day. Officials chosen in Pickens, as in Anderson and Oconee, were all white and mostly Democrats; Republican O. C. Folger, won as constable. Oconee's Democratic majority was 350, grown significantly since only 140 presumably all-white voters opposed the convention seven months earlier. W. S. Grisham bragged to Orr, "Radicals [were] beaten fairly." Evidently the "organize" slogan was taking effect.[8]

Doing their own organizing, blacks registered additional voters, expanded Union Leagues, and worked in other arenas. Sixteen churches formed the Rocky River Baptist Association in August. And the Reverend James Rosemond was busily establishing Methodist churches. Political pressures intruded onto both black churches and white-controlled church attitudes about retaining black members.

"Ku Kluks" warning to blacks posted in summer 1868. Black Heritage in the Upper Piedmont, S.C. Department of Archives and History

Intense intimidation marked much of 1868. It included Ku Klux Klan threats, terror, attacks on black and white Republicans, and murder of a Union League official. The first-reported Klan action in Anderson, Oconee, and Pickens counties targeted white Oconee Republicans during the summer. Nineteen white men complained to Governor Scott that the Ku Klux Klan was "very bold and alarming" in countering Union Leagues. Posted on a white-identified church door, a KKK notice advised "Niggers" and "league Devvels and leaders take warning at once." Mary A. Sharp urged Governor Scott in August to help establish a freedmen's school in Walhalla as support for people being intimidated.⁹

Other harassment occurred elsewhere. In rural Eastatoe Township (Pickens), where there were sixty-five white voters but only six registered blacks, the League president and vice president—both white—begged Scott that same month for assistance as they "received informaiton to Disband" and were "in a perilous conditn." The governor did not have to rely on Republican claims; a white Pickens Democrat wrote Scott bluntly, "I object to any one of them voting in this state."¹⁰

Anderson white Republican E. I. Pinson later testified about his experience. A few days before the election, he found at his gate "a pasteboard coffin with a Republican State ticket appended, and marked 'K.K.K. is about'; also coffin lid, with

'K.K.K., E.I. Pinson, ere two weeks.'" He was so fearful that he slept with his weapons for a year, he said. At the same time freedman Jack Scott received through the post office a letter "containing a note notifying him his conduct had been reported to [Klan] headquarters as obnoxious and would not be tolerated, and threatening to put him two feet under ground."[11]

Several Anderson and Oconee men between August and November renounced in newspaper advertisements their Union League or Republican membership. Anderson County's Pleasant Grove League members felt so threatened in October 1868 that they destroyed their books and papers. And some white-controlled churches cited or expelled members who belonged to Union Leagues.[12]

A week before November elections Grace Cochran, alarmed wife of white Republican county chair John R. Cochran, wrote Scott: "we expect an attack [on our house] to night from the Ku Klux Klan." She named several white and black people who had been beaten and added that "a week or two ago, the night was set apart by the K. K. K.'s to visit us in order to force my husband to leave the country." The Klan, thwarted then, rescheduled for the night she was writing. So, Cochran was "now awaiting their coming with a band of ten men well armed." He already had fortified their house with sheet iron; he also "bought ammunition and armed a guard of colored men for my protection at night." Husband and wife stayed elsewhere that evening.[13]

Of all upper-piedmont white Republicans, Cochran presents the most fascinating story. His family came from an unpretentious background. Entering Republican politics in 1867 while in his midtwenties, Cochran soon became Anderson's Republican county chairman. Somehow he acquired financial resources to buy much land being sold for debts. He then sold 4157 acres to the State Land Commission, and bought other property from it, evidently as a front man for Governor Scott.[14]

Quickly becoming the county's most conspicuous Republican, Cochran incurred much white hostility for his association with "colored Republicans." He collaborated politically with neighbor Richmond Payton, a U.S. Census assistant marshal in 1870; Napoleon Gaillard, a leader among Anderson County's black Baptists and Republicans; and Henry Kennedy. The *Intelligencer* often printed barbed comments about Cochran's political roles. Nevertheless he won election to the state house in 1872 and to the state senate for two terms in 1874 and 1876. He was a state Republican committeeman in 1868–74, Republican county chair 1868–76, and a colonel on Governor Moses's staff. Yet he also won office as warden and then mayor of Anderson, which required numerous white votes in addition to his black supporters.

J. P. Reed and James Hoyt emerged as Anderson's major white Democratic leaders. Both would have important statewide roles, in contrast to Oconee and Pickens white politicians. Running as Democratic candidate for U.S. Congressman, Reed won in November 1868, only to have his election overturned by Republican challenger Solomon Hoge. Reed also spoke to a Democratic club at Shiloh, attended by about 150 whites and 45 to 50 blacks.[15]

That same week Elias Kennedy, an Anderson minister and Union League officer, was murdered at Ruckersville, Georgia, about twenty miles to the west. There, another black minister warned him of white retaliation if he tried to organize a league, and whites ordered him to leave within an hour. Although complying, Kennedy was killed only a mile away. Going to claim his body, fifteen black men carried letters from Anderson's leading white citizens asking that the men be granted protection. That these white endorsers realized the danger even in retrieving Kennedy's body tells much about racial tensions and violence. Many whites attended his burial at Mount Tabor Church near Anderson town. Despite other harassment this evidently was the only verified political murder in Anderson, Oconee, and Pickens counties of an African American during Reconstruction. Murders of other preachers, especially those belonging to the African Methodist Episcopal and Methodist Episcopal denominations, occurred elsewhere in the state.[16] The summer's problems were omens of concentrated white harassment in the fall.

November 1868 Elections

Even more intense intimidation surrounded Anderson County's November 1868 presidential election. Oconee and Pickens likely had their share, but Anderson's is well documented. Outright coercion in many upstate counties came under scrutiny by the General Assembly's Committee of Investigation. Testimony by twenty-eight Anderson black men and three women along with forty-two whites—mostly Democrats and some Republicans—tells a forceful story. The committee heard accounts —encompassing all voting precincts—from many white election managers, constables, or other peace officers. The collective impact of official testimony is often gruesome, brutal, and chilling.[17]

On election day, white intimidation turned away potential Republican voters, mostly black. Many who intended to vote later testified that they were deterred by whites who obstructed voting sites, displayed weapons, made death threats, and in some cases destroyed their Republican ballots. Some roads were blocked to prevent Republicans from traveling to the polls. Candidates had their own ballots, called "tickets," printed and distributed by party recruits. Voters did not need ballots dispensed by an official election manager. Both sides, then, already possessed ample tickets, varying in color by party and visible to all, for supporters or coerced men to use.[18]

In Williamston "a man stood by, and when a black man voted, he took out a paper and pencil, and wrote" down their names. There a white county commissioner of elections, Jesse Pickerell, "was deterred from voting [Republican] as I desired. I voted a Democratic ticket, out and out, against my will, because I thought it was the only way I could save my life and get my goods and chattels from Williamston." Similarly, Adam Waites said that whites Sitton, Robinson, and others at Pendleton "wanted me to put the [Republican] tickets away . . . they said I ought to be killed."

Sometimes Democrats would not allow a man simply to walk away without voting, instead forcing him to cast a Democratic ballot. Black John Wesley Sherrard, voting at Holland's store, reported that Thomas Holland "said if I didn't vote the Democratic ticket I might possibly lose my life . . . and that if I went away without voting [at all] I should be bushwhacked, and . . . turned out of the County and have no home." Peter Brooks, who was black, specifically named Stephen Leverett and Elias McGee as having made such threats.[19]

White Democrats did not wait until election day to employ coercion. They made frequent threats in advance that men voting Republican would likely lose their jobs and thus their houses. Numerous whites denied that such threats occurred, despite abundant references in the local press. Crawford Keys, released from prison two years earlier, was one who made threats.[20] At night black people often heard men riding about, sometimes in white KKK garb with some horses draped in white also, and firing guns throughout the night. Edmund Pickens remembered the "tramp of horses riding in all directions." The following accounts indicate quite graphically the brutality involved.

Terror intruded into homes as night riders burst in, destroyed furniture and clothing, made threats, and brutalized men, women, and children. Harriet Freeman, then living on Alfred Neal's place five miles from Anderson town, told of her horror: "About 11 o'clock one Saturday night prior to the election, five white men came to my house, broke open the door, . . . and told us if we didn't leave before Sunday night they would kill us. They stripped us naked and whipped us with a leather strap. They gave us both nearly one hundred lashes and told us, while whipping us, that they would have no d—d Radical men or women about there." "The next day," her husband said, "my wife and niece were bruised and scarred so much, they could scarcely move." Despite torture and threats, he voted Radical; Neal forced him to leave the area.[21]

Stewart and Winnie Moore suffered an even more brutal experience. Prior to the election they lived for only a year at Samuel Emerson's, ten miles from Anderson town. Stewart Moore recalled one night, "some men . . . came in, took one of my children, threw it in the fire, and choked one, and pulled my aunt out of the house by the leg. . . . [I ran out,] loaded my gun, and shot at them." Moore recognized his attackers, who hadn't bothered to disguise themselves: Stacy McCully, Frank McKinney, and Bob Clinkscales. Even after this, Moore voted at Anderson Court House precinct.

Winnie Moore was even more disturbingly graphic: "They kicked and stamped my children, (one ten years old, and one eight, and one eleven,) and choked them with their knees, stamped the ten-year-old boy in the forehead with the boot heel, knocked him in the fire, . . . said they had a good mind to kill every damned one of us, jerked a woman out of bed with a young baby only two weeks old, attempted to throw the baby out of door. . . . I now live in town, because I am afraid to live in the country, as they have since said they would kill me for reporting them." Her testimony was exceeded only by the boy's appearance a year after the attack: "scars from burns were plainley visible, disfiguring the child's forehead, nose and lips."

This committee inquired, not very successfully, about the KKK. A Captain Wells from Newberry reportedly spent a month recruiting KKK members in Anderson. In response to most questions, white Democrats answered—no doubt in fear of reprisal—"I know nothing about it." Committee members sought information about Wyatt Aiken's public threat that leading Republican and Congressional candidate B. F. Randolph would be killed in Anderson; but en route to Anderson on October 15, Randolph was murdered at Hodges Depot in Abbeville.[22]

The legislators gathered ample information to prove that league officials and members were special targets. Jackson Humphreys confirmed that "they were more severe on the officers than the privates. I was an officer, and did not go [to the polls], as I knew I could not vote as I wanted." W. R. Redmond, Belton's Union League president, testified that "Dr. Carl Brown . . . [and] Mr. Milton Elgins said I would be killed and the place I lived at be destroyed by fire." And the Reverend Frank Morris and his congregation were ejected from a white church building in Williamston. "Accused of voting the Radical ticket, and carrying handbills and Radical tickets to the colored people to influence them," he "was ordered not to enter the church any more."[23]

Governor Scott's sworn testimony said that laws could not be enforced in Anderson County and that political organizations, such as the KKK, defied the law. The *Keowee Courier* responded, "Libel." The committee described Anderson County as inflicting more widespread intimidation and harassment than did either Newberry or Abbeville. The committee found no evidence that authorities sought or arrested any white men doing so.[24]

Evidently these travesties were the most vicious widespread harassment of individual voters in Anderson, Oconee, and Pickens counties for almost a century. Economic intimidation, already launched, would force many families to submit or to move often. And there was a pervasive atmosphere of white control, especially after 1876. But no comparable evidence exists of such widespread physical brutality as that perpetrated in November 1868. Even then, in contrast to other areas, there are no known killings in the tricounty area to retaliate for political views or actions. The one victim, Elias Kennedy, was slain in neighboring Georgia. Some men from Abbeville County, from elsewhere in the state, and from Georgia contributed to Anderson's terrorism in 1868. Several families of Anderson men who threatened voters would be suspects thirty years later in scandals for imprisoning blacks.

Determination to vote, often against enormous odds and in the face of threats, remained strong. Some black men walked ten to fifteen miles overnight to vote; Samuel Green said he "wouldn't have missed it for fifty dollars." When told "'you are a damned fool for voting a Radical ticket,'" Green replied "I vote with the men who set me free." Cochran secretly organized blacks in Anderson's town precinct to vote as soon as polls opened before whites, mostly from out of town, arrived to harass them. Union Leagues, energizing voters, also became conspicuous targets. Coercion reduced black voting by more than a half in Anderson and about a fourth in Pickens compared to a year earlier. After the November 1868 election, the area's political scene was relatively calm and normal until 1876, when white Democrats effectively dominated the election. Growing political maturity characterized intervening years.[25]

1869–72: Republicans Dominate State Government, but Not the Upper Piedmont

Based on Republican control of South Carolina's state government and on some federal protection, African Americans had many opportunities for political activity. Between 1869 and 1876 they voted in sizable but fluctuating numbers, participated in county organizations, ran in a few cases for local offices, and petitioned Reconstruction governors. While benefiting from their party's control of state government, Republicans in Anderson, Oconee, and Pickens counties were also tainted by state government corruption. Their minority status presented a continuing barrier, as they could win an election only with sizable white support or absenteeism. All elected county officials and legislators in the tricounty area were white, and most town elections brought white Democratic victories.

Participation in politics from 1869 through 1876 can be only partially charted by white newspaper accounts, voting statistics, and petitions to the governor. Federal reports on intimidation ceased, not because intimidation had ended but because troops and the Freedmen's Bureau were no longer present to document it. Still, there seems to have been relatively little compared either to 1868 or 1876, or to elsewhere in the state.[26]

Activity is easier to reconstruct than are attitudes. A few pithy instances show the range of expressed political thought, little of it recorded in the white press. A fundamental starting point seemed to be that expressed by Samuel Green: "I vote with the men who set me free." Elias Kennedy's son Henry Kennedy advocated in 1870 that "votes of the colored people be cast for men of their own race." Oconee's Independent Republicans, black and white, allied themselves with the United Workingmen of America. Much more pointedly, W. R. Parker proclaimed in 1877 that the "county was as much the black man's as the white man's, because blacks had cleaned and drained it, and worked for the white people until emancipation." Collectively these excerpts hint at a well-developed political and racial philosophy. Unfortunately not much survives of its fuller exposition.[27]

Predominantly black Republican parties functioned capably, if not very successfully, in all three counties through 1876 and somewhat later. They did field some black county candidates at each election through 1878; all running for county office lost, but some won town-council seats. Black Republicans served among state-appointed election managers between 1870 and 1876, typically filling one of three positions per Anderson precinct, less often in Pickens and Oconee.

The 1870 political scene involved Republican campaigning in the late summer and fall, establishment of the state's first black militia, and some victories in town elections. Early activity began on July 4, which quickly became a ritual celebration of black independence, all the more since southern whites hardly participated anymore. Although nobody planned formal observances, blacks casually congregated near Anderson's town square. Politics soon became the focus as "several [unnamed] prominent negroes"—Henry Kennedy and Samuel Johnson, candidates for the legislature—spoke. Kennedy urged that his audience "overthrow the carpetbaggers and set up for them selves . . . [and] that votes of the colored people be cast for men of their own race."[28]

The Republican party—chaired by Cochran, an election commissioner—held numerous meetings to energize voters. Oconee's county convention attracted between two hundred and three hundred attendees, mostly black according to the press. Republicans fared poorly in Pickens, where many white men subscribed to the Union Reform Party, a hybrid conservative effort. Reform was such a compelling message in 1870 that Kennedy, advertising his candidacy as representative, opposed bribery and corruption in the General Assembly.[29]

Campaigning held secondary interest for whites and blacks, both far more preoccupied with militia demonstrations. Creation of numerous units, authorized by the state and supplied with state-issued weapons, resulted from Governor Scott's initiative. Walhalla's "colored militia," organized in August 1870, seems to have been the first in the three-county area. Its captain, Baptist minister James Keith, marshal of league guards, was one involved in the Miles Hunnicutt affair. Other units followed shortly in Pendleton and Anderson as well as in Dark Corner and Williamston townships. On Saturday, August 27, Anderson's town militia marched with Springfield rifles. The following summer a contingent provided full military honors for a member who accidentally drowned. The few press references to militia activities strongly suggest that they played a limited role in Anderson, Oconee, and Pickens counties.[30]

Militia demonstrations seemingly produced higher voter turnout among whites. While numbers of blacks remained virtually the same, many more whites voted in October 1870 than in April 1868—nearly half again in Anderson and double in Oconee and Pickens. Black men for the first time served as election managers, appointed to eighteen of Anderson County's twenty precincts, and Samuel Johnson was one of three appointed election commissioners. Kennedy and most county Republican candidates lost. Scott won a second term and the legislature remained overwhelmingly Republican with a 55 percent black majority. Reflecting both a complicated and fragmented political scene, the upper piedmont's total delegation of nine whites included four independents, three Union Reformers, and two Democrats, among only five in the senate; the house had none.[31]

Black Republicans Moses Chamblee and Richmond Payton, along with white J. R. Cochran, won seats in 1871 on Anderson's town council, whose mayor was white Republican J. Scott Murray. Pendleton, however, chose an all-white council. Blacks—although constituting a 54 percent majority in that precinct, abandoning their white-identified Methodist church en masse, and creating a militia—never won a single council seat for reasons that remain obscure.[32]

Sporadic references to voting intimidation that appeared in the press most likely understated it. By contrast, Laurens's black militia, led by white Republican Joe Crews, brought out a heavy "Radical" vote totaling 1900, to which whites cried "fraud," saying only twelve hundred blacks voted. In small-scale conflict one of the militia was killed, two others and three whites were wounded. Colonel A. T. Smith, earlier stationed in Anderson, and his troops kept order, but Smith's garrison was soon withdrawn from the state.

Congress, however, passed two Enforcement Laws in reaction to that fracas, harassment of black voters, and widespread Klan activity in nine upstate counties lying south and east of Greenville. The May 1870 act allowed federal intervention when people were deprived of voting rights based on race or previous servitude; an additional April 1871 "Kuklux" law gave the president even more power. These two acts underpinned anti-KKK trials and federal supervision of congressional and presidential—but not state—elections.[33]

The 1870 Enforcement Law was soon applied. In December the U.S. Commissioner arrested four Anderson whites for interfering with Oconee voters, who made a complaint.[34] Reacting to later harassment, Alonzo Folger wrote Moses on May 11, 1873, that federal troops should remain "for the sake of the peace and the poor downtrodden white Republicans of our upper counties." Someone fired into his brother's house a few days earlier and yelled, "Poke your head out, you damned nigger loving son-of-bitch and I will kill you," and another man shot at the young son. Subsequently, federal officers jailed one suspect under the Enforcement Act and were pursuing another, Alonzo reported.

While Republicans dominated state politics, upstate whites groped for an effective mechanism to oppose them. One was an 1870 Union Reform Party of South Carolina; Hoyt was a member of its executive committee. Poor election results throughout the state that fall led to its early demise. Whites occupied a position statewide exactly opposite that of local black Republicans. Coming from one of the few white-majority areas, various men—especially Hoyt, Orr, and Reed—had critical roles in these experimental groups, state parties, and the Masons. These organizations had little impact. Local whites, preserving all elective county offices for themselves, swayed few black voters. Some whites belonged to Republican clubs, and perhaps a hundred typically voted Republican in each county election.

Blacks enthusiastically sustained Republicanism in Anderson, Oconee, and Pickens counties. Their July 4, 1870, Anderson events signified that this was a homegrown phenomenon, not directed by outside forces. Black roles already extended to militia and town council seats in Anderson, and broader participation through petitions. During 1872 elections blacks took sides between party factions and served as election managers. Internal Republican feuds would soon test their political mettle.

1872–75: Divided Republicans Still Control the State

Fissures in the Republican party on local, state, and national levels led to a new coalescing. Widespread charges of corruption and extravagant spending tainted Reconstruction officials soon after they came to power. Areas of malfeasance included high legislative salaries, terms extended to provide more per diem expenses, several "rings" that manipulated state funds for private wealth, large unfunded debts with high interest, excessive printing costs, and incompetent and corrupt State Land Commission transactions. Both legislative and executive branches were incriminated, as were private financial interests, especially issuers of bonds and railroad officials. This all increasingly became a political liability in 1872 on national as well as state levels since major financial scandals also surrounded President Grant's cabinet and his friends.

These problems helped cause a Republican split. One dominant state-level group still controlled South Carolina's official party. Dissenters—referring to themselves as "Reform" and "Independent" but also labeled "Bolters"—sought reforms and opposed corrupt leaders of their own party; so doing, they attracted white allies. Former Governor Orr, who led this group, argued that, as Republicans with black votes dominated South Carolina, reform could come only by joining forces with them, which he did personally. Each Republican faction, offering its own slate of candidates, campaigned in 1872 on rival "reform" platforms. Bolters probably were genuinely offended by corruption and other problems among Republicans in power, but also realized that their objections could win additional white support. Gubernatorial candidates Reuben Tomlinson ran on the Reform slate, Franklin Moses Jr. on the official Radical ticket.[35]

This statewide rupture had repercussions in each county, as competing factions held county conventions. Prominent white Anderson leaders, supported by two hundred men, mostly whites, sought to bring together "Liberal" Republicans and Democrats into a new movement, New Departure Democrats. Several men including J. P. Reed briefly dabbled with the Republican Party but returned to the Democratic fold. There was no overt Democratic slate in 1870, 1872, and 1874; white candidates ran under Reform, Independent, or Conservative labels.[36]

Both Democratic and Republican county conventions in August 1872 began campaign plans and continued exploring new forms of party organization. At Anderson's Reform meeting, which drew a large attendance of both white and black, Orr and Samuel Johnson attacked the Moses party for corruption. In turn, Anderson's Radical rally attracted about three hundred black people in early September. Cochran, Henry Kennedy, and Green D. Williams allied themselves with the Radicals. Conflict occurred also among Oconee Republicans, who were courted by William Keith and James Hoyt, both white Democratic leaders and newspaper editors. Moses got 411 votes, roughly the same Republican and black vote as in 1868 and 1870.[37]

Whites, Democratic at heart, dominated almost all races in October 1872 state elections in the upper piedmont. However, Republican John R. Cochran won as state representative. Benjamin L. Roberts, antebellum free person of color and Anderson's only black Reconstruction candidate to run statewide, carried Anderson and Oconee—but not Pickens—as Reform state educational superintendent. The solitary black nominee to win *Intelligencer* endorsement, Roberts is "well known as an honest man . . . has a good education, and speaks fluently, without indulging in vituperation or abuse of any class." But his slate lost statewide, and Moses became governor with promises to end corruption.[38]

Other candidates did not fare well. Napoleon Gaillard, running for county commissioner, and Elias Webb, seeking to become clerk of court, seem to have been Anderson's only black county candidates; neither won, although Gaillard gathered 1289 votes. In Oconee preacher Tenus Maxwell ran for county commissioner, as did Johnson Wright; David Singleton and John Reed competed—splitting the black vote between them—against several whites running for state representative. No local black candidates won there either.[39]

This October state election brought a record number of area black voters but represented a poor showing by whites, roughly the reverse of 1870. Nearly 95 percent of the black electorate voted, the Anderson newspaper reported, while almost one-third of registered whites stayed home. Ulysses S. Grant, with a thirty-one-vote majority in Anderson's presidential tally, gained at least forty-six white votes.[40]

Following both state and federal elections, local politicking again largely disappeared from newspapers in Anderson, Oconee, and Pickens counties for another twenty months. Local groups affiliated with the National Grange began appearing in fall 1873; by summer 1874 there were twenty-five chapters (white) in Anderson County and smaller numbers in Oconee and Pickens. They surely offered occasions for ongoing political discussion, even though Grange policy forbade group political involvement. Nevertheless Anderson members agreed not to hire any laborer already contracted with another member; anyone doing so might suffer expulsion. Gen. M. F. Gary proclaimed that "God has destined the Caucasian race to rule the other."[41]

Informal discussions at white Masonic lodges, which included many men active and influential in politics, likely served as another opportunity for political contacts. Shortly after Orr left the governor's office in 1868, he spoke at Walhalla's Masonic celebrations. That year Orr headed the state's grand lodge, while editor James Hoyt, occupying leading positions in Anderson, gave prominent attention to meetings and yearly elections in his newspaper. After holding statewide Masonic offices between 1871 and 1874, he headed South Carolina's grand lodge in 1875. *Keowee Courier* co-owner R. A. Thompson, Oconee's county Democratic chair, was also a Masonic officer. On the opposite side of the political fence, new Republican newspapers began publishing in Anderson, Abbeville, Edgefield, Aiken, Lexington, and Union, among other locations.[42]

Splits, both state and local, that were more contentious than in 1872 nearly fractured the Republican Party in 1874. Rival Republican factions in Oconee and Anderson chose delegates for competing state conventions, and each tried to swing voters behind them. At Walhalla's August meeting a splinter faction calling themselves Independent Republicans quickly emerged, chose their own delegates to a separate state convention, and embraced the United Workingmen of America. That such connections were made is amazing; how is unknown. Both Oconee groups submitted reports; reprinted by the *Keowee Courier*, these provide an unusual firsthand account. Divisions continued to play out in Anderson, where Cochran led the official Republicans. Chamberlain's faction proved an effective draw in Oconee, as approximately a hundred black men and many white conservatives turned out for Walhalla's official Republican meeting in early October.[43]

Divided Republicans held two separate state conventions, each nominating its own slate of candidates. Official Republicans (Radicals) needed conservative white votes, which neatly complemented their national executive committee's desire to vindicate Republican integrity. Holding an early-September state convention in Columbia, they nominated as governor Daniel Chamberlain, thus denying Moses a second term. Independents (Bolters) a month later chose white native South Carolinian John T. Greene to head their slate. They opposed corrupt rings and disliked carpetbaggers; virtually everybody now voiced these sentiments. Democrats in 1874 did not offer a statewide slate, or even officially endorse county candidates. "Conservatives" did, however, run legislative candidates—including most winners in the three-county area—and two congressional nominees.[44]

Chamberlain, winning 80,403 votes to Greene's 68,404 in South Carolina's largest turnout since 1868, led his party to another state victory. Anderson, Oconee, and Pickens counties went in the opposite direction, 4517 for Greene, 2935 for Chamberlain. Only Cochran, having at least 25 percent of Anderson's white vote and perhaps all of the black, won as a Republican candidate there. More Anderson whites voted than ever before, and the black vote too was high. Candidates Hiram Greenlee for county commissioner and Harvey Gaillard, Emery Arnold, and W. R. Parker for state representative all lost.[45] Black men continued to serve as election managers at most Anderson precincts and at several Oconee ones, as well as election commissioners appointed to Anderson, Oconee, and Pickens counties by the governor.

Excepting Anderson's town elections in August 1875, that off-year was again devoid of reported politics. Cochran won as Anderson's mayor with an all-white council. He was "supported by almost the entire colored vote" as "the negroes will stick together . . . [and] are controlled by one man," according to defeated candidate Hoyt's newspaper. Cochran replied, however, that he did not run by any ticket, party or race, and won a third of the white vote. Louise Vandiver claimed that Cochran "was greatly anathematized" by whites.[46]

Divisions, confusion, and corruption shaped political attitudes in the state and Anderson, Oconee, and Pickens counties between 1869 and 1875. Despite the 1868 intimidation of black men, they continued to vote in large numbers and some ran for office. A few won in town elections. African Americans provided the bulk of Republican votes. Although Cochran and other whites held top leadership positions, these were shared with blacks, who ritually spoke at Republican meetings. This must have been a heady, liberating experience for those enslaved only a few years before. Little violence or harassment accompanied campaigns in the three counties during these years; at least little got reported in the press or in private correspondence to Reconstruction governors. The next year would be dramatically different.

Other Avenues of Political Activity

Although a minority unlikely to win elective office, African American men in Anderson, Oconee, and Pickens counties involved themselves in additional political arenas between 1865 and 1876. Hundreds appeared in jury pools during these years, and twelve served in Anderson during 1876. Among other political acts, blacks exercised in large numbers their right to petition Reconstruction governors, a surprising and striking political role for these newly freed men. None of the state's Reconstruction studies has analyzed petitions, which show widespread involvement, previously unnoticed. Additionally, about a hundred men served as appointed election managers or Republican poll supervisors. A smaller number ran for office, a few won, and others got appointive positions. Approximately three hundred also contributed to community development by 1876 as ministers, elders or deacons, and teachers.[47]

Sometimes African Americans added their names to petitions circulated by and for white candidates, but they also advocated their own specifically black concerns. Two of the earliest black petitions came in 1867 when seventeen men convicted in the Hunnicutt case appealed for clemency and fifty-seven "Colored Citizens of Pickens District" independently supported their plea, as did numerous whites, separately. Black men in Anderson town petitioned in August 1868 to get a school there. They also sought in February 1873 to have Trial Justice G. W. Hammond removed "as he is the most active in keeping up strife and is a Willing tool to oppress the poor." Moses, however, refused to comply. And on several occasions petitions sought clemency for convicted blacks; almost always these requests included signatures of prominent whites, often the solicitor and jury members and occasionally Judge Orr also. Some white candidates succeeded in getting black endorsements. Three Anderson white men, each hoping to be appointed county treasurer, circulated petitions in December 1872 that, ranging from 25 to 219, together got a total of 373 black names.[48]

Collectively, nearly 1,225 black men joined petitions. Anderson's more than 900 petitioners equaled 64 percent of registered black voters in 1868 and over 60 percent of adult black men. Sizable numbers of those involved, or their families, were also religious or educational leaders. Petitioners included many of Anderson's sixty-eight

Portion of a petition for a governor's pardon, 1870; subscribers include Reconstruction leaders Cochran, Gaillard, Johnson, Kennedy, Morris, Thompson, and Jenkins. S.C. Department of Archives and History

election managers and Republican supervisors, several ministers and teachers, and church officers. At least 10 percent of the total were Baptist deacons. Craftsmen participated at substantial rates, 70 percent of those in Anderson, Oconee, and Pickens counties.[49]

Anderson ministers—thirteen or more—had various levels of political involvement. Elias Kennedy, a Union League organizer, was murdered in 1868; W. R. Parker (Snow Hill Baptist) is discussed below. Eight specifically identified themselves as "Rev." when signing an 1874 request to have white A. O. Norris appointed county treasurer. They included Frank Morris, founder of several Baptist churches in 1865–68, and Methodist minister Elijah Carlisle. Milton Lindsey (b. 1840), both minister and blacksmith with more economic independence than other clergy, supported petitions and served numerous Baptist churches.[50]

Considerable age variations marked specific political roles. African American registered voters in 1867 ranged from twenty-one, the minimum, to their seventies. Those who endorsed petitions, given their large number, probably came from similarly diverse ages. But candidates, election supervisors, managers, and ministers were mostly in their forties, fifties, or older. By contrast most teachers were younger. Those Union League officers whose names are known were mostly in their thirties, forties, or fifties; most Walhalla League officers were craftsmen and landowning farmers. Contrasted to them, the youngest group was those men arrested for Hunnicutt's murder in October 1867, in their late teens and twenties.[51]

Although concentrated in the town of Anderson, petitioners also came from Honea Path, Belton, and Williamston, as well as from rural areas. Numbers of Anderson's politically active men far outpaced those in either Oconee or Pickens. There, many Walhalla-area blacks joined petitions, and others came especially from Dacusville, "Old Pickens," and "New Pickens" vicinities. Pickens had considerably less black political activity compared to Anderson. Only 135 blacks petitioned, over a third of them for the 1867 prisoners. Based on a smaller population, they still equaled only 35 percent of registered black voters. Few Pickens blacks served as election managers or Republican supervisors and evidently none ran for elective office. As happened in Oconee and Anderson, whites in Pickens, competing against each other, tried to line up black supporters.[52]

Dominating Pickens Republican party offices, whites pursued intense personal rivalries. They included brothers Alonzo and O. C. Folger, son-in-law Perrin O'Dell, W. A. Lesley, and Jeremiah Looper. Alonzo Folger said that he "can show" that his father was loyal during the late war, and Fredman's Bureau officer William Stone verified that Loopers "are loyal men and were so throughout the war." The Eastatoe Union League indicates white Republican support in the county's upper region. Some blacks recommended for appointive office were passed over, as was Thomas Cannon for election commissioner. Alonzo Folger, Jeremiah Looper, and black minister D. C. Owens held those posts from 1870 through 1874. When Owens left the state, Pickens had no black commissioner in 1876.[53] Both Pickens and Oconee attracted proportionately more white Republicans, probably wartime Unionists, than did Anderson.

Republicans were more active in Oconee and had more black leadership than in Pickens. Oconee's 176 blacks who supported petitions amounted to 40 percent of registered voters. Twenty-three black men served as election managers and supervisors between 1872 and 1876, fifteen ran for office, and several wrote letters to governors, as did minister James Keith in November 1874. Keith held one of the most significant roles among early Republicans in the Union League and as captain of the earliest black militia in Anderson, Oconee, and Pickens counties (1870). By 1872 David Singleton, Elias Jenkins, and others surpassed him in party standing.[54]

Election commissioners, as state officials, held gubernatorial appointments. Commissioners verified election results and appointed managers for each precinct.

Between 1870 and 1876 they were usually balanced, Democrats and Republicans, white and black. Elias Jenkins and Johnson Wright each held two terms in Oconee along with white Republicans. Samuel Johnson served from 1870 through 1876 in Anderson; part of that time Cochran was also a commissioner. N. B. Gaillard, appointed in 1876, continued through 1880.

Fifty-three Anderson black Republicans were election managers for twenty precincts between 1870 and 1876. Over half served just one election year; only three men had appointments all four election years. Many of these managers came from politically active families—four Lees, two Sampsons, and two Reeds were among them—and often had leadership positions in churches and schools also. In some cases rather than teachers or ministers themselves, members of their families petitioned or worked as election staff.[55]

Several politically involved men served in multiple roles. Taking those who were both election managers and petitioners as a core leadership, it becomes clear that no single factor united them. Some came from towns, disproportionately so, but many lived in rural areas. A few were skilled craftsmen, but many worked as farm laborers; and some could not read or write. Almost all, however, had children who were literate or attending school. Many served as ministers or early church officials and a few as teachers.

Many key leaders living within Anderson city had mostly been slaves (whose owners are unknown) in the town, supported Greeley Institute, and formed an extended clique in the same area of town. They included Napoleon Bonaparte (N. B.) Gaillard (1826), a tanner, who served as Republican officer, election manager, and Rocky River Baptist Association clerk for several years. From rural areas, Allen (1840) and Carey (1844) Pickens, grandson of Jemima Pickens, were petitioners and, respectively, a Brushy Creek Township election manager and John Wesley Methodist Episcopal trustee. Elsewhere in the county, sixty-year-old Jack Mance, an illiterate Hall Township farm laborer, was a three-time election manager. A Pleasant Grove Baptist Church charter member, he endorsed two petitions, and most likely belonged to the Union League there.

The most controversial minister earned the headline "Nigger Parker Rules in Fair Play." That referred to a Reconstruction-era leader still living in the community. Born in 1839, enslaved in Georgia, William R. Parker came to South Carolina during the war. Evidently working for Benjamin Holland in 1867, Parker by 1870 lived with his second wife, Emeline, a South Carolina native, in Anderson's Fork Township near Oconee's unincorporated Fair Play community. Owning two hundred dollars' worth of land in 1870, he taught an early freedmen's school, served as minister at several churches, participated in Reconstruction politics, and likely was a Union League officer. An active Republican, he was a delegate to the 1874 state convention and unsuccessful legislative candidate. Parker served several times as election manager and Republican supervisor.

Although only a few contemporary newspaper accounts mentioned him, clearly Parker did not find favor with local whites. The highly prejudiced *Intelligencer* reported an open debate in 1876 between Republican Parker at his church and co-editor E. B. Murray, representing Democrats. Parker delivered "a bitter speech appealing to the worst prejudices and feelings of the colored people," according to the writer. Three months later officials charged Parker with embezzling school money. In 1877 he "attacked the white people of this county, and claimed that the county was as much the black man's as the white man's, because they had cleaned and drained it, and worked for the white people until emancipation." Later, however, Parker precipitated clashes among Pickens and Oconee black Baptists.[56]

Parker articulated a more radical argument than any other black leader in the three counties. Yet, as shown earlier, other snippets suggest dimensions of black political thought. Determination by many men to vote and to undertake other actions that might well lead to retaliation emphasizes their compelling drive to improve conditions for freed African Americans.

Parameters Affecting Black Political Activity

While many Republicans participated actively in politics and hundreds more petitioned their Reconstruction governors, they all did so in the midst of vitriol and overt intimidation. A broader view should take into account these factors. One, economic intimidation, left little hard evidence. Most people depended on white employment and housing, so opportunities to suffer economic pressure, stated and unstated, were abundant.

Another complication was limited and distorted news coverage of African Americans, which affected and reinforced many white views. Bias of newspapers virtually eliminated that conventional vehicle for literate blacks to reach their own community. Rather, newspapers often carried notices urging landlords to inform tenants of a forthcoming Democratic rally that they should attend—advice not likely offered on an indifferent or benign basis. Further, the press repeatedly stressed black crime and each "Negro Outrage," almost a running headline locally as throughout the nation.[57]

Some alleged crimes may have been fabricated for harassment. In 1870, 1871, and 1872 four Republicans involved in the 1867 Hunnicutt incident were arrested. Other arrests targeted Anderson County men. Samuel Johnson—constitutional convention delegate and Anderson town property-owner—was charged in fall 1871 with disturbing a religious service, which resulted in four weeks' demeaning work on Anderson's streets. Even less credibly, W. R. Parker was arrested in 1877.[58]

Arson was an additional factor during Reconstruction. Newspapers reported numerous burnings of buildings, suspected as "incendiary." So little information exists that it is now impossible to make definitive judgments. Yet it seems clear that some fires were political retaliation, such as that at Cochran's building in 1875. J. B.

Sitton's Oconee gin house burned in 1873, as did one in 1875 belonging to A. J. Sitton, credited with Pendleton's 1876 use of red shirts (see chapter 16). A. M. Neal, who evicted laborers following their Republican vote in 1868, lost his gin house with three bales of cotton and machinery in January 1874. And several Honea Path stores burned six weeks after 1876 elections.[59] Economic frustrations may have motivated some fires, such as G. W. Rankin's mills and Mark Prince's cotton house, both in 1873. Two white men were arrested for the Rankin incident without racial or political connotations.

Arson involved black-on-white and white-on-white incidents for a mixture of political, economic, and personal motivations. Countered to these, there were joint white-black efforts to put out accidental fires. Among other occasions, that happened when "both white and colored people worked with the utmost energy and skill" to stop fire spreading at Dr. J. H. Maxwell's building. And several whites tried to save black children from fires. Numerous black families lost their houses by fire; if they voted Democratic, white neighbors sometimes helped rebuild and replace lost possessions.[60]

Some black families benefited from a Reconstruction program that was surrounded by many problems, the State Land Commission. If not the proverbial "forty acres and a mule" as partial compensation for their previous labor and servitude, commission sales enabled numerous families to acquire some affordable land. State funds got siphoned off in the process. Carol Bleser has effectively traced commission incompetence and corruption that often deprived intended beneficiaries.

Especially in Oconee, however, dozens of families bought parcels, many of them near Walhalla. Forty-seven buyers, including five black women and perhaps ten whites, bought twenty-one hundred acres at an average price of $3.50 per acre. As occurred elsewhere in the state, some buyers failed to make payments and lost their property through delinquent land sales. That happened to several Oconee buyers as soon as 1874–75, but over 40 percent of them or their families still owned land in 1880, and about that many in 1900. Black families did not fare as well getting State Land Commission land in Anderson or Pickens.[61]

African Americans made political choices that indicate a rapidly developed consciousness as they decided to express publicly their views, chose among factions, and calculated alternatives. They divided among themselves along 1872 and 1874 statewide factional lines. These roles and widespread involvement in petitioning show a greater mobilization than has been assumed for the upper piedmont. Since references to their actions are widely scattered, it has been easy to overlook these activities.

Organizing energetically to influence political decisions in Anderson, Oconee, and Pickens counties, blacks there shaped skills applied also to developing churches, schools, and communities. Virtually all political leaders and candidates were tri-county natives with hardly any "outsiders." Only Richmond Payton, his nephew Joberry (Jr.)—teacher, election manager, and supervisor—and Benjamin Roberts came from antebellum free families. Eager and effective leadership quickly emerged within the three counties from those recently in bondage there.

Between 1867 and 1875, African Americans shared in most traditional roles including some direct benefits and favors, such as State Land Commission land and appointments. Whites continued to display a mixture of paternalism—"we know what is best, so vote Democratic with us"—and oppression—"if you don't, leave our land." After 1868 little violence or overt harassment accompanied political campaigns, or at least got reported in newspapers or in private letters to the governors. But 1876 would be critically different.[62]

SIXTEEN

Black Politics Curtailed, 1876–90

DRAMATIC ALTERATIONS MARKED Reconstruction politics during 1876. It would be poor historiography to say that changes were inevitable, or that "they were in the air." However, reading 1876 newspapers yields a palpable sense of white momentum, determination, and effectiveness. Fierce resolution obviously drove Democratic capture of South Carolina from Republicans and blacks. To achieve that goal, white Democrats employed intense intimidation. In Anderson, Oconee, and Pickens counties, at least, it was usually generalized pressure rather than direct whipping or harassment as marked the November 1868 election. On the other hand, no investigation documented what transpired in 1876. Some Republican letters shed light on specific incidents.

White Democrats not only recaptured state government. They succeeded also in getting federal troops withdrawn from the state only, however, by casting South Carolina's votes for the Republican presidential candidate. These events put a brake on black political activity, which slowly decelerated over the next two decades. Outside forces again shaped African American lives. Whites controlled state government again as well as land, resources, and public institutions.

The 1876 Campaign

Campaign maneuvering began early in 1876, a striking contrast to recent election years. Republicans in state politics seemed increasingly vulnerable due to corruption and internal factionalization. The presidential election added yet another dimension, as Grant was not running for a third term. A changed political climate nationally also offered hope for white southern Democrats. And a late-1875 furor over state Republican judges especially angered Democrats.

On January 6 the Democratic State Central Committee, laying plans to reclaim the state, vowed to run a Democratic slate, as demanded by "Straightouts," for the first time since 1868. The Democrats' pronouncement, not surprisingly, emphasized Republican evils and spoke of what "people of South Carolina" must do "for their own salvation."[1] The state Democratic committee assigned county chairs—including James Hoyt, R. A. Thompson, and R. E. Bowen—a special duty to organize and energize local clubs in every precinct. The *Keowee Courier* in its first 1876 issue and in subsequent weeks resumed its theme that whites must organize. Doing just that, several groups calling themselves Reformers met in Anderson County during January, and local Democratic clubs began enrolling new members. Activity and momentum began unusually early in the year.

Both Democrats and Republicans convened spring meetings, first county then state, to choose delegates to their national conventions. Oconee Republicans, led by David Singleton and Elias Jenkins, met in mid-March 1876. United this time, they chose blacks Robert Goode and David Sanders and two white alternates to their state convention. Meanwhile, unnamed blacks in Anderson reportedly vowed not to work for Democratic club members. That led to a counterthreat that Democrats would not hire Republicans. Whites repeated such comments throughout the year as a potent threat.[2]

As viewed by the public, the upper-piedmont political scene remained relatively quiet after these spring meetings. Events in late summer and early fall hint at widespread white plotting to recapture the state from Republican control. South Carolina was one of only three states not yet "redeemed"—the term white southerners used for ousting Republican governments—which led to intense efforts in each of them. The mid-July Democratic national convention at St. Louis, attended by Hoyt and others, afforded private political negotiations that likely provided much encouragement to South Carolina Democrats.

"Redemption" became a major campaign slogan and a term used later to characterize an era. At the same time Anderson Republicans announced that they would not nominate legislative or county candidates unless the Democratic nominees were offensive. Straining their nonpolitical constitution, Grange societies often supplied their halls for Democratic meetings, and in August the Rock Mills Democratic Club and the Grange held a "united demonstration." Obviously richly varied political activities were in play.[3]

Deadly conflict erupted during the summer, most of it elsewhere in the state. The *Keowee Courier* on June 9 virtually endorsed the lynching of an Abbeville black man for "savage butchery" of a white couple. Six weeks later fourteen armed black men pursued John Wilson from Abbeville into Anderson County. They had a warrant for his arrest, but failed to capture him, and wounded instead a black man at Belton. The *Intelligencer* complained that "their conduct was unlawful and seditious . . . [and] insolent."[4]

More violence occurred farther south. Conflict leading to the "Hamburg riot" began on July 4. Captain Doc Adams was drilling his militia company when two young white men, arriving in a carriage, demanded passage through the blocked and "deserted street." According to one partisan account the soldiers "cursed and vilified them in the grossest manner" and beat their drums around the horse's head to frighten it. The father of one of the white fellows secured services of General M. C. Butler, Confederate hero, attorney, and leader of Edgefield County rifle clubs.

On July 8 Butler approached black legislator, Hamburg mayor Prince Rivers, also formerly captain of that company, asking for an apology and disarmament. As trial justice, Rivers negotiated between Butler and Adams.

Adams refused these requests, which evidently pleased Butler and other Edgefield whites. According to Joel Williamson's *After Slavery*, their intent "apparently was the disarming of the Hamburg militia.... Militant Redeemers were set to provide the Negro voter with a horrible example of the awful force which lay behind the white man's threats." After Butler got reinforcements—men and cannon—from Augusta, his forces attacked the militia in the armory where they retreated. They returned fire from a window and killed one white man, the first death. Whites retaliated with cannon. Two of the militia trying to escape were killed, nearly thirty more were captured, and leaders were deliberately separated and shot. In some areas, especially Charleston, "among Negroes indignation rose to the danger point." Upper piedmont's black reaction was probably both angered and fearful. During the next two months whites throughout South Carolina deliberately avoided further armed conflict, but any remaining Conservative ties to Chamberlain dissolved.[5]

It is worth considering why upper-piedmont whites were so concerned, even before these events, to reclaim "their" government. As a majority, they held virtually all local elective offices, Democrats with rare exceptions, and the legislative delegations from the three counties were all white. Republicans dominated appointive offices, especially treasurers and auditors, and had a sizable number of trial justices and notary publics, virtually all of them white. And Republicans, including blacks, could shape the district's Congressional choice. Yet whites clearly were determined to eliminate even these limited roles. Fundamentally, they considered black involvement in politics as too much independence, even insolence. This required complete black political subjugation as attempted in 1868 but now done on a statewide basis.

Most whites throughout South Carolina concurred, the political scene seemed favorable, and Democrats found a viable gubernatorial candidate. Meeting in Columbia on August 15, the state Democratic convention followed six weeks after the Hamburg riot, which thus intensified delegates' emotions. They selected Wade Hampton, who periodically after 1865 appeared at various public meetings and in letters and speeches reproduced in the press. Addressing reunions of his own and other Civil War brigades, Hampton kept his name before the public. On July 4, 1876, he led a Charleston procession marking the nation's centennial. The Democratic platform pledged "genuine and thorough reform" in government and invited "all citizens, irrespective of race, color or previous condition, to rally with us to its redemption." The *Pickens Sentinel* proclaimed that "if any man in the State can command the full white vote, it is Hampton."[6]

Shortly after becoming Democratic nominee, Hampton took his campaign upstate into white-majority counties. He traveled the Columbia–Anderson–Walhalla railroad route, with stops at Belton and Pendleton and speeches at most towns. His September 2 appearance in Anderson was called the "grandest political demonstration" there in fifteen years, that is, since celebrating secession. The rally included, as elsewhere, rifle clubs and Hampton guards, both illegally armed.[7]

"Red Shirts" quickly became Hampton's campaign insignia. Many parts of the state claimed to have originated the symbol. One local version, which the *Columbia Register* supported in April 1877, attributed it to Pendleton men, choosing red flannel as their rally insignia. Hampton campaigned to recapture state government but tried also to appeal to black voters. Hampton boasted that he was the first southern white man to support black suffrage; however, his views then sharply limited it. He also, in words of a later era, appealed to "bring us together," susceptible of more than one interpretation.[8]

Juxtaposed against these Red Shirts, often mounted, black Democratic clubs and Red Shirts advertised Hampton's position that he would serve both black and white. Presumably these men fell to their landlords' intimidation and coercion. Combined paternalism and intimidation evidently became more difficult to withstand during fall 1876. Especially in Pickens and Oconee, however, it should have been clear to black Republicans that, with only 25 percent of the voting population, they could not achieve any electoral victory. They may, then, have been pragmatically susceptible to white cajoling. In mid-October the *Intelligencer* reported that five hundred black men rode with the Anderson "rifle clubs." Although associated with Hampton's 1876 campaign, black Democratic clubs survived in Anderson at late as 1878.[9]

Democrats feverishly created and publicized black clubs during September and October. Former Governor Perry, speaking to the Walhalla club in early September, urged those present to vote with whites. Two weeks later Hampton spoke to fifty African Americans; the *Keowee Courier* listed their names as members of Walhalla's Democratic club. The next day both men addressed a Honea Path crowd in what the *Intelligencer* called a grand finale to Hampton's personal upcountry campaign. Reportedly two thousand mounted, uniformed men attended—almost exactly the total of all white-owned horses in Anderson County—as did two hundred blacks. Although reporting a "Hampton colored club" in Anderson town, the *Intelligencer* gave no hint of its membership numbers.[10]

Enormous pressures bore down on black men during the campaign. Hints appeared in the September 28 *Pickens Sentinel:* "We hear that . . . colored voters have commenced renouncing Radicalism.—Look for a stampede about the 7th of November. . . . Give the colored men who vote with you employment and good wages, and protect him in all his rights, but let those who vote against you take care of himself, or go to his carpet-bag friends for help and protection." Two weeks later William Turner felt obligated to deny rumors that he organized a Dacusville-area rifle team. An early-October public Democratic meeting in Seneca included several black speakers.

Most contemporary accounts come from the *Intelligencer,* recounting only pressure against black Democrats, not any against Republicans. Hoyt's newspaper charged on August 17 that they, trying to prevent others from joining Democrats, "will inaugurate mob law." The guilty must be punished and "adequate protection given the colored men who seek to unite with the Democrats."[11] Frequent appearances of mounted Hampton guards seem to have had just that effect.

White influence on black Democratic clubs coupled with mounted displays of force accurately reflect the mixture of paternalism and oppression that characterized white reactions to black voting. Frequent requests appeared in the upper-piedmont press for landlords to read announcements—virtually orders—to tenants. The *Pickens Sentinel* on June 22 argued that as a class, "colored" voters were "not capable of comprehending or appreciating newspaper arguments." But, the editor contended, these voters would more readily believe their employers than newspapers. Ten weeks later the same editor described the "Campaign in the State" as encouraging for Democracy: "The negro, for the first time since emancipation, has an opportunity of having his old master and friend talk to him on the political issues of the day."

Similarly, the October 26 *Intelligencer* said that "every citizen should endeavor to induce the colored men of our County to attend the Consolidated meetings next week." And the *Sentinel*'s November 2 mandate was unmistakable: "Let every colored man in this County be visited by some influential Democrat before the election, and explain to them the importance of voting for Hampton."

A lull in armed conflict following the Hamburg riot ceased by September. Then more confrontations occurred in both Charleston and Ellenton (Aiken County), and another near Cainhoy (Charleston County) in October. Chamberlain, citing these and other disturbances, urged Grant to send troops to South Carolina. Based on the governor's description of "lawlessness, violence and terrorism," Grant on October 17 ordered troops to prevent "insurrection and domestic violence." His action and the army's presence angered white Democrats. All circuit court judges and many grand juries—including a unanimous decision by Anderson's, consisting of both white and black jurors—condemned Chamberlain's characterization of the state. No similar violence marked Anderson, Oconee, and Pickens counties, partly because of paternalism combined with discreet pressure and potential force by whites.

A New York *Herald* reporter in Columbia described South Carolina's politics as volatile as nitroglycerin. Certainly the next six months were explosive. Using different terms, the *Pickens Sentinel* told of a Republican meeting held in Pickens, Monday, October 23, when about two hundred people attended. Democrats, asking in advance for equal speakers' time, were refused. But "two hundred and fifty mounted Democrats [equaling half the county's white-owned horses], in their [red shirt] campaign regalia" arrived early. Then "a circle was formed around the improvised Republican stand, completely closing in all the Republicans." Democrats gave "three rousing cheers" for Hampton and "frequently interrupted" Republican speakers. The *Sentinel* editor left little to the reader's imagination or that of black voters.[12] Hampton supporters perfected their intimidation tactics while neatly avoiding bodily harm except in calculated situations such as Hamburg.

Other intimidation and resulting fears echoed in black and white Republican letters to Chamberlain. On October 10 twenty-one black men from lower Anderson County wrote the governor: "Collored leaders of the Republican party [want] some protection from the unlawful violence & threats that is being forced on us by the Democrat Clubs coming to our houses calling us out & threatening our lives, taking us out of our fields & making us promise to vote for Hampton & leaving bunches of switches near our houses with threats what they will do if we don't vote for Hampton." That same day white J. E. Nevill declined Chamberlain's appointment as election commissioner due to "politicks high in this country 180 [degrees] in the shade."

Some public complaints may be exaggerated, like Reconstruction rhetoric by all sides, but similar themes appear in private letters. After the election, E. R. Brown of Belton wrote: These are "hard times with the Poor colord people that voted Republican tickets[;] the democrats will not let them have any thing to Eat or any work to do I don't see how we are to live they say [we] shal not work thar land if we work anybodys land it will be Mr. Chamberlains land who we voted for."[13]

More violent attacks rang through Alexander Bryce Jr.'s December 15 account, informing Chamberlain of "some trouble in this county and Pickens." Arriving while Bryce was writing, James Goldman—probably a former Calhoun slave—brought news of a white man telling others "to go upt in the Mountain and get his Rifle Demmocat Clube to come down Kill the dam chamberlian negros." A group of fifteen to twenty white men shot black Jacer Buttle in the arm, Goldman reported. "They got hold of Buttles daughter beat and abused her. . . . Shamefully and drew thier guns on Buttles wife and threatened her with Violence." They dragged Fred Vance from his hiding place into the yard, beat him, and said "dam you if you Ever vote again you will vote for Hampton." Badly battered, Vance was expected to die. Bryce said other black men, hiding fearfully in the woods and at his house, "are a fraid to go back near Pendleton at a place call fort Hill in this County."

Views of black males can be deduced only from their actions, the white press, and a few letters to Reconstruction governors. Newspapers reported many conflicts between Republicans and other blacks who publicly endorsed Hampton. Among the most active Anderson Republicans, Samuel Johnson publicly announced that he would support Hayes for president but vote Hampton Democrats for state offices. Following Johnson's line, an October 30 black meeting in Anderson's courthouse passed a resolution for peace between the races.[14] The *Intelligencer* predicted on November 2, "If one-half of the white voters in Anderson County will vote one colored man for Hampton, his majority in Anderson County will reach over FOUR THOUSAND! This fact alone should be sufficient incentive to a powerful and united effort next Tuesday." Such a result of white enthusiasm would hardly occur without enormous pressure, intimidation hardly veiled.

Because men dominated politics, it is difficult to determine women's attitudes. Like Buttle's wife and daughter in 1876 and Henrietta Moore in 1868, they suffered fear, humiliation, and physical abuse. Regardless, some endured, insisted that their husbands vote Republican, and beat a few husbands who did not do so, according to the *Intelligencer*. One aged woman—fearful because of rumors that if Hampton was elected, blacks would be returned to slavery—went to see Cochran. Otherwise opposed to Hampton, he assured her that the story was false.[15] Knowing their wives' fears and dangers may have kept many men from voting. They were also eager to protect their livelihood and homes against potential evictions of their families.

Election and Aftermath

Despite much intimidation throughout the state and pitched battles in numerous locations, locally voting day itself passed calmly. Cochran and Hoyt, usually opposed, worked together to prevent both disturbances and federal troops being present at polling booths. Agreeing, the sheriff sent constables—evidently all white marshals, including some Republicans—to each precinct. Military personnel remained available if needed, but were not called in Anderson, Oconee, and Pickens counties. Most precincts had one black Republican manager plus a black federally designated Republican supervisor for the presidential election; there were also white Democratic and Republican staff.[16]

The November vote hardly settled the campaign. Rather, it precipitated five more months of controversy and chaos. Chamberlain challenged Hampton's claim to have won the election. Upper-piedmont newspapers printed only sketchy reports of the vote. According to figures they did publish and interpretations based on them, sixty to a hundred blacks voted for Hampton in Oconee and Pickens and nearly seven hundred did so in Anderson. White votes in Oconee were nearly double, but in Anderson one and a half times those of 1870. There, Chamberlain won a majority only at one Anderson town precinct. Area newspapers soon reported blacks as saying they now thought Hampton would do a good job and that, although casting

Table 16.1 **Eligible Voters and Votes Cast by Race and by Party, 1876**

	Anderson County		Oconee County		Pickens County	
1. males 21+	3329 W	2215 B	2046 W	703 B	1814 W	545 B
2. Nov./race	3465 W	1858 B	2018 W	631 B	1926 W	512 B
3. gov./party	4155 D	1124 R	2083 D	524 R	2002 D	406 R

1. numbers of adult males, white and black, from 1875 state census;
2. numbers of white and black voters in November, by race; and
3. numbers of Democratic and Republican votes in gubernatorial race.

W = White; B = Black; D = Democrat; R = Republican

Sources: According to these figures, 136 more white men voted in Anderson than were 21 or older in the 1875 census. Figures for (1) and (3) come from various Nov. issues of *AI, KC*, and *PS* in 1876, 1878, and 1880, plus *Reports and Resolutions, 1877; PS* and *AI*, both Nov. 23; *KC* printed full results; racial composition for Anderson voting from data in S. M. Pegg, *General Descriptive Map of Anderson, S.C.* (New York: Charles Hart, 1877).

a ballot for Chamberlain that year, they would vote for Hampton next time. The *Intelligencer* advised whites to be magnanimous in victory and continue to hire men who voted Republican, but to offer them lower wages. Whites confidently reveled in their continuing electoral supremacy, which they held for nearly a century.

South Carolina's gubernatorial election was challenged as part of the Tilden-Hayes presidential toss-up in the electoral college. Newly redeemed Louisiana, Florida, and South Carolina all faced contested U.S. House of Representatives seats; the disputed presidential selection rested on these choices. Within South Carolina rival state houses, one Democratic and the other Republican, claimed to be authentically elected and installed. Disputed elections in both Edgefield and Laurens would tilt the state balance.

Chamberlain had federal troops at the state capitol protecting him and his electoral claim. The dual governments of legislators and governors competed as Hampton and Chamberlain both had swearing-in ceremonies. Many Hampton supporters during early 1877 paid their taxes into a special fund rather than to Republican county treasurers. Newspapers contained long columns of those doing so, including 155 Anderson and nearly 50 Oconee blacks, most likely under pressure.[17]

Both parties demanded rights to appointive offices. Hampton's auditors in Oconee and Pickens seized records from their Republican predecessors, who did not yield willingly. Retaliating, Bryce broke into the Walhalla office to recover his books, which led to his arrest. Both gubernatorial claimants made black appointments, Chamberlain of W. R. Parker as trial justice and Hampton of Samuel Johnson as election commissioner. Johnson's appointment occurred despite Anderson County Democratic Club objections and later earned a grand-jury protest.[18]

Meanwhile, national politics surrounding the Tilden-Hayes decision subsumed South Carolina's controversies. High-level deals by southern Democrats, acting also for Florida and Louisiana, allowed Hampton to take office while delivering South Carolina votes to Republican Rutherford B. Hayes. He then withdrew troops from both the capitol, effective April 10, and the state; Chamberlain surrendered office to Hampton on April 11.[19]

Broader conflicts had little impact on northwestern South Carolina whites. Months earlier they celebrated Hampton's victory—and, they thought, that of white people in general—with torchlight parades and other festivities. Had they known the hymn, they would have appreciated its lyrics, "Redeemed, how I love to proclaim it!" Hampton's election also inaugurated a new period of sharply reduced black political impact. G. D. Williams, however, wrote in May 1877 that "colored people will be so well pleased with him as Governor" that they will help elect him again. "I sincerely believe that Hampton will protect your rights," he said, a sharp turn from his own posture six months earlier.[20]

From 1877 until the 1895 constitution, black men in decreasing numbers continued to vote, to express publicly their political opinions, to appear in jury pools, to serve on coroners' juries, and to prop up a greatly weakened Republican party.

However, they would not regain similar prospects of significant political influence envisioned between 1865 and 1876. Moreover, black people no longer had any support from the state government, now virtually devoid of black legislators and state officials, or any active federal protection. Hampton's regime quickly disbanded black militia units throughout the state. Blacks might have found "slough of despair" a more appropriate slogan than "redeemed."

After 1876: Declining Political Roles
Although black men still voted throughout the remaining quarter of the century and participated in Republican clubs, their roles declined. When four black voters were disqualified following August 1877 Anderson town elections, loss of those ballots changed the original Republican majority into a Democratic victory. Major W. W. Humphreys now won by two, and Anderson had an all-white Democratic town council again, as did Honea Path. Verbal assaults paralleled political machinations; that same month an *Intelligencer* reprint complained of a not-guilty "nigger verdict" by a "nigger jury."[21]

Many societal issues surrounded Hampton's victory and redemption of the state. They occurred during the years that harsh weather conditions produced smaller crops of both cotton and foodstuffs, and cotton prices declined. Both black and white were experiencing religious fervor, revivals, camp meetings, and substantially increased church membership. Whiskey wagons and lewd women in bawdy houses provided ample targets for moral outrage. Several white men in 1870 burned an Oconee house, "one of ill fame[,] and the raid was made" to drive the white woman and her daughter out of the neighborhood. Interracial couples often encountered neighborhood ire, and Greenville County's courts accused five interracial couples of adultery in 1881–82.[22] Both the *Anderson Intelligencer* and the *Keowee Courier* began using more racist language.

Hampton personally avoided sharp statements against blacks and often made verbal assurances that he was their friend. His followers exercised less restraint. As both black voting and the Republican Party's fortunes declined, conditions for African Americans at the state penitentiary quickly became oppressive under Hampton. Increasingly its population was mostly black. In 1877, 108 black convicts died, compared to 13 in 1870. Only 20 black prisoners were pardoned contrasted to 46 under Orr in 1867 and 112 under Scott in 1870. As the prison system began leasing convicts to farmers and to railroad companies, many convict laborers died. Convict presence throughout the state reinforced an image of "negro crime."[23]

While harsh attitudes by whites gradually intensified, black political participation waned. By contrast, white Oconee Red Shirts celebrated their second anniversary in 1878 with a barbecue, addressed by Murray, Orr, and others. Pendleton festivities included Hampton's cavalry officers. There General E. W. Moise "told the colored people . . . that they were freer, happier and more prosperous under Democratic rule than they were under the government of their own choice."[24]

That same day a "Radical Pow-Wow at Townville," originally planned for Saturday at nearby Parker's Church, was shifted to Friday. Altering their meeting date on short notice, Republicans hoped to prevent mounted Democrats from attending. However, three Red Shirt companies at Pendleton's celebration learned of this change, then quickly rode to the rally. Hoyt and new *Intelligencer* editor E. B. Murray, both Hampton colonels, led the dash to Townville. Democrats effectively took over this Republican rally, as they frequently did in 1876. Murray instructed "colored people" that, as a minority, they were wasting their time on politics. He verbally attacked Parker repeatedly and got him to admit using a church collection for travel to the Radical state convention. Murray, in the same issue reporting Parker's meeting, editorially commended black Presiding Elder James Rosemond (Methodist Episcopal, North), who told his district ministers that they "were desired not to meddle with politics, but to give their whole attention to their ministerial duties."[25]

Various political meetings continued throughout the fall. Approximately fifty Oconee Republicans gathered at the courthouse to discuss candidates. Red Shirt companies hovered nearby but made no overt effort to disrupt this late-September meeting. The newspaper praised chairman Johnson Wright, who "has a good record as a slave, and since freedom he has shown himself to be a thrifty and industrious colored man." At a Democratic mass meeting two weeks later the chairman told the crowd, "The Caucasian race has ever and will ever rule, unless it fritters away its opportunities by divisions." A few days later the *Intelligencer* more bluntly advised "colored people" to vote Democratic, in appreciation for good rulers, that is, Hampton and his followers.

This barbed advice failed. Numbers of black voters dropped significantly compared to 1876, but racial vitriol followed anyway. Reporting that Williamston black men voted for "Radical Parker" as legislative candidate, an unsigned letter in the *Temperance Standard* said to let Republicans find land for them to work, it won't be mine.[26] And on October 31 the *Keowee Courier* used a filler containing the word "nigger," not yet its normal practice.

Elections occurred in two stages in 1878. At varying October dates Pickens, Oconee, and Anderson held Democratic primaries; unfortunately newspapers reported only sketchy results. Over three hundred black voters participated in Pickens, the *Keowee Courier* said; both Pickens and Oconee ballots had only white candidates. As a Republican, Parker appeared only on Anderson's November 5 general election ballot; then he lost. That year black men still served among federally appointed Republican supervisors: twenty in Anderson; four in Oconee with white Republicans at ten other precincts; and only whites in Pickens. The Republican candidate for U.S. Congress garnered 550 votes in the three counties, only 25 of them in Pickens, despite the report noted above. But Belton voters in early 1879 chose black James Robertson among its six-member town council.[27]

General election results have not been found. Oconee blacks voted only in the congressional race and bypassed all Democratic county and state candidates according to the *Keowee Courier.* Parker's candidacy and the presence of black supervisors may have encouraged more voters in Anderson. Generally, however, 1878 had the last significant black participation. Almost simultaneously Alexander Bryce Jr., a contentious leader of Oconee Republicans and the one white defendant in the Hunnicutt case, was murdered.[28]

Tools to dissuade black voters included the white primary and other innovations. Use of Democratic primaries soon effectively guaranteed election of individuals that the white power structure sanctioned as whites united behind one candidate in general elections. In a black-minority area, then, this virtually nullified black votes. Primaries afforded Democrats another advantage; they were free from federal supervisors. Further, the 1882 "eight-box law" forced voters to cast separate ballots for each position and deposit them in the proper box. Other statutes made the process even more complicated. Redistricting in 1882 guaranteed that a gerrymandered third congressional district, sprawling from Newberry to Oconee but excluding Anderson, would have a white-majority vote and thus a white, Democratic congressman. Pickens's black/Republican vote shrank from 512 in 1876 to about 100 in 1884.[29]

Black Republicans sustained some efforts throughout the 1880s with meetings, barbecues, and votes in federal elections. Two national guard companies in Pickens in 1879 had black men and officers, including teachers C. T. Miller and W. D. Jenkins. In post-Reconstruction years only a few black Republicans served as town officials, gubernatorially appointed election or jury commissioners, or election managers, and few as party supervisors. Although blacks continued to appear in jury pools in the 1880s, only a tiny number served as jurors except for coroners' inquests, where county officials meticulously included them whenever the deceased was black. Voting and jury service become more difficult to trace.[30]

Clearly polarized Anderson politicking and pressure to vote Democratic occurred in 1884. When Democrats had a "Grand Rally" with all "white and colored, old and young" invited, reportedly two thousand turned out to hear Hampton speak. Only black men attended the Republican county convention to choose state convention delegates. But after elections "two enthusiastic colored Democrats paraded" on muleback in Pickens with an American flag and red flannel hatbands as they cheered for Cleveland. "They are sensible darkies and are entitled to the respect and confidence of the white Democrats of the County," the *Sentinel* editor exuded. Meanwhile the *Keowee Courier* lambasted the "treachery" of seventeen black men who participated in the Democratic primary, then attended the Republican county convention.

Political involvement slowly dwindled. C. T. Miller served in 1891 as a federal juror. A Pickens Republican meeting in October 1892 drew four white and forty black attendees; they sent three black delegates—men not involved in politics during the 1870s—to their state convention. New leaders similarly dominated Anderson's Republican party.[31] The 1892 Republican presidential and congressional candidates garnered 745 votes in Anderson, Oconee, and Pickens counties. White attitudes led to a new, restrictive "Jim Crow" constitution by 1895, eight years after the first lynching in the three-county area. Although their political roles and impact on elections eroded markedly after Hampton's 1876 victory, African Americans pursued community building in other avenues. Williamson observes in *Crucible of Race* that political and other "energies that were encountering rejection in the broad white world were now being vested in local and very tangible enclaves."[32]

SEVENTEEN

Community Building ∻ Churches and Schools

AS EXPRESSIONS OF THEIR FREEDOM, African Americans soon established their own churches, which drew on antebellum experiences, and schools.[1] Churches were the first institutions freed blacks created in the upstate, as in Charleston and Columbia. Leadership often came from those who were deacons, elders, and lay preachers during slavery, as well as from men who were literate. Three of eight men incorporating St. Paul Baptist Church in 1870 had been slaves of attorney J. P. Reed, and a fourth had been owned by Samuel Earle. Although not moving immediately and massively from white ones, Baptists in Anderson, Belton, and Honea Path established churches—all called Liberty or Freedmen—within months after emancipation. Most people, however, remained within former churches for another year or two, some even longer.

Freed people also eagerly sought education for themselves and their children. The Freedmen's Bureau and northern philanthropic organizations helped provide buildings, teachers, and books. Hundreds of African Americans, many of them adults, flocked to schools beginning in spring 1866. Both men and women—local and northern, white and black, military and civilian—taught in these schools. In some cases, notably Anderson and Pendleton, freed people created their own boards and controlled institutions themselves.

As with Reconstruction politics, most educational and religious leaders came from long-standing local families; they included Jemima Pickens's grandson and George and Betty Wiggins's sons. Churches and schools, centrally located within the community, frequently shared facilities and sometimes leadership. Numerous ministers or their family members served as teachers.[2] Families often collectively invested in church and school property before they could afford their own.

Locally a minority, African Americans were almost always circumscribed by whites. Over 99 percent of blacks who worked did so for white employers or landlords in the 1870s. Schools and churches, distinctly black, became important cornerstones for the community.

Postbellum White Churches and Freed People
Although some areas of the state had black congregations during antebellum years,[3] upper-piedmont churches included slaves, free people of color, and whites. Racial

attitudes of these churches, increasingly white-identified soon after emancipation, are a surprisingly complicated story. Departures from these churches—often called an exodus—were not simultaneous and followed no single pattern based on denomination, geography, or timetable. Although churches were not yet wholly white, church authorities were—many of them former slave owners, now landlords for whom freed people worked. No other issue so clearly demonstrates ambivalent attitudes between freed people and former owners during the 1865–70 period.

Documentation for Anderson County is much more abundant than for Oconee or Pickens, so Anderson is our primary focus. Virtually all information comes from "white" church minutes and association records.[4] Anderson's church leadership adopted quite different postures toward their freed congregants. Some demanded that freed people leave and establish their own; others offered help if they wished to organize new churches; and a few "white" churches still included black members as late as the 1880s. First Creek Baptists (Anderson) during 1869 and 1870 offered their old pulpit to a nearby black church, dismissed five black members by their request, and restored a black woman to membership. There seems to be no easy explanation for these varied patterns within just one county.

Generally, few freed people left white-controlled churches in 1865; some did so in 1866, and even more in 1867; and most, but not all, departed by 1870. Several deterrents slowed the process of establishing new churches. Freedom brought few changes in the overall social structure in 1865 or 1866; physical survival—shelter, food, and work—was a more immediate priority for most people than were new churches. Moreover, whites did not initially eject freed members; retaining them provided scrutiny and supervision. And starting new churches encountered obstacles of limited education, logistics of church organization, and money. Establishing churches, however, moved so rapidly during freedom's first decade that by 1877 Anderson County already had forty black Baptist and Methodist churches and over four thousand members, exceeding the black population aged twenty-one or older.[5]

The war's end had little immediate impact in Anderson, Oconee, and Pickens counties, and churches acted in ambiguous ways. Big Creek Baptist Church, with sixty-seven black members (20 percent), made on September 30, 1865, the area's first formal statement regarding freed people: that whenever "colored members . . . leave their former owners without leave, they shall notify the church" and "apply for letters of dismission within the space of six months or their names shall be erased from the church book." The church that had enjoyed Caesar's preaching in the 1820s became the first to begin clearing its roll of black members. The church in March 1866 required freed people wishing to remain to declare their intentions; only six complied. This device of compiling a new roll and requiring freed people to request to remain members would be followed by other churches.[6]

Anderson's Mount Pisgah Baptists went through several attitudes, eventually stern, toward former slaves after happier relations earlier in the year. The church in March 1866 authorized its pastor to hold services for "colored members," and in

May offered "the privilege of dismissions from the church in order to form a separate church." Or, if they preferred, they could remain, vote on their own new members, and—if charged with offenses—be tried by "there own collar." Mount Pisgah in June granted use of its building for a Sabbath school "if properly conducted"—permission was revoked two months later. But three blacks joined during the protracted August meeting, and in September there was another sermon for freed people. This strange ambivalence continued for another year—black reception of new members and supervision over straying ones and white-imposed restrictions; at the same time blacks comprised almost 40 percent of the congregation.

Although only Big Creek and Mount Pisgah expressed hostility or sternness toward black members in 1866, other churches purged membership rolls. Mountain Creek (Anderson) called its freed people to a February 1866 meeting and then in May inserted into the minutes "Names of the Colored members . . . [with] names of their former owners," that is, fourteen individuals, by their personal names and their former owners' surnames. Also in May Hopewell Presbyterian had its clerk compile a new membership list; after purging absentees, its result was a decline to 28 percent blacks from their antebellum figure of 39 percent.

Given widespread confusion and perplexity on how to deal with freed members, the South Carolina Baptist Convention urged constituent associations to draft standards. Edgefield Baptists in fall 1865 decided to "disapprove of their being organized into separated Churches, or assemblages apart from the usual meetings, to be under the guidance of ignorant, unqualified, and unauthorized persons."[7] Some "unauthorized" leaders may have had enthusiastic interpretations of freedom and political ideas unpalatable to the white establishment.

Saluda Baptists, grappling with this same issue a year later, found it more complicated. Deacons confessed in 1866 that they had very little experience for a matter involving "the future church relations of the colored people." The association recommended in August 1866 that if "colored people prefer to remain . . . it will be better for them to do so." But if freed people "prefer to be organized into separate churches, . . . it will be wise, regularly to dismiss them for the constitution of separate churches, to aid them by kind counsels, and, as far as possible, other means, and to persuade them to secure for themselves, the benefits of an intelligent ministry." As in politics, whites sought to determine the paths blacks should follow. Generally, churches acted along these guidelines, but association and South Carolina Baptist Convention resolutions had no binding effect.

Churches throughout the post-May 1865 period continued to exclude individual black members, as did Mount Pisgah, even while receiving new ones. First Creek Baptist removed Cudjo, "formerly a slave of Tucker May," in June 1866 for stealing, cursing, and swearing. Cases involving theft or issues generally grouped as immorality—drunkenness, dancing, card playing, adultery, and fornication—do not seem to have varied from their antebellum level, and whites were also being excluded for similar offenses. Congregations now, however, used additional charges to expel lapsed freed members who were not attending or who joined another church. Old Westminster Baptist (Oconee) in September 1866 excluded five for joining the black Methodist church. Mountain Creek Baptist in 1868 dropped one who joined an "irregular" black church; one church noted in 1868 that among "colored communicants . . . all quit."

Like several other churches, Varennes Presbyterian in September 1869 passed a resolution "That the names of the coloured people, except those who . . . signified their desire to remain, . . . be erased from our roll"; three people "desire to remain in This church Sept 13 1869." At least four had "gone to the Negro baptist church" and one to the Methodists; five others moved to Georgia, Florida, and Arkansas; and one died. The next fall most remaining members left by choice over a four-month period.

Major disruptions, by contrast, occurred between freed members and Pendleton's Presbyterian and Methodist churches in 1867–69. Hopewell, which in 1858 had thirty-nine black congregants, evidently two of them free, dropped to twenty-nine after its 1866 purge of absentees. The following year the church noted that twenty-nine "have removed without letter of dismission." Others must have joined as nine people remained, including one free black woman. Pendleton's white Baptists there lost nearly 60 percent of their black members between 1867 and 1869 but retained some until 1874. St. Paul's Episcopal Church was still confirming new black members and marrying freed people.

A sudden rupture, however, occurred among Pendleton's Methodists. Sparse information comes from a statement seventy years later to a WPA interviewer that, when the church refused to "funeralize a colored member," the others all left. Walking out of a white-controlled church holds an important role in Methodist legacy, as when Charleston's Trinity Methodist Church black members in 1865 followed their leader, who said, "there will be no galleries in heaven." Pendleton's white congregants, evidently not expecting a sudden reaction, were clearly startled. Their supervising body, the Cokesbury District, quickly created a separate Pendleton "colored circuit," one of several.[8] It soon had 230 members, and 310 a year later, more than a third of all Anderson County's black Methodists. By 1870 African Americans had in Pendleton both a black Methodist (northern) church and the area's first African Methodist Episcopal (AME) one; and "colored circuits" were disbanded. As AME work, concentrated along the coast in 1865, moved upstate slowly, Pendleton became a major AME foothold in the upper piedmont.[9]

Methodists were not the major drawing card. Just as several Varennes Presbyterians joined a Baptist or a Methodist church, freed people often chose churches for proximity and family reasons as for denominational preference, as whites often did. Especially in the 1860s and 1870s, few locales had more than one denominational option. Black Presbyterians and Episcopalians often joined Baptist or Methodist congregations as there were no black Episcopal churches in Anderson, Oconee, or Pickens counties, and only four small Presbyterian ones as late as 1900. By 1868 there were thirteen Baptist churches in Anderson County, several in Pickens and Oconee, and industrious black Methodist endeavors. More freed people began leaving their former churches as they had opportunity to join a new one.

Churches that African Americans attended as slaves took increasingly divergent, ambiguous, and conflicted attitudes as political events and attitudes often converged with sterner church postures. Mountain Creek Baptists authorized James Williford in July 1867 to use his religious gifts, presumably as exhorter. Political tensions soon escalated. During the November 1867 election period, James Williford and Major Williford "declared their determination to renounce the Union League and remain with the church," a decision not likely reached without enormous pressure. Not completely penitent, both Willifords continued to attend league meetings and were cited the following May. The church in June 1868 excluded James for "disorderly and unchristian conduct," specifically for being ordained by "some coulered men" without Mountain Creek's approval and for his new church not being regularly established. Mountain Creek veered into the political realm, using its power of exclusion for reasons other than religion, and First Creek excluded Mulberry Mauldin, recently approved as an elder.

Although white Baptists both expressed support throughout the next two decades and offered assistance in training black ministers, their sentiments were not entirely altruistic. Whites wanted close scrutiny of clergy, as shown in Edgefield's 1865 resolution and during the Miles Hunnicutt inquest, when obtaining names of preachers involved in politics was a special topic of interrogation. Complaints about James Williford's "irregular ordination" meant that he should have received not only proper spiritual sanction of his work but also—using a regular ecclesiastical process—probing into his views.

Big Creek enacted the sternest, most hostile posture toward freed people continuing in a church. It said, in essence, "get out!" The "colored membership . . . distinct people . . . [s]hould have their own Church organizations, and attend to their own Business in their own Churches." Mount Pisgah adopted in April 1869 a briefer, milder version; by autumn, the church had only one remaining black member. Those who left organized New Mount Pisgah, located nearby on land from white Ezekiel Long. Its 126 members in 1874 were more than double those who left the old church.[10]

Not all wanted to leave, however, and black members remained in perhaps a dozen churches until the late 1870s. After purging its rolls again in 1868, Hopewell Presbyterian still had six active black members. Anderson Presbyterian had sixteen, and in Belton, the Presbyterians had four. At least seven Saluda Baptist churches collectively retained more than fifty black members in 1874, and three still had some in 1878. By then all upper-piedmont white churches and denominations stopped reporting racial breakdowns of membership. Among those still in mostly white churches more than twenty years after emancipation, a man who joined First Creek as "C Wakefields Sanders" in 1863 withdrew on September 25, 1886—

Silver Spring Baptist Church, Pendleton, built ca. 1870s; perhaps AOP's oldest-surviving black church building. Black Heritage in the Upper Piedmont

evidently its last black member. After St. Paul's Episcopal Church performed eleven black marriages in the early 1880s, Margaret Maverick's death in 1885 was the final reference to a black member.[11]

Hostility or relative peacefulness of departures seem to fit no particular pattern, nor does timing. Most white-identified churches did not begin to push black members out until 1868 and 1869, but at quite different times. Denominations did not act uniformly—Hopewell Presbyterian purged its rolls in 1868, but Roberts kept most black members until autumn 1870, when they left slowly and willingly. Geography alone does not fully explain matters either. Hopewell's exclusion of absent members in Pendleton coincides generally with the flare-up at the Methodist church, but Episcopalians and Baptists there had no similar experience. Baptists did not establish a church there, Silver Spring, until 1874. Many local conditions, most of them now unfathomable, evidently affected these varied patterns.

Timing seems a more critical factor than location or denomination. Most efforts by white-identified churches to reduce or end their black membership occurred between fall 1867 and 1869. Pendleton Methodist and Presbyterian withdrawals and sanctions on Williford and Mauldin all coincided with the 1867–69 formation of Union Leagues (especially at Pleasant Grove), voter registration, fall elections, the Hunnicutt crisis, and spring 1868 elections.[12]

Yet some churches retained black members into the 1870s; the Saluda Association continued sporadic training for black leadership in later decades; and some all-white churches still allowed black burials in their cemeteries fifty years later—truly divergent and not easily explained currents amid substantial local variations. The African American exodus from specific white-controlled churches spanned barely three years. Blacks moved as rapidly and energetically to establish their own churches as they did to unite families and to vote.

Black Churches, 1865–1900

Chronicling the process of establishing churches is not easy. Virtually all lack contemporary records or any histories written prior to 1920, and white-owned newspapers made only sporadic references. For Anderson County, however, there are numerous, if incomplete, sources including that compiled by a WPA researcher in the 1930s. New churches in 1865–67, according to their later histories, began in three towns: Liberty Baptist in Honea Path; Freedmen's Church, later called New Hope Missionary Baptist, just outside Belton; First Freedmen's, later St. Paul Baptist; and a Methodist congregation in Anderson. The fourteen others founded prior to 1870 were all Baptist. More than half of them were either in towns or within four miles of towns, others were in dense black clusters, such as New Light Baptists on Adger land near Pendleton.[13]

Baptists thrived in immediate postemancipation years partly because white Baptists dominated. Contrasted to more hierarchical Methodist and Presbyterian churches, Baptist congregations could organize without conference or synod sanction. Similarly, ministerial appointments did not require credentials or higher approval. Frank Morris (b. 1817) and his son Philip (b. 1841) founded several Baptist churches, three each by 1868, and served additional ones during the next decade. Frank Morris became embroiled in early internecine squabbling. St. Paul Baptists in June 1868 expelled him for "immoral and unchristian conduct" following a church trial and publicized it in a paid Anderson newspaper advertisement. Clerk Napoleon Gaillard was deeply involved in politics, so the conflict may have been partly political—especially likely since the trial occurred shortly after county elections and because Morris's reputation survived despite the censure.[14]

Literate, both Morrises led in organizing on August 14, 1868, the Rocky River Baptist Association. Frank Morris served several years as president. Delegates from thirteen Baptist churches in or near Anderson County jointly founded the association, only the second black Baptist association in the state.[15] During its first decade the Rocky River Baptist Association spawned the Enoree Baptist Association (1869; including Greenville County churches), and hosted the Baptist State Convention. When launched in 1868, Rocky River's 10 Anderson churches had 234 members; 16 churches in 1874 reported congregations totaling 1,643; and by 1879 its 23 Anderson churches had 3,196 members.

Ten other churches withdrew cordially that year to form the Seneca River Missionary Baptist Association, which covered primarily Oconee and southern Pickens counties. Ministers J. W. Keith became its first moderator and W. R. Parker its clerk, both of Reconstruction-era fame, and S. H. Oglesby, the treasurer. Twelve churches established in 1885 the Oolenoy Baptist Association, centered mostly in northern Pickens County. Walhalla had one of Oconee's earliest churches, and black Griffin Ebenezer Baptist was New Pickens's first church, white or black.[16]

White men helped organize the Rocky River Baptist Association and initially held membership by its constitution, but their guidance soon became less welcome. Although in 1874 "our white brethren—Elder Thomas Dawson, J. C. Watkins, G. W. Burriss, H. R. Vandiver, and others—assisted us nobly in our undertakings," black ministers intended in 1879 to direct their own affairs. At that time "white brethren" were "invited to aid in the labors of the association, but not in the meeting." Other people also assisted churches. At least two-thirds of those begun between 1865 and 1869 received, by their own accounts, either land, other contributions, or organizational guidance and training. One congregation, Pleasant Grove Baptist, held services in the white Hebron Methodist building for years.[17]

No record of white opposition to black churches has been found. Since few black congregations owned land in the early years, they usually met on white-owned property, in either tenant houses, brush arbors, or white churches, all expressly or tacitly tolerated. The Rock Springs Baptist Church and school (Oconee) in 1870 used land belonging to S. E. Maxwell, formerly a wealthy slave owner. Describing their early church histories to a WPA interviewer, blacks frequently mentioned or even praised early white support given seventy years earlier. At least a quarter of black churches between 1865 and 1890 received gifts of land and sometimes buildings from whites, often former owners. Even a 1990s publication by black Andersonians, intended almost exclusively for themselves, repeated these connections. Quite a few deeds refer to a church already being on the land before legal transfer to the black congregation. Several churches adopted names from their white donors.[18]

White cooperation during the 1870s was closer than assumed by many people who read back into this era attitudes from a period of greater racial polarization. Typical of such cooperation, several white clergy attending the December 1870 Presbyterian Synod of South Carolina, meeting in Anderson, preached at black churches. Frequently the white Saluda Baptist Association invited delegates from Rocky River, and itself sent representatives to Rocky River association meetings. Sporadically during the rest of the century both Saluda and the South Carolina Baptist Convention appointed white ministers to preach during their annual sessions to nearby black congregations. State black Baptists noted these good exchanges, "promoting good feelings," and assistance from "white brethren" who held institutes for ministers and deacons.[19]

As Anderson's freed people organized new churches, they chose names that reflected their values. The earliest names were Freedmen and Liberty, the latter "because of the Liberty given the coloreds just after the war," as a member told the WPA. Eight others began with the word "New." Several titles included Canaan or Mount Sinai, from which Moses viewed the promised land. For congregations often forced to meet outdoors, names often referred to groves, creeks, scenic views, forests, or a rock hill, and "pleasant" recurred often.

Finances dictated early settings. Many accounts describe church origins in brush arbors, cleared outdoor areas, often with benches. Although brush-arbor lore evoked romanticized images of their beginnings, many congregations initially could not afford a building. Especially during summers, a shaded outdoor site may well have been more pleasant than a hot building: "The Brush Harbor was rebuilt with fresh tree tops whenever necessary in order to provide shade for the worshippers. A nearby [white-owned] sawmill provided sawdust for a cool soft carpet for the ground floor also, seats for pews were made from slabs obtained from the same sawmill. Hymn books were unknown and the whole congregation was one big choir."[20]

Between 1865 and 1874 all new Anderson County churches with their own buildings had log structures. Other arrangements involved several meeting in tenant houses, a black Methodist church sharing its facilities with Baptists, and another using a store room. Those early churches took an average of nearly eleven years to construct a more substantial building, usually wood-frame, typically with dimensions ranging from twenty-five to forty feet on each side. None has survived due to flimsy structures, fires, tornadoes, or cyclones. Churches that began between 1874 and 1899 started with substantially better structures, and managed to upgrade to a wood-frame church somewhat quicker than did earlier ones. In Anderson city Salem Presbyterian (1892) and St. Paul Baptist (ca. 1900) built the county's first brick edifices for black congregations.

Resources for buildings and clergy were limited severely by individual congregations' poverty. Most held services only one Sunday a month, as did most rural white churches, and consequently paid their ministers very little, one hundred dollars per year per church being a typical salary as late as the 1890s. Ministers usually served several churches, sometimes meeting two on a Sunday—one in the morning, another in the evening. S. H. Oglesby, meeting seven churches concurrently in 1888, listed his occupation in 1880 as farming. Seldom deriving their primary income from ministerial work, ministers often lived some distance away. One Abel Baptist (Pickens) minister in the 1890s traveled by train one weekend each month from Seneca, nearly fifteen miles away. Frequently changing addresses of both ministers and teachers between 1865 and 1900 demonstrate the vicissitudes of their work, income, and lives. Between 1885 and 1907 Will Anderson, serving both Mountain Spring (Anderson) and New Olive Grove (Pickens) Baptist churches, had six post office locations in two counties. Some ministers held teaching positions; many farmed; and a few had other work.[21]

These churches suffered also from belonging to impoverished associations or conferences that could not afford to extend them help. Some northern support came from the Presbyterian Church in the U.S.A., the AME, and the Methodist Episcopal Church, cited here as ME(N), distinguishing it from ME, South—all white by the 1870s.

Kings Chapel African Methodist Episcopal Church, Pendleton; built ca. 1900, replaced by a 1960s brick building (taken by Lewis Moorhead). Black Heritage in the Upper Piedmont

Methodist efforts lagged chronologically and numerically behind Baptists, and the Presbyterian more so. Northern Methodists organized four Anderson County congregations between 1865 and 1874, five in the next decade, and five more by 1900, when they constituted almost 20 percent of the county's black churches. The Reverend James Rosemond, a preacher during slavery, began fifty ME(N) churches in northwestern South Carolina, fourteen of them—including the first, Centennial —in Anderson, Oconee, and Pickens counties. At least four congregations belonged to the Colored Methodist Episcopal (CME) denomination, encouraged by white southern Methodists to compete with ME(N) churches.[22] The ME(N) had several congregations in Oconee and Pickens, and the CME at least one in Pickens. Because of hostilities between the northern and southern Methodist Episcopal churches, there evidently was no cooperation between them or their local clergy as there was between black and white Baptists.

The AME made some headway in South Carolina's northwestern corner, while the separate AME, Zion, denomination thrived in north-central counties. The AME attempted mission posts in Pickens and Oconee as late as 1900, but none of them survived. It fared better in Anderson with nine churches—one organized in 1870, seven, 1880–97, and one, 1912—and did even better in Greenville city and county with many in Anderson and Greenville counties still in existence.

Anderson's first AME church, Kings Chapel in Pendleton, resulted from white Methodists' refusal to "'funeralize' a negro," which precipitated a mass withdrawal.

The leadership, better-educated and less impoverished than most ME(N) congregations, preferred AME although both groups evidently worshipped together in the ME, South "Colored Circuit" for two years. George Maxwell served Pendleton's ME(N) members by 1870. Pendleton's AME leaders likely had prior contacts with Charleston churches. Silas Jefferson, their first minister, arrived in 1870, but stayed only one year; he taught school also. Jefferson rose rapidly to become presiding elder, trustee of AME's Allen University (Columbia), and member of both conference and national AME educational committees.

Almost all other AME congregations—primarily semirural except for one, founded 1883, in Anderson city—were begun by different ministers. A later Kings Chapel minister, William David Chappelle, supervised its first building, an attractive wooden-frame structure. During his appointment "the cause of African Methodism took on a new lease of life in that section," and he helped persuade students to attend Allen University. Chappelle, also a rising AME star, became a bishop in 1912.[23]

Both the AME and ME(N) denominations required training and a probation period for their clergy. They established institutes and colleges, located in Charleston initially and later in Columbia and Orangeburg, respectively. Following Methodist practice of rotating ministers, those serving Anderson, Oconee, and Pickens counties often came from elsewhere in the state and typically remained only one or two years. By contrast, Baptist clergy might stay for decades and had a more enduring personal impact.

The Board of Missions for Freedmen coordinated northern Presbyterian work. Slowly over three decades it organized and funded upper-piedmont schools, taught by white missionaries, while its theological school in Charlotte, Biddle University, trained clergy. E. B. Craig, a Pickens County student, graduated from Biddle and joined its faculty around 1880. Presbyterians organized Salem church by 1890 and shortly afterward Salem Industrial School in Anderson city. Local members chose as minister John Peter Foster, an Abbeville native, educated at Howard University, in preference to white missionaries who taught at the school. Salem is the only surviving black Presbyterian congregation in the three-county area. Shortly before 1900 Presbyterians launched their first Oconee and Pickens efforts.[24]

Growth of these early churches raises interesting questions. Since only a third of adult slaves in Anderson, Oconee, and Pickens counties were church members in antebellum years, did other freed people join postemancipation churches just because they were among the few black organizations? Or had many of these people been Christians, not institutionally affiliated? This raises, once again, a big question in a small place, the query "Why join?" in chapter 6. Not surprisingly, no data exist to answer it definitively. Typically most new churches started with only twenty to thirty charter members—often fewer—who belonged to antebellum churches. By 1869 Rocky River Baptist Association church memberships exceeded the area's 1860 slave membership. Whatever individual motivations may have been, many men found that church connections reinforced their roles in Reconstruction politics and in the community.

Anderson County's ten Baptist churches in 1868 baptized 309 people, almost 60 percent of their total membership, indicating that they had not been church members during slavery. That year Wilson's Creek Baptists baptized 96 of its 130 members, and Parker's church, 170 in 1869. Rocky River's Anderson churches in 1869 accepted 46 percent of its new members by baptism. Twenty-three Baptist churches from 1874 to 1879 baptized 1117 people, 35 percent of their membership then. In Pendleton and Anderson towns, which had sizable antebellum slave attendance, a much smaller number, about 25 percent, of new Baptists were admitted by baptism. Comparable AME and ME(N) figures are not available. Rocky River Baptist Association churches baptized 1148 people in 1891–93, a boom period for new members.

Who constituted the early clergy? In contrast to other areas of the South, no northern black ministers came to the upper piedmont. Mostly, then, they were South Carolinians, many—especially Baptists—from Anderson, Oconee, and Pickens counties and adjacent counties. Founding clergy were likely to be literate and mulatto. The earliest ME(N) clerical appointments in the three-county area, short of full ordination, consisted entirely of local men. Anderson County ministers, active in the 1870s and listed in the census, had an average age of thirty-seven, Silas Jefferson at twenty-two being by far the youngest; evidently all were literate. The census described only one as a minister. Others were farmers, farm laborers, teachers, and a blacksmith. Many of Oconee's early clergy, elders, and deacons—some also among early black landowners—came from large plantations. Clergy and deacons often helped launch more than one church. Evidently many lay preachers during early decades were illiterate and untrained.

Although African Americans had their own clergy and congregations, white toleration and control affected church activities. Virtually all churches, like their members, were surrounded by white landowners. Typically white men transferred an acre, while their land continued to adjoin church property on at least two sides. Town churches in the latter 1800s were never more than two to four blocks from white houses, churches, or businesses. It was difficult, if not impossible, to escape white onlookers. The Adger family "at night enjoyed hearing the Negroes sing their old-time hymns at a tenant house not far away." An Adger descendant asked a member there to help transcribe their song lyrics.

Many deeds from white grantors, requiring that the premises be used only for educational and religious purposes, included a reversionary clause. Anderson's earliest-such provision was 1873; another one added a requirement that good order be observed. Even more restrictive language appeared after 1876. One 1883 deed donated the land only "as long as they have Good Behavior and not to be used for political purposes." The most restrictive provisions were recorded in 1887. Robert Adger required that land he gave for New Light Baptist Church be used "solely for

Kings Chapel AME stewardesses (mid-1900s), with the minister. Left to right: Mrs. Rebecca Reese, Mrs. Rosa Robinson, and Mrs. Cora Reid (sitting); Mrs. Mamie Crawford; Mrs. Essie Fisher; and Mrs. Williams. Black Heritage in the Upper Piedmont

religious and educational purposes and exercises and no political social or secular meeting of any kind to be held there."[25]

Like their white counterparts, black churches seem to have had no interdenominational squabbles, saving their quarrels for internal purposes. In unusual cooperation Mount Sinai Methodists had Mt. Olive Baptist members worshipping jointly around 1870. By contrast some internal conflicts resulted in splits, as happened around 1885 when some members left New Light Baptist to establish Holly Springs Baptist about a half mile away. Some churches, such as Sweet Canaan Baptist (1871), sprang up as people tired of traveling to the nearest one, often up to ten miles away.[26]

Women's roles in churches are poorly documented. Often they were charter members, but all deacons, trustees, and clergy were men, who wrote the records. Anderson's pentecostal church in 1920 would have the upper piedmont's first woman minister. In many other locations women have been the majority of members, as was likely true for area churches. Women helped with fund-raising and undoubtedly with church dinners. By 1900 they took an active role in Sunday schools and on educational committees; numbers and percentages of women who taught public school increased during the late 1800s also. They headed five of twenty-one Methodist Sunday schools, and Georgia Reeves joined a mission in Sierra Leone in 1895.[27] Ministers' wives had a respected community role; Rocky River Baptist Association referred fondly to Mother Morris, widow of its founder.

As churches gained land and grew in both members and facilities, several distinct periods of growth characterized Anderson's Baptist churches. Political events sometimes coincided with spurts in church membership. The year 1868 had both statewide Republican victories and a boom in baptisms, the largest number of total baptisms until 1879. Sixteen Rocky River churches, adding nearly five hundred new members, grew by over 25 percent between 1875 and 1877; Hampton's 1876 political victory, coinciding with more black members, may have driven them into churches for refuge. Later peaks occurred in 1881–83 and 1891–93, followed by a decline until a 1904–7 surge. During the 1890s South Carolinians, among others, joined pentecostal churches and launched the Fire Baptized Holiness denomination (predominantly white), the South Carolina Conference of Wesleyan Methodists (white), and the earliest black Fire Baptized Holiness churches, including one in Seneca.[28]

By 1900 Anderson County's churches had grown significantly in numbers, reaching a total of seventy-one. They included forty-three Baptist churches with approximately 6,700 members; eighteen Methodist and Colored Methodist, 1,600; eight AME, 700; and two Presbyterian churches, totaling perhaps 50. Baptist churches in or within a four-mile range of towns averaged nearly 100 more members per congregation than did rural ones. St. Paul in Anderson claimed 755 members, making it the largest church in Anderson, Oconee, and Pickens counties, white or black; Pleasant Grove, just outside Starr, 665 members, Belton's Mount Zion, 600, and Honea Path's Liberty, 435. Trains may well have brought some congregants from a wider area to town churches. Oconee and Pickens together had about thirty churches with over 4,600 members, the largest individual congregations and totals being Baptist.[29]

Increased numbers of churches derived from several factors. Black population by 1900 was more than double that of 1870. Some churches began as new population centers grew, including Mount Sinai AME (1889), near Piedmont, for workers constructing a cotton mill. A new Southern Railroad line through Oconee and

Table 17.1 **Estimates of Black Church Members, 1900**

	Anderson	Oconee	Pickens	Total	Percent
Baptists	6,715	1,544	1,500	9,759	71 %
ME(N)	1,320	448	614	2,382	17
AME	700	50	250	1,000	7
CME	250	—	100	350	3
Presbyterian, USA	50	—	20	70	1
FBH, estimated	—	50	50	100	1
Totals	9,035	2,092	2,534	13,661	100 %

Sources: RRBA, E&M, AME, and ME(N) reports; figures substantially higher than shown in Census Office, *Report of Statistics of Churches in the United States at the Eleventh Census: 1890* (Washington, D.C.: GPO, 1894); Bureau of the Census, Special Reports, *Religious Bodies: 1906* (Washington, D.C.: GPO, 1910); and Middleton.

Pickens counties led to new towns begun from scratch: Westminster, Seneca, Calhoun, Central, Norris, Liberty, and Easley, with black Baptists established in all of these and Methodists in several. And intensified denominational efforts produced more ME(N), AME, CME, and Presbyterian congregations.

Much was accomplished between 1865 and 1900. Although primarily religious organizations, churches occupied a pivotal position in communities and their development. Churches spoke against perceived evils, and Rocky River Baptist Association minutes abound with attacks on drinking and gambling. Member churches each year collectively excluded dozens of members, typically over a hundred per year in the 1880s.[30]

Churches were also connected with larger organizations, including their own regional, state, and national denominational bodies, which provided contacts with black accomplishments and ideas elsewhere. Churches furnished space for many other groups, including at times Republicans and often benevolent societies. They dealt with broader issues that concerned African Americans such as their Africanness as well as missions to Africa; and they especially supported educational efforts through facilities, financial aid to students, overlapping staffs, and higher educational standards for their own clergy.

Churches repaid in many ways community efforts to establish them, to buy land, and to help fund the clergy's training, a fruitful symbiosis. African Americans reaped bountifully from seeds they planted.

Schools, 1865–1900

Freed people worked as zealously to obtain education for their children as to support churches.[31] Building on limited antebellum literacy, the community eagerly embraced educational opportunities. Schools, however, needed more resources, including an educated teacher, books, and a facility. They also deprived families by removing their children from field or other work to attend school. Both the Freedmen's Bureau in 1866 and after 1868 the state Department of Education aided early endeavors. Contemporary bureau correspondence, school attendance reports, and complimentary accounts in white newspapers testify to postbellum African Americans' strong impulse to acquire an education, as was observed across the South. D. M. Minus, a young Colleton County man who would become a teacher and preacher in Pickens, Oconee, and Greenville, hired white tutors at four dollars a month to help him learn how to read and write. By 1900 he headed several large schools.[32]

Schools began in 1866 with Freedmen's Bureau assistance. The bureau in 1869 helped repair Belton's school building and supported a school in Walhalla, where "the masses [of whites] are opposed to any movement that will tend to elevate the freed people." In 1870 Frances Tudor, a "young [white] lady from Vermont," was the teacher, well received by students and much disliked by local whites. In response, "a number of white men decided to use their efforts to break up the school [within its first two or three months]. They hired a drunken vagabond negro to attend its sessions, and accompany the teacher home. . . . A Northern gentleman residing there heard of the plan, and prevented the performance of the last part of the scheme [perhaps rape?]." After one year Tudor, pleading for full payment of her salary, was "very anxious to leave for the North," a victory for local whites.[33]

By 1870 the bureau shut down its operations throughout the South as state governments assumed full responsibilities. J. K. Jillson, elected state superintendent of education in 1868, was an educator from Massachusetts who escaped bitter criticism and charges of corruption heaped on other state Republican officials. "He was well and favorably known in this State during the Republican regime," the only Republican executive official to serve all four terms.[34]

During the 1869–70 transition when the Freedmen's Bureau still rendered substantial support, student figures dramatize both an intense desire for education and hardships that it often entailed. Eleven schools meeting for varying terms, mostly in Anderson County, had a total enrollment exceeding two thousand; about eight hundred individuals were represented. Anderson town had both the largest number and highest percentage of older students: at least fifty in 1869–70 were over 16 years old. Supplementing formal education at established schools, some occurred informally at churches and within homes. Often a family could spare only one or a few of their children for school while others worked. Sometimes a child who went to school taught siblings who could not attend, as happened in William Pickens's family. Many children aged six to sixteen, reported in the 1870 census as being able to read or write, were not enrolled in school; they must have learned through these alternative means. Unfortunately many, although attending school, could not read or write—not surprising since most schools had only one teacher with fifty, a hundred, or more students and terms of only a few weeks, while some children attended only a few days. During that same year Pickens County had only one black school, its eleven pupils were taught by a white teacher.[35]

The 1869–70 schools collectively had about two-thirds of their students attending on an average day, with the highest figures in towns. A higher proportion of black school-age children attended Anderson schools in 1874 than did whites. Then, as in later years, Oconee and Pickens—more rural and mountainous—had a much smaller percentage enrolled, 41 percent, and 55 percent, respectively, of school age than did Anderson, 80 percent. More males than females attended during the 1870s. Men predominated in South Carolina's schools, almost 60 percent for the state's white teachers, and nearly 70 percent for blacks. Anderson, Oconee, and Pickens each had 60 to 75 percent males among their black staff in 1874 and 77 percent in 1885. Gender balances for students and teachers changed later in the century.

Teachers received little compensation, partly because terms were short. In Anderson, Oconee, and Pickens counties average salaries for white and black teachers ranged from eighteen to twenty-five dollars a month, with men typically higher than women. Black teachers made as little as ten dollars a month in the 1870s and

1870 "Teacher's Reports" by S. H. Jefferson, Pendleton, April 1 and October 31, 1870, listing names of students, attendance, and owner of school house (J. B. Sitton). Black Heritage in the Upper Piedmont, S.C. Department of Archives and History

1880s and not quite twenty dollars by 1900.[36] Terms averaged only four months statewide for all students; local figures, not published, were probably shorter than two months for blacks. Teachers certainly had to earn much of their living elsewhere. Since schools closed during planting and harvesting time, teachers were as likely as students to be found in the fields. D. B. Finlay's 1880 Williamston Township (Anderson) census listing, "Farmer & Teacher," could well describe many others.

Early school records show only a small number of teachers available. Unlike ministers and deacons, few took part in politics, although some of their relatives did. And teachers were mostly younger than ministers. Faculty drew more heavily on antebellum free families than did church leadership, and teachers—or their families—were disproportionately mulattos, skilled craftsmen, and property owners. Already, religious and educational leaders overlapped.

Pickens certification registers begin in 1870, and those for Anderson County in 1872. Only two Pickens black men qualified in 1870; four women and two additional men did so in 1871–72. Ranging from seventeen to twenty-eight years old, they averaged twenty-three years. Joberry Sizemore came from an antebellum free family. Only one of these eight taught in Pickens more than three years, Warren D. Jenkins, still active at the end of the century. Among free persons of color, five Sizemores and two Paytons taught in Pickens County between 1870 and 1890.

Ten Anderson black people who qualified for county certification in 1872 included six males, two married females, and two single females—aged seventeen to sixty-four and averaging twenty-nine. Three were farmers, three farm laborers, and one a minister; one woman was a housewife. Seven had personal property; one also owned land. Fifteen more black Anderson teachers were certified in 1873, and more each succeeding year. Ten of twenty-five approved in 1872–73 taught for more than three years; they included, among others, Joberry Payton (Jr.), Hiram Greenlee, Martha Johnson, and Tabitha Morris, daughter of minister Frank Morris.

Both literacy and teaching often depended on family. At least some other household members of teachers with spouses and/or children could read or write. Often several teachers came from a single family. Anderson's two oldest teachers, Hiram Greenlee (sixty-seven) and Isaac Greenlee (sixty-two), likely were brothers, as probably were three Williams men (thirty-two, twenty-eight, and twenty-two years old); Cornelia Williams, a wife, and William Thompson, a grandson, also taught.[37]

Soon after emancipation, African Americans were often able to control their own schools. A building sometime served as both church and school, perhaps with the same man leading both. In Pendleton, for example, the community chose its own school board, provided a building, and approved the teacher, initially AME minister Silas Jefferson. Pendleton's first school in 1870 drew seventy-seven students. Two-thirds of 1869–70 schools in Anderson, Oconee, and Pickens counties used black-owned properties, sometimes private houses or lots. Pickens's only black school that year, Graball School House, was locally run and supported: "condition very bad, owned by colored citizens of the vicinity."[38]

Pendleton and Anderson community boards acquired land for their schools, in the latter case buying fifteen hundred dollars' worth of State Land Commission land that Reconstruction politician John R. Cochran obtained. Eight black men, constituting that board in 1870, averaged forty-six years old and were disproportionately literate and mulatto. Seven could read and write, as could the wife of the eighth. They came mostly from the crafts—a shoemaker, two carpenters, a brick mason, and a gardener; three were farmers. Richmond Payton belonged to an antebellum free family; Tabor Warren and Franklin Morris were pioneer Baptist clergy, as was George Maxwell among Methodists. Four owned personal property, and two of them land. Payton and Morris families would supply several Anderson teachers. Known as Greeley Institute, this school was the tricounty area's only private black-owned school prior to 1899.

Churches often provided facilities for schools, either the church building itself or space on its lot. Even in 1870 the "Colored Methodist Church" owned Cedar Grove's "wooden log house." For decades many white and black schools, especially in rural areas and small towns, stood on church property. Although churches provided facilities, teachers received their salaries from county funds.

Support for education came in other ways besides land. Many clergymen had wives or children who taught. The Rocky River Baptist Association in the 1870s repeatedly expressed its concern that ministers be educated. By the 1880s the educational committee of the Rocky River Baptist Association supported both ministerial and other students financially; the association also established its own educational group. The state's black denominations provided additional opportunities: Baptists at Benedict Institute (later, Benedict College; Columbia); AME, Allen University (Columbia); and ME(N), Claflin University (Orangeburg). Allen was the only postbellum college in South Carolina named for a black person and the only one controlled by African Americans.[39]

Black education benefited also from statewide educational improvements, though never as much as white schools did. The 1868 Reconstruction constitution established, as one of its enduring contributions, free public education, a novel concept for the state. Terms were short, teacher salaries low and pupil ratios high, while facilities seldom reached the level of adequacy, let alone surpassed it. Later in the century state educational leaders would push for graded elementary rather than one-room schools. As late as the 1890s, Pickens County's average term for both black and white schools was only two and a half months, and the county had only one high school, white. Half of Clemson Agricultural College's five hundred young men during its 1893 inaugural term enrolled in the high-school program, clear evidence of the state's paucity of even white high schools. Public black high schools would be established even more slowly, only a few of them throughout South Carolina before 1920.

Terms typically followed the agricultural cycle with breaks for planting and harvesting, as they often did for white schools too. Many terms lasted only a few weeks; a year's schooling of two or three months often consisted of even shorter periods separated by agricultural work. Town schools, whose students were less likely to be needed for farming, had longer terms, higher attendance records, and more funds. Students in both Anderson and Pickens counties by 1885 achieved high attendance averages, 82 percent and 91 percent respectively, approximating those for whites. That for Oconee blacks, 73 percent, exceeded a white average of 65 percent. Short Pickens terms, creating less conflict between school and farm work, may have boosted average attendance there.

Teachers—laboring under difficulties of low pay, short terms, and crowded one-room ungraded schools—often had many more pupils per teacher than did white counterparts; in Anderson, black teachers taught an average of 60 students in 1874, double the number in white schools. Those in Oconee and Pickens averaged 44 and

47 each, with 35.7 the statewide average. Daily attendance was somewhat lower. Well into the twentieth century most black and white schools had only one teacher to accommodate all enrolled students except in towns and cities, and sometimes there as well. Anderson's 150 schools, black and white, matched 150 teachers in 1884.

After initial Pickens county certifications in 1870-72, only five more black people qualified in 1873 and 1874, with an average age of twenty. One was Clark T. Miller, who had the longest career of any Pickens black teacher prior to 1920. He taught from 1874 through 1909 at varied locations including Anderson County. Miller and his son John Miller, who attended Howard University, were Pickens's first black teachers to receive state certificates. At least eight Pickens families each contributed five or more teachers between 1870 and 1900. During that time over three hundred teachers were certified, although many served only one or two years.

Similarly, fifteen families each supplied five or more teachers to Anderson's staff. Most among Anderson's nearly five hundred black teachers during those same years likewise taught only a year or so. Only eighteen could be considered long-term, serving more than a decade, and only two more than twenty years: Henry H. Johnson and Jacob J. Martin. C. T. Miller and family, several Jenkinses, and several Thomases taught in both Anderson and either Oconee or Pickens. At least seventy-seven Anderson teachers from 1888 to 1895 earned certification elsewhere.[40]

Despite the 1868 constitutional provision for free public education, it would be almost one hundred years before county educational boards would provide substantial buildings for most black schools. Meanwhile, many were one-room school houses, some hardly more than shacks, often of log construction. The county seldom paid even for them; rather, churches or community groups erected these buildings out of their own meager funds. Oconee had fewer county-owned school buildings than did Anderson or Pickens. Photographs taken well into the twentieth century and descriptions by county superintendents of education document often poor conditions of school buildings. Most black schools were still log cabins as were some for whites, although most of theirs by then were wood-frame.[41] Lacking any other building in 1894, the Easley-area "Colored School #12" held classes at Mr. Chapman's tenant house.

John Starks, attending rural Greenwood County schools in the 1880s and 1890s, left a vivid account: "The school building was a one-room log cabin of rudest type. There was no ceiling of any kind. The floor was of rough unmatched, unsized, random-width boards. The seats were of slabs with auger holes bored through them in which were inserted sawed off saplings for legs. These schools were ungraded. Spelling, geography, reading, grammar, history, and arithmetic made up the course of study." Rural students trying to get an education in town faced special hardships. When Starks left home for Greenwood town in the 1880s, he had to walk because the train fare was beyond his family's means. He hauled, on his back, bedding, clothing, and provisions for the week. Each weekend he walked home for clean clothes and another week's food. His second year was easier as he could afford to ship his load by freight but still had to walk.[42] Starks later would preside over Seneca Institute, Morris College, and Benedict College; at each place he put a high emphasis on quality buildings erected by black labor.

The family of William Pickens, one of the best-known men from Anderson County, reflected rural educational limitations. His parents as adults began to learn to read with a New Testament sold by book agents, he wrote. His older sisters took him along to "a characteristic Negro schoolhouse built of logs, with one door and one window, the latter having no panes.... There were no desks; the seats were long board benches with no backs." Like the Pickens family who moved into Pendleton, Jane Hunter's father "decided that he wanted to live near a school, so that his children could attend." He sold his farm equipment and moved into Pendleton also. Hunter's school, "conducted by the Silver Spring Baptist Church," did not go "beyond the 'First Reader.'"[43]

With few exceptions the best opportunities for education were found in towns. Most black schools between 1865 and 1870, and many early churches, were in towns, especially Anderson, Belton, Williamston, and Walhalla. White newspapers commented favorably and frequently about black schools in Pickens and Anderson, but the *Keowee Courier*, like Oconee's school board, gave little encouragement or support for black education.

Located about four blocks from Anderson's courthouse, Greeley Institute received many compliments from the *Intelligencer* editor like that of January 27, 1881: "The colored people of Anderson have done nobly in subscribing to the repair of their town school house the sum of about one hundred seventy dollars." Benevolent societies soon raised funds, $20 by the Good Samaritans and $52.38 from a Good Templars hot supper.[44] M. H. Gassaway served as principal.

Until after 1900 blacks—and most whites—had to go out of the tricounty area for postgrammar studies, available primarily at Benedict, Allen, Claflin, and, after 1896, State College, or at proprietary high schools, mostly in lower parts of the state. Students attending these institutions, mostly in high-school programs, often received financial help from area religious groups.[45]

Lack of high schools, let alone nearby collegiate facilities, handicapped teachers. State superintendents commented frequently on limited training and caliber of both black and white teachers, few of whom even attended high school. This theme persisted among all state superintendents—regardless of political party or faction from 1868 until 1900—who called for additional training to raise standards. By the 1880s state-funded summer institutes helped upgrade teaching; most of these were county based, though at only a few sites each year.

Local teachers had their first opportunity in 1891, when thirteen from Pickens attended a Greenville institute. Two years later thirty-six teachers participated in Anderson's four-day institute, held at Greeley, and fifty-eight teachers in 1895 enrolled in another session there. The white instructor, Prof. J. E. Wallace of Columbia, observed that these teachers were "making rapid strides as educators"

Vineland school, Pickens County; probably early 1900s. Pendleton District Commission

and worked with "heart and mind." Others followed in subsequent years. College-level studies for a few teachers greatly improved their qualifications.

Teachers, excluded from white county organizations, launched their own. Oconee County's Educational Association in February 1887 met at Walhalla's Methodist Episcopal church (North); the *Keowee Courier* called it a "commendable undertaking" deserving "the encouragement of our white people." Two years later C. T. Miller and others launched a similar Pickens Colored Teachers Association.[46]

Despite a second-rate status for black schools and discriminatory public funding in the late nineteenth century, an expanding emphasis on South Carolina education gradually upgraded these schools with more funds, longer terms, and larger attendances. In the process, however, educational reform for unified county and district boards often eliminated black control of grammar schools, even when communities were expected to provide buildings.[47]

Teacher training and pay certainly improved. Certification records for both Anderson and Pickens counties from 1870 into the twentieth century document that school teachers were trained and qualified; nevertheless they earned far less than white counterparts. By 1900 more had high school and college training but only somewhat better pay. College graduates got first-class certification.

Children often acquired at least a basic education despite poor facilities and county funding due to racist attitudes. That half, or more, of them attended school in these circumstances again testifies to black determination to gain education. Clearly they worked hard at it. Dependence on sharecropping often forced children into agricultural labor instead of school rooms, especially in years of good crops. Nevertheless black school enrollment climbed dramatically between 1866 and 1900. Anderson, which in 1874 had 80 percent of its school-age children enrolled in school, increased from 2,094 that year to 5,039 in 1900. Oconee and Pickens, with approximately 50 percent of black children enrolled in 1874, made more striking increases from 310 to 1,258 for Oconee, 375 to 1,252 for Pickens County.

Ironically, bad as well as good crop years could reduce attendance. Less money in bad crop years meant less available to pay for textbooks—not provided by the state—and clothing. Marked gains in attendance are all the more striking as the state would not have a compulsory-attendance law until after 1910. In many black families and white families students had to work in the fields.[48]

Table 17.2 **Official State Superintendent of Education Reports—AOP Black Schools**

	% School Pop Enrolled		% Att. of Enrolled	School Pop.	% Lit 10+	Teachers		Schools
	1874	1900	1900	1910	1910	1874	1900	1900
Anderson	64%	65%	63%	55%	63%	35	66	58
Oconee	36	63	78	47	69	6	32	31
Pickens	49	79	41	55	70	8	26	25
State of S.C.	40	61	71	56	61			

Enrollment, Class Sizes, and Terms

1900 Schools	Anderson	Oconee	Pickens	AOP
students, black	5,039	1,093	1,202	7,334
av/teacher, b. cf. w.	76 cf. 51	34 cf. 49	47 cf. 58	
av. weeks, b. cf. w.	19 cf.	24	7 cf. 14	11 cf. 21
(blacks compared to whites)				

Attendance/Enrollment, 1900

black	63%	78%	75%
white	67	90	63

Highest Black Literacy Rates, 1910

Marion	73.7	Sumter	67.9	Greenwood	66.5
Pickens	69.9	Charleston	67.3	8 others	—
Oconee	69.1	Dillon	67.3	Anderson	63.1
Newberry	69.1	Orangeburg	67.3		
Richland	68.9	Greenville	66.7	S.C.	61.3

Sources: 1874 is the first year for which this data is available; "attendance" was reported then, "enrollment" in 1900–figures not strictly commensurate. The 1875 state census lists the "Number of Children between 6 and 16 years of age," which I have taken as the potential enrollment, then calculated the percentage of people 6–16/those 6–20 (74%) for South Carolina and to derive an approximate figure for AOP's 6–16. The 1900 *Annual Report* gives student enrollment and attendance numbers. The 1900 census in *Population*, part 2, lists figures for "persons 5 to 20, inclusive," and the 1910 furnishes U.S. Census "Supplement for South Carolina" for attendance data and for "Negro, Percent of illiterate." Cf. "Total Illiterate Population 10 Years of Age and Over, . . . by Counties: 1900," table 84 of the 1900 *Population*, part 2, 2:483.

By the century's end Jim Crow–era racism affected superintendents also. John J. McMahan in 1899 said that county boards "strain their consciences and grant certificates to negroes upon examination papers that would not be considered if handed up by white applicants. . . . 'We must have teachers for the negro schools—it would not do to close them,'" boards say. "There is no opening for the negro in the learned professions. . . . If the cravings of intellectual tastes could be awakened there is little opportunity to gratify them." Far better, then, to prepare "negro children" to work in occupations that are available, that is, farming and crafts, he said. McMahan argued that "the best type of the negro of intelligence and character is a mechanic educated in that best of schools the well governed plantation before the War." Book learning may carry "negroes" to the penitentiary as ambition and desires are frustrated. Their "teachers are often so devoid of both character and learning that the so-called education of the pupils is actually hurtful." If we provide more industrial training, there will be "fewer vagabond loafers around country stores and railways depots, and fewer thieves in towns."[49]

Anderson's black institutes had previously been described in highly complimentary terms. But the 1900 director's report read, similar to McMahan's views, "that the indolent has been aroused, the smart 'Alicks' have found it necessary to study a little more, and the studious and thoughtful teacher has been quickened."[50] Clearly racism permeated not only the general public but professional educators as well. Statistics dramatically illustrate improvements in black literacy under deprived conditions despite McMahan's rhetoric.

Black education had significant successes although handicapped by poor facilities, ill-paid teachers, and many families who could not or did not send their children to school. Anderson's black schools in 1900 ranged from a five-week session in one district where whites attended twenty-eight weeks, to another where both white and black students had a thirty-week term. The county's black average age was nineteen but twenty-one for whites. Given one-teacher schools, a wide array of situations occurred, including one rural district whose white teacher had ninety-two students, its black school thirty-eight. Pickens showed similarly unequal white-black variations. For both races Pickens had fewer schools and more students per school and per teacher. Some districts—especially those in Pickens's and Oconee's northern tier of mountainous areas—had no black schools and virtually no black population. Oconee's average session for blacks was seven weeks, while Pickens had eleven; those for whites were twice as long. Black teachers in Anderson, Oconee, and Pickens counties were paid about one dollar per day, white teachers about $1.25.[51]

By 1900 over half of the counties' blacks ten and older could read and write, a major achievement during difficult financial times for freed families with limited state support. Anderson schools, county and town, were among the state's best educational systems and had higher percentages of black literacy. In 1910 Pickens and Oconee had the state's second- and third-highest black literacy rates, 69.9 and 69.1; the state average was 61.3. Anderson with 63.1 percent ranked twentieth.

More than a thousand teachers in the three counties passed examinations between 1870 and 1900. Many stayed only a few years, some moving elsewhere; some younger women left when they married, and others had to quit for full-time work. Hundreds of students in Anderson, Oconee, and Pickens counties attended Benedict, Claflin, and Allen; many of them received some local financial support; and over a hundred teachers between 1888 and 1900 had licentiate or bachelor's degrees. Several families contributed numerous teachers and constituted a core leadership for the community.

EIGHTEEN

Black Communities, Town and Rural

TOWN COMMUNITIES HAVE BEEN IMPORTANT, perhaps crucial, to African Americans. Significant institutions could be found there: many of the larger churches and better schools, as well as benevolent and fraternal associations, bands, and businesses. Towns usually offered more and better jobs as well—all due to population clusters that sustained them. Little analytical material is available about African Americans in the nation's small towns, partly because so little information is readily accessible.

Studies of major urban centers such as New Orleans, Philadelphia, or Charleston cannot begin to reflect conditions where only fifty or a hundred blacks lived among a few hundred whites. Examining upper-piedmont towns provides insights into racial relations—which often shed light on "white" town history—and into technological change. African Americans gained from railroad expansion, manufacturing and business in railroad towns, and increased job opportunities there. As railroad facilities spurred growth of cotton mills, in or near towns, this impacted rural areas.

Most upper-piedmont towns centering around railroad lines were founded only in the 1850s, 1870s, or later. Benefiting from these new centers, African Americans found land and houses more affordable than in rural areas and job opportunities more varied. Taking advantage of these factors, blacks created their own communities, institutions, and organizations. This chapter deals with twelve incorporated towns, excluding Anderson town (chapter 19), overshadowing the others with greater population and opportunities.[1]

Racial relations were more harmonious in towns than in some rural areas. That may have resulted from many of these towns and their black communities developing simultaneously. Certainly black and white constituted distinctly separate groups, but they lived near each other, shopped at the same stores, and shared public events. Even William Pickens, later to be an NAACP field-worker, described Pendleton: "there was extraordinary good feeling between the white and the black race. . . . Race antagonism seemed not to touch our world." And the Reverend Harrison Watkins, celebrating Griffin Ebenezer Baptist's thirtieth anniversary in 1902, said that the town of "Pickens is made up of a generous set of white people" and thanked them for contributions for a new church building. But in both towns and rural areas there seems to have been less collaboration between black and white skilled crafts people than in earlier years. There were joint black-white enterprises, including Pickens saw mill partners, and some illegal distilling.

Good racial relations, however, were subject to quick change. When an Easley "negro . . . sent an offensive letter to a most estimable young [white] lady," her male friend beat the black man about the head and had him arrested. Although a "strong delegation" of white men seemed bent on lynching him, armed blacks protected the accused, who decided to flee. A "large mass meeting" of whites notified "all the negroes [including the town's black Baptist minister] who went to the court house to leave the town within twenty-four hours. . . . Much bad blood between the two races has been engendered. . . . The town is being patroled tonight." Relations that appeared placid could easily become volatile.[2]

Town Origins

Compared to rural areas, towns usually afford more opportunities for upward mobility and varied occupations and crafts, especially for minorities. After 1870 similar advantages, if on a small scale, expanded in northwestern South Carolina. Earlier, however, towns played a relatively minor role there and offered little for African Americans. As late as the 1840s, the only towns were Pendleton, Anderson, and Pickens, all incorporated just in that decade.[3]

Area towns increased in number and importance for blacks and whites during far-reaching post–Civil War change. Increasingly in the 1870s, 1880s, and 1890s, African Americans were deeply affected—often to their disadvantage—by technical and societal changes sweeping the country. When the Southern Railroad route was demarcated in the early 1870s, its tracks passed through the densest black sections of Oconee and Pickens. New towns quickly emerged along this route. So did numerous cotton mills, taking advantage of easy rail shipment of their products. Sharecroppers then had to raise more cotton, soon the mainstay of cropping agreements. Rising rapidly, the state's production more than doubled between 1870 and 1880, rose more slowly by another 25 percent during the 1880s, and 50 percent by 1898. Cotton itself depended on fertilizer, such a booming industry that the 1895 state handbook carried a full-page illustration of a fertilizer mill.[4]

Expanding rapidly in the late 1800s and early 1900s, many new mills consumed huge quantities of sharecroppers' cotton and drove up the demand for it. At Pelzer Mills since 1881 there "has grown up as if by magic a thriving and prosperous town of fourteen hundred inhabitants. In it stands one of the finest cotton mills in the South," the *News and Courier* reported in 1885. The seventeen cotton mills operating in Anderson, Oconee, and Pickens counties in 1900 employed 8,528 hands, or approximately 25 percent of whites over fifteen years old. These include Pelzer and Piedmont mills; although the latter was located on Greenville County's side of the river, many workers lived in Anderson County.[5]

"Mill towns" became distinctive settlements where textile operators lived mostly in company-owned housing. These grew from scratch and consisted almost entirely

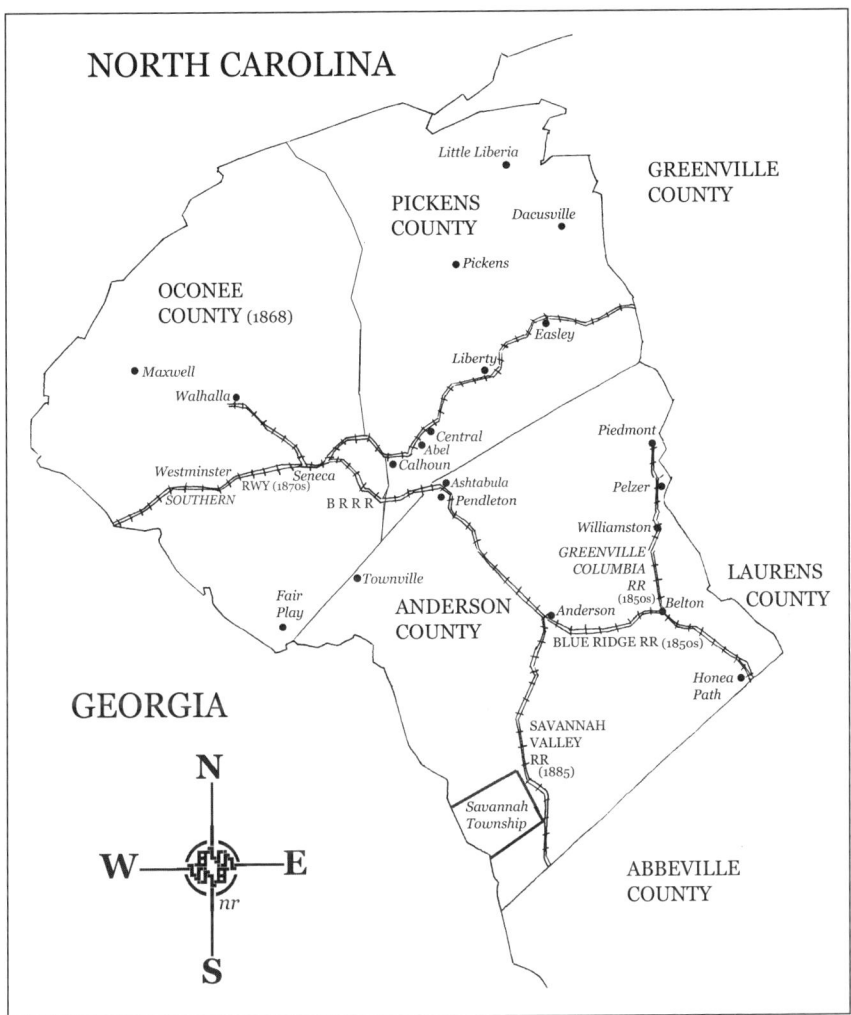

Anderson, Oconee, and Pickens, 1868–1900

of white people, as was the case with Catechee and Newry; Piedmont was a conspicuous exception. The mill just outside Central's town limits accounted for fifty consecutive census households, all whites. These towns had company housing, company-supported schools in their own separate districts, and sometimes company-sponsored churches.[6]

Rapid growth of these enclaves and of their residents, living there under strict company rules, led to social turmoil. Workers from mountainous areas had little prior experience with black people. Regarded by other whites as lower-class, "lintheads" became especially antagonistic toward African Americans. By the 1900s mill workers constituted several lynch mobs, although usually led by well-established whites.[7] Mill people remained a distinctly different population outside traditional local relationships. White townsfolk shared more contacts with blacks than with white mill people.

Railroads, Related Occupations, and Other Town Employment

Railroads, major technological developments beyond black control, changed the area's slower rural nature as it led to the founding of new towns. Existing ones—Anderson, Pendleton, and Walhalla—benefited from the Blue Ridge Railroad's construction in the 1850s. Three new Anderson towns sprang up along that Blue Ridge route—Williamston, Honea Path, and Belton. Belton thrived as connecting link with the Greenville and Columbia Railroad; waiting for transfers, passengers utilized hotel, restaurant, and tavern facilities. Railroads carried mail, Atlanta and Greenville newspapers, packages, and general store merchandise. Rail service became such an integral part of town life that testimony about an 1887 lynching in Central centered around the time the night train came through.

Two decades after the Blue Ridge Railroad opening, the Air Line Railroad—a firm known during most of its history as the Southern Railroad—laid a new route between Atlanta, Charlotte, and Richmond, connecting to Washington, D.C. The 1870s, then, saw another spurt of new railroad towns, this time in Oconee: Westminster and Seneca; and in Pickens: Central (literally the Atlanta–Charlotte midpoint), Liberty, and Easley—all developed solely because of the railroad. Entrepreneurs in each case bought agricultural land and sold parcels to ready buyers. When reading about activities of the 1880s or 1890s, remember that these Southern Railroad towns were barely one or two decades old, and that all black residents chose to move there.

African Americans benefited directly from railroads in varied ways. Initially, men worked helping to lay the tracks; the Blue Ridge in the 1850s hired some who were slaves. Railroads needed constant maintenance, and hundreds of black men in the three-county area in the 1870s, 1880s, and later serviced tracks and trains. Laying and repairing railroad lines was difficult labor, as related by one Sizemore relative: "My father was working on the railroads.... Only paid one dollar a day.... It was rough back then. It wasn't no play. Pick and shovel all day long. Bringing in those rocks and pulling out cross-ties, ... some of them weighed 150 pounds.... it wasn't nothing but man killer."[8]

Divided into relatively short "sections," railroads had separate maintenance crews every few miles. White engineer Paul Smith in 1880 headed a Pendleton household—probably a "section house"—with twelve black Blue Ridge workers. Ranging in age from eighteen to thirty-five, most were unmarried. Westminster in 1880 had four black railroad "hands." Heading their own family households, they averaged twenty-seven years old; two were illiterate. Contrasted to Pendleton's crew, these men had settled family lives. Two blacksmiths in town probably derived some livelihood from services for the railroad as well.

Postcare of railroad workers: Prince Nash (Pendleton) and coworkers. Black Heritage in the Upper Piedmont

Table 18.1 **Town Populations and Occupations, 1880**

Location Town	Population			Literacy/School			Employment		
	Black Pop.	Total Pop.	Black %	R/W #	R/W %	No. in School	Farm %	Laborer %	service
Pendleton	361	672	54	85	34	22	36	10	12
Honea Path	90	279	32	36	58	08	43	0	22
Belton	145	317	46	51	50	6	63	8	16
Townville	39	105	37	7	29	0	26	68	0
Pickens	75	214	35	7	58	18	44	0	20
Easley	78	327	24	26	61	1	31	6	24
Liberty	43	149	29	4	16	0	26	30	13
Central	50	186	27	8	22	4	17	8	38
Seneca	99	382	26	38	56	1	2	2	31
Westminster	40	171	23	8	32	1	40	5	0
Walhalla	212	789	27	50	36	7	23	4	35
Fort Madison	15	38	42	2	29	2	33	0	17
Total	1247	3629	34	322	27	70	32	12	19

Other men throughout Anderson, Oconee, and Pickens counties loaded and unloaded cargo at depots. A few men had jobs on the trains themselves, mostly tending coal, fire, and brakes. Firms directly serving the railroads and their customers also required employees at blacksmith shops, livery stables, and hotels, which offered both rooms and restaurant service. A history of Central recalled "John Stokes . . . [whose] courteous manner of welcoming passengers to the hotel dining room was impressive. 'Come right in, ladies and gentlemen, this is where you get blackberry pie and fresh Seneca River Salmon.'" Elsewhere, one Pendleton hotel proprietor employed in his home a cook, a porter, and a nursemaid. Several men worked for the local sawmill, which existed primarily because the railroad could cheaply haul its products.[9] Collectively these firms and the railroad utilized more blacks in towns than did any other type of employment. And mills depended on railroads, and thus workers, to ship finished products.

Oconee centers—Seneca, Westminster, and Walhalla—had more skilled black craftsmen and professionals than did Pickens or most Anderson ones (table 18.1). Even Belton, with a larger black population than either Seneca or Westminster, did not match them. Only Anderson and Pendleton had more professional and skilled black workers; Westminster had the highest percentage compared to its black population. Pickens County came up short, with no more than four professional and skilled workers in any one town.

Created in 1892, much later than other Southern Railroad towns, Calhoun—known later as Clemson—and Clemson Agricultural College provided for most nearby blacks their first alternative to farm work, domestic service, or labor for the railroad. As college employees they still worked as servants—cooks, waiters, or janitors—or farm laborers, but wages were somewhat higher and steadier than elsewhere, and some were allotted homes. Even at that, Robert Reid did not make fifteen dollars per month, about seventy-five cents per day—somewhat above the going wage for manual labor—until he married.

Edward Dorsey and Elbert Walker worked at the college hotel as butler and servant, while Mary Owens cooked. Two women were cooks for white families in town. Laundress Frances Dupree—Milly Dupree's granddaughter—often did her washing for college faculty in a creek behind the Cold Spring plantation house. Only two of Calhoun's ten wives in 1900 had to take gainful employment. Work not dependent on cotton crops provided attractive and stable alternatives for town people.[10]

Town Neighborhoods, Schools, and Churches

Advantages offered by towns drew people there. One family demonstrates a deliberate, fortuitous decision—"sacred," William Pickens called it—to move into town, as others also chose to do. Sharecroppers, Jacob and Mary Pickens relocated from an outlying rural area to obtain better education for their children. Jacob Pickens, becoming a wage earner for the hotel, got its owner to advance money for their move. A bartender, he also worked as a railroad section hand, brakeman, and fireman and served as Baptist Sunday school superintendent. Mary Pickens cooked and cleaned for white families, considered decidedly preferable to her working in the fields.[11]

Many larger churches and better schools were centered in towns whose concentrations of population and of community leaders supported them. Belton and Anderson had two of the larger black churches in the mid-1870s. Most black clergy and educators held several positions at one time, and clergy especially had to derive their livelihood from some other source. Ministers and teachers often lived in towns, where they found both employment and train service to outlying churches or schools.

Educational opportunities developed rapidly in some towns, especially Anderson and Pendleton, as did most freedmen's schools, but slowly in others. Most black town residents in 1880 had significantly higher literacy rates than did rural counterparts. Seneca with 50 percent, Pendleton with 54 percent, and Easley with 56 percent had the highest, but Pickens and Liberty—both with smaller populations—dropped below 20 percent. School facilities and literacy varied substantially among twelve towns. Excluding Anderson and Williamston, the three counties' towns collectively had only seventy black students in 1879–80. By 1900, however, these towns would all have black schools, larger student attendance, and higher literacy rates. Black postgrammar schools in Anderson, Oconee, and Pickens counties in 1920 were all in towns.

Neighborhoods—determined by land prices—sprang up simultaneously with new railroad towns' beginnings. Houses, schools, and churches clustered there. These areas lay slightly away from the town center, usually the hub of white businesses and fashionable homes. Black people often got less desirable land with gullies, ditches, or creeks. When Pickens District was divided in 1868 into Oconee and Pickens counties, the latter created that same year New Pickens, located about fifteen miles from Old Pickens. As whites abandoned the old one, black people quickly established a rural community there and soon had one of Oconee's early churches.

Black sections similarly developed early in other towns. Liberty's community lay on the town's eastern side. Southern Railroad tracks formed Calhoun's east–west artery, and black residences were to the northeast and southeast. Their land was a poorer quality for crops or gardens and the terrain, more rugged than in the town's core white section, was also cheaper. Landowners in Calhoun frequently had to mortgage their homes, then lost them when repayment became impossible. Walhalla's black area is primarily to the southwest, especially along John Street. Each of these neighborhoods remains black occupied today, with younger generations of original families still owning homes there.

Surprisingly, it was easier to buy a house in town than in the country. Although houses in town typically cost more, rural land usually involved purchasing many acres, while in these new towns one could buy a small lot when heirs of deceased

Gassaway bedroom suite, Seneca, S.C, belonging to Larkin Gassaway, a farmer in the Seneca area, who owned his property free of mortgage in 1900. Black Heritage in the Upper Piedmont

Middle-class furnishings of an AOP black middle-class family; the home and contents still belong to descendants a century later. Black Heritage in the Upper Piedmont

whites sold large tracts in towns. That happened in Pendleton during the 1880s; part of John S. Lorton's property became a black area known as Belmina, the one place in town exclusively their own. Later, deaths of R. A. Cochran, Aaron Boggs, and other owners opened up land for Abel residents to purchase plots and build homes of similar style.

Half of Oconee's eighty black landowners in 1880 had property in towns. Twenty years later town holdings were valued as 27 percent of Oconee's black-owned land, 25 percent in Pickens. Property ownership reached a high level in Pendleton town: by 1900 nearly 40 percent of black households owned their house or farm.[12] Only 14 percent of these properties were mortgaged, well below national, state, or local averages. By contrast, fewer than 10 percent of the surrounding Pendleton Township black households owned land.

Churches formed the locus of small-town communities. There, churches, as elsewhere, offered meeting space for community events and served as solidifying forces. Many schools were located on or adjacent to church property, as were several fraternal orders, especially Masons. All town ministers could read and write, which reinforced their roles as community leaders.

Town Populations and Occupations

Virtually all towns in Anderson, Oconee, and Pickens counties—except Anderson, a conspicuous exception—were too small in total population to sustain black businesses before 1900. Twelve others in 1880 had a total population ranging from 38 in Fort Madison to 672 in Pendleton and Walhalla's 789. Easley and Seneca, nearly in the middle, had 327 and 382 respectively (see table 18.1). Only three of them had more than 100 black residents: Belton with 145 (46 percent of town population), Walhalla, 212 (27 percent), and Pendleton, 361 (54 percent), which had both the largest black number and highest percentage. Those in nine other towns ranged from 23 percent, Westminster, to 37 percent, Townville.[13]

Few records or oral traditions have been found of black businesses, other than skilled crafts, in these towns prior to 1900. Later small neighborhood stores—likely with pre-1900 antecedents—would sell snacks, tobacco, and sometimes school supplies, but none substituted for the white-owned general stores, patronized for most other needs. The 1880 census indicates only one black-owned store, Benjamin Keels's confectionery in Pendleton, which probably served the whole town population. Several craftsmen advertised, as did P. S. Little for his Central shoe shop and school, and Ben Griffin for his butchery in Pickens. *Smith's South Carolina Business Directory* for 1876–77 carried only one Pendleton black listing, June Lewis, blacksmith, and none for other towns except Anderson.[14]

African Americans worked as blacksmiths in nine towns, shoemakers in five, carpenters in four, barbers in three, and painters in three. Other skilled occupations found in only one or two towns included tinsmith and brick mason. More barbers and butchers would emerge by 1900, then almost dominating their fields. Other late-1800s employers included railroads, livery stables, and hotels, using waiters and porters. Central resident Philip Green's well-digging services were utilized throughout the area.[15]

These 1880 occupations appear diversified when compared with rural areas (table 19.2, pp. 343–44), where workers consisted almost entirely of farmers, farm laborers, and laborers, based on two sample townships in each county. Additionally, there were five blacksmiths, one minister, and one teacher; the one cook and twenty servants all lived in white households. One person each worked for the railroad, was a railroad laborer, worked in a saw mill, and was an assistant cook. These thirty-two men and women were the only exceptions to agricultural labor among 2,357 rural people sampled. In rural Anderson County, an 1884 report stated that "colored women and children out of the towns generally work in the fields."[16] Relatively little change occurred in rural occupations by 1900, or perhaps even by 1950.

Women in towns, like Mary Pickens, had gainful employment primarily in service: laundresses, cooks, maids, household servants, and "nurses" tending children. A combination of Williamston's female academy, mineral-resort visitors, and a nearby mill provided employment for sixty-four laundresses. In Walhalla, Central, and Westminster, women in service held 35 to 38 percent of all black employment there. Anderson employed 42 percent of its black workers in service positions. By 1900 women's fields expanded to include seamstresses and a few teachers.

Many white families of middle or higher socioeconomic status expected to have domestic help. Pendleton's families with live-in cooks or servants included, among others, a general-store proprietor, a blacksmith, a carriage manufacturer, the Episcopal rector, and several widowed women.[17] When Clemson Agricultural College was established nearby in the 1890s, it built servants' houses behind faculty homes on campus. All women employed in Pendleton, 22 percent of its black labor force, held jobs as cooks or servants. Ten percent of white households there had a live-in cook, and a partially overlapping 15 percent, a live-in servant. A nearly equal number of cooks and servants resided in their own households. Most were married, but some were widowed or single, and several were young girls. Some cooks and servants worked at the town's hotel. Nearly 20 percent of white households, then, employed cooks, and almost 30 percent, maids.[18]

"Laborers" in the mid-1800s formed one of America's largest categories of employment. Only Liberty (30 percent), Anderson (42 percent), and Townville (68 percent) in the 1880 census had more than 10 percent of employed blacks who described their work simply as "laborer," almost all men. Some of these had regular employment; many more found odd jobs as day laborers. With town boundaries often only one-half mile in radius, agriculture, not surprisingly, employed many men, women, and children. Their figures in 1880 ranged from 2 percent among black workers for Seneca to 63 percent in Belton. Some farmers lived in towns, which reinforced a sense that town and rural communities were not entirely separated.

Although other occupational choices grew by 1900 (see table 19.2, pp. 343–44), agriculture shrank significantly. In 1900 there was only a fourth as many farm workers living in towns as in 1880. On the whole farmers were more literate than black townspeople, even more so when two illiterate men both aged seventy (b. 1830) are not counted. Nine families owned their homes or farms.

Black Organizations and Festive Occasions

Increased prospects of owning land and obtaining diversified employment other than farming attracted many families into towns, as did wider social, religious, and educational offerings. More social opportunities occurred in towns than in the countryside, although special occasions drew people from outlying areas as well. Bustling traffic occurred each fall when farmers hauled their cotton to sales. Photographs of these crowds exist for many towns, and maps show large cotton platforms at train depots. Presumably these days, with hundreds of farmers in town, involved—for black and white—much socializing, shopping, and drinking.

Several events brought black and white together in ways unimaginable in later decades. Black people in 1878 attended performances at Anderson's white Masonic Hall, and blacks in Pickens joined whites for McFowler's magic lantern show in December 1887. Until the early 1900s circuses and fairs drew black and white at the same time. Great Eastern Circus's 1873 Anderson event attracted between five and six thousand white and black, equaling over a third of the county's population.

Cotton hauled to the Greenville market, 1899, photograph by C. L. Baley. Courtesy Schomberg Center for Research in Black Culture, New York Public Library

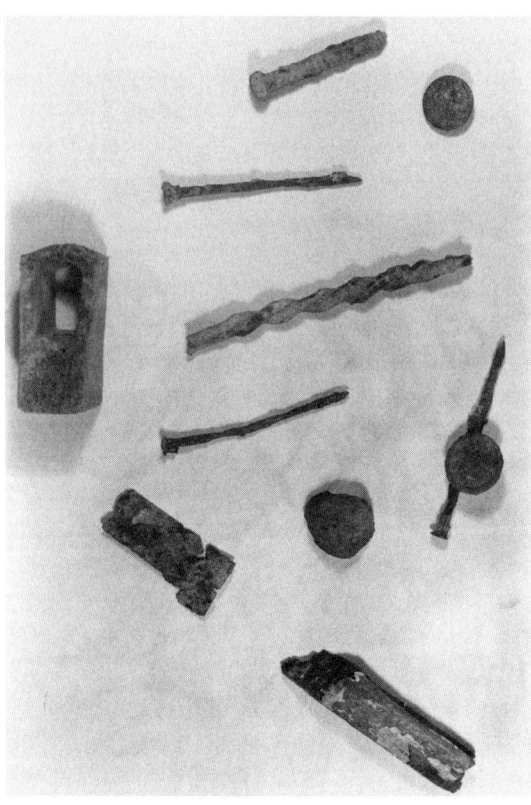

Left: Sidney Burt's blacksmith shop artifacts (excavated from the backyard of a descendant). Black Heritage in the Upper Piedmont

P. S. Little's advertisements for school and shoe work, Central, S.C.; reprinted from November 1, 1888, advertisements in the *Populace* (Central). Black Heritage in the Upper Piedmont

P. S. LITTLE'S SHOE SHOP
On Corner Main and Watkins Street.
FIRST-CLASS WORK, REPAIRING AND MAKING
AS LOW AS THE LOWEST.

CENTRAL COLORED SCHOOL.
TAUGHT BY P. S. LITTLE,
Six months each year. Bring your children to me if you want them educated.
West End, Central, S. C.

G. M. BOWLING,
Central,   S. Carolina,
Fashionable Hair Cutting, Shampooing, etc. Shop on West End.

Many people combined business with entertainment, as two hundred bales of cotton were sold that same day. Similarly county fairs in Anderson, Walhalla, and Pickens served their whole population until the early 1900s. Fairs, then held in Pickens town, drew both black and white as late as 1907, although there were racially separated dancing and wrestling competitions.[19]

School exhibitions, usually held as closing exercises, attracted sizable crowds and were often accompanied by parades and dinners. Usually at least the county school superintendent and commissioners attended, as often did other white men as well. Contests rewarded students for the best accomplishments, term grades, and attendance. A black minister usually provided prayer and remarks. A typical announcement in a September 1897 *People's Journal* issue reported that closing exercises would be held for Pickens's black school with everyone, "white and colored," invited. Churches also sponsored joint Sunday school conventions and singing schools.[20]

Participation in public political celebrations, both Republican and Democratic, continued in the 1880s and perhaps later. Such occasions often involved parades and picnics or barbecues. Other events occurred on Emancipation Day and July 4. In 1867, Independence Day observances, by then almost exclusively black, held deeply personal significance and drew a large attendance in Anderson. Republicans periodically held July 4 celebrations in Anderson and Walhalla, and, to recruit members, a union organizer held a July 4, 1887, meeting in Dacusville (Pickens County), likely with food and festivities. A crowd of 150 included about 30 blacks, none of whom enlisted. The first Emancipation Day references in Anderson, Oconee, and Pickens counties are from Pendleton's 1900 service, which attracted a large crowd.[21]

Excursions to nearby cities followed a special October 1878 train from Walhalla to Charleston. White and black occupied separate coaches, as on a "colored excursion" train from Charlotte to Atlanta that picked up local passengers. Special coaches in August 1894 brought almost eight hundred Newberry blacks to Anderson on a Thursday for competition between black firemen, a dance, and a late-night return trip. It is hard to imagine that many black people arriving there fifty or a hundred years later without causing concern among white residents. A year later Andersonians including a brass band traveled to Greenville, "warmly welcomed" by Greenville's black community. Other trips followed in subsequent years, primarily to or from Anderson, with baseball games added. Festive excursions continued into the 1900s.[22]

Northern soldiers reportedly introduced baseball into South Carolina in the 1860s. Black teams, organized by towns, began as early as 1879 in the three-county area, but earlier in Charleston and Columbia. Pickens town resident, veterinarian, and butcher Ben P. Griffin, who "promoted ball games, sold food while the game was playing. He would also kill beef to sell. He would have these games on Saturday," his daughter recalled. In the early 1900s Anderson's Taylor family played and managed teams in the Negro League. Pool halls provided yet another form of recreation.[23]

Fraternal organizations developed slowly with most Masonic, Eastern Star, and Knights of Pythias lodges being organized after 1890. Anderson had an Odd Fellows lodge by 1895, when it laid the cornerstone for the new AME church. Both the Sons and Daughters and Good Templars owned land in Pendleton before most families did. Anderson's Good Samaritans chapter offered mutual aid during illness and distress, as did Anderson's Good Templars. G. D. Williams led its July 1879 anniversary celebration, which featured a "colored band" and procession, begun at Greeley Institute. Anderson, Oconee, and Pickens counties had no black funeral homes until the 1920s and perhaps no burial insurance firms there, as often found in larger cities.[24]

Darker events also attracted large crowds, as they did throughout the nation's history. The three to four thousand people, many of them black, who watched Shedrick Webster's hanging in 1871 were called Anderson County's greatest attendance at any public event. Webster, a black man, was convicted of killing the black woman with whom he was living.

Towns as well as the countryside often had both black and white houses of prostitution and vendors of illegal whiskey. A black "low bawdy house" in Greenville made the newspaper when a murder occurred there. The victims, assailant, and madam were all black, but white men also patronized the house. Several complaints about whiskey wagons and prostitution—both white and black women were named—reached Oconee's 1878 grand jury.[25] References appeared to black prostitution in early 1900s Greenville and tricounty railroad towns.

Little contemporary information survives about black music of the era. What bands played is unknown. Whites commented on and enjoyed black religious music. Printed hymnals, like other religious literature, came from white denominational presses—except AME materials, and its hymns were largely those also used in white churches. Concert performances at association meetings likely followed these same texts, as certainly did hymns sung at Rocky River's annual meetings. Jane Hunter, however, liked to hear "the rich voices of the cotton pickers, singing 'Swing Low, Sweet Chariot,' and . . . 'Walk Together, Children, Don't Get Weary.'" Sporadic comments refer to work songs. She recalled her aunt, "often when she reached the end of the row [of cotton] . . . singing, 'We are climbing Jacob's ladder.'" When Jane Hunter wanted "to shock 'proper folk' and be abysmally wicked," she turned to "Georgia Gal," "Swanee River," and "Old Black Joe."[26]

Music played an important role in many social, religious, and educational activities. Bands provided spirited music for parades, an 1874 celebration at Cochran's house, and an 1879 Good Templars celebration. Several black musicians performed in Pickens town in February 1900; entrepreneur and town butcher Ben Tolbert managed the event, drawing a "very large crowd of both white and colored," all paying a dime for admission. Blacks could also enjoy occasional white outdoor bands, as happened in Easley and at Clemson.

Right: Masonic regalia worn by Frederick Washington, early 1900s, Seneca. Black Heritage in the Upper Piedmont

Von Hasseln 1897 map of Anderson County; Pendleton inset clearly shows black-owned homes and churches; the curved road on the right is still black-occupied Belmina Street. Black Heritage in the Upper Piedmont

Performers included "Uncle Jack Calhoun." Reported to have been John C. Calhoun's slave, he performed in Clarksville, Georgia, in the 1870s: "Jack Calhoun fiddling—Joe Alston and his boys and another darky with a guitar. Such music! . . . the 'Virginia Reel' . . . and the 'Lancers.'" Later, he led the Slabtown String Band in an 1887 Central performance, evidently for both white and black. Anderson's Rough and Ready fire brigade had a band that often played for white, black, and shared events. Accompanying various excursion groups, bands played at host cities. A Pickens town band included four harmonicas, fiddle, drum, and triangle.[27]

Camp meetings, usually held in a rural setting, drew large crowds from cities and surrounding countryside. Pickens County's black Union Campground, which evidently had antebellum roots, operated throughout subsequent decades. Mid-July 1879 Methodist Sunday School celebrations at Providence—a site that whites also used—included groups from eight churches. An upper Anderson County meeting drew several thousand attendees. "The singing was distinctly heard five miles away," the newspaper reported.[28]

White and black town folk separately enjoyed rural picnics. There, they probably were joined by friends, relatives, and joiners-on from the countryside. Singing schools often evoked a similar atmosphere as attendees were urged to bring bulging picnic baskets. Black picnics usually made the news when they turned raucous, as did one at Garvin's Springs near Central on a May 1882 Saturday, but an "orderly" August 1894 event at Fowler Creek also got a brief press notice.[29]

Community life developed considerably wider resources in towns than in the country, especially where there were both large town and black populations. Approximately a hundred black people seem to have been a critical dividing line marking towns that had many more opportunities, but even those with at least fifty blacks achieved more than in rural areas. A concentration of fifty to a hundred black people within less than a mile radius supported churches, schools, and community activities. Similarly, white businesses afforded more, and more diversified, black job prospects than in rural areas.

Lines between town and country, or between black and white, were not sharp. Townspeople often had relatives who lived there too. People from throughout the surrounding region would come into town for special events. Church association or conference meetings rotated sites among town and rural churches. By the early 1900s Knights of Pythias town lodges had members throughout the surrounding countryside.

Although black and white entertainments were not yet totally separated, distinct areas for standing or seating might well apply, as certainly occurred on excursion trains. Some events identified as black, such as school exhibitions or church dinners, often included white guests, who had a separate seating area or table. White delegates, guests, or speakers attended regional black church meetings, and vice versa. Given the small size of towns, even Anderson as late as the 1880s, any white or black family in town lived within a short distance—no more than a quarter mile—from a

Richard & Clarissa Addison at home, Grandchildren and all.

Addison's family cabin on the outskirts of Greenville, 1899, photograph by C. L. Baley. Courtesy Schomberg Center for Research in Black Culture, New York Public Library

A flash-light result. Note fire in hearth and grandchild & cigarette.

Addison cabin interior view of Richard and Clarissa Addison's cabin at Camp Wetherill, photograph by C. L. Baley. Courtesy Schomberg Center for Research in Black Culture, New York Public Library

family of another race. Jane Hunter referred to "the white and colored people in the neighborhood" where she worked in Anderson. Since virtually all employed blacks worked for whites and many lived in white-owned houses, contacts between races persisted on a daily, if highly unequal, basis.[30] Skewed evidence comes from the white press, not well informed on some all-black events.

Towns did not guarantee a better life. Poverty and squalid dwellings were unfortunate fates for some people. In later decades upper-piedmont newspapers—all white—would stress "negro crime" in cities and towns. Black Baptists and African Methodist Episcopalians lamented these crimes also. As early as June 1879 the *Intelligencer* complained that many "colored people" in Anderson were too lazy to work and spent their time gambling; the police arrested five last Saturday night, the paper reported. The Rocky River Baptist Association in 1893 proclaimed that the Gospel pulls "men out of the bar-room, the pool-room, the gambling den, and many other such places." Both whites and blacks contended, at times, that black people belonged in the countryside rather than in towns, as did the 1906 Colored Baptist State Convention. Increasingly in those same years more professionals, home owners, and businesses demonstrated positive advantages of town life.[31]

Beyond Towns

Communities flourished also in rural areas, such as Little Liberia, the Tenus Maxwell vicinity, and Abel. Emerging mostly from centers of slave population, they offered a sense of belonging, that is of community and mutual support. The vast majority of southern African Americans lived in the countryside—in Anderson, Oconee, and Pickens counties, 95 percent in 1880, reduced to 86 percent in 1900. There, "the setting was on a 200-acre farm of poor red clay hills, and soil, lots of woodland and a BIG DEBT. There were no welfare, social security, or salaried jobs."[32] Serving the bulk of blacks in the three-county area, these communities provided primary collective identity and associations, even more critical there than in towns.

Yet rural and town communities during the 1870s and 1880s sometimes joined larger movements or organizations to improve their lives. Oconee Republicans in 1874 formed a connection with a workingmen's association. During 1887 blacks joined local Cooperative Workers of America organizations in nearby Spartanburg, Laurens, and Greenville counties, and perhaps Dacusville. And black farmers near Liberty and Easley, creating local alliances in the late 1880s or early 1890s, had enough support to purchase their own building in Liberty. G. D. Williams of Anderson city, vice president of the state black farmers' alliances in 1892, presumably helped to spread local units throughout the upstate. Further, a benevolent society had its headquarters in rural Anderson County near the Mount Sinai campground.[33] Only sketchy information is available on each of these endeavors.

Hardly any surviving material reveals details of black rural life in Anderson, Oconee, and Pickens counties. Harsh economic realities suggest that it was often dreary. Even elsewhere in the state, WPA interviewers—focusing their attention primarily on antebellum years and on Reconstruction—mostly ignored postbellum rural conditions. Two studies on Abbeville and Mars Bluff provide some insights.[34]

More information is available on African American Christmas seasons, corn shuckings, and other rural social life during slavery than afterward. Sporadic newspaper tidbits refer to picnics, camp meetings, church services, Sunday schools, and singing conventions. "Hot suppers" were popular rural events. Camp meetings and excursions occurred during August, when the crops needed little attention, and year-end festivities followed their antebellum customs.[35]

Medical care for postbellum rural African Americans is a virtually undocumented subject. At least two men appearing in the census were likely traditional or herb doctors, as were Forch Allen and some Sizemore relatives. Entries in 1880 mortality schedules show both a sizable number of blacks who received some medical attention and many who did not. That care may have begun, in some cases, only during a last illness. Generally, babies who died and people who lived in rural areas were less likely to have had any doctor in attendance; people in towns were more apt to receive some care.[36]

Churches and schools were especially important for rural folk, who were mostly too impoverished to enjoy excursions or circuses and lacked clothing for dress-up events. Jane Hunter and John Starks had to borrow suitable garb for their graduations, and a 1908 photograph of Seneca's Gassaway family hides the sons' feet, as none of them owned shoes. And, for those living in more distant locations, travel to town by foot, mule, or buggy took at least an hour or two. A Thompson family member reported, "Our longest day was our getting up in the morning by four o'clock to go the distance of fifteen miles (driving the mule and buggy) to Anderson to see the parade of the Ringling Brothers Circus . . . we never had enough money to buy tickets and go in the show."[37]

Rural people sometimes provided overnight lodging for travelers. Many late-1800s blacks and whites, lacking a horse or mule and either not affording or having any train nearby, traversed rural areas on foot. Simply asking often yielded overnight lodgings. John Starks begged a ride to Hartwell. The driver was not going that far but told Starks to stop with "his daughter and son-in-law . . . and tell them that he said let me spend the night"; that family refused any payment. Several years later, Starks "saw a man and his wife ploughing. . . . I stopped, approached the man, and asked if I might stay with him for the night. He kindly consented." Censuses for rural areas show numerous boarders living with families, occasionally with whites. Rural folk often had to live together to meet expenses.[38]

WPA photographs throughout the South document poor-quality often shabby houses for sharecroppers. Sometimes these houses appear disorderly outside as well. Jane Hunter, referring to "the filth and squalor in which many of the Negroes lived," wrote that her mother instead compulsively maintained a clean home: "The house in which we lived was a two-room frame dwelling which stood at the edge of a sloping field . . . [and was] surrounded by 'house leeks' which she had dug up in the woods. . . . [We children] scrubbed the floors of the cabin, not forgetting to wash between the chinks of the boards, for mother was a scrupulous housekeeper and trained us early in habits of neatness and cleanliness. . . . As there was not enough chairs, we sat on the floor to eat our cornbread and milk out of tin cups; but the scrubbed planks were as clean as a dining table in the finest home." Her "squalor" comments, along with those by Baptist ministers and other black writers, indicate that some people kept their crowded, ill-furnished sharecroppers' houses in disarray and "filth." Occupying, perhaps for only a year, a house owned by a landlord, families had little incentive to improve its condition, and—with prospects of soon moving again—practical as well as economic reasons to have few possessions.[39]

Rural Communities

Three communities, two of them especially isolated, illustrate rural life. Their black populations between 1870 and 1900 may each have approximated a hundred. Contrasted to towns, these people often were long-term residents, having lived in these areas as slaves. Traces of two still survive today, and another, a vibrant force, acquired a city-funded community center in the 1990s.

African Americans residing in a remote foothills section of Pickens County, north of Pumpkintown, created a community called Little Liberia. Some black families evidently moved there from other rural Pickens areas. A church and a school were key institutions. Founded in the late 1870s, Soap Stone Baptist Church, called Little Durby, served also as schoolhouse. Teacher C. T. Miller produced a dramatic closing exercise there in 1896 with "panorama, chants, dialogues, trios and gymnastic" displays.[40]

Personal names and titles sometimes had political connotations, as did "Little Liberia" itself. Willie Owens called his boy, born in 1876, General George Washington Independent Centennial Owens. One family named their daughter Queen Hagood, another their son King Ferguson. One man added the surname King to his slave name Pompey; later a boy was called King Terrell.[41]

Despite these names that some might call "black nationalism," the community seems to have functioned harmoniously with local whites most of the time. Post–World War II books and newspaper articles by whites have stressed this harmony. These reports stated that four white landowners gave five acres of land to each of their freed families—Little Liberia's original black settlers—including Talleys, Keiths, Chastains, Gowans, Terrells, Glenns, Owens, and others.[42] Less kindly, Oolenoy Baptist Church, several miles to the west, adopted a blunt policy in February 1868: "colored people can . . . set up their own meeting house. We will not grant them the privilege of holding meetings at this place [nor let them be members]."

Memories have blurred both dates and basic facts of land that whites deeded to black families. Tax records for 1899 show only two men, whose holdings totaled 630 acres, in the area considered Little Liberia; for most families supposed to have been early black owners, such as Owens, no deeds were recorded until a decade or more later. Some propertied families bought land rather than receiving it as gifts. Throughout the entire township, land is very hilly, poor in quality, and cheap in price, its 1899 black-owned holdings being appraised at 90 cents an acre compared to $4.15 in Savannah Township (Anderson County).[43]

Other factors suggest relatively peaceful black-white relationships. A sizable number of African American surnames matched those of slave owners, probably a higher proportion than elsewhere in Anderson, Oconee, and Pickens counties. When black Matthew Ferguson, described as old and respected, died in 1894, he was buried in the white Ferguson graveyard. And when Andy Gowans, then the oldest black resident, died in 1928, the *Pickens Sentinel* said that "he had the esteem and respect of neighbors, both black and white."[44] Even a century later some whites still felt protective and paternal toward black families with personal relationships extending over generations from the nineteenth century.

Several recent sources refer to a peak population of three hundred blacks, but some moved away, as a 1928 newspaper referred to the "once popular negro settlement." Staying there the rest of their lives, Christopher and Lula McJunkin Owens, both born in the 1890s, celebrated their fiftieth wedding anniversary in 1975 and their one hundredth birthdays in the 1990s. The small church there, housed in a new building, still holds services for a handful of worshipers, and the Little Liberia name survives in local conversation, periodic newspaper articles, and oral tradition.[45]

Both Little Liberia and the Tenus Maxwell community lay in remote, semi-mountainous parts of Pickens and Oconee. John Starks described "my mountain church" that he served in a similar setting "near the foot of the Blue Ridge mountains. I remember that a certain deacon told me that his 84-year-old father had never joined the church because he lived back in the mountains and had never heard the gospel. He brought the old man to one of our revival services, one of ingathering old people.... There were but a handful of members ... poor and ignorant."[46]

Tenus Maxwell, formerly a slave on S. E. Maxwell's plantation, led his local, very rural Oconee community, not quite as remote as Little Liberia.[47] S.E., who owned a home in Pendleton, also bought in 1851 a plantation of rugged terrain north of the Chauga River. The August 22, 1857, *Keowee Courier* called Maxwell "one of the best farmers in the country." Selling part of the plantation to G. K. Keels in 1871, S.E. described that land: "15 acres are good and 15 acres poor, bottom 125 acres cleared upland and rather thin and the balance (662 acres) verry broken and unfit for cultivation."[48]

When people freed on the Maxwell plantation completed a labor agreement in September 1865, seventy-four of them had signed on, which along with children may have covered virtually all of S.E.'s former slaves. More than any other local group they perpetuated African practices of using days, Wednesday, or months, October, as names. Others, African derived, such as Tenah and Cuffe, appeared as well. Reconstruction activist December Gadsden probably had been a slave there and likely was married to Tenus Maxwell's daughter.[49]

The plantation's contracted laborers included a dozen or more men who registered to vote in 1867. Tenus Maxwell, one of them, became an election manager and in 1874 a candidate for county commissioner. By that time he owned sixteen hundred dollars' worth of land, 817 acres of S. E. Maxwell's plantation. That was an incredible amount of money for an Oconee man, free less than a decade, to have earned, let alone saved. Although listed in the census as a "farmer," Tenus Maxwell also owned blacksmith and carpentry tools; he may well have occasionally practiced both crafts, which would have increased his earnings considerably. Maxwell in 1880 possessed Oconee's highest-valued black-owned property. Acquiring surviving cabins —twenty-three on the whole plantation in 1860—he provided housing for perhaps a dozen families.[50]

This land served in effect as a community center, as did its cemetery. Secluded in the woods, it could be reached only by a long, steep climb, and had over one hundred black burials between 1865 and 1900, years after it passed into white ownership again. Oral tradition tells of processions, accompanied by spirited singing, up the hill to the cemetery. It may have originated before 1865; its "1865 M PRST" stone is probably the upstate's earliest surviving postemancipation tombstone.

Maxwell's tombstone shows that he became an early Baptist minister: "For 20 Yrs a Baptist Preacher." He likely held services in a brush arbor not far from the cemetery. Although the census reports him as able to read and write, he had little if any training as a minister. Maxwell probably helped found the Seneca River Missionary Baptist Association in 1879, and reportedly was St. Mark's first minister.

Typical of many families in that community, most of Tenus Maxwell's (b. 1818) adult children moved away, several of them into Georgia. When he died in 1883, a four-page accounting of his personal property showed many items being sold to black neighbors. But a court-appointed administrator sold his land for debts. Three white men who bought it permitted black burials to continue for another fifteen years; why they then ceased is not known. Called "If These Stones Could Talk," a ceremony held by white and black, descendants of Maxwell slaves, neighbors, school kids, and clergy rededicated the restored cemetery in 1997. It evokes memories of a community that has long since disappeared.

Twenty miles away the Abel community now thrives within the city of Clemson just a few hundred yards from Central's town limits. Completely rural in early postbellum years, its population probably came from those formerly enslaved on nearby plantations, just east of John C. Calhoun's land. By 1870 most were sharecroppers, some still on Calhoun property owned by his daughter and son-in-law Anna and Thomas G. Clemson. His white neighbors James W. Crawford, Aaron Boggs, and R. A. Cochran—two of them relatively recent arrivals in the immediate area—had sharecroppers working for them.

Typical 1870 census entries form a periphery of sharecroppers surrounding white landowners, as William Pickens described. Similar geographic, economic, and power relationships existed throughout Anderson, Oconee, and Pickens counties, and

Susie Haywood, daughter of Harrison Haywood and long-term clerk of Abel Baptist Church. Black Heritage in the Upper Piedmont

indeed much of the South. Despite black roles as sharecroppers, most wives in the Abel area, as in some others, did not formally participate in farm work, nor did most daughters.

None of the people listed there could read or yet owned land. Only James Watkins had any personal property, $150 worth; evidently he rented land for cash since he is one of only six black men listed as "farmer" in the township. Abel's black land ownership evidently began mostly in the 1900s when white owners died and their land was sold in small lots, as in Pendleton.

Community residents established several formal institutions, one quickly and others slowly over several decades.[51] Abel Baptist Church began in 1868. Several black men, perhaps already holding informal services in a brush arbor, met with a white friend, J. C. "Pet" Watkins, who helped them organize the church. Founding deacons included Billy Holmes, a former Colhoun slave; Washington Haywood, whose son Harrison was involved in an 1887 lynching; John Singleton, chairman of the board of deacons for many years; and Jimmy Watkins, whose family produced two ministers. According to the church's history, a white woman donated land, evidently not until 1876. Like many other churches, its congregation worshipped for years on land it did not own. The original structure lasted until 1928, when it was destroyed by fire, and a brick one replaced it. The church invited Pet Watkin's daughter to attend centennial ceremonies in 1968.

Abel, an early Rocky River Baptist Association member, became in 1879 one of the new Seneca River's founding churches. Like Tenus Maxwell's, Abel's land served as community cemetery, whose earliest-surviving tombstones date from the 1880s.

Hundreds of 1870s–1920s fieldstones have disappeared, either as plunder for nearby buildings or as hindrances to mowing in recent decades. Milly Dupree was likely buried at Abel; her granddaughters Fanny, Tena, and probably Amelia also are buried there, as are Fanny's son Tom Dupree, his wife, one of their daughters, and other family members. Abel's ministers included Harrison Oglesby, who served 1889–99.

Abel's land also provided sites for both a community school, called Abel, and the Banneker Masonic lodge, founded circa 1910. "Mother Abel" spawned several additional churches, called "Little Abels." Some people withdrew in 1874 to form Pendleton's Silver Spring. Goldenview Baptist, two miles to the west, separated peacefully after the town of Calhoun was founded, and its members still retain burial rights at Abel. In later years Abel would add a community center; a short distance away thrived a "juke joint," also a part of the community. In the 1990s the city built on that site a new center, which serves the still-intact Abel community. Abel, absorbed into rapid late twentieth-century urban growth, has flourished, but rapid growth and economic development gobble at the fringes of Abel. The church's role has been so pivotal that its name describes the surrounding community, as in many other rural areas.

Whether rural or urban, these communities provided a sense of identity and mutual support. Camp meetings in the countryside and festive occasions in towns drew people both ways, so neither rural nor urban people were completely isolated from each other. Similarly, numerous town dwellers worked on farm land, and country folk drifted into towns for jobs. Although the countryside held most of the upper piedmont's population, towns sustained most larger churches and better schools. Increasingly, they would also furnish the base for diversified jobs and for black businesses, as in Anderson city.

NINETEEN

Anderson's Urban Community

THE CITY OF ANDERSON far exceeded other local towns in total population as well as numbers of African Americans.[1] Anderson, South Carolina's sixth-largest city in 1900, had a well-developed black community. The city's sizable African American population made possible development of their churches, graded school, and other educational institutions. It also provided a consumer base for black businesses, which in turn enabled some people to purchase land and homes. Various organizations such as the Women's Christian Temperance Union, Masons, and Odd Fellows functioned because of the growing community. The city's size attracted people who came to work on a temporary basis. At the core, however, long-term families provided stability and led the community, many of them highlighted in Gwendolyn Anderson's *Profiles of Black Folks in Anderson County*.

Rapid growth of the city resulted largely from industrial progress and dominance of cotton. This included railroad service, new mills, and factories. Although Anderson's mills consumed much cotton, the city also served as a major shipping

Workers building a road near Anderson, early 1900s. Pendleton District Commission

point for that being sold elsewhere. African Americans benefited directly from these changes and the city's expansion.

The Town's Early Decades

Like nearby towns, the village of Anderson had a sudden birth, induced in this case by the legislature's subdividing Pendleton District into two independent units, Anderson and Pickens (including Oconee), both populous enough by 1826 to stand alone. Like later towns, Anderson village sprang from farm land bought from several owners, divided into lots, and sold to new arrivals and speculators. Anderson remained small during antebellum years. Hardly anything is known about African American residents then, other than names of a few free people of color, notably the Paytons, and numbers of slaves. Progress came slowly and unevenly. In a bizarre case the Paytons were accusing of dumping a dead horse in the city well; in 1874 Anderson got gas lights while the newspaper complained about cows roaming town streets.[2]

Service beginning in the 1850s by the Blue Ridge Railroad and in 1886 by the Savannah Valley Railroad spurred growth. To route the Blue Ridge Railroad through town, Crawford Keys had his slaves dig a "cut" north of the town square. Anderson in the late 1800s developed the country's first capacity to transmit electricity over a long distance and quickly acquired manufacturing plants including several textile mills. By 1890 Anderson became the state's eighth-largest city, rising to sixth in 1900 and fifth in 1910. Between 1860 and 1920 piedmont cities—Anderson, Greenville, and Spartanburg—were the state's fastest growing, with Anderson leading at times.

Postbellum Anderson became a likely place for African Americans to find diversified employment and to build a strong community. Between 1865 and 1870 townspeople organized St. Paul Baptist Church and a northern Methodist Episcopal congregation as well as Greeley Institute, a freedmen's school with a nine-member local board. St. Paul's minister and officers led in establishing the Rocky River Baptist Association in 1868. Already Anderson had an energetic, effective leadership, likely based on a core of antebellum skilled town slaves. The town—the tricounty political center in Reconstruction years—had an active Republican leadership, a Union League in 1867–68, and an 1870s militia unit. Several black men served on the town council between 1870 and 1875, while 358 registered men constituted 47 percent of total town voters.[3]

Soon Anderson would afford more educational and religious opportunities than found elsewhere in the county or adjacent Oconee, Pickens, and Abbeville. Large numbers of blacks moved to Anderson for these reasons. Incoming residents evidently came primarily from nearby areas, including Georgia.

An 1880 Snapshot

The first clear description of life and work for postbellum residents emerges from the 1880 census. That year's 810 blacks constituted 27 percent of the city population and nearly 40 percent of all black townspeople in Anderson, Oconee, and Pickens counties. Although town draymen and haulers had neither prestigious nor well-paid jobs, these provided alternatives to sharecropping.

Despite a variety of job titles, most Anderson black workers in 1880 fell into two large, traditional categories: domestic servants and laborers. Household heads accounted for roughly equal numbers of each. Although women dominated domestic service, some were laborers. Virtually all employed female heads of families held jobs as servants, cooks, nurses, or "washer women." Many wives and daughters, doing similar work, swelled the number of servants, whose life could be very hard. Jane Hunter described her work in Anderson: "I was ten years old, and cooked, cleaned, washed and ironed for a family of six; in addition I looked after two younger children. . . . There were times when the white and colored people in the neighborhood were moved to protest my mistreatment at the hands of my [female] employer."[4]

Cooks tended to be younger and more literate than laundresses. Over 60 percent of cooks lived with white households, mostly those considered the town's leading citizens. The forty-one live-in cooks had a total of sixty-three additional family members—children or husbands, some of them laborers or servants—living with them. Half of Anderson's white households employed a cook. Servants with a 35 percent literacy rate and cooks with 16 percent surpassed laundresses, 10 percent. These variations derived partly from age differences as there were many young servants, while sizable numbers of laundresses were older. All laundresses had their own residences, often rented. A large percentage of either laundresses or their parents were born outside of South Carolina, many in Virginia.

Table 19.1 **Anderson City, 1880: Distribution of Black Occupations**

Classifications by gender for all workers and for household heads

	All Black Workers				Heads of Households			
	M N189	F N190	M % of Total	F	M N91	F N20	M % of Total	F
Agriculture	2	0	1.1	0	2	0	2.2	0
Laborer/day lab.	125	10	66.1	5.3	47	0	51.6	0
Other labor	7	0	3.7	0	3	0	3.3	0
Railroad	1	0	0.5	0	0	0	0	0
Skilled labor & semiskilled	42	0	22.2	0	31	0	34.1	0
Professions	7	5	3.7	2.6	4	0	4.4	0
Domestic service	5	175	2.6	92.1	4	20	4.4	100
% employed of all black population	46.8							
Female/male ratio	100.5						22.0	

Source: 1880 census

"Laborers" rivaled domestic service as a dominant work classification. Totaling 182, they formed the single largest specific category and encompassed over half of employed black male heads of households. No information exists on their particular employment, some as day laborers. Others probably worked for small-scale manufacturers. This figure must also include men who had jobs in livery stables, on the railroad, and as draymen, otherwise not accounted for in the census. An 1884 report said that Anderson County had 747 whites and 178 blacks employed in manufacturing firms, among them lumber mills, wagon factories, and cotton seed oil plants. Over 10 percent of laborers lived with whites and presumably worked for their businesses. So did a black tinsmith and a harness maker, each living with a similar white craftsman; additionally, two shoemakers lived adjacent to white counterparts. Nearly a third of laborers who had their own residences had wives in domestic service; almost as many wives had no gainful employment listed; and many women were single.

Opportunities created by Anderson's rapid growth drew laborers from other states as well. Eleven percent of 1880's black population was born in Georgia, North Carolina, or Virginia. Since Georgia-born residents averaged twenty-four years old, some would have come to Anderson in the 1870s. Not all of them were laborers; one each was a shoemaker, a brick mason, and a carpenter, Samuel Johnson.[5]

Although relatively small in numbers, men in skilled and professional occupations emerged as economic, social, educational, and religious leaders. Craftspeople included nine blacksmiths plus two apprentices, twelve carpenters, six shoemakers, three brick masons, one tinsmith, and one mechanic; several of these were free before the Civil War. The city had about half as many skilled and professional workers as all other towns in Anderson, Oconee, and Pickens counties combined. There were also small numbers, one to three each, of other occupations: barber, tailor, baker, butcher, harness maker, butler, porter, and clerk. Professionals included three men and seven women teachers plus three ministers, two Baptist and one Methodist—"Rev. Geo. Maxwell, Shaving, Hair Cutting, Dyeing and Shampooing Saloon," Anderson's only black display listing in *Smith's South Carolina Business Directory* for 1876–77, along with a one-line entry, "B. Collins, Barber"—neither identified as black.

Many who held a leadership role were active professionally in 1880. They include three young blacksmiths, aged twenty-one to twenty-two years old: Quincy Leverett, David Dooley, and Napoleon Gaillard. Gaillard's father played a significant role in Anderson's Reconstruction politics and in the Rocky River Baptist Association, and Leverett and Dooley would be community leaders within a few years. Families of three other men had a significant impact, although none then lived within the city. Minister E. V. Gassaway and farmer Henry McGowan served as president and treasurer, respectively of the Rocky River's Educational and Sunday School Convention. Mark H. Gassaway, E. V.'s brother, was Greeley Institute principal in the 1890s, until he became head of the county's first black graded school, located only a few blocks away. Their education and families illustrate opportunities available to a few. McGowan, a farmer living a few miles outside of the city, became the county's most prosperous African American. He built a store and hall that provided meeting space for many organizations.[6]

Community Development, 1880–1900

Information concerning social and economic development during the 1880s and 1890s is also limited. Newspapers provided only sparse coverage of black events, and the 1890 census was accidentally destroyed. Fraternal orders and religious groups, however, furnish clues about what was happening. These include the recently organized Good Templars and Good Samaritans orders, along with large churches such as St. Paul, whose membership grew from 364 in 1881 to 755 in 1900, and Royal, Anderson's second black Baptist church, exceeding 150 members in the early 1890s. Named in 1876 for the nation's celebration, Centennial Methodist Episcopal Church expanded as it baptized thirty-six people on one Sunday in 1884 and later that year dedicated a new building, its entire cost of one thousand dollars already paid. Unlike rural white and black counterparts, Anderson's churches held services each Sunday. Their membership, drawing from outlying areas as well as the town, helped link Anderson city to nearby rural communities. Joining the reform movement against liquor, a black contingent of forty-three charter members organized a Women's Christian Temperance Union chapter in 1880.[7]

Anderson's black community also established fraternal organizations, among them the Odd Fellows, who in 1895 laid the cornerstone for the AME's new building. Both the Odd Fellows and the Lawrence Jones (Masonic) Lodge, No. 57, F.A.M., met at McGowan's Hall on South Main Street. By 1900 Anderson also had two Knights of Pythias lodges: Lincoln, No. 37, and Beulah, the state's eighteenth lodge. Dooley's Hall, a brick structure that also included Dooley's blacksmith shop, provided an additional facility for community events besides McGowan's. Officers of the Women's Christian Temperance Union, Masons, and Odd Fellows in 1905 included Earle, McGowan, and Thomas family members.[8]

The business community's gradual emergence can be traced through the statewide *South Carolina Business Directory*. As early as 1880 it listed Greeley Institute and Rev. J. E. Carlisle, (Centennial) Methodist Episcopal minister. By 1886 several businesses had entries, among them Elias Terrell, shoemaker, and B. C. Collins, barber. It also included two blacksmith firms, those of Dooley and Leverett and of Guyton and Guyton (father Ben and son Elbert). When the northern Methodist Episcopal South Carolina Conference held its annual meeting in Anderson in 1886, several businessmen advertised in its program. Elias Terrel publicized his restaurant at Main and Market streets, Julius Thomson his "Groceries, Confectionary, County Produce," and Barton & Smith (evidently whites), their lumber yard, "Invit[ing] the Patronage of Their Colored Friends."

Fifteen people, mostly craftsmen and professionals, owned homes by 1885. They included Dooley, Leverett, both Guytons, Baptist minister Frank Morris, and carpenter–Republican politician Samuel Johnson among others. Besides their homes, the two Guytons and Dooley owned five other buildings, probably their blacksmith shops and some rental houses. They were among the area's earliest black landlords.

Various new social opportunities emerged. They included train excursions that occasionally took Anderson's black people to Greenville, Newberry, Spartanburg, Charleston, or Atlanta, and brought groups from other towns to visit Anderson. These events involved competitions, a parade, and a large dance, all of which usually drew many white spectators. A popular band often performed for black as well as interracial events. It was part of the forty-member newly formed Rough and Ready black fire brigade, which served primarily black residential areas. "Colored" baseball teams by 1879 supplied additional occasions for travel and social activities.[9]

Greeley Institute continued both to educate town and area students and to host varied organizations and public meetings. An 1875 conflict erupted among the black leadership, which was split over denouncing or defending a teacher. Although Republicans used the courthouse in the 1870s, Greeley opened its doors for even more controversial assemblies, such as one that excluded whites in January 1877 following Hampton's election, as well as most subsequent Republican meetings.

Nevertheless Greeley consistently won compliments from the white press. In 1881, for instance, the *Intelligencer* reported of Anderson's blacks "nobly . . . subscribing . . . one hundred seventy dollars" for Greeley's repair. But now, the *Intelligencer* said, it is the "duty of those in more fortunate circumstances to help them," the otherwise increasingly racist paper argued. Greeley, other schools, and churches always got favorable reportage, as Greeley did in 1886 when the *Pickens Sentinel* listed it among Anderson's outstanding features.[10]

By 1900 many conditions for Anderson's black population changed substantially for the better and for the worse. Although the new state constitution restricted voting rights and a "Jim Crow" mentality was sweeping into the political realm, other areas of life improved. The black population more than doubled since 1880, from 810 to 1737; their literacy rate increased significantly; more families owned homes; and their array of employment categories expanded.

Launching of several industries brought many new arrivals to the city. The 1895 *South Carolina Hand Book* described Anderson as "probably the most prosperous little city in the South. It enjoys trade from a larger area of surrounding country than almost any other . . . [and] buys more cotton from wagons than any town of its size east of the Mississippi [River]."[11] New facilities included several cotton mills, a cotton seed oil mill, a railroad to Augusta, an ice factory, a mattress factory, an iron foundry and machine shop, lumber mills, and an electrical power company. These all provided employment for blacks, who moved into town in numbers evidently exceeding available jobs. A June 1900 *Intelligencer* article commented that scarce labor throughout rural sections meant that many black people were moving to towns, even though few could find work there. Black population increased in both numbers and percentages of total city population: 27 percent in 1880, 32 percent in 1900, and 35 percent in 1910.

1900 Households, Employment, and Literacy

The year 1900 serves as a useful benchmark indicating further accomplishments. Rapid city growth and industrial development occurred due to this technological change. Black people seized opportunities for personal advancement with diversified jobs, a fruitful symbiosis for businesses that needed laborers. African Americans also increased their rates of home ownership and literacy through hard work—personal advances that supported community development. Anderson's black population doubled since 1880, employment opportunities expanded, and other gains were obvious. The state handbook failed to note, let alone celebrate, that black landowners in 1900 reached eighty-four, almost one-fourth of black households.[12] Half held their forty-one houses and five farms free of mortgage. Several families who could not yet afford to build a house owned and farmed land while renting houses elsewhere.

That year's census provides further insights into home ownership, structure of households, and employment. Owner-occupiers covered a wide span of employment from professional to unskilled. They included carpenters, painters, blacksmiths, barbers, teachers, shoemakers, and farmers, as well as cooks, laundresses, "haulers" (draymen and hackmen), and day laborers. Women, mostly widows, constituted nearly 20 percent of resident owners; a few evidently inherited land from their parents. Some who owned land in Anderson lived outside the city while renting their town houses to tenants. Anderson's black-owned savings and loan association, one of only thirteen in the United States, helped provide means to buy a home.

Despite increased opportunities, most African Americans in Anderson still held traditional jobs. As we already saw in chapter 18 for towns in general these included domestic service (cooks, servants, laundresses, and "nurses," that is, those providing child care) and laboring (day laborers, laborers, draymen, hackmen, and teamsters). Thirty percent of family heads—excluding spouses and dependents, many of whom also worked—held jobs in these types of labor. Women too worked as both day and regularly employed laborers. Nearly 35 percent of women held jobs in service; two cooks and several servants were men. Most black people who lived with white families were cooks, servants, or laborers, as in 1880. However, both numbers and percentages in white households shrank dramatically since 1880, from 18 percent to 4 percent (tables 19.1, 19.2, and 19.3).

Family heads, however, held a variety of positions, some of which were relatively new for Anderson blacks. These included nineteen ministers and teachers and one physician, 7.5 percent of jobs held by male household heads. Two men operated restaurants, and two others were merchants. Several black-owned businesses, including barbershops, restaurants, and blacksmith shops, also served as employers. Others in town had jobs as gardeners and hostlers as well as in the crafts—blacksmiths, shoemakers, tinsmiths and stonemasons. These occupations, held by only a few, further diversified job opportunities and accounted for over 10 percent of employed black family heads. A disproportionate number of them were homeowners.

Building trades—carpentry, bricklaying, masonry, and painting, each with 12 to 19 men—accounted for more than 10 percent of all black employment, and almost 20 percent of that among men. Elijah Blassingame (b. 1874) was a bricklayer after earlier years as a hod carrier and as an apprentice. Later, he would have his own business and build, among others, the Calhoun Hotel and Royal Baptist Church.[13] Additional occupations included one or two each: butcher, butler, cab man, coach man, electrician, engineer, "errand boy," harness repairer, telephone lineman, machinist, mattress builder, planer, plasterer, soap maker, tailor, well digger, and wood sawyer. The city council employed a watchman, hack driver, fireman, and bill poster. Several laborers plus a porter, a stewardess, and a handful of hackmen worked at railroad depots. Some women supported their families as seamstresses.

Many wives, children, and other dependents worked as domestics and laborers. Nearly half of all wives were in domestic service; two were teachers. Families often had offspring living at home who held full-time jobs; for those ten and older, 43 percent of daughters and 63 percent of sons worked, mostly in domestic and laboring jobs, respectively. Figures drop to 3 percent of daughters and 55 percent of sons aged ten to nineteen.

Besides children with jobs listed in the census, many others undoubtedly performed occasional chores or seasonal work for pay. Often the oldest daughter had to tend her younger siblings while their mother took outside employment. A total of 292 family dependents—constituting three-eights of Anderson's black work force—were listed with jobs that helped make up family income.

The 1900 census provides no specific description of work done by hundreds of men, women, and children as "laborers" or "day laborers." But Anderson's first *City Directory* does name employers for most people, excluding day laborers who took different chores as they were available. Not only is this 1905 directory more informative about specific employers, but it also reflects Anderson's nearly 50 percent growth since 1900.

Day workers, totaling 177 in the 1900 census, made up a large labor force, living precariously. They included 107 heads of households, five of them widows. Children in their early teens worked as day laborers, and others even younger as errand boys; another day laborer was a sixty-two-year-old woman. The 1905 directory listed even more day laborers, 233, without fixed jobs.

Distinctions between those working regularly for one employer and "day laborers" sharpen the focus for this broad spectrum covering hundreds of workers. The directory, which excluded wives and children living at home, lists 1112 employed black people. Categories such as blacksmiths, laundresses, draymen, and unspecified laborers agree largely with similar census entries. Laborers with or without regular

Table 19.2 **Distribution of Black Occupations, 1880 and 1900**

By location, gender, and classification of work; Anderson, Oconee, and Pickens

All employed blacks	1880 Rural		1880 Town		1880 And. City		1900 Rural		1900 Town		1900 And. City	
	M N344	F N168	M N343	F N211	M N189	F N190	M N532	F N139	M N223	F N150	M N421	F N381
Agriculture	91.9	89.9	55.1	22.7	01.1	0	92.1	79.0	36.8	16.0	08.1	01.3
Laborer/day labor	2.9	0	8.5	7.1	66.1	5.3	1.1	0.7	4.0	4.7	37.5	0.5
Other labor	0.6	0	4.4	0	3.7	0	2.6	0	26.5	2.0	18.1	0.3
Railroad	1.2	0	9.9	0	0.5	0	0.9	0	10.3	0	0.5	0
Skilled labor and semiskilled	0.8	0	13.1	0	22.2	0	2.2	0	11.7	0	24.7	0
Professions	0	0	2.3	0	3.7	2.6	0.6	2.2	4.9	4.7	5.5	0.8
Domestic service	2.3	10.1	6.4	70.1	2.6	92.1	0.8	18.1	5.8	72.7	5.7	97.1
employed as % of all black population	40.2%		43.8		46.8			40.9		36.8		44.5
Female/Male ratio	48.8%		61.5		100.5		26.1		67.3		90.5	

Heads of households only	1880 Rural		1880 Town		1880 And. City		1900 Rural		1900 Town		1900 And. City	
	M N167	F N21	M N161	F N40	M N91	F N20	M N221	F N20	M N122	F N20	M N254	F N109
Agriculture	93.4	95.2	52.2	17.5	2.2	0	92.8		35.2	15.0	09.4	00.9
Laborer/day labor	3.0	0	5.0	12.5	51.6		1.4		1.6		34.6	3.7
Other labor			3.7		3.3		1.8		27.9	10.0	14.6	0.9
Railroad	1.8		9.3		0		0.9		13.1		0.0	

Table 19.2 (continued)

Heads of households only:

	1880						1900					
	Rural		Town		And. City		Rural		Town		And. City	
	M	F	M	F	M	F	M	F	M	F	M	F
	N167	N21	N161	N40	N91	N20	N221	N20	N122	N20	N254	N109
Skilled labor and semiskilled	0.6		23.0		34.1		2.3		9.8		28.3	
Professions			6.2		4.4		0.5		8.2		7.1	.9
Domestic service	1.2	4.8	0.6	70.0	4.4	100.0	0.5	20.0	4.1	75.0	5.9	93.6
Female/Male ratio	12.6		24.8		22.0		9.0		16.3		42.9	

Totals approximate 100% due to rounding.

Sources and notes: 1870, 1880, and 1900 manuscript census schedules for the city of Anderson (not separately reported in 1870; partially included in Varennes Township); Oconee: Keowee and Seneca (including Seneca town in 1880 and 1900) Townships; Pickens: Pickens Court House (including town of Pickens, not specifically designated in 1870) and Central (including town of Central in 1880 and 1900; Calhoun town excluded from sample) Townships; and Anderson: Pendleton (including town of Pendleton), Varennes, and—for 1870 only—Savannah Townships.

Sampling in 1880 and 1900 rural township areas was based on an effort to include 150 or more people (about 30 households) per township by taking every nth household (including any headed by white families) that included one or more African Americans; the result ranged from 115 for Keowee Township in 1900 to 455 for Pendleton Township in 1900.

My division of specific occupations into broader categories mostly parallels Burton and the 1880 census grouping. I have not divided agriculture into "farmer" and "farm laborer" as does Burton; usage of these terms varies by year and census enumerator. Similarly, I grouped unskilled and skilled railroad labor together as terminology often is not clear. The more critical factor is the role of railroad labor; perhaps 10% of it consisted of brakemen and other skilled workers. For "skilled," Burton's and census classifications omit female cooks, milliners, and dressmakers, and for "semiskilled" omit laundresses, a misleading and skewed gender separation.

employers account for almost half of all working blacks and nearly 60 percent of males listed. Wives without employment generally are not included, and virtually all other women fall under the headings of cooks and laundresses. A few seamstresses, nurses (child care), and teachers complete a limited array of women's jobs.

Many employers for those called "laborers" in the census were relatively new Anderson businesses. The 1905 directory lists eight textile mills, which utilized 68 black laborers plus 3 firemen and 3 drivers; Brogan's Mills's 12 was the largest black textile work force. None of these dealt with weaving processes. Twenty-six laborers worked for railroads and city transit, as did 2 brakemen and 3 porters. The depot itself had one worker but also a barber, a blacksmith, and a waitress; several hackmen operated there as well. Anderson Fertilizer Works hired the most black laborers, 25; five other firms, using a total of 45, ranged from 6 to 13 each. The Farmers Oil Mill, processing cotton seed oil, had 5. Seventeen men worked for the city, Anderson Telephone Company, and Anderson Water, Light, and Power Company. Only one full-time fireman staffed the city's Rough and Ready unit. Several blacks served on Anderson's police force also.[14]

Two businesses illustrate varied jobs available at a single firm. J. E. Dobbins's livery stable employed four laborers plus a drayman, a driver, and a hostler. Anderson's new Chiquola Hotel hired a bellman, two porters, and a maid; its restaurant had one chief cook (male), two cooks (male), one head waiter, and four other waiters. The Chiquola Drug Company, also on the premises, used a porter and the Chiquola Barber Shop a laborer.

The directory also lists a few positions that did not appear in the census: a packer, janitors—three at schools and one each at a bank, post office, and opera house—a house mover, a fish dealer, well diggers, and a confectionist. Coca-Cola and the city cemetery employed a few men. Three women held positions described as "trained" or "sick" nurses in the health care field.

Although 95 percent of blacks working were dependent primarily on white employment, regular or occasional, several professionals and businessmen created a niche relatively independent of whites. Black professionals were limited to a physician, two officers of the Anderson Building and Loan Association, and six ministers; plus three principals (all males) and eleven teachers (ten females) at Greeley Institute, Salem (Presbyterian) School, and the public Grammar School No. 4. Several men held dual professions: one loan officer was also a physician, the other a minister, and another minister (J. P. Foster) doubled as Salem's principal.

An increased number of businesses in the past decade served the community and provided additional black-controlled jobs. Several men had their own firms that employed other blacks: Quincy Leverett's, David Dooley's, and J. Dupree's blacksmith shops; the Jenkins Brothers' grocery; James W. Mitchell's barbershop; and Lawrence Edwards' poolroom. Collectively these firms hired about fifteen workers. Other black-owned businesses included barbershops, restaurants, and shoemakers' and tailors' shops. Located mostly within a block or two of the town square, each adjoined white businesses. West Market structures near Centennial Methodist Church were all new; by 1911 the church itself would have a brick building. Businesses began to settle on East Church Street, which would soon become Anderson's black commercial center until the 1980s. Collectively twenty-one professionals, thirty-seven shopkeepers, and their employees in 1905 comprised slightly more than 5 percent of the city's black work force. These businesses would have drawn not only city customers but also many from the countryside on weekends.[15]

Increasingly the professions attracted people from elsewhere in South Carolina to work as teachers and ministers. Many of them were recent college graduates. Professional development would soon include participation in two state organizations, the Palmetto Medical Association and the Colored Teachers Association. The state department of education periodically sponsored summer Colored Teachers' Institutes in Anderson.

Anderson's schools and literacy rates for both blacks and whites far surpassed state norms. Graded schools were rare when mostly one-room schools dominated. Moreover, Anderson's Grammar School No. 4, one of South Carolina's few black graded schools, offered the only nine-month instruction in Anderson, Oconee, and Pickens counties. Known as Reed Street School, Grammar School No. 4 enrolled in 1900 nearly 600 students, almost one-third of the city's black population; they were taught by five teachers. The staff soon grew to one principal, Mark H. Gassaway, and nine teachers, including Gassaway's wife and daughter. Still operating under its own board, Greeley Institute with one principal—G. W. Hill in 1905—and one teacher provided high-school instruction. Salem school in 1900 had 190 students.

Church endeavors complemented the schools' advancement of literacy. St. Paul Baptists, for example, made the third-largest church contribution to the 1894 state Baptists' education collection. Rev. E. V. Gassaway and Anderson educators similarly took leading roles within the Rocky River Baptist Association and its Sunday School affiliate. The association helped students with small scholarships.

Decades of education since the city's first freedmen's school in 1866 clearly produced dividends. Much higher than the state average, 78 percent of Anderson's black people ten years and older were able to read, write, or both. Although older people were less likely to read and write and the oldest illiterate person was ninety-three, one ninety-five-year-old man was listed as able to read and write. Literally dozens of illiterate household heads made sure that at least some of their children got educated; only five literate families did not have at least one child in school. Often older children had to forgo schooling to help support the family while younger siblings attended school; but daughters by 1900 went to school more often than sons. Cooks and female servants, then, often had more education than males. And parents helped teach their own children at home.

Anderson's black population contained a disproportionate percentage of people born out-of-state. Still, the percentage shrank significantly since 1880. Sixty of them, about 3 percent, were born mostly in Georgia (thirty-one), Virginia (ten), and North Carolina (nine). Most Virginians, including ninety-nine-year-old Roseanah Smith, were old enough to have come to South Carolina as slaves, although three were born after 1860. A few originated from seven other states ranging from Maryland to Florida (someone with South Carolina–born parents) and Louisiana (evidently newly relocated to Anderson). Those from Georgia, averaging twenty-five years old, were mostly recent arrivals; only six were born before the Civil War. Della Young was born in South Carolina in 1845, lived in Georgia circa 1892–95, and then moved to Anderson. Two brick masons, born in Georgia and sharing a house, arrived in Anderson within the past year.

Residential Patterns

The core of Anderson's community advanced significantly in their occupations, home ownership, and literacy. New professional arrivals joined their number. Others, however, formed a more transitory group who came into the city for job opportunities but often did not stay long. Increasingly the ingredients that distinguished community leaders, or their opposites—low-paying jobs, illiteracy, and temporary status—shaped where people lived.

Beginning with Anderson's first Sanborn Fire Insurance map, 1884, the census's first listing of Anderson street addresses in 1900, and the earliest city directory, 1905, black residential areas become clearer.[16] The 1884 Sanborn map includes only the downtown area, barely more than a block in each direction from the town square. It shows just a few premises specifically designated as black occupied. Two larger dwellings on Church Street (later the black business center) and on McDuffie, a block from the town square, had a "servants' house" behind them. Church Street had two brick "Negro Tenements," one behind a drug store and another evidently with eight rooms; a third "Negro Tenement" was on McDuffie.

More extensive maps in 1890 and 1896 include several of these same buildings plus those labeled "Negro Dwelling," "Negro Tenement," "Negro Quarters," and three shanties. Two black Methodist churches appear, one of them "new"—Centennial Methodist Episcopal Church, built in 1886. Sanborn's 1896 edition also has Salem Presbyterian Church without racial notation. For the first time black businesses are shown, all in one South Main Street structure: a "Negro" barbershop, restaurant, and shoe shop.

Each subsequent edition of Sanborn maps covers a wider area, reflecting the city's growth, construction of new churches and schools, and recognition of black business. The 1901 edition includes, along with most of these buildings, a "Negro boarding house" on Whitner—evidently that headed by Sylvia Williams with six lodgers—backing onto a "Negro shanty" on Benson; a "Public School (Colored)" on Reed Street; and the "A.M.E. Church" on West Market—a mistake, actually northern Methodist Episcopal.

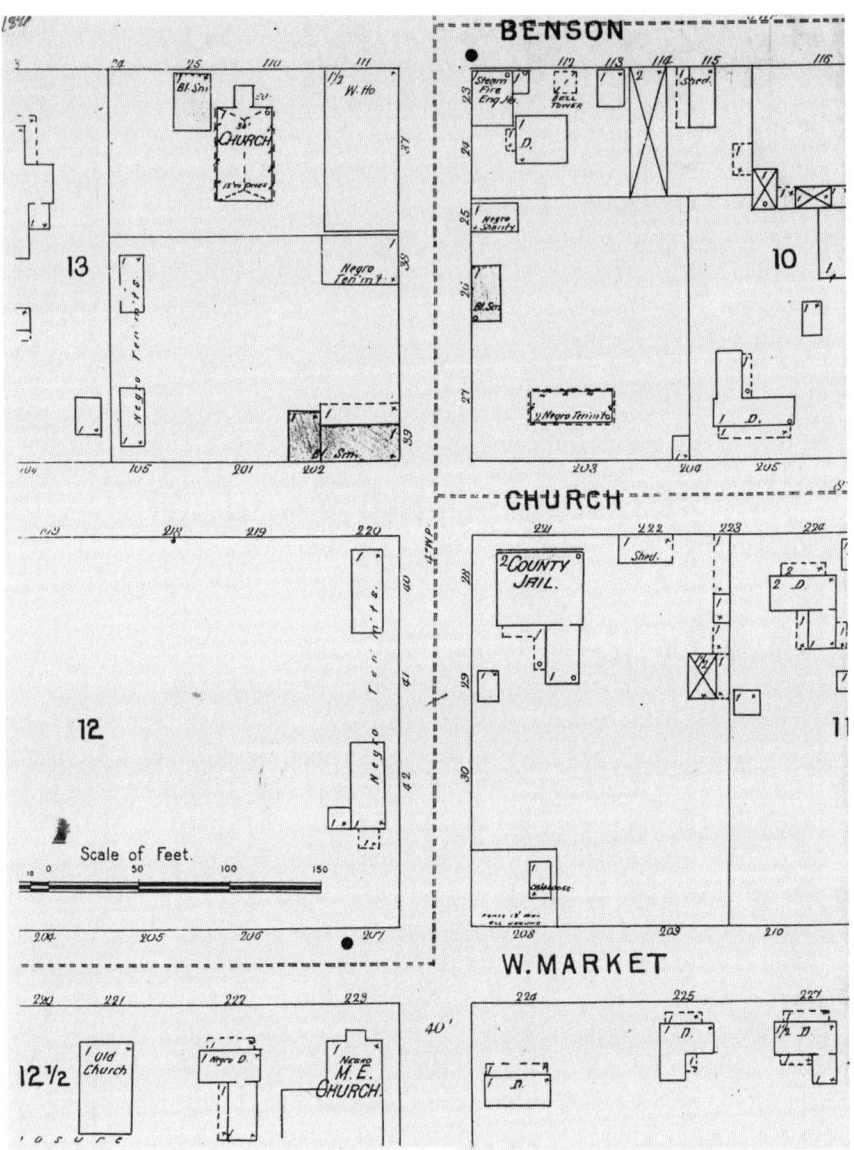

Sanborn Fire Insurance Company 1901 map, showing part of city of Anderson. Note, at bottom, the ME(N) Church and various "Negro Tenem't" and "Servants" buildings. Black Heritage in the Upper Piedmont

Anderson street scene in the early 1900s as children ride on the ice wagon.
Pendleton District Commission

Anderson's expansion, chronicled by Sanborn maps, appears more dramatic by 1906. Increased to fifteen sheets since the 1884 one-page version, the 1906 version includes special pages for mills. Now—coupled with census and city directory listings—varied residential patterns appear clearly. Dozens of domestics lived in homes with white families; nearly thirty other black residences were separate servants' quarters. Other households occupied tenements and shanties in the city's center, where older buildings remained as black housing while population and nicer residential sections spread to areas farther away. A "negro dwelling" and a "cabin" burned one late-December 1899 night, evidently accidents.[17] A few families, such as the Dooleys, owned fine houses in predominantly white sections of town.

Relatively new black neighborhoods developed mostly on the town's fringes or in less desirable areas where land and rent were cheaper as Anderson's population grew by nearly 50 percent between 1900 and 1905. Increasingly by 1906, Ligon "Row" and Murray "Alley" symbolize narrow, crowded clusters of black residences. Spring and Railroad streets near the train tracks and Reed and McCulley streets, backing onto Whitner Creek typify less cramped but still less desirable sites. Land near mills provided similarly unattractive but affordable areas. An 1894 newspaper account of murder in "Nickel Row" indicates attitudes toward these sections of town, considered by many whites to be poorer and seed beds of crime. Other racist epithets appear in newspapers, and similar comments sprinkle white testimony whenever a coroner's inquest dealt with a death in these areas.[18]

Residential patterns and family structure tended to merge. Virtually all "rows" and "alleys," lacking owner-occupiers, were white owned. Few nuclear families were found in the poorest areas. Instead, many nuclear and home-owning families lived

Table 19.3 **Analysis of Black Households and Population, 1870–1900**

By household type

	1870	80R	80T	80A	00R	00T	00A
N =	555	260	300	184	311	241	411
Nuclear	61.5	54.2	42.7	34.8	61.4	58.9	49.4
Extended	14.2	21.9	18.3	10.9	19.6	13.2	17.8
Augmented	13.2	11.1	8.3	19.0	6.4	10.4	5.6
Irregular	11.1	12.7	30.7	35.3	12.5	17.4	27.3

80T, 00T = 1880 and 1900 towns, specifically designated and counted in toto.
80A, 00A = 1880 and 1900 Anderson (city), counted in toto.
totals range from 99.9 to 100.1 due to rounding

By people

	1870	80R	80T	80A	00R	00T	00A
N =	2059	1273	1260	813	1555	1023	1733
Full Nuclear	46.2	44.1	33.3	30.3	45.4	55.8	36.1
Nuclear + Older Generation in One Household	4.3	5.6	7.5	4.3	8.2	6.5	4.4
With Whites	7.8	4.6	11.6	19.6	1.6	5.1	3.6
Female Headed	20.9	11.9	22.9	25.9	6.0	22.4	22.4
Singles	9.1	1.0	3.2	0.1	1.9	2.0	1.0
Born outside S.C.	3.2	4.9	5.2	5.1	1.0	2.0	3.6

Sources: Based on seven complete townships in 1870 (including two towns and part of the city of Anderson), all of Anderson (city) in 1880 and 1900, and sampling of six townships (including three towns) in 1880 and 1890; see table 21.1.

in established residential sections. Reed Street had many black residents, as did property-owning families on West Franklin Street, a block nearer town. Reed Street became a major center with the school and St. Paul Baptist Church, situated in a new brick building.[19]

Nearly 40 percent of Anderson's black population lived in nuclear families, either couples only or couples with children and no other residents. Such families accounted for more than their proportionate share of home ownership. Two blocks of East Market Street immediately off the square had five homeowners, mostly nuclear families, and several businesses. Five black-owned homes were located on Thomas Street, also with a preponderance of nuclear families. An additional 10 percent of blacks lived in extended families—a nuclear family plus other relations: siblings, nieces, nephews, cousins, and spouses of their married sons or daughters without any children. These families lived almost entirely in older, established black neighborhoods. Another nearly 5 percent lived in three-generation extended households.

Approximately 4 percent of the black population lived with white households, almost entirely in older, more socially prestigious neighborhoods. As in 1880, most were either single, single with one or two children, or widowed; there were a few couples and a few elderly people, such as ninety-two-year-old Morris Cherry, a "gardener," probably maintained with little work on his part. Nearly 1 percent of black people consisted of convict laborers and county prisoners.

Several city areas had racially mixed blocks where whites and blacks of similar socioeconomic status lived side by side. An entire block bounded in part by McDuffie and Morris had residences for both black—notably David Dooley—and white middle class, plus Greeley Institute and the African Methodist Episcopal church. Several black families lived on River Street's farther extent near John R. Cochran, a white Republican politician. The eastern part of Calhoun Street, South Market Street near A. T. Broyles, and other areas also were mixed. So were F Street near Orr Mills, Orr Street near the railroad, and Spring Street by the gin—tenant houses owned by J. E. Barton—areas of mixed lower socioeconomic groups, both white and black. The nature of most black areas—servants' houses, alleys, and streets along creeks or railroad tracks—meant that virtually all blacks in Anderson lived within a block or two of whites. By 1920 population shifts would create more racial separation.

Both household and residential patterns reflect transitory aspects of life, family structure, economics, and mobility. Fifty-nine widows headed their own households, some alone, some with other family members present. One section of West Boundary Street consisting of twenty-five houses had 11 widows, most of them laundresses. Elsewhere other households were headed by single women with children or married women whose husbands were not present in the household. Gender skewing appeared with 105 widows compared to 24 widowers.

Boarding houses similarly show changing circumstances, both for paying residents and for those taking in boarders. Forty-four black households included fifty-eight boarders, primarily, or lodgers. These houses were mostly headed by people who did not own the building, had no nuclear family, and lived in less-established areas of town. Most people who took in boarders or lodgers were single, divorced, widowed, married without spouse present, or elderly; presumably most did so to supplement their income. Many who had boarders were laundresses, cooks, day laborers, and draymen. Although found throughout black areas, they were concentrated largely in newer and more transitory sections. However, most people with boarders also had several relatives with them, and thirteen household heads owned their homes.

Boarders were more transitory than their landlords. A disproportionate number of boarders were young, some in their teens or younger, or without spouse. A few boarders under the age of sixteen evidently were sent into town by parents for schooling; others may have been placed there by relatives unable to care for them. Most young boarders including students had jobs as servants or errand boys. Only a handful of the 1900 boarders could be found in the city directory five years later. Given low wages for laborers, it was often necessary for two families to share a house. In some cases white landlords seem to have rented out separate rooms in an otherwise-undivided house to unrelated individuals. There were neighborhood clusterings of households with unrelated people, either young men working for the same employer, or female heads, such as the grouping of widowed laundresses.

Even heads of households moved in large numbers. Nearly half of those in the 1900 census do not appear in the 1905 city directory. Fewer than one-fifth still in Anderson lived at the same address. Migrations within the city were even greater for single people, especially day laborers, and for boarders. Similarly, the 1910 census would show a substantial turnover as well, a trend evident elsewhere. Calhoun, a nearby small town, had a population of about two hundred white and black people in 1900, as it did in 1910; but over two-thirds of the 1900 population moved away, to be replaced by a nearly equal number.

Rapidly changing, Anderson had a fluid population. A combination of more job opportunities, many of them lower paying, brought into town people who stayed a short while and left. Established families and their neighborhoods, however, provided stability and leadership that allowed the community to thrive and progress.

Racial Relations in the City

Racial relations in Anderson were complicated in ways difficult to assess. On some levels white and black interacted well. Certainly that applied to joint festive occasions, including parades and Rough and Ready band concerts. The press lauded educational and religious accomplishments. The white Saluda Baptist Association periodically offered training for Rocky River ministers and teachers, and these groups frequently exchanged delegates for their meetings.

Several churches and Greeley Institute appealed to "white friends" for help with building expenses and gratefully acknowledged such contributions. Whites praised such individuals as Greeley principal and educator M. H. Gassaway, who is "recognized as one of the best teachers of his race, and is doing a good work." Like Centennial's and Greeley's thank-yous to "white friends," periodic notices by white men appeared, such as Joseph E. Burton's 1884 "thanks to my friends of the city of Anderson, both white and colored," for putting out a fire and saving his planing mill. And "Anderson's firemen, white and colored, fought fire bravely" when forty bales of cotton began burning at the Savannah Valley Railroad depot.[20]

But other attitudes also are evident. Although whites enjoyed black bands playing in parades for free, they paid to see frequent minstrel shows, some of them traveling performers, others local amateur productions. A "shooting affray" occurred at the Orr Cotton Mills one weekday night in 1900 when a young white fellow demanded that black Will Leslie play music for him. Refusing, Leslie shot the man harassing him. Most individual confrontations occurred near mills and in mixed lower socioeconomic neighborhoods.

Always supporting black schools, the press also ridiculed black ignorance. Ambivalent attitudes appeared in the March 13, 1884, *Intelligencer*, which claimed that "there is not a County in the State where the negroes, as a whole, are in better condition than those of Anderson County." That same issue, however, carried a headline "The Nigger and His Day." Two weeks later the newspaper referred to "darkies."

Other comments from 1895 indicate the type of black people the white community might consider kindly. The *Intelligencer* wrote on January 9 about a local black man, Wade Hampton, who though paralytic, was running the city's delivery wagon: Hampton is "worthy . . . give him your patronage." A few issues later an obituary appeared for a thirty-seven-year-old man: "Henry Burch, a well known shoemaker, died at his home in this city last Monday, after a brief illness. He was a polite, courteous negro, and had the confidence and good will of his white friends."

Polite, even friendly, attitudes by white people during peaceful interracial events and toward certain favored individuals formed a generally pleasant face that turned ugly at times. During the first six months of 1903 the *Intelligencer* ran repeated stories, not for the first time, of Negro arrests, weapons, liquor, rapists, and accidents—at least one story each issue, but often more. It also bemoaned on February 25 a move to Arkansas by W. T. Mattison, a "well-known and respected, hard working, honest citizen." Two weeks later ninety-five-year-old Moses Cherry, a Methodist clergyman who died, was described as a "good man and highly esteemed by his white friends."[21] But the predominant theme in the early 1900s was increasingly critical, and "negro crime" was described in far more racist language than appeared earlier.

Anderson's population growth along with more skilled craftsmen and professionals, schools, churches, and fraternal organizations made it one of the state's better-developed black communities. There were now more homeowners, landlords, and businesses, some of them providing employment. By the early 1900s, there were significant achievements with their own organizations, a savings and loan association, a county fair, and professional associations for both teachers and doctors. Growing racism throughout the state may well have induced the community to pull more closely together. African Americans simultaneously benefited from manufacturing and business growth but suffered from this racism—problems reflected in development of black thought.

TWENTY

Divergent Views of Blacks

DIVERGENT VIEWS OF AFRICAN AMERICANS abounded, even within the press. Local newspapers, all controlled and published by whites, lamented black voting, highlighted black crime extensively, and spoke well of certain favored individuals. Black people themselves held diverse views about their community and means to improve it, terms to describe themselves, and "race consciousness." Viewpoints changed over time, responding partly to increasingly white-dominated politics, but also to development of black newspapers and organizations elsewhere in the country with lively debates on Booker T. Washington's and W. E. B. DuBois's views. Additionally, growing black population in towns, more education, stronger churches and regional associations, and an emerging leadership helped shape local views and institutions. Grappling with major issues such as race consciousness, improvement, and ties to Africa, blacks informed their own community's concepts.[1]

Coverage in the White Press

Newspaper coverage—whether good or bad—about black people and events of importance to them was more extensive than might be imagined. Coverage fluctuated over time in both tone and quantity. Editors often spoke kindly of well-respected people, reported some marriages and deaths, especially of the aged, and frequently included school exhibitions, camp meetings, or other religious events. Most of these consisted of a sentence or two, typical of most local news, black or white. Varied over time, formats usually consisted of "Local Items," filling one to three columns on page three of a four-page paper, and short notes from community reporters, all white, throughout the county. Most black items appeared in the main block, prepared by newspaper staff.

Four weeklies constituted the press in Anderson, Oconee, and Pickens counties from 1865 to 1900. They were the *Keowee Courier*, published at Walhalla, Oconee's county seat, beginning in 1868; the *Anderson Intelligencer*, Anderson; and the *Pickens Sentinel*, launched at "New Pickens" in 1871; it absorbed a later rival, the *People's Journal* (1894–1903). A few additional newspapers had short runs seldom lasting more than a year or so; hardly any issues survive.

The most extensive reportage involving blacks occurred in the 1870s, due partly to Reconstruction politics and also because of calmer racial relations than would occur later. An intensive analysis of that decade's reportage falls short of completeness due to gaps for each newspaper: issues are missing for all these, and *Sentinel* files survive for only a few of those ten years.

If African Americans had only these newspapers as a mirror for their own lives, they would have seen a very distorted image. Their references were small in comparison to white news, were often negative, and omitted many things of particular interest to blacks. But the numbers of names would have surprised later generations. At least 570 people, mostly men, were cited by name in the 1870s, plus nearly 100 others as an unspecified "colored man" or "colored woman." Other people appeared without racial designations in reports of teachers' pay, county payments to jurors and witnesses, and others among people tried before the courts, whose reports often omitted racial identification. These 570 names exceed 15 percent of the area's adult black men then. Press focus on crime, politics, and the clergy heavily skewed reportage toward men, which male editors tended to do anyway.[2]

Nearly a third of references to named individuals appeared in a context related to crime. Although local newspapers had not yet launched a major campaign of "Negro Crime" headlines and reportage as appeared in later years, accounts of black people did have a heavy connection with crime. Specific accounts followed rather much the same style as that concerning white people. The major difference was that reported crime constituted a much higher percentage of all black individuals, contrasted to considerably more extensive reporting on whites otherwise; that implicitly placed white offenses in a much smaller proportion. And theirs were not flagged as "white crime."

Nearly equal numbers of criminal references fall in three broad subcategories: people accused of or arrested for a crime, or both; those found guilty; and others found not guilty, people killed, or those involved in some way with crime-related activities. The latter includes those in fights or shooting "affrays" where charges evidently were not filed. One convicted man was executed and another was pardoned by the governor. No single charge predominated; the largest number consisted of assault and battery or simple assault, 25 percent of all guilty verdicts; a similar percentage included larceny and receiving stolen goods. Ten percent dealt mostly with manslaughter or with murder. Seven men were convicted of riot in an 1878 Townville incident. A variety of other offenses included, in smaller numbers, forgery, bigamy, breach of peace, littering, burning a mill, and rape. All victims of murder, manslaughter, or rape by black men were also black, except perhaps one.[3]

Along with disproportionately many people listed as criminals, others were victims of crimes and of accidents. These included attacks—assault and battery and manslaughter—inflicted on them by other blacks plus a small number by white perpetrators. Most white-on-black violence escaped both reportage and legal consequences. And newspapers showed blacks as victims of many diverse accidents: drowning, accidental killings including railroad incidents, lightning, children burned in house fires while parents were absent, and brawls. A third of all these people survived.

Reconstruction political matters including elections collectively accounted for 45 percent of all names mentioned. Lists of men selected for jury pool or for duty included at least sixty blacks, while 144 names (including multiple references to some individuals) appeared for those serving as election managers and supervisors, all for Anderson and Oconee counties. Three Anderson County men served as election commissioners and one as jury commissioner, while eight others were appointed as trial justices or elected to various town offices in Anderson and Belton. Nine men ran unsuccessfully for office, and one declined a nomination to run. These references, appearing so seldom and so overwhelmed by crime reports and black victims, probably had little impact on readers, white or black.

Given the political climate of the 1870s and the opportunities for blacks in Republican organizations, it should be no surprise that nearly 10 percent of those cited were Republicans. About half of these named men who held offices in county organizations and served on committees or as delegates to state conventions, mostly duplicating the officers. Another half mentioned people attending meetings, facing intimidation for voting Republican, or other connections. Nine articles concerned black militia in Anderson and Oconee counties.

By 1876 the emphasis shifted considerably. Due to the political climate and intense intimidation, nearly as many black men appeared as Democratic club members or as otherwise supporting Hampton and the Democratic party. Some reports dealt specifically with intimidation by other blacks to support either Hampton or Chamberlain. After Hampton's term began but before he gained access to the state capitol, Democrats collected taxes independent of Republican officers; forty-eight Oconee blacks paid into this pool. Without identifying any individuals the *Intelligencer* said that sixty Anderson black men similarly paid.[4]

The remaining contexts covered a wide field. About 4 percent referred to black deaths due to old age, pneumonia, typhoid, malaria, accidents, suicide, and other causes not inflicted by another person. These all had a neutral or mildly sympathetic tone. Nearly 10 percent dealt with education and religion in neutral or positive terms: teachers, preachers at camp meetings, church deacons or officers, attendees at Sunday School conventions or institutes, Rocky River Baptist Association officers, and African Methodist Episcopal and northern Methodist Episcopal appointments. An additional group, nearly 6 percent, spanned matters too diverse to be classified individually: marriages; agricultural accomplishments—records for picking cotton, outstanding yams, other crops; severe illness; three men listed in an advertisement as owning Singer Sewing machines; land transactions; and officers in benevolent associations. Slightly more than 1 percent reported black people helping to put out fires at white houses or businesses.

Reportage about specific individuals was mostly matter-of-fact with little derogatory language or slant except for a few criminals. Since "white" was seldom added, whites seemed to be the norm, African Americans the variant. "Colored" was used most frequently, followed by "black" and occasionally by "negro"—almost always in lowercase type, as quoted throughout this book. At times all three appeared on the same page. Newspapers had yet to resort regularly to more offensive terms, printed in greater frequency by the 1890s and early 1900s. The *Intelligencer* ran on October 10, 1872, a paid advertisement, "Bought a Nigger."[5] Discussing an all-black jury's freeing an accused black murderer of white Levi Brown in 1877, a white writer complained, "it was a nigger murder, a nigger jury and a nigger verdict." By mid-1879 the word showed up more often in material reprinted from sources in Charleston, Chicago, Des Moines, and other cities, though local newspapers still generally avoided that term in their own writing. Like other dual attitudes, editors retained a discreet posture themselves while willingly carrying more racist material and language from other newspapers.[6]

Coupled with many items referring to black people as perpetrators or victims or in crime-related contexts, then, newspapers had a negative effect, not so much in individual personal descriptions as in overall impact. Few references to specific African Americans contained negative wording. But a strong message emerged among many more general articles attacking perceived black domination of South Carolina's Reconstruction, with frequent stories about political scandals traced to white or black Republicans and accounts of black crime throughout the state. Even reports of Anderson's black elected council members and most accounts of local Republican meetings carried at most only mildly negative tones, W. R. Parker being a conspicuous exception. Periodic articles about schools, churches, camp meetings, and their teachers and ministers were almost always favorable. They were, however, surrounded by other material.

Further, white organizations and the press adopted terms that implicitly excluded blacks. The Pickens County Teachers Association was a group of white teachers, just as the Oconee County Democratic Club by 1880 included white men only. Church, school, and Masonic lodge listings typically encompassed only white institutions. Rather like a sideshow mirror, then, newspapers presented different images, depending on the facet viewed, and delivered resulting distortions.

During the 1880s coverage changed significantly. Although political involvement waned, more black men appeared in other spheres as numbers of ministers and teachers increased, as did the frequency of camp meetings. As churches could afford new buildings, newspapers reported dedication services, often with laudatory language. The *Pickens Sentinel* praised New Olive Grove Baptist Church's new building near Norris in 1888: "It is an honor to them, and a credit to the country, as the members are mostly poor."[7] As more individuals bought land and homes, occasionally these accomplishments were noted in the paper, but so were delinquent taxpayers. There were increasing numbers of teachers' pay accounts and certification results.

Coverage included social opportunities, including fraternal groups, parades, excursion trips, and baseball games. Unless crime was connected with any of these, press reports were neutral or, usually, favorable. Occasionally a writer mentioned that all was "peaceful" or "orderly," a subtle reminder that at times they were not, in the editor's judgment. Press accounts provide much of the documentation on political activity, towns, Anderson city, schools, and churches.

Both the newspapers' own posture in the 1880s and 1890s and that of many letter writers carried more negative tones than were printed—though not necessarily felt—in the 1870s. Lurid articles about black crime elsewhere in the state or nation appeared frequently, as did reports about lynchings throughout South Carolina. *Pickens Sentinel* issues carried these early 1881 items: in Prosperity, South Carolina, David Spearman and Sam Fair, believed to have committed the "most horrible crime ever reported," infuriated whites, who shot the men immediately. There also a black woman—even though "half-witted"—was lynched three months later for attempting to burn J. S. Blalock's premises. Collectively these items portrayed blacks in very negative tones. Attitudes toward lynching follow in chapter 21.

Besides associations with crime, African Americans often appeared as stereotypes or as victims. Oddly, that often happened while somebody was walking on, lying on, or sleeping on railroad tracks. So many such incidents occurred that one has to be suspicious of their frequency and supposedly innocent nature. Other accidents included lightning, house fires, and illness. Stereotypes also associated blacks with music or distorted them in minstrel shows. The Pickens local columnist fostered a stereotype in 1882: "a negro picking a banjo, with forty school boys around him is one of the pictures of happiness." When "Blind Tom . . . negro musical prodigy" performed in both Pickens and Anderson during 1884, the *Intelligencer* said his "highly enjoyed" performance attracted the largest attendance ever at any hall in Anderson.[8]

While portraying blacks collectively in these images, newspapers used special language to describe favored individuals. Pickens editors regularly reported on C. T. Miller's and W. D. Jenkins's schools as well as church activities at Griffin Ebenezer and Cold Spring Baptist churches. One minister attending Claflin University, the Reverend E. E. Jenkins from Walhalla, won praise for his speech at a black barbecue. Both individuals and churches in towns or nearby got much better coverage than those in outlying rural areas.[9] In 1887 the *Sentinel* chronicled with growing sympathy four Rosamond family deaths within seven months. And Pickens newspapers by the 1890s reported more black marriages, often with courtesy titles, and deaths than in earlier years.

Viewed as a whole, coverage of African Americans is greater than most local people would have expected at that time. But their emphases on blacks in crimes, as victims, and as stereotypes would create a cumulative effect. By the early 1900s the result was, at best, poisonous.

Black Thought, 1865–1900

Better informed than their portrayal in the local press might suggest, area black people clearly were familiar with many racial issues discussed and argued on a state and national level. Perspectives quite different from those in the white press appeared within the black community; only a few traces of this dialogue made it into print and survived. If quoted accurately, a black Methodist minister, speaking at Anderson's Good Templars event in 1879, said that the "Good Samaritan" in scripture was a "Negro."[10]

Racial and political considerations affected some festive events as well as the names of individuals. After emancipation a few families chose Sherman as their surname; Sickles, after the general, was the first name of one Pickens County youth; and an Anderson County son was named Greeley, after the institute in Anderson. Dozens of babies born in the 1870s, 1880s, and 1890s were called Ulysses after Civil War hero and President Grant.

Early communal celebrations of freedom involved special days throughout the South to commemorate liberation from slavery. Independence Day, July 4, was favored in Anderson as elsewhere; Pendleton and Anderson events appeared in newspapers between 1867 and the 1880s. Anderson Methodists honored the nation's one-hundredth birthday by naming their congregation Centennial Methodist in 1876. Such July 4 festivities continued well into the 1900s, but southern whites generally abstained from publicly celebrating the day. Emancipation observances in Anderson, Oconee, and Pickens counties began decades later, at least by 1900. Students who participated in Benedict, Allen, and Claflin commemorations may have brought that practice back home. Anderson services evidently continued regularly, and other communities also held them with parades and distinguished speakers from Columbia, Orangeburg, and Charleston. Anderson's best-reported event celebrated 1915's fiftieth anniversary of the war's end. By contrast, a strange gathering of former slaves occurred in Pickens in 1910.[11]

As with celebrations, enough information survives to provide strong clues as to what black people thought about issues involving racial matters. A strong racial strand underlay much black political activity after emancipation. Not surprisingly, race played a major part in support of Reconstruction governors. There is just enough material to trace broad outlines without sufficient evidence to determine when specific ideas began to be discussed locally or how wide an audience they reached. It is even more difficult to figure out how late nineteenth-century blacks in the tricounty area learned of issues initially articulated far beyond the area. Somehow Abel Masons knew about eighteenth-century black mathematician Benjamin Banneker and named their lodge for him.[12]

As sources of printed information were limited, much was conveyed orally; press coverage was sadly lacking. Local newspapers, all white, barely touched on developing African American organizations and concepts. Few 1865–1900 South Carolina black papers—almost all published in lower parts of the state—endured for more than a year. Many of these, moreover, served as official or unofficial denominational organs. John Starks (Seneca) in 1900 was subscribing to the *People's Recorder,* one that survived the longest.[13]

Schoolbooks and church literature contained, in most cases, no specifically black content. Schools used standard, state-sanctioned textbooks. Other coverage in classrooms had to come from teachers who, using their own knowledge and resources, could share stories about Frederick Douglass, Sojourner Truth, the Underground Railroad, or Banneker. South Carolina's black Baptists and Methodists used white-controlled American Baptist or ME(N) published literature. Only the AME Church produced resources with specific black interest. Even its materials were printed by ME, South presses until 1900, when W. D. Chappelle took over direction.[14]

How many of these AME publications reached Anderson, Oconee, and Pickens is another matter. Its newspaper, *Christian Recorder*, carried local congregational accounts throughout the country each week, as well as accomplishments and verbal or physical assaults on African Americans. It featured news of interest, including major addresses, conferences, and arguments among black leaders on a variety of issues. Henry M. Turner, an Abbeville native and first black U.S. Army chaplain, edited the *Recorder* between 1876 and 1880. His work may have increased local interest in the publication.[15]

Many, though not all, AME ministers would have subscribed to the *Christian Recorder*, as did some lay people. Ministers could then disseminate news and ideas to their congregations, formally or informally. Since AME and ME(N) clergy rotated assigned posts frequently, they gleaned ideas throughout the state and passed them on to successive congregations. Fledgling AME ministers trained in Charleston during early postbellum years or later at Allen University, and ME(N) ministers at Claflin University, where they had exposure to black news and ideas.

Such was the background of Silas H. Jefferson, the first AME minister in the upper piedmont. From later posts Spartanburg, Newberry, and other towns he sent notices of his churches' problems and accomplishments to the *Recorder*, as did other Pendleton successors, G. T. Strickland and W. D. Chappelle. All three later became presiding elders and Chappelle a bishop; Pendleton was getting some of the up-and-coming AME leaders and their ideas. While serving in 1883 as presiding elder of AME's Abbeville District, including Anderson, Oconee, and Pickens counties, Jefferson published the *Journal of Enterprise*.[16] Anderson and Pendleton people likely got at least some issues of these papers by someone once serving them.

Church conferences provided significant contacts for AME, Methodist, and Baptist men. Both AME and Methodist ministers held quarterly district and annual conference meetings. Because these followed a prescribed formula, their minutes provide little other content of those meetings. Baptists met annually in the Rocky River, Seneca, and Oolenoy associations; two hundred or more men participated each year. These minutes and committee reports, providing considerably more insight into black thought, are used extensively below. Smaller numbers of delegates attended annual conventions of the Baptist Educational, Missionary and Sunday School Convention of South Carolina (E&M), established in 1877 for Baptists statewide. Anderson's Philip Morris joined its board in 1879. Several other local men later served, H. Watkins as vice president, and E. V. Gassaway as secretary.[17]

Some men attended statewide political meetings, and a few traveled as delegates to national church conferences and political conventions. There they learned from and exchanged ideas with others throughout the country. Delegates Elias Jenkins and David Singleton, Oconee Republicans, attended the 1874 state convention in Charleston, and two other Oconee Republicans got the opportunity in 1876, as did W. R. Parker and Henry Kennedy from Anderson. Anderson's contingent to the 1892 state Republican convention included teacher W. A. Clark. And Wilson Cooke —Greenville political leader and ME(N) trustee—was one of eight blacks among fourteen delegates to the 1880 national Republican convention.[18] Additionally, the state's major leaders such as Richard Carroll, E. M. Brawley, and AME and ME(N) presiding elders and bishops attended and presented their ideas to upper-piedmont denominational gatherings. Baptists and Methodists held statewide meetings in Anderson. Knowledge of national developments in black thought and organization fostered local groups and discussions about race and its terminology.

Choices of terms describing themselves collectively show evolution, or at least fluctuations. "Rocky River Colored Baptist Association" was in 1868 the full constitutional name of Rocky River Baptist Association; its preamble began, "We, the United Colored Baptist Churches." The word "Colored" continued to be the choice in Baptist minutes and other records in Anderson, Oconee, and Pickens counties. When a conflict arose in 1877 within the association, its minutes referred to "a tedious debate . . . between white and colored." That same year the E&M was launched as "Colored Baptists of South Carolina have felt the importance of united action."[19]

The term persevered. Gassaway in 1886 posted an *Intelligencer* notice entitled, "Attention, Colored Citizens." Ironically, by that time Rocky River adopted a new constitution that dropped "Colored" from its name and text.[20] The state convention likewise omitted its description as being specifically for "colored" churches. But E&M's printed minutes in the 1890s carried an unofficial slogan, "Of the Colored Baptists of South Carolina," and in 1904 founding president Gassaway's rival group adopted the name "Colored Baptist." "Negro," however, became increasingly popular by 1900.

Racial matters became a frequent subject for discussion in the 1880s. Issues linked, at least implicitly, terminology, race improvement, and ties and responsibilities to Africa, as well as attitudes toward it. Arguments surged among local, state, and national groups about emigration to Liberia and about missions to Africa while European countries were increasing their imperialistic control over that continent. Late-1800s emigration to Liberia evidently did not include anyone from the tri-county area, although the local white press covered major events such as the *Azor*'s departure from Charleston in early 1879. Its passengers included several Abbeville

County emigrants. A few people went to Liberia in earlier years, and two Hallums —a woman and her mother, both born there—came to live in Pickens County.[21] Although relatively little local interest seems to have developed about emigrating to Africa, its imagery evidently grabbed attention as a rural, northern Pickens community proclaimed itself "Little Liberia."

African ties lingered; the area still had several African-born residents and more people whose parents were born in Africa. In 1849 Saluda Baptists reported $2.24 "by colored people" for African missions, clear evidence of a continued awareness of Africa. A few elderly, African-born people survived in the upper piedmont in 1880, and nearly seventy sons and daughters of African-born parents lived in the area. Even in 1900 there were still at least fifteen tricounty residents who reported that one parent was born in Africa. Skills, foods, and names maintained some African traditions. Periodic area press reports of current African events added knowledge of recent happenings.

Attitudes about Liberia, Africa, and race contained mixed undertones. In 1879 the E&M referred to Africa as "the land of our fore-fathers," and an 1881 resolution deplored the "sad condition of the many millions of heathen in Africa." Once, "all there was of civilization was in Africa. . . . But now a great portion of Africa stands absorbed in ignorance and degradation." And an 1885 report said that "our people in Africa . . . are in a savage, degraded condition."

Three years later the Rocky River association again emphasized a need to support work in Liberia, "now recognized among the civilized nations of the world, while other parts [of Africa] still grope in darkness." E&M, Rocky River, and state AME leaders stressed their distinctive ability and obligation to support African missions: "the blackness of our skin has allied us to the inhabitants of this vast country [Congo]. . . . To the African anything but a black face is generally the face of an enemy." American blacks were well suited to the climate, they said, an ironic parallel to stereotypes held by whites. Attitudes remained mixed, as a Rocky River report spoke of the "gross darkness of Africa" with its "ignorance and superstition."[22]

Anderson natives Georgia Ann Reeves and husband Jim Anderson in 1895 joined over two hundred people sailing from Savannah to become missionaries in Sierra Leone, where she worked in a Freetown girls' industrial school. Six years later, after her husband's death, she returned home. She raised funds by speaking to many organizations, including a white women's group of Anderson's First Baptist Church. Encouraging immigration to Sierra Leone, she returned there herself, having married another missionary.[23]

Rocky River Baptists articulated more racially conscious ideas in the early 1880s, as did area AME. A late-1881 AME resolution deplored "the tide of prejudice which flows against the race," and W. D. Jenkins talked about "improvement of the race" in an 1882 Pickens address. By 1886 the word "race" itself appears frequently. A Rocky River educational committee said that "as a race we can never go onward without education." An 1886 report praised Greeley Institute as "an institution for the education of the negro," perhaps Rocky River's earliest "negro" reference in surviving records. The association's usage of "race" and "blackness" indicate new consciousness and language for the group.[24]

Rocky River's Educational Committee, energetically urging more and better education, increasingly merged that goal with racial improvement. The association in 1891 said once again, "Come, each one who has the interest of the race question at heart, and put forth more strenuous efforts to raise the educational standard of the people." This appeal was expanded a year later: "When we can come into the possession of property and have our doctors, lawyers and some little independence, our success will be in our own grasp." Gassaway and Belton teacher F. J. Washington dominated the committee for years; Gassaway's brother, M. H., an educator and a Methodist, likely pursued similar goals in ME(N) meetings.

Both Rocky River and state Baptists provided small sums to help further students' education, often at the high-school level since that was not widely available. But a few people were going further in collegiate and professional studies. Anderson's first doctor and first pharmacist both benefited from this aid at the turn of the century.[25]

Clearly help was not forthcoming from state or federal government or from whites in general. As with efforts to create high schools, blacks also began to establish other organizations for advancement. The *Intelligencer* on September 10, 1891, first reported "Colored [Farmers] Alliances" being organized in Galveston and demanding one dollar in wages for each one hundred pounds of cotton picked. Although the *Intelligencer* called these alliances "futile," the *Pickens Sentinel* almost simultaneously observed that Pickens had a dire shortage of pickers, and by November the *Intelligencer* was reporting black alliances throughout Anderson County. G. D. Williams served as general manager of the Anderson Alliance and state vice president. A few years later Pickens County men organized Turner's Hill Farmers' Aid Society, located near Liberty. It is not clear what either of these organizations intended or accomplished, as is true for Oconee and Pickens black teachers organizations in the same period.[26]

Resulting from increasing racial pride as well as separation induced by whites, there developed both a State Colored Fair in Columbia in the 1880s and an Anderson County Colored Fair organization around 1900. Several Anderson men created in 1899 an Afro-American Real Estate Association, indicating awareness of growing "Afro-American" usage nationwide.[27]

Increasing racial consciousness and conflict appeared in relations between the white-dominated American Baptist Convention (ABC) and the new National Baptist Convention, an independent, black-controlled organization established in the 1880s. Rocky River became deeply involved in a growing rift as the state's black Baptists disagreed with control of Benedict College, still staffed by a white president and faculty. A movement began around 1900 to create—perhaps at Anderson—a new black-controlled college.

Left: Racist stereotypes, found increasingly during the late 1800s. Black Heritage in the Upper Piedmont

Seneca Institute trustees (ca. 1905–1910); seated (left to right): Cicero F. Harrison, Prof. W. J. Thomas, and A. E. Dupree; standing: Wiley Ferguson, Dr. N. A. Doyle, George C. Scott, Rev. J. S. Steward, J. H. Haywood, Dr. B. S. Sharp, and Tom D. Southerland. Black Heritage in the Upper Piedmont

People in Anderson, Oconee, and Pickens counties increasingly delved into a broader question of how to improve their conditions; occasionally, but rarely, they spoke out publicly and formally on racist political issues. A statewide conference of what the *Intelligencer* called "Prominent Negro Leaders" met to deal with an urgent crisis of lynchings in 1893, a peak year for South Carolina and for the upper piedmont. In May alone the *Pickens Sentinel* carried articles about four incidents, one of them near Pelzer. Leaders, who met without a formal organization, included four from the three-county area: E. V. Gassaway, teachers E. A. Saxon and A. R. Bacote, and AME minister W. D. Chappelle. The group issued a lengthy appeal to Confederate veterans, ministers of any race, and other white leaders that they demand a halt to the "judge lynch." Copies went to the governor and to the press.[28] This was one of the few occasions on which upper-piedmont or state groups spoke publicly against racist attacks.

Racial improvement continued to pervade Rocky River's emphasis on education, as it did again in 1897. "The education of the race is a pressing necessity," the association said. It advocated studying systematically rather than getting a smattering of education, and reading more books and newspapers, "or we can never advance far above the present status." That same year Rocky River Baptists, who previously used the *Intelligencer* press to print yearly minutes, found other printers. And the association in 1900 stated, "We cannot, as a race, hope to rise . . . without intellectual development."

Education became the issue on which Baptists first challenged a state official. An E&M resolution in 1901 criticized State Superintendent of Education McMahan for appointing white faculty to conduct the 1900 state-paid summer teachers' institute. In blunt language this resolution criticized his choice of "white teachers who have never shown interest in the race, and Whereas the State Superintendent of Education has thus raised the color question along lines hitherto free from it, and Whereas, We have in South Carolina colored men fully competent to fill the places in said school, . . . Resolved . . . we believe in Negro men for Negro women, Negro churches for Negro preachers, Negro teachers for Negro public schools."[29]

Five years later the new Colored Baptist State Convention condemned lynching and assaults on women, both white and black. It asked "whites to make a difference between the industrious, law-abiding and self-respecting element and the criminal and worthless element in the Negro race," almost an excuse for rough handling of this "worthless element." "Industrious, law-abiding and self-respecting" people, especially through religious organizations, grappled with and criticized the less-savory elements "in the Negro race." In his presidential address that same year Gassaway acknowledged the existence of some bad members within the community. But, he said, "there is no people on earth who deplore the crimes laid at the door of the criminal class more than the good colored people."[30]

Rocky River Baptists and African Methodist Episcopal leaders frequently attacked drinking and emphasized the importance of a stable home life. Writing Rocky River's

1890 annual message, Gassaway addressed this issue: "As a race much depends on the way our homes are conducted." Homes should not be places of strife or contention, he said, and "mothers, wives, and sisters must make homes as pleasant as possible." Men ought not spend time in questionable places; if they stayed home at proper times, they would avoid intoxicating drink. Rocky River Baptists frequently denounced dancing, barrooms, and "hot suppers," events often associated with drinking and brawls. The association, noting in 1890 that "as a race much depends on the way our lives are conducted," said three years later that the Gospel pulls "men out of the bar-room, the pool-room, the gambling den, and many other such places."

Many ministers, themselves with rural churches, believed that towns provided too many chances for evil activities, idleness, and unemployment. The same resolution that condemned lynching advised people to stay out of cities, remaining instead in the country where they could make an independent living and could own homes and property. Black men reportedly discussed plans in 1879 to rid Pickens town of tramps and black refugees from Georgia who were committing crimes, some of which evidently were being blamed on the local community.[31]

One form of self-improvement was to leave for areas believed to offer better wages and more opportunities. Some people departed in the first year or two of freedom, some to cities such as Charleston, Columbia, and Atlanta; others, farther west. Larger numbers left in the 1880s, drawn especially as organizers recruited labor for Arkansan and other southwestern farms. William Pickens's family was one among many who followed that route. On one March 1884 day forty Anderson blacks boarded a train for Little Rock, with their first change at Seneca; more followed the next week, and then more two weeks later. Local black leaders who encouraged emigration westward got paid. Although those who migrated received a "free" ticket, it had to be paid for after they began work in Arkansas. Quite a few people were stranded in Seneca when organizers accepted only families, not single people. According to the newspaper, some migrants decided within three months that they wanted to return home. White families throughout the upstate also went to Arkansas and Texas during the 1880s. Newspapers began carrying the headline "Negro Exodus," which they repeated in subsequent years.[32]

No other large groups left comparable to those departing for the southwest. But families and individuals moved, one by one. Dozens of upper-piedmont families by 1900 lived in Atlanta and Washington, D.C., where they likely had government employment. At least two men had military duty in the Philippines during the Spanish-American war. Some people went north for education, then returned, as did John I. Miller: a few weeks after graduating from Howard University with honors in 1901, he began teaching in Pickens. Similarly, Anderson native D. C. Hill, educated at Shaw University's medical school (North Carolina), came back to Pendleton where he practiced in 1900. Later, Willis Ignatius Peek and E. J. Thomas, future Anderson businessmen, graduated from Tuskegee Institute (Alabama) in 1915 and 1916.

Individuals moved to other places as well. Jane Hunter went first to Virginia, where friends encouraged her to move to Ohio. Other families also went to Ohio, although most people followed the major railroad line, which ran to Richmond, Washington, and New York. A. R. Robinson, who served Pendleton and Anderson Baptist churches, accepted a Philadelphia pastorate in 1906. Several families would go to Pittsburgh and other northern cities, but nothing resembling significant numbers moving north from Anderson, Oconee, and Pickens counties would occur before the late 1910s and 1920s. Options of leaving the area, staying there and moving into a town, or otherwise working for personal advancement all contributed to racial and community improvement. Race gradually became a major issue for both white and black in the 1880s and 1890s. Later, Jane Hunter, J. J. Starks, and William Pickens, among other writers from the upper piedmont, would talk specifically in terms of "race pride."[33] Race was increasingly the order of the day and is the focus of part 6. While African Americans expanded their own opportunities, whites took others away.

PART 6 ↣ *Changing Conditions, for Better, for Worse*

Introduction to Part 6

JUST AS SOCIETY, railroad lines, towns, and manufacturing changed dramatically during the 1870s and 1880s, so did racial attitudes. Lacking any significant landmark, the landscape of attitudes and politics by the 1890s looked quite different. As during Reconstruction, national issues and societal change deeply affected African Americans, still a minority caught up in larger forces.

Racism, more specifically white racist views toward blacks and other nonwhites, permeated society in Anderson, Oconee, and Pickens counties, the nation, and the world before the century's end. This strong undercurrent manifested itself locally in barbed epithets and slogans, stronger and uglier than in earlier decades; a greater emphasis on "negro crime" as deviant and dangerous to white society; political discrimination enshrined in an 1895 "Jim Crow" constitution; the white Democratic primary in 1896; and lynchings. Though small in number, these murders spread terror and served as ominous warnings. Sexual exploitation was a more frequent, more pervasive reminder of white male domination and black vulnerability.

African Americans, who became politically subordinated to a dominant white supremacy and to discriminatory laws, also formed an economically subjugated class. Blacks, mostly sharecroppers, seldom made more in a year than they spent; more often they sank deeper in debt. Liens on their crops, obligated to the landlord, unpaid balances at the general store, and fertilizer advances—all of these pulled blacks further into poverty. Either "Another day older and deeper in debt" or, as in slavery, "Nobody knows the trouble I've seen" equally characterized their dilemma.

Many analysts would describe these conditions as structural oppression. Not only did individuals suffer, but the whole system of white-dominated government, laws, and economy was oppressive. The "white supremacy" slogan and a "Jim Crow" constitution based on that premise illustrate oppression's political thrust. The economic and personal plight of sharecroppers effectively shows other oppression. Instances of whites whipping a black man, forcing him to leave the county—let alone lynchings and sexual violations—further solidify the argument.

Complicating this dismal portrait, however, was the fact that more families owned land than ever before. More were literate—dramatically more so than in 1870—and hundreds pursued education beyond local, one-room schools. An emerging middle class, defined mostly by status rather than by prosperity, included teachers, ministers, a few merchants, and skilled craftsmen. Some families moved away to escape. Oppression led to out-migration, which produced opportunities for some. Those who left were too few to alter significantly numbers of the local population or continuity of their community. Much larger numbers suffered deeper political and economic subjugation at home. And abundant examples show continued interpersonal relationships on some levels between black and white and at times kind and friendly interactions. Perhaps they were a polite veneer overlaying economic and political subjugation.

TWENTY-ONE

Societal Attitudes and Oppression

HEIGHTENED RACIAL CONSCIOUSNESS among upper-piedmont African Americans and their awareness of black developments elsewhere in the country came during the same decades when whites sharpened, and harshened, racial distinctions. Intensified labeling frequently produced offensive barbs in language, stereotypes, and brutal lynchings.[1] Attitudes, gradually developing for two decades, hardened into a set of laws and an era known as "Jim Crow," a racist term itself. Although many of these changes originated far beyond the boundaries of Anderson, Oconee, and Pickens counties, they still had significant impact there.

The nearly fifteen-year period between Wade Hampton's and Benjamin Tillman's gubernatorial elections, not clearly defined, lacked major landmarks. Otherwise, it might not be described only by gubernatorial names, themselves shorthand signals. Like the course of Anderson's urban growth, that period reflected concurrent trends of increased business and more racism. The 1880s were an exceptionally ill-defined decade in South Carolina and across the nation. Business and manufacturing expanded, continuing growth spurred by the Civil War. Textile mills, including several local ones, required more cotton. And racist views became more widespread. These all had reverberations in local, state, national, and even worldwide arenas. New towns along the Southern Railroad line provided opportunities for white merchants, black employment, and relatively cheap shipping for cotton. Not all benefited economically or politically. Gradually, disgruntled whites, especially upstate farmers, coalesced into a group that would "play the race card." Intensified racism contributed directly to oppressing blacks in Anderson, Oconee, and Pickens counties, as elsewhere.

As business boomed, religious and other reformers complained about alcohol, immorality, and prostitution. The temperance movement's zealousness sometimes involved direct action against offenders. Intensified white concerns included fornication, adultery, and especially interracial sex; meanwhile white sexual exploitation of black women continued without public outcry. Although business growth depended on stability, the 1880s saw much violence, both local and national. Vigilante justice, especially along America's western frontier, and many lynchings occurred. Directing violence against blacks, white men also fought, shot, and killed one another and occasionally turned against white women also.

Larger numbers of lynchings, local and statewide, and institutionalized political discrimination against African Americans—both fully developed in the 1890s—had yet to come. The tricounty's first lynching, which occurred in late December 1887, combined unusual circumstances and convoluted white attitudes toward lynch law. These years for African Americans saw a mixture of oppression, opportunities, and small-scale out-migration. Although diminished, voting continued. Relatively small numbers of blacks—mostly men—sought opportunities elsewhere. In Anderson and other towns, communities developed significantly, due partly to more and somewhat improved schools and to more property ownership. Many leaders—ranging from Booker T. Washington to Anderson's clergy—advocated racial improvement through education and hard work.

Intense political and economic subjugation of the 1890s, chronicled in chapter 22, are interwoven with this chapter's societal attitudes and harsh implementations of them: stereotypes, sexual exploitation, and lynchings. Creating fear among African Americans, these became very personal extensions of political subjugation.

After Hampton: Changing Political and Societal Landscape

Both Governor Wade Hampton's election in 1876, accompanied by strong pressure on black people to vote Democratic, and decline of most federal interest in the state held bad omens for African Americans. The end of Reconstruction has long been understood as closing an era of black political activity and societal advances. Hampton's top staff and party leaders were all Confederate generals. The two decades following his victory were a brake on black politics and an escalator for white racial attitudes. Blacks voted in remaining years of the century but mostly in presidential and congressional, rather than in Democratically controlled state and county, elections.[2]

Whites since 1865 had many conflicting attitudes toward emancipated people. One goal of whites was to reduce their dependence on black workers. While favoring European labor as an alternative to black workers, newspapers in Anderson, Oconee, and Pickens counties derided blacks who emigrated westward. Recruiters in Abbeville faced hostile, even brutal, opposition as they tempted workers into leaving the state. The *Pickens Sentinel* described them as having been enticed by "flaming advertisements which have been so profusely scattered amongst them by emigrant agents." Similarly, while ridiculing ignorance, whites complained about supporting a school system to educate African Americans. Abbeville's *Press and Banner* said it "turned their heads" and led them to loaf around train depots. It argued that blacks should instead acquire a good house, furniture, and an intelligent conviction of right and wrong. "It requires time to bring the colored race to our standard."[3]

Those same years saw gradually rising racial tensions especially when they involved interracial sex. A black woman teaching in Pickens was "caught in bed with a (white) man," and a South Carolinian writing for the *Atlantic Monthly* referred to interracial couples found in each county. The legislature in 1879 passed South

Carolina's first law formally prohibiting interracial marriages. The issue of such relationships arose especially during poor agricultural harvests and distressed financial conditions. Pickens County in 1883 tried a mixed-race couple for adultery. Two years later four white men drove an Anderson black tenant family from their house and shot at homes of another tenant and the white landowner. The *Intelligencer* editorialized, "We must, in the most emphatic manner, denounce the perpetration of these outrages" and see that the guilty are punished.[4]

Local attitudes and discrimination were part of a wider web. Never were Anderson, Oconee, and Pickens counties and South Carolina more in vogue than with their late-1800s racism. Its antiblack character found manifestation elsewhere as anti-immigrant sentiment in the Northeast and Midwest, European imperialism in Africa and Asia, Russian slaughter of Jews, and Japanese subjugation of Korea. Racial attitudes permeated laws and literature from South Carolina's 1895 constitution through the Supreme Court's *Plessy v. Ferguson* decision to Rudyard Kipling's *White Man's Burden*. There was, in fact, increasing racial consciousness by whites, blacks, and others, in the three counties and around the world.

Contempt for so-called less-fit and unfit peoples flourished worldwide. Following in Charles Darwin's and Herbert Spencer's footsteps, pseudoscientific theories by whites found other peoples to be inferior: darker "races" of southeastern Europe, Gypsies, Asians, Jews, and black peoples in Africa and in America. Local newspapers carried stories as Europeans fought and conquered darker peoples—described contemptuously in the press—in Africa and Asia. Newspaper columnists in Anderson, Oconee, and Pickens counties popularized racist theories of the day. Increasingly these ideas took root and permeated both language and subconscious of politics, a slow and hardly perceptible process.

Cumulative indications of changing attitudes can be found in the white press. Increasingly in the 1880s, more so in the 1890s, and even more often after 1900, area newspapers used "nigger," "darkie," "son of Ham," and other racial epithets as well as stereotypes. Hardly appearing earlier in this text, they come frequently in these final chapters reflecting prolific contemporary usage.[5] Shortened names were another derogatory means of addressing blacks. Pinckney, long a personal name for black and white, now became almost universally "Pink" for African Americans. Others, listed in the 1870 census as James, now were almost always called "Jim."

South Carolina's governing elite did not support this cultural trend. While riding into office on antiblack and anti-Republican sentiments, Hampton and his close associates did not actively endorse policies of oppression. "Bourbons," as they have often been described, paid more attention to their romanticized views of antebellum life and to their current economic interests in railroads, phosphate, textile mills, and insurance. Similarly, successive governors pursued prosperity rather than racial polarization.[6] Following expensive, often lavish, and occasionally corrupt Reconstruction government, Bourbons sought to cut finances drastically and to pay off most state debt. Education, especially that for black children, clearly could not thrive in such a climate. Discounted teacher pay claims in Anderson, Oconee, and Pickens counties and elsewhere affected blacks more severely than whites.

Crime, although one of many factors, serves as a convenient thread to weave together white attitudes and their consequences. Crime increasingly bore a black face, at least as far as laws defined, and courts punished, it in South Carolina. Newspapers, having long denounced what they perceived as Republican evils, easily continued a tirade against black crime in subsequent years. Immediately following Hampton's April 1877 accession to the governor's office, the *Intelligencer* began May 1877 with a headline "The South Carolina Senate Wrested from the Thieves"; a few days later Hampton had a victory ball in Pendleton; and later in May the *Intelligencer* ran a half-page editorial supporting leasing of convict labor to railroads or farmers to reduce expensive penitentiary costs. Advocated by Hampton and passed by the legislature, it began that summer. Seven years later, Anderson's first group arrived, one hundred shackled black men with ten white guards, to undertake Savannah Valley Railroad construction. Railroad expansion and punishment of black crime merged, while some Andersonians on the penitentiary staff and prosperous local farmers also would benefit from convict leasing.

By 1900 the penitentiary was 88 percent African American. Public labor displayed the blackness of convicts, as did county chain gangs. More and more of these men showed up in prison garb throughout the state under watchful eyes of their armed guards and of curious onlookers. Chain gangs, appearing in Anderson and Oconee as early as 1887, later in Pickens, worked especially on roads. When Clemson College obtained prison labor in the 1890s to help build its campus, trustees requested that the penitentiary send only black convicts. Several hundred worked there at one time, making quite a public image. Death rates among leased convicts and on county chain gangs were horrendous, a toll increased by numbers reported shot or killed while attempting to escape.[7]

As we've already seen, the phrase "negro crime" itself immediately set black people apart as offenders; newspapers never used a "white crime" headline. And lynchings demonstrated what could happen to blacks who erred. What they did wrong was to violate community standards, as defined by whites. These expectations and punishments derived from white arrogance, epitomized in Peter Harris's banishment from Anderson County. Such acts stemmed from a fundamental presumption that whites had the prerogative to define standards and punish offenders. Whites did it by whippings, lynchings, and—legally—employing convict labor. At the same time South Carolina's Lunatic Asylum housed a disproportionate number of black "inmates." Among possible explanations, black people might have had more mental problems; white families were better able to care for their relatives; or the state used its asylum as a means to confine more black people. Several from Anderson, Oconee, and Pickens counties were sent there between the 1880s and early 1900s, but so were at least two men from well-known white families in one lower Pickens County town.

Chain gang of prisoners, as seen in the late 1800s; they often built public roads or worked on private farm land, with a heavy death toll. Pendleton District Commission

"Next to last legal hanging in Pickens Co., c. 1910–20" (no name or date but perhaps Henry Jones, scheduled to be hanged on Aug. 25, 1904). Courtesy of the Pickens County Museum of Art and History

These attitudes toward convicts, "lunatics," and blacks evolved as many whites expressed generalized hostilities and groped for a new cohesive political force. Although united in 1876 to "redeem" the state, whites had little common agreement afterward. With relatively prosperous times following 1877, their divisions initially were neither sharp nor critical. Following a mid-1880s agricultural recession, frustration grew among those not prospering from thriving sectors of the economy. Grumblings began among farmers and political dissidents, excluded from a ruling "Bourbon" elite—including Martin W. Gary, John Irby, and Benjamin Tillman, mostly Confederate veterans from South Carolina's midlands.

New economic difficulties resulting from poor mid-1880s harvests, high railroad rates, and a national depression created problems for both farmers and businessmen, but the state party offered no solution. Upstate whites, who earlier tried various political venues, turned to new alternatives, the Grange in the 1870s and Farmers Alliances in the 1880s. A joint May 1884 Grange and Democratic club meeting at Providence Camp Ground in Anderson County—one of several—linked politics and farmers' interests.[8]

Other unsettling change accompanied rise of textile firms. Driving up the demand for white farmers' cotton, raised mostly by sharecroppers, mills consumed huge quantities of the crop. Mills expanded rapidly in the late 1800s and early 1900s. Textile operators, virtually all white, lived mostly in company-owned "mill towns" with their own schools and churches, standing apart from local society.

The Rise of Tillman

"Pitchfork" Ben Tillman launched a new farmers' movement to rival the more elite Grange and to provide himself with a political base. As politician, governor, and later U.S. senator, he began to symbolize and unite upstate white farmers and other disaffected groups. Like Hampton's 1876 victory, Tillman's rising political success began during a period of bad crops and other economic problems—also an era favoring populism and opposition to established financial interests, as did that of William Jennings Bryan. Tillman skillfully blended interests and frustrations shared by many upstate whites. While the upstate's political leadership and prosperous farmers endorsed him, many fervent supporters came from a lower socioeconomic level who psychologically needed an underclass below them; it was not hard to find.[9] Like a slow camera fade-out, that change was a gradual regression for blacks without major landmarks between 1877 and 1890. By then, diverse, discontented elements would come together.

While Tillman's political stature grew and racial tensions escalated, Atlanta's *Constitution* editor Henry Grady articulated a different message. Grady's historic "New South" speech, carried in the January 1887 *Keowee Courier*, envisioned an industrialized, business-oriented South that would leave such problems behind. He and others advocating a New South believed in "this glorious sunny South," its unlimited potential, natural resources, and cheap labor. Northern investment and development of industries would be necessary but desirable—an attitude different from that of much of the "Yankee-hating South." Delivering a different message, *Constitution* columnist Bill Arp contributed much racist verbiage, especially as his columns were widely reprinted. One, appearing in an 1897 *People's Journal* issue, said that "we will have to . . . establish the whipping post."

As well as "rednecks," many prosperous farmers, often descendants of antebellum farmers' society members, experimented with various nonpolitical agricultural organizations after the Civil War. Thomas Clemson served as president of several short-lived societies and also urged establishment of agricultural education. When he died in April 1888, bequeathing Calhoun's former plantation for a state agricultural college, several issues merged: agricultural education, farmers' concerns, and Tillman's political campaign. Clemson's will named as lifetime college trustee Ben Tillman and R. W. (Dick) Simpson. Elected governor in 1890 amid increasingly racist statements in the press and in political discourse, Tillman relied on political followers who got the retrospective label "rednecks" and believed in white control. The *Pickens Sentinel* wholeheartedly endorsed him: "Vote that ticket, it is democracy; vote that ticket, it is white supremacy; vote that ticket, it is the solid South; vote that ticket, it is the bulwark of our freedom."

Its rival *People's Journal* reported in 1894 the state Democratic party's lament that the "colored voting population" had increased 40,000 more than had whites since 1876 and urged a new constitution to disenfranchise the "negro vote" and the "evils of mongrelism." "White supremacy" became a central plank of Tillmanite attitudes that would lead in 1895 to demolishing the Reconstruction constitution. Tillman described his own victory in 1890: "The triumph of Democracy and white supremacy over mongrelism and anarchy is most complete." Tillmanites often spoke graphically. Anderson County fan J. W. Earle, writing Tillman in October 1892 from "Holland's Store P.O.," complained about the ratio of "precinct voters . . . 200 of them being Niggers & 150 Whites." Earle opposed one Republican politician who "has been heading meetings & making speeches to the Niggers at night in every Nigger church & school hous in the township one, two & three times a week." Earle blasted "the Nigger con.[stitution]," "Yankee books" for schools, and "abusive coroner's inquests" that cost too much money, that is, those for blacks. Jonas Armstrong from Honea Path told the governor, "Believe me to be a Simon pure Tillmanite Democrat until death."[10]

Tillman's four years as governor and the 1895 constitutional convention occurred during extensive Civil War commemoration and celebration. For months Anderson, Oconee, and Pickens counties newspapers in every issue carried articles about the war, its veterans, and reenactments, as well as obituaries of deceased veterans and notices of regimental reunions. Elaborate accounts of Chickamauga and other battles periodically consumed up to two pages of four-page weekly editions, and "Blind Tom" incorporated his "Battle of Manassas" rendition into performances, including an 1891 appearance in Anderson. Enthusiasm continued into the next decade.[11] The Civil War was still very much a part of the general culture, as most white males over the age of forty-five were former Confederate soldiers, and many of those in power served as officers. Younger whites were nurtured on family stories and decades of reunion events. By contrast, most African Americans older than thirty remembered their years as slaves, accounts passed on to younger blacks.

This virtual mania created another reason why white southerners felt the need for a victory; their easiest available target was the black population. African Americans felt the brunt not only by constitutional exclusion of themselves as voters and thus as officeholders, but also through harsher sufferings.

Personalized Oppression: Sexual Exploitation and Lynchings

Lynching served as the most dramatic, most public, and most dreaded form of racial oppression for many decades. Usually a group or mob activity, it almost always was a visibly public murder, sometimes with crowds of up to two hundred involved. But convictions for lynching were incredibly rare. Ironically, in 1900 the State Lunatic Asylum had numerous inmates committed for masturbation, although the courts tried, let alone convicted, hardly anyone for lynching.

Other forms of intimidation existed, of course. The threat of lynching itself no doubt drove many people into fearful submission or into exile. White men individually killed black men without being caught or punished. Although some of these deaths were personal disagreements or unplanned shootings by drunken white men, many were racially motivated; most went uninvestigated, some not even reported.

And many white men sexually exploited black females. Approximately thirteen years old, Jane Hunter, working at Clemson's hotel, reported that college staff and businessmen staying there frequently tried to lure her into their bedrooms: "[My] effort at earning my living had hazards. . . . It meant constant battle against unwanted advances, a studied ignoring of impudent glances, insulting questions. Whenever I entered a room to clean it, I pushed the door wide open. . . . Frequently I had to bolt my door, for the proprietor was as shameless in his pursuit of pretty mulatto girls [including herself] as were any of his patrons." Her aunt Caroline was so disturbed that she walked several miles to warn Jane Hunter's mother about "stories she had learned of young colored girls who had met disgrace in such establishments."[12] Such warnings shared by women helped protect others.

Other women reported dangers facing young females, and some suffered them personally. Lucinda Reid Brown, nearly a hundred years old, said in 1988, "What all they did to those black girls, I don't want to think about it." Aside from forced sex, some women were prostitutes with white clientele. One homeless young girl around 1900 moved into an upper-piedmont railroad town where she survived through prostitution. At one depot a drunken white fellow in 1906 yelled to a black man, with whom he was gambling, "I'm going to the nigger whorehouse in Greenville."[13]

Lynching and sexual exploitation of black women occurred in an atmosphere of broader violence. Numerous cases of white men's violence against white women appeared in newspapers, and black men sometimes abused and beat black women or even children. On several occasions in 1900 alone, angered blacks pursued a black man who abused or raped a young black girl. Black men also killed each other, especially during quarrels or when drunk. Three Easley blacks in 1883 murdered another one, a witness in a federal trial; influenced by whiskey, they knifed him at a Greenville "low bawdy house." Coroners' inquests recorded murders resulting from arguments over sums as small as a quarter or allegations that another black man was involved with one's wife. A Baptist church offered a reward leading to the arrest of a black man who murdered another in Central.[14] Quarrels, fights, and murders among blacks were reported in the press. White violence against blacks virtually never was.

Contrasted to numerous white men frequently and systematically molesting black girls and women, lynchings arose out of immediate emotions deliberately inflamed among a larger crowd. Although most were public, it is still difficult to determine firm numbers. Lists compiled by different people vary in both entries and totals. Major efforts include NAACP's *Thirty Years of Lynching*, covering the entire South as did a Tuskegee Institute compilation; Jack Mullins's reinterpretation of these in his 1961 thesis, "Lynching in South Carolina, 1900–1914"; and recent research by E. M. Beek and Stewart E. Tolnay. Even with established criteria that emerged out of a 1940 Tuskegee conference, these lists still remain inconsistent and tentative. Tables 21.1 and 21.2 combine most of their entries, cast doubts on some, and add a few others from newspapers.[15]

There seem to have been thirteen lynchings in Anderson, Oconee, and Pickens counties—plus three in Greenville that originated in Anderson, and another in Abbeville that also originated in Anderson—with sixteen victims between 1887 and 1914. Of these, one killed a white man, another a white woman accused of adultery. Tuskegee and the NAACP classified specific allegations for lynching: rape, murder, white racial prejudice, race riot, and others. Several reported instances lack verification or specific information. Lynchings occurred in scattered sites around the three counties, most of them in Anderson County, and all in rural areas, although sometimes victims were hauled out of town to a tree farther away. Most victims were lynched at night, but some by day; times of several are unknown. Two lynchings involved more than one victim: an unverified Six Mile lynching of "two negroes" around 1895–98, and extensively reported 1914 lynchings of three men near Fair Play.

Rapid population growth in Anderson County—25 percent between 1890 and 1900 but 52 percent in Williamston Township and 82 percent in Anderson city—and related societal pressures may have contributed to the rise in lynchings. Although details of most lynching groups are not known, those from Williamston, Piedmont, Pelzer, and Honea Path may well have included mill workers. However, rural men were also active, such as those at Six Mile (Pickens County) and Fair Play (Anderson), both small, unincorporated, mostly agricultural settlements.

Only three local lynchings—those in 1887, 1914, and 1930—have lingered in oral tradition. Each involved numerous people as lynchers; only in 1914 was the victim killed with guns; and all three resulted in statewide attention and well-publicized trials. Public officials led lynch crowds in two of these, plus another one in a "short story." In 1947, one of the nation's most famous lynchings, targeting Willie Earle, originally from the Abel community, attracted national media attention, and intense scrutiny by the NAACP.[16]

A White Victim in 1887

Lynchings went far beyond structural oppression to very personal murder of specific individuals. Yet they played a central role in systematic terror as did sexual violation, both acts emerging out of white arrogance. The first lynching in Anderson, Oconee, and Pickens counties occurred near Central, still a relatively new and sometimes raucous railroad town. Remarkably, its victim was white, its mob black, and those accused, though tried, eventually were pardoned. Thousands of white and black people throughout the state, including city and state officials, petitioned the governor to secure their release.[17]

A white fellow, described at the time as a "lunatic," savagely raped black Etta Lula, Cato Sherman's thirteen year-old daughter, on December 29, 1887. She died a day later, and that evening a coroner's inquest judged Manzeo Waldrop guilty. The trial justice, serving also as acting coroner, got Waldrop arrested during the inquest, secured his confession, and turned him over to local constables. They scheduled him to be moved from Central's holding cell to Pickens, about fifteen miles away. His transfer involved a mule-drawn wagon, an unusual starting time around midnight—two hours after Waldrop's formal charge, and limited security for him. Acting Constable Gaylord Eaton (who was white), according to later testimony, drank heavily, said that "Waldrop ought to be hanged anyhow" and bragged that he "would tie the rope to hang him if he could get three negroes to help."[18]

A short distance from town, twenty black men seized Waldrop and shot him. Although mortally wounded, he survived a short while, denying still that he assaulted the girl. While Eaton was returning Waldrop to Central, black men again grabbed him. The next morning his "body was found hanging to a tree not far from the roadside."

Authorities, aided by informants, quickly picked out six men as primary culprits. Solicitor James L. Orr Jr. presided at an inquest over Waldrop's body, whose verdict accused six black men: Cato Sherman, Henry Bolton, John Reese, Foster Knox, William C. Williams, and Harrison Haywood; it also named Eaton as accessory. Inquest jurors further alleged that several white men instigated Waldrop's lynching. The six men and Eaton, those actually arrested, were bound over for a grand jury, to meet two weeks later.[19] Central whites denounced the lynching, thanked Orr for helping to identify its perpetrators, and stressed their wish to uphold civil law.

The *Keowee Courier* on January 12, 1888, summed up press reaction elsewhere in the state. The editor proclaimed, "It is generally conceded that the act is the natural result of a precedent established by the whites in like cases of offence," a theme resonating through subsequent petitions. The editor further said, without evidence, that "no law abiding citizen will deny but lynch law is wrong." But, taking a quick switch, he believed that some crimes are "so revolting to man's moral nature, so destructive to society, so awful in their consequences to individuals and by sympathy to communities, that neither human nor divine law ever has or even can stay the hand of vengeance in their punishment. Of these crimes[,] fiendish and brutal violence to respectable women is the highest. . . . Summary punishment of a brute, black or white, who assaults a pure woman, we cannot condemn, and yet we cannot deny it is a dangerous precedent . . . playing with fire."

This waffling position, that lynching is "wrong but . . . ," typified much of the tricounty press coverage throughout three decades. Elsewhere, the case attracted wide attention. Black groups in both Greenville and Charleston raised money for the defense, and a black attorney from Charleston visited the prisoners, as did a *News and Courier* reporter.

Circuit Court Judge Norton, who in 1867 defended black men accused of murdering Miles Hunnicutt, and the grand jury responded without any ambivalence. Norton said, "It is the duty of every city and county in the State to suppress riots and prevent violence or injury to any person accused of crime." The grand jury returned true bills of murder against five black men and against Eaton as accessory. Somehow the black defendants acquired services of R. W. Simpson, noted partner in the Broyles and Simpson law firm. He won a postponement from January 1888 until the July term. Unlike Eaton, Simpson's clients could not post bail and remained imprisoned. "Dick" Simpson (Civil War letters in chapter 11) would soon become Clemson's first chairman of its board of trustees, not the most likely champion of black lynchers.

The July grand jury dismissed charges against those white men who supposedly instigated this lynching, while the petit jury deadlocked, resulting in a mistrial for the defendants. They remained in jail during another postponement until March 1889. Then the jury acquitted Eaton, Sherman, and Reese. Finding Williams, Haywood, and Bolton guilty, jurors recommended them to the court's mercy. That seemed not to be forthcoming, as Norton sentenced Williams and Haywood to be hanged a month later, but granted Bolton a new trial.

Now public reaction was far less ambiguous, but the *Keowee Courier* editor still rode two horses. Clearly he did not expect the men to be hanged: "If the white man lynches for rape, we must expect the black man to do the same thing. . . . We are opposed to lynch law and so are the people of the country. . . . What we object to is, that an exception should be made in the case of the negro." The *Pickens Sentinel* went further: "Public sentiment is against their punishment, and public sentiment will have its way." Implicitly, the *Courier* described a widespread atmosphere of violence.

Harrison Haywood home; he was one of six black men charged with lynching a white man in 1887. Black Heritage in the Upper Piedmont

Elsewhere, an immediate outpouring of protests complained about the verdicts. The general theme began as prominent whites in Pickens and Oconee signed petitions. Like the *Courier*, they said, in essence: we do not approve of lynching, but if white people are not prosecuted for similar episodes, neither should these men be. Similar versions circulated around the state, notably in Columbia and Charleston. Overwhelmed by thousands of signatures, including many prominent officeholders, Governor John Peter Richardson pardoned both Williams and Haywood. The latter subsequently served as Abel Baptist Church clerk from 1894 until 1925. Henry Bolton, working as an Southern Rail Road brakeman, was killed in an 1891 train accident at Seneca; Williams was working as a railroad hand in Central in 1900, as was his son.[20]

Ironically, the first lynching in Anderson, Oconee, and Pickens counties involved a white victim, a distinct variation from most in South Carolina, even more so because perpetrators were black. Widespread support for lynchers, some of it coming from leading officials, foreshadowed later events. So did their escape from death, but imprisonment for over a year did not happen with white defendants; in fact, few whites were ever accused, let alone arrested and imprisoned for lynching black men.[21] Tragically, exculpation of the Central six came at a mentally retarded fellow's expense.

Short Stories

Several lynchings in the 1890s and early 1900s deserve brief mention. Newspaper accounts provide the only information available, which leaves no means of verifying these versions. The word "alleged" applies to all of these accounts. Charleston's *News and Courier* reported several instances that the upper-piedmont press did not mention.[22]

Table 21.1 **Lynchings in Anderson, Oconee, and Pickens: A Tentative List**

Date	Name of Victim	County	Alleged Offense	Newspaper Reports	Notes
1881 Nov. 3	Williams, Bob	Greenville	rape	KC, PS	victim of mob; Williamston
1887 Dec. 30	Waldrop, Manse (white)	Pickens	rape	PS	Central
1890 Dec. 3	Johnson, Henry Welsby, Henry	Pickens	rape	PS	Central; cremated
1894 Dec. 19	Sullivan, Ed (age 14)	Anderson	murder	AI	en route, Williamson to Anderson; newspaper date
1895 July 15	Jackson, Ira	Greenville	alleged rape	AI	Piedmont
ca. 1895–97	unnamed negro(es)	Pickens			Six Mile vicinity; oral trad. KC 12/10/02
1898 May	Harris, Elbert	Anderson	burning gin house		N&C 3–10–01; arrested, seized, whipped, died in jail; 1901 suit
1901 Nov. 24	Ladison, John Ladderby	Anderson	murder; "attempted" adultery	AI	Rock Mills; Coroner's inquest; sheriff in pursuit
1901 Nov. 24	Powell, Rachel ("Mrs."; white)	Oconee			Salem
1901 Dec. 7	Greer, Oliver	Anderson	rape		Belton
1903 July 1	Elrod, Reuben	Greenville	race prejudice; adultery	AI	Piedmont; Coroner's inquest
1905 Sept. 17	Pendleton, Allen	Abbeville	murder	AI	Honea Path pursuers; N&C source

Table 21.1 (continued)

Date	Name of Victim	County	Alleged Offense	Newspaper Reports	Notes
1911 Oct. 10	Jackson, Willis	Anderson Greenville	rape	AI	Honea Path, near Greenville
1914 Dec. 20	Spight, Tom (varied spellings)	Oconee	attempted arson; race prejudice	ADI	Fair Play; died in GA
1914 Dec. 20	Gibson, George	Oconee	race prejudice	ADI	Fair Play; died in GA
1914 Dec. 20	Gibson, Green	Oconee	attempt to save son's life	ADI	Fair Play
1930 April 23	Green, Al	Oconee	adultery with white woman	KC	Walhalla

Sources: Jack Mullins, "Lynching in South Carolina, 1900–1914" (M.A. thesis, University of South Carolina, 1961); NAACP, *Thirty Years of Lynching in the United States, 1889–1918* (1919; New York: Arno Press, 1969), 88–91; Tuskegee Institute unpublished lynching statistics for South Carolina, 1900–1914, as supplied to and cited by Mullins; and Stewart E. Tolnay and E. M. Beck, *A Festival of Violence: An Analysis of Southern Lynchings, 1882–1930* (Urbana: Univ. of Illinois Press, 1995); and Tolnay and Beck research lists. Newspapers, as cited; listings are not complete; they do indicate whether a lynching was reported locally or not. Sources cover different time periods (starting 1882, 1889, and 1900); none of these lynchings was cited by all of them.

Abbreviations: *ADI = Anderson Daily Intelligencer*; *AI = Anderson Intelligencer*; *KC = Keowee Courier*; *N&C = News and Courier*; *PS = Pickens Sentinel*.

Table 21.2 Alleged Lynchings—Anderson, Oconee, and Pickens*

Date	Name of Victim	County	Alleged Offense	Newspapers	Notes
1889 Jan. 6	Brewington, Wm.	Pickens	murder	Hale	"Uncertain"
1891 Aug. 7	"Unnamed Negro"	Pickens	assault	PS	N&C 08-07-91
1893 May 30	Lincoln, Isaac	Oconee	insulted woman		N&C 06-02-93
1903 Jan. 1	negro and wife	Greenville	murder	People's Journal	Troy area
1903 March	Turnbull, William	Greenville	murder		unverified
1904 Mar. 20	Oglesby, Harrison	Pickens	creating disturbance		unverified; [evid. no KC, People's Journal ref.]
1905 Dec. 18	Thompson, Andrew	Greenville	rape		unverified
1909 Dec. 26	Fuller, Jesse (white)	Greenville	murder		unverified, "attempted"; Greenville
1909 Dec. 26	Barker, Joe	Greenville	murder		unverified, "attempted"; Greenville
1914 Dec. 20	Gibson, Will	Oconee	race riot		unverified; Fair Play
1914 Dec. 20	Earle, Bud	Oconee	race riot		unverified; Fair Play

*Table 21.1 omits eleven entries, which complete the list of all those found in AOP newspapers for those counties, or in the cited compilations. This set also includes several Greenville lynchings; the only Greenville ones in the main list involved Anderson mobs. Dates for those based on N&C are usually newspaper dates rather than dates of the incidents. Beck and Tolnay cite only Isaac Lincoln among all those in this list.

Sources: Same as those for table 21.1; only two of these alleged incidents were reported by AOP newspapers. The "Unnamed Negro" may refer to an incident reported in PS, July 30, Aug. 6, and Aug. 27, 1891; in the latter article, the supposed perpetrator was said to be alive, "lurking in the woods."

Abbreviations: KC = Keowee Courier; N&C = News and Courier; PS = Pickens Sentinel.

Central again was the setting for the tricounty area's second lynching, nearly three years after Waldrop. On December 3, 1890, black Henry Welsby was accused of assaulting a white woman. Escaping, he was captured in Oconee County and brought back to Central by a crowd of two hundred. There he confessed, the newspaper said, was tied to a tree, and was shot. Surviving until the following morning, Welsby was shot again, then burned. Only one foot survived, according to the *Pickens Sentinel*, which called Welsby a "fiend in human form."[23] Earlier found guilty in 1886 for criminal assault, he then served one year's hard labor at the state penitentiary. The *Sentinel*'s "Judge Lynch's Court" headline was typical for the period.

One other lynching reportedly occurred in Pickens County. Only two sentences written in 1902 tell about that 1890s event, although descendants of white perpetrators recounted it in interviews decades later. According to their family tradition, a small group of whites lynched one or two black men, whose supposed offense and names are not known. Evidently whites simply wanted to rid their community, Six Mile, of black residents. Following this alleged killing, black people did move away. The victim or victims were lynched, then burned, as in Central, and buried so that their bodies would not be discovered. Evidently the lynch party did not then tell other people what they had done, and nothing appeared in newspapers until a few years later, and then only two sentences. It marks a strange contrast to typically public displays, meant to intimidate the black population generally.[24]

John Laddison, a former convict from Newberry, became another victim. After early release he went to the Crafts' home in Rock Mills (Anderson County) asking for food. Not satisfied with what he got, he shot, but did not kill, the nineteen-year-old wife. While fleeing, he was wounded by her relatives. Using bloodhounds, Anderson's sheriff pursued him to the Savannah River, where a black man told officers that Laddison was hiding in his house. A crowd of nearly two hundred, including several "leading citizens" and fifteen black men, lynched Laddison, then pinned a placard to his body: "This negro was hanged for shooting a white lady in this settlement without cause, November 24, 1901." According to the press, "some of the negroes expressed a desire to burn the prisoner, but this was not permitted."[25]

Each story has differences. Two very public cases had crowds of "200"—an oft-reported figure—pursuing a suspect. Both involved an immediate, alleged offense by a former convict. According to the white press, the black community cooperated against Laddison and wanted to burn him, as was done to Welsby. Six Mile's lynching stands out for lack of any publicity. Upper-piedmont newspapers did not condemn any of these events, as they similarly failed to do in virtually all other local instances, a major exception occurring in 1914.

Varied Press and Official Attitudes

As with Laddison's case, officials often took part in and supported these murders. Tillman declared in an 1892 stump speech that "Governor as I am, I would lead a mob to lynch the negro who ravishes a white woman." That same year "Citizen Josh

Ashley," who figured in at least three lynchings, won election as Anderson's state legislator. Ashley, who joined Tillman's movement, was arrested in 1904 for disorderly conduct and also was indicted by a federal grand jury on twenty counts of peonage involving four black farmhands. But he escaped conviction. Supporting a lynching of what he called a "bad negro" killing a good white boy, he said in 1905 that "we live in a white man's country."[26] Surpassing typical official support, Ashley headed a 1911 lynching at Honea Path. Although he may not have handled rope or guns, he certainly led and encouraged that large mob. And in 1914, then sheriff, he gave his blessings to Fair Play lynchers, among them notably a magistrate; Governor Cole Blease also praised that event. Ashley was the only official in Anderson, Oconee, and Pickens counties to advocate lynch law publicly, but Blease often did so on a statewide level. Although words cannot contain the full horror of the act of lynching, nevertheless the reader may wish to avoid reading the following graphic account.

Two gruesome episodes involving Piedmont, a mill town straddling the Anderson/Greenville boundary, occurred in 1895 and 1903. Although Anderson men took part in the first, the deaths occurred in Greenville County. Ira Jackson, according to the crime charged against him, "brutally assaulted" an eleven-year-old white girl, who escaped and later identified Jackson—also called Johnson—as her attacker. Arrested and awaiting trial in 1895, he was seized and brutalized: "The dead man was naked to the waist, having on only a pair of cotton drawers which were once white but in which the red of his blood and of clay were mingled so as to make them a brick dust color. The face in death was nearly white and down the naked breast were many long streaks of red where the blood had trickled down in different streams, crossing and interlacing each other. The back was punctured from neck to waist with bullet holes, looking like some horrible eruption, so thick were they. . . . Johnson had been drawn a few inches from the ground and there were two hundred wounds, some from buckshot, some from revolver bullets of different sizes. There were also a number of bullets in the side and back of the head. A few of the heavier caliber had gone through and through the body . . . some of these had penetrated the bark of the tree."[27] This text is typical of many other graphic descriptions; in later years they would be supplemented by photographs.

Another Piedmont-area lynching, done with guns rather than by hanging, not only killed Reuben Elrod but also involved whipping several women. Charleston's *News and Courier* reported that fifty to one hundred men, all "unknown" according to a coroner's inquest, killed Elrod in his home. They then whipped three black women found in the house and warned them to leave the county. Although the article described Elrod as a "respected old negro . . . the general supposition is that the women were objectionable to the people of the community," that is, alleged prostitutes. Reportedly, local white residents strongly condemned this action and would likely demand a thorough investigation. But nothing further happened.[28]

Still another Piedmont lynching was narrowly averted in May 1900. It involved James Martin, accused of assaulting a three-year-old white girl. Arrested locally, he was taken to the Greenville jail, or he "would have shared the fate of all other characters of that kind," the *Piedmont Sun-Herald* said. And in 1911 another lynching involved pursuit into Greenville from an Anderson County mill center near the boundary. Ashley led a crowd that seized Willis Jackson from Greenville law enforcement officials and brought him to Honea Path, where reportedly over two thousand people watched him hanged.[29]

Several bizarre cases of nonlynchings—attempts abandoned or falsely reported—appeared in the press.[30] Contrasted to several standard lists refer to "unverified" cases, these incidents evidently never happened. Oral circulation of these stories highlights widespread belief than any black suspect may have been lynched.

Editorial attitudes varied throughout the period. Newspapers frequently carried reports of lynchings elsewhere in the state, throughout the South, and even more enthusiastically when in the North. Eight months before black men in Central killed Waldrop, the *Keowee Courier* called a York County lynching of five men "A Disgusting and Disgraceful Scene." There was "no excuse for the act . . . [which] deserves universal condemnation," especially as the court was in session and could have handled the matter, the editor contended.[31] Soon, however, he would excuse Central's black lynchers.

Although newspapers often condemned such acts on a theoretical basis or when it occurred elsewhere, they only rarely attacked one in their own backyard. The *Keowee Courier* on March 10, 1892, referred to "a lurking danger of greater harm occurring from the widespread reign of mob law than from the acts of criminals who receive such summary punishment." Three months later the June 9 *Intelligencer* deplored a Laurens lynching. The *Pickens Sentinel*, which at times opposed such acts, took a different posture a year later: "What is the matter with the colored people? The recent lynchings ought to teach them that it is death to lay violent hands on our white women." Columnist Bill Arp, expressing similar views as reprinted in the *People's Journal*, supported lynching in 1899, calling such mobs a large jury. But the *Intelligencer*, condemning Ira Jackson's 1895 Greenville County lynching, called it "inexcusable . . . diabolical outrage" resulting from the "wild, unbridled and criminal talk in which some of the political leaders of the day have indulged."[32] If any local white ministers publicly opposed lynching, that did not merit newspaper coverage.

Public moralism dealt only with selective topics. These included lynchings elsewhere, drunkenness, adultery, fornication, and a few other offensive acts. But white moralism, coupled with racism, evidently was content with derogatory comments about black people, disenfranchising black voters, and economic subjugation. African Americans were now not only a numerical minority but also a stigmatized class. As whites controlled the legal apparatus, they provided themselves immunity to lynch and authority to write a new constitution. Owning land and resources—fertilizer, supplies, and food—they, in essence, controlled sharecroppers. Structural oppression was institutionalized, and the South was "solid" in more ways than Democratic voting.

TWENTY-TWO

Political and Economic Subjugation

AFRICAN AMERICANS' POLITICAL and economical subordination, although not new, worsened in the 1890s due to increasingly racist attitudes. Owning most of the land, dictating conditions on which it could be used, and eliminating most black voting rights, whites solidified a monumental system of structural oppression based on "white supremacy." It shared the same attitudes that excused sexual exploitation, whippings, and lynchings.

Changes in the 1890s altered political roles of the past thirty years. Although slavery technically ended in 1865, blacks soon found themselves labeled "servants" as emancipation did not bring economic freedom, and many people initially remained laborers exactly where previously enslaved. Although gradually opting to move onto other land, most became sharecroppers locked in an elaborate and complicated system, in effect economic bondage.

Constitutional revisions produced a Jim Crow document that all but revoked black voting rights gained during Reconstruction. Subsequent laws forbade interracial marriage and integrated railroad passenger cars. The grip of racist attitudes, lynchings, sexual exploitation, and economic and political subjugation tightened.

Constitutional Change

Escalating racism occasionally led to suggestions that South Carolina's Reconstruction constitution should be altered, following Mississippi's lead. In 1894 Ben Tillman, thriving politically on his racist views, called for a new constitution. Demand for a new document received sudden impetus when a state judge in spring 1895 invalidated state voting laws. Many whites feared a return to sizable black voting, and editorials and letters flooded the newspapers in Anderson, Oconee, and Pickens counties. White Carolinians acted quickly. Swiftly paced, a call for a convention, election of its delegates, their assembly, and formal adoption of a new constitution all occurred within a few months.[1] Though now in the U.S. Senate, Tillman was still the constitution's guiding hand and spirit. Its preamble, "for the preservation and perpetuation" of "our liberties," was exactly opposite of its impact on black people.

To achieve that goal—preservation of liberties (for whites, understood)—voting requirements led to virtual disenfranchisement of black men as accomplished by Mississippi's 1890 constitution. South Carolina imposed new restrictions, including a literacy test, for voting: one who could read and write any constitutional section, or paid taxes on property worth at least three hundred dollars. Even when literate men applied, registrars in practice could offer complicated sections. Poll taxes now had to be paid not only for the current year but also for previous ones before a man could vote. He had to have resided in the state for two years, his county for a year, and precinct for four months. Sharecroppers who moved from one farm to another might not qualify for their four months' precinct residency; most had no money to pay poll taxes at any time. The avowed purpose of election laws, to prohibit "all undue influences from power, bribery, tumult or improper conduct," summarized how their white authors viewed Reconstruction years. David Duncan Wallace stated that "the elimination of the negro from politics as effectively as this could be accomplished by constitutional enactment was the one object . . . of this distinctly anti-African document."[2]

Some Tillmanites feared that literacy tests could boomerang against illiterate whites, especially those in the upstate and "the unlettered among the Confederate veterans." To protect those voting rights, delegates inserted a "grandfather" clause: any man already voting and able to explain a constitutional section, without being required to read it, qualified for lifetime voting. The primary system, solidified in the 1895 text, now reigned supreme as a constitutionally protected method that the legislature could regulate. Wallace's 1914 school textbook observed that "all the white people in South Carolina, except a very few, are Democrats. Only a few colored people vote at all and nearly all of them are Republicans." Literacy tests and poll taxes were not required for voting in primaries, which was based entirely on party membership. And a 1896 "School Law" tightened the governor's control over the Department of Education.[3]

For over two hundred years South Carolina as colony and state had no law prohibiting interracial marriage or no legal definition of "Negro." Imprecise and varying judicial decisions fell short of settling the question decisively. The state now incorporated constitutionally its first antimiscegenation law, passed in 1879. Moreover, the constitution legally defined who was a "Negro" for the first time in South Carolina's history: anyone with "one-eighth or more of negro blood." That proved the convention's most heated issue, especially when some proposed a "one-drop" definition. Evidently many "white" South Carolinians had some black antecedents, as even George Tillman asserted that no "white" man sitting in the convention could claim exemption.[4]

Although continuing an 1868 provision for a "liberal system of free public schools for all children," the new constitution required them to be segregated, as they already were in practice. But some sections arguably could help African Americans. Any law enforcement official who allowed a prisoner to be seized and lynched would be suspended and removed from office if found guilty—of a misdemeanor. Any county where a person was lynched had to pay the victim's heirs two thousand dollars as compensation. Few claims were ever filed, fewer paid. A 1901 suit for compensation from Anderson County failed.[5] Women did benefit from a provision that a married woman retained property rights, whether possessed by her beforehand or acquired during marriage. On totally unrelated issues, regulations on corporations and railroads satisfied other Tillmanite demands. Appealing to several broad constituencies, the constitution gained wide approval among whites. Convention delegates, adopting it by their own authority, forestalled opposition and a popular referendum. A myriad of additional, later laws imposed most well-known racial restrictions.[6]

This new constitution significantly altered the state's 1868 racial and voting provisions. Black voting did not end immediately. The state house retained low-country black members until 1902, but voting declined sharply in 1896 due to the formalized "white primary." In substantially reduced numbers some African Americans voted for another decade or two, as some upper-piedmont men evidently did into the early 1900s. Hard figures and dates are virtually impossible to find; Wallace in 1914 acknowledged that some still did vote. But most black voting—a major accomplishment of immediate postbellum years—soon perished, not to be resurrected in the South until the Civil Rights Acts of the 1960s.

Local communities took additional actions to limit black voting. Pendleton in 1898 voted to remove a black portion of the town from the official limits, which denied some black voters the right to vote in town elections. Fifteen years later the town would enact segregated residential restrictions.[7]

Racism, 1890s-style, in South Carolina and Far Afield

As black voting dwindled to a halt, a wider body of discriminatory actions reflected deep-seated and widely ranging white attitudes, both homegrown and also far-flung around the world. These attitudes underpinned Tillman's election, the 1895 constitution, local harassment of blacks, and economic subjugation. Even the state superintendent of education's annual reports include harsher racial statements after 1895. The statewide summer institute for black teachers had its first exclusively white faculty in 1900. That induced black Baptists to make a public protest. As late as 1897 its director Professor Wallace described "untiring and eminently successful efforts of the teachers" at the state institute. But Superintendent John J. McMahan said that he desired such an institute to be "taught by the ablest white educators in our State" to "give these negro teachers a high order of instruction which they have never had the opportunity to receive," that is, while previously under black instruction. "The good negroes before the war were brought up and trained by their masters, through the well ordered discipline of the plantation. The ruling class should now look well to the schools," McMahan contended.

He also justified use of white instructors as "missionary work" and "scientific investigation," that is, checking accomplishments of blacks when taught by whites. Yet the summer faculty's white chairman attributed the institute's success to a black college professor "whose presence and influence was inspiring and helpful." Local upstate institute directors had been complimentary for many years, but Anderson's white leader in 1900 described his group condescendingly.[8]

South Carolina, although a skilled practitioner, did not have a monopoly on racist oppression. Changes in racial attitudes occurred worldwide; they also found their way into U.S. Supreme Court decisions. An early indication came in 1883 when the court ruled part of the 1875 Civil Rights Act unconstitutional. Later, a federal judge in 1888 declared that all children born in slavery were deemed illegitimate, something even South Carolina's Black Codes denied. Going considerably further, the U.S. Supreme Court's 1896 *Plessy v. Ferguson* decision upheld Louisiana's segregated transportation law. The court, proclaiming that "legislation is powerless to eradicate racial instincts," legitimized, virtually sanctified, the "separate but equal" principle that governed judicial decisions for nearly sixty years. While vigorously enforcing the "separate" phrase, South Carolina's government ignored the equation's "equal" part.

Just three years after enactment of South Carolina's new constitution, the nation turned its attention to "colored races" elsewhere in the world. C. Vann Woodward clearly connected both projection of racism abroad and domestic attitudes. Quoting the *Atlantic Monthly*, Woodward noted, "If the stronger and cleverer race . . . is free to impose its will upon 'new-caught, sullen peoples' on the other side of the globe, why not in South Carolina and Mississippi?"[9] If not acquainted with the *Atlantic Monthly*, many upper-piedmont whites acted on these principles. Description of the constitution, Jim Crow laws, and official views should not mask much oppression that occurred outside the law. "Uppity" sharecroppers could be evicted at the season's end, or sometimes earlier. Lynchings served as a powerful mechanism of control and terror by whites. And many other incidents frequently plagued black people.

Immediate danger faced Jane Hunter's uncle. Having abandoned her precarious life at Clemson's hotel, she lived with Aunt Caroline Milliner and worked at nearby Woodburn farm. There, she recounted, "Uncle Abe served as race horse breeder . . . [and as] foreman of the field workers. On one occasion, one of the white men came to work quite intoxicated. He had a jealous disposition, and over a minor disagreement called Uncle a bad name. This so roused the latter's ire that in his anger he threw a stone at the drunkard. Within a short time, all the poor whites from adjoining farms assembled to incite a lynching party against Abe. The overseer wired [Woodburn's owner] Major Smythe for advice. Before the lynchers could effect their organization, Major sent orders to rush Uncle Abe out of the state until the white man could be dismissed."[10] Fortunately "Uncle Abe" Milliner had Smythe's support. But this incident, escalating quickly, could easily have ended Milliner's life due to white arrogance following a white man's drunken insult.

Landlords, if less kindly disposed than Smythe, were able to impose their will on most tenants or sharecroppers through economic controls, aided by laws that served property interests but failed to protect workers. And whites could resort to direct, individual threats and terrorization, often done by landless whites. This system economically subordinated African Americans even more effectively than a Jim Crow constitution did politically. While lynchings effected immediate terror, sharecropping was a continually numbing, degrading system of impoverishment and subjugation, economic and otherwise.

Economic Subjugation, Sharecropping, and Crop Liens

"From Slavery to Serfdom" describes concisely African Americans' economic plight soon after emancipation. Lacking resources of their own, most were forced to work a white man's land on his terms. White dominance of political and judicial structures after 1876 guaranteed that sharecroppers had no legal recourse.[11]

William Pickens's description of his family's moving twenty times in fewer years dramatizes their distress as does the lyric "another day older and deeper in debt." The population in Anderson, Oconee, and Pickens counties in 1900 was still 85 percent rural and agricultural, and somewhat more so for blacks. Moreover, they did not on the whole rent land as tenants but worked it as sharecroppers, which was more perilous. Businessmen in Anderson city, a growing middle class in Pendleton, and small numbers of town craftsmen and professionals—although important to their communities—were very much the exception. And while hundreds of black families owned land in 1900, most did not. Moreover, most of this small minority of owners had to mortgage their land.

An ensnaring system virtually guaranteed increasing, cumulative debt. Without any legal rights, sharecroppers had to surrender most or all of their crop. Impoverished, most could plant their cotton each spring only by borrowing money for fertilizer and other supplies. In the meantime they bought—on credit—food and clothing from the general store. Literally, almost everyone could say "[I] owed my soul to the company store." Some stores also sold fertilizer, doubling their hold over customers. Laws forbade farm workers, whether tenants or croppers, to sell any of their harvest before paying a landlord's share; fertilizer suppliers likewise had a lien. Surprisingly, when Cary Pickens in 1895 was accused of selling mortgaged property, that charge was dismissed.[12] Sharecroppers did not have friends who could help financially, unlike depression-era Harlem "rent parties." And there were too many destitute people for their churches, themselves poor, to provide assistance. On January 3, 1900, the *Intelligencer* reported that "many tenants, both white and black, are changing residences" as the year began. There was no economic emancipation to celebrate.

An especially clear example of ensnaring conditions concerns Joe Watson. Working for a new landowner, Watson "was immediately taken sick." But the employer, asked by Watson's wife "to furnish them provisions," refused. When Watson recovered he went elsewhere "to gain a living for his wife and children." The employer sued, and Watson, imprisoned, "can't gather his crop and his family will either suffer for food and clothing or become a charge upon the County." Leading Andersonians,

Jack Carter's 1881 mortgage of his cotton crop to J. T. Hunter for $99.45. Clemson University

including the former governor, recommended a pardon. Watson's employer had other men similarly convicted.[13]

Some whites shared these woes and in that capacity had no more legal rights than did blacks. One white family interviewed in 1993 and asked about cropping contracts said they never saw one and had to move frequently. Perhaps 75 percent of white rural households did not own land; they had to work that belonging to other family members, rent a farm, or become sharecroppers.[14]

Several sets of data help illustrate sharecroppers' precarious conditions and their frequent relocations. Analysis of Honea Path Township in the early 1870s shows that many families moved often. Only half of 166 black men listed in the 1870 census as household heads or as living with white families could be found in township tax rolls a year later. Another quarter were not there in 1873. Occasionally some returned; six were in Honea Path in 1870 and 1875, but not intervening years. Evidence twenty-five years later for Savannah Township yields similar results.[15]

White economic control reinforced this often-temporary nature of farm work. Landlords could, at will, dismiss agricultural laborers, who had no legal protections safeguarding them. Post-Reconstruction legislatures, virtually all white, passed laws that sanctioned landowners' absolute rights. Only a federal law against peonage offered recourse, one not easily available to an impoverished, dispossessed, hungry family that had to take the first available offer, no matter how harsh. Lawrence Perry, not yet having a contract in early February 1900, said he would work land belonging to either "J. E. Horton or anybody else" who would take him.

White perceptions evidently distinguished four strata of black farmers: landowners; other long-term residents and well-known families, many of them working the same land for many years; known sharecroppers living in an area semipermanently but, like Pickens's family, shifting often within a small radius; and very transitory workers, often unknown locally. Anderson tax assessor's schedules for 1900, compared with census and lien agreements, demonstrate these categories.[16]

Viewed as transitory, nearly two thousand sharecroppers were identified by their landlords' names in Anderson County's 1900 tax rolls. Newspapers, especially when reporting "negro crime" or accidents, typically linked black men with their white landowners. A nineteen-year-old black fellow who lived on John P. Green's land, the *Intelligencer* said, accidentally killed a young black boy in August 1900. Later that year, young Martha Smith died while living on Benjamin Holder's property. Newspapers periodically omitted names of black people: in December 1894 a "negro house" on Joe Martin's land, near Anderson city, burned, and an "old negro" and two children—none named—nearly died, the *Intelligencer* reported.[17]

Classifying black households in one area, Savannah Township, will show their varied standings. Without any town, Savannah remained virtually all agricultural. Only two blacks, a minister and a blacksmith, had other employment. Like Abel's community, black sharecroppers surrounded the township's landowners in 1900. Tax rolls linked 153 black men in the township with their white landlords' names. Families headed by women would likewise have been so identified if they had had to pay taxes. Workers who moved virtually each year had the least regard by whites.[18]

Blacks with highest standing, as treated in tax records and evidently in white attitudes, consisted of eighteen families who owned land. They included McGees, Pickens, Sherards, Wakefields, and Willifords—all established, long-standing, and well-known families, most of whom lived in Savannah Township in 1870, and probably earlier as slaves—plus Keowns, more recent arrivals.[19] At least thirty-eight additional men heading farming households did not own land but appeared in tax rolls in their own right. Many of these came from other long-standing Savannah Township families, and some likely rented rather than cropped. They occupied a slightly lower rung than did owners.

The township's socioeconomic character, probably similar to most of rural Anderson, Oconee, and Pickens counties, centered around well-to-do white landowners. Not only did four times, proportionately, as many white households own land, but also their acreage averaged nearly double that of blacks. Thirty-nine white families —four of them nonresidents—owned land; dozens of nonlandowning whites had to rent land as tenants or work as sharecroppers.

Wealth was especially concentrated in eight white families, owning nearly half of Savannah's land. Besides their own residences, these eight had seventy-seven buildings—stores in some cases but mostly rental houses; fifty-six men were listed in tax rolls as their workers. P. B. Allen owned more than a tenth of the entire township. Savannah Township's second-wealthiest holding—one and a half square miles with eight houses—belonged to absentee C. D. Watson, who lived in Anderson city, as did R. W. Pruitt, who had the township's third-highest value of land and six houses. Not included among these eight families, the white McGee brothers, while having smaller separate holdings, collectively owned one and a half square miles (about 7 percent of the township) with five tenant houses, and had seventeen men working for them. The McGee family perpetuated long-term dominance, as shown by their political clout against potential voters in 1868.[20] Through siblings, in-laws, and cousins, similar landowning families exercised pervasive influence throughout Anderson County and could create serious problems for any farm worker they evicted by blacklisting his name elsewhere.

Most larger landowners also loaned fertilizer money. Forty-three black Savannah Township farmers in 1900 borrowed an average exceeding one hundred dollars for fertilizer and other supplies; two firms provided nearly half of this, totaling almost two thousand dollars. Typical of many others, Jim Watson borrowed seventy-five dollars from a Brown firm on January 26, 1900, while working McGee land; two months later he got a fifty-dollar loan from J. H. Sanders, for whom he also worked.

Borrowers in 1900 reflected migratory characteristics of many sharecroppers. Only slightly more than a third could be found on the same farm in three consecutive years. Of forty-three Savannah Township borrowers in 1900, only thirteen worked identical land in 1899, 1900, and 1901, and four of them owned their land. Five additional men, whose locations are known for each year, worked the same farms in 1899 and 1900, but had different landlords in 1901. And twenty-seven men —nearly 60 percent—had agricultural liens in several townships in 1900, but not in 1899 or 1901. Rather than being less financially distressed those years, most probably moved elsewhere and borrowed money there. How they were trapped by debts to landlords yet moved to other land at the same time is not clear. There are stories from Fair Play and from Abbeville of families, hidden under a wagonload of hay, escaping during the night. In 1898 Dave Sherard, reneging on his labor agreement with W. T. Dean, fled across the country and joined the army in San Francisco.[21]

Agricultural liens reveal further complications for borrowers. Like Jim Watson, many had to borrow more than once during a year, especially when working different lands but sometimes even for just one plot. It was not unusual for two or more men, especially when related, to farm jointly an owner's land and for them all to apply for loans, as did "J. H. Brock et al" for two February 1900 advances. Elsewhere,

T. H. Williamson had to work for three Pendleton landlords that same year in order to earn enough to survive. Even some black landowners "would always borrow money to do a new crop" or worked other land to make ends meet.[22]

An additional factor contributed to Savannah Township's farming: convict labor. The Penitentiary Board inspected P. B. Allen's stockade in 1899 and a grand jury investigated it two years later. Its eleven black prisoners in summer 1900 ranged from twenty-three to thirty-nine years of age. Allen also had sixteen single males, mostly aged eleven to thirty-four, living in one household and working as farm laborers. Four more, eleven to twenty-five years old, had another house; and two inmates, perhaps trustees, lived with still another farm laborer.

Evidently it was Allen s stockade from which York Goodlett heard prisoners crying out. A Methodist minister, Goodlett had just taken charge of Savannah Township's Mount Sinai ME(N) church. Screams of chain-gang convicts woke him one night. He heard a prisoner's plea, "Please, Captain, please, I didn't do it, please," followed by more "sounds of whip lashes." Goodlett prayed, "Lord, something has to be done. I can't stand this happening most every night. Please, free my people from this bondage." He must have believed that settling men on their own property would improve conditions. Putting their concerns into action, Goodlett got church leaders to organize the Afro-American Real Estate Association for families to buy land. They acquired 435 acres of land, but very few buyers benefited.[23]

A combination of wealthy landholdings, money loaned for fertilizer, and sharecroppers indebted to the landlord afforded much power and control. Adding convict labor enhanced one's wealth and power for minimal investment. The nexus of landownership and its economic power made it a measure of authority for whites, mostly men. And it served as further leverage for political and sexual subordination of those they dominated. A sample of agricultural liens throughout the county yields results similar to those for Savannah Township alone. One third of a hundred borrowers worked the same land (some of it their own) for three years—1899, 1900, and 1901; about 20 percent borrowed only two years, staying on the same farm, and 15 percent, different land those two years; nearly 25 percent were found in lien records only for 1900. Impoverishment and forced relocations marked lives of many sharecroppers.[24]

Hunter's General Store in Pendleton illustrates such an establishment's clout through its multiple influences over borrowers. Like most general stores of that era, it allowed customers to buy on credit, with many—white and black—not paying until after harvest, and sometimes not even then. Some people had year-old unpaid bills and a few had balances lasting several years. Only after a year did store owners usually add interest.[25]

The Hunters loaned money for fertilizer as well as for their purchases. With a lien against fall crops, the store acquired many bales and much cotton seed each autumn. Debtors typically surrendered their cotton in the early fall even though prices were low, while better-financed white producers, often holding theirs until spring, got higher prices. Many customers delivered cotton only to find it just canceling their prior debts; they then immediately acquired new ones. The store sold cotton hulls for livestock feed, and cotton seed went to a local company that pressed it for oil. Hunter thus made multiple profits from cotton, but customers often had it only serve to pay their debts.[26]

Impoverished blacks knew far too keenly that their debts constituted what later would be called a "vicious cycle." As rent, general store purchases, and fertilizer led to mounting indebtedness, sharecroppers found that their crop hardly met these obligations. Truly they had fallen into economic bondage, a plight that led to further complications. Their debt and difficulties in moving meant personal subjugation to whites and left women even more vulnerable to sexual exploitation. And it may be that a "Jim Crow" constitution that inhibited voting had less impact than its reputation suggests. A greatly indebted man could easily be intimidated not to vote or certainly not to vote the "wrong way," specifically, Republican. Sharecroppers seemed to be locked irrevocably in a dependency relationship.[27]

"This system was the successor and heir of the slave system," William Pickens wrote. "The landlord was perfectly secure in these advanced outlays: the tenant was bound by this debt and local law would enforce it against his very person.... If he sought to escape, any justice of the peace could fine him and then jail him in default of payment of fine. But of course the fine would be paid by his magnanimous and benevolent (?) landlord and added to his former debt,—thus binding him the closer. In fact it was better for the landlord when a peon attempted to escape and failed, for after the matter was reviewed by the 'court' of justice, it gave the aggrieved landlord a better claim, a sort of adjudicated title to this Negro's brawn." Later, federal authorities would document similar control—peonage—that a white landowner near Fair Play exercised over a debtor.

Whites sometimes used other mechanisms to clear unwanted people from their neighborhood. Among these, Peter Harris, labeled by the *Intelligencer* as a "notorious bad negro," suffered in July 1900 a severe whipping only a few miles west of Anderson for insulting a white woman and was forced to leave the county. And the 1890s lynching in Six Mile was reportedly done to rid that vicinity of all black people.[28]

Given sharecroppers' economic difficulties and frequent relocations, it is a wonder that their children got much education at all. Yet black adults in Savannah Township could read and write at a level exceeding state averages. Nearly four hundred black children attended one-room school houses for a twenty-six-week term in 1900. It is also incredible that churches, having poor and migratory membership, managed to survive. Savannah had one of the upper piedmont's earliest Methodist churches, Mount Sinai, along with its campground; two small Colored Methodist Episcopal congregations; and two Baptist churches organized in 1871 and 1885. Collectively church membership of all five approximated 800.

On the other hand, it is not surprising that clergy increasingly talked about owning land as a means to personal as well as racial improvement. Ministerial references to home values, including both cleanliness and the loyalty of men to their families, dealt with forms of stability much needed in the midst of an otherwise subjugated and impoverished life.

Stockade Scandal

An especially clear demonstration of oppressing workers spread across *Anderson Intelligencer* pages in 1901. Prominent white men were the culprits; several had close ties to penitentiary officials and guards, also from Anderson. This dramatic exposé involved not only maltreatment of leased convicts but also incarceration of free men contracted to work for the same farmers. That scandal, attracting statewide and even northern attention, was initially dismissed by local press. But a grand jury investigated then charged several prominent men with harming both convicts and free laborers. Other public officials and the press complacently defended those accused. Racism and respectability went hand in hand.

The *Intelligencer*, in the midst of this scandal, ridiculed an article recounting "negro reports" about Anderson's "slavery." It apparently forgot many articles about abuses and deaths carried in the past decade. An escapee from the Clemson College stockade said that convicts were so ill-treated that he preferred returning to the penitentiary. Three weeks later the *Pickens Sentinel* reported conditions of South Carolina convicts, and the *Intelligencer* printed a "County Convict Camp" drawing. Its accompanying article contained no criticism; rather, it showed camps as assets to the county's economy.[29]

During spring 1899 at least eight Anderson men had convicts working for them; only nine other men throughout the state did so. The Anderson group collectively had slightly more than half the total hired to private individuals; this seems to have been a cozy arrangement made through Anderson County connections at the penitentiary. Those in Anderson included both Hammonds, Newell, Watson, Fowler, Neal, Allen, and E. P. Earle—all but one was investigated in the scandal. Three convicts died in these camps in 1899.[30]

J. S. Fowler's stables, Anderson city; Fowler was indicted by a grand jury in 1901 for incarcerating free black men on his rural plantation. Pendleton District Commission

Other newspaper accounts dealt with escapes from and deaths in these camps. Anderson's D. H. Cooley, who employed many sharecroppers and used convict labor, was tried for killing several in April 1891, but a mistrial resulted. A neutral statement in late 1899 noted that "Neal & Newell are working about twenty State convicts at their brickyard." Various articles told of convicts escaping from W. A. Neal's farm, which had several sharecroppers in Hopewell Township; J. S. Fowler's stockade; and W. Q. Hammond's lands, where an escapee was killed and his death ruled justifiable homicide. Others died from heat on W. Q. Hammond's and J. S. Hammond's farms on July 4, 1900.[31]

Corruption, or at least its appearance, ran rampant. Two related offenses occurred in 1901. Anderson's W. A. Neal, former state penitentiary superintendent, was charged with not forwarding to the state all payments for convict leasing; further, state constable and Anderson native W. S. Newell, tried for murdering a convict, won a not-guilty verdict in less than a day. No official investigations probed into these related events as a whole.

Then the Anderson scandal erupted, drawing national attention. It had little to do with leased convicts themselves. The specific problem was that men, freely contracting to work for some landowners who leased convicts, were treated like prisoners—forced to live in stockades, prevented from leaving without permission, given poor food, and otherwise subjected to indecent treatment. After initial reports in February 1901, Judge Benet issued warrants against several landowners for assault and battery and false imprisonment.

Anderson's grand jury appointed a special committee. Its members found abuse of free labor at seven stockades on farms in the county. In the worst case, although the state earlier seized J. R. Miller's convicts, he kept his "free" labor in stockades, using whips and shackles on those men. He got contracts—often with blanks instead of specific times and payment—signed and witnessed. Elias McGee and W. Q. Hammond also used stockades for freely contracted labor. The *Intelligencer* tried to play down this matter and printed favorable material about Hammond. After initial hoopla, nothing happened to accused landlords, and the issue disappeared from both press and official scrutiny, a "conspiracy of silence."[32]

Complications, Again

None of these matters should suggest a simplistic story. During this same period the *Pickens Sentinel*, which supported Tillman and reprinted Bill Arp's columns, reported more news than before of black marriages. Both it and the *People's Journal* occasionally used courtesy titles "Mr." and "Miss" when mentioning black marriages. Newspapers continued to report and praise endeavors by teachers and ministers. And numerous incidents involved white neighbors helping black people whose houses burned. Minister C. T. and wife Anna E. Miller in 1896 paid for a "Card of Thanks" in the newspaper "to both white and black during the trying times of our crippled baby."[33]

In one week alone, both the *People's Journal* and the *Intelligencer* praised well-regarded blacks. White "Mr. Ferguson did not forget his faithful old servant," Tony Ferguson, and supported him for several years when he was too sick to work, according to the notice of Tony Ferguson's 1884 death. That same week Annie Cherry died; she was "one of Anderson's most worthy colored citizens" and had the "respect and confidence of all, white and black." But Arp's columns in both Anderson and Pickens newspapers pondered whether blacks had souls.[34]

Shortly after 1900 the new Seneca Institute girls' dormitory burned. President Starks recorded that white families took girls into their homes and white merchants helped replace lost clothing. By contrast the local press usually reported black crime at great length and used racist stereotypes and caricatures. Reports of "negro crime" often included references to attacks on or insults to white women, followed by an escape; the culprit was sometimes pursued by bloodhounds—often called "nigger hounds"—such as E. P. Earle's, which reportedly caught thirty fleeing criminals. Stereotype was piled on top of stereotype. The newspapers' multifaceted attitudes seem to have been as follows: we like our good "darkies" at home; we hate colored crime, at home or elsewhere; and we oppose "negro rights" in general. Frequent fluctuations in these attitudes make them almost impossible to disentangle, let alone understand.[35]

Like white attitudes toward black people, crime was not a simple issue. Whites requested the governor to pardon or commute sentences of specific black men. An 1888 petition to pardon Albert Bird, for instance, contained signatures of nine among twelve jurors who convicted him. John S. Goodman, employed at Clemson College, proclaimed to Tillman in 1892 that I "am not [a] negro lover but wish every negro in the state was in [the country of] guina . . . but I do want the negro Wm. Washington pardoned," referring to a convict working on college land. And in 1901 the governor pardoned John Murphy and Lee Owens, both convicted with a white man in 1895 for arson; Anderson's solicitor joined a lengthy petition for their release.[36]

On some levels white-black relations were more skewed than in antebellum years. A larger percentage of white families now had blacks working for them—as sharecroppers or maids—than did so during slavery. And white landlords no longer worked side by side with the black men laboring for them.

While neither simplistic nor sudden, racist attitudes affected newspapers in Anderson, Oconee, and Pickens counties, the state's "Jim Crow" constitution and laws, and national views. For people who remember the completed twentieth-century enshrinement of these attitudes and laws, it is difficult to realize how gradually they developed. Descriptions in South Carolina's 1712 law of African Americans—having "barbarous, wild, savage natures, and such as renders them wholly unqualified to be governed by the laws, customs, and practices of this Province"—now found new life as, varied slightly, they returned as newspaper themes of the 1890s and later. Continuous and poisonous usage, accompanied by white acceptance of lynching, made discriminatory laws, as well as a personal economic subjugation of sharecroppers, seem reasonable.

Yet, as other chapters show, opportunities existed. There were more black landowners, bigger churches, more literacy, and more and better-funded schools. Out-migration provided opportunities for some. Blacks continued to obtain more education, gain better and more diversified jobs, create more community organizations, and otherwise improve their lives. That happened more effectively in towns than in its rural areas. The story was still a complicated, multifaceted one. Booker T. Washington's self-help arguments, widely attacked during his lifetime and later, were being implemented in Anderson, Oconee, and Pickens counties. An overview of life and accomplishments in one year, 1900, personalizes and further illustrates these issues.

TWENTY-THREE

1900 ⚡ One Year in the Life of a Community

PENDLETON'S AFRICAN AMERICANS celebrated Emancipation Day on January 1, 1900. That year marked no special event, occasion, or movement for them. It serves, however, as a convenient landmark, the approximate ending date of this story, and the dawn of a new century. But it was the Jim Crow constitution's fifth year, more darkness than a dawning light, especially given its curtailment of black voting. Comings and goings of several people—many already familiar names—and their transactions at Hunter's General Store in Pendleton illustrate both a typical yearly cycle and conditions for African Americans at the turn of the century. The year also left an abundant paper trail of these store accounts, Baptist minutes, individual census and tax entries, educational reports, and brief newspaper items.[1]

The Year's Cycle

As the year began, Milly Dupree reflected on her life, which encompassed most of the past century. Sadly, however, Elbert Guyton's and Sidney Burt's families mourned their passing. Burt had served his community not only as a blacksmith but also as a founding trustee of Kings Chapel African Methodist Episcopal Church and the school next door. Working for a long time, he saved enough money to buy property adjacent to the church lot, but he needed still more income to afford a house.

Sidney Burt's daughter and family, Pendleton, 1902: parents Martha Burt Vance (seated, front) and Augustus Thomas Vance (holding Bible), and their children. Black Heritage in the Upper Piedmont

NOTE and MORTGAGE

No. 122

Calhoun, S.C. April 4, 1906

On the 15 day of Oct 1906 I promise to pay to the order of R B Cochran

Twelve ———————————— Dollars.

Value received. Interest at 8 per cent. per annum from maturity until paid; with ten per cent additional for attorney's fee should this note be collected by an attorney, by suit or through Court. Witness my hand and seal.

Terrel + Wright

STATE of SOUTH CAROLINA
County of Pickens

WHEREAS, I am indebted to R. B. Cochran in the sum of Twelve ———————————— Dollars, and have given my note therefor, of even date with these Presents, payable on the 15 day of Oct A.D. 1906.

NOW, in order to secure the payment of said note, and in consideration of the sum of Five Dollars to me in hand paid, I do hereby grant, bargain and sell unto R B Cochran the following goods, chattels, crops and stock, to-wit: One cow Jersey Color name Red about five years old Also one hog weight about 100 lbs

TO HAVE AND TO HOLD, all and singular, the said goods, chattels, crops and stock unto the said R B Cochran and his assigns forever.

PROVIDED, NEVERTHELESS, That if the said Terrel shall pay, or cause to be paid, unto the said R B Cochran the note herein above mentioned, when due, then this mortgage is to be void; otherwise to remain in full force and virtue.

AND PROVIDED FURTHER, That Terrel Wright retain possession of said goods and chattels until default be made in the payment of said note, and if before said note is due, he shall attempt to dispose of or remove said goods and chattels, or any part thereof, from the place where they now are, then R B Cochran or his agent, shall have the right, without suit or process, to take such as may be necessary, at public auction, for cash, after giving notice of the time and place for three days, and shall apply the proceeds of said sale to the discharge of said debt, and if there be any surplus, pay the same to Terrel or his assigns.

IN WITNESS WHEREOF I have hereunto set my hand and seal this 4 day of April 1906.

R B Cochran

Signed, sealed and delivered in the presence of

Terrel + Wright

Terrel Wright's 1906 mortgage of his cow. Black Heritage in the Upper Piedmont

Hunter General Store charge account: Jim Evans, 1895. Black Heritage in the Upper Piedmont, Clemson University

After only a few years in this new house, his family celebrated his life while lamenting its end.

Many families who owned no land had to move to a new landlord's property. Anderson's newspaper observed on January 3, "many tenants, both white and black, are changing residences." Relocated, they would begin the year impoverished, just as they would likely conclude it twelve months later. Abel resident John Cannon knew that problem far too well. Buying two cords of wood and a few small cash payments. Still, he owed fifty dollars from the past year even though he gave up his gray horse for a forty-dollar credit toward his arrears. He could sympathize with Terrel Wright, who bought bacon and four gallons of molasses plus 225 pounds of tobacco, but, unable to pay anything, would later have to mortgage his cow.

Sharecropping, a continuing fundamental condition, was in many ways more devastating than the new 1895 constitution. Unusually rich material available on black employment and expenditures at the turn of the century—as well as cropping data—allows an especially convenient and useful gauge of life then, and of changes since 1865. Work, primarily sharecropping, emerges as a dominant theme, as does the agricultural cycle—both of which weave throughout this account, as they did throughout black lives. Dependency on white jobs, houses, and general stores becomes painfully clear, as it did to African Americans experiencing it then. A larger percentage of whites had African Americans working for them in 1900 than during slavery. But advantages of town life, skilled crafts, and improved education are also evident, as are the important roles of churches and schools.[2]

Hunter's General Store customers—drawn from the town of Pendleton, outlying rural areas, and nearby towns—present a microcosm of the black community in Anderson, Oconee, and Pickens counties. Sales and payments at Hunter's store varied throughout a given year. When Julia Crooks paid her account in early March she learned that the value of her cotton exactly met her balance due—until weighing charges were added, and she was still in debt. She did not settle that fee until October. By contrast, Alf Adams managed to pay his store bill in March with credits against Ashtabula farm for his wages. Working regularly at the store also, Adams could afford to buy grits, lard, sugar, tobacco, and a water bucket.

As the year's poll tax became due in March, Pendleton's Jim Evans paid by charging it against his account. He also bought tobacco, jeans, a half bushel of corn, and fifty pounds of flour but returned a pair of shoes. After Evans and others paid poll and property taxes, auditors prepared their yearly reports. Implicitly these showed that keys to economic independence involved skilled crafts, professions, and owning farm or town property, which increased significantly between 1865 and 1900. These annual tax returns included nearly eight hundred tricounty families—one in twelve—who owned land.

Although only 7 percent of household heads owned homes, that rose to nearly 40 percent in some towns. Average property values did not quite reach two hundred dollars, as many families—like Sidney Burt's—had to wait several years before they could afford to build. Until then, it made sense to farm their land and to rent a house elsewhere. Others simply preferred living in town. In Anderson, Pendleton, and other towns, a few families owned rental property as well as their own homes.[3]

Residents enjoyed advantages of living in town. Maria Pinson on an April shopping spree bought grits, salt, sugar, coffee, her weekly pound of lard, kerosene, and many sewing items. She got 13 yards of checks, 6 yards of homespun, and 10 of calico; plus a coat and vest, which alone cost her a week's work. Like most other townspeople she seldom needed to buy vegetables, as many families raised their own. Keeping a few animals, customers seldom had to purchase chickens, eggs, or milk. But provisions were running out by the spring, and some people had to buy items they would not purchase again during the summer. Then, however, more people would buy bacon as their reserves dwindled. Even in town, life and store purchases reflected the agricultural calendar.

While some blacks found more varied and better employment in towns and cities, agriculture still dominated beyond town boundaries. As Jacob and Mary Pickens clearly knew, most folks—black and white—lived in rural areas where work for black men and women was overwhelmingly agricultural labor. It consumed the energies of rural blacks who were employed, nearly 80 percent for women and 92 percent for men. Black dependency on whites for land, work, and homes was especially critical in the country. Over 850 Anderson white landowners worked an average of two taxpayers each, but P. B. Allen had twenty Savannah Township men working for him in 1900.

Exercising a complex web of white domination, extended families had far-reaching influence over black workers. Burriss families employed forty men in nearly half of Anderson's townships. With such a wide network, views by any landowner that a sharecropper was disrespectful or disobedient—let alone politically active—could reverberate against any worker, as well as against his father, brothers, brothers-in-law, sons, and cousins elsewhere in the county. Three black Humphreys men worked for landlord Julia Burriss; five Welborn men and women for J. T. Dean; and four Ligons for R. B. Kay. These ties could be multiplied. Clearly Welborns or Ligons could ill afford to offend a landowner, or they and their families could be evicted from the land they worked. Memories lingered of harassment of black voters during and after 1868 fall elections, and individuals still continued to suffer expulsions when landlords perceived that their workers were insolent or negligent. Oral culture quickly spread accounts of families harassed or expelled from the land they tilled.

Only a tiny number of rural blacks did nonagricultural work. Less than 20 percent of women employed in rural areas found positions as cooks and as laundresses, compared to 73 percent in towns. Limited alternative work for rural men included a few professionals such as teachers and ministers, and skilled craftsmen such as blacksmiths, carpenters, and stonemasons. Others worked as railroad hands or at saw mills as laborers, firemen, or engineers. Clearly, job choices in the country were still limited.[4]

Farm labor demanded many family members beyond household heads. Dependents added hundreds of additional people—nearly a third of the total—to the rural work force. Overwhelmingly, 87 percent of them labored in agriculture too. These additional workers included some wives and many others: sons and daughters, brothers and sisters, nieces and nephews.

Jobs available in smaller towns still fell mostly into traditional categories, primarily as laborers. Even within towns, over a quarter of families were involved in agriculture, and it impacted other townspeople too. Among household heads, one-fourth were farmers and farm laborers; a nearly identical number were domestic workers; and 15 percent were day laborers. Railroads, brickyards, and quarries afforded other employment. Smaller numbers of men worked as butlers or as store porters, as teamsters or carriage drivers, or at saw mills and in woodcutting. But Lucy

Crayton Sloan paid her store bills by milking the Hunters' cows. With spring's arrival, Philip Green cleaned the Hunters' well, for which he earned $1.25 against his store account. While farmer Henry Oliver got a hoe and cattle powders, Rufus Crew bought a plow stock and two plows, which cost him about three days' pay.

Professionals and craftsmen—more abundant in towns than in the countryside —made up most of the remaining work force, about 15 percent: teachers and ministers; craftspeople, including blacksmiths and shoemakers; and building trades— carpenters, housepainters, brick masons, and bricklayers. Townspeople growing their own vegetables, those who worked on farms, and others in building trades—all felt keenly the agricultural cycle.

In May, before any new crops would come in, several people ran short of both money and provisions. Butler Reid—Easter Reid's son—from Calhoun made a new note at Hunter's for $42.54, the equivalent of three months' work. His balance included $3.15 interest, a charge the Hunters usually did not impose until after a year's lapse. Bob Sanders knew too much about that problem. Although owing $150, he would not be able to make a payment until the following year. In the meantime he bought only a few foodstuffs—sardines, crackers, and candy—plus tobacco and socks and shoes. And he borrowed 10 cents from the store each week. Unlike Reid and Sanders, Clemson College's laundryman Ed Haywood made only one charge during the year—a saucepan and an agate pan—and paid three weeks later by money order. College staff received steadier wages than most area blacks.

During the spring Butler Reid and many others honored the women who raised them in special church services. Women had to bear much of the brunt of family life, as Jane Hunter's mother clearly recognized. Women had to stretch meager budgets to feed the entire family and had to work hard to keep their children clean for school and church. Before indoor plumbing and with dirt or mud roads, that was not easy. When husbands worked ten or twelve hours in the fields, they had little time for young children. Women, then, had to hold the family together as fathers strove to keep its members from starving. Churches paid tribute to mothers; in some, there were special seats and dresses for "mothers of the church," or, as at Kings Chapel, stewardesses.

Census enumerators trekked throughout the area during the summer. Collectively they gathered valuable data on families, landownership, and occupations. These census workers undoubtedly worked hard to complete their forms, which were valuable contributions to the year's documentary legacy and provide rich insights today into those lives in 1900.

The summer months were brutally hot especially for those hoeing weeds in the red baked soil of the upper piedmont. Abe Milliner, who a few years earlier narrowly escaped being lynched, bought two straw hats for his sons. Three hundred black convicts laboring on nearby Clemson College lands certainly felt the heat. July 4, an occasion for festive celebrations, was also the day convicts died from heat on W. Q. Hammond's and J. S. Hammond's farms. And that same month Peter Harris,

Convict labor at Clemson Agricultural College, ca. 1890–93. Black Heritage in the Upper Piedmont, Clemson University

suffering a severe whipping by white men only a few miles west of Anderson, yielded to pressure and fled the county for supposedly insulting a white woman.[5]

Even amid this harshness, some folks had opportunities for parties, group socializing, worship, and reading. Sue Brown bought one hundred pounds of flour plus soda and bacon in August, and L. N. Williams bought melons and twenty-nine pounds of bacon. Major Jenkins purchased Anlet's third reader, and Winsome Bibbs got a grammar book but returned it a few days later for 75 cents credit.

As the lay-by season began in late summer, Methodists opened camp meetings and Rocky River Baptists held their annual meeting. Baptists, ME(N), and the AME maintained a near-monopoly on area religion. But William Fuller already sparked a few groups soon to develop into Fire Baptized Holiness churches; other pentecostals too found a ready if small audience. Baptists still dominated, however, followed by Methodists and, more distantly, AME, CME, Presbyterians, and Fire Baptized Holiness. Over a hundred Anderson, Oconee, and Pickens churches continued to anchor community life and to spur educational improvement.

The Rocky River Baptist Association met August 14–16 at Pleasant Grove Baptist Church. Representatives attended from thirty churches, which were served by fourteen ministers. Most held several pulpits; they included A. Walker, four churches totaling 1,008 members; S. J. Jones, four churches with 572; and S. Oliver, three churches with 1,638. The association gave a small pension to Jennie Williford, aged widow of minister James Williford—excluded from Mountain Creek Baptist Church in 1868. As they often did, Rocky River Baptists stressed education, partly through stipends to students—five men and four women. Pendleton's minister chaired the education committee, whose report stressed that "we cannot, as a race, hope to rise ... without intellectual development."

Silver Spring Baptists expanded their building in Pendleton by adding a vestibule and a Sunday school room. Anderson Smith, Tenus Winston, and minister A. R. Robinson all bought lumber, nails, and shingles for the church, which got fancy sateen cloth for dedication services when the additions were ready. John Williams and Lewis Webb earned credits against their store accounts by working on St. Paul's Episcopal Church, which the Hunters attended, and for cleaning it. Webb was probably the same "Lewis" who as a young man served the Simpson brothers in Virginia during the Civil War.[6]

A few weeks later Patsy Adams's purchases at Hunter's store reflect her domestic service in Pendleton, like many other townswomen. Rather than tending a white household, however, she was a seamstress. She paid for her many pieces of cloth and notions by taking in the Hunters' washing. Forty percent of Anderson's employed women were laundresses, as were one-fourth of those in other towns. Laundress Julia Crooks was one of a few black townspeople to pay store accounts in cash, as did Philip Green and several ministers. In late November she bought a shotgun.

The autumn brought unneeded reminders of white domination. Although the term "structural oppression" would appear only decades later, its reality enveloped blacks. Shut out of the September Democratic primaries, most men also would not be able to vote in November general elections. And throughout the fall many found that their summer's cotton would just pay their store and fertilizer charges. Too many other people learned that once again they fell short of paying their current year's debts. Joe Hamilton, however, settled his account with 300 pounds of pork, and Dave English earned 50 cents a day working for the Hunters at both their cotton gin and their mill.

Farm managers at Ashtabula, a plantation just outside Pendleton owned by the Pelzer family, placed intense demands on labor to pick its cotton crop in the fall. Sixty-five people—including fifteen women and several children—labored there; in the process they nearly shredded their hands on the sharp bolls. They included four members of the Conley family and eight Reids. Nearly forty of these sixty-five worked at Ashtabula only in the fall; a few of them came just in December to plow up the cotton fields after picking cotton for themselves and other employers.

Aaron Mansion earned $182.26 for his year-round labor there; working periodically, his wife and three children added $31.07 to the family's coffers. The second-largest pay for the year, $156.12, went to Tom Brown, whose family similarly earned additional sums. Both in towns and in rural areas it often took many hands, even those as young as seven, to make ends meet; workers under twenty years of age amounted to 44 percent of employed rural folk.

Farm labor and sharecropping involved many complicated arrangements. Some men managed to combine other work with their farm labor; others needed their children to pick cotton and sometimes hired other blacks too. Tinsmith Jim Evans, renting his shop from the Hunters, also worked for them at their store. Evans earned six days' pay, 60 cents each, and paid the Hunters 50 cents for his shop's weekly rent. As a farm laborer, he paid four men and women to help him in September; rather than hand them cash, Evans had the Hunters charge his account for the wages he owed and credit his helpers with these same amounts. Other men paid their taxes and their insurance premiums by charging them at the store, which in essence functioned as an early-day credit card and ATM. Similarly, white landowners could pay their farm laborers through store credits, as did Ashtabula managers, and as B. Harris did for Jane Hunter's Uncle Abe Milliner in August, September, and October.[7]

Blacksmith Tenus Winston stayed busy throughout the fall, as in the spring, repairing Ashtabula farm tools for a total of $87.51. He earned additional money from other employers and at his shop, as well as from two houses he rented to tenant families. Three single Winston daughters lived at home: twenty-four-year-old Mary, a recent Benedict College graduate who taught public school; a twenty-year-old laundress; and an eighteen-year-old farm laborer. Like Winston, Ben Keese made ends meet by varied methods. He operated a confectionery store and served hot meals to customers. Keese also repaired machinery at Ashtabula and elsewhere in town. And he paid his Hunter account with possums.

Students usually returned to school after picking cotton. As a new term began, public-school teacher J. A. Richie visited Hunter's store to buy history and spelling books plus chalk, for which he paid cash. Also during the autumn, the state superintendent of education compiled his annual report for the legislature. It told an ambivalent story, depending on the point of view. One evident fact was a dramatic increase in literacy rates since 1865, especially for younger people. Despite limited teachers' salaries, short terms, and often shabby school houses, more children learned to read and write and more sought advanced education.

Black children had more schools, longer terms, and better-educated teachers than before, but conditions still were inferior compared to white schools, as J. J. McMahan's figures clearly demonstrated. Black students totaled 7,334 children in the three-county area who attended mostly one-teacher, one-room schools. In Anderson County there were seventy-six black students per teacher (much higher than in either Oconee, thirty-four, or Pickens, forty-seven), half again as many as Anderson's white students, fifty-one. The slogan should have been "separate forever but equal never."

Terms varied among districts; poorer funding and more rural areas meant shorter terms in Oconee and Pickens; in Anderson they were longer and came closer to matching those for whites. Many children did not attend school regularly. The area's general culture did not stress education, and families needed them to work in fields or as day laborers. Only Anderson, Easley, Honea Path, and Pendleton offered "town" schools for black children with a combined enrollment of 1086, about one of seven black students in Anderson, Oconee, and Pickens counties.[8]

Teachers in fall 1900 had better training and credentials than their predecessors in the 1870s and 1880s. Women still held a minority of certifications, 22 percent in Pickens and 38 percent in Anderson. Anderson and Pickens county boards of education approved 119 black certifications between 1899 and 1901; 22 among them held licentiate degrees.

Between 1897 and 1901 about fifty upper-piedmont students attended colleges including Benedict, Claflin, State, Leonard Medical College, and Spelman Seminary. G. W. Hill became in 1899 Anderson County's first black teacher to win permanent certification by the state board of education. Those few who managed to go to college had prospects of a professional career. But most African Americans found work only in farming, domestic service, or labor.

Seneca Institute, opened in 1899, was the second black-controlled school in the tricounty area, supplementing Greeley Institute in Anderson city. Seneca Institute operated as a newly founded private school under Seneca River Missionary Baptist Association control. Nearby, Greenville Methodists sponsored the new Sterling Institute. These schools' respective presidents, ministers J. J. Starks and D. M. Minus, differed in their attitudes toward whites.

Both earned respect from the white community and maintained friendly relations with white leaders. Minus praised such support. He hoped that readers of his autobiography would "see the good feelings that existed between the two races," the successful joint black-white board of trustees, and their working "together in perfect harmony" as whites "gave their money and their time to help a negro school." Although Jane Hunter and Starks expressed similar views, Starks insisted on black people building their own school, and Seneca Institute operated under an all-black board. Harrison Wiggins and A. E. Dupree, two trustees, had been Colhoun slaves.[9]

Despite the dreariness of debts and hard work, families turned to Christmas celebrations. Jack Jordan bought rice and a turkey, perhaps one of those that Stewart Thompson sold to Hunter's store. L. N. Williams purchased currants, citron, sugar, and eggs for a cake, and on December 25 preacher Robinson took home raisins, coconuts, five pounds of meat and a pound of cheese, plus shoes and hose as practical gifts for his wife—another recent Benedict graduate—and children. Despite meager resources his congregation gave him a love offering.

African Americans in Anderson, Oconee, and Pickens still formed something of a community, and even more so in specific locales, where most people would have recognized each other. Many had lived in the same vicinity for decades. Area blacks, as in the state as a whole, were 98 percent South Carolina–born; the few "outsiders" lived in rural areas, where only 1 percent came from elsewhere, mostly from nearby Georgia. By contrast, 3.6 percent of Anderson's city population was born in other states, but in-migration had declined in the past two decades.

Similarly, there was limited out-migration to Arkansas and later to Atlanta, Richmond, and Washington; more went to nearby Greenville and to adjacent Georgia counties. But most students who attended out-of-state colleges—especially Spelman (Atlanta), Howard (Washington), and Mehery Medical College (Tennessee)—returned home to work.

Another type of mobility occurred within towns. Whites and blacks were slowly separating geographically. The growing population of the city of Anderson led to new white sections being established farther from the city's core, where many black residents remained. These newer white areas lacked both servants' houses and alleys, as found in the city's center. Further, thousands of whites lived in mill towns where virtually no blacks were present. Some rural antagonisms evidently caused separations also.

Some families would begin the year 1901 by moving yet again, as they had the previous January. Yearly cycles, especially for those who worked the fields and tended cotton, had little variation. For many, events would resemble very much those of the past year. A scandal in the spring revealed the plight of some farm laborers being forced to live in prison stockades. Although a grand jury investigated, hardly any change resulted. Even more tragic news occurred in 1901 when two Anderson black men and an Oconee white woman were lynched in late November and early December. This followed a surprising six-year lull between 1895—the year of the new constitution—and 1901, which would see the largest number of lynchings in Anderson, Oconee, and Pickens counties in any one year. By contrast, in late December a "crowd of both whites and blacks" on Ashley's plantation were throwing dice together.[10]

African Americans still were constrained and buffeted by circumstances beyond their control. One of these was the economic domination of cotton, closely connected in their lives to their lack of "means of production." That kept many sharecroppers indebted to the landlord, general store, and fertilizer supplier. And fluctuating cotton prices—mostly downward recently—often cheapened their year's labor, as could bad weather. Yet, creating rural communities, people in an isolated Pickens area had their own "Little Liberia," and Anderson County entrepreneurs launched an Afro-American Real Estate Association.

One change improved conditions for some families. They benefited from the growth of railroads, manufacturing and business in towns, and more job opportunities. Starr and Iva were recently booming due to the new Savannah Valley Railroad, built by black labor and opened in 1886. People with skills and resources could achieve more autonomy and success in towns; even day laborers would often fare better working there than on rural farms. Certainly towns afforded more social advantages, better schools, larger churches, and a more interesting life. In Anderson, Calhoun, Pendleton, Pickens, and Seneca, among others, there was a rising, educated middle class in relatively comfortable circumstances that often included home ownership.

Continuities, Past and Present

A minority status, coupled with lack of effective political or economic power, surrounded all black advances. Several twentieth-century episodes demonstrate continued complexity of white-black relationships, some friendly, but others hostile, even brutal. Whichever, they were virtually inevitable. As whites and blacks lived around and near each other and as their families often had generations of shared experiences, they had a commonality that marked their daily lives and deaths. For example, sometimes white people sent flowers and sympathy after a black death, and an occasional "Tribute of Respect from Colored Citizens" was placed in newspapers for whites, like Malinda Hollingsworth, called "a fast, true and loyal friend."[11]

Susan Richardson, a former Calhoun slave, provides insight into long-term interpersonal relations among some whites and blacks. Her story, originating in Pendleton District, spans eighty years and three extended white families. "Aunt Susan" was the daughter of John C. Calhoun slave Daphne and her husband Bill Lawrence. Calhoun gave Daphne to his daughter Anna Maria Clemson as her personal servant; Thomas Clemson then bought Daphne's daughter Susan from John Ewing Colhoun (Jr.) to keep them together. Clemson later sold Daphne, Susan, and Bill [Lawrence] to Alfred Dearing.[12] Susan and husband Billy Richardson had six children. Working after emancipation for a family near Saluda, she for decades tended Edwards children, some of their grandchildren, and one great-grandchild.

Susan Richardson wrote in intensely personal tones to one of those grandchildren, Myrtle Harlong, on April 6, 1910: "I only wish I was so I could run in and help you . . . but I doubt if much work would be done as I think I could sit down and talk to you for a week. . . . First I want to tell you how gratefull and thankfull from my heart I feel to your Brother," who arranged transportation for Richardson's dying son Tucker to stay with her. "Give my love to all," she wrote. "I guess your mother is back home by now. I was just thinking about whether your grandmother is living or not. . . . I hope you will write again soon. Remember me kindly to each one of the family. . . . With much love to you from your Mammy."

Myrtle Harlong in 1958 recorded her own recollections. "I used to love to sit with Aunt Susan evenings as she relived some of her past life, especially in the homes of the Calhouns and Clemsons." As a young child Harlong received a reprimand from Aunt Susan, who told her that "the Lord is going to think a lot more of you if you do . . . [your] churning chores now" and read the Bible later, as the Lord "doesn't like folks who neglect their duties." Harlong decades later recalled Richardson's counsel.

Susan Richardson's relationships with five generations of white families extending over eighty years is repeated in other stories throughout the South. The sentiments expressed in such accounts contrast sharply with white dominance through the press, economic control, and societal pressure.

On the other hand, pleasantries could suddenly disappear. A year after Richardson's letter, state legislator Joshua Ashley led a lynch mob that spilled out Willis Jackson's blood and life at Honea Path. Two years after that, Pendleton's town council passed a segregated residential law, likely the upstate's earliest. It forbade blacks and whites from living on the same block except for servants occupying part of the white family's premises.[13]

M. H. Gassaway, teacher and principal of Anderson public schools, had perhaps as much respect as any black man in the area. Local newspapers often commented kindly on his accomplishments as well as those of his brother, the Reverend E. V. Gassaway. Circumstances took a sharp turn in 1918. When one of M. H. Gassaway's staff was accused of stealing small amounts of money, he stood up for her. Doing so, he encountered white ire and hastily obeyed threats that he leave town within a few hours. Moving to Ohio, he worked there as a laborer.[14]

Two episodes from later in the twentieth century continue the story of shared experiences and acquaintance with the same circle of people. One day in the 1970s Viola Williams, a black woman in Clemson whose grandmother had been enslaved to the Calhouns, went to the post office. There she found a wallet with one hundred dollars, left behind by Mamie Crawford, a white woman of similar age, whom she knew. Williams left immediately, found Crawford and returned her wallet. Crawford hugged and hugged and thanked her, according to Williams.

Similarly, during the 1998 Tenus Maxwell cemetery rededication, a black woman and a white woman—evidently unknown personally to each other, both in their seventies with roots in the neighborhood, though since moved away—began chatting and catching up on news of families whom they both knew. Their lives, and even more so those of their parents, had been dramatically different, but there were shared interpersonal relationships, a factor that marked the area for two hundred years, for good and for ill.[15]

As he retired in 2001, Dr. Spencer Crew, whose father Rufus Crew moved from Norris to the North, could walk through the Smithsonian Museum of American History and see his *Field to Factory* exhibit. It explores the movement from southern rural areas to northern cities. There comforting continuities were often provided by religious communities and a network of friends and relatives who moved to the same northern city. Many people, however, found relocation unsettling as they lost their traditional moorings. Most local people did not move north. "Those who remained" labored and collectively enriched their communities. Doing so, they provide rich insights into a limited view of honor.

Assessments of nineteenth-century white South Carolinians emphasize "honor," a pride in one's self and reputation. It sometimes led to conflicts and duels. When a community's "honor" was at stake, vigilante justice—against either antebellum abolitionists or supposed criminals in the latter 1800s—led to whippings, expulsions, and lynchings. Hardly any account refers to black honor or mentions "dignity." Yet

Ruthie Guyton, Anderson. Pendleton District Commission

upper-piedmont African Americans not only persisted and persevered, many also did so with highest dignity.[16]

Milly's laundress granddaughters, Frances and Amelia Dupree, took pride in their quality work. Equally, blacksmiths James Rosemond, his son James Jr., and Miles Perry, who helped found Seneca Institute, received widespread recognition for their skills. Recent college graduates Rena Jones, Alec Dupree, and John Miller all taught competently and successfully for many years. And as a young man, Robert Reid had limited skills but meticulously cleaned Clemson College's buildings and enjoyed talking with both students and faculty, while John Reese and John Stokes worked hard and well as butlers at Clemson and Central hotels.

Already widowed at thirty-two, Rosa Morris persevered. A dressmaker, she supported her two daughters, seven and nine years old, sent them to school, and took in four boarders to help pay bills and to make sure that her daughters got educated rather than entering domestic service at such young ages, as others had to do. Similarly, widowed Charity Guyton worked as a laundress to keep her thirteen- and fifteen-year-old sons in Anderson's eight-month school, just a few doors away. Both she and widowed sister-in-law Ruth Guyton, also a laundress, owned their homes free of mortgage.

Brick mason John Payton, thirty-nine, continued his family's skills in Anderson, as did N. B. Gaillard as a blacksmith. Morris Cherry still worked as a gardener at the age of ninety-two. One of George and Betty Wiggins's grandsons applied his mining expertise in Seneca Township. And both George Gary and Lawrence Rutledge, held demanding, skilled, responsible jobs, Gary as a saw mill engineer in Seneca and Rutledge as a fireman at Anderson's planing mill. Working hard and well, all these people earned respect from black and white alike. And these diligent workers supported their churches, sent their children to school, and enriched their communities.

Milly Dupree herself could look with pride, honor, and dignity at her decades of hard work and at the many accomplishments of her sons, granddaughters, and their children.

Abbreviations

ACH	Anderson Court House
AI	*Anderson Intelligencer*
AME	African Methodist Episcopal Church
AND + number	Anderson MFH trial number
AOP	Anderson, Oconee, and Pickens counties
BHUP	Black Heritage in the Upper Piedmont (project)
CU	Clemson University
DB	deed book
E&M	South Carolina Baptist Educational, Missionary, and Sunday School Convention
FMB	Freedmen's Bureau
FPC	free person/people of color
GO	General Order (military; FMB)
SO	Special Order (military; FMB)
JCC	John C. Calhoun
JEC	John Ewing Colhoun
KC	*Keowee Courier*
ME(N)	Methodist Episcopal Church (North)
MFH	Magistrates and Freeholders
OR	*Official Records, War of the Rebellion*
PDC	Pendleton District Commission
PKNS	Pickens
PM	*Pendleton Messenger*
PS	*Pickens Sentinel*
RG	Record Group
RRBA	Rocky River Baptist Association
SCBC	SC Baptist Convention
SCDAH	SC Department of Archives and History
SCHM	*SC Historical Magazine*
SCL	South Caroliniana Library, University of South Carolina
SHC	Southern Historical Collection, University of North Carolina at Chapel Hill
SRMBA	Seneca River Missionary Baptist Association
USCT	United States Colored Troops
WPA	Works Progress Administration
WSC	Western South Carolina

Notes

Prologue

1. I have used Milly's photograph in workshops where several participants believed that she had some Native American ancestry. There is no specific information about her death date or burial site. For a detailed analysis of the Keowee plantation, see "African Americans on the Colhoun and Calhoun Plantations, 1790–1865" in chapter 9; chapter 18 for more about the cemetery in Abel, where other Duprees are buried; and note 12 about her grandson in "Black Thought, 1865–1900" in chapter 20. All notes cited by chapter number refer to the notes to this volume.

2. "Thirteen" stated for her children reflects those identified with her in the ledger and in the 1870 census; some may in fact have been grandchildren, nieces, or nephews. A white contemporary who lived near Milly had twelve children, so thirteen may be accurate for Milly herself.

3. Interviewed in 1990, Tom Dupree (born ca. 1900) recalled that his mother Frances (Fanny) Dupree had this old photograph of a woman she called Aunt Milly, someone Tom Dupree had not known. The only Milly found in the 1870 census for Anderson, Oconee, and Pickens who could possibly fit is Milly Dupree.

Introduction: A Piedmont Setting

1. Charles Joyner, *Shared Traditions: Southern History and Folk Traditions* (Urbana: University of Illinois Press, 1999), 1. Similarly, as Timothy Fulop says, the "earlier presumed 'invisibility' of African Americans was more a result of scholarly neglect than the paucity of sources." *African-American Religion: Interpretive Essays in History and Culture*, ed. Timothy E. Fulop and Albert J. Raboteau (New York: Routledge, 1997), 1; cited as *African-American Religion*. Like one of the anthology's articles, my study is "An Exploration in Neglected Sources" (Lawrence W. Levine); "withheld" in Teri Holbrook, *A Far and Deadly Cry* (New York: Bantam Books, 1995), 57. Stephanie McCurry refers to historical invisibility of lowcountry yeoman in contemporary travel accounts as well as scholarly studies; *Masters of Small Worlds* (New York: Oxford University Press, 1995), 37–43, ch. 2, and throughout her book; cited as McCurry. Her goal of "rendering the yeomanry visible is, then, the first and necessary step" (37) to studying their households and other relationships, an argument equally applicable for upper-piedmont slaves. Source materials have previously been neglected, partly because, piecemeal, they have not been very informative; bringing together many types of sources—most never before used for upper-piedmont African Americans—for this study has been essential to render a richly textured story. "Small" may be a comparative matter. Pendleton District was about 15% larger than Edgefield District, studied by Orville Vernon Burton, approximately the size of Delaware, and double that of Rhode Island.

2. Charles Joyner presents a brief argument for local context, the need for examination of a "*particular* slave community" and demonstrates its value superbly in *Down by the Riverside: A South Carolina Slave Community* (Urbana: University of Illinois Press, 1985), xiv. Robert L. Hall points out the importance of being specific about variations dependent on time and locale, comments appearing in a Symposium on Southern History (University of Mississippi)

volume edited by Ted Ownby, *Black and White Cultural Interaction in the Antebellum South* (Jackson: University Press of Mississippi, 1993), 50–51; cited as *Cultural Interaction*. A shortcoming of most studies that draw heavily from WPA interviews is that too few of them indicate, let alone develop, the local context.

3. John Hope Franklin, *From Slavery to Freedom: A History of Negro Americans* (New York: Alfred A. Knopf, 1967); Winthrop D. Jordan, *White over Black: American Attitudes toward the Negro, 1550–1812* (Chapel Hill: Institute of Early American History and Culture, 1968); Eugene D. Genovese, *Roll, Jordan, Roll: The World the Slaves Made* (New York: Random House, 1972); John W. Blassingame, *The Slave Community: Plantation Life in the Antebellum South* (New York: Oxford University Press, 1972); Peter H. Wood, *Black Majority: Negroes in Colonial South Carolina from 1670 through the Stono Rebellion* (New York: Alfred A. Knopf, 1974), cited as Wood; John C. Inscoe, *Mountain Masters: Slavery and the Sectional Crisis in Western North Carolina* (Knoxville: University of Tennessee Press, 1989); Bernard E. Powers Jr., *Black Charlestonians: A Social History, 1822–1885* (Fayetteville: University of Arkansas Press, 1994), cited as Powers, *Black Charlestonians*; and Harold A. McDougall, *Black Baltimore: A New Theory of Community* (Philadelphia: Temple University Press, 1993).

4. Charles Joyner, *Down by the Riverside: A South Carolina Slave Community*; Joel Williamson, *After Slavery: The Negro in South Carolina during Reconstruction, 1861–1877* (Chapel Hill: University of North Carolina Press, 1965); Francis Butler Simkins and Robert Hilliard Woody, *South Carolina during Reconstruction* (Chapel Hill: University of North Carolina Press, 1932); George W. Tindall, *South Carolina Negroes, 1877–1900* (Columbia: University of South Carolina Press, 1952); Margaret Creel, *A Peculiar People: Slave Religion and Community-Culture among the Gullah* (New York: New York University Press, 1988); and Orville Vernon Burton, *In My Father's House Are Many Mansions: Family and Community in Edgefield, South Carolina* (Chapel Hill: University of North Carolina Press, 1985), cited as Burton. Others dealing with South Carolina inland regions are noted in "Beyond Towns," ch. 18 of this book.

Starting from a lowcountry viewpoint, McCurry states (47) that "the demographic predominance of black slaves is the crucial context for every other calculation and inquiry with respect to slave society." It should follow, then, that understanding a minority slave population and a white-majority culture shed light on each other.

Two pioneering studies, paying little attention to the upstate or to local context, emphasize conditions that apply more to lower parts of the state: Asa H. Gordon, *Sketches of Negro Life and History in South Carolina* (1929; Columbia: University of South Carolina Press, 1971), and I. A. Newby, *Black Carolinians: A History of Blacks in South Carolina from 1895 to 1968* (Columbia: South Carolina Tricentennial Commission, 1973), cited as Newby.

5. Numerous articles and conference papers have dealt with specific aspects; these have yet to lead to cohesive, continuous studies. Most backcountry scholars focus primarily on whites in the 1700s; see note 11, below. One recent study of an area with demographics similar to those of Pendleton District is Ted J. Smith, "Slavery in Washington County, Arkansas, 1828–1860" (M.A. thesis, University of Arkansas, 1995). Lacy K. Ford Jr. illustrates this point in *Origins of Southern Radicalism: The South Carolina Upcountry, 1800–1860* (New York: Oxford University Press, 1988), viii (note that AOP would fit within a narrower part of Ford's "broad, arcing Southern Piedmont"), 47, table 2.2, and elsewhere; cited as Ford. *Mountain Masters*, above, deals primarily with white-majority Appalachian counties for a shorter period of time than does this present study. Another study focuses on one specific aspect: Wilma A. Dunaway, *The First American Frontier: Transition to Capitalism in Southern Appalachia* (Chapel Hill: University of North Carolina Press, 1996), 57; cited as Dunaway.

Efforts to treat this general "swath" as a whole have occurred with classifications in Charles S. Johnson, *Statistical Atlas of Southern Counties* (Chapel Hill: University of North

Carolina Press, 1941), and more recently the Appalachian Regional Commission studies. The *Statistical Atlas* compiled 1930s-era statistics, including crop type, percentage of black population, black educational and tenancy characteristics, and number of lynchings, 1900–1931.

One study, treating the southern backcountry as a whole, grew out of a 1993 conference, "The Southern Colonial Backcountry: Beginning an Interdisciplinary Dialogue" at the University of South Carolina: *The Southern Colonial Backcountry: Interdisciplinary Perspectives on Frontier Communities* (Knoxville: University of Tennessee Press, 1998). The word "beginning" is a significant key to both book and conference, as each essay deals with a different perspective and geographical locale. With one exception the book's thoughtful essays mention slaves or African Americans only in passing.

6. 1860 comparisons: Joyner, *Down by the Riverside*,19. Ford, 40 (table 1.1), 46 and 47 (table 2.2), and passim.

7. Philip D. Morgan has contributed significantly to 18th century comparisons between Carolina and Virginia colonies, primarily their coastal regions: *Slave Counterpoint: Black Culture in the Eighteenth-Century Chesapeake and Lowcountry* (Chapel Hill: University of North Carolina Press, 1998) and "The Development of Slave Culture in Eighteenth Century Plantation America" (Ph.D. diss., University College, London, 1977); cited as Morgan, "Slave Culture." By contrast, see Robin Blackburn, *The Making of New World Slavery: From the Baroque to the Modern 1492–1800* (London: Verso, 1998), in which the British North American mainland colonies play a minor role. A valuable contribution deals systematically with the various periods of slavery: Ira Berlin, *Many Thousands Gone* (Cambridge: Belknap Press of Harvard University Press, 1999); cited as Berlin.

Cf. Hall's emphasis (note 2 above) on specifying variations dependent on time, as well as locale (Joyner in that same note). Combining Hall's observations, those by Berlin ("Families" in note 1, ch. 9) and by Herbert G. Gutman (*The Black Family in Slavery and Freedom, 1750–1925* [New York: Vintage Books, 1976]), and two of my own (but not uniquely), four types of periods emerge:

(1) Focusing on a long-range view, one—forming the structure and analysis in *Many Thousands Gone*—deals with the major periods of enslavement in North America, coupled with chronological and geographic shifts in settlement and thriving plantations on the continent.

(2) Gutman stresses periods in the owners' lives, which include accumulation of slaves, a mature plantation holding, and much later dispersal to adult sons and daughters, as well as potential owner debts, also leading to dispersal.

(3) Neither Gutman nor Berlin placed much emphasis on the stages within the slaves' own lives, families, and their troubles—a subject difficult to address en masse, but critically important to the individuals in bondage; cf. my case study on the Keowee plantation, "African Americans on the Calhoun and Colhoun Plantations, 1790–1865," ch. 9, p. 147–156.

(4) Further, there were fluctuating times of societal, agricultural, and economic stress, discussed in chs. 5 and 11. Thus, there were multiple types of "periods" that need to be kept in mind but are difficult to address simultaneously.

8. This partially meets some observations, perhaps objections, that many studies of slavery deal primarily with the late antebellum era, mostly 1840–60. Pendleton District sources about African Americans (other than deeds of sale and owners' estate records) are sparse for the 1784–1820 period, but provide enough to construct broad outlines. My account provides some pointers to their prior enslaved conditions in Virginia, the lowcountry, and other American regions.

9. Bernard Powers's *Black Charlestonians* is the best account that spans more than fifty years. Covering an even longer time than Powers does, this study benefits from recent Old Pendleton District local accounts; most have dealt with specific towns or subjects. However,

they cumulatively demonstrate a wealth of materials yet to be systematically mined. So does an increasing abundance of data being placed on internet web sites. No overall history of the three counties exists—nor to most nearby counties as well, nor is there any specialized account of its religion, agriculture, economy, or demographics, other than Lacy Ford. A major exception is Archie Vernon Huff Jr., *Greenville: The History of the City and County in the South Carolina Piedmont* (Columbia: University of South Carolina Press, 1995); cited as Huff, *Greenville*.

Several accounts that are either brief or narrowly focused provide some comparative insights. These include Joseph D. Mathis, "Race Relations in Greenville, South Carolina, From 1865 through 1900, As Seen in a Critical Analysis of the Greenville City Council Proceedings and Other Related Works" (M.A. thesis, Atlanta University, 1971); Dwain Pruitt, *Things Hidden: An Introduction to the History of Blacks in Spartanburg* ([Spartanburg, S.C.]: City of Spartanburg Community Relations Office, [1995]), cited as Pruitt, *Spartanburg;* William Cinque Henderson, "Spartan Slaves: A Documentary Account of Blacks on Trial in Spartanburg, South Carolina, 1830 to 1865" (Ph.D. diss., Northwestern University, 1978); and studies based on postbellum Abbeville and Greenwood counties, cited in note 34, ch. 18.

A study, sadly lacking, that would both complement and enlighten this present work is one about African Americans in Abbeville, immediately to the south of Anderson. Cf. Lowry Ware, *Old Abbeville: Scenes of the Past of a Town Where Old Time Things Are Not Forgotten* (Columbia, S.C.: SCMAR, 1992), esp. his ch. 7, "Abbeville and Its Slaves: Paternalism and Fear," and 54–57, 145–50; cited as Ware. Allen B. Ballard's *One More Day's Journey: The Story of a Family and a People* (New York: McGraw-Hill, 1984) also presents useful interpretations; see also Charles E. Orser, who quotes two letters to James Edward Calhoun about the South's depressed economy in *The Material Basis of the Postbellum Tenant Plantation: Historical Archaeology in the South Carolina Piedmont* (Athens: University of Georgia Press, 1988), cited as Orser.

10. Joyner, *Down by the Riverside,* xiv.

11. In *Black Carolinians,* Newby (x) said that "the study I have written is not the one I set out to write. My original intent was to focus exclusively upon black Carolinians giving scant regard to whites or race relations. This proved impossible," as I also found. He continued: "Black and white Carolinians have been rigidly segregated since 1895," which certainly did not apply to earlier decades in the upstate. Newby emphasizes "repression, poverty, powerlessness, and efforts to accommodate to it or withstand it."

Burton stresses white-black involvement in his Edgefield study. Although variations are important to consider, Gutman finds striking similarities among African American families across divergent geographic and cultural areas of the South (*Black Family*). Morgan, "Slave Culture," 427. Two classic studies of southern whites are Frank Lawrence Owsley, *Plain Folk of the Old South* (Baton Rogue: Louisiana State University Press, 1949), and Bertram Wyatt-Brown, *Southern Honor: Ethics and Behavior in the Old South* (New York: Oxford University Press, 1982).

A recent study that treats the subject specifically for South Carolina's upper piedmont is Stephen West, "From Yeoman to Redneck in Upstate South Carolina, 1850–1915" (Ph.D. diss., Columbia University, 1998); cited as West, "Yeoman to Redneck." See "Upper Piedmont" in this book's "Selected Bibliography: An Essay" for West's forthcoming volume.

As shown throughout this text, contemporary white opinions of friendly relations with blacks should be considered cautiously; these abounded especially during early postbellum years. W. K. Easley said in May 1866: "Apart from the natural sympathy we must feel for a people with whom we have been familiar from the cradle, with whom we have had such long and such intimate social relationships, from whom we have received and to whom we have extended so many offices of kindness . . . [we all] should live together on terms of mutual kindness and good will." The May 26, 1866, *Keowee Courier* uses the word "national," but "natural" surely must have been intended.

Although federal mortality censuses required owners to specify names, dates, ages, and other information, some lowcountry planters reported more ambiguously, as in Georgetown's 46 "Negroes not named," died of cholera, or similar Beaufort groupings of 50–70; indicating many deaths from a single disease, such entries also suggest that coastal masters were far more detached from their slaves, often not personally knowing them by name. South Carolina Mortality Schedule, 1850, 113, 293–97.

By contrast, the extended Calhoun-Colhoun family correspondence referred to at least 50 slaves by name—residing on at least eight different premises in four states—clearly understanding that recipients would know the individual African American mentioned.

12. Newby (2–3) wrote in 1973 that "history-as-actuality has conspired to leave a largely 'white' body of historical source materials in the state. . . . The historian of black Carolina thus faces problems of bias and imbalance which are built into his source materials." He then criticizes the SCDAH, SCL, and SCHS, all of which have endeavored in recent decades to enrich their black holdings and access to them. The story is not as dismal now as Newby found it in 1973.

All of AOP's known antebellum letters and documents (except a forged pass) were written by whites. Some church minutes record slaves' actions. Transcripts of 500-plus slave trials come closer than anything else to contemporary black expression, even though written by whites within a white-controlled environment. If any black families have letters, diaries, or other accounts written between 1865 and 1900, they are not in depositories and have not emerged in two earlier projects—except Sidney Burt's late-nineteenth-century notebook (owned by a descendant) of his charges and payments at the Hunter General Store.

Many families, having to move often, lost possessions, and fires destroyed many black homes and family treasures. Bethel Methodist Church records perished when the clerk's house burned in 1929; later in the century Viola Williams lost her formerly enslaved grandmother's personal account in a fire; and Jim Benson similarly lost decades of family documents and photographs the same way.

By contrast there is a rich, barely tapped oral tradition. In 1989–90 I directed a Black Heritage in South Carolina's Upper Piedmont, 1865–1920 (BHUP) project, funded in part by the South Carolina Humanities Council (now Humanities Council SC). A major component was interviews with over fifty elderly black people, many of them in their 80s or 90s. John M. Coggeshall, *Carolina Piedmont Country* (Jackson: University Press of Mississippi, 1996) uses a number of these taped interviews; cited as Coggeshall. Additionally, Gwendolyn Anderson's *Profiles of Black Folks in Anderson County* (Spartanburg, S.C.: Reprint Co., 1993) contains family accounts that trace ancestors back to the early 1800s; cited as *Profiles of Black Folks*. The few black newspapers in the area, published briefly, have left behind no copies (see note 11, ch. 20). The Rocky River Baptist Association (RRBA) *Minutes* (1868–1915) provide the best contemporary insight into black thought, which is explored in my ch. 20.

A few antebellum or later-1800s charcoals or photographs of African Americans survive, along with some tools and other artifacts. Evidently the earliest black photographer in the immediate area was Edgar L. Thomas, who had a studio in Anderson by 1909 until at least 1923, according to Harvey Teal, *Partners with the Sun: South Carolina Photographers, 1840–1940* (Columbia: University of South Carolina Press), 287; cited as Teal, *Partners with the Sun*. Earlier photographs of AOP black people, then, would almost certainly have been taken by white photographers, either in studios or by door-to-door work. The earliest photographs found in the BHUP project appear in this book: the Thompson family (Pendleton), ca. early 1880s; the Frusters, included with Thomas Clemson, early 1880s; Milly Dupree, ca. 1890s; Clemson convicts, ca. 1894; and the Vance family (Pendleton), 1902. Additionally there are 1899 photographs taken at a Greenville army camp. Several earlier charcoals survive, including perhaps the illustration of Easter Reid.

13. An increasing body of literature—and some law—deals with victimization of slaves, psychological damage, and continuing effects generations later. See comments by Lawrence T. McDonnell in *Cultural Interaction*, 127–28. One plantation owner, James Henry Hammond, devised a list of offenses (quoted in West, "Yeoman to Redneck," 105) that he thought merited whippings; these ranged from neglect of work to running away. On the Hammonds, see Carol Bleser, *The Hammonds of Redcliffe* (New York: Oxford University Press, 1981) and *Secret and Sacred: The Diaries of John Henry Hammond, A Southern Slaveholder* (New York: Oxford University Press, 1988).

14. For a late-1990s analysis, although focused primarily on religion, see three articles, grouped as "Models for Studying African-American Religion," in *African-American Religion*. African American archaeology and material culture have become rich fields of study. Two pertinent books are Leland Ferguson, *Uncommon Ground: Archaeology and Early African America, 1650–1800* (Washington: Smithsonian Institution Press, 1992); and Kym Rice's exhibit and catalog, *Before Freedom Came: African-American Life in the Antebellum South* (Richmond: Museum of the Confederacy, 1991). See "Houses and Household Items" in ch. 10, pp. 160–63; and Sobel, "Personal Ethics in a Slave Society," *Cultural Interaction*, 55–56. A significant approach, divergent from those dealing with harmonious black-white exchanges, may be found in Sterling Stuckey, *Slave Culture: Nationalist Theory and the Foundations of Black America* (New York: Oxford University Press, 1987).

15. Boles, *Black Southerners, 1619–1869* (Lexington: University Press of Kentucky, 1983); an essay in Charles Reagan Wilson, ed., *Religion in the South* (Jackson: University Press of Mississippi, 1985); and, as editor, *Masters and Slaves in the House of the Lord: Race and Religion in the American South, 1740–1870* (Lexington: University Press of Kentucky, 1988). Fox-Genovese, *Within the Plantation Household: Black and White Women of the Old South* (Chapel Hill: University of North Carolina Press, 1988); Ownby's *Cultural Interaction;* and Joyner's *Shared Traditions*. See also Joel Williamson, *The Crucible of Race: Black-White Relations in the American South since Emancipation* (New York: Oxford University Press, 1984); cited as *Crucible;* he says (25) that "black and white southerners . . . continued to swap recipes and cultural styles, songs and stories, accents and attitudes." John Hammond Moore, *Southern Homefront, 1861–1865* (Columbia, S.C.: Summerhouse Press, 1998), ch. 5, discusses convoluted attitudes toward slaves during the Civil War.

16. John Hammond Moore's *Columbia and Richland County: A South Carolina Community, 1740–1990* (Columbia: University of South Carolina Press, 1993) uses the term even more loosely; cited as Moore, *Columbia*. Despite titles, neither editors nor authors define "community" as used in the following works: Orville Vernon Burton and Robert C. McMath Jr., eds., *Class, Conflict, and Consensus: Antebellum Southern Community Studies* (Westport, Conn.: Greenwood Press, 1982); and Vincent P. Franklin, *The Education of Black Philadelphia: The Social and Educational History of a Minority Community, 1900–1950* (Philadelphia: University of Pennsylvania Press, 1979). "Community" appears frequently in titles of African American studies—as well as other subjects—since the 1960s; it seldom gets defined, however. Cf. Williamson, *After Slavery*, ch. 9, "The Negro Community," referring to all African Americans in South Carolina.

17. See Joyner, *Down by the Riverside*, 59, 89; he uses slightly different language about slaves manipulating the system and even modifying their work pace to suit their own style.

18. As described to me by trained observers (folklorists, a cultural historian, and anthropologists) who have variously lived in, studied about, or briefly visited the area. None was systematically researching the subject of African continuities; all expressed only impressions. The fact that they observed few, if any, continuities does not necessarily mean that these do not exist. But if they do, they are not as readily apparent as are many lowcountry ones.

One person has spoken publicly on the subject. Carrel Cowan-Ricks, an African American archaeologist, described a different, piedmont style, where black burials more nearly resemble those of European Americans than those of Africa;cf. her unpublished "Cemetery Hill Archaeological Project: In Search of John C. Calhoun's Pre-Emancipation African Americans," 8.

Among the many studies that describe white culture, two by piedmont South Carolina natives are especially useful: Burton, *In My Father's House Are Many Mansions: Family and Community in Edgefield, South Carolina*, and *Crucible*. Williamson's family comes from Anderson County, so he is not only an insightful, but also an especially appropriate, observer to inform the present study. See note 1, ch. 6, on Afro-Christianity and my qualified dissent.

19. A few notable exceptions include testimony about harassment and intimidation during 1868 and 1876 elections (chs. 15, pp. 257–60, and 16, p. 279); white sources on lynchings (ch. 21, pp. 382–90 [and notes] passim; and other late-1800s harassment (chs. 21, pp. 374–82 [and notes] passim, and 22, pp. 392–401 [and notes] passim). Some accounts of brutality and whippings do come from white sources. Black sources prior to 1900 consist largely of Baptist minutes (chs. 17, pp. 292–300 [and notes] passim, and 20, pp. 358–67 [and notes] passim).

Chapter 1. The Early Years, 1784–1810

1. Since most deed, tax, and church records are missing for 1784–89, the 1790 census provides the first broad insight into settlement and slaveholding. All references to population and slaveholding, unless otherwise cited, come from my reading and analysis of the Population Schedules of the U.S. Census for 1790–1900 plus Slave Schedules for 1850 and 1860, as well as Mortality, Agricultural, and Industrial Schedules for 1850 through 1880. Published indexes for all South Carolina Population (1790–1870) and Slave Schedules, plus the 1850 and 1860 Mortality Schedules are available in printed volumes.

2. The Massachusetts Supreme Court, ruling that slavery was incompatible with that state's constitution, ended enslavement there. Other northern states also abolished slavery, and heated debates about abolition preoccupied the country's 1787 constitutional convention. Methodists, Quakers, and others opposed slavery for religious reasons. Still other people contended that a declining market for American cotton made slavery economically unproductive.

3. A tiny number of white and black people connected with Native trade and affairs lived there when the Cherokee controlled the area; itinerant white traders passed through on periodic selling endeavors. Old Stone Church cemetery historian, Peggy Rich, described for me its area of slave graves. Native Americans: Robert Mills, *Statistics of South Carolina, Including a View of Its Natural, Civil, and Military History, General and Particular* (Charleston: Hurlbut & Loyd, 1826); cited as Mills, *Statistics*.

4. Population cited for both Pendleton and Greenville Districts. One researcher estimates that about ten landowners accounted for 52% of the total acreage owned in Pendleton in 1790–92. Dunaway, 57; cf. Betty Willie, *Pendleton District, S.C. Deeds, 1790–1806* (Easley, S.C.: Southern Historical Press, 1982), 196; cited as Willie, *Deeds*; Clyde R. Ferguson, "General Andrew Pickens" (Ph.D. diss., Duke University, 1960).

5. Colhoun Papers, Special Collections Library, Duke University.

6. Over 75% of all 1433 heads of households had at least one counterpart with the same surname. Genealogists, including William Stewart, have tracked clusters of neighboring, though not necessarily related, families who moved from the same areas in Pittsylvania County, Va., Wilkes County, N.C., and other sites. Pendleton District wills and deeds throughout four decades refer to parents, in-laws, land, and slaves still in Virginia or North Carolina. See William C. Stewart, comp., *1800 Census of Pendleton District, South Carolina* (Washington: National Genealogical Society, 1963); and Stan McGaha, *Pendleton District, S.C., Deeds,*

1807–1810 (privately printed, 1993); cited respectively as Stewart, *1800 Census* and as McGaha. All references to "DB" (deed book) prior to 1828 apply to Pendleton District (filmed along with Anderson deeds) unless otherwise stated; after 1828, "DB" refers to Pickens or Anderson and after 1868 to either of them plus Oconee.

7. Judged by surnames, 15% of all 1790 households left before 1800; relatively few of them owned slaves. A typical deed transferring 253 acres showed four owners in 22 years. Departure rate was highest, nearly 33%, for those household heads who were the only ones of their surname. Local researchers believe that substantially more than 15% of white settlers left the area before 1800. Whites blithely ignored some laws. They did not rigidly enforce required passes for slaves and had a thriving but illegal distilling industry in later decades. Later, officials often failed to submit required reports to the state superintendent of education; similarly, Baptist church clerks—white and black—often did not send annual statistics to their respective associations. And in the 1870s AOP counties sometimes were not represented in various white and black statewide political groups. The word "maverick" derives, in fact, from a prominent Pendleton slave owner, who moved to Texas.

8. That area north of the geographic fall line and west of the Broad River constituted a new Ninety Six Judicial District. Rapid population growth prompted the creation of six counties in 1785 within Ninety Six, then two more counties, Pendleton in 1786 and Greenville in 1789. The Cherokee lands ceded in 1777 were temporarily attached in 1785 to Abbeville, Laurens, and Spartanburg counties. During the 1780s the Court of Common Pleas and General Sessions serving Pendleton was based at Ninety Six as part of the Ninety Six Judicial District. Two years later Pendleton and Greenville together constituted in 1791 a new district, Washington, whose seat was at Pickensville. Useful maps showing these changes appear in Beth Ann Klosky, *The Pendleton Legacy* (Columbia, S.C.: Sandlapper Press, 1971), 30; cited as Klosky.

In the late 1790s the legislature abolished the term county (and county courts) and made most existing counties, including Pendleton and Greenville, into independent judicial districts (eliminating Washington District). Legislation dealing with land grants, courts, and county and district organization appears Thomas Cooper and David J. McCord, eds., *The Statutes at Large of South Carolina* (Columbia, S.C.: A. S. Johnston, 1836); cited as Cooper and McCord; see 4:590–710; 5:191, 240; and 7:211–300.

9. Thus including both the 1780s before Pendleton was separated from Abbeville and the 1790s when it functioned as Pendleton County, while courts served the larger Washington District. Although Oconee was not created until 1868, that area was by 1800 a separate militia regiment; most antebellum records are fairly clear as to which parts of Pickens District—the later Oconee or Pickens counties—are being treated.

10. Forts: Ninety Six farther south in Abbeville County, Rutledge in the area later known as Clemson, and Prince George farther up the Keowee River.

11. "Charleston and Hamburg are the two principal markets of this district [Pendleton]"; Mills, *Statistics*, 611.

12. Wood, 106–7; "Journal of General Peter Horry," Wood, 97. Anne McCuen et al., comp., *Abstracts of General Sessions Court Case Rolls: Washington District, South Carolina, 1792–1799; Greenville County, South Carolina 1787–1799* (Greenville: Greenville County Historic Preservation Commission, 1994), 193; cited as McCuen.

13. Colonel John Moffett (Revolutionary War), the major exception, had fewer slaves (7) in 1810 than in 1800. Dunaway (70) projects a very large percentage of landless persons in Pendleton District from 1790 to 1810, figures higher than those by local researchers. Her calculations for later decades are higher also than those in West, "Yeoman to Redneck." Dunaway and Thomas D. Russell are both contributing to the study of South Carolina's antebellum economic structure and its relationship to the law and to slavery. See, e.g., "The

Antebellum Courthouse as Creditors' Domain," *American Journal of Legal History*, July 1996, 331 ff.; cf. Willie, *Deeds*, 380.

14. The average land holding (whether owned or not) in 1800 seems to have been about 24 acres—both cleared and uncultivated—per person, or 160 acres per household. Records of taxation appear in annual volumes of the legislative *Reports and Resolutions*. Families known to have grown rice—McElhenney and Colhoun—came from the lowcountry, as did their slaves, already familiar with its production.

15. Punctuation added; John Ewing Colhoun Papers, Southern Historical Collection (SHC), the University of North Carolina at Chapel Hill; cited as Colhoun, SHC. Andrew Pickens, April 7, 1802, to Colhoun, Pickens Family Letters, SCL.

16. DB C–D, 35; Willie, *Deeds*, 90; for further on Gilliland, see "Reasons for Emancipations" in note 11, ch. 3.

17. William A. Schapter referred to "gentlemen planters" with $50,000 to $100,000 worth of property "holding their own plows or driving their own wagons to market laden with the produce of their own fields." Schapter, *Sectionalism and Representation in South Carolina* (1901; New York: De Capo Press, 1968); cited as Schapter. But as recently as 1995, McCurry felt it necessary to state this point (48): "Surprising as it might seem, farmers could well have owned as many as nine slaves and still have found themselves dependent on family members even for field labor." Even a holding of twenty might include only four or five adult men, "full hands." McCurry's "nine" seems low to me; among Earle's 24 field hands, only one was a man; cf. table 2.4. Houses: McElhenney's and Pickens's wood-frame houses and Richards's brick house at Oconee Station, all still standing.

18. Dates based on church minutes (table 6.2) and histories: T. H. Garrett, *A History of the Saluda Baptist Association* (Richmond, S.C.: F. B. Johnson Publishing, 1896); George Howe, *History of the Presbyterian Church in South Carolina* (Columbia, S.C.: Duffie & Chapman, 1870), cited as Howe; and information from local historians. Since a specific reference can be readily found by date, further citations are not given. For early Methodists, see Francis Asbury, *Journal and Letters* (Nashville: Abingdon Press, 1958), vol. 2, passim; cited as Asbury, *Journal*. Shoal Creek church was perhaps then in what is now Georgia. Aside from these denominations, there were only a few antebellum Associated Reformed Presbyterian, Universalist, and Lutheran (Walhalla) churches.

19. No Pendleton District churches regularly reported separately white and black membership prior to the 1840s; numbers and percentages deduced from membership lists (often undated), minutes, and rare statements of figures. Hopewell was built circa 1797–1802.

20. *Pendleton Messenger*, Feb. 27, 1819; July 2, 1808; cited as *PM*. Hardly any other local instances of runaways involved more than one or two. Anthropologist Will Goins, whose ancestors lived in Pendleton District, is continuing research on Native Americans in the area.

21. McCuen, 69–70, 127–28; cf. A. Charles Cannon, "The Maxwells, A Pioneer Greenville Family," *Proceedings and Papers of the Greenville County Historical Society* 8 (1984–90): 187–97.

22. Colhoun Papers, SCL; cf. lists of "Negroes at the Mountain," 1795, SHC, and "Negroes to work" on 1797 "12 Mile Memorandum," SHC.

23. These concentrations have to be deduced from church minutes, land holdings, census records, and oral tradition. Additional clues come from polling locations; appointments of justices of the peace; and names of election managers and grand jurors. There is also a petition "The Senate and House of Representatives of the United States in Congress Assembled" (by residents of lower Anderson and upper Abbeville counties to have a post office established in lower Anderson), 2 Jan. 1802 (SCL); and a separately cataloged letter of same date in Colhoun Papers (SCL). Also some references and estate appraisals indicate where stores were located. Robert Mills discussed some early communities; cf. his *Statistics* and his adaptation

of an earlier Pendleton map in *Mills' Atlas: Atlas of the State of South Carolina, 1825* (1825; Easley, S.C.: Southern Historical Press, 1980).

The upper region of Pickens County, populated by folks who migrated through the mountains from North Carolina, has been traced (primarily on oral tradition, it appears) in Bert Reece, *History of Pumpkintown-Oolenoy* ([Pickens, S.C.?]: Miracle Hill Print Shop, 1970).

Descriptions: Klosky, *Pendleton Legacy*, 77; Frank A. Dickson, *Journeys into the Past: The Anderson Region's Heritage* (Anderson, S.C.: Frank A. Dickson, 1975), 51–52, cited as Dickson; summary of Hartwell (Ga.) *Sun* 1889 article in Rudolph E. Lee, "List of Old Time Suburban and Rural Homes in the Vicinity of Pendleton, South Carolina" (CU); and Klosky, "Varennes Tavern," *South Carolina History Illustrated* 1 (Nov. 1970): 15–19. Andersonville was destroyed by flooding in 1840. A large percentage of blacks lived in these concentrates as slaves and later as freed people; Mills, *Statistics* (675).

24. Based on analysis of 1790 and 1800 census listings. In fact it is usually impossible to know exactly who owned slaves listed with the head of household; I am treating slaves as if they all belonged to the head of household. Nearly one-third of slaves sold between 1790 and 1800 involved family transactions; based on Willie, *Deeds*. In 1790 there were 22 sets of households whose heads, sharing the same surname, owned the same number.

25. Jno. Green, 12 Mile River, March 6, 1792, Colhoun Papers, SCL.

26. Early FPC are discussed more fully in chs. 3 and 4; ca. 1800 Shoal Creek's 8 FPC. Local historians are researching a migration pattern of families from counties lying to the northeast into Pendleton District and subsequently into Georgia. It appears that this cluster had a significant percentage of craftsmen. Dacusville residents in the 1990s compiled an album of their community, a product focusing mostly on whites: *Down Home: Dacusville Yesterday, Today and Tomorrow* (Easley, S.C.: Dacusville Community History Project, 1995), SCL.

Chapter 2. Piedmont Peoples, Their Environment, and Their Work

1. Numerous early obituaries and tombstones indicate an Irish place of birth. See "Surnames" in ch. 14, pp. 237–39, about black usage of Scots-Irish surnames after emancipation. Pendleton District family names are taken from the 1800 census. In the 1850s arrivals of Germans who created the town of Walhalla slightly altered the composition, as did other Germans and Irish who worked on the railroad there.

Of the 125 AOP owners with 20 or more slaves in 1860, 99 families were already living in AOP by 1810. Of the 40 Pendleton District owners in 1800 with 10 or more slaves, only 4 seem to have left the district by 1810; in nine other cases the owner died and slaves were divided among heirs; in most cases the result was smaller holdings. Figures are based on identical surnames (usually male); if names of all wives' parents, as well as married daughters or remarried widows, were known, even more continuity would likely appear.

As size of holdings increased in AOP and other upstate regions, "a statewide planter community had emerged—a fact of crucial importance in the state's subsequent political history." John Barnwell, *Love of Order: South Carolina's First Secession Crisis* (Chapel Hill: University of North Carolina Press, 1982), 11; cited as Barnwell. Rachel Klein developed this argument for the latter 1700s: *The Unification of a Slave State: The Rise of the Planter Class in the South Carolina Backcountry, 1760–1808* (Chapel Hill: University of North Carolina Press, 1990); cited as Klein. Barnwell further notes (13) that non–slave owners were overrepresented in white out-migration of the 1820s–40s; that "increased the proportion of slave owners in South Carolina's population and concentrated the state's interest in preserving slavery."

2. Major sources about Pendleton District families appear in the bibliography ("Antebellum Anderson, Oconee, and Pickens Counties and Slaveowners") as well as Stewart, *1800 Census*. Others that have been published include Ackers, Alexanders, Blassingames, Browns,

Calhouns, Earles, Kays, Maxwells, and Pickens; available at either Anderson County Library, CU, PDC, or SCL. The PDC and Faith Clayton Room at Southern Wesleyan University (Central) have numerous donated family files, not always authenticated.

See ch. 8, "Broader Horizons: Charleston Connections and Literacy," pp. 137–38. It is easier to calculate the numbers of blacks who moved into AOP after 1865—or at least were born outside of South Carolina, about 2%—than to estimate the numbers who moved away. See table 14.2 for number of blacks living in AOP in 1870 who had been born elsewhere, about half of them in Va. and nearly 10% in N.C. Note also "Cotton, Not Yet King," pp. 45–47, for lowcountry ties to the area's rice production.

3. Rachel Klein (235) suggests that owners who in the 1760s lived in areas of South Carolina farther to the east and southeast bought sizable numbers of newly imported slaves. But Pendleton masters, arriving later, do not seem to have done so. There, slaves most recently arrived from Africa probably came by way of Virginia after one or more generations there.

Monemi and Polydore, shown in various lists made by John E. Colhoun (Sr.) in the 1790s, previously belonged to his father-in-law (Samuel Bonneau, d. 1792); 1792 and 1797 listings include seven of their children. Owning more than 100 slaves, Colhoun mentioned in his will only twelve as specific bequests, four of them Polydore's children. "Old Monimia" was probably the woman listed as 110 years old in the 1850 census. *The Papers of John C. Calhoun* (Columbia: University of South Carolina Press; various editors) 17:14, cited as *JCC*; New York *Herald*, July 26, 1849. Cf. "African Americans on the Colhoun and Calhoun Plantations" in ch. 9, pp. 147–56.

4. The oldest in 1880 was Colign Ombero Taylor (b. 1770); Charity Bozeman, Anderson County Coroner's Inquisition, June 11, 1880 (SCDAH). Over 50% with one parent from Africa had another born in Virginia plus a few from Maryland and the District of Columbia. Most other parents were South Carolina natives, but one came from Alabama, another from France.

Apparently many of these Africa-born parents were brought to South Carolina from Virginia and Maryland, perhaps in the 1820s. They were acquired by a few eastern and central Anderson County owners, a clustering strongly suggesting a specific migration or large-scale purchases at one time. A former slave from Chester told of his father being "bought out of a drove of slaves from Virginia," which evidently happened between the 1820s and the mid-1840s. WPA 2, pt. 4, 51; see note 5, ch. 8, on WPA citations: George P. Rawick, *The American Slave: A Composite Autobiography* (Westport, Conn.: Greenwood Press, date varies). Both Charles Ball and Solomon Northup, although free, tell of being seized by traders and brought to South Carolina and Louisiana, respectively: Charles Ball, *Fifty Years in Chains; Or, The Life of an American Slave* (1858; Miami: Mnemosyne Publishing, 1969); Solomon Northup, *Twelve Years a Slave: Narrative of Solomon Northup* (1853; Baton Rouge: Louisiana State University Press, 1968).

A York County man, John Springs, went to Maryland in 1821 and "returned with 41 likely Negroes 19 Men and boys and 22 Women & Girls about $10200[.] Sold the whole to Judge Smith amounting to 15425." Springs Day Book in Davidson Family Papers, SHC; see also Templeman & Goodwin (a Richmond firm), "Account Book," 1849–1851, SHC. Numerous respondents in WPA interviews and depositors to the Freedmen's Savings Banks reported that they or their parents had been sold by traders from Virginia. Oral tradition among black families in many states recalls ancestors' fears of being "sold South," something repeated to me as late as 2001. Cf. WPA, Maryland, 53.

5. Elizabeth Donnan, *Documents Illustrative of the History of the Slave Trade in America*, 4 vols. (1930–35); Philip D. Curtin, *The Atlantic Slave Trade: A Census* (Madison: University of Wisconsin Press, 1969); Walter Minchinton, Celia King, and Peter Waite refined Donnan's

figures and extended them into later decades: *Virginia Slave-Trade Statistics 1698–1775* (Richmond: Virginia State Library, 1984). Daniel C. Littlefield's *Rice and Slaves: Ethnicity and the Slave Trade in Colonial South Carolina* (1981; Urbana: University of Illinois Press, 1991) reflects a trend to combine statistical information with a cultural context. Both Curtain and Littlefield, among others, have tables of African origins for specific time periods and New World destinations. John Barnwell (4) observes that South Carolina imported more slaves directly from Africa compared to other North America mainland colonies. See also *Family across the Sea*, a 1991 documentary produced by S.C. Educational Television, that traces links between Sierra Leone and the lowcountry, as have exhibits at Charleston Museum and South Carolina State Museum.

6. Joseph Africanus: DB L, 401; "Names of Slaves" in ch. 9, pp. 145–47. George Washington Boggs sent Celia to Liberia in 1832; George Washington Boggs to brother Thomas G. Boggs. A temperance pledge in the same collection lists "Celia Boggs" with a later notation, "gone to africa." Thomas Gilliland Boggs, Family Papers, SCL.

7. Harris's "boys making baskets," Feb. 12, 1858; David Golightly Harris, *Piedmont Farmer: The Journals of David Golightly Harris, 1855–1870*, ed. Philip N. Racine (Knoxville: Univ. of Tennessee Press, 1990), 74; cited as *Piedmont Farmer*. Elbert Brown (b. 1895), a Pendleton resident, was selling fish baskets of African derivation (with perhaps some Catawba influences) in the mid- to late-1900s; see photograph of him and his basketry in Clyde H. Smith, *South Carolina: A Scenic Discovery* (Durham, N.H.: Foremost Publishers, 1984). Williamson in *Crucible* (37) emphasizes adaptation by Africans relocated in North America to the local environment, which resulted in local variations among African Americans.

See sociologist John Coggeshall on "complex relationship of mutual avoidance coupled with mutual dependency" and African Americans' "white companions, often working alongside them, shared stories and beliefs about ghosts and gardens and often ate the same goods prepared by the same black cook." Indicative of recent trends in scholarship about southern culture, Ted Ownby's *Black and White Cultural Interaction in the Antebellum South* has several articles that analyze inter- and cross-cultural relationships. Collectively the authors argue that much cultural transmission took place in both directions. They also, as a group, comment on how much we do not yet know about the subject.

Two observations by Joyner (*Cultural Interaction*, 12–15) provide useful insight, although I am applying them in a different context than he intended. Discussing the varied African backgrounds of slaves "of such places as the Carolina and Georgia lowcountry," he indicates that in these locations they met "more Africans from more ethnic groups than he or she would encounter in a lifetime in Africa." And then their "varied African cultures were fused increasingly" in "a new culture, predominantly African in origin." I suggest, however, that in AOP with a small black population, that this "new culture" had stronger elements from the dominant white contribution than in the locations Joyner describes. If, in the lowcountry, "European settlers far more often encountered old African cultures there than African settlers encountered old European cultures," as Joyner argues, then it seems likely that the reverse occurred in AOP, where most white and black—and the latter in many cases several generations American-born—arrived at the same time. Coggeshall, 34, 223; Wood, 97.

Williamson (*Crucible*, 37–41) talks about interchanges of black and white culture from gumbos to miscegenation. Like many others, Joyner (*Down by the Riverside*, 202 and elsewhere) talks about the mingling of cultures, including the blending of English words and African grammar. Various observers note that some supposedly "black" expressions are derived from English and Scots-Irish usage; these lingered among blacks past widespread white usage.

8. Ch. 9 includes a case study of Calhoun-Colhoun family slaves, their sources, and relocations; table 9.2 also shows fluctuations throughout a year. Cf. "Intermarrying Families of

Pendleton District," Craig Thompson Friend, "Frontier and Plantation, Pendleton, South Carolina, 1780–1830" (M.A. thesis, Clemson University, 1990), 79; cited as Friend.

9. John Durant Ashmore's "Book, 1853–59" (SHC) is available on microfilm (Records of Ante-Bellum Southern Plantations, series F); cited as Ashmore. Entries are arranged chronologically.

10. See late-1800s discussion about clout of interlocking landlord families in chs. 22 and 23. Daughter Sarah, on marrying Dr. O. R. Broyles, received 11 slaves from her father. Lucy married David S. Taylor; Mary, Richard F. Simpson (their sons and servants appear in ch. 11; he served in U.S. House of Representatives); and Caroline, Dr. H. C. Miller. Genealogies of these families appear in Simpson, *History of Old Pendleton District*. Lewis (ch. 11) seems to be Lewis Webb, household 280 in Pendleton Township, 1870 (near R. W. Simpson, household 277). Webb descendants still live in Pendleton today.

11. Robert Maxwell was Greenville's first representative to the state General Assembly, 1791; he was followed in 1794 by Elias Earle. Robert's son John Maxwell served in the General Assembly in 1828–37, 1844–45, and 1853. Elias Earle was one of the wealthiest men in Greenville and Pendleton Districts, Greenville member of the state Senate in 1798–1804, and U.S. Representative for five terms between 1805 and 1821. Two of his nephews also served as U.S. Representatives (*Biographical Directories*). Their 1860s holdings constituted about 2.5% of all AOP slaves, a much smaller percentage than for large lowcountry owners. Further on Maxwells in "Rural Communities" in ch. 18, p. 331 and notes 47–48.

12. Calhoun: The farmer hired "steadily, but one [free] Negro fellow at $5 per month" and other additional labor at harvest time for under $20. *JCC* 6:392. On Oct. 7, 1865, J. J. Norton made a similar observation: "If the Yanks can make a living without the negro, why cant we"; Norton Papers, SCL. Achates [General Thomas Pinckney], *Reflections Occasioned by the Late Disturbances in Charleston* (Charleston: A. E. Miller, 1822), 29–30. For more data and sources on life span and mortality, see "Mortality" in ch. 9, pp. 144–45; ch. 7 treats more fully the concept of slaves as property. "Servants": Mary Stevenson, *The Recollection of a Happy Childhood by Mary Esther Huger* (Pendleton: Foundation for Historic Restoration in Pendleton Area, 1976), 37 ff.; cited as Huger; Burton, 145. Compilers of the *Biographical Directory of the South Carolina House of Representatives* and *Senate* companion volumes routinely listed slaveholdings as a measure of wealth.

13. Wendy Overly in 1990 wrote and directed "Telling the Old, Old Stories," based on BHUP oral history interviews. As I carefully watched the audience, most people—black or white—over 50 understood references that younger whites or blacks did not grasp. Cf. "Shared Experiences" in ch. 10; Lay: *Wills*, 92; Zion: Edward W. Simpson and Guy R. Everson, eds., *"Far, Far from Home": The Wartime Letters of Dick and Tally Simpson Third South Carolina Volunteers* (New York: Oxford University Press, 1994), 129–30; cited as *"Far, Far from Home."* A fuller exploration of a plantation as extended family appears in chapter 10.

14. Gassaway: 1880 Anderson, Honea Path Township, household 246; and Rice: Martin Township, household 192. Thompsons trace their ancestry to Irish-born George Seaborn and his slave Elizabeth (Betty), who "called her son by her maiden name, Thompson, instead of by Seaborn. Reuben married Martha Jones, a black woman from Mexico, according to oral sources." A younger woman, Mary—born 1850 in Texas—is listed as Reuben's wife in 1880. Evidently Martha died in the early 1870s and Reuben married Mary ca. 1874, as a son was born in 1875.

Reuben and Martha Thompson's son Stewart married a woman fathered by another slave owner. She was called Martha Ann Josephine Grisham. William Grisham, her owner, "was madly in love with" Nancy. Nancy's mother was Anna Knox (of "Indian and 'Other'" ancestry), whose husband was Martin Harris. Grisham "tried many times to seduce her [Nancy] when his wife, Josephine, was away. . . . He finally carried out his aim . . . [by] rape" that resulted in Martha Ann Josephine Grisham's birth. Nancy married (ca. 1867) John Reed, who lived near Walhalla.

Sources: Josephine Sherard Davis, "Facts from the Family Tree of the Thompsons of Pendleton South Carolina," July 1977, and "The Thompson Family Reunion, Pendleton, South Carolina, July 1–14 1985" (comp. not stated); both SCL. The 1870 census lists Reuben as a carpenter, and descendants still have some of his tools; Edinburg (b. ca. 1818) indicated his ancestor's foreign birth in the 1880 census and probably was Reuben's brother; there was also a Moses (b. ca. 1805). The 1880 census shows Mary, wife of Reuben Thompson, as born in Texas ca. 1850.

15. C. Vann Woodward, ed., *Mary Chesnut's Civil War* (New Haven: Yale University Press, 1981), 29; cf. quotation from William Pickens and other comments on slave mistresses and mulatto children, "Interracial Sex" in ch. 10, pp. 171–72.

16. *Wills*, 28, 65, 87, 92; cf. Helen H. Catterall, ed., *Judicial Cases Concerning American Slavery and the Negro*, vol. 2 (Washington: Carnegie Institution of Washington, 1929), 381–83; cited as *Judicial Cases*; and E. M. Lander, *The Calhoun Family and Thomas Green Clemson: Decline of a Southern Patriarchy* (Columbia: University of South Carolina Press, 1983), 156–57; cited as Lander.

17. At Anderson Presbyterian Church, Allen (W. Harrison) was "under censue & Sold by his Master & removed from state" (notation on church roll); cases of banishment appear in ch. 5; *JCC* 11:232, 668–69.

18. *JCC* 5:152. Virtually no analytical information exists about AOP's antebellum agriculture, with not much more for the 1865–90 period. Scattered information appears in estate records, correspondence (esp. John C. Calhoun's), and newspapers. Four men recorded some details about their farming practice; they are (in descending order of information) David Golightly Harris (cited as *Piedmont Farmer*), John C. Calhoun (cited in "Introduction: A Piedmont Setting"); Washington Taylor, *A Diary of Transactions of Washington Taylor, 1835–1855, Greenville County, South Carolina* [Frederick, Md.: H. G. Taylor, 1988], cited as Taylor; and John D. Ashmore (cited above). See also Joseph Davis Applewhite, "Some Aspects of Rural Society in South Carolina in 1850" (Ph.D. diss., Vanderbilt University, 1949); cited as Applewhite; Anderson is one of three counties in his study.

Statistics in this chapter on antebellum agriculture and manufacturing production come from my calculations based on the 1820–60 censuses, especially from printed summary figures. I have used AOP's full 1850 and 1860 Agricultural Schedules. Occupations are listed in the Population Schedules.

19. Williamson observes that Africans were shaped, in various parts of America, partly by diverse geographic regions and "created lifestyles that had least to do with color of skin." *Crucible*, 37; cf. notes 23 and 24 below on local self-sufficiency, defined in various ways. Quotation from Lawrence T. McDonnell, "Work, Culture, and Society in the Slave South, 1790–1861," *Cultural Interaction*, 129; he also refers to labor in industries; see note 24 on *Mountain Masters*.

20. Pendleton and Anderson in 1850 each had only a few hundred inhabitants; Pickens was a small village of perhaps one hundred. Each had a hotel or two, one or two general stores, lawyers' and doctors' offices, a blacksmith's shop, a few specialty stores, churches, and, except Pendleton, courthouse functions. Some current research, such as that by Wilma Dunaway, argues that there was more distant trading than earlier authors have suggested. *JCC* 25:433; and Pendleton County Court Minutes, 30–31. Robert Mills discussed (1826) Pendleton District's navigable rivers and streams: *Statistics*, 675–76; see also Ford, *Origins of Southern Radicalism: The South Carolina Upcountry, 1800–1860*, 15–19.

21. For a complete survey of Oconee and Pickens 1850 free craftsmen and professionals, see W. J. Megginson, "1850 Pickens District Professions, Skilled Crafts, and Trades," *Pickens*

District . . . 1850 Census (Central: Old Pendleton Genealogical Society, 1995), 2 vols. The 125 men owning slaves had a rounded average of ten each, with lawyers having 21, merchants 16, physicians 14, clergy 8, carpenters 5, blacksmiths 4, and teachers 4. Two-thirds of physicians and clergymen and almost as many merchants owned slaves. Burton's chapter 2 portrays a similar agricultural dominance in Edgefield. On white occupations, see also West, "Yeoman to Redneck," ch. 1, and esp. 36, 42, 57, 72–78; his table 1.1 (36) shows an increase in Pickens-Oconee's white agricultural work force between 1850 and 1860.

22. 1870 census: Honea Path Township, household 80, and Centerville Township, household 33, both Anderson County; Wagner Township, Oconee, households 130 and 131. Pendleton's white employers Cyrus Stephens, Chancey Stephens, and Jno. B. Sitton hired, collectively, 20 "hands" (Industrial Schedule). It is not clear how many were black. Ch. 3 explores FPC occupations.

23. Those lacking land equaled nearly 40% of farmers in Pickens, 45% in Oconee (1850); 900 households in farming, but not listed in the Agriculture Schedule, evidently were tenants (enumerators did not use terms such as "farmer," "planter," or "farm laborer" consistently among counties or in different years). Five hundred Pickens and Oconee "farmers" had real property valued from $100–$1000 but no slaves. Several farmers without land owned slaves, worked presumably on rented or family land. Some men who did not own land at any given time were sons or sons-in-law of landed families and expected to inherit a plantation that they in many cases already occupied and worked. But many were truly landless; see Burton, McCurry, and West.

Burton, Ford, and West—among others examining upstate South Carolina agricultural production—have used various "self-sufficiency" formulas, based on earlier scholarly constructions. These may be useful indicators for entire counties or districts, but less so for specific cases.

It is impossible to estimate the number of people involved in a nonslave farm, as hired farm laborers and, based on census listings, unlanded relatives may have shared work and produce on some farms—complications ignored in several published works.

Using a traditional definition of "planter" as someone owning 20 or more slaves, I have followed in the footsteps of Klein, Ford, and Burton; some scholars have argued different standards. Although 20 seems a reasonable dividing line among layers of white slave owners. it hardly seems appropriate to describe an owner with only, say, 5 or 6 adult male field hands as a "planter." Burton adds a higher level, "wealthy," for those with 50 slaves or more. (Burton, Joyner—19, 35—and McCurry, among others, divide holders of wealth into quadrilles; and McCurry—54, 95—adds additional categories of planter elite and great planters.) By that standard, 9 men in 1860 qualified in Oconee, 6 in Anderson, and 4 in Pickens. But Elias Earle, with 44 slaves in Anderson County and 46 in Oconee, certainly belongs to that class. Four Norris men, together owning 105 slaves in holdings that ranged from 23 to 30, were more prestigious and perhaps more affluent than some "wealthy" owners. These figures all ignore the amount of debt that many owners incurred. Quantifications obscure extended families and perceived community standing.

My figure 40%–45% applies only to those listed in the agricultural census; the previous paragraph refers to 35% of "all households," including those without occupation or those with skilled crafts but no land. Philip Racine calculates that 44% of those listed in the Spartanburg Agriculture Schedules did not own land; *Piedmont Farmer*, 505, note 19. See also Burton, 48–52, 109–14.

24. Price ratios clearly illustrate what was local and relatively cheap, or what had to be shipped and was more costly; see table in Friend, "Frontier and Plantation," 72. *Mountain Masters* discusses the business of raising and moving livestock for sale. "Self-sufficiency" takes on more specific definitions. Farmers raised much of what they needed, then bartered with

neighbors for other items (even newspaper subscriptions); currency was often in short supply. *Keowee Courier* (cited as *KC*), Jan. 5 and 12, 1850, cited in West, "Yeoman to Redneck," 65.

25. By 1840 Anderson had the state's second-largest wheat production, approximately 6 bushels for each person, while Pickens and Oconee raised about half as much per capita; similar figures applied in 1850. "Basic": R. A. McLemore, ed., *A History of Mississippi* (Jackson: University and College Press of Mississippi, 1973), 343; cited as *History of Mississippi*.

26. John Ewing Colhoun operated a distillery on his plantation in 1802, when there were 900 gallons of liquor on hand. AOP's apparent later decline in distilling is suspicious; early agricultural and manufacturing statistics in the census schedules are incomplete and perhaps not accurate; cf. West, "Yeoman to Redneck," 176. See Broyles estate advertisement including a stiller, *PM*, Nov. 7, 1845; labor contract with a freedman for distilling, by Cooley & Cauldin, Jan. 1, 1866 (National Archives RG 105/3073; ch. 12); and postbellum black-white distilling in ch. 18.

27. Taylor; *Piedmont Farmer*, 81.

28. MFH, PKNS, Kin, 1839 (see note 1, ch. 5, for MFH citations); *JCC* 10:257; 11:556; 15:417; 24:535, 469; Mills, *Statistics*, 684; and for Hunt, Pauline Young, *A Genealogical Collection of South Carolina Wills and Records* (Greenville, S.C.: Greenville Printing, 1955, and Easley: Southern Historical Press, 1984), 1:204; 2 vols.; cited as Young, 1 and Young, 2.

29. Donna Roper, "To Promote and Improve Agriculture: A Study of Four Antebellum South Carolina Farmers' Societies" (M.A. thesis, University of South Carolina, 1989), 17, 20–21 (opposition to manuring), 33, 40, and passim; cited as Roper. Illustrated advertisements for machines appeared occasionally in the *PM* and in the 1850s *Farmer and Planter* and *KC*; see also *JCC*: 10:46; 11:260, 556; 21:598; 24:395; *Wills*, 341, 386–87; DB M, 201; cf. *KC*, Dec. 7, 1867.

Reflecting social standing, these "farmers" groups had physicians and clergy among their members; 1854 *Farmer and Planter*, quoted in Roper, 6, 7. Other agricultural journals, most short-lived, are mentioned in a draft MSS on agricultural history, William Hayne Mills Collection, CU.

30. Non-slave owners Daniel Simms sold two cotton machines along with his livestock in 1804, and James Edmondson Jr. sold "one 32 saw cotton gin," livestock, and corn a year later. When Elias Earle bought land in 1813, his purchase included a cotton machine as well. Packing: Alex. Noble to JEC, 12 Aug. 1802, Colhoun Papers, SCL.

31. A belt of upcountry counties somewhat to the south of Pendleton and Greenville did support cotton monoculture in the early 1800s, until the soil became depleted by later antebellum years. They include Laurens, Union, Abbeville, Edgefield, Chester, Newberry, and Fairfield; Charles F. Kovacik, *South Carolina: A Geography* (Boulder, Colo.: Westview Press., 1987), 88–90; cf. Mills, *Statistics*. AND 6, 7; for cotton's rapid postbellum dominance, see "Town Origins" in ch. 18, pp. 312–14.

32. As early as 1800 a "cotton wheel and cards" began to show up in estate records and deeds; one household also had a flax wheel. DB F, 185; and J. S. Buckingham, *The Slave States in America* (London: Fisher, Son, 1842), 2:166, referring to an adjacent county in Georgia; cited as Buckingham.

33. Nobody compiled regular, systematic figures on the state's antebellum agricultural production; federal census data on agriculture and Lieber's reports are among the few sets available. Despite the critical importance of agriculture, the state first created a department of agriculture in 1880. Antebellum statistics on cotton come primarily from shipments at Charleston (thus excluding upstate cotton shipped to Hamburg and Augusta) and, except for federal censuses, ignore domestic consumption. Schapter, 16–57, observes a much broader

"curious ratio of the colored population to the white for regions raising certain crops." For details on Calhoun family, land holdings, and divisions, see ch. 9. Note, however, that increased late-antebellum holdings evidently resulted primarily from natural reproduction and from white marriage alliances rather than by large-scale purchases. More slaves, however, may have enabled larger cotton production rather than the opposite cause-and-effect process.

34. Rich cotton-growing Mississippi Delta plantations were producing 6 to 8 bales per hand (evidently based on "full hands," probably no more than a third of a total holding). If its figure (*History of Mississippi*, 312, 340) of an average hand picking 150 pounds of cotton per day holds true for AOP, that would mean each field hand picked cotton for about eight days. References to "farmers" apply to those listed in the agricultural schedule. Only 25 out of 351 Pickens-Oconee farmers with cotton in 1850 netted ten or more bales. Only half of Taylor's 56 or Sloan's 25 slaves would have been over 16 years old, and half of them women. *JCC* 15:318.

35. Calhoun, in 1836 netted $2192.19 from a shipment of 49 bales. In 1837 he and neighbors William Sloan and Elisha Lawrence "have between us two full boat loads," shipping their previous fall's cotton after holding it until the price rose. *JCC* 13:258, 499, 514–15, 645, 17:778; accounts, folder 2, Norris and Thomson Families (SCL) for examples of sales through Hamburg.

36. *JCC* 11:260, 470, 13:645, 16:636, 18:42, 26:383–84.

37. Nearly 450 of over 3000 farmers grew some tobacco, but only 27 had a crop of 350 pounds or more. Nine of them had slaves; only the four farmers with 1000 to 1200 pounds—AOP's maximum—owned more than 15 slaves. Phillips, *Transportation in the Cotton Belt*, 54–57, cited in Norman Gasque Raiford, *South Carolina and the Issue of Internal Improvement, 1775–1860* (1974; Ann Arbor: University Microfilms, 1993), 63. Buckingham (2:174), touring AOP in 1839, mentioned tobacco.

38. Much of it was grown by one farmer, perhaps a mistaken census entry. Four coastal: Beaufort, Charleston, Colleton, and Georgetown.

39. Payments by Harris (246) for supplies and white help appear in the back of the book (both his original and the published edition), evidently July 29–Oct. 4, 1853. Although Taylor and Harris, both with holdings of approximately 10 slaves, worked along with them, neither owner did so regularly. By contrast W. R. Colhoun (son of J. E. Colhoun Jr.; see ch. 9) sometimes spent weeks or months away from his plantation; his holding of approximately 70 warranted an overseer, however. Ashmore, Harris, and Taylor—each having 10 slaves—shed light on a median-sized holding and its agricultural scale. See Burton on white agricultural work, passim, esp. 63–64, 115; Brackenridge: Young, 1:205; *Wills*, 92.

40. Calhoun cared deeply for his land and often directly supervised work. *JCC* 17:268; similar comments in Charles M. Wiltse, *John C. Calhoun* (Indianapolis: Bobbs-Merrill, 1944–51), 3 vols.

41. A "real good overseer" was hard to find; "there is little prospect to get one in this quarter," Calhoun wrote; *JCC* 24:597, 22:746–47. The Hammonds also changed overseers frequently (information from Carol Bleser); cf. Burton, 48, 52, 59, 61, 136, 145. See "Overseer's Day Book of a Small Plantation, 1822–1917" (Abbeville County), CU; cf. "Management of Negroes upon Southern Estates," *DeBow's Review*, n.s., 10:622, and advertisement for an overseer in the Abbeville *Whig and Southern Nullifier*, Feb. 28, 1833.

Affleck's *Plantation Ledger* contained forms for inventories and advice to planters on obtaining, supervising, and keeping a good overseer; published in New Orleans in the 1850s.

42. *PM*, Dec. 15, 1837; table 2.4 itemizes Samuel G. Earle's slaves, their occupations, and values, as shown in his 1848 estate appraisal; the 49 (including 6 infants) average $415.31 each, totaling $20,350. Blanks indicate that no occupation was listed. See note 13, ch. 17, in

about this Taber and a postbellum minister, Taber Warren. His 1870 Varennes Township (Anderson) household included wife Flora and son John.

43. *PM*, Feb. 10, 1819, Nov. 16, 1825. Similarly, Harris frequently referred to Ann, evidently around 20 years old, working in the fields and plowing; *Piedmont Farmer*, 15, 36, 57, 71, 140.

44. The types of documented, local skilled crafts were somewhat limited. For a much broader survey, see James E. Newton and Ronald L. Lewis, eds., *The Other Slaves: Mechanics, Artisans and Craftsmen* (Boston: G. K. Hall, 1978). Blacksmiths: AND 322; they may be Charles Gambrill and Solomon Perry in the 1870 census. Hand prints: information from Zachary Rice, an architectural consultant to the church; more about slave labor on railroads appears in chs. 5 and 8; "Occupations" in ch. 14, pp. 244–45, and table 14.4 deal with skilled freedmen.

45. Pickens, Oconee, and Anderson led at various times in fur hats and in value of hats produced. The 1850 census lists no tanners and only 11 men for AOP in the currier, sadler, or harness-making crafts; it appears, then, that much of the work was done by slave labor. See Mills, *Statistics*, 674–75; "Changing Population and Slaveholdings, 1800" in ch. 1, pp. 27–29; *JCC* 11:xxxii. Colhoun advertised (*PM*, Jan. 21, 1842), among several slaves for sale, "Mary, good Factory hand."

Chapter 3. The Puzzling Free Persons of Color

1. Samuel Lorenzo Malone, *The Sizemore Family Tree: One Man's Search for His Roots* (n.p.: privately printed, 1980), 93, 116.

2. Documentary sources for FPC include censuses for 1790–1880, wills, deeds, estate proceedings, civil cases, MFH trials, church minutes, guardianship files, and petitions to the General Assembly.

Studies dealing with FPC in S.C. include Wikramanayake's *World of Shadow* (Columbia: South Carolina Tricentennial Commission, 1973); H. M. Henry, *The Police Control of the Slave in South Carolina* (Emory, Va.: privately printed, 1914), cited as *Police Control*; Larry Koger, *Black Slaveowners: Free Black Slave Masters in South Carolina, 1790–1860* (Jefferson, N.C.: McFarland, 1985), cited as Koger; John Livingston Bradley, "Slave Manumission in South Carolina, 1820–1860" (M.A. thesis, University of South Carolina, 1964), cited as Bradley; sources on slave laws cited in note 2, ch. 5; an article by Philip Racine, "The Trial and Tribulations of Jesse Hughey, Free Negro," *Proceedings of the South Carolina Historical Association* (1985), 29–39; Powers, *Black Charlestonians* and *No Chariot Let Down*; Burton, ch. 5, "The Free Afro-American in Antebellum Edgefield"; and personal correspondence and visits with descendants of several FPC families (Oglesbys-Allens, Sizemores, Dukes, Hallums, and Paytons).

Anne McCuen has diligently searched for Greenville County documentary material on FPC. See her *Abstracts of General Sessions Court Case Rolls: Washington District, South Carolina, 1792–1799; Greenville County, South Carolina 1787–1799* (Greenville, S.C.: Greenville County Historic Preservation Commission, 1994; along with co-comps.) and *Abstracts of Extant Greenville, South Carolina, Newspapers concerning Black People, Free and Slave, 1826–1865* (Greenville: Greenville Chapter, S.C. Genealogical Society, 2000); cited as McCuen, *Greenville Newspapers*; further references to the *Greenville Mountaineer* (*GM*) come from McCuen's book.

3. Birth states were not included in census records prior to 1850, so this section is skewed toward those still living at that time. Others from Va. with approximate birth years are: Solomon Davison, 1770; Leonard Gwin, 1775; Ama Pugh, 1780; FPC Priscilla Timbers's free white mother, 1780; and Jemima Packett, 1789. Birth dates are calculated from censuses, which were often far from accurate.

4. Caesar's emancipation is reported in an 1813 petition to the Clerk of Court of Pendleton District by Jacob Chamblee to be appointed his guardian; but see note 11, ch. 6, on Caesar and Robert Maxwell. Hudnal: DB I, 51; additionally, he had "two negroes Charles and Violet [who were] to work to raise my small children"; freed Dennis Waters was to get "learning" and to be bound to a trade. O'Neal: 1850, 1860, and 1870 censuses offer conflicting information.

5. *Judicial Cases*, 269, 350, 357, 386, 400–401, 404; and by other jurists, 344, 358–59. O'Neall wrote in 1846 that "it would be difficult, if not impolitic, to define by . . . inflexible rules the line of separation" between FPC and whites; O'Neall, *Negro Law of South Carolina* (Columbia, S.C.: John G. Bowman, 1848), 6, 9. Cited as *Negro Law*.

6. Agusta: March 19, 1808, in McGaha, 35; Priscilla Timbers: Greenville DB P, 266; Q, 85; R, 38, 279; S, 13; Sizemore, PKNS DB R, 245. Payton MFH cases AND 92, 101, 103–4 (note 1, ch. 5, explains MFH citations). Jeffries's "oath" is unusually emphatic: "she is clear blooded and no mixture of any kind of blood is in her more than any other white person"; A. Seasor's will of 1804; Mary Jeffries's affidavit in 1808; and Ezekiel Holly's 1838 guardianship, Greenville DB S, 382. White Burdines were "ancient Methodists." Asbury, *Journal*, 2:266, 309; Sarah and A. Elizabeth Delany, *Having Our Say: The Delany Sisters' First 100 Years* (New York: Kodansha International, 1993).

One author, descended partly from Oconee black sharecroppers, has a lineage nearly as varied at the Delany family. Her forbears include a wealthy white Englishman, who bore a child by a slave woman, their son who married a white woman, and a black man with a Native American wife. Sheila Ferguson, *Soul Food: Classic Cuisine from the Deep South* (New York: Grove Press, 1989); genealogical information appears in small tidbits throughout her book; cited as Ferguson, *Soul Food*.

7. AND 299; one Greenville (DB X, 504) FPC, Nelson Patterson, proved his free status in 1856 with 1843 documentation from Virginia.

8. Peter in 1811 bought one lot of farming tools, a saddle, and bridle from James Hallum's estate for $9. Hallum's estate proceedings and DB H, 70: "When the negro found he was not free he runaway and was not got untill he died." Coats: "Early FPC" in ch. 4, p. 60; his are the only land deeds I have located for any Pendleton District FPC other than Hudnal's. No law forbidding black land ownership has been found—perhaps custom and common law rather than a legislative act.

9. Bradley (22 and passim) cites cases in which the owner's parentage of a slave was stated in petitions to the General Assembly. Thomas Farrar (DB O, 505–6) owned 9 slaves in 1810.

10. Ruth Oglesby's 1813 emancipation for her husband was not recorded until 1824. Racine, "Trial and Tribulations," 29–39.

11. Burdines and Douthets, who housed FPC, were early Methodist leaders; Asbury, *Journal* 2:264–65, 309, 744–45. Schapter says that about 1200 Quakers left South Carolina for Ohio and Indiana between 1805–19, partly as a protest against slavery; Klein, 250–51, 275; *Minutes*, Presbytery of South Carolina. According to. A. L. Pickens, Gilliland, the minister in the 1795 case, moved to Ohio a few years later; *Anti-Slavery and Other Memories of Old Richmond* (Paducah, Ky.: Meridian States Research, 1943), 35–41.

12. Many Pendleton, Greenville, and Abbeville District FPC had surnames of white Virginia families; cf. Paul Heinegg, *Free African Americans of North Carolina and Virginia* . . . (Baltimore: Genealogical Publishing, 1997).

13. Hopewell Presbyterian elder Robert Anderson indicated that he intended to write about slavery. Whether he would have opposed it—while owning 26 slaves—is not known, but his will did require heirs to treat slaves kindly, not to sell them away from his extended Anderson relatives, and not to break up slave families; for more on this, see ch. 7, this volume.

14. Rates and upper age limits varied; Anderson has summary lists for 1835 until the Civil War (with gaps).

15. The 1823 act was selectively ignored; Bernard Powers's *Black Charlestonians*, ch. 1; more about Vesey's revolt in "The Tense and Brutal 1820s" in ch. 5, p. 80.

16. AND 13.

17. Young, 1:205; Burdine (1841): PKNS. Courts ruled in several cases that patrollers exceeded their authority; *Judicial Cases*, 313, 321, 329, 365.

18. James E. Wooley, ed., *A Collection of Upper South Carolina Genealogical and Family Records* (Easley: Southern Historical Press, 1983), 1:28; 3 vols., cited as Wooley, 1, 2, or 3. See Tannery estate proceedings (1846; PKNS).

19. Lydia, 51, and Lucinda, 27, probably Lydia's daughter. See Koger and G. Carter Woodson, *Free Negro Owners of Slaves in the United States in 1830* (Washington: Association for the Study of Negro Life and History, 1925) and *Free Negro Heads of Families in the United States in 1830* (Washington: Association for the Study of Negro Life and History, 1925). In 1835 "Cesar Free man" was the only free man of color listed in Anderson's tax rolls. Roberts, missing from most AOP records, reappears in 1870, living in Greenville, and in 1872 as candidate for state superintendent of education, ch. 15. Payton debts: Anderson Inventory of Wills, Appraisements, and Sales, 4: 19 (SCDAH).

20. Applewhite (246–49) has several tables on Anderson's FPC farmers; cf. my table 16.1. The villages and towns were Pendleton, Anderson, and Pickens, and, after 1850, also Walhalla, Belton, Honea Path and Williamston.

21. Demonstrated by Bernard Powers; cf. a survey of FPC occupations—thirty types—in Charleston in 1819, E. Horace Fitchett, "The Status of the Free Negro in Charleston, South Carolina," *Journal of Negro History* 32 (Oct. 1947): 435; cited in Bradley, 90. For Edgefield FPC occupations, see Burton, 213–15; some FPC and slave occupations in Columbia are described by Moore, *Columbia*, 130–31.

22. Although parents of mulatto children enumerated in white households are not identified, numbers of these children in the 1850 and 1860 census suggest an increased incidence. If these children were legally free, their mothers had to have been also; cf. "Color within the Community," Burton, 216–17.

23. *Sizemore*, 48, 92, 93.

24. Declines not likely attributable to natural causes occurred between 1820 and 1830, when the state's number of FPC grew 16%; but Chesterfield dropped from 171 to 124; Greenville from 90 to 32; Marion from 86 to 44; Marlborough from 142 to 55; Orangeburg from 64 to 6; and Williamsburg from 57 to 26. Spartanburg's gain of 43 may reflect Greenville's loss; and Barnwell's increase possibly came from Orangeburg. Several districts rebounded during the 1830–40 decade. Burton (204–7) discusses numerical changes in Edgefield's FPC. Figures for 1850–60 (statewide gain of 11%) show further striking variations: "Population by Counties, South Carolina," U.S. Census, 1870, *Population*, 60, also used as source for the following:

District	1850	1860
Charleston	3861	3622
Chesterfield	218	132
Edgefield	285	173
Georgetown	291	183
Richland	501	439

25. "Cato Hallum" evidently is "Cato (free)," listed without a surname, sharing his house with a free woman of color near Anderson village in its 1830 census. Cato Hallum figures

again in ch. 13; he is mentioned in 1872 (Young, 1:16) and in a Common Pleas suit in Dec. 1873 (Pickens, Lucas Papers, SCDAH; see note 15, ch. 5).

26. Kenneth A. Whitney, *A Documented Afro-American Family History, Carey Pickens and Mary Hallums (1765–1910)* (N.p., n.d.); see photograph and references (12–13) to "Mary, who was as fair in complexion as any Caucasian" and could pass as white.

27. Michael P. Johnson and James L. Roark, eds., *No Chariot Let Down: Charleston's Free People of Color on the Eve of the Civil War* (Chapel Hill: University of North Carolina Press, 1984); *Sizemore*, 108, 117.

Chapter 4. Those Who Were Free Persons of Color

1. According to an affidavit in Coats's estate file (Anderson), John Owen of Granville County, N.C., owned Mary; evidently Coats bought her, as another affidavit says that he "did give Mary Smith her freedom."

2. Estate, Anderson District.

3. There is only one free Morris—Joberry Payton's son—in the 1860 census for AOP, Greenville, or Abbeville. AND 209, 309; see Anderson District, Coroner's Inquisitions, Jan. 7, 1858, on Morris. Bricklayer Morris Payton was the 18-year-old son of Joseph and Lucinda Payton, and grandson of Fanny Payton; AND 366.

4. See "Those Who Had Been Free Persons of Color" in ch. 14, pp. 236–37, and throughout ch. 17.

5. Correspondence and interviews with Elsie Taylor Goins and her son Dr. Will Goins.

6. Doctor Tom, according to the 1820 census, was over 45 and had his own household with twelve other FPC, perhaps including the Oglesbys. He lived near Aaron Terrell (white), a Shoal Creek member, as were the Oglesbys. "Doctor Tom" may have been the Tom freed (DB M, 401), along with wife Sukey, by John T. Lewis in 1815. Tom's story ends with his death in 1829 at James C. Griffin's house.

7. Routine papers documenting these legal affairs raise more questions than they answer; Dennis appears in only one record, and for most Oglesbys there are no surviving guardianship papers.

8. Young, 1:24; cf. households 49, 667, Pickens District, Western Region [Oconee], 1850; W. K. Easley's 25-page brief in his papers at SCL; the MFH file was found among Pickens District, Mixed Provenance papers (Lucas Papers, SCDAH).

9. In 1846 E. P. Verner, as administrator of Moses Shannon's estate, rented land to Jesse Oglesby for $7.50. Involvement of the two Verners and Johns is puzzling. Although they lived near Oglesbys for several decades, 1856–59 is the only period when they had recorded difficulties. Names of "others" are missing from surviving papers.

10. *KC*, Oct. 29, Nov. 5, 1859.

11. Dr. J. N. Lawrence, petition (SCDAH: 1852/112) to General Assembly Nov. 19, 1852, for payment for autopsy on Rachel Oglesby.

12. Born in Georgia in 1785, he was described as mulatto with a free mulatto wife, Patsey. A Shoal Creek Church member in 1812, he had his own household in 1820 with three other FPC and in 1830 with six others. Alphin/Olphin joined Shoal Creek the same year as some of the Oglesbys. His name was written as Allen Fosh in 1840 and as Alphin Force in 1850 Franklin County, Ga., censuses. Family genealogical charts show him as father of the younger Forch Allen.

13. Mary Allen's 1860 household included several, mostly younger, members. In 1860 Alfred worked for the Blue Ridge Railroad, while Mary, daughter Elizabeth, and Alfred's wife Martha were farmers; they owned $300 worth of land.

14. Punctuation altered with family consent.

15. Malone, *The Sizemore Family Tree: One Man's Search for His Roots*, 11; cited as *Sizemore*. The book consists of documents, photographs, census entries, genealogical charts, and transcriptions of oral history interviews (1977–79). Malone is the great-grandson of William Duke Sizemore.

16. The family's ancestor appeared in Pendleton District's 1800 census as Lovina Seyemore with three white children. Only ten FPC by the Sizemore name are in the 1850 census among three Pickens households, those of Rhoda Duke, of Sarah, 52, and of Polly, 28, the last two both black. In 1850 there were four FPC Sizemores in Anderson. None of the 1850 FPC Sizemores in Pickens or Anderson are in 1860.

William Duke was born 1804 according to the 1870 census, where he is listed as black, with Melinda and four mulatto children. "A black minister," William could have been Rhoda's son; *Sizemore*, 16, 120–36.

17. *Sizemore*, 49, 65, 132. According to the 1890 census of former Union soldiers (Pickens County, Special Schedule) William Sizemore was a 2nd Corp. in the 2nd U.S. Inf.; he enlisted Oct. 6, 1864, and was discharged Nov. 1, 1865.

18. *Sizemore*, 15, 33, 111.

19. Three older Arters, described in 1850 as black, were born in Greenville County in the early 1800s.

20. Henry, Temperance, and Isaac had moved into the Queensboro area quite recently, and other white folk were alarmed about their lack of livelihood, their morals, but mostly their associating with slaves. Anderson MFH-Vagrancy.

Supposed-vagrant Thomas Sizemore was treated as white. His charge was filed on the same day as was that of slave Abram (James Wardlaw) for misdemeanor; some of the same jurors sat on both cases, which suggests some connection. AND 247, 246. Sarah Sizemore in 1860 charged slave Cyrus (Joshua Sith) with stealing money from her purse. One witness did "not feel bound to believe prosecutor on her oath, has heard it rumored that pros[ecutrix] had a coulard child." AND 411.

21. John William DeForest, Freedmen's Bureau agent in Greenville, wrote about two women "living in the same cabin with a black family, the negroes occupying one end of the building and the Anglo-Saxons the other" and of white women with "mulatto children, others who were maintained by Negroes, and one who had a Negro husband." "The Low-Down People," *Putnam's Magazine*, June 1868, 704–10; included in *A Union Officer in the Reconstruction* (1948; Baton Rouge: Louisiana State University Press, 1997), 135–58.

22. AND 92, 101, 103, 104.

23. Richmond first appears in AOP records as a witness in 1824 for a slave trial, AND 9; cf. Fenton Hall (Sr.) estate. Nothing more is known about Narcissa; Mary Jane married Elijah Rice, a 38-year-old day laborer in the 1870 Honea Path census. Later generations of that family moved to Abbeville and then to Ohio.

24. The court affirmed Fanny—born of a "free white woman" (in Pendleton District according to an 1870 affidavit)—as a free person of color. AND 92, 101, 103, 109, 112, 349A; see Fanny Payton case in "Other Resistance" in ch. 5, p. 86.

25. Joberry was a witness in 1849. He periodically charged items and got cash advances from the John P. Benson Hotel, virtually adjacent to the Payton home. See its Registers (Anderson County, Master); Payton vs. John B. Moore, Payton vs. Wm. M. Osborne, Rolls 2429 and 2430, Court of Common Pleas, Anderson District, 1860; AND 349A; Payton, Sale Bill, 1867, Estates; all SCDAH.

26. A grandson said that "some of the Sizemores were radicals. . . . a few of them left town and went somewhere else to live." *Sizemore*, 90–91.

27. Earle petition to General Assembly.

28. A plausible match is Dinah Grant, who died in Feb. 1870 of "old age" at 100; other Grants appear to have been Lorton slaves in Pendleton; 1870 Mortality Schedule, Oconee County, Wagener Township. Also in Pendleton village, Margaret Maverick's surname and status suggest that she was free, so indicated only by the word "free" in vestry records (d. 1885). The census does not list her among FPC; neither of them paid FPC taxes.

29. Daniel Greer, 24, was listed in Newberry County in 1850 as a free black carpenter with wife Maria, 22 (Mary Jane Elliott evidently a second wife), and son J.C., 5. Mary Elliott acquired 122 acres of land, in 1827, and in 1850 was listed in Jane Smith's Pendleton household. See her will, dated Feb. 3, 1858, and proved Nov. 10, 1860. Both Margaret Maverick and the Mary Jane Elliott–Daniel Grier marriage appear in Edwin H. Vedder, *Records of St. Paul's Episcopal Church of Pendleton, South Carolina* (Greenville, S.C.: A. Press, 1982).

Chapter 5. Laws, Courts, and Resistance

1. Although all S.C. counties had MFH courts, only a few have surviving records. Approximately 550 cases—one of AOP's best sources for African Americans prior to 1865—span 1819–65 with a few for earlier years. Unfortunately files are both incomplete and somewhat scattered. Some references to what must have been MFH trials appear occasionally in other sources.

Cases for Pendleton District and its successor Anderson have been filmed by the SCDAH and are accompanied by an inventory. I cite these as AND plus number without repeating "MFH." Roughly 105 cases (plus 5 inquests and 3 cases dealing with white men), widely dispersed, have been found for Pickens District, even more incomplete. Some trial papers (1828–48) are still in Pickens courthouse storage; SCDAH has about 30 files; I have cited these as PKNS (for those held in Pickens) and PKNS SCDAH plus number (for those at SCDAH). Other cases appear in printed materials by Pauline Young (mostly 1850–65; cited as Young, 1 or 2).

Generally I have treated MFH verdicts as valid except when the stated evidence or other circumstances conflicted with the verdict and sentence; otherwise, it is impossible to verify their substance.

2. Since England's legal system did not encompass slavery, such measures were a New World innovation. South Carolina borrowed heavily from laws developed by Barbados and Virginia. The most convenient summary of South Carolina's "Slave Code" is that section of vol. 7 of Cooper and McCord, *Statutes at Large of South Carolina*, which ends in the 1830s; afterward one can consult annual *Acts* of South Carolina or use periodic compilations. Wood discusses most early laws in *Black Majority*, and many are referenced in Henry, *The Police Control of the Slave in South Carolina*. John Belton O'Neall treated the slave code briefly in *Negro Law*. Appellate cases appear in Helen H. Catterall, ed., *Judicial Cases Concerning American Slavery and the Negro*, vol. 2 (Washington: Carnegie Institution of Washington, 1929), cited as *Judicial Cases*. For white fears elsewhere, see essays in Orville Vernon Burton and Robert C. McMath Jr., eds., *Class, Conflict, and Consensus: Antebellum Southern Community Studies* (Westport, Conn.: Greenwood Press, 1982); and Ray Granade, "Slave Unrest in Florida," *Florida Historical Quarterly* 55:18–36. See also *Vogues in Villainy: Crime and Retribution in Ante-bellum South Carolina* and *Lynch-Law*, both cited in "The Tense 1850s" in note 2, ch. 11, as well as West, "Yeoman to Redneck" for a fuller exploration of crime that focuses primarily on white violence and other misdeeds.

3. Among these are Z. Taliaferro (ch. 2), Isaac Clement (1802), William Hunter (undated; SCDAH [n.d.]-1569-01), William May (1817), and James Liddell (1817). According to Douglas R. Egerton, *He Shall Go Out Free: The Lives of Denmark Vesey* (Madison: Madison House, 1999) 96, it was pressure from "upcountry agriculturalists" that induced the legislature to

reopen legal slave trade in 1803; it ended Jan. 1, 1808, by federal law. It seems unlikely that many of the 39,075 "Africans" (Egerton) who entered South Carolina during those few years actually reached the upper piedmont. A large majority of AOP blacks in 1880 with an African-born parent also had a Virginia- or Maryland-born parent, suggesting a port of entry farther north. Since foreign importation had been illegal for ten years, buying slaves from other states was the only source of additional quantities, other than natural reproduction. Conveniently there was a surplus in Virginia; note 4, ch. 2, and "Mobility" in ch. 14, p. 234, and table 14.2.

4. There is no single source for Pendleton District executions; no official file of judicial papers exists for that era. Will's hanging is documented in the John Ewing Colhoun Papers, SCL; the remaining ones are found mostly in owners' petitions (SCDAH) to the General Assembly for reimbursement: Barnett (Kennedy); Lew (John B. Earle); Wiley (James Anderson); Dot (Thomas Adams); Dave (John Burress); name omitted (Jeremiah Forester, Greenville, 1825); and Bob (Alexander Calhoun, Abbeville, 1825). Tildy's and Ben's trials appear in Pendleton's MFH files, 15 and 16. Lew's 1828 trial and execution begin Pickens's MFH records.

5. Highter, 60–70 years old, had a remarkable scar on his upper lip, other identifying marks, and spoke so badly that he could not be understood. An 1808 warning of five runaway slaves from one Abbeville owner—an unusual circumstance—surely indicates their intent to flee the state. Shoal Creek Baptist and Old Liberty Baptist churches, both located near the Georgia border, excluded two slaves for running away.

6. Kershaw MFH, folders 19 and 20; *Judicial Cases*, 307, 316 (original ellipses); cf. L. Glen Inabinet, "'The July Fourth Incident' of 1816: An Insurrection Plotted by Slaves in Camden, South Carolina," *South Carolina Legal History*, ed. Herbert A. Johnson (Columbia: Southern Studies Program, University of South Carolina, 1980), 209–21; and *Crucible*, 19. Joyner (*Down by the Riverside*, 233) discusses alleged insurrections, and Pearson in *Designs against Charleston* (76–77, note 7) deals with the depressed economy in Charleston.

7. There were MFH trials before execution, done by hanging; a slave who informed about the revolt was rewarded with emancipation; *JCC* 7:220–21. A flurry of books in the late 1990s set the revolt in a larger world of resistance: Edward A. Pearson, ed., *Designs against Charleston: The Trial Record of the Denmark Vesey Slave Conspiracy of 1822* (Chapel Hill: University of North Carolina Press, 1999); David Robertson, *Denmark Vesey* (New York: Alfred A. Knopf, 1999); Egerton, *He Shall Go Out Free*; and Michael P. Johnson, "Denmark Vesey and His Co-Conspirators," *William and Mary Quarterly* 58 (Oct. 2001): 915–71; each cited by author's surname. AME: Bradley, 17, 18, 46–48; Egerton, ch. 5.

8. For both church and MFH trials there may be some skewing simply because records are more complete in the mid-1820s than earlier.

9. Several instances of 1820s executions appear; see pp. 80–81 and notes 10–11, below. Quote from John Quincy Adams diary of November 30, 1824; *JCC* 9:xxii, 10:382. Orser, 28.

10. AND 15 and 16 for Tildy and Ben; Burress, Colhoun, and Forester Petitions to General Assembly; MFH files have not been found for those cases; for more on Free Hannah's murder, see "Glimpses" in ch. 4, pp. 63–64.

Caroline Olivia Laurens, who was visiting Greenville, recorded the 1825 event: *SCHM* 72:172; *Columbia Telescope*, May 23, 1825, by a Greenville writer; quoted in Lowry Ware, "The Burning of Jerry: The Last Slave Execution by Fire in South Carolina," *SCHM* 91 (April 1990): 100–107. I have not found any complete account; see the Charleston *City Gazette*, July 7, 1825, on governor's reward (proclamation of June 16); and Niles's *Weekly Register*, Aug. 27, 1825, reprinting from *Philadelphia Gazette*. The *PM* reprinted the Niles reprint. John Campbell was 15 years old when the event occurred; Greenville's *Enterprise and Mountaineer*, Aug. 16, 1882.

11. Ware, "Burning of Jerry." Gov. Manning opposed burning as a means of execution in his message to the General Assembly, Nov. 28, 1825, 21). Charles Ball, *Fifty Years in Chains; Or, The Life of an American Slave* (1858; Miami: Mnemosyne Publishing, 1969), 297.

12. PKNS SCDAH 4.

13. Any white person hiding a runaway could be prosecuted, fined up to $1000, and sentenced to one year in prison. Runaway slaves likely being harbored: *GM*, May 24, 1844, May 7, 1847.

14. West, "Yeoman to Redneck," 115–17; *PM*, April 21, 1827.

15. No MFH records for Dave have been found. Mattison: Anderson, Lucas Papers, SCDAH; more on the Mattison case appears below in "Influences," pp. 82, 94. During the earlier years of my research, SCDAH had several unsorted cartons of "Lucas Papers." Some of these papers have subsequently been transferred to "Mixed" or "Uncertain" Provenance files.

16. *AI*, March 9, 1865. Jane Edna Hunter, *A Nickel and a Prayer* (n.p.: Elli Kani Publishing, 1940), 46 (cited as Hunter, *A Nickel and a Prayer*); *Highland Sentinel*, Feb. 10, 1843; *KC*, April 27, 1861.

17. AND 133–35. Passes and attempts to reach a free state: *GM*, Sept. 10, 1830; July 30, 1831; July 23, 1847; and July 7, 1848. 70-year-old Tim fled from Greenville; March 11, 1852, *Southern Patriot*; reprinted in McCuen, *Greenville Newspapers*.

18. Pendleton Farmers' Society, Committee on History, *Pendleton Farmers' Society* (Atlanta: Foote & Davies, 1908); the story reflects great attention to the Civil War and subsequent romanticizing of slaves (often called "old time darkies") as with Essex, p. 84.

19. AND 128, 136, 139, 151; 1853 PKNS: Willis, Big Henry. A story, perhaps exaggerated, is found in a WPA narrative (Tom Hawkins, born Belton, South Carolina), Georgia, pt. 2, 131: "Niggers didn't run to no North. . . . One . . . lived hid out in dat cave 'bout 15 years." Treatment of black dialect is one criticism leveled against the WPA interviewers; see George P. Rawick, among other critics.

20. AND 208, 257; H. A. Johnson, *Sword of Honor: A Story of the Civil War* (Hallowell, Maine: Register Printing House, 1906), 33, cited as Johnson, *Sword of Honor*; A. Cooper, *In and Out of Rebel Prisons* (Owego, N.Y.: R. J. Oliphant, 1898), 156.

21. *On the Old Plantation: Reminiscences of His Childhood* (1924; New York: Negro Universities Press, 1969), 7–30.

22. AND 270–71; Sarah: PKNS SCDAH 7; Phillis: First Creek, Jan. 22, 1831.

23. Lathan Algerna Windley, *A Profile of Runaway Slaves in Virginia and South Carolina from 1730 through 1787* (New York: Garland Publishing, 1995); Gutman, 238–39, 262–69; cf. Joyner, *Down by the Riverside*, 21–22, 27–28, 85, 225, 233.

24. This was AOP's most serious case of large-scale antebellum collective arrests and punishments; AND 101; cf. runaway slave inventoried in table 2.4. Court language: *Judicial Cases*, 434, 436. There were substantially fewer black McFalls in 1870 than slaves to the McFalls in 1860.

25. AND 252; muddled testimony. The formal charge involved insurrection; another defendant, Ned, was hanged. Mattison received Anderson MFH's most severe punishment—other than hanging—to date.

26. See ch. 2 on slaves' vested interests in producing food; cf. Joyner, *Down by the Riverside*, 50–51, slowing the work pace; AND 174. Dot was executed in 1818 for murdering her "child," perhaps older than an infant.

27. Neither Hester nor Massey was a popular surname for freed people. Hester families owned 33 slaves in 1860; there was only one household of 4 black Hesters in 1870. Two Sittons owned 22 slaves in 1860; three black households in 1870, including 6 people, used the

name Sitton. See "Parameters Affecting Black Political Activity" in ch. 15, p. 272, for arson of two white Sitton premises in 1873 and 1875; note burning of a Sitton house, discussed on p. 92. 1855 incident: PKNS SCDAH 5; PKNS, 1845, 1855; AND 352, 224; AND 191, 122, 72; PKNS. Adam, AND 92, 122.

28. AND 109, 112, 187, 226, 263; cf. *Judicial Cases*, 373.

29. One black man in 1811 said "I do not consider it stealing when a person eats, where he labors without compensation both night and day." Quoted in *Cultural Interaction* (72); cf. Joyner, *Down by the Riverside*, 106.

30. "Promise Land" quoted in WPA 1, pt. 1, 33 (Marlboro). There is a rich body of literature on black music beginning with Hampton Institute's collection and research after the Civil War. See, among many others, Albert J. Raboteau, *Slave Religion: The "Invisible Institution" in the Antebellum South* (New York: Oxford University Press, 1978), 243–66; and Joyner, *Down by the Riverside*, on use of music, language, and stories to disguise slave attitudes and resistance: 132–33, 172–95, 209.

31. *GM*, Aug. 24, 1849; *Carolina Spartan*, Aug. 16, 1849; Massey's slave, 1851, "Convergences"; pp. 87–88, and a successful murder in Spartanburg, MFH 1855.

32. "Relatively calm" if one does not count the nullification crisis, which was serious for South Carolina politics and its relationship to the nation.

33. See *JCC* passim, specifically 22:66–67, 453.

34. Jerry's execution in 1852 was for successful rape (record missing from Pickens MFH papers, evidenced only by executioner's application to be paid); Sam: *Yorkville Miscellany*, April 26, 1851; James F. Sloan Diary, SCL.

35. Governor Manning's 1825 message to the general assembly recommended that trials be held at the district courthouse "where the correcting influence of the public eye, and of public opinion" would be a safeguard; *Judicial Cases*, 404; Bradley, 100.

36. Writing his mother on Jan. 15, 1848, H. H. Townes reported execution of three slaves in Abbeville (Sept 7, 1835, Townes Family Papers, SCL). Cf. James F. Sloan, diary, July 6, 1855; James F. Sloan Papers, SCL.

37. 1850s: AND 234, 252; Jerry, Solomon, and Oglesby, all PKNS. Sam Oglesby's abortive execution in "The Oglesby Family" in ch. 4, pp. 63–64; cf. "The Tense 1850s" in ch. 11, p. 182.

38. Buckingham (2:168–69), writing in 1839, reports that the sheriff (Pickens District) a few months earlier hanged a slave for killing three white people. I have not found any relevant MFH case or claim by an owner for compensation. In late summer 1835 an Abbeville slave woman was executed for attempting to poison her master; her accomplice was cleared. Sept 7, 1835, Townes Family Papers, SCL; PKNS SCDAH 24; AND 325, 419.

39. Free Morris, mentioned as one of her sexual partners, was not charged with any offense; AND 309; Greenville MFH 32, May 26, 1860 (SCDAH).

40. AND, 279, 353, 181, 331; O'Neall, *Negro Law*, 28.

41. Patsy, 1852, PKNS; AND 74, 175; PKNS; AND 255, 273; Townes Family Papers, SCL; Narcissa Clayton Papers, SCL.

42. AND 56, 88, 61, 101; a total of 16 were convicted in the 1839 case (101) under two different charges; Andrew: AND 129.

43. AND 287; PKNS; AND 265, 266, 339. All cases in this and next paragraph from PKNS: James, 1861; Young, 1:175; and one case, divided in PKNS SCDAH 11 and 17. Mary E. Lyons, *Letters from a Slave Girl: The Story of Harriet Jacobs* (New York: Charles Scribner's Sons, 1992), 62.

44. Alexander in 1856 got 300 lashes and 12 months in prison for assault and battery with intent to kill. Further, Hamp in 1857 suffered 1,029 for burglary, Henry in 1864 had 700 for assault and battery, and that same year Harriet, as an accessory to murder, received 600 lashes. AND 20, 409; Willis, PKNS; Alexander, PKNS SCDAH 10.

45. AND 274; a case cited earlier led to more than 176 lashes—not counted in this context as official documents for that case do not survive; rather it appears in an unofficial source.

46. Total costs for several owners in one Anderson case ran $41.44; typical fees for whipping were one or two dollars; AND 101; cf. a Hagood-Hester civil suit, "Legal, Religious, and Moral Standards for Treating Slaves" in ch. 7, pp. 120–21 and note 24, ch. 7.

47. In 1842 Young Sawney "ran away," but actually only tried to accompany other Calhoun slaves being sent to Alabama. After Young Sawney was apprehended, "Mr. Calhoun writes me to have him sent out in chains to Andrew . . . [for] wearing a durk . . . to kill our Overseer . . . he might set fire to the gin house . . . Old Sawney, is at the bottom of all . . . a dangerous old Negro . . . . " Young Sawney was not on the Fort Hill plantation in 1854, although Old Sawney was. Floride C. Calhoun to Margaret M. Calhoun (Ala.), Feb. 8, 1842. *JCC* 15:116, 22:213–14, 24:311–13. F. W. Pickens to James Edward Calhoun, Aug. 4, 1833 (SCL).

Izzy and Young Sawney were children of Old Sawney. That name had both Hausa and Bini origins. Sawney, born ca. 1792–95, belonged to Calhoun's father and appeared as a boy in the elder Calhoun's 1797 estate. Reportedly he and Calhoun grew up together and worked Calhoun's father's land together. Irving H. Bartlett, *John C. Calhoun: A Biography* (New York: W. W. Norton, 1933), 37, 282–83; cited as Bartlett.

48. Broyles and Brown: AND 349, 350. Wade Dennis appellate case, *Judicial Cases*, 400.

49. Between 1822 and 1835 there were six such examples two to four months after alleged incidents. But Leah Moore's Buck was charged on Aug. 1, 1840, with stealing boots 18 months earlier; a patroller complained only on Feb. 15, 1847, that Handy had hit him on Dec. 29; and Robert Chamblee charged in Nov. 1860 that Massey's slave Thornton burned his still three years previously. AND 90–91, 190, 374.

Chapter 6. Churches, a Shared Setting

1. Antebellum midwives and skilled craftsmen also had special standing, but not as ritually sanctioned as those with religious titles. This discussion diverges from studies of low-country slave religion, which emphasize African continuities, and other studies of African American religious beliefs, not the focus here. Both the approach and conclusions also vary significantly from Randy Sparks, who presents a rosier picture of biracial religious worship in "A Mingled Yarn: Race and Religion in Mississippi, 1806–1876" (Ph.D. diss., Rice University, 1988).

This chapter—linked to control mechanisms including the MFH, societal convergences, and the slave communications network—uses a wider lens and consequently captures a different view. I have taken all available deposited AOP church minutes (see table 6.2), imposing, then, no selectivity of my own. This also grounds the story firmly within a geographical context, missing from most studies of antebellum slave religion. Cf. Henry S. Stroupe, "'Cite Them Both to Attend the Next Church Conference': Social Control by North Carolina Baptist Churches, 1772–1908," *North Carolina Historical Review* 53 (April 1975): 151–70.

Contrasted to the works cited in the bibliography ("Antebellum Religion"), I do not attempt to describe slaves' religious *beliefs*, for which I find too little AOP evidence to assess. My emphasis on their affiliation and practice may shed some light on that broader subject, especially given continuities after 1865. Religion forms a part of virtually all studies of southern whites; for areas nearby, see Burton, 21–28, 57–60, and passim; Vandiver's chapter on churches; and Huff, *Greenville*.

Joyner, as in many other areas, also sheds light on the subject. Although he and other highly regarded authors speak of Afro-Christianity, I am reluctant to describe upper-piedmont black religious practice by that term. A reading of postbellum black Baptist minutes and printed sermons (ch. 20) shows little variance from white Baptists. Certainly there is an articulated racial consciousness, especially by the 1880s; but rituals, sermons, hymns, and even exclusions

450 / *Notes to Pages 96–100*

of members for various offenses show a strong continuity from what blacks experienced in shared antebellum church settings.

2. A list appears as table 6.2. As these are available at depositories or archives and as minutes usually include only a page per monthly session, further citations are not usually necessary. *Minutes* of regional Baptist associations (notably Saluda, covering primarily Anderson County) and South Carolina Baptist Convention are similarly deposited. Anderson is best represented, Oconee second, and Pickens least. Most, 24, are Baptist. All 11 records for 1796–1830 are Baptist; the earliest Presbyterian one starts only in 1832. Ten Presbyterian churches are included, all from Anderson County. No Methodist church's records are known to be deposited. Fortunately vestry registers of Pendleton's St. Paul's, the only AOP Episcopal church with many slaves, have survived. Coincidentally, available records concerning early postbellum black churches are similarly concentrated for Anderson County Baptists.

Published church records include Edwin H. Vedder, *Records of St. Paul's Episcopal Church of Pendleton, South Carolina* (Greenville, S.C.: A. Press, 1982), cited as *Records of St. Paul's;* and Richard Newman Brackett, *The Old Stone Church, Oconee County South Carolina* (1905; [Clemson, S.C.?]: Old Stone Church and Cemetery Commission, 1972); cited as *Old Stone Church.*

3. Leroy F. Beaty, *Work of South Carolina Methodism among the Slaves*, 1901; and H. B. Browne, *Methodist Sunday Schools after a Hundred Years*, 1911, both pamphlets. Beaty, 3, 6–15; Browne, 3–5.

4. Keowee statistics: see Holstein Conference, Minutes (Wofford College).

5. By Richard Furman; printed in Charleston by A. E. Miller, 1823; SCBC minutes do not mention this message or convention discussion.

6. T. H. Garrett, *A History of the Saluda Baptist Association*, (Richmond: F. B. Johnson Publishing, 1896), 34; *Old Stone Church*, 53 (Dec. 1833); see also "Broader Horizons" in ch. 8, pp. 137–38; treasurer's accounts, "Pendleton Sunday School Society, Records, 1819–1824," WPA typescript, CU; for more on W. B. Johnson, see comments in Burton and in Joe M. King, *A History of South Carolina Baptists* (Columbia: General Board of the South Carolina Baptist Convention, 1964).

7. Shoal Creek's 1806 episode: "Interactions in Churches" in ch. 1, p. 26. Benjamin's owner is not named; he seems to be Benjamin Terrell; also missing is the owner's name for Mulberry (probably Mulberry Mauldin, "Postwar White Churches and Freed People" in ch. 17, p. 290).

8. Hopewell, June 1847, June 1850, and Aug. 1855: "Sarah (Rev. J. B. Adger's) rcvd on suspension from 2nd Presbyterian" in Charleston.

9. At least half a dozen Pendleton owners had some slaves attending Hopewell Presbyterian, but others baptized at St. Paul's. The undated pledge has approximately 150 subscribers, including 13 slaves, among them "Celia Boggs" (with a later notation "gone to africa") and "Jema[,] Pickens slave" (ch. 1). Thomas Gilliland Boggs, Family Papers, SCL.

10. Lot: Holstein Conference, Minutes (Wofford); cf. May 1848 "Sermon by frank a colored man," Mount Pisgah Baptist; and "Public Service by brethring Dolton & our colered brother," unnamed, November 1847, Old Westminster.

11. Caesar, according to affidavits and a twentieth-century newspaper account, was freed by Thomas Winslow of Randolph County, N.C.—date unknown, probably late eighteenth century. But Robert Maxwell also filed an affidavit about his slave Caesar who, for "peculiar circumstances," lived apart and was de facto free. These may be two men. Preacher Caesar's emancipation is reported in an 1813 petition to the clerk of court of Pendleton District by Jacob Chamblee to be appointed his guardian. "Caesor (free negro over 50)" and "Caesar's Polly" are among Anderson FPC paying taxes in 1844. *Wills*, 367–69. Maxwell's 1859 petition to the legislature referred to "Caesar Bennett." Caesar, who had died, bought land (with

Maxwell's permission) according to Maxwell's petition to have its proceeds given to "Polly Bennett and her children, the objects of Caesar's bounty." "Caesar had also purchased" Abram and his wife Polly, according to Maxwell. The court agreed. Anderson District, Court of Equity, June 1859; *Anderson Independent*, May 27, 1938. Spence: Big Creek, Aug. 1824; Aug. and Sept. 1825.

12. Jim (b. 1820 in Greenville) was converted in 1854, he said, and soon got an exhorter's license; his story continues in ch. 17. James A. Tolbert, *Christ in Black, Or the Life and Times of Rev. James R. Rosemond* (Greenville: Shannon & Co., 1902), 21–23; Rosemond's photograph is reprinted in Huff, *Greenville* (160ff.); *GM*, Feb. 17, 1897 (not from McCuen).

13. *Old Stone Church*, 15. Another elder, Andy [Cherry], appears in "1867" in ch. 13, p. 224.

14. SCBC, *Minutes; AI*, June 17, 1896.

15. Quoted from his book in Mary Stevenson, ed., *The Diary of Clarissa Adger Bowen, Ashtabula Plantation, 1865* (Pendleton, S.C.: Foundation for Historic Restoration in Pendleton Area, 1973), 48; cited as *Diary of Clarissa Adger Bowen*.

16. "The Hunnicutt Murder Crisis" in ch. 13, 225–28.

17. *Old Stone Church*, 59; AND 352.

18. Anna W. Marshall, *First Baptist Church, Belton, South Carolina, 1861–1961* (Belton: First Baptist Church, [1961?]), 18; AND 170; 169, Aug. 1845.

19. *JCC* 23:450. Friend (55–56) has tables of slaveholdings among the first ten elders at Hopewell Presbyterian and the first ten vestrymen of St. Paul's. In a WPA narrative Tom Hawkins (from Belton, South Carolina) said that the preacher told slaves that "'it's a sin to steal; don't steal Marster's and Mist'ess' chickens and hogs;' and such lak. How could anybody be converted to dat kind of preacher?" WPA, Georgia, pt. 2, 131. Pinckney: Susan Markey Fickling, *Slave Conversion in South Carolina, 1830–1860* (Columbia: University of South Carolina Press, 1924), 13–15.

20. Fair was an attorney, 38, in the 1860 census. *Southern Presbyterian Review*, 154–55; Clarke, *Wrestlin' Jacob*, which also features John B. Adger; cf. O'Neall, *Negro Law*, 23, original emphasis. Jones earlier published *The Religious Instruction of the Negroes, in the United States* (Savannah: 1842).

21. Second Presbyterian Church, "Records, 1847–1845," WPA typescript, CU, and newspaper clippings in same file; *Wrestlin' Jacob*; and Adger, *My Life and Times* (Richmond, Va.: Presbyterian Committee of Publication, [1899]), 348. "Adger" was a popular postbellum family and personal name.

22. Dickson, *Plantation Sermons* (1856) and *Lessons about Salvation* (n.d.); both published in Philadelphia, Presbyterian Board of Publication.

23. Exclusions: First Creek, July 1835, "Black Brother Dick" (Wakefield) for marrying while his first wife was still living; and Mount Carmel Baptist (Pickens), Joanna (William Bowen), April 1844, because she "had a living husband and has married to another man." Similarly, Bethesda Baptists (Anderson) cited in Sept. 1834 a "Black sister . . . brought to childbed" without a husband.

24. Evidently his slave Jude, excluded for "teling lies to injuer her master," instigated the story. According to Tom (John Harrison), Jude said that Cleveland committed adultery with Easter. Cf. Ben (David Barton), Shoal Creek, 1827; Judy: "Legal, Religious, and Moral Standards for Treating Slaves" in ch. 7.

25. Church minutes refer to the whipping; AND 85.

26. Based on those churches for which it is possible to track specific slaves over time. Membership rosters, initially created at specific times, later had names added to them without dates; often dates of deaths and exclusions were omitted in such lists.

27. Fifteen is used more specifically as an age bracket in published census reports of FPC and slave ages; Williamson (*Crucible*, 21) reaches a similar figure for the entire state.

28. 12 Mile River's earliest-available report, in 1867, was 7%, probably somewhat lower than in prewar years. Old Liberty Baptists got a sudden boost in 1812 when 120 people joined, 16.7% of them slaves, almost exactly their proportion of Pendleton's 1810 population.

29. 1842: itemized by slave name and date in *Records of St. Paul's*. An especially clear example of owner choice appears with Mrs. J. L. North; 10 of her slaves were baptized on Dec. 12, 1852; no additional ones until 7 infants and one old man, Nov. 18, 1855; another lapse until 7 on Jan 7, 1858; and no more until 5 on July 29, 1860.

30. Extended account of Bethel camp meeting in *Old Stone Church*, 52–54; Bethel's minutes recount the "solemnity."

31. A Sizemore (153) descendant described early 1900s events near Gaffney, South Carolina.

32. Jacob: Roberts minutes; cf. Charles A. Johnson, *The Frontier Camp Meeting: Religion's Harvest Time* (Dallas: Southern Methodist University Press, 1955).

33. Berry was sentenced to 39 lashes. MFH file, Anderson County, Uncertain Provenance, SCDAH; cf. references to snakeroot as a Pendleton District export to Savannah, Mills, *Statistics*, 675.

34. *Saluda*, 37.

Chapter 7. Ambivalent Interactions

1. I have relied heavily on wills and estate proceedings throughout this chapter. Unless otherwise noted, dates given are those when wills were written, as intentions are more important here than the owners' deaths. All wills and estates prior to 1828, unless noted, were in Pendleton District and are available on microfilm (SCDAH) and in WPA typescripts. Abstracts of all Pendleton and Anderson wills and summaries of estate proceedings after 1838 appear in *Pendleton District and Anderson County, S.C. Wills, Estates, Inventories, Tax Returns, and Census Records*, cited as *Wills*.

Pickens wills and estate records (including those for what would become Oconee County after 1868) are available at the Pickens probate office and on microfilm at SCDAH. Some wills and estate proceedings for Pickens and Oconee from Pauline Young appear Young, *A Genealogical Collection of South Carolina Wills and Records*, 2 vols., cited as Young 1 or 2; and from her records by James E. Wooley, ed., *A Collection of Upper South Carolina Genealogical and Family Records* (Easley: Southern Historical Press, 1983), 3 vols.; cited as Wooley, 1, 2, or 3. Appellate: *Judicial Cases*, 267–78.

2. Quoted in Roper, 36; West quotes Hammond's prescriptions for offenses he thought merited whippings, "Yeoman to Redneck," 105. See Joyner on the white owner as patriarch, dispensing rewards and punishments; 50–51, 56; cf. West, 43–44 and references.

3. 1843, Abbeville: F. W. Pickens, in Pickens Family Letters (typescript), ?; in 1813 William Hillhouse, transferring 8 slaves, described parents Dick and Catherine as "the stock from which the six (6) succeeding have sprung," DB M, 176.

4. Jan. 2, April 16, 1808; other hiring out, ch. 8. Contentious lease agreements: Samuel Maverick vs. Lewis & Gibbs, which reached an appellate court in 1825; 3 McCord 211–17. *PM*, Sept. 27, 1826; T. J. Pickens Papers, CU, f2.

5. *Wills*, 39, 54, 78, 97, 105.

6. Lucy: William Simpson's estate (PKNS). By contrast Wm. Clayton in 1858 did "warrant to be sound in body and mind and free from any incumbrances" two boys; loose paper in Faith Clayton Room, Southern Wesleyan University; Chapman: DB R, 180.

7. Samuel Earle's 1833 estate appraisal similarly list diverse roles; cf. table 2.4, Samuel Earle's Slaves and Their Occupations.

8. *JCC* 22:570; Henry W. DeSaussure to Floride Bonneau Colhoun, June 18, 1807, Colhoun Papers, SCL. Cf. ch. 23 for a slave family held, then sold, by Clemson.

9. Townes Family Papers, SCL: Jan. 31, 1839; Dec. 7, 1834; Jan. 13, 1836; Nov. 21, 1837; *JCC* 25:436.

10. *PM*, June 23, 1842 and March 14, 1845; Sitton Papers, SCL; cf. (note 13, ch. 1) Thomas Russell and Wilma Dunaway. Most data on individuals both owing and being owed money come from estate records; also Calhoun's and Thomas G. Clemson's published and private correspondence (CU); Calhoun's debt: "African Americans on the Colhoun and Calhoun Plantations" in ch. 9, p. 150.

11. People wishing to buy slaves could do so at sheriffs' or private sales; individual owners sometimes advertised one or more slaves for sale; and law firms found themselves holding and selling slaves for individual clients or for estates. "Negro traders" and dealers passed through the area, evidently at sporadic times.

12. Son John C. Kilpatrick Jr. died in 1840, leaving a wife and two infant children under 5 years of age; father John C. Sr. was executor of his son's will but died in 1843. Although the estate was not divided until after John Jr.'s son F. W. died in 1863, its managers sold several slaves in 1844 and leased out others. John C. Jr. willed several slaves directly to his wife Eliza Amanda Whitner; when she married John S. Lorton ca. 1842, he assumed management of the estate.

13. Mansell: Young, 1:72; Wooley, 3:74.

14. Anderson: WPA; *Judicial Cases*, 297 (quotation), 362, 367.

15. McCann: *Wills*, 71–72; Norwood: Wooley, 1:235.

16. *Wills*, 60, 69, 111; Asbury, *Journal* 2:264, 309, 744–45.

17. Neither Grief nor Peggy Pres(s)ly has been found in South Carolina in 1870—perhaps a covert emancipation; Hembree: estate proceedings.

18. Anderson: *Wills*, 44; Caradine: *Wills*, 54, 55; Reid: PKNS; Reeder: Wooley, 1:261. Greenlee: Wooley, 2:104; Reeder: Wooley, 1:262. Support: Greenleas, 1802, *Wills*, 28; cf. West, "Yeoman to Redneck," 51.

19. A complicated case involved a marriage settlement, leasing, other debts, removal from South Carolina, and several Pendleton families: Arthur S. Gibbes [trustee] vs. Jesse Cobb, E. M. Cobb, George Seaborn, and A. C. Campbell; South Carolina Equity Reports, Richardson, 7, Appeals in Equity, 55–76. Cf. Eaton estate, Young, 1:83–84, and *Judicial Cases*, 355.

20. Fears of families being so broken up at such a time run throughout WPA interviews with former slaves. "De ole plantation be sold, and de hands sold too, or we be divide.' . . . neber lib together no more." Joyner, *Down by the Riverside*, 230–31.

21. Like Hester and Sitton, Massey was not a popular postbellum black surname; 8 freed people were called Massey, compared to his 1860 holding of 22 slaves; cf. Vandiver, 266. On good/bad masters, see sketch (unsigned) of Winston Sherard in *Profiles of Black Folks*, 320; and Josephine S. Davis, "Origin and History of the Black Sherards in South Carolina" (typescript in Anderson County Library); conversations by the author with Viola Williams in Clemson, South Carolina, 1988–90.

22. McCurry (her chs. 4, 5) thoroughly explores the concept of family with a white male head to whom both white females and slaves were subordinated. James: 1853 PKNS.

23. Cresia: AND 239; Nero 93, 141; Baptist: Anderson District, Coroner's Inquisitions, March 10–12, 1863, slave Jane (Rev. Albert A. Moore); SCDAH. Whitner was not a popular surname for freed people after 1865: 19 black Whitners compared to 43 Whitner slaves (1860). O'Neall, *Negro Law*, 19; Cooper & McCord, 12:629–30.

24. Hester's slave Amy died ca. 1837. Hagood evidently said that she periodically ran away, that Hester turned his dogs on her (and perhaps killed her), and that Hester tried to prevent

her body from being examined. Hester then sued Hagood for slander. Attorney Benjamin Perry called three slave witnesses to support Hester. *KC*, June 6, 1857; AND 69; PKNS SCDAH (no no.); and Dr. O. R. Broyles, undated (1850s) petition to the General Assembly. Some Anderson slave inquests appear in the regular Coroner's series; two Pickens inquests are in Young, 1:94, 164; Racine, *SCHM*: slave Catharine "bears the marks of laceration and the scars on her limbs shew cruel treatment."

25. *Piedmont Farmer*, 140; Davison McDowell Papers, SCL; cf. Ashmore's flogging of his slave, "Other Resistance" in ch. 5, p. 86; Spartanburg MFH 271, cited and quoted by Racine, *SCHM*; WPA, Georgia, pt. 2, 130.

26. Blair, Abbeville, 1813: Young, 2:158; Douthet: *Wills*, 111.

Chapter 8. Carving out a Niche

1. Cf. Joyner, *Down by the Riverside*, 80: "Together they created and maintained, against frightful odds, a slave community." Important studies that deal with the same concept include Eugene D. Genovese, *Roll, Jordan, Roll: The World the Slaves Made* (New York: Random House, 1972), and John W. Blassingame, *The Slave Community: Plantation Life in the Antebellum South* (New York: Oxford University Press, 1972). Among others, Joyner, *Down by the Riverside*, talks about forging an Afro-American culture from varied African origins along with factors of European culture and the geographic environment.

2. "Run," quoted in Pruitt, *Things Hidden: An Introduction to the History of Blacks in Spartanburg*, ch. 4 (unpaginated).

3. Anderson County, Coroner's Inquests. Recent studies on Denmark Vesey, esp. Pearson (56–57), emphasize the gap between laws and daily variations.

4. Note Joyner's caution (*Down by the Riverside*, 231): "the matter of relative proportion is both important and elusive," poignantly true words; on withholding, see p. 4 in this volume.

5. Trial records contain a white person's summary of testimony, sometimes by ten or more slaves in a given trial. These accounts, often recounting information incidental to a trial's purpose, are the nearest approximation to contemporary AOP slave experiences. A much fuller understanding of their daily lives in South Carolina emerges in ways possible for only a few counties with surviving MFH records.

During the 1930s the Federal Writers' Project of the WPA conducted thousands of "exslave" interviews throughout the South, including over three hundred in South Carolina, mostly near the coast and in the midlands. Only one South Carolina interview dealt with AOP, a few more for Abbeville, Greenville, and Laurens, and a somewhat larger number for Spartanburg. Some interviews in other states concerned former AOP residents.

George P. Rawick in his general introduction to the series he edited, *The American Slave: A Composite Autobiography* (Westport, Conn.: Greenwood Press, date varies), explores numerous problems in interpreting these materials. References below to WPA interviewees without further geographic description all come from South Carolina.

6. The spelling of "patrolling" as "pateroling," used for antebellum and postbellum activities, recurs often in WPA interviews. Antebellum patrol and postbellum KKK activities evidently merged in African American memories; cf. Harris's usage (164, 239).

7. Contacts on plantations and on railroads are cited throughout this chapter; for contacts at a Williamston hotel, see Anderson Coroner's Inquisition, Sept. 17, 1857, Lewis Green [FPC]. An inquisition on Sam (J. W. Harrison), Oct. 5, 1854, shows slaves of several owners, while working for the railroad, sharing sleeping quarters. John P. Benson Hotel Registers (Anderson County, Master, SCDAH) include charges for "servants" who stayed overnight. Egerton in his chapter 3 has a rich exploration of slave money and acquisitions.

Note esp. John Campbell, "As 'A Kind of Freeman'?": Slaves' Market-Related Activities in the South Carolina Up Country, 1800–1860" in Ira Berlin and Philip D. Morgan, eds., *Labor and the Shaping of Slave Life in the Americas* (Charlottesville: University of Virginia Press, 1993).

8. Ruth Oglesby freed her husband in 1813; cf. Caesar in "Exhorters and Preachers" in ch. 6, p. 100. "Thomas Guerrin," a slave in 1856, paid $420 to William C. Porter for 140 acres near Twelve Mile River; Porter held title, then transferred the property in 1873 to the man, then called Thomas Cannon. Pickens DB B-2, 300. For a Laurens County slave who bought property, see W. B. Bell, statement of Feb. 15, 1878, Simpson Young Dean and Coleman Families (SCL).

9. WPA 1, pt. 1, 185 (near Florence?); 2, pt. 3, 159 (Florence), 200 (Beaufort).

10. *Diary of Clarissa Adger Bowen*, 77.

11. *Piedmont Farmer*, 294; Ashmore, "Plantation Journal"; *AI*, Feb. 28, 1867; WPA, Georgia, pt. 2, 131 (cotton patch for slaves' own use, near Belton, South Carolina); Thornton: AND 334; guns: AND 121, 336; PKNS 1842 Tom, and 1843 Alse & Seborn.

12. Americus (b. 1831) presumably sold baskets slightly later. Runaway Henry (1848), ch. 5; Harris (74); Seaborn's slave not mentioned by name: Pendleton Farmers' Society Minutes, Oct. 14, 1853, and Feb. 12, 1858; AND 129, 142, 208.

13. Pendleton Farmers' Society Minutes, 1824–1833; Treasurer's Book, 1828–1853; Henry received $10 in 1830. St. Paul's financial records (copies at PDC); cf. Joyner, *Down by the Riverside*, 74, 87; cf. *Judicial Cases*, 311.

14. J. N. Boggs leased Milly from Joseph Whitner (1824), W. K. Clement employed Silas Holloway's Anthony (1845), and Samuel Hutchinson hired Mrs. Groves's Levi from Abbeville (1855); AND 5, 168, 287. Ashmore, July 1856; Kilpatrick estate.

15. Symmes's estate proceedings: "Mid wife," unnamed, and 4 children.

16. *Anderson Gazette*, June 21, 1854; AND 272, 420; *Anderson Intelligencer*, Sept. 10, 1860; *Profiles of Black Folks*, 110.

17. AND 335; 1860 Census, Pickens District, Western Division.

18. PKNS SCDAH 25; see Gilbert in "Runaways, 1820s–1865" and "Broader Horizons: Charleston Connections and Literacy," in ch. 8, pp. 82–83, 138. AND 185, 157, 191; and *JCC* 12:156.

19. Parris, PKNS, 1850; AND 321, 354, 412, 342, 3; undated mss. in hand of W. D. Simpson; Simpson Young Dean and Coleman Families Papers, SCL; details on earning money are given in the text that follows.

20. AND 90–91, 412, 157.

21. AND 130, 132, 157, 245, 253, 282, 350, 349.

22. AND 165, 246, 259, 113.

23. AND 7, 127, 236, 238.

24. WPA 2, pt. 3, 234.

25. AND 93, 127, 302, 403; loose papers in Anderson, Mixed Provenance (SCDAH); Young, 1:14; *KC*, May 30, 1857. McCurry describes (5, 112) widespread "illicit traffick" with lowcountry slaves.

26. AND 176, 326, 187.

27. *JCC* 12:156; AND 142, 221; 141, 222, 232.

28. Ashmore, April 30, 1857; several examples by Anna Calhoun Clemson survive in the Thomas Clemson Papers, CU. In 1800 William Steele billed J. E. Colhoun for postage, with several entries noted "Sent per your Negroe Boy," Colhoun Papers, SCL. The Ravenels sent items and money by a servant to Mrs. Andrew P. Calhoun, Sept. 9, 1863; Calhoun Papers,

SCL. That servant was Priest; he may be the Priest Osborn in 1870, household 181, Seneca Township, Oconee County. Books on Denmark Vesey emphasize the importance of African American oral culture and the wide geographic range that it might encompass.

29. That many contacts would have been available only to slaves on larger plantations who also left their premises on errands. But Egerton (140, 150) cites Charleston city authorities who believed that "as many as 9,000 slaves at least heard of the [Vesey] plot," a figure that he finds plausible for an area extending up to 60 or more miles from the city. And that applies to a *secret* plot.

30. *Judicial Cases*, 312; WPA 1, pt. 1, 28, Ballard (b. ca. 1849). Gutman (note ?, ch. 9) about husbands hauling soiled laundry and provisions on trips to their wives.

31. Burton, 152. Coming and going: AND 170, 179, 222, 232; 1855, PKNS (Gill, Nero); *Piedmont Farmer*, 154, 210; *Judicial Cases*, 276; Beech Island, quoted in Roper, 37.

32. WPA 1, pt. 2, 2 (near Winnsboro); cf. episodes at FPC homes in "Legal Standing," in ch. 3, p. 56

33. Serving MFH warrants, constables itemized mileage for reimbursement; the totals sometimes were more than 50 miles to the defendant's owner, jurors, and witnesses.

34. AND 264, 335, 322, 279.

35. "The Tense and Brutal 1820s" in ch. 5, p. 81, and "Celebrations and Life Cycles" in ch. 10, pp. 166–67.

36. Calhoun's grandson had a servant at South Carolina College; Jan. 24, 1861, Calhoun Papers, SCL; Kilpatrick daughters took servants to Charleston (estate proceedings).

37. *Diary of Clarissa Adger Bowen*, 23; the Calhouns may have trusted these slaves, but also knew how to punish family members if one escaped or got into trouble during such trips.

38. Surely Jack was cautious about approaching any slave for food or shelter, but unlikely to make the long journey without some help; "Runaways, 1820s–1865" in ch. 5, p. 83. John W. Philpot estate, 1863: Wooley, 1:251.

39. WPA 2, pt. 4, 52–53.

40. See "Freedom: Food and Work, but No Land" in ch. 12, p. 205, on the potential uprising; and accounts of voter registration and petitioning in ch. 15, passim.

41. The best survey is "Summer Migrations of South Carolina Planters" in *Historical Papers* (1947; New York: AMS Press, 1970), esp. ch. 4, "Discovering the Up Country." Among numerous books dealing with Pendleton District, wealthy lowcountry families' plantations around Pendleton village, and Charleston connections, two based on good scholarship and prolific use of diaries and other materials were edited by Mary Stevenson. Both published in Pendleton by the Foundation for Historic Restoration in Pendleton Area, they are *The Diary of Clarissa Adger Bowen, Ashtabula Plantation, 1865* (1973) and *The Recollection of a Happy Childhood by Mary Esther Huger* (1976), cited as Huger; Foundation newsletters often reprint original materials.

Three books of varying quality deal with the area; those by Vandiver and Dickson lack documentation. Beth Ann Klosky, *Pendleton Legacy* (1971); Louise Ayer Vandiver, *Traditions and History of Anderson County: History of Anderson County* (1928), which aptly stresses traditions (topically organized); and Frank A. Dickson, *Journeys into the Past: The Anderson Region's Heritage* (Anderson: privately printed, 1975). R. W. Simpson's *History of Old Pendleton District* contains useful family histories—often with Charleston connections—and genealogies, which can be supplemented by *Old Stone Church* and *Records of St. Paul's* (Episcopal Church).

Two freedmen involved in the "The Hunnicutt Murder Crisis" in ch. 13, p. 225, used surnames rarely found in AOP but were those of men connected with Vesey's plot and may have been have deliberately chosen.

42. Merchants William Turpin and Samuel Maverick acquired property and operated trading firms in the area, utilizing upcountry associates including William Steele in Pendleton

village. Turpin certainly and Maverick evidently emancipated slaves, and Turpin bequeathed funds for educating some freed Charleston slaves and for abolition groups. Turpin: *Wills*, 80–83.

43. Charleston was the nation's 11th largest city in 1850, and, following New Orleans, encompassed the South's second-largest urban African American population. Its 3500 FPC in 1850, about half of all those in South Carolina, exceeded all FPC in either Alabama, Georgia, or Missouri. As late as 1900, it ranked eleventh in the country's number of urban blacks. James Dunworthy Brownson DeBow, *Statistical View of the United States* . . . (Washington: A. O. P. Nicholson, 1854), 63; cited as DeBow, *Statistical View*.

44. Mills, *Statistics* in 1826, quoted in *Diary of Clarissa Adger Bowen*, 34; Huger, 16, 18; *Records of St. Paul's;* and Sarah Edith Ann Smith Mills, "Reminiscences," CU.

45. In 1850 approximately fifty of the area's FPC could read, that is 25% of all over 20 years of age, higher for those between 20 and 50. Based on census records for 1850 and 1860.

46. "Pendleton Sunday School Society, Records, 1819–1824," WPA typescript, CU. George W. Boggs, superintendent in 1822, sent slave Celia to Liberia in 1832. See also WPA 2, pt. 3, 53 (Spartanburg town). Abbeville: General Assembly petition N.D. 1561, SCDAH.

47. Baptists: *Minutes;* WPA, Georgia, pt. 2, 131: "When Dr. Cannon found out dat his carriage driver had learned to read and write whilst he was takin' de doctor's chillun to and f'um school," the doctor had the man's thumbs cut off and replaced him with another driver (from Tom Hawkins, near Belton). But Louisa Gassaway "was taught to read by her father, who was white," *Profiles of Black Folks*, 133.

48. Young, 1:83–84; cf. F. W. Pickens on Dec. 7, 1841: slave "Peter had written" to say he was coming for Christmas. Pickens Family Letters, vol. 2, SCL; Caesar: Big Creek Baptist, Minutes, Sept. 1825.

49. Stone, June 1, 1866, Letters Sent, Anderson Court House, RG 105/3065; *KC*, April 7, 1866.

Chapter 9. Families, Mortality, and Names

1. Although specific examples document each combination just described, it is impossible to determine their relative frequency. For detailed exploration of slave families, based on owners' estates, see ch. 7 and "Families and Households" in 1870, ch. 14, pp. 239–43. Gutman deals extensively with slaves separated by sale for an owner's indebtedness and occasionally as control mechanisms. Cf. Burton (159, 169, 171–75), esp. ch. 4, "The Slave Family," and in this context his reference to "unidentified fathers."

2. Registers of Signatures of Depositors in Branches of the Freedmen's Savings and Trust Co., National Archives, Freedmen's Bureau RG 101. Atlanta 2544, 785; 606; Charleston 3097. Although in enormously different circumstances, white Elizabeth Halbert's adult sons and daughters were "scattered in Indiana, Missouri, Mississippi, Alabama, Tennessee, and South Carolina" (willfully, one presumes); see ch. 2.

3. Wooley, 1:41; cf. fear quoted by Joyner, *Down by the Riverside*, 230–31; see note 20, ch. 7. John Ewing Colhoun (Sr.) highly regarded Polydore and Monemi, but in 1802 specifically willed four of their children to four of his own, thus separating a favored African American family.

4. Gutman demonstrates that many slave couples were divided between two plantations, even on plantations of 100 or more slaves, as a large slave owner might divide families.

5. Households in the 1870 and 1900 censuses demonstrate the same point for later time periods. The 1900 census inquired how many children a woman had borne, and for those females older than 55, inferential calculations are possible.

6. Figures here are not actuarial life expectancies, but the average of all slaves living in Pickens in 1850 and 1860. The figure is distorted because of high infant mortality; a child who survived infancy and made it to the age of 5 had a much higher life expectancy than 18.

7. "Orphans" here should be taken in the most literal sense of both parents having died; typically such children were incorporated into an extended family; later examples, *Sizemore,* 37, 56, 132.

8. One former slave in Spartanburg was not sure of his age, but "I settled it as 80 years old. Dat give me respect from everybody," he said. WPA 2, pt. 4, 12. Cf. U.S. Census Bureau, *Negroes in the United States* (Washington: GPO, 1904), 36; Joyner, *Down by the Riverside,* 63–64. Two Colhoun slaves, Cyrus and Moses, were cited as 100 years old when they died but should have been 78 or 79 based on the plantation ledger; *Records of St. Paul's; Pickens Sentinel* (cited as *PS*), June 18, 1891.

9. "Analysis of Labor Agreements, 1865–67" in ch. 12, p. 210, shows mothers of adult workers; cf. "Families and Households" in ch. 14, pp. 239–43.

10. A former slave from Belton told about his parents living on different plantations, a mile apart, as did his grandparents. WPA, Georgia, 1, pt. 2, 127; Simpson letters, "Enforced Slave Contributions to the War Effort" in ch. 11, p. 192.

11. Quotation from Ernestine Richerson, 1978, in *Sizemore,* 48. The frozen river anecdote comes from the author's interview with Lucinda Reid Brown, Aug. 15, 1988; Gutman, 136–39.

12. The published version omits some information found in the original manuscript (photocopies at PDC); moreover, the editor used the word "unknown" for some slave parents, but the original simply omits those names; in one case, the mother had died. *Records of St. Paul's.*

13. Bethesda Association (Baptist) Minutes, 1793.

14. Robert Anderson noted in 1813 that "I traded for Jesse, the Husband of Hannah, at considerable disadvantage." Wooley, 2:67; *PM,* Sept. 12, 1845; Louisa Rebecca Hayne McCord, "Recollections," SCL; for a case involving Calhouns in Abbeville, see *Judicial Cases,* 461, and Richardson 19, Appeals in Equity, 362 ff.. Gutman specifies stages of an owner's life in which varied separations were more likely to occur. He does not deal with small holdings where separations were virtually inevitable.

15. J. W. Hunter to Lt. Col. Andrew Pickens [Jr.], Oct. 5, 1812, Pickens Family Letters, SCL; and *PM* obituaries; Capt. John Calhoun's family in Abbeville; and 1856: *Records of St. Paul's;* cf. "Health" and "Celebrations and Life Cycles" in ch. 10, pp. 165, 168.

Data on mortality come from the 1850 and 1860 federal census, Mortality Schedules; 1850 and 1860 compilations of federal census data; and 1857–60 Mortality reports to the state legislature. Calculations on ages of living persons are derived from the 1850 and 1860 Population and Slave Schedules, including Anne Sheriff, *1850 Federal Slave Census of Pickens District, South Carolina, Eastern Division: Present-day Pickens County* and *1860 Federal Slave Census of Pickens District, South Carolina, 5th Regiment: Present-day Pickens County.* In 1850 average ages of slaves who died 1849–50 were 15.8 in Pickens County, 19.2 in Oconee, and 17.2 in Anderson.

16. The 1880 Mortality Schedule, Pickens Court House Township.

17. "Registrar's Report, Relating to Births, Deaths, and Marriages," 58–65, in 1860 *Reports and Resolutions.* By 1859–60 the average age for living slaves in Pickens was 18.3.

18. DeBow, *Statistical View,* 51. No comprehensive data on ages of slaves or their deaths exists prior to 1850; inferential figures can be drawn from the white population. In 1820 half of Pendleton District's slaves were under 14; some clerics in Charleston pointed out that half of the black population there was too young or too old to attend services. "2nd Presbyterian Church, Charleston, Records, 1847–1848," CU.

19. Murray Heller, ed. (Boston: G. K. Hall, 1975); cited as *Black Names.* Based on material collected by Newbell N. Puckett in the 1930s, this list covers both slave and free black names from 1800 to 1860. The *Black Names* study draws from all slave states; South Carolina's 475 are only about 3% of the total.

20. Cf. Cheryll Ann Cody, "There Was No 'Absalom' on the Ball Plantations," *American Historical Review* 92 (June 1987): 563–96.

21. Findings shared by Gutman, 180–86. A sample Pendleton transaction in 1811 that sold fifteen slaves included Tombo, Marshac, Quammasey, and Cumba; DB L, 88.

22. *Black Names* found Quash to be the second-most frequent name of African usage for men (11 instances). By contrast, there were virtually no Quashes in 1866–69 AOP sources and none among 1870 heads of households. The Maxwell and Calhoun plantation Quashes evidently were both listed as Wash in the 1870 census.

23. The plantation evidently included Sandy [Reed], born in Africa in 1770; his presence may have helped perpetuate African naming practices there, some of which could still be found in the 1900 census.

24. Generally, names known for FPC come from a somewhat later period than those for many slaves. Colhoun (Sr.) prepared lists—evidently annually—of slaves he controlled (SHC and SCL). Colhoun (Jr.) lists are those compiled as part of his estate and also in the Affleck ledger (below). Most of John C. Calhoun's slaves were itemized by name and age when his family sold Fort Hill and 57 slaves to Andrew P. Calhoun in 1854. Perhaps 13 of James Edward Calhoun's may have been his father's, based on age and name (lists kindly supplied by Charles Orser).

25. My observations vary from Gutman (185–94, 230–56), who found few daughters named for their mothers and most sons who were Junior to be first- or second-born. Note two wills, 1797–98, that show names passed to the younger generation, including females; "Changing Population and Slaveholdings, 1800–1810" in ch. 1; also a sale notice in the April 24, 1840, *GM*; it included "Seven Negroes" "Cato sr., Cato jr., Patty sr., Patty jr."

26. I have had approximately equal success with the Kilpatrick, Maxwell, and Calhoun plantations and have matched some St. Paul's members with their postbellum surnames and locations.

Sources for the families include the published *Papers of John C. Calhoun* and his manuscript collections at South Caroliniana Library (Univ. of South Carolina) and CU Special Collections as well as those of John Ewing Colhoun (Sr.), James Edward Calhoun (SCL), and Thomas Green Clemson (CU). Other documentary sources are deeds, wills, estate records, census listings (including 1870 for freed African Americans), *PM* newspaper files, and records relating to the Court of Common Pleas, including sheriff's sale books and execution books. E. M. Lander's account of the family is invaluable: *The Calhoun Family and Thomas Green Clemson: Decline of a Southern Patriarchy* (Columbia: University of South Carolina Press, 1983), cited as Lander; the Affleck ledger is available on microfilm at SCL.

27. Scots-Irish, the Calhouns moved along traditional routes from Pennsylvania to Virginia, spending several years there, then lived a few years in the Waxhaws near South Carolina's border, as did Andrew Pickens, a relative. *JCC* 23:448; *Biographical Directory . . . House*, 3:146–48.

28. Each year Colhoun carefully detailed which slaves were his own (52 in one listing), which belonged to his wife (42 that same year), perhaps in trust for their children, and which he utilized on behalf of allied partners. Jan. 8, 1793, purchase in Colhoun Papers, SCL. Operations at Keowee included a mill and a distillery. See B. Green to JEC, Jan. 15, 1802; Colhoun Papers, SCL; and note 3 on "Old Polydore" in ch. 2.

29. James Edward Colhoun, the youngest sibling, owned land farther south in Anderson, but settled in Abbeville. Occasional insights into his holdings and life may be found in his collected papers (SCL) and in Orser's *The Material Basis of the Postbellum Tenant Plantation* about Calhoun's plantations.

30. John C. Calhoun invested heavily, using borrowed funds, in an Alabama cotton plantation along with son Andrew P. Calhoun, who dragged Calhoun's son-in-law Thomas G.

Clemson into this financial quagmire. For twenty-five years they quarreled (by letters), often angrily, over the debt. After Calhoun died, his wife sold Fort Hill and 54 slaves to son Andrew, who borrowed from his mother and siblings to finance the purchase. Those included in his mortgage were each listed by name and age in what appear to be family groupings.

Mrs. Calhoun, retaining several slaves as her personal property, moved them with her to Pendleton, while Anna and Thomas Clemson took others to Maryland—evidently freed when that state abolished slavery in 1863. That same year Andrew brought back slaves to Fort Hill, where he died in March 1865. Fort Hill slaves: "Celebrations and Life Cycles" in ch. 10, and New York *Herald*, July 26, 1849, reprinted in *JCC* 26:526–35; cf. Irving H. Bartlett, *John C. Calhoun: A Biography* (1993), 300–301, 368, 371, 374.

31. See Peggy and an unnamed man in "Slaveholdings, 1790–1860" in ch. 2, and Izzy in "Influences, Neighboring and Farther Afield" in ch. 5. Only two years before JCC's death, his wife acquired "a very fine cook," Nelly, from Mr. Moses, by selling Nancy and Aleck. "Robert is also sold to Mr. Moses, he takes them all to Louisiana, and sells them on one of the larger plantations." Floride C. Calhoun to son J[ames] E. Calhoun, Nov. 12, 1848, SCL. Calhoun, deeply in debt primarily because of his Alabama plantation, borrowed even more in 1848. When a prominent Anderson doctor wrote asking Calhoun's advice about how to invest funds, Calhoun replied, in essence, "Loan them to me!" *JCC* 25:44, 220–21, 306–7, 325, 357, 383; cf. 26:45–46, 89–90, 200, 308, 370–72, 383–84. Andrew P. Calhoun likewise fell into large debt. Ultimately he died bankrupt in 1865, and Fort Hill was later sold at public auction, to be bought by Thomas Clemson.

32. In 1816 he bought 16 slaves, part of Ezekiel Pickens's estate, they cost $4690, averaging $295. In 1829 the family agent and cousin John Bonneau, located in Charleston, bought Colhoun a male cook, 45–47, for $350, and promised to look for a chambermaid and a gardener; Bonneau to JEC, John Ewing Colhoun (Jr.) Papers, SCL.

33. Cf. "Good Land for Sale," p. 79. Colhoun tried to sell still more slaves to a relation, F. W. Pickens, who, having exhausted his own funds, recommended selling them through public "out-cry." Pickens Family Letters, typescript, 2, Jan. 16, 1843, and Feb. 7, 1844; *JCC* 12:371, 16:582, 591, 17:142; and quotation about Edgefield slaves: note, "The Plantation as a Family" in ch. 10; Cf. Mechal Sobel, *Cultural Interaction*, 78.

34. Some of Colhoun's income came from selling nearly 1000 acres of his father's land for $3800 in June 1843 and then in July 1844 the 700-plus–acre plantation where his mother had lived, Cold Spring, for $4850. *JCC* 25:425. Margaret Colhoun to James Edward Calhoun, Sept. 10, 1843, Calhoun Papers, SCL. Following Colhoun's death his family was forced to sell more land in 1849. See JEC to James Edward Calhoun, Dec. 10, 1842, and Feb. 10, 1843; Colhoun Papers, SCL. Burton (151 and quotes, 381) refers briefly to JEC's sale of slaves but does not mention Susan, Daphny's daughter whom Clemson bought from John Ewing Colhoun Jr. Clemson in 1851 sold 51 slaves—including this family—to Alfred Dearing, father-in-law of Francis W. Pickens. *JCC* 23:338; Edgefield DB G, 9, 170; Colhoun estate in Pickens Equity, box 1, case 31.

35. This ledger (SCL), the basis for the rest of this chapter, is supplemented by the 1850, 1860, 1870, and 1880 censuses, including Slave Schedules for 1850 and 1860, as well as 1865–68 Pickens District tax records, the vestry register of St. Paul's, and family information. Colhoun's entries include calculations and abbreviated information for himself. Additional problems of interpretation include difficult handwriting, varying usage of formal or diminutive names, conflicting ages, and names omitted for many babies. Several lists lack a clear purpose or date.

36. Jack (47), Lenah (37), and their children Becky (13), Frank (7), Peggy (9), and evidently John Flander (12). Colhoun offered them for sale in 1844, but "Jack's family & himself have not yet been sold"; *JCC* 17:842.

37. George bore his father's name, George (b. 1792). The elder George may be the same one found in J. E. Colhoun (Sr.)'s 1793 inventory. George, wife Fanny, and eight children (including son George) were advertised for sale in 1842 (*PM*, Jan. 21) but retained.

38. Ralph Beaumont Leonard, "The Graveyard of the Keowee Plantation" (photographic report, CU).

39. Cf. Keowee freed people in "Analysis of Labor Agreements, 1865–67" in ch. 12. In 1885 Harrison Wiggins sold property to Edward Dupree, Isaac Dupree, and Ephraim Wiggins, trustees of the Mount Nebo Baptist Church; clearly the families remained closely associated; Oconee DB K, 414–15. J. J. Starks's autobiography paid tribute to A. E. Dupree (Milly's grandson) and Rev. H. Wiggins (Betty's son) for assistance in establishing Seneca Institute: *Lo These Many Years: An Autobiographical Sketch* (Columbia, S.C.: State Co., 1941), 68. Harrison Wiggins received a pension for wartime service to Ransom Colhoun; cf. "Enforced Slave Contributions to the War Effort" in ch. 11.

Chapter 10. Material and Emotional Conditions

1. "Pair of copperas coloured striped pantaloons, a mixed blue, red, and white homespun jacket, a blue and white hunting shirt, a large hat with a high crown," advertised by Levi Robbins; *PM*, July 7, 1810; note also clothing in cover photograph for Gutman, *Black Family* (paperbound); cf. 1735 "Act for the Better Ordering," Cooper & McCord, 7.

2. Typescript labeled "Plantation Manual of James H. Hammond of Beach [sic] Island, South Carolina, About 1834," University of South Carolina Medical College's historical Waring Library; cited as "Plantation Manual."

3. Mary Esther (Mrs. H. A.) Huger, "Plantation Book of 1858," in the Habersham Elliot Papers, SHC; punctuation added.

4. Kilpatrick estate papers, Pickens; cf. Senator J. E. Colhoun's estate accounting, 1804.

5. *Diary of Clarissa Adger Bowen*, 24, 37; and *The Recollection of a Happy Childhood by Mary Esther Huger*; cf. Colhoun's textile factory, "Other Slave Labor on Plantations and in Towns" in ch. 2.

6. AND 45, 113.

7. Rawick, p. 134; bill from Henry & Co., Mobile, Ala., Dec. 22, 1849 (Calhoun Papers, SCL).

8. AND 129, 131; PKNS SCDAH 17.

9. Greasy: PKNS SCDAH 13.

10. AND 240, 251, 299, 88, 30, 120, 129, 292. Andrew Oliver inherited Candas and four other slaves (two of them witnesses in AND 120) from his father (d. 1830).

11. The definitive study of antebellum plantation outbuildings is that by John Michael Vlach, *Back of the Big House: The Architecture of Plantation Slavery* (Chapel Hill: University of North Carolina Press, 1993). Vlach's 1930s–90s photographs represent only the most substantial ones, especially those made of brick. Incidental information on slave Jane's lodgings in Coroner's Inquisition, March 10–12, 1863 (SCDAH); calculations from 1860 Slave Schedules. One long-enduring cabin, reported to have been used for slaves, appears in Piper Peters Aheron, *Oconee County* (Charleston: Arcadia, 1998), 100. *JCC* 14:501, 22:635.

12. *Piedmont Farmer*, 31–32, 38, 75, 212–14, 263, 413, 530.

13. AND 264; my observations during visits to locations cited and discussions with staffs there. Cf. Orser's study of James Edward Calhoun's Abbeville plantation: *Material Basis of the Postbellum Tenant Plantation*.

14. Table 9.2; 1867: "The Hunnicutt Murder Crisis" in ch. 13.

15. Hammond's "Plantation Manual"; Calhoun Papers, CU.

16. Featherstonhaugh, quoted in Huger, 30; Thomas B. Keys, *The Army and Crawford Keys: Aftermath of the Brown's Ferry Outrage* (privately printed, 1974), 17.

17. *Wills*, 108; Freedmen's Labor Agreements, Anderson, RG 105/3073, National Archives.

18. Huger, 22, 37 ff.; note also Goober Jack's raids on "old time kitchens" in "Runaways, 1820s–1865" in ch. 5.

19. Vlach, "Slave Quarters as Bi-Cultural Expression" in *Cultural Interaction*, 110; for examples of "neat row," see Vlach, 174–75 (figs. 11.9 and 11.10), and jacket for Berlin.

20. For a brief overview along coastal Carolina, see Vennie Deas-Moore, "Home Remedies, Herb Doctors, and Granny Midwives," *World and I* (Jan. 1987): 474–85, and its bibliography. Tyson Gibbs, Kathleen Cargill, Leslie Sue Lieberman and Elizabeth Reitz, in "Nutrition in a Slave Population: An Anthropological Examination," *Medical Anthropology* 4 (spring 1980): 175–262. See also Hammond, "Plantation Manual."

21. *Diary of Clarissa Adger Bowen*, 77; *Piedmont Farmer*, 139, 162, 379, 394.

22. PKNS 1843 (Alse), 1850 (Waddy), 1852 (Tom), 1853 (James & Toney); 278, AND 252, 292, 303, 336.

23. Museum of York County's 2002 exhibit on Scots-Irish in the Carolinas indicates that barbecue had roots in that culture also; Rawick, 130; AND 151, 299.

24. South Carolina slaves, following African traditions, sometimes ate dirt, which they believed had nutritional values that they otherwise were missing; two Anderson slaves died from this practice in 1850. Oconee had 3 doctors, Pickens, 3, and Anderson, 27, in 1850. Dr. William Robinson, Papers, CU; Charles Middleton Lay, 1863: Wooley, 1:185; and J. E. Colhoun's estate accounting, 1804: $10.91 to Dr. Hunter "in full for Medicine & attendance on Negroes," in Gen. Andrew Pickens Record, 1787–1858 (SCL photostats). 1850 Mortality Census, Anderson, Western District, p. 4; see *Judicial Cases*, 392; Dr. William Jenkins Day Book (CU, photocopy).

25. *Piedmont Farmer*, 50–51.

26. *JCC* 7:1; *Piedmont Farmer*, 54; and Maria Calhoun, writing John E. Colhoun (Jr.) in 1844, about Edward Calhoun losing nine negroes and his own children being near death; Colhoun Papers, SCL.

27. Lander, 156–57; WPA, Georgia, pt. 2, 133; *Piedmont Farmer*, 346. Poore (130) used roots, leaves, and ashes.

28. The 1802 episode involved James Collins, in Mechal Sobel, *Cultural Traditions*, 64–68, 212. Collins traveled to Pendleton to be treated by a white "eminent physician," who referred Collins to the black practitioner. Walker: Centerville Township, Sequence 1, household 16; Doctor: AND 3; *Sizemore*, 72, 14; and *PM*, Oct. 1828. Berry: "Why join?" ch. 6.

29. *PM*, Oct. 24, 1845.

30. WPA 1, pt. 1, 1–2; 2, pt. 3, 73 (Union) and 244 (Marion); and pt. 4, 10; AND 103, 104.

31. Griffin: "Not only did he furnish music for his own people at their annual 'cake-walks,' but he helped often to furnish music at the dances of the white race." Clinkscales, *On the Old Plantation*, 12; WPA 2, pt. 3, 115 (Summerton) and 242 (Marion); *Crucible*, 69.

32. *AI*, Jan. 3, 1900.

33. *Piedmont Farmer*, 94–95, 122–23, 315; 355 (Emily). Several slaves at Calhoun's Dahlonega, Ga., gold mine came to Fort Hill for year-end festivities with other Calhoun slaves; cf. *JCC* 15:403, 581. AND 129, 292; William Pickens, *Bursting Bonds* (Boston: Jordan & More Press, 1923), 9–11; cited as Pickens, *Bursting Bonds*.

34. Coroner's Inquest (Anderson), Henry, 1831; AND 176, 277, 292. White drinking: J. J. Norton wrote his father on Feb. 6, 1860, about "a great many drunken [white] men about town this evening." Norton Papers, SCL; cf. West, "Yeoman to Redneck," esp. 176, 182, 187–92, 468.

35. AND 189, 190, 216; Solomon, Tom: PKNS.

36. 1900 census listings (which asked month and year born) and death certificates.

37. Waddy (Thomas Blassingame) mentioned in 1851 having been to a wedding, PKNS SCDAH; WPA 2, pt. 3, 115 (Summerton); New York *Herald*, July 26, 1849.

38. Mary Frances Boxley, comp., *Gravestone Inscriptions in Amherst County, Virginia* (Amherst, Va.: privately printed, 1985); Carrel Cowan-Ricks discussed a piedmont-style burial pattern, distinct from lowcountry burials ("Cemetery Hill Archaeological Project: In Search of John C. Calhoun's Pre-Emancipation African Americans," unpublished paper, p. 8); cf. Burton, 142–45, on Edgefield white attitudes toward death and rituals surrounding it; Ashmore: Aug. 20, 1857.

39. *Piedmont Farmer*, 158, 333. Hunter, *A Nickel and a Prayer*, 46. Gabriel Ferguson in 1890 was buried in the "colored ground" near his Glassy Mountain home; whether it had antebellum burials is not clear. *Pickens Sentinel* (cited as *PS*), March 10, 1890.

40. Alfred Hester's slave, mentioned in ch. 7, was buried in a church cemetery. Secona Baptist Church ("new" Pickens) buried slaves in a separate area farther from the church than that for whites. The rector at St. Paul's (Pendleton) recorded a number of slave interments, but there are no markers. At Bethlehem, postbellum tombstones, mostly for families that had been FPC, appear beyond this area on its far side. I am indebted to Carrel Cowan-Ricks for sharing her expertise during our visits to Oolenoy, Secona, and Soapstone (ch. 18) cemeteries.

41. Most White memorials in nearby St. Paul's cemetery were made for the Bee family, who came from Charleston. Markers at the Presbyterian church at Old Pickens of relatively recent vintage were erected for graves relocated due to construction of Lake Hartwell. One is an individual commemoration ("Henry Craig, Last Slave of Craig Family, Died July 1927"), the other a collective one ("In Memory of Our Faithful Colored Friends"). Of 468 graves in black cemeteries relocated in the 1950s, 262 were specifically considered slaves, based (presumably) on oral tradition. Seven of ten cemeteries from Anderson County were added to the New Prospect Baptist Church cemetery. Corps of Engineers Cemetery Relocations, Corps of Engineers Hartwell Dam and Reservoir Project [n.d.]; reprinted in *Carolina Genealogist*, summer 1971, 21–28.

42. Calhoun's agent wrote in 1828 that "the whole family have been down with it [the Dangue]—whites & blacks, not a solitary exemption." *JCC* 6:751, 10:411; Lay in *Wills*, 92. Some white households also included white servants, Benjamin Franklin Perry Letters, Dec. 11, 1838 (SCL); *JCC* 17:867.

43. Huger, 45.

44. *Piedmont Farmer*, 137, 156, 221, 317, 74, 204.

45. *Piedmont Farmer*, 333, 346, 135, 191.

46. *JCC* 10:254, 15:391; JEC to William Clark, Jan. 27, 1825, and Anna Clemson to Patrick Calhoun, June 24, 1850, Calhoun Papers, SCL. Cf. concerning slaves at the Edgefield plantation, Anna Calhoun Clemson, "quite unhappy, lest they should be neglected, or ill used, being left so entirely in charge of an overseer." *JCC* 22:503–5.

47. "*Far, Far from Home*," 39, 84, 138, 199, 123, 256, 244; cf. Zion, Lewis, and James in ch. 11. *JCC* 17:135; Anna Clemson to James Edward Calhoun, May 26, 1872, Calhoun Papers, SCL.

48. William Pickens, *The Vengeance of the Gods* (1922; New York: AMS Press, 1975), 15; WPA 1, pt. 2, 14 (Marion). Williamson talks about the interchange of black and white culture from gumbos to miscegenation, and mulattos in *Crucible* (37–43) and his *New People: Miscegenation and Mulattoes in the United States* (New York: Free Press, 1980); cf. Burton, 185–89.

49. *PS*, Dec. 2, 1886. A woman, descended from at least Native American and Oconee African American forebears, was called "Red Jenny . . . because of her sandy-colored hair,"

Ferguson, *Soul Food*, 37. Color seems to have been an important issue in the early 1800s; cf. Jeffries's oath (ch. 3, note 6), "clear blooded," reference to "Yellow Sall." An 1808 sale referred to Cornelius Keith buying "Mulattoe slaves . . . born of a Negro woman," i.e., evidently fathered recently by a white man. McGaha, 55, 105, 110.

50. Court of general sessions, Roll 2064 (SCDAH); see ch. 6 for churches' attitudes.

51. AND 414; PKNS 1853; AND 212.

52. Even during the Civil War Abe was found not guilty of trying to get into bed with a white woman. AND 228; PKNS undated; AND 393.

53. Hester: PKNS Pleadings & Judgements (Nov. 14, 1845), 245–47; cf. *Judicial Cases*, 450; Young, 1:24; WPA typescript, 70.

54. Other references to the Reid family appear elsewhere. Other examples of white ancestry include the Thompsons (table 2.3) and Jane Hunter; cf. an owner forcing sex on some of his slaves; AND 76.

55. *Piedmont Farmer*, 354, 357; Edward Bell, *Slaves in the Family* (New York: Farrar, Strauss, Giroux, 1997).

56. These include slave Andrew and FPC William Robertson in 1846–47. AND 129, 264, 9, 40, 205, 354, 81; PKNS, SCDAH 11, 17.

57. AND 321, 374; Vandiver, 266; cf. Joyner, *Down by the Riverside*, 97, 104.

58. Four slaves allegedly threatened Ned with one hundred lashes when they burst into his house and attacked him in 1854; in 1846 fourteen men from ten plantations were charged with fighting, rioting and unlawful assembly; and four slaves, seized Jack (Mrs. E. Rogers) from his house and beat him in 1862. AND 268, 377, 189, 167, 261, 300, 368, 371; Young, 1:205; Reuben, 1841, PKNS; Willis, 1846, PKNS; *PM*, Jan. 8 and 27, 1853; Greenville, Coroner's Inquisitions, 1856, "Dead Body of Slave Henry"; *York Enterprise*, Feb. 19, 1857; and Spartanburg MFH 271.

59. AND 381; Anderson Town Council Minutes, WPA typescript, 69–70; "Slaveholdings, 1790–1860" in ch. 2. Mechal Sobel has written that "the nature of the experiences that blacks and whites often shared in early childhood, provided a basis for the sharing of significant values throughout life" (*Cultural Interaction*, 81); cf. Elliott J. Gorn, ibid., 86; and Benjamin Franklin Perry Letters, Dec. 11, 1838, SCL. From white Maxwell family tradition; see notes on Tenus Maxwell, "Rural Communities" in ch. 18; will of Robert Anderson; cf. Easley's May 1866 statement in "Introduction: A Piedmont Setting," note 11.

60. Quoted in *Diary of Clarissa Adger Bowen*, 46.

61. *PM*, Oct. 30, 1813. Three white men and a "negro boy" camped overnight near Pickens in 1858 (Wooley, 3:107); specific circumstances are unfortunately unknown. Similarly, we know nothing about the spatial and social circumstances when white and slave men ate lunch in the field—together, completely separate, or in proximate but distinctly separated spaces— or relieved themselves while working.

62. *Christ in Black*, 39; see also Susan Richardson and cross-racial expressions of sympathy, both in ch. 23.

63. Quoted by Bill C. Malone in *Cultural Interaction*, 150.

Chapter 11. War Years, the Home Front, and African Americans

1. There is no good source for the war's impact on AOP, with virtually no diaries or newspaper holdings for 1862–1864. John Hammond Moore's *Southern Homefront, 1861–1865* (Columbia, S.C.: Summerhouse Press, 1998) sketches the major military actions in South Carolina; cited as *Homefront*. Cf. *"Far, Far from Home": The Wartime Letters of Dick and Tally Simpson Third South Carolina Volunteers*, cited as *"Far, Far from Home"*; and *Piedmont Farmer*. Other major sources for this chapter are MFH trials and church minutes.

2. Stephen West has well explored the concept of violence and its role in the upper piedmont in "Yeoman to Redneck"; note esp. 142 and 148–49 for antebellum, and 355–468 for postbellum violence. He includes "vigilance committees" (117 ff.), the patrol, KKK, and lynching within this context.

The legacy included pre–Revolutionary War Regulators (both North and South Carolina), Pendleton District hangings in the 1790s of those thought to have been Tories, 1830s vigilance committees, and temperance societies. In 1852 a Pickens Sons of Temperance group seized W. Hagood "without any warrant," tied him and his wife, "Breaking her arms from tieing her With the same Rope" (loose paper "found in the Court of Equity minutes book," Pickens County Clerk of Court's office). The family of future governor Benjamin Tillman provides an excellent example of violence as it "combined the characteristic lawlessness of 'bloody Edgefield.'" Francis Butler Simkins, *Pitchfork Ben Tillman, South Carolinian* (Baton Rouge: Louisiana State University Press, 1944), 8–11, 25–35.

For other explorations see Jack Kenny Williams, *Vogues in Villainy: Crime and Retribution in Ante-bellum South Carolina* (Columbia: University of South Carolina Press, 1959), and James Elbert Cutler, *Lynch-Law: An Investigation into the History of Lynching in the United States* (1905; New York: Negro Universities Press, 1969).

3. *Abbeville Independent Press*, May 21; *Abbeville Banner*, May 27, in *Police*, 154–64; *Abbeville Independent Press*, Feb. 11, 1859; Burton, 146; O'Neall, in *Police*, 77–78. Pendleton whites expelled the Caseys ("Thefts, Illegal Sales, and Bartering Stolen Goods" in ch. 8) in other vigilante action; another mob action against a white man trading with slaves there in 1859 appears in West, "Yeoman to Redneck," 119; cf. Ware, 52–53, and McCurry, 6.

4. *KC*, Dec. 10, 17, 1859; *Abbeville Banner*, Dec. 1, 1859. *Abbeville Independent Press*, Nov. 2, 9; son J. C. Calhoun to his father A. P. Calhoun, Oct. 17, 1860, SCL; and Huff, *Greenville*, 131. But see West, "Yeoman to Redneck," 233, on "lethargy"; cf. *Anderson Intelligencer* (cited as *AI*), May 2, 1861, notice "To Members of the Evergreen Vigilance Association."

5. *Piedmont Farmer*, 161; son J. C. Calhoun to A. P. Calhoun, Oct. 22, 1860, SCL; see chs. 5 and 10 on MFH controls; cf. 1850 and 1860 census entries. Throughout the country shifts in sexual and religious mores, growth of town population, and westward expansion, among others, occurred before, during, and after the war.

6. In January 1861 a Unionist militia was proposed in Spartanburg, while several hundred of Greenville's Union sympathizers planned to march on Columbia; James T. Otten, "Disloyalty in the Upper Districts of South Carolina during the Civil War," *SCHM* 74 (1976): 104, quoting Ashmore; cited as "Disloyalty." Wallace, *The History of South Carolina*, 2: 151–69 (cited as Wallace); Lander, 200–201; Harris: Dec. 17, 1860: *Piedmont Farmer*, 166.

7. *Homefront*, 41, 49, 66.

8. R. Y. H. OSheals taught a Pickens District school in 1864, evidently for five months; Wooley 2:228.

9. April 16, 1862, was the first Confederate draft act (18–35 years old), then Sept. 27 (18–45); and Feb. 17, 1864 (17–50, but 17 and 45–50 only for service in own states); from Wallace, vol. 3; cf. *Homefront*, 113–34. Calculations based on AOP's 1860 population, specifically males then between 10 and 40, and lists of soldiers in Louise Matheson Bell, *Rebels in Grey: Soldiers from Pickens District, 1861–1865* (Seneca: Greys of Oconee Chapter No. 1783, United Daughters of the Confederacy, 1984); cited as *Rebels in Grey*. Not all AOP men who served did so in the units listed, which included some men from Abbeville, Laurens, and elsewhere. George Benet Shealy, *Walhalla: A German Settlement in Upstate South Carolina*, "The Garden of the Gods" (Seneca: Blue Ridge Arts Association, 1990), 63, 99; *Compendium of the Confederate Armies*, vol. 8, *South Carolina and Georgia* (New York: Facts on File, 1995), 56.

The standard documentary source for military events is *A Compilation of the Official Records of the Union and Confederate Armies* (Washington: GPO, 1893), cited as *OR*. For a survey of units, including federal troops occupying South Carolina in 1865–68, see Frederick H. Dyer, *A Compendium of the War of the Rebellion* (New York: Thomas Yoseloff, 1959); *South Carolina Confederate Soldiers, 1861–1865*, ed. Janet B. Hewett (Wilmington, N.C.: Broadfoot Pub., 1998); and Facts *Compendium*, above.

10. *Piedmont Farmer* 243 (April 23, 1862). One-fifth of Anderson County white families qualified for distribution of relief supplies in late 1863; see West, "Yeoman to Redneck," 242; and on starvation reported in Greenville, *Homefront*, 33; Long, Probate, July 1, 1863; *Wills*, 142. In contrast to conscription of soldiers and of slave labor, both under state authority, the Confederate Congress in April 1863 imposed a demand for "one-tenth of all agricultural product"; additionally, the state collected cash for its own "war tax." See Racine in *Piedmont Farmer*, 542, note 46; Andrew Pickens Calhoun receipts (Calhoun Papers, SCL); *Abbeville Press*, July 31, 1863; *AI*, Aug. 24, 1865; cf. *Homefront*, 75; diaries of Floride Clemson, Ella Lorton, Emmala Reed, and Clarissa Adger Bowen are cited and used extensively in notes, 3, 4, and 7, ch. 12.

11. Floride was the oldest child of Anna Calhoun Clemson and Thomas G. Clemson, and thus the granddaughter of John C. and Floride Calhoun. She was staying with her mother and grandmother in Pendleton. E. M. Lander has edited daughter Floride's writings in *A Rebel Came Home*. *Rebel*, 74; entry of Jan. 8. See also Stribling Family Papers, SCL; J. E. Hagood Papers, SCL; and Calhoun Papers, SCL, 1861–65 passim.

Overseers on large plantations were exempt from the draft; AOP had few who qualified (three from Anderson and one from Pendleton); S.C. Office of the Adjutant and Inspector General, "Overseers Exempt from the Draft, 1862" (SCDAH); cf. Moore's *Southern Homefront*, 28, 29 (re: S. E. Maxwell).

12. *Piedmont Farmer*, 277, 307, 343.

13. "Disloyalty," 103; see Ashmore, Aug. 25, 1863; *OR*, ser. 4, vol. 2, 769–72; *Charleston Daily Courier*, March 23, 1864. Cf. an observation by Floride Clemson in April 1865, ch. 12; and *Homefront*, ch.4, "The Draft, Desertion & Dissent." Some of these men wrote Gov. Orr in 1866 complaining of persecution then by other whites; "1866: Violence, Limited Military Force, and White Preoccupations" in ch. 13. Cf. accounts by escaping federal officers, cited below; one referred to these men hidden in the mountains and also to a cluster of "some twenty Union women" who provided help as did some South Carolina deserters who moved into Tennessee during the war; H. A. Johnson, *Sword of Honor: A Story of the Civil War* (Hallowell, Maine: Register Printing House, 1906), 34–36, 44; cited as Johnson.

14. Roberts, March 10, 1865; *Rebel*, 77, 137; Belton Presbyterian, Nov. 1861, July 1864.

15. Cf. references to changing morals in DeForest, "The Low-Down People" (esp. 705), cited in "The Sizemore Family" in ch. 4, and in *Homefront*, 25, 38, 70, and its ch. 3, "Shortages, Speculation and Self."

16. Cf. *Homefront*, 31.

17. *Piedmont Farmer*, 165; Lander, 201. In an unsigned and undated account of "May Day 1865" (Papers of the Maverick & Van Wyck Families, SCL), the white author states that Norris slaves supported the white family during the war and grieved for their young master Lt. William C. Norris when his body was returned from Richmond.

18. Francis Marion Tucker to wife Addie, undated [spring 1861]; Papers of the Duncan, Kinard, Sanders, and Tucker Families, SCL. *Piedmont Farmer*, 235, 258; Chesley (b. ca. 1813), *Pickens Sentinel* (cited as *PS*), Nov. 12, 1891. Such comments, written in the "Jim Crow" era and romanticizing happy owner-slave relations, should be viewed skeptically.

19. These episodes evidently had connections with the African Americans' weeklong holiday at Christmas. Greenville MFH, folder 33, no. 3, SCDAH; Spartanburg MFH 231, SCDAH.

20. Smith letter reprinted in *Rebels in Grey*, 105; AND 377, 378; *Homefront*, ch. 5, deals with slave awareness of the war's events, its potential impact on themselves, and increased disregard for pass requirements and laws.

21. General Assembly Petition, 1862, no. 28, House Committee on Claims; AND 372, 373. Joyner, *Down by the Riverside*, 54, 171, recounts slaves running for freedom and praying for freedom; *Homefront*, 44, note 5; cf. Sylvia Frey about African American Christianity as a millenarian movement, *Cultural Interaction*, 25.

22. Pickens and Oconee records for war years survive only in fragmentary form, published in Wooley's and Pauline Young's books. A complete file might tell a different story; three executions (below) are missing even from these printed fragments.

23. Phil (R. B. Hutchinson), who in 1864 solicited a white woman and touched her, got 500 lashes and then was banished from Anderson; AND 419. Previously Anderson's highest numbers of lashes were 175 in 1843 and 1854, 300 in 1848, and 425 in 1852 (MFH 138, 198, 252, 274). Appeals include MFH 363 and 381. Alfred was lynched: "Capital Crimes" in ch. 5, p. 95.

24. AND 361, 382, 358; cf. ch. 5; Anderson Town Council, Minutes (WPA typescript, SCDAH), Dec. 8, 1862; home after dark: Vandiver; cf. Ware, 53.

25. AND 357, 360, 362, 374, 386, 428; *Rebel*, 81; *Piedmont Farmer*, 351; "Disloyalty," 104.

26. AND 363, 375, 381, 388, 396, 410; Abbeville: Clinkscales, *On the Old Plantation*, 75.

27. An official account is missing; Narcissa Clayton Papers, SCL; cf. *KC*, Nov. 12 and Dec. 10, 1902. Anderson's Town Council (70) issued a complaint against one white woman on March 9, 1865, for trading with slaves, selling them liquor, and keeping a house of ill fame.

28. PKNS SCDAH 1. Spartanburg charged five FPC and found three guilty.

29. The U.S. military, accusing Keys in 1866, said that Keys took Horn, who "was loyal to the United States . . . [and did] publicly beat and whip with a horsewhip." One Keys supporter said that Horn's punishment "was authorized by a meeting of citizens." John Wilson said that "I heard that [John J.] Horn . . . had been using his influence to excite insurrection among the colored people." *AI*, March 27, 1861; Thomas B. Keys, *The Army and Crawford Keys: Aftermath of the Brown's Ferry Outrage* (privately printed, 1974), 12–13, 27, 29, 69, 80; cited as *Army and Crawford Keys*; *KC*, April 27, 1861; Pillsbury, Jan. 23, 1867; cf. West, "Yeoman to Redneck," 125.

30. Her letter, Nov. 17, 1871, to Gov. Scott (SCDAH); cf. "Disloyalty," 96; Gen. Gillmore's GO 102, June 27, 1865 (*AI*, Aug. 10); Freedmen's Bureau (FMB) officer Stone, letter of Sept. 1, 1866 (RG 105/3065); FMB Neide report of May 25, 1866 (RG 105/3227); and DeForest letter about "a good Union man during the war" (J. K. Stone. RG 105/3227). See "Civil War and Early Reconstruction" in bibliography for explanation of FMB (RG 105) and military (RG 393) references. J. E. Hagood referred to those "who were always good Unions, during the war" in an April 25, 1867, letter to Governor James L. Orr (an Anderson native); Governor Orr, Letters Received, SCDAH.

31. Johnson, 34; A. Cooper, *In and Out of Rebel Prisons* (Owego, N.Y.: R. J. Oliphant, 1898); A. O. Abbott, *Prison Life in the South* (New York: Harper & Brothers 1865); Emily Harris in *Piedmont Farmer*, 353; and Charleston *Daily Courier*, June 22, 1864.

32. Some "boys" fled from Burdine's plantation in Pickens in late 1864. *Rebel*, 43; letter to J. E. Hagood, Jan. 14, 1865, Hagood Papers, SCL; AND 401; and table 14.2.

33. "An Ordinance to provide for the removal of Negroes and other property from portions of the State which may be invaded by the enemy"; South Carolina, Commission for Removal of Negroes, SCDAH. FMB RG 105/3065: Letters Sent, Anderson Court House, April 5 (Williams), May 15 (Chester refugees), and Aug. 31 (Jockey), 1866.

34. Knight, and in succeeding paragraphs Black, Hampton, and Wright, are postbellum surnames, as perhaps is Rosemon. On *Progress* newspaper stationery, Union, South Carolina

(SCDAH); cf. sketch of Jerry Anderson, which refers to his grandfather Dick Lewis in *Profiles of Black Folks*, 11; cf. table 2.2.

35. *"Far, Far from Home,"* 64 (RWS); not suffer: TNS, 76. RWS = Richard Wright Simpson; TNS = Taliaferro (Tally) N. Simpson. Cf. Robert Harley Mackintosh Jr., ed., *"Dear Martha . . .": The Confederate War Letters of a South Carolina Soldier Alexander Faulkner Fewell* (privately printed, 1976).

36. TNS, *"Far, Far from Home,"* 167–68, 259, 188, 86, 244; cf. *Piedmont Farmer*, 542, note 43.

37. TNS, *"Far, Far from Home,"* 139; total of 7 paragraphs; Stribling Family Papers, SCL.

38. When soldier Samuel Wilkes was killed in July 1862, Jim Hampton "came home with the body." RWS, *"Far, Far from Home,"* 68; Wooley, 1:251. In 1878 Wright would chair a meeting of the Oconee "Radical Convention"; *KC*, Sept. 26, 1878; cf. Louisa Rebecca Hayne McCord, "Recollections," SCL. Sam Rosemon, "who had made it to Pittsburg," wrote a March 1867 letter mentioning family living in Anderson District; reprinted in Gutman (5) from DeForest (118). Thomas A. Tobin to Harry Miller, Camp Near Chattanooga Tenn; Rev. John M. Carlisle to R. F. Simpson, Ringgold Geo[rgia] R R; *"Far, Far from Home,"* 290–91, 284–85. *A Faithful Heart: The Journals of Emmala Reed, 1865 and 1866*, ed. Robert T. Oliver (Columbia: University of South Carolina Press, 2004),; cited as *Reed*.

39. *"Far, Far from Home,"* 114; WPA 2, pt. 4, 14; Norton, memorandum book, 1861–62; Joseph Jeptha Norton Papers, SCL; Chesnut, 398; Pickens District, Commissioners Report, Oct. 17, 1863; loose paper in Pickens County, Clerk of Court's files. *Report of the Auditor of South Carolina of Claims against the State for Slaves Lost in the Public Service* (Columbia, S.C.: Charles P. Pelham, 1864) does not include names of the slaves who died during coastal service.

40. South Carolina enacted legislation in 1923 granting pensions, awardable in 1924. Alexia J. Helsley, "Black Confederates," *SCHM* 74 (1973): 184–87; cf. her *South Carolina's African American Confederate Pensioners, 1923–1925* ([Columbia, S.C.]: SCDAH, 1998). A list of eleven black men from AOP claiming benefits appears (with more details) in my *Black Soldiers in World War I: Anderson, Pickens, and Oconee Counties, South Carolina* (Clemson, S.C.: Oconee County Historical Society, 1995); another version appeared in *SCHM*, April 1995. They are: Jake Crayton (owner: Gus Lewis; role: servant); Ben P. Griffin ("___ Griffin"; laborer); Jim Hampton (Samuel Wilkes; servant); Henry Harris (Sam Hester; laborer); L. Knight (Dr. J. R. Knight; cook); Marshall Mattison (Wyatt Watson; cook); Starling Owens (B. L. Thompson; cook); John R. Smith (Wm. and Jesse Smith; cook & attendant); Harrison Wiggins (Ransom Calhoun; servant); James Willson (Captain Langston?; cook); and Johnson Wright (Capt. Kilpatrick; cook).

41. How he joined the USCT is unknown; nor is it clear whether he lived in Pendleton before the war or made it his home later. Richard Green, 42, Pendleton, waiter, in USCT 33, Company C (from "Black Union Soldiers Company C 33rd Infantry Regiment," SCHS; handwritten [modern] list); also Stephen Murrill, 53–year-old plowman, Greenville (county).

42. *Piedmont Farmer*, 356; cf. Adger's 1863 deed for a black church on his land, "Black Churches, 1865–1900" in ch. 17.

43. Floride Clemson, April 4, *Rebel*, 80.

Chapter 12. Reconstruction's First Months, 1865

1. Most serious issues relating to Reconstruction did not arise in AOP as early as 1865; an overview of major studies appears in note 1, ch. 15. As on other issues, West's "Yeoman to Redneck" provides useful insights. *A Compilation of the Official Records of the Union and Confederate Armies* (Washington: GPO, 1893). Major General Schofield to Sherman, May 5, 1865; *OR*, ser. 1, vol. 47, pt. 3, 404; cited as *OR*. See FMB Circular 15, Oct. 19, reprinted

in *KC*, Nov. 11, and FMB Circular (unnumbered), Nov., ACH, Letters Sent, FMB RG 105/3065, reported in *KC*, Dec. 9. The figure 57% refers to 1860 population.

See "Civil War and Early Reconstruction" in bibliography for explanation of military accounts in RG 105 and RG 393. To avoid numerous personal names not essential for these chapters, letters are styled to "HQ" unless addressed specifically to Gillmore, Sickles, or Canby. I have also omitted changing titles of Department of the South, Department of South Carolina, and 2nd Military District. Other RG 393 citations are to HQ except those specifically noted as WSC or the Anderson or Greenville posts.

Tax records for 1865–68 list most adult black males, as do 1867–68 voter registration books; state 1868 agricultural and 1869 population censuses (Oconee's is missing); 1870 federal census, specifying all black people by name for the first time; and thousands of labor agreements. All of these along with newspapers, military and Freedmen's Bureau correspondence and school records, governors' papers, and church minutes supply almost overwhelming source materials, but hardly provide answers for many important questions.

2. "Humiliation" appears, among other places, in an unsigned, undated account of "May Day 1865" in Maverick and Van Wyck Papers, SCL.

3. *Rebel*, 81. Stoneman commanded the U.S. Volunteers, District of East Tennessee. His orders of April 27 (following directives from Secretary of War E. M. Stanton) appear in *OR*, ser. 1, vol. 49, pt. 1, 546–47. An atlas accompanying *OR* shows Palmer's and Brown's routes; reprinted in *The Diary of Clarissa Adger Bowen, Ashtabula Plantation, 1865*, 27; hereafter *Diary of Clarissa Adger Bowen*.

4. *Diary of Clarissa Adger Bowen*, 73, 53–55. Numerous WPA interviewees spoke both of Yankee pillage (e.g., 1, pt. 1, 151) and of whites having slaves bury silver and other items or hiding it in their own cabins (2, pt. 4, 225); cf. 1, pt. 2, 26; Ferguson, *Soul Food*, 106; Reed, 60–70.

Nancy Ashmore Cooper, "When the Yankees Sacked Greenville: Stoneman's Raid, May 2, 1865)," *Carologue*, Spring 1994, 8–12; and *The Life and Times of Ella Lorton, A Pendleton SC Confederate*, ed. Ernest McPherson Lander Jr. (Clemson, S.C.: Clemson Printers, 1996), 76; cited as Lorton; cf. Emily Harris's entry (366) of March 3 about Confederate soldiers wanting overnight lodging.

5. *OR*, ser. 1, vol. 49, pt. 1, 547–50; further on Palmer's troops, vol. 47, 3:609; and vol. 49, pt. 2, 488–91, 539, 549, 555–56, 615, 850, 864. Letters Sent, ACH, April 28, 1866, RG 105/3065; McMurden, Endorsements Sent, WSC, 222, Oct. 25, RG 393:3/865; Affidavit of 26 April 1872; Commissioner of Claims, Settled Case Files, Southern Claims Commission, 217/file 19356 (the only case for AOP).

A retrospective by one participating federal regiment, the 13th Tennessee Cavalry, recorded in 1903: "in the Palmetto State, . . . we did not at that time have any scruples about despoiling the country." On April 27, 1865, Assistant Adjutant-General, acting on Sherman's instructions, issued Special Field Order 65 against looting or "foraging." *OR*, ser. 1, vol. 47, pt. 3, 322, 338–39, 342; orders repeated on April 27 specifically for Brown's troops: vol. 49, pt. 2, 491. Reed, 65 (Manuel), 70 (Henry); *Diary of Clarissa Adger Bowen*, 55–56, 73. Military reports from northwestern South Carolina are scarce. Solicitor J. P. Reed's report to General Assembly 1865 (SCDAH) detailed destruction in the courthouse to official documents and jury box by raiding parties as well as damage by the garrison quartered there later in the year. Cf. Vandiver, 244 ff., and Thomas Bland Keys, "The Federal Pillage of Anderson, South Carolina: Brown's Raid," *SCHM* 76 (April 1975): 80–86; cited as Keys, *SCHM*.

6. Keys, *SCHM*, based on *AI*, May 3, 1866.

7. *Diary of Clarissa Adger Bowen*, 73; Reed, 88–94; Floride Clemson, *A Rebel Came Home: The Diary and Letters of Floride Clemson, 1863–66*, ed. E. M. Lander (Columbia: University of South Carolina Press, 1961), 87; cited as *Rebel*.

8. Commanding the Department of the South, Gillmore was based in Hilton Head, South Carolina, and had served under Sherman. *OR*, ser. 1, vol. 47, pt. 3, 362–63, 498–99; *Piedmont Farmer*, 377–78; Anderson Town Council, Minutes. Toney: quoted in Joel Williamson's *After Slavery* (Chapel Hill: University of North Carolina Press, 1965), 33; cited as Williamson; cf. Henry W. Ravenel and his slave Edward in ibid., 51, and Emily Harris, *Piedmont Farmer*, 367.

9. *AI*, Aug. 24; *KC*, Oct. 14.

10. One commander in North Carolina expressed qualms: "What is to be done with the freedmen . . . requires prompt and wise action to prevent the negro from becoming a huge elephant on our hands." Military views toward freedmen: ACH, Letters Sent and Letters Received, RG 105/3065 and RG 105/3231. John William DeForest, *A Union Officer in the Reconstruction* (Baton Rouge: Louisiana State University Press, 1997), 46; cited as DeForest; *Diary of Clarissa Adger Bowen*, 74. Thomas B. Keys, *The Army and Crawford Keys: Aftermath of the Brown's Ferry Outrage* (n.p.: n.p., 1974), 53, 55–56; hereafter, *Army and Crawford Keys*.

Sherman: *OR*, ser. 1, vol. 47, pt. 3, 410–11. "Phobia" from Jas. M. Trotter, 55th MA Vol., writing from Orangeburg, May 27, to E. W. Kinsley, Boston; see also Trotter to Kinsley, July 1, 1866; Edward W. Kinsley Correspondence, Duke University. Gutman (366–85) chronicles hostile, nasty treatment in Kentucky—where Palmer was in charge—toward freed blacks, even soldiers, by white Union soldiers. Cf. *Homefront*, 41–42; *OR*, ser. 1, vol. 47, pt. 3, 560–61; Joseph T. Blatthaar, *Forged in Battle: The Civil War Alliance of Black Soldiers and White Officers* (New York: Free Press, 1990), 185, 218.

11. For general background see Eric Foner, *Reconstruction: America's Unfinished Revolution* (New York: Harper & Row, 1988); cited as Foner.

12. *AI*, Aug. 28, 1865, Oct. 18, 1866; ACH SO 41, Dec. 15, 1865.

13. Orangeburg was chosen for occupation as early as May 3. Gillmore created four military districts by SO 164 on June 23 then reaffirmed them as part of the new Department of South Carolina structure by GO 103, June 27, establishing the four districts. Technically, the command at Anderson was a subdistrict, not a post, until May 1866 reorganization (ch. 13). *OR*, ser. 1, vol. 53, 109–10; vol. 47, pt. 3, 669–70. The process of occupying South Carolina was ill-organized. Dept. of the South, SO 164, 179, 189; RG 393:1/4128; and WSC, SO 12, and WSC GO 1; RG 393:3/869 and 871.

The troops allocated to Trowbridge were units of the 56th NY Volunteers; other units occupied Greenville at the same time (III/871, WSC SO 1); other insights about Trowbridge in Susie King Taylor, *Reminiscences of My Life in Camp with the 33rd United States Colored Troops Late 1st S.C. Volunteers* (Boston: privately printed, 1902).

14. *Diary of Clarissa Adger Bowen*, 77; Vandiver, 249–50; *AI*, June 21, 1866.

Several officers in chs. 12 and 13, including Capt. Alfred T. Smith (Brvt. Lt. Col.) and Capt. Charles Snyder (Brvt. Capt.), were part of the 8th U.S. Infantry. "Register of Station of Officers," RG 393:1/4140. Correspondence from WSC July–Sept. 1865; RG 393:3/863. On Trowbridge and Brown, see WSC, Letters Sent, RG 393:3/863: Acting Asst. Adj. Gen. on Aug. 28 to Trowbridge; Acting Asst. Adj. Gen. to C. S. Brown, Sept. 18; GO 8, Sept. 15 to Brown, RG 393:3/869. Further on withdrawal of USCT, Sickles SO 34, 49 of Aug. 16 and 29; RG 393:1/4128. See also WSC SO 26, Sept. 2, and SO 13 (new series), Oct. 2, RG 393:3/871. Brown's initial unit was the 1st ME Batt. *Sword of Honor*, 45–62; *OR*, ser. 1, vol. 46, pt. 3, 1040, 1189.

Brown remained in Anderson nearly a year until Aug. 1866. He was replaced by Capt. A. T. Smith, who served from Aug. 1866 until Dec. 1867, when he was reassigned to the new regional headquarters at Laurens (ch. 13). Endorsements Sent, RG 393:3/865; *Diary of Clarissa Adger Bowen*, 80; see note 2, ch. 11 about a tradition of local violence.

15. May 12, GO 91, War Department; May 18, SO 238 assigning assistant commissioners, see *OR*, ser. 1, vol. 46, pt. 3, 1139, 1170; vol. 47, pt. 3, 468. The classic account of the FMB's prototype is Willie Lee Rose, *Rehearsal for Reconstruction: The Port Royal Experiment* (New York: Oxford University Press, 1964); cf. Laura Josephine Webster, *The Operation of the Freedmen's Bureau in South Carolina* (Northampton, Mass.: Department of History of Smith College, 1916), and Martin Abbott, *The Freedmen's Bureau in South Carolina, 1865–1872* (Chapel Hill: University of North Carolina Press, 1967); these general accounts have little AOP material. A seminal book on the FMB's operations and their relationship to its purposes and to the law is Donald G. Nieman's *To Set the Law in Motion: The Freedmen's Bureau and the Legal Rights of Blacks, 1865–1868* (Millwood, N.Y.: KTO Press, 1979).

16. A brief sketch of Orr appears in *Rebels in Grey*, 1–10; Roger P. Leemhuis, *James L. Orr and the Sectional Conflict* (Washington: University Press of America, 1979), cited as Leemhuis; and Lillian Adele Kibler, *Benjamin F. Perry, South Carolina Unionist* (Durham: Duke University Press, 1946). See, among other statements, Perry in *AI*, July 17, Aug. 14, 1867. Orr: *AI*, Oct. 23; cf. Governor's Papers, Orr, Letters Sent, SCDAH.

17. *AI*, Sept. 14; *KC*, Sept. 23. Sickles replaced Gillmore in Nov. 1865. For Johnson's program, oaths, and pardons, see Foner, 159, 183–84, and 190–91. In contrast to Anderson's attitudes toward Trowbridge, Walhalla's white citizens expressed to Capt. Niles G. Parker their "esteem" for the "quiet, order, and good discipline of his command." 1034 oaths were administered in Walhalla from ca. Aug. 31 through Sept. 5 and an additional 1295 oaths through Dec. 31; "Oaths of Allegiance . . . Walhalla, SC," RG 393:2/3363; Resolution of Aug. 26, 1865, following the murder of Lt. Furman; *AI*, Aug. 31. Taylor in *Reminiscences of My Life in Camp* said (44) that 1st Lt. Jerome T. Furman "and a number of soldiers were killed by these South Carolina bushwhackers at Wall Hallow."

18. *Piedmont Farmer*, 379, 389; *OR*, ser. 1, vol. 49, pt 2, 1041–42; *Diary of Clarissa Adger Bowen*, 77–78, 89–90; cf. Henry Ravenel, quoted in Williamson, 247; WPA, Georgia, pt. 2, 133; narrator Tom Hawkins came from Belton, South Carolina.

19. Entry of July 29, *Rebel*, 92; *Diary of Clarissa Adger Bowen*, 78–79; Vandiver, 250–51.

20. Letters Sent, WSC, RG 393:3/869. On Feb. 7, 1866, the WSC Asst. Adj. Gen. noted that Furman was shot while trying to arrest Jolly. WSC Letters Sent, RG 393:3/863; cf. Sickles's (Nov. 12, 1867) statement in *Report of the Secretary of War* (1867), 1:414. The army later identified Sargent as Furman's assassin.

21. Vandiver, 244 ff.; see also E. Don Herd, *The South Carolina Upcountry, 1540–1980* (Greenwood, SC.: Attic Press, 1981–82), 2:401 ff.; cited as Herd. *Army and Crawford Keys*, 80; Jolly: Sickles in ibid., 80; General Assembly of South Carolina, Committee of Investigation, Third Congressional District, August 18, 1869, in *Reports and Resolutions, 1869–70*, 1326–27; cited as *Reports, 1869–70*, DeForest, 14–16. A prominent Pendletonian wrote a supposedly fictional account, "Bushwhacker's Retreat, an Incident of 1865"; Papers of the Maverick and Van Wyck Families, SCL.

22. *Diary of Clarissa Adger Bowen*, 79; Sarah Mills, "Reminiscences," 16.

23. A family member's account of the trial is Thomas B. Keys, *Army and Crawford Keys*, based on 1400 pages of RG 153, Records of the Office of the Judge Advocate General, which includes all of the trial testimony and related documents. *KC*, Oct. 21, 28.

24. Ames to HQ, Nov. 4, Letters Sent, WSC, RG 393:3/863.

25. *AI*, Aug. 17; *Rebel*, 98.

26. Freedmen's Bureau Circular 5, October 19, and unnumbered, Nov. 22; in *KC*, Nov. 11 and Dec. 9, 1865; Jan. 13, 1866.

27. *Rebel*, 96, (98); Sickles to Orr, Dec. 17; Orr, Letters Received.

28. Ames, WSC, to HQ, Dec. 27, Letters Received, Department of the South; RG 393:1/4109.

29. Huger, 44. This caveat ("Introduction: A Piedmont Setting") deserves repeating: "contemporary white opinions of friendly relations with blacks should be considered cautiously; these abounded especially during early postbellum years." GO 1 of Jan. 1, 1866, ordered planters to support the elderly and infirm, but it seems to have lapsed within a few months.

30. *Reports and Resolutions, 1866*, 286; *KC*, Feb. 17, 1866. The Pickens delegation was considerably more moderate than the rest of the state; *Acts*, 1866. Francis Butler Simkins and Robert Hilliard Woody, *South Carolina during Reconstruction* (Chapel Hill: University of North Carolina Press, 1932), 37–52, 57; cited as Simkins; and John Schreiner Reynolds, *Reconstruction in South Carolina* (Columbia, S.C.: State Co., 1905), 106–8; cited as Reynolds; *AI*, Sept. 14.

31. *Rebel*, 90–91; *AI*, Nov. 2; Lorton, 78; cf. "Mobility" in ch. 14.

32. *Diary of Clarissa Adger Bowen*, 77.

33. From Ralph Ely, FMB, Letters Received, Department of the South, RG 393:1/4109; see "1866: Freedmen's Schools, Social Welfare" in ch. 13; Adger, *My Life and Times*, 348–49.

34. Agents (presumably the landowners) often paid taxes owned by adult black men. These lists provide significant clues as to where specific black people lived between 1865 and 1868. Comptroller General, Tax Returns, 1865, 1866, 1867 (SCDAH) for Pickens-Oconee and Anderson. GO 10 in *AI*, April 24, 1867, dealt with taxes.

35. The 1870 federal agricultural census and 1871 Anderson personal property tax schedules confirm ownership.

36. Sickles to Asst. Adj. Gen. Ruggles, Dec. 14; Dept. of the South, Letters Sent, RG 393:1/4088; similar expressions in *Reed* diary.

37. Adger, quoted in *Diary of Clarissa Adger Bowen*, 45; ibid., 77, 79; Sarah Cromer's diary is owned by the Bethesda Methodist Church, Powdersville, South Carolina.

38. F. M. Burgess, Dec. 31, 1865, to J. E. Hagood, SCL; Norton: Oct. 7, 1865, Norton Papers, SCL.

39. Beginning in Dec. 1865 the FMB required weekly regional office reports; RG 393:2/2382, WSC, General and Special Orders.

40. "Labor Contracts" are filed as RG 105/3073 for Anderson and RG 105/3240 for the Greenville office, which in 1867 included Pickens and Oconee in its jurisdiction. Signed by the thousands just for AOP, these documents form the most voluminous source for what happened to individuals in the immediate postemancipation era. For a broader study see Lewis C. Chartock, "A History and Analysis of Labor Contracts Administered by the Bureau of Refugees, Freedmen, and Abandoned Lands in Edgefield, Abbeville and Anderson Counties in South Carolina, 1865–1868" (Ph.D. diss., Bryn Mawr College, 1973); cf. Williamson, chs. 3 and 5.

I sampled about 325 contracts on the following informal criteria: preference was given to 1865 contracts, forms that listed ages, landowners who were known to have made contracts in other years, those including large numbers of names, and landowners who had been large slaveholders or for whom other information was available.

41. *Diary of Clarissa Adger Bowen*, 89–90; George Seaborn, no. 133, 1865; unnumbered FMB Circular, Nov. 22; printed in *KC*, Dec. 9, 1865. Julie Saville, *The Work of Reconstruction: From Slave to Wage Laborer in South Carolina, 1860–1870* (New York: Cambridge University Press, 1994), passim; cited as Saville. WSC GO 3, July 15, 1865, canceled any contract provisions that included power to punish; *AI*, July 27. Sickles GO 1, Jan. 1, 1866, forbade punishments; reprinted in *KC*, Feb. 3, 1866. See "Early 1866" in ch. 13, and Sickles to Orr, Oct. 25, 1866; Letters Sent, RG 393:1/4088.

42. None of the 1865 contracts sampled offered a percentage; all were for fixed amounts. By contrast virtually all 1866 agricultural contracts included a percentage of at least one crop. "Best," H. D. Colhoun, no. 805, Jan. 1, 1866.

43. *Diary of Clarissa Adger Bowen*, 77, 89–90; cf. "Freedom: Taxes, Black Codes, and Churches," p. 206; Saville, 54; J. P. Reed, Jan. 30, 1866 (no no.; box 50A), with his former slave.

44. Additional hands: Frances C. Williams, Feb. 10, 1866 (no no., box 51A); relocations: J. W. Harrison, Nov. 9, 1865, no. 284C; and W. T. Smith, March 6, 1867, no. 81; see Adger's help to freedman Charles, "Freedom: Departures," p. 206.

45. Livingston 1866 contracts, nos. 426–29; Alex. Ramsey, Oct. 2, 1865, no. 111; Ella F. Lorton, Aug. 16, 1865, no. 412; R. J. Gilliand, Dec. 18, 1865, no. 59, with an invalid and five children; Jeptha Norton estate (by J. B. Sitton), Aug. 30, 1865, no. 131, whose fourteen people included "Bella, has sore leg & unable to work or walk about." Harrison: Dec. 26, 1865, no. 268. GO 1 of 1866 required owners not to evict destitute elderly blacks; it is not clear how long that order remained in effect.

46. Elvira Norris, for Charles Keown's wife, Mar. 23, 1866, N-7; John R. Cochran, Jan. 22, 1866, no. 365; and Mrs. S. E. Calhoun, Sept. 9, 1866 (apprentice bonds, for 9 years until 18); Elias Earle, March 31, 1866, E-8, for a saw mill, with Frank Delight; Reed: no no.; box 50A.

47. Obedience: J. R. Shelor, Dec. 2, 1865, no. 134; J. B. Sitton, Aug. 30, 1865, no. 131; Martha Boggs, Jan. 1, 1866, no. 20; profane: J. B. Sitton, Dec. 25, 1865, no. 271; no company: G. R. Cherry, Dec. 18, 1865, no. 157; Kenon Breazeale, Jan. 10, 1866, no. 220. Prohibitions against firearms, liquor, and "drunkenness or other gross vices" come from the standard 1865 and 1866 FMB forms.

48. Typically 1866 contracts called for penalties of 50 to 75 cents/day missed; but G. R. Cherry charged $1 per day (Jan. 30, 1866, no. 136); and A. F. Lewis demanded $2 (Jan. 18, 1866, no. 418). See on school or church B. F. Hammond, Jan. 1, 1866, no. 360, and J. P. Reed, Jan. 22, 1866 (no no.; box 50A). One of Carlisle's contracted laborers was Elijah Carlisle, soon to be a Methodist minister.

49. J. P. Reed, Jan. 1866 (no no.; box 50A); Ella F. Lorton, Aug. 16, 1865, no. 412.

50. Stone to McDougall, Letters Sent, ACH, Sept. 1, 1866, RG 105/3065; DeForest to Thompson, Letters Sent, Greenville, Feb. 5, 1867, RG 105/3227; testimony in "November 1868 Elections" in ch. 15.

Chapter 13. Reconstruction Evolves, 1866–68

1. *KC*, Feb. 3; June 28, GO 8, *AI*, July 19; *Rebel*, 98. This may be the first editorial use of the term "niggers" in an upstate newspaper. Conversations with Anne McCuen, John Hammond Moore, and Stephen West. Many freed people had no labor agreements and others worked without fixed or written conditions. Sonte, ACH, Letters Sent, March 23, and GO 4, RG 105/3065; J. Chase Jr., Asst. Provost Marshall, Anderson, notation on Report on Contracts, March 7, 1866, RG 105/3070; *KC*, March 31. Note sources in note 1, ch. 12.

2. Bray's entry for Report on Contracts, March 7, 1866; Letters Sent, WSC, Ames to HQ, RG 393:3/863, March 10, 1866.

3. Based on a review of nearly forty cases, March–June 1866; reported by Stone, Letters Sent, ACH, RG 105/3065.

4. Lorton, 88; Williamson, 49; *AI*, Oct. 30, 1866.

5. Norton to Orr, Letters Received, Feb. 1, 1866. The FMB provided no clue about what instigated this brutality. Testimony taken May 15, 1866; two months afterward, Amaziah Payton was murdered ("Violence Again," pp. 216–17).

6. Gov. Orr commuted sentences to lifetime hard labor on Feb. 25, 1867, and on May 1, 1867, remitted the balance of James Perry Looper's sentence. Official documents in Pickens County, Lucas Papers, SCDAH; cf. DeForest, 165–67.

7. Testimony April 2; held by Keys's lawyers to be the culprits; *Army and Crawford Keys*, 32; DeForest, 1–15; Ames, WSC, to HQ, March 13, 1866; Orr to Sickles, March 5; Department of South Carolina, Letters Received, RG 393:1/4109; see below on "Cato Hallums." Other bushwhackers: *Reed*, 94, 234, and Jolly photograph, following 150.

8. Sickles to Ames, Letters Sent, Feb. 12, 1866, RG 393:1/4088; GO 1, ACH, *AI*, March 1, 1866; cf. GO 90: "energetic means will soon result in the capture of Jollie alive or dead." WSC, Letters Sent, RG 393:3/868; GO: WSC, Letters Received, RG 393:3/867; cf. *Reed*, 246.

9. Charges against the other three accused men were dismissed. R. F. Simpson complained in 1866 that this "is the first case in our state where Negro testimony has been taken where both parties were white." Keys, *Army and Crawford Keys*, 37, 43, 51; additional materials in "Keys & Stowers Case," Trescot Papers (SCL).

10. *Army and Crawford Keys*, 56; Ames to HQ, Letters Sent, WSC, March 31, 1866, RG 393:3/863; Stone to Acting Asst. Comsr., Letters Sent, ACH, March 23, 1866, RG 105/3065.

11. Letters Received, WSC, RG 393:3/868; *AI*, July 27; cf. Returns from U.S. Military Posts, Anderson, S.C., May 1866–December 1867 (National Archives and Records Admin. Microcopy 617). Ames reported on March 31, 1866, that one-fourth of the 25th Ohio unit had deserted. WSC, Letters Sent, RG 393:3/863.

12. *AI*, Aug. 9; Letters Received, Department of the South, RG 393:1/4109; Coroner's Inquest, Anderson.

13. *AI*, Aug. 2, Aug. 16.

14. Estate records; Letters Sent, Anderson, July 20 and 26, RG 105/3065; *AI*, July 19, 26.

15. What then happened is not clear, but Hallum appears in the 1867 voter registration, 1869 state census, and a Sept. 1873 petition to Governor Moses; DeForest, 1–13; and "Report of Outrages, Greenville District, October 1866" and for "November 1866"; other DeForest letters in Letters Sent, Greenville, RG 105/3227.

16. Stone to Lt. Snyder, Comd. Post, ACH, Letters Sent, June 26, RG 105/3065; Smith (ACH) to HQ, Letters Received, Dept. of the South, RG 393:1/4109; *KC*, Oct. 20, Nov. 10; *AI*, March 8, Oct. 18, Dec. 6, 1866. Cf. *Reed*, 293.

17. Niles to HQ, June 14, RG 393:1/4107–8, June 18, RG 105/3227; ACH GO 1, June 16; *AI*, June 21; Stone, Sept. 1, Letters Sent, RG 105/3065; National Archives and Records Admin. guide to RG 105 shows replacement of staff.

18. Forwarded to Gov. Orr, box 3, folder 27, SCDAH.

19. *AI*, Oct. 11.

20. *AI, KC*, summer 1866; lodge notices throughout 1866–67; *AI*, Nov. 27, Dec. 11, 18, 1867.

21. *KC*, Oct. 6, p. 1, enclosed with Capt. Goodman at Greenville to HQ, Letters Received, Department of the South, RG 393:1/4109. Sickles report, included in the *Report of the Secretary of War* (1866), 59; reprinted in *AI*, Dec. 13, 1866.

22. DeForest to Intendant Doct. R. D. Long, Greenville, Letters Sent, RG 105/3227; Cheatham: Letters Received, Department of the South, RG 393:1/4109.

23. The following (Orr letters) from Sarah Calhoun, handwritten by her on November 4, 1867, puts the blame on what evidently was a black servant: "the one that kep hous for me the time that the crime was comited is the gilty one . . . me and hir made agreement for me to come out the way that I did to confess anything but the truth." Other infanticides: *KC*, Oct. 27, Dec. 8, 1866; RG 393:3/4305 Report of Crimes.

24. *DeBow's Review*, N.S. 1 (March 1866), 550–52 (quoted in Simkins, 17); cf. a similar statement by W. K. Easley in "Introduction: A Piedmont Setting," note 11. Fifteen hundred people equaled about 16% of the county's black population. Stone, June 20, Sept. 1, Letters Sent, RG 105/3065; Smith to HQ, Sept. 30, Letters Sent, and Letters Sent, Anderson Court House, Oct. 31, RG 393:4/520; GO 20, Sept. 20, reprinted in *KC*, Oct. 13.

25. Technically, the title was *intendant* for AOP towns; I am substituting the more familiar term, *mayor*. Letters Received, 2nd Military District, Aug. 31; RG 393:1/4111.

26. "An Act [4798] To Declare the Rights of Persons Lately Known as Slaves and as Freed Persons of Color," Sept. 21, 1866; Sickles to Orr, Aug. 14, and Oct. 24, Dept. of the South, RG 393:1/4088; Leemhuis, 193 ff.. Orr received favorable coverage in the *AI* (May 8) and *KC* (May 2) when he died and in subsequent issues. Sickles to Orr, Aug. 14, Letters Sent, Department of the South, RG 393:1/4088; Sickles to Orr, Oct. 4, 8, Abstracts of Letters Received, no. 750, no. 764, Orr Papers, SCDAH. Provost Marshall General E. W. Dennis created detective forces. GO 34; *Report of the Secretary of War, 1867, House Executive Doc. No. 1, Part 1, 40th Congress, 2nd Session* (Washington: GPO, 1868), 300, 308; cited as *War Report*. Required monthly reports on crimes: RG 393:1/4300, 4304, 4305, 4307.

27. Contemporary records of FMB educational efforts may be found in semiannual reports of John W. Alvord, Inspector of Schools and Finances; published as *Freedmen's Schools and Textbooks* (1865–70; New York: AMS Press, 1980); cf. Martin Abbott, "The Freedmen's Bureau and Negro Schooling in South Carolina," *SCHM* 58 (1956): 65–81. Stone, March 26, to W. J. Knauff, Letters Sent, ACH, RG 105/3065.

28. Letters Sent, ACH, March 27, May 28, 1866, RG 105/3065; Petition of Aug. 13, 1868, to Scott, SCDAH.

29. Neither Crawford, Williams, nor Austin (below) has been found for AOP in the 1870 census. Williams was twice driven off the land on which he was contracted; Stone intervened. Schools included those at Anderson Court House Presbyterian Church (100 attending), Seneca (15), Andrew Norris's plantation (15; taught by himself), Belton (25), and Shiloh Church (10–15). Letters Sent, ACH, May 31, June 1, June 6, June 14, July 3, July 28, 1866, RG 105/3065; cf. also "Miscellaneous Records," including school reports, RG 105/3076. P. L. Walker (white) was listed in Anderson's 1860 census as a 60–year-old teacher born in Virginia.

There is a curious emphasis on "color" in the Freedmen's Schools student lists and in Freedmen's Savings Banks depositors' records (ch. 14) with special emphasis (it seems) on "mixed blood."

30. Freedman Charles Austin tried to establish a school on his own place in Pickens, had his house broken into, and received warnings to quit the county before sunrise, which he did. Teachers secured by the Freedmen's Bureau for another Pickens school were subjected to such annoyances that they too left. Carroll Neide, Greenville, Letters Sent, July 31, 1868, RG 105/3227.

Favorable *KC* article, April 7; RG 105/3065: Letters Sent, ACH, April 1, 4, 17; May 28; Stone, May 31, to Dr. T. G. Wright, Supt. of Freedmen Schools, Western District; June 6 to Rev. Stratton, ACH Presbyterian Church; June 11, Stone to Dr. Wright; July 25–Aug. 31, 1866, Stone to Snyder; and "Negro melee," *AI*, July 19, 1866.

31. From P. L. Walker, July 13, 1866, ACH, Letters Received, RG 105/3067; FMB "List of Schools under Patronage of Societies" (RG 105/2964); ACH, Letters Sent, Sept. 17, 1866; Jan. 3, Jan. 31, March 31, 1867.

32. Letters Sent, ACH, March 30, May 6, and May 17, 1866; RG 105/3065. Memphis case: DeForest to Officer in Charge, FMB, Memphis, Dec. 30, 1866, Letters Sent, Greenville, RG 105/3227.

Perhaps as much as 80%–90% of FMB activity in AOP focused on black men, usually the ones whose names headed labor contracts, who were involved in conflicts with, or assaults by, white men, or who were arrested. New research on women during Reconstruction and FMB attitudes is being done by Carol Faulkner and Hannah Rosen, among others.

33. Stone: *KC*, Aug. 11; Letters Sent, ACH, RG 105/3065.

34. RG 105/3227, Letters Sent, Greenville: July 30, Niles to Lt. Thomas Britton; Aug. 7, to Lt. Charles Snyder, Comdg. Post Anderson; Sept. 3, to Snyder. See also Aug. 1, Geo. R. Cherry to Orr, urging FMB aid for poor whites and blacks, Orr Letters, SCDAH; RG 105/3065, Letters Sent, Anderson Court House; Stone, "Monthly Report," Sept. 1, RG 393:4/520; and *AI*, Oct. 18. Stone reported on June 9 that more than a hundred white families in Anderson County needed food. Letters Sent, RG 105/3065; *cf.* "List of Destitute Persons in the Eastatohoe Beat 5th Regiment Pickens District" (June 11, 1867), which included 36 whites, 5 "colored."

35. DeForest to Board of Commissioners for the Poor, Pickens District, Jan. 5 and 7 and Feb. 4; to R. A. Thompson, Feb. 5, 1867; to Col. Smith, May 15; to Dean, Aug. 8. Letters Sent, Greenville, RG 105/3227.

36. "Drunk": Pillsbury to Congress in *Army and Crawford Keys*, 79–80, 93; the House Select Committee on the Murder of Union Soldiers in South Carolina was established on Dec. 6. HR, *Report* No. 23, 39th Cong., 2nd sess.

37. *War Report*, 1867, 299; Sickles, GO 1, March 21, in *KC*, March 30, 1867; Sickles address to Charleston freedmen, *KC*, April 6, 1867; Foner, 271–91. Greenville fell under Anderson's command in this reorganization.

38. Canby proposed the change in his annual report to the Secretary of War, Oct. 24; Orr to Canby on Nov. 29 and Dec. 18 and from Canby, Nov. 30 (SCDAH); these exchanges occurred during the "The Hunnicutt Murder Crisis," below. Canby's GO 145 effected the changes, *AI*, Dec. 11, 1867; tribute to Lt. Col. A. T. Smith, *KC*, Dec. 21, 1867; Max L. Heyman Jr., "'The Great Reconstructor': General E. R. S. Canby and the Second Military District," *North Carolina Historical Review* 32 (Jan. 1955): 52–80; cited as "Canby," *NCHR*. Vandiver, 257; DeForest to Robert A. Thompson (*KC* editor), Feb. 5, 1867, RG 105/3227, Greenville, Letters Sent.

39. April 15 public meeting [Walhalla?], Gossett (April 18) to Orr enclosing *KC* report, Orr Papers, SCDAH; also *AI*, April 24; quotation from Hagood to Orr, April 25, 1867; Leemhuis, 174, 181, 189.

40. *AI*, July 17, 1867.

41. Reynolds, 61; *KC*, Aug. 3, 1867; J. B. McGee to Orr, March 17, 1868; Pickens-Oconee and Spartanburg were not represented.

42. Saville, 188, on Walhalla's Union League; RG 105/3227, Greenville, Letters Sent, Aug. 26; cf. July 10 to Mason Pickens, informing him that he could not dismiss any freed men for political reasons.

43. *KC*, Aug. 10, 17; *AI*, Sept. 4, 18, 25.

44. Leemhuis, 186–87; *KC*, Sept. 21, 28.

45. "Canby," *NCHR*. GO 63, detailed "Regulations for Registration," and GO 64, reprinted in *AI*, Aug. 1, and *KC*, Aug. 18.

46. This is the first published analysis of the Hunnicutt crisis, although Joel Williamson and Julie Saville both refer to it; despite numerous sources available, they are highly dispersed. The major documents are the Coroner's Inquest on Miles Hunnicutt and the General Sessions Journal of the trial, incorporated into the *Report of the Secretary of War* (1867), vol. 1.

Voluminous correspondence between Canby and Orr is found in Orr's correspondence (SCDAH), and Canby's letters, RG 393:1/4089 and 4410. Orr also received several petitions and exchanged numerous letters with J. J. Norton, Sheriff Lemuel Thomas, J. W. Livingston, J. E. Hagood, and others. *KC* and *AI* coverage, although incomplete, adds some details not found elsewhere. There are a few relevant letters from the Anderson post to Canby in RG 105/3065 and RG 393:1/4089. Pardons appear in *Reports and Resolutions* for 1868 and subsequent years, as well as the Central Register of Prisoners, 1867–1872 (SCDAH). Robert Smith's capture and trial: *War Report*, 457–58 and 465–67.

47. Grand-jury indictments (dropped) for murder also included James W. Keith and Green Cleveland Sr. According to a Dec. 5, 1986, newspaper history of Flat Rock Baptist Church, James Keith (ch. 15) helped organize that church in 1866 and became its first minister; charter members included family members for 3 of the 10 accused men. Elias Kennedy was murdered in 1868 ("Spring to Fall 1868" in ch. 15).

48. Those found not guilty of murder were Adams, Brackenridge, Bryce, and Dean; Dean and Brackenridge were found guilty of riot, false imprisonment, and assault and battery—the latter two for "vigilante" pursuit of Smith; Bryce was found not guilty of the same charges; and Adams was not charged on riot and assault and battery. Charges against about thirty other men were dropped.

49. *KC*, Oct. 19. Post reports show a total (including officers) of 49 men at the end of Sept.; 37 at the end of Oct.; 73 on Nov. 30; and 32 when the post was evacuated on Dec. 24. Orr on Oct. 31, Nov. 11, Nov. 28, and Dec. 3 to Sheriff Thomas, Orr Papers, and Anderson County, Lucas Papers, SCDAH; Dec. 1867 "Monthly Returns of Prisoners," RG 393:1/4300; and *AI*, Dec. 18, 1867.

50. Orr to Canby, Oct. 31; G. F. Slieferr(?), Diamond Hill, Nov. 8; Abstracts of Letters Received, no. 1282, Canby to Orr, Nov. 25; all Orr Papers, SCDAH; "Canby," *NCHR*, 59–60.

51. Other trouble in that vicinity: "The 1876 Campaign" in ch. 16.

52. Evidently the first white support for the condemned men, Calhouns to Orr, Nov. 1, 1867; Livingston to Orr, May 1, 1868, SCDAH. Attorneys were Norton, McGowan and Adams, and Easley—not further identified.

53. "Canby," *NCHR*, 74–76.

54. Orr to Sheriff, Nov. 2; J. E. Hagood to Orr, Nov. 8; Norton to Orr, Nov. 15; Orr letter to Canby, Nov. 29 (followed by telegram); Orr to Norton, Dec. 3; Orr to Sheriff, Dec. 9; and Orr to Canby, RG 393:1/4110, Register of Letters Received.

55. Orr's personal role is indicated all the more by his conveying to Sheriff Thomas in Jan. 1868 (undated letter) $50 for Elias Kennedy's fine. Other white support: former owner Capt. William Sanders for Elias Sanders (also supported by prominent Norris, Broyles, and Simpson families); petition to Orr, March 18: undated letter to Orr (filed with March 1868, box 12), SCDAH; and former owner A. W. Lowery for Jack Walker (to Orr, May 15, 1868, and Orr notation on the cover, SCDAH). See Sarah Calhoun's plea for executive clemency in "1866: Violence, Limited Military Force, and White Preoccupations," above. Frazier seems to have lacked much support, white or black, in the local community, and, evidently too young, did not register to vote and or pay taxes in 1865–67.

Orr in Dec. 1867 commuted sentences of five men to two to five years' hard labor: Gadsden, Cleveland Jr., John Keith, Henderson, and Walker; "Monthly Returns of Prisoners," RG 393:1/4300, for Sarah Calhoun and for those arrested in connection with Hunnicutt's murder. Not commuted: one, released earlier, and another died earlier in the penitentiary; Central Register of Prisoners, 1867–1872 (SCDAH).

56. One researcher argues that Anderson's 77%–79% registration of blacks fell well below both 90% statewide or even the piedmont average (not stated); Saville, 166–67. My calculations for Anderson and Pickens-Oconee—93.3 and 101.5% respectively—run higher than hers. I compared official voter registration figures (from Canby) with the number of black

males over 21 reported in the 1869 state census; cf. Saville's methodology, 166–67. The 853 blacks registered in November 1867 in Pickens-Oconee exceeded the 840 reported to be 21 and older in 1869! Peggy Burton Rich and Frederick C. Holder, *Oconee and Pickens Counties, South Carolina, 1868 Voter Registration* ([Clemson, S.C.?]: Pendleton Chapter of the South Carolina Genealogical Society, 1990).

In Anderson there were 1988 registered whites; 1932 registered voters did not cast a ballot for or against the convention; the vote against it was only 79. Pickens-Oconee registered whites totaled 2038; 1728 registered similarly did not vote for or against the convention, but 254 men voted against it. "Recapitulation of registration and elections on convention," *War Report*, 1868; black turnout, note 59, below, and page 229 in text. "Abundant": Wesley Pitchford to Orr, Jan. 14, 1868.

57. Oconee was part of Pickens District until 1868, when the constitutional convention divided the district into separate counties. Walhalla became Oconee's county seat; the old town of Pickens (located within Oconee's boundaries) was mostly dismantled and removed, and New Pickens was established several miles to the east. Jane Boroughs Morris, *Pickens: The Town and the First Baptist Church* (Pickens, S.C.: First Baptist Church, 1991); cited as Morris, *Pickens*.

Neither Zuczek (see note 2, his ch. 3) nor Reynolds gives party affiliation for whites; those from AOP at least cooperated well with Republicans, but it is not clear that they ran under, or accepted, that label. Richard Zuczek, *State of Rebellion: Reconstruction in South Carolina* (Columbia: University of South Carolina Press, 1996); cited as *Zuczek*; *KC*, May 29, 1868; Morris, *Pickens*, 11.

58. Details involving the official change appear in "Canby," *NCHR*, 71–74, 77. One further procedure was necessary: approval of the 14th Amendment to the U.S. Constitution, done by late July in both states. Canby relinquished his command of troops in North Carolina and South Carolina on August 5. GO 136, 145, printed in *AI*, July 22 (special issue), and *KC*, July 24.

59. Pickens-Oconee's figure seems to be 102.7%. The constitutional vote evidently won some white support, which would reduce slightly the apparent 91.4% of all adult black men voting in Anderson.

Chapter 14. Panorama of Black Families in Freedom

1. The major source for this chapter is the 1870 census for AOP. I have examined every black household (Population, Agriculture, and Mortality Schedules); checked for professionals, literacy, and out-of-state births; and sampled intensively seven townships on family structure. Figures on S.C. blacks and whites come from the published Census Bureau volumes.

Black leaders at times urged their congregations to acquire property as a means of establishing independence and protecting themselves (chs. 20, 22): AME minister James T. Baker in Abbeville in the early 1870s; dozens of Oconee black families buying State Land Commission land ("Parameters Affecting Black Political Activity" in ch. 15); and in 1881 Silas Jefferson urging black people to acquire homesteads; Abbeville [AME] Singing Convention, *Minutes* (Abbeville, S.C.: Hugh Wilson, Printer, 1889), 13–14; AME *Minutes*, 1881: 34 (SCL).

2. Burton (327–32) gives the 1870 census for Edgefield a high level of confidence for different reasons.

3. *Reports, 1869–70*; Honea Path: "Economic Subjugation, Sharecropping, and Crop Liens" in ch. 22.

4. Pickens, *Bursting Bonds* (Boston: Jordan & More Press, 1923), 8; Jane Edna Hunter, *A Nickel and a Prayer*; and William Pickens, *The Vengeance of the Gods* (1922; New York: AMS Press, 1975), 12–13, cited as Pickens, *Vengeance*; cf. *Crucible*, 46.

5. *Piedmont Farmer*, 454–55, 486–87; Pickens was listed in *Who's Who in Colored America* (New York: Who's Who in Colored America Corporation, Publisher, 1927), 158.

6. Jerry Anderson (b. 1861) "was tenderly cared for by his mistress whom he remembers with love and tenderness." *Profiles of Black Folks*, 11; 1870 Census, Dark Corner Township (Anderson), household 56; cf. mulatto Amy Ferguson, 25, "deaf & dumb," living with Judge Ferguson but without employment; Pickens Court House Township, household 110; see table 14.3 for sample townships and below for blacks with white "Families and households."

7. Calculations based on published data in the 1860 *Compendium* and the 1870 *Agriculture* volume. Total improved and unimproved land in the Agriculture Schedule dropped by one-fifth between 1860 and 1870. Some enumerators interpreted the term *farmer* narrowly to exclude sharecroppers; others used it for most people involved in agriculture.

8. *AI*, Dec. 24, 1891, June 17, 1896; cf. references to two Fergusons in "Rural Communities," both Little Liberia and Tenus Maxwell vicinity, in ch. 18; and note 29 of this chapter on blacks (7.8% in AOP) shown in the 1870 census as living in white households.

9. Greenville's *Southern Enterprise*, Jan. 10, 1867; DeForest, 130; cf. Burton, 237–38; Williamson, 108 ff. One AOP family, that of Jack Young, evidently left in late 1866 or early 1867 for Liberia; Stone (Anderson) to Lt. Col. Smith, Oct. 15, 1866; RG 393:3/3065.

10. Three-fourths of those born elsewhere came from North Carolina, Virginia, and Georgia. Others in the state included 1653 people born in New York, Massachusetts, and Pennsylvania, presumably mostly army men still remaining in South Carolina or people who came as teachers, preachers, or politicians after the war. Rosa Lawhen, b. ca. 1780 in N.Y.; her son or grandson, Capt Lawhen, b. 1826 in South Carolina; Anderson County, Pendleton Township, 2nd sequence, household 55.

11. Jane Barnes, born in Alabama in 1843, birthed children in Texas between 1860 and 1866, but her youngest was a 1–year-old South Carolina native. Mississippian Sylvia Reed (1825), who had one child born there in 1858, was living in South Carolina at her youngest child's birth in 1866.

12. Others include Pendleton natives Anna Victoria White (1848), her parents and siblings, and Joseph Perry (1852) to Atlanta; Frederick Purse (1845) from Pendleton with parents for Charleston, where he became a painter; and Peter Johnson (1836) from Anderson County, as a waged farm worker in the Augusta area. These represent most area-born residents who lived in Atlanta and Charleston and opened deposit accounts. Registers of Signatures of Depositors in Branches of the Freedmen's Savings and Trust Co., National Archives, Freedmen's Bureau RG 101. Atlanta 26, 96, 206, 220; Charleston 2280, 2691, 3138, 6493; and Augusta 2342.

13. Charleston County reported nearly 20,000 more blacks, while Columbia city and Richland gained almost 4,000; but Beaufort lost nearly 3,000, and both Georgetown and Orangeburg about 5,000 each. Many of the latter may have gone to nearby Barnwell County, which increased by an almost identical number. Cf. antebellum "Changing Locations and Surnames" of FPC in ch. 3. On Abbeville, see Ballard's *One More Day's Journey*, which chronicles intimidation in Abbeville, especially that targeted against Union Leagues and militia; cited as Ballard.

14. When adult black men had to pay per capita taxes but could not afford to do so, "agents" (presumably landowners) paid taxes for them. These lists provide significant clues to where specific black people lived between 1865 and 1868. Cf. study of Honea Path Township blacks, 1870–75, "Economic Subjugation, Sharecropping, and Crop Liens" in ch. 22. Peggy Burton Rich and Margaret Ogle, *Pickens District, South Carolina 1866 Tax List* ([Clemson, S.C.?]: Old Pendleton District Chapter of the South Carolina Genealogical Society, 1991). WPA, Inventory of Church Records, South Carolina, Anderson County (SCHS microfiche); "Black Churches, 1865–1900" in ch. 17.

15. Benjamin Small was listed as 84 years old in the 1870 census, Pendleton Township; the family working for Hillhouse has not been identified. RG 105/3073: Wyck, May 16, 1866, and Hillhouse, Jan. 13, 1866. David Golightly Harris's tenants in Spartanburg County built their own new houses on his land in 1866 and 1867.

16. Quite a few landowners as shown in the census cannot be found in deed books; in other cases their purchase did not occur until years after 1870, a curious circumstance. Figures here come from the Population Schedule of the 1870 census; those in chs. 18–23 are taken from tax records, which should be more accurate.

17. *Sizemore*, 77.

18. AME *Minutes*, 1881, 34 (SCL).

19. Three Oglesbys were described as farming, and a young mother's status was "keeping house." Forch Allen's farming household had ten people including several described as white. Polly Allen, 76, living separately, was the only Oglesby or Allen over 50. In 1900 younger Payton generations were still living in Anderson; one man continued the family tradition as a brick mason; another one owned property. Oglesbys were still active in the late 1900s and early 2000s in church and business roles and were still holding annual family reunions at Cross Roads Baptist Church.

20. The 1869 Oconee census has been lost.

21. One account, repeated in 1978, said that one man's "father was named Keith and about four more brothers and three daughters . . . each one took a different name. One of them said I want to be named a Cannon because it makes a big noise." *Sizemore*, 47.

22. Curiously, few of the Ashtabula surnames could be found in AOP's 1870 census. One sample consists of early enrollees at Charleston's Freedmen's Savings Bank. On the first form used there, asking for the former owner's name, there was an approximately 50% match with the freed man's surname. My own compilation of AOP former slaves for whom there is definitive information on their owners' names has similar results.

23. Cannon: *Sizemore*, 118; cf. above; Scott: interview by Yolanda Harrell with Velma Childers, Jan. 4, 1990 (BHUP). The count includes only those names beginning with "Mc," not any other Scottish derivations; those 103 households included nearly 400 people.

24. Most South Carolina blacks with these lowcountry names lived in the lowcountry; for numbers of Pendleton-area people to choose them further suggests ongoing Charleston connections.

25. See ch. 5, notes 21 and 23, for samples of unpopular surnames and likely reasons.

26. Williamson describes a time span of freed people beginning to use surnames, as I have; *After Slavery*, 310–12. Yankee Bonaparte, born ca. 1865, Anderson's Garvin Township (household 145).

27. Additionally, there are perhaps 100 out of 1068 sampled households (including those headed by whites) in which brothers or other siblings lived together without parents, who may have died. Another pattern is found frequently: a nuclear family unit plus young children—often under 6—with a different surname. Some of these may be nieces or nephews; others could be foster children.

I am using "family" to apply to people related by blood or by marriage; however, the census omits terms of relationships.

28. Specifically, I began by counting numbers of *people* who lived in various family groupings; by contrast both Burton and Gutman calculated percentages of *households*. My approach presents specific segments not addressed by Burton or Gutman, as shown further in my text; among them are three-generational families (lumped together by Gutman and Burton among "extended" or "augmented" families).

As Burton (328) says, in a different sense, "I devised" categories of people that "maintained the consistent delineations I needed." I have grouped my classifications into a framework that permits direct comparison with Burton's Edgefield figures while allowing other segmentations. (See Burton, 109–14, 260–68, for his definitions.) My figures are, unintentionally, skewed somewhat toward town settings (Pendleton and Anderson towns), where more people lived alone than did so in rural areas. Burton surveyed all residents in households headed by blacks; my 1870 sample covers 31% of AOP blacks, including those living in households headed by whites.

Percentages immediately below apply to households, omitting black people who lived in white households. Burton (261) uses a bar graph from which I have estimated his percentages. Except for this note and table, all results of my study refer to percentages of people, including those in white households.

For "female-headed family units," I have calculated the total number of people in nuclear families, husband absent; extended families, female headed; and augmented families, female headed. To them I have also added female-headed family units within augmented families headed by somebody else, and female-headed family units within white households.

Comparisons of Households, Edgefield and AOP

classifications of households	AOP	Edgefield
Nuclear	62%	65%
Extended	14	12
Augmented	11	15
Irregular	13	7

29. Among seven sample townships, the percentage living with whites ranged from 7.5 to 12.9%. Many living in white households were the only African American present, but sometimes there were black families. Many were domestic servants or farm laborers; a few had other occupations. A surprising number of blacks residing in white households had no occupation, were "at home," often sharing the white family's surname and listed as a continuation of that family. Some may have been disguised interracial relationships or children of the white head of household.

See note 28 on "singles" in table 14.3 and note 27 above on "family units."

30. I have calculated "nuclear" families in three ways. One method includes a father or mother whose spouse is absent plus children, as well as couples without children present, plus a "full nuclear" family. That yields a total of 61.5%. A narrower standard (labeled "full nuclear" in the table) consists only of households that include both parents and children, but nobody else. That result is 46.2%. On the other hand, extended and augmented families, as well as some blacks in white households include a nuclear unit within the expanded household. By including them as well, the figure exceeds 75%.

31. Both Dilsey and Amanda appeared in Benjamin Hagood's estate appraisal, March 1865.

32. *Sizemore*, 124. References to marriages (or to couples) in this text refer to settled relationships, regardless of ritual or ceremony involved. The minister at St. Paul's conducted six black marriages from June through Dec. 1865, and others into the 1880s. Some later marriages received a short notice in the newspaper, especially in Pickens. These (fifty over a fifteen-year period) involved services performed by a black or occasionally a white minister or by a justice of the peace. A white Presbyterian minister's record of marriages performed between 1876 and 1882 included six black couples. A white Pickens minister recorded his 480 "white" and 150 "black" marriages; *People's Journal*, Feb. 6, 1896; cited as *PJ*.

33. Greenville, Letters Sent, Feb. 6, 1867; FMB, RG 105/3227.

34. The oldest Hiram Greenlee and Isaac, probably a brother, were early Anderson County teachers and church officers; chs. 15 and 17. Greenlee: households 106, 130. "Beyond Towns" in ch. 18, and "Residential Patterns" in 1900 Anderson in ch. 19.

35. Many wives would have participated in farm chores, even if they were not specifically called farm laborers.

36. See chs. 18 and 19 on towns. Although no FMB school evidently operated in Savannah Township (SVT), the township's black literacy rate substantially exceeded the AOP average. Surnames and other information suggests that a sizable number of SVT blacks who could read came from larger plantations, such as those owned by the Earle, McGee, Norris, Simpson, and perhaps Holland families. Black Sherards were literate and became major black landowners in SVT; Andy Simpson, the Dooley family, and both Humphreys and Cunninghams were literate and important in Reconstruction or Anderson city town life.

37. "Broader Horizons" in ch. 8, pp. 137–38; "1866: Freedom's Schools, Social Welfare, and Protection of Freedmen" in ch. 13, pp. 220–21; "Schools, 1865–1900" in ch. 17, pp. 300–302.

38. The 10–14 age bracket used by the U.S. Census, covers only five years, while the 21-plus bracket spans over sixty years. U.S. Census, 1870, *Population*, 427–28, plus my literacy figures. Pickens had a similar average age, 28.0. Among whites more men than women over 21 could read in AOP and South Carolina, the same skewing that applied to blacks over 21. The skewing for those 21 or older toward male literacy for AOP blacks applied also for AOP and S.C. whites. Sizable numbers of literate blacks in Seneca Township came from the Colhoun, Kilpatrick, and Maxwell plantations.

39. "1866: Freedmen's Schools, Social Welfare, and Protection of Freedmen" in ch. 13.

Chapter 15. Black Political Activity, 1867–75

1. I have dealt with Reconstruction from an AOP perspective, primarily as it involved and affected African Americans. My two major sources have been local newspapers and governors' papers, the latter underutilized by other writers on the period. They especially show the extent of black support for petitions—one measure of political participation—and private communications. They also reveal factional conflicts among AOP's white Republicans. Governors' Papers (Orr, Scott, Moses, Chamberlain, and Hampton), which include petitions and pardons, are filed chronologically at SCDAH.

Woefully lacking in studies of South Carolina from 1865 through 1877 is the role of the military, incorporated into my chs. 12 and 13, and the impact of its withdrawal from the state. Although source material is limited, I have provided brief sketches of some black political leaders and rank-and-file members. See West, "Yeoman to Redneck," for a setting of white violence, including that by the Klan targeted against blacks; he finds little evidence of it occurring in AOP or Greenville.

2. Only Powers and Burton, and on a much briefer basis Huff and John Hammond Moore, provide a sustained local account. Both Willie Lee Rose and Saville deal primarily with coastal areas during war years. Ballard provides good material about Abbeville; cf. Edmund L. Drago, *Hurrah for Hampton! Black Red Shirts in South Carolina during Reconstruction* (Fayetteville: University of Arkansas Press, 1998); cited as Drago, *Hurrah for Hampton!*

3. *KC*, Feb. 28, 1868; the newspaper had just relocated from (old) Pickens Court House to Walhalla.

4. Reynolds, 86–87, 93, 106–8.

5. Carroll Neide, Greenville, Letters Sent, May 25, RG 105/3227.

6. *KC*, June 29. The *AI* in virtually every issue beginning April 27 carried reports of new Democratic clubs created in Anderson County; *AI*, July 18, 1868, Sept. 25, 1867, and Sept. 16, 1868.

7. FMB officer DeKnight, April 30, Monthly Report, Greenville, RG 105/3227. Two earlier attacks on Cato Hallum are discussed in "1866: Violence, Limited Military Force, and White Preoccupations" in ch. 13.

8. Morris, *Pickens*, 10; lists of AOP officials appear in respective WPA guides to county records; *KC*, June 19 (quoting from Charleston *News*).

9. Petition by 19 Oconee white men (enclosing KKK notice, evidently copied by one of the signers) to Scott, Aug. 19, 1868; Sharp to Scott, Aug. 13, 1868; *KC*, March 27, 1868, cited in Henry Johnson Eldor, "Educational Development of Oconee County, South Carolina" (M.A. thesis, University of South Carolina, 1934), 11–12.

10. August 9 letter to Scott from "Estoee League," by whites Alfred McCrarey, president, Alston J. Beezley, vice president; Joseph D. Ferguson to Scott, Dec. 17, 1869.

11. *Reports and Resolutions, 1869–70*, 1400–1405, cited as *Reports, 1869–70*.

12. *AI*, Oct. 7; Saville, 183; "Postbellum White Churches and Freed People" in ch. 17.

13. Mrs. John (Grace) Cochran to Scott, Oct. 27, 1868; John R. Cochran, *Reports, 1869–70*, 1422 ff..

14. Grandfather Daniel Cochran was a "peddler" (Vandiver's term) who bought land near Anderson's courthouse and moved there around 1828; *Biographical Directory, Senate*. See one foreclosure suit by Anderson's County clerk of court against Cochran, Scott, and J. W. Harrison on a 565-acre "Gold Mine Tract" in Oconee; *KC*, April 12, 1872. Transactions appear in annual State Land Commission statements in *Reports and Resolutions* and in deed books; Carol Bleser, *The Promised Land: The History of the South Carolina Land Commission* (Columbia: University of South Carolina Press, 1969), 48, 54–56.

15. *AI*, Aug. 26, Sept. 2 and 9.

16. Kennedy: *AI*, Sept. 2; see also his role in summer 1867 and in 1867 "The Hunnicutt Murder Crisis" in ch. 13; *AI*, Sept. 25, 1867; see note 25 below on Rosemond; and AME histories cited in ch. 17.

17. Testimony below comes from the investigation in *Reports, 1869–70*. Beginning pages for each person's account follow in the same sequence as this text: Pickerell, 1405; Waites, 1410; John Wesley Sherrard, 1414; Peter Brooks, 1409; Gailliard, 1378; Harriet Freeman, 1415; Joseph Freeman, 1416; Stewart Moore, 1418 (cf. Williams, 1388); Winnie Moore, 1419; Morris, 1393; Redmond, 1410; and Humphreys, 1387. W. R. Parker is the most conspicuous Republican who did not testify. Ballard's *One More Day's Journey* chronicles intimidation in Abbeville, especially against Union Leagues

18. No one testifying said that the men who obstructed or intimidated them were election officials, despite intense committee interrogation; cf. *AI*, Oct. 21, 1868, list of election managers.

19. Freedman William Gailliard testified about political and physical coercion inflicted on him by Elias McGee and William Long, as did Dump Sherrard at a different precinct about a Mr. McGee—evidently Jesse, related to Elias—and Mr. Cook. Greenville, Letters Sent, March 31, 1868, to Neide, RG 105/3227. References to attacks on Sherrard and others: Grace Cochran to Scott, Oct. 27, 1868.

20. *Reports, 1869–70*, 1417.

21. Several laborers, including Harry, Neal's former slave, challenged their contract terms with Neal in spring 1866; in each case the FMB ruled against Neal. ACH, Letters Sent, no. 30, no. 44, RG 105/3065. Other Neals are included in "Economic Subjugation, Sharecropping, and Crop Liens" in ch. 22.

22. Zuczek, 50–54; Ballard (ch. 9) sets this in a wider context of murders in Abbeville County.

23. Cochran to Scott, April 20 (2 letters), April 29; and C. M. Hicks to Scott, April 27; *KC*, spring 1869; Mrs. John Cochran to Scott, Oct. 27, 1868; E. I. Pinson, *Reports, 1869–70*, 1400–1405. Harassment of church leaders: "After 1876" in ch. 16.

24. *KC*, April 9, 1869.

25. *Reports, 1869-70*, 1332, Green; 1422, Cochran.

26. Voting statistics are difficult to compile and reconcile as newspapers printed voting figures in inconsistent forms and at varied times; some issues are missing; and some voting results never were published. Ones in this chapter are a combination of those carried by the newspapers and official results in *Reports and Resolutions*. Because the federal government required registration by race, it is usually possible to determine—with reasonable accuracy—the number of black voters through 1876, but not afterward.

27. *AI*, July 7, 1870; Workingmen: *KC*, Aug. 28, 1874; Parker: *AI*, Jan. 27, 1877.

28. *AI*, July 7.

29. State convention delegates included Cochran, W. Everson (white), and Henry Kennedy; *AI*, June 30, July 28, Sept. 30; *KC*, Oct. 13.

30. *AI*, Aug. 18, *KC*, Aug. 19; cf. Williamson, 262; "The Hunnicutt Murder Crisis" in ch. 13. A black militia guard attended S. Webster's execution in 1871, *AI*, July 27, 1871. I found no subsequent references to AOP's black militia until *AI*, Aug. 30, 1877.

31. Official newspaper notices of election managers typically appeared during the month preceding elections; race usually is not indicated. The governor appointed election commissioners, whose names appeared in official notices, appointments in the governors' papers, and *Reports and Resolutions*; Reynolds, 154–55.

32. Strangely, only 14% of Pendleton's black registered voters endorsed petitions compared to a county average of almost 65%. *AI*, Aug. 4, 11, Sept. 15, Oct. 13, 27, Nov. 18, 1870. This information comes from Vandiver and the *Biographical Directory, Senate*.

33. *AI*, Oct. 27. The incident became the subject of major inquiries and trials. Among those who testified—often dealing with the general background of S.C. Reconstruction—are Orr (1–25), Tomlinson (86–87), Butler (1185 ff.), and Hampton (1218 ff.); in *Joint Select Committee to Inquire into the Conditions of Affairs in the Late Insurrectionary States, South Carolina* (1872; New York: AMS, 1968); cf. Williams, *The Great South Carolina Ku Klux Klan Trials, 1871–1872* (Athens: University of Georgia Press, 1996); Foner, 271–91.

34. Reynolds, 191–200; *AI*, Dec. 15, 22; reprinted in *KC*, Dec. 23.

35. Leemhuis, 191, 236; Francis Butler Simkins and Robert Hilliard Woody, *South Carolina during Reconstruction* (Chapel Hill: University of North Carolina Press, 1932), 464–73; cited as Simkins. Orr received favorable coverage in the *KC* and *AI* when he died; see May 2 and 8, 1873, respectively, and subsequent issues.

36. Foner, 412–21, 505–6, 511, 547–48; plus 264, 347 on Orr; *AI*, Aug, 2, 29, 1872; Vandiver, 256; *KC*, Aug. 26, 1872.

37. *AI*, Aug. 22, 29, and Sept. 12; *KC*, Aug. 23, Sept. 20, 27, Oct. 11, and Nov. 1, 1872.

38. *AI*, Oct. 3, 24.

39. For state House, David Singleton received 320 votes and John Reed, 102; for county commissioner, Tenus Maxwell, 437, and Johnson Wright, 235, compared to a total black vote approximating 500. The *AI* mistakenly reported the "colored" candidate as Elijah Webb, Oct. 24; *KC*, Oct. 25; "Rural Communities" in ch. 18.

40. *AI*, Oct. 24, Nov. 7 and 14; *KC*, Oct. 25.

41. Jerald West's careful study of several York County white organizations shows overlapping memberships among them, which extended there also to the Klan. Supplement to Feb. 26 issue, *AI*; Feb. 12, 19, March 12, 25, July 16, 1874; Jerald L. West, *Political Actions of York County, South Carolina, Conservative Clubs in 1868* (Hickory Grove, S.C.: Broad River Basin Historical Society, 1996); further information from West, who has forthcoming studies on York's voter registration and on the KKK. Further evidence may be found in the SHC collection of Sally Elmore Taylor papers (information from Bruce Baker).

42. *KC*, Dec. 6, 1872; *AI*, June 12, 1873; and others. Three of sixteen Masonic grand lodge officers in 1876 were state Democratic delegates.

43. *KC*, Aug. 28; *AI*, Sept. 10; *KC*, Oct. 2, 9.
44. Simkins, 464–73; Reynolds, 279–85; *AI*, Oct. 22; *KC*, Oct. 1, 1875.
45. Simkins, 464–73; *AI*, November 12; cf. 1872; *Reports, 1875*, 91; *KC*, Nov. 13.
46. *AI*, Aug. 12, Sept. 2; Vandiver, 255.
47. Information on political candidacy and service as campaign officials or supervisors comes from newspapers and petitions and letters in the governor's papers. Data on families comes from the 1870 census, and from my calculated percentages of craftsmen represented (ch. 14); see note 1, ch. 17, on "Schools, 1865–1900," for teacher certification records. I matched lists of petitioners with known ministers, teachers, deacons, and elders (references in ch. 17). For 1876 Anderson jurors, see *AI*, Jan. 20 and Nov. 16; that same year five black men were among the Pickens County grand and petit jury pool; *Pickens Sentinel* (cited as *PS*), March 2.
48. Altogether, 70 petitions (1867–77) included black names. Petitions varied in style regarding race. Some were labeled specifically as "Colored Citizens" or an equivalent; others exclusively by black men did not state that fact. Still, others had separate columns labeled "White" and "Colored," but some intermingled the names, with either "c" or "colored" after names of black men. Other petitions—more often in Pickens than in Anderson—neither separated races nor indicated races of individuals. Treasurer petitions in 1872 for Robert Wright, Ballard Dean, and A. O. Norris.
49. They varied from 60% for carpenters to 75% for blacksmith assistants and apprentices; 77% for blacksmiths; 80% of shoemakers and bootmakers; and 83% of brick masons, who had the highest percentage. Surprisingly, 29 of 53 managers (below) did not petition.
50. Additional Baptist ministers including Samuel Sampson (Liberty Baptist) signed petitions; for the Norris one, John Rice, Joseph Robinson, Tabor Warren, James Williford, and James Young. Those endorsing other causes included George Maxwell, a Methodist minister, and Joberry Payton, a manager and teacher who also filled some Methodist pulpits. *AI*, Sept. 14, 1874.
51. "The Hunnicutt Murder Crisis" in ch. 13.
52. Especially in petitions, as O. C. Folger did in late 1874 against W. A. Lesley.
53. Stone, May 5, 1866, FMB, RG 105/3065; 1870 census: Pickensville Township (Pickens); DeForest, 165–67; see 1887 reference to Republican J. M. Looper in "After 1876" in ch. 16.
54. Evidently having been a slave of a prominent white family, Keith was one of Oconee's first black ministers. A shoemaker, he rented a shop from Alexander Bryce. At 47 years old, he was a Union League marshall in 1867 and one of those accused of Hunnicutt's murder. The first moderator of Seneca River Missionary Baptist Association in 1879, Keith served along with W. R. Parker (below), clerk.
55. Of 68 managers and supervisors, 14 were teachers, and 4 others had teachers among their relatives. One was a Baptist minister, 6 were founding Baptist deacons and/or early leaders in the Rocky River Baptist Association (RRBA), another a founding Methodist elder; one was evidently related to an AME minister.
56. His churches included one named for himself, Parker's Chapel, as well as Shiloh and Snow Hill Baptist. Parker's Chapel hosted RRBA's annual meeting in 1871. In 1874 he polled only 399 votes compared to Cochran's 2498 votes for the Senate and black Hiram Greenlee's 1396 for county commissioner. *AI*, Nov. 5 and 12, 1874; Oct. 12, 1876; *Anderson Daily Intelligencer*, Cheshire, Dec. 30, 1914. G. M. Maret, Trial Justice, Fair Play, to State Supt. of Ed., Aug. 1876; Correspondence: General; SCDAH. *AI*, Jan. 25, Feb. 1, 1877. West cites an incident in which Murray acted even more violently; "Yeoman to Redneck," 381–82; Parker's political role in 1878: "After 1876" in ch. 16. I have been unable to find the "Nigger Parker" article; friends reliably remember its headline. Baptist trouble: *PS*, Feb. 5, July 16, 1891; 1898

Minutes, Baptist Educational, Missionary and Sunday School Convention of South Carolina (ch. 20); cited as E&M. Parker also appeared as a controversial figure in a 1914 lynching.

57. *AI*, July 27, 1871; black crime: *AI* beginning Aug. 1871.

58. Oconee: earlier a Union League sergeant of guards, December Gadsden was sentenced to five years' hard labor in the penitentiary for burglary, and Clark Cleveland Jr., a guard, was convicted of petit larceny. Jackson Henderson, the local League's vice president in 1867, and Clark Cleveland Sr., president then, were arrested for violating the federal Enforcement Act. *AI*, July 27, 1871.

59. See references to Sitton (initials not given) in "Nov. 1868 elections," above; and note 27, ch. 7, that few freed people used "Sitton" as surname. Note also an arson attempt on Blalock's barn in early 1881 (Laurens County); a black woman, the alleged culprit, was lynched. Blalock contracted for penitentiary convicts later in the century; cf. "Stockade Scandal" in ch. 22, and Neals in that account and in "November 1868 Elections," above. *PS*, April 21, 28, 1881.

60. *AI*, Feb. 27, March 27, Nov. 6, 1873; Jan. 15, 1874; June 24, 1875; Dec. 21, 1876; Jan. 23, April 10, Aug. 14, 1879; *KC*, Feb. 22, 1877.

61. The largest Oconee tract, 1045 acres of J. O. Lewis's estate near Walhalla, initially cost $3000 in 1869; passing through several hands, including those of Scott and Cochran, within two years it reached a price of $10,000. Bleser chronicles similar hanky-panky throughout the state. Mostly whites bought Anderson's 645 acres. And the State Land Commission reported in 1873 that, of six Pickens County tracts containing 1500 acres, "these lands are exceedingly poor, and no purchasers can be found at one dollar per acre." See *Reports and Resolutions* for the 1870s and 1880s; the quote comes from 1872–73, 150.

62. Paternalism during elections in the 1870s: *Crucible*, 82–84.

Chapter 16. Black Politics Curtailed, 1876–90

1. Legislators elected W. J. Whipper and Franklin Moses Jr. as circuit court judges to displace J. P. Reed of Anderson and A. J. Shaw of Sumter, both holding unexpired elective terms. The state Supreme Court upheld Reed's and Shaw's continuing right to office. Reynolds, 320–26, 337–39; cf. Zuczek's coverage (his chs. 7 and 8) of related 1875 events.

2. *KC*, March 10, March 17, April 7.

3. *KC*, March 10, 17, April 7; *AI*, Feb. and March; April 13, Aug. 3.

4. *AI*, July 20 and 27.

5. Reynolds, 374–82; Williamson, 267–71; *KC*, July 20; Chamberlain probably incurred additional stigma for his command of USCT during the war. A study by Samuel J. Martin, *Southern Hero: Matthew Calbraith Butler, Confederate General, Hampton Red Shirts and U.S. Senator* (Mechanicsburg, Pa.: Stackpole Books, 2001), uses sources primarily favorable to Butler.

6. Throughout this section, see Simkins's ch. 20, "The Campaign of 1876"; *KC*, Aug. 24; *AI*, July 6, Aug. 24; *Pickens Sentinel* (cited as *PS*), July 13.

7. *AI*, Aug. 24, 31, Sept. 7; *KC*, Sept. 7.

8. *KC*, Sept. 14; Columbia's *Daily Phoenix*, Aug. 28, 1867; cf. Simkins, 37–43, and Hampton Jarrell, *Wade Hampton and the Negro*.

9. *KC*, Sept. 7, 14; 1875 state census; *AI*, Oct. 12; for more on black Democrats elsewhere in South Carolina, see Drago, *Hurrah for Hampton!*.

10. *AI*, Sept. 28; the crowd probably drew also from Abbeville and Laurens.

11. *AI*, Aug. 17, 24, 31; *PS*, Oct. 12; *KC*, Oct. 5; and Turner's Hill Farmers' Aid Society in "Black Thought, 1865–1900" in ch. 20; it is not clear whether it was named for this Turner.

12. Reynolds, 381–87; *KC*, Oct. 19, quoting from a New York *Herald* correspondent based in Columbia; *PS*, Oct. 26.

13. Brown to Chamberlain, Dec. 10.
14. *AI*, Oct. 26, Nov. 2; G. D. Williams, *AI*, May 10, 1877.
15. *AI*, Nov. 9, Sept. 14.
16. *AI*, Nov. 2; cf. Oct. 2, 1876 on Spartanburg.
17. *AI*, beginning Feb. 15, and *KC*, beginning March 1, 1877.
18. *AI*, Feb. 1, March 29, Sept. 20, 1877; *KC*, Feb. 8, March 15.
19. Reynolds, 456–60.
20. *AI*, May 10, 1877.
21. The best statewide assessment remains George W. Tindall's *South Carolina Negroes, 1877–1900* (Columbia: University of South Carolina Press, 1952), cited as Tindall, *Negroes*; *AI*, Aug. 23, 30, Sept. 13; the reprint from the *News and Courier* concerned a Kingstree trial (Williamsburg County).
22. Orr (July 8, 1871) recommended that Scott pardon the men; cf. Greenville Court of General Sessions rolls 3918, 3919, 3929, 3932; information from S. West.
23. Based on *Reports and Resolutions, 1870–71*, and Central Register of Prisoners, 1867–1872 (SCDAH); in 1877, 38 successfully escaped; and 22 others were recaptured.
24. *KC*, Aug. 29; *AI*, Aug. 29.
25. Rosemond held no services during the winter of 1870–71 for his "country congregations in Spartanburg County for fear of bodily harm. Many of his members had been brutally whipped." *AI*, Aug. 29, 1878. Nearby AME Zion minister Lewis Thompson was whipped, mutilated, and thrown in the river; cf. *KC*, Oct. 17, 1878. Parker: *AI*, Aug. 29.
26. Reprinted in *AI*, Oct. 31; *KC*, Sept 26, Oct. 17.
27. Nearby, Greenwood and Spartanburg still had a black council member into the 1880s and 1890s, and Greenville and Spartanburg, like Anderson, had black policemen. *KC*, Oct. 3, 17, 31; *AI*, Oct. 24, 31. *AI*, Jan. 16, 1879; John Hammond Moore, *South Carolina in the 1880s: A Gazetteer* (Orangeburg, S.C.: Sandlapper Publishers, 1989), 139, 151, 239.
28. *KC*, Nov. 7, 14, 1878; *AI*, Aug. 14, 1879. Bryce: *KC*, April 18, Aug. 22, 1878, Aug. 14, 21, Sept. 11–Nov. 20, 1879; Jan. 1, 1880. The murder attracted national attention, including the New York *Daily Times* and an Iowa newspaper; *KC*, Mar. 11, 1880.
29. Primaries, not standardized until after the 1895 constitution, had been scheduled by county organizations, also establishing their own regulations; scholars have mostly ignored this earlier period of primary elections. *AI*, Oct. 30, 1884; *PS*, Feb. 16, 1882, July 13, 20, Nov. 9, 16, 1882. Referendum issues: *AI*, June 11, July 2, 1874; June 21, July 26, Aug. 9 (suggesting coercion) and 23, 1877; Aug. 29, 1878 (Parker's views); *PS*, Aug. 2 (allegedly a black writer), 16, 23, 1877; *KC*, Jan. 1, 1880, Nov. 10, 1881; West, "Yeoman to Redneck," 529. During fall 1880, Oconee and Pickens together had more than 1000 black/Republican votes, about 5% more than in 1876. *AI*, Nov. 11, 1880; cf. *Reports and Resolutions*.
30. AOP newspapers stopped reporting numbers of black voters and identifying jurors by race and hardly ever printed names of coroners' jurors. New voter registration in 1882 and 1896 omitted racial identification (required earlier by federal orders). *AI*, Dec. 1, 1881; *PS*, May 23, 1882, and Jan. 7, 1886.
31. *AI*, Nov. 13; *PS*, Nov. 20, 1884; *Greenville Enterprise and Messenger*, Oct. 13, Nov. 3, 17, 1880; Coroner's Inquisition on Perry Cox; *KC*, Sept. 18, 1884. AOP newspapers covered 1884 county Republican meetings; that year seems to be the last recorded appearance of black Democrats. "Report of the Adjutant and Inspector General, 1879" in *Reports and Resolutions, 1879*; *PS*, Oct. 28, Nov. 4, 1880; Oct. 2, Nov. 20, 1884; *KC*, Sept. 18, 1884; *AI*, Sept. 25, Oct. 6, 1884; Oct. 7, 1892; from Morris, *Pickens*, 111–12, 327.
32. *Crucible*, 53.

Chapter 17. Community Building: Churches and Schools

1. Relatively little has been written about the history of South Carolina's education, specifically black schools, or of black churches; see, however, Tindall, *Negroes*. An extensive "Sketch of Education in South Carolina" appears in Harry Hammond, *South Carolina: Resources and Population, Institutions and Industries* (Charleston: Walker, Evans & Goswell, 1883). Changes, especially in funding and in legislation, can be followed in the Superintendent of Education's *Annual Reports*. For both schools and churches, cf. Burton, 242–59.

2. Cf. "Families and Households" in ch. 14, pp. 242–46, and "1872–75" in ch. 15, pp. 264–67.

3. For antebellum black churches, see Clarke, *Wrestlin' Jacob*, 116–34; John Hammond Moore, *Columbia*, 134; Leah Townsend, *South Carolina Baptists, 1670–1805* (Florence, S.C.: Florence Printing, 1935), 255–60, and Joe M. King, *A History of South Carolina Baptists*. See also Larry G. Murphy et al., eds., *Encyclopedia of African American Religions* (New York: Garland Publishing, 1993).

4. Sources are the 35 minutes in table 6.2. References in this section to *only, first, last*, or *probably* aptly apply; cf. note 2 in ch. 6 on interpreting these minutes. Statistics for black churches drawn from black association or conference minutes; see notes 13 and 15 in this chapter. The earliest contemporary black sources are one 1867 deed, an 1868 newspaper notice, 1868 RRBA minutes, and 1869 legislative testimony.

5. The larger white population had only 67 churches. Data from Pegg's 1877 map of Anderson County. Baptists dominated with 26 churches and 3590 members (averaging 138), the 13 Methodists churches were second with 632 (averaging 48), and AME, 200; memberships collectively exceeded Anderson's black population over 20 years of age. These figures compare favorably with RRBA, ME(N), and AME records. Saluda Baptist Association churches had 1414 black members in 1865 (31% of its total). The 1877 map itself shows sites of 15 named black rural churches; many more appear on von Hasseln's 1897 map. In RRBA's 1875–77 reports, 23 Anderson churches had a total of 2908 members. Pegg, *General Descriptive Map of Anderson, S.C.*; cf. *Map of Anderson County, South Carolina* (Anderson: privately printed, 1897).

6. Almost all churches periodically updated membership lists, although sometimes at intervals as long as 20 or 30 years. The frequency of 1865–70 revisions and specific references to the "colored" members indicate that this was not a routine activity.

7. Laurens, 9; the association had 26 churches with 1855 "colored" and 2508 "white" members; Edgefield: Item no. 34 in the minutes.

8. Also Richard Allen's exodus (to launch Bethel AME) in 1787. Powers, *Black Charlestonians*, 194; Clarence E. Walker, *A Rock in a Weary Land: The African Methodist Episcopal Church during the Civil War and Reconstruction* (Baton Rouge: Louisiana State University Press, 1982), 73; cf. James A. Tolbert, *Christ in Black, Or the Life and Times of Rev. James R. Rosemond* (Greenville: Shannon & Co., 1902), 25.

The Rev. J. L. Stroudemire (white; previously appointed to Summerville) for nearly two years tended this circuit, including several congregations beyond the town. Information on "Colored circuits": 1868, 1869, and 1870 ME, South Conference *Minutes; KC*, Aug. 14, 1868, and Feb. 19, 1869.

9. Abbeville in 1867 became AME headquarters for northwestern South Carolina. Nancy Vance Ashmore, "The Development of the African Methodist Episcopal Church in South Carolina, 1865–1965" (M.A. thesis, University of South Carolina, 1969) 24–27; Abbeville [AME] Singing Convention, *Minutes*, 13–14, and its summary of the life of Rev. James T. Baker; and Thomas Henry Jackson, *Sketch of the Life and Character of Rev. Simon Miller* (Columbia, S.C.: Union-Herald, 1875). The AME *Christian Recorder* provides useful details; cf. Ballard for Abbeville's early AME history.

10. Fairfield Colored Methodist Episcopal Church was also derived from nearby (white) Mount Pisgah.

11. See entries in *Records of St. Paul's* and "Glimpses" in ch. 4, p. 69.

12. Cf. Oolenoy Baptists' Feb. 1868 resolution in "Rural Communities" in ch. 18, p. 330.

13. My dating combines data from WPA Inventory of Church Records, each church's first land deed, 1877 and 1897 maps, and other sources, especially RRBA minutes; a reasonably accurate account emerges. Both AME and ME(N), more active in Anderson than in Oconee and Pickens, left brief but helpful conference proceedings.

St. Paul (somehow omitted from the inventory) claims 1865, when meetings occurred in a brush arbor; *Profiles of Black Folks*, 419; Liberty cites Sept. 1867 (473) and New Hope, 1873 (490). The earliest contemporary reference to St. Paul is in FMB correspondence. When First Freedmen's Baptist (St. Paul) in summer 1870 submitted a petition for incorporation, trustees were: N. B. Gailiard [sic], clerk, Benjamin Guyton, Julius Thomas, W. H. Morris, Henry Kennedy, Henry Reed, and McDuffie Singleton; Taber Warren, moderator. *AI*, Aug. 25, 1870. New Hope applied five years later; *AI*, July 1, 1875.

Much information in this section depends on John A. Middleton, *Pre-1900 Statistical Table of S.C. Black Baptist Churches* (Columbia, S.C.: J. A. Middleton, 1992); cited as Middleton, *Black Baptists*.

14. "One of the most faithful ministers of the State, died September 1st, 1887." *AI*, Aug. 12; July 14; see "November 1868 Elections" in ch. 15, p. 260; Little River Baptist Association, 1888: 17.

15. Following after Nov. 14, 1867, Gethsemane Baptist Association, composed primarily of coastal and midlands churches; introductory essay in Middleton, *Black Baptists*, supplemented by conversations and correspondence with Middleton; *AI*, Dec. 9, 1876.

16. Ascertaining dates for Oconee and Pickens churches has been considerably more difficult than for Anderson ones; there are few contemporary records, no WPA reports, and no surviving 1800s SRMBA and Oolenoy minutes. See *Seneca River Missionary Baptist Association, Centennial Yearbook, 1878–1978* (privately printed, cited as *SRMBA*) for early history; cf. *Seneca River*, cited below, and *Observance of the Griffin Ebenezer Baptist Church*, 1979; and *Oolenoy River Education and Missionary Baptist Association of Pickens County, South Carolina, Centennial Celebration*, 1982.

17. "History," *Rocky River Baptist Association, 100 Years* (1968); SRMBA, *the Centennial Celebration of the Sunday School and B.T.U. Convention* (1986), 20.

18. Including Brown-Salem Methodist Episcopal and Evergreen Colored Methodist Episcopal Church (both Anderson); *Profiles of Black Folks*.

19. Black Benedict College's white president at SCBC in 1873; exchange of delegates in Spartanburg; and SCBC welcome to RRBA delegates in 1876 at Greenville; Baptist Educational, Missionary, and Sunday School Convention of South Carolina, *Minutes*, 1878, cited as E&M (SCL photocopies, from Middleton); *KC*, Nov. 16, 1870.

20. WPA Inventory of Church Records, Anderson County; *Profiles of Black Folks*; SRMBA and RRBA publications (cited above); *Sizemore*, 38; and Pleasant Hill Baptist Church, Westminster, *SRMBA*, not pag.

21. *KC*, Dec. 8, 1887; 1880 Census: household 31, Center Township; cf. correspondence (SCL) of Rev. J. W. Robinson, an AME, Zion minister elsewhere in the state; and an 1888 example in "Coverage in the White Press" in ch. 20, p. 35.

22. *Christ in Black, Or the Life and Times of Rev. James R. Rosemond*; and Warren M. Jenkins, *Steps Along the Way: The Origin and Development of the South Carolina Conference of the Central Jurisdiction of the Methodist Church* (Columbia, S.C.: Socamead Press, 1967). Rosemond served the Greenville District in 1867 and in 1868 had charge of Anderson also. Anderson had, and still has, more Colored Methodist Episcopal churches than does Pickens or Oconee.

Whites sometimes inserted "Colored" or "African" in deeds and other records, using these words in a racial sense rather than as a proper title, which confuses efforts to identify specific affiliations.

23. Silas's brother Paul W. Jefferson also rose quickly, taught in Abbeville, and would later pastor Charleston's Morris Brown AME. See sketches of both brothers in Benjamin Arnett, *Proceedings of the Quarto-Centennial Conference* ([Charleston, S.C.?]: [AME], 1890); cited as AME, *Quarto-Centennial*. Allen graduate Chappelle began serving in Pendleton in 1888. John R. Wilson, *A Brief Sketch of the Life and Career of the Right Rev. William David Chappelle* (n.p.: n.p., [ca. 1913]), 19–20; Anderson Teacher Certification Records, SCDAH. Allen catalogs include Rena J. (Clark) Jones, who taught for many years in Pendleton. Cf. Chappelle, "Black Thought, 1865–1900" in ch. 20, p. 360.

24. Craig, *Pickens Sentinel* (cited as *PS*), May 24, 1883. The Presbyterian Historical Society (Philadelphia) holds Board of Missions records, minutes and accounts. Foster was born in Abbeville County ca. 1860, graduated from Howard University in 1887, was ordained in 1888; was stated supply at Salem Church (Anderson) and Andersonville, beginning in 1887; and organized Iva church and was stated supply there, beginning in 1897; Edgar Sutton Robinson, *The Ministerial Directory* (Oxford, Ohio: Ministerial Directory, 1898), vol. 1.

25. Jefferson Chapel ME and Oak View Baptist; similar reversionary clauses appeared in black school deeds. Adger's deed is most curious; dated 1863, it was not recorded until 1887. Its restrictive language sounds more like the 1880s than the Civil War years. Unlike most S.C. deeds during the war, it refers to the 87th year of (American) Independence. If Robert Adger did in fact deed his slaves property in 1863, he evidently did not expect the Confederacy to survive; it is not clear whether the intended African American recipients knew of it then.

26. *Diary of Clarissa Adger Bowen*, 87; nearly a century later New Light and Holly Springs reunited.

27. Lucinda Whitner deeded her land for Abel Baptist Church (Pickens); Reeves, ch. 20. Due to late-1800s creation of denominational women's organizations, women were holding offices in the Women's Auxiliary or similar titles, and in young people's organizations. Also assuming major offices in Sunday school organizations, women increasingly attended, and spoke at, previously male-only meetings; e.g., Mary J. Washington, a teacher, at 1886 RRBA; numerous others followed.

RRBA in 1889 commended Sister Ella McGowan for raising funds and appointed a missionary representative for each church; more than half were women, all single. Women sometimes served as clerks (mostly after 1900), as would Abel's Susie Haywood, or charter members of their churches. Changing gender roles nationwide, and increasingly better education for women helped expand their places within churches. Numbers of ministerial wives taught, supplementing (and sometimes exceeding) the family income from their churches.

28. Only "negroes" came to a holiness tent services in Pendleton (*AI*, June 17, 1896). Some pentecostal believers created in 1898 the Fire Baptized Holiness Church (FBH), the only religious denomination founded in South Carolina. William Fuller, the only black attendee, was ordained, elected to the general board, and assigned to reach black believers. Vinson Synan, *The Holiness-Pentecostal Tradition: Charismatic Movements in the Twentieth Century* (Grand Rapids: William B. Erdmans Publishing, 1997; orig. 1971). Mt. Zion in Seneca, and Mount Moriah in Central, were AOP's first black FBH to acquire property.

Another black pentecostal group, the Universal Pentecostal Holiness Church, began in North Carolina shortly after 1900 and soon had congregations in AOP. In South Carolina a group thrived with a significant base in Seneca; leaders included A. J. Brown (b. 1895, Pickens County), who became Universal Pentecostal Holiness bishop. *Profiles of Black Folks*, 36,

80–82, 254; *Encyclopedia of Religion in the South* (n.p.: Mercer University Press, 1984), 253–54; *Encyclopedia of American Religions* (Detroit: Gale Research, 1993), 411; and the Garland *Encyclopedia of African American Religions*.

29. Baptist figure based on Middleton, *Black Baptists*.

30. Even in August 1868, when most churches were still fairly new, they reported excluding 15 members during the previous year; St. Paul often led in number (24 in 1874, more than 10% of its membership). Church exclusions continued: 155 in 1878, when six churches each ousted more than 10% of their members; 120 members were ejected in 1885, 141 in 1895, and 196 in 1900.

31. Most data in this section come from the State Superintendent of Education's *Annual Report*, published as separate volumes. Certification records for Pickens County survive in the county superintendent's office, those for Anderson at SCDAH; I have not been able to locate any for Oconee. G. Anne Sheriff, *Black History in Pickens District, South Carolina*, vol. 2, *Teacher Certification* (Easley, S.C.: Forest Acres Elementary School, 1993).

32. D. M. Minus, *The Struggling Boy* (Greenville: privately printed, [1923]). Robert Reid was taught privately by Clemson College faculty while he worked there in a janitorial capacity, "Railroads, Related Occupations, and Other Town Employment" in ch. 18, p. 316.

33. *Freedmen's Schools and Textbooks* (semiannual reports of John W. Alvord, Inspector of Schools and Finances; New York: AMS Press, 1980), Jan. 1, 1870: 26. Frances Tudor to Scott, July 10, 1870, and endorsement by Oconee County school commissioner; Supt. of Education, Teacher Reports, 1869–70; SCDAH. Her transportation was paid by the ME(N), Freedmen's Aid Society.

34. *PS*, Dec. 22, 1881.

35. "Over fifty" at Anderson's school in 1870 exceeded 20% of the town's black population over 16; note report in "Broader Horizons: Charleston Connections and Literacy," in ch. 8, p. 138, about books available among Anderson's FMB students.

36. Racial breakdowns were not published until late in the century. The average black teacher's yearly salary in 1900 for Anderson city was $108 (for 19 weeks; whites $160 for 24 weeks); for Anderson county $42 (10 weeks; whites $96 for 14 weeks); for Pickens, $85 (11 weeks; whites $205, 21 weeks); Oconee figures, 1899. These salaries are barely more—and sometimes less—than wages for common labor. 1900: 175, 201–6, 217, 245–47.

37. Hiram Greenlee (67), a founding deacon of Belton's Baptist church and of RRBA, and Isaac Greenlee (62) were two of Anderson's earliest teachers, evidently brothers literate during slavery with a religious background; cf. Eli Greenlee (1810), who indicated a Virginia-born father.

38. Betty Hendricks, "History and Present Status of the Negro Schools of Pickens County, South Carolina" (M.A. thesis, Furman University, 1949), evaluation, ca. 1950, of Pickens County in "Negro Schools"; she includes her own snapshots of each school; cited as "Negro Schools."

39. Brief sketches of these schools appeared in *Annual Reports* and in the *South Carolina Handbook*, various years (including 1883 with a variant title). Avery, Benedict, Claflin, Penn, Schofield, and Sterling were named for northern white benefactors, as later were Rosenwald schools. Cf. Rev. H. Watkins's "Greater Necessity of a Trained Ministry," RRBA, 1882.

40. W. J. Thomas also served as first director of Seneca's Ebenezer Baptist Sunday School.

41. Most publicly financed buildings for AOP students by 1900 were wood frame; evidently most log cabins were church buildings and community-supplied schools; 1892: 34; 1893: 164–65; 1897: 123.

42. J. J. Starks, *Lo These Many Years* (Columbia, S.C.: State Co., 1941), 19–25, 39; cited as Starks.

43. Hunter, *A Nickel and a Prayer*, 24–25, 29; Pickens, *Bursting Bonds*, 9–19.
44. *AI*, April 28, 1881; more reports in chs. 18 and 19.
45. "State College" was initially established as the Colored Normal, Industrial, Agricultural and Mechanical College but called by a variety of names. Hunter, 37–44.
46. *PS*, May 2, June 13, and July 25, 1889.
47. Sporadic, very brief references to local boards indicate some continued black control, at least of property and perhaps veto over prospective teachers.
48. *Annual Report, 1883*, 32; *People's Journal (PJ)*, Sept. 20, 1894; and *KC*, Oct. 4, 1877.
49. 1899: 13–15; cf. *AI*, May 15, 1884.
50. 1900: 117, J. C. Martin.
51. Picket Post; *Annual Report, 1900*, 201–2; *1885*, 5; *1900*, 175, 201–2, 205–6, 217, 241–43, 245–46; figures much higher in counties with high percentages of African Americans. Black schools statewide in 1900 had longer terms, but still wide variations: an average of 86 students per school, 76 per teacher, compared to a white school's 69 students, 51 per teacher.

Chapter 18. Black Communities, Town and Rural

1. I am using "town" as an informal term as it appeared in many newspaper references and in most contemporary legislative charters. Sources for this chapter include 1870–1900 census entries for towns; maps, including those by Sanborn; deeds; newspaper articles; RRBA minutes, church and school statistics, cited in ch. 17; and autobiographies by Jane Hunter, William Pickens, and J. J. Starks. I have visited and explored these towns and the three rural communities and greatly benefited from a trip through other rural Pickens areas with Sidney Durham. Similarly, I am indebted to dozens of families in town and rural areas who welcomed me into their homes. Data on town population, literacy, school attendance, and occupations come from my calculations based on the census; and property ownership from deeds, county tax records (held at SCDAH), and mortgage books (retained at AOP courthouses).

Studies of AOP towns appear in "Towns" in the bibliography, where full citations are given. See also *Profiles of Black Folks* on the city of Anderson; and Tindall. Although he includes very little on northwestern South Carolina, let alone AOP, his work should be considered in relation to my chs. 15–23.

Von Hasseln's *Map of Anderson County, South Carolina* (1897) has city inserts; among them Pendleton and Anderson show several black property owners, churches, and Greeley Institute (most not identified by race); cited as von Hasseln, 1897. Additionally there are maps in town histories, later Sanborn maps, and a 1915 property map of Calhoun.

2. Pickens, *Bursting Bonds*, 15; *PJ*, Jan. 9, 1902. Black-white joint distilling: white partner, James J. Holliday, killed John P. Crew, black; see pardons in Governor Tillman Papers, 1891; *AI*, June 27, 1872, June 11, 1874; *Pickens Sentinel* (cited as *PS*), Aug. 16, 1877, May 14, 1891; *PJ*, May 2, 1901. Easley: *PS*, Jan. 5, 1893.

3. All of its towns in the 1800s were deliberately created at a specific time from rural land. Like state and national capitals, several towns were established to serve judicial and political functions. After 1828 Anderson and Pickens became courthouse towns, and following Oconee's 1868 creation, Walhalla (organized in the 1850s mostly by Germans from Charleston) became its county seat. Shealy, *Walhalla*; West, "Yeoman to Redneck," 221–22, on late antebellum Anderson and Williamston businesses, and 331 on postbellum links.

4. Calculations based on data in *King Cotton*, as reprinted in Julian Jay Petty, *The Growth and Distribution of Population in South Carolina* (Spartanburg, S.C.: Reprint Co., 1975); cf. Huff, *Greenville*, for the impact there. For more on cotton, mill towns, and postbellum agricultural practices including sharecropping, see West, "Yeoman to Redneck" passim; note esp. 18–21, 229 (table), 303, 315, 325, 333, 338, and 345. See Walter B. Edgar, *South Carolina: A History* (Columbia: University of South Carolina Press, 1998), maps 21, 22, and 23.

5. John Hammond Moore, *South Carolina in the 1880s: A Gazetteer*, 203; cited as Moore, *South Carolina in the 1880s*. See Melton McLaurin, *Paternalism and Protest: Southern Cotton Mill Workers and Organized Labor, 1875–1905* (Westport, Conn.: Greenwood Publishing, 1971), 86, 88, 122, and 174, about labor trouble in the Piedmont mill. Statistics for the 17 cotton mills in South Carolina, Department of Agriculture, Commerce, and Immigration, *Handbook of South Carolina: Resources, Institutions and Industries of the State* (Columbia, S.C.: State Co., 1908), 457–60; cited as *Handbook of South Carolina*. Unable to find comparable figures for 1900, or a nearer year, I counted employment only for mills operating in 1900.

6. Numerous studies and exhibits have emerged in recent years; the most helpful for this account is David L. Carlton, *Mill and Town in South Carolina 1880–1920* (Baton Rouge: Louisiana State University Press, 1983); cited as Carlton.

7. On mill workers' origins, see John M. Coggeshall, *Carolina Piedmont Country*, Folklore in the South series), 20–23; he cites WPA, *South Carolina Guidebook*; see also Carlton, 10, 66, 121, 133, 146–49; Moore, *South Carolina in the 1880s*, 203; and West, "Yeoman to Redneck," 21–22, 341, 345–48. West implies, without developing the point, that earlier mill workers (1880s) came from nearby farms, and later (early 1900s, perhaps) from farther away, especially from the mountains.

8. *Sizemore*, 5.

9. *AI*, June 22, 1876; Mattie May Morgan Allen, *Central: Today and Yesterday* (Taylors, S.C.: Faith Publishing, 1973), 88.

10. Comparable to records for nearby black labor hired in the 1880s by Thomas Clemson and by Aaron Boggs; cf. "good field hands receive from fifty to sixty cents a day without board, or from $6 to $10 a month with board"; *Health Resorts of the South* (Boston: Geo. H. Chapin, 1891), 152. These figures also accord with entries for various Hunter General Store accounts; street hands in Anderson made about 50 cents per day in 1870 (*AI*, Sept. 15, 1870); and Jane Hunter's (23) father made $1.25 on a good day digging ditches. Reid: American Association of University Women, Clemson Chapter, "Clemson: A Glance at the Past" (1973; CU); servants' quarters: Mrs. F. H. E. Calhoun, "Long, Long Ago" (CU). I found no contemporary AOP records for compensation to black women in full-time domestic service, let alone differentials for those who lodged with their employers. Hunter Store records show payments to women for milking and for laundry (ch. 23). Cf. Reid's (b. 1884) grandmother Easter Reid (ch. 10) and father Butler Reid (below and ch. 23).

11. Pickens, *Bursting Bonds*, 12–17.

12. Pickens County tax records do not exist for 1880, those for Anderson do not designate race, and the 1880 census does not indicate home ownership.

13. Williamston is not included, as its town population was not specifically demarcated in the census. Fair Play (not incorporated) was just inside Oconee's boundary with Anderson.

14. Decades later Keese's son Ben had a small eatery, store, and antique business. Information on small neighborhood stores resides almost totally in oral tradition. Further on Griffin in note 27, ch. 3.

15. Anderson barbers Benjamin Roberts and Sam Black moved to Greenville, whose "radical" barbers were more numerous and better organized than those in AOP; *PS*, June 1, 1882. Another Central well-digger was Cato Sherman, a key figure in an 1887 lynching story (ch. 21).

16. Samples: Keowee in Oconee, Central in Pickens (excluding the town of Central), and Varennes in Anderson; *AI*, Feb. 7, 1884.

17. In six sample townships (ch. 14), there were only 13 black females living alone, excluding Pendleton; cf. Savannah Township, ch. 22; and Burton's concluding chapters.

18. Pendleton's figures probably would have been higher, as maids often worked two or three days a week each for several families.

19. *PS*, Nov. 17, 1887; *AI*, Aug. 1, 1878; Oct. 25, 1866; Oct. 21, 1867; Nov. 6, Dec. 4, 1873; Nov 6, 1901; Oct. 9, 1873; *Anderson Daily Intelligencer*, March 31, 1915; Abbeville [AME] Singing Convention, *Minutes*, 15; and ch. 10, "Celebrations," for antebellum examples. On Greenville's circus day in 1881, police arrested more than thirty men, roughly equally divided between black and white; West, "Yeoman to Redneck," 517; see note 32, below. Cotton sale day: ca. 1890 photograph in Teal, *Partners with the Sun*, 128; *Reed*, f150.

20. *KC*, Oct 5, 1876, Aug. 12, 1877; *PS*, Sept. 6, 1877, June 16, 1881; and *PJ*, Sept. 9, 1897.

21. Williamson, 49–50; *AI*, July 10, 1867, July 7, 1870, July 4, 1872, and July 6, 1876; *PS*, June 30, July 7, 1887; Jan. 5, 1900; *AI*, Jan. 3, 1900; "Black Thought, 1865–1900" in ch. 20.

22. *KC*, Oct. 10, 1878; *PS*, July 28, 1887; *AI*, Aug. 29, 1894, Oct. 20, 1881, and Aug. 7, 1895; June 24, 1896; *PS*, Aug. 3, 1899.

23. *PS*, summer 1877; *AI*, Sept. 12, 1878, May 15, 1879, Sept. 1, 1881; *Sizemore*, 91. Taylors: *Profiles of Black Folks*, 343–45; *Chicago Defender*, March 24, 1922; James Riley, *Biographical Encyclopedia of Negro Baseball Leagues* (New York: Carol & Graf, 1994), 763; and information from writer Paul DeBono.

24. *AI*, July 24, 1879. White-owned businesses supplied coffins and burial preparation for African Americans into the 1900s. Among these were G. F. Tolly and Sons Funeral and Furniture (Anderson) and the Gassaway firm (Central; later known as Duckett Funeral Home). Seneca's Adams Mortuary seems to have been AOP's earliest one outside of Anderson city. Duckett ceased handling black burials in the late 1920s. For Peek and PBA, *Profiles of Black Folks*, 87; Committee to Commemorate Black Businesses, comp., *The Legacy of Black Pioneers* ([Anderson, S.C.]: privately printed, 1982), 42–46; and Edgar Wallace Biggs Papers, SCL, for Greenville ones.

25. *KC*, Feb. 29, 1878.

26. Early postbellum songs for baptisms, wood chopping, and cotton picking; WPA interview in Wooley, 3:3; Hunter, 25–26, 38, 47–48.

27. *PS*, June 30, 1887; *PJ*, Feb. 8, 1900; *AI*, July 5, 1900. Calhoun: quoted in *Foothills Folk Tales* (Greenville, S.C.: Piedmont Branch, National League of American Pen Women, 1976), 15; *PS*, Aug. 4, 1887. "Uncle Jack" would seem to be the man reported as 42–year-old J. Washington, violinist, in the 1870 census (Pendleton) and as 52–year-old Jack Calhoun, farmer, in Anderson's Garvin Township, 1880. Young black "Blind Tom, the Musical Phenomenon," toured in AOP and much of the state in the 1880s and 1890s. *AI*, Sept 18, 1873, Jan. 8, 1874, and March 22, 1877; *PS*, March 9, 1882; *PJ*, Feb. 8, 1900.

28. *PS*, Nov. 3, 1877; *AI*, Aug. 16, 1877; July 17 & Aug. 14, 21, Sept. 11, and Oct. 2, 1879; Sept. 8, 1881; RRBA, 1895: 5–6.

29. *PS*, May 18, 1882, Aug. 16, 1894.

30. Prince Hall Free and Accepted Masons, Jurisdiction of South Carolina, *Bicentennial Journal, 1776–1976* (Columbia, S.C.: privately printed, 1976); further in SRMBA publications and in biographies of individual members; see *Profiles of Black Folks*; Records of the Knights of Pythias, Grand Lodge of South Carolina, 1904–1941, SCL. Hunter, 29.

31. *AI*, June 12, 1879; cf. Baptist and AME critiques, "Black Thought, 1865–1900" in ch. 20, and quotation about sinful "bar-room, the pool-room, the gambling den" places from RRBA, 1890, in "Black Thought, 1865–1900" in ch 20.

32. Willie Thompson McLaughlin, "A Collection of My Childhood Memories" (typescript prepared for a 1985 reunion, SCL), 2; cited as McLaughlin, "Childhood."

33. Bruce Baker, "The 'Hoover Scare' in South Carolina, 1887: An Attempt to Organize Black Farm Labor," *Labor History* 40 (1999): 261–82; *AI*, Nov. 12, 1892. "Prior to the end of the 19th century," a Turner's Hill Farmer's Aid Society (FAS) was organized in Liberty. By 1900 it "had a large membership of males and females"; the lower floor was "for *school*

purposes," and the lodge used the upper floor; the Baptist church owned the adjacent lot; Julia Jean Woodson and G. Anne Sheriff, *Liberty, South Carolina: One Hundred Years 1876–1976* (Central, S.C.: Faith Clayton Family Research Center, 1992), 40, 82–83. At Easley the FAS, Masons, and Good Samaritans all shared a building. Benevolent society: von Hasseln, 1897; this may be the Afro-American Real Estate Association.

34. Elizabeth Rauh Bethel, *Promiseland: A Century of Life in a Negro Community* (Columbia: University of South Carolina Press, 1981); Allen R. Ballard, *One More Day's Journey: The Story of a Family and a People* (1984), cited as Ballard; and Amelia Wallace Vernon, *African Americans at Mars Bluff, South Carolina* (Columbia: University of South Carolina Press, 1995).

35. Corn shucking, *AI*, Dec. 3, 1874; "A Christmas frolic" in June 1875 letter to Chamberlain; Hunter, 79.

36. Dick Walker (Centerville Township, Anderson County), a "doctor," 1870 census; and 84-year-old "physician" Abraham Pickens (Liberty Township, Pickens County), 1880. Mortality Schedules (esp. 1880) and coroners' inquisitions provide useful insight. Some black estate include medical bills; cf. John Andrew Robinson Papers, SCL.

37. McLaughlin, "Childhood," 23; cf. early 1900s all-day rural church events with lunches, *Sizemore*, 153.

38. Starks, 36–39, 43; 1900: Keowee (Oconee), Central (Pickens), and Varennes (Anderson). Incidental information on lodging arrangements appears in coroners' inquests; cf. boarding arrangements in Anderson city, "Residential Patterns" in ch. 19.

39. Hunter, 13–14, 25 ("leaks" in the original); more Gassaway comments appear in ch. 20.

40. *PS*, Oct. 28, 1880; *PJ*, Feb. 6, 1896.

41. Other areas, including Beaufort, had Little Liberias; a "Little Africa" in Spartanburg County (Pruitt, *Spartanburg*); and in northern Greenville County and primarily across the North Carolina border, a Happy Kingdom. Huff, *Greenville*, 167; Sadie Smathers Patton, *The Kingdom of the Happy Land* (Hendersonville, N.C.: privately printed, n.d.); and "The Kingdom of Happy Land," *Echoes: Reflections of the Past* (Travelers Rest, S.C.: privately printed, 1985), 15–24. Pumpkintown: Mills, *Statistics*; *KC*, July 12, 1916; March 3, 1881.

42. Bert Reece, *History of Pumpkintown-Oolenoy* ([Pickens, S.C.?]: Miracle Hill Print Shop, 1970). This story, repeated in various later forms, does not name specific recipients. See also Alma Lynch, *Echoes: Oolenoy-Pumpkintown* (Easley, S.C.: Pace Printing, 1980). The black families I name come from a March 23, 1983, *Greenville News* article, which seems to rely on an interview with Chris Owens and on Soapstone tombstones.

43. *PS*, Feb. 8, 1894. The township's twenty black landowners, barely exceeding those in 1900, owned land appraised at $2.39 per acre in 1920; only seven families owned homes. Savannah Township (Anderson): "Economic Subjugation, Sharecropping, and Crop Liens" in ch. 22.

44. *PJ*, Feb. 4, Nov. 7, 1894.

45. The Greenville and Pickens newspapers published several articles each between 1979 and 2000; all featured the Owens couple.

46. Starks, 140; sequence reorganized with a few words omitted.

47. Sources include: census listings; Tenus Maxwell's estate papers; S. E. Maxwell's advertisement of land for sale; SRMBA publications; deeds and property tax records; and my attendance at the cemetery's 1997 rededication. See Pat Pritchard, ed., *"If These Stones Could Talk," The Rediscovery of the Old Maxwell Cemetery* ([Westminster, S.C.]: Fair Play Camp School, 1997), a report on the cemetery project and rededication with an introduction by Megginson; and Pritchard, "When History Speaks, Can the Heart Listen: Affective Responses of Emotionally Disturbed Adolescent Males to a Local History Project" (Ph.D. diss., Clemson

University, 1998). All readable tombstones have been transcribed and all graves plotted in *"If These Stones Could Talk."* Maxwell's tombstone is one of the best surviving African American ones from the nineteenth century.

48. Oconee DB B, 130. S.E. retained 3000 acres, "there being now fourteen families on the place."

49. Gadsden is listed among Maxwell's heirs (estate proceedings, Oconee). When Tena Frierson died in Sept. 1872, the *KC* reported that she was over 100 years of age and had been with the (white) Maxwells since 1811, and earlier with Major Keels (Maxwell's father-in-law). Maxwell praised her "irreproachable character for honesty, fidelity and truth." She still lived with the Maxwells, "whose confidence and affection she had won by her faithfulness."

50. S. E. Maxwell sold 817 acres to G. K. Keels in 1871 in exchange for canceling a debt (owed by S.E.) of $1250.25; Tenus Maxwell's price was nearly $400 more. Oconee DB B, 130; DB D, 324.

51. It is not clear when Abel's school was established, probably not until the 1890s or perhaps the 1880s. Students earlier might have attended a black school in Central (P. S. Little's, earlier in this chapter). Abel's school in 1900 had an enrollment of 72, taught by one person, Hendricks (32–35) says; the school was held from 1899 until 1928 in an old dwelling, which evidently burned in 1928 when the church did. See also souvenir booklets published by Abel, *History of Abel Baptist Church, 1868 to April 11, 1985,* and by Goldenview Baptist, 1981, *Mortgage Burning Service;* photocopies at SCL and PDC from author's originals. In 1989–90 Abel's cemetery supervisor, James Benson, and I inventoried all legible tombstones there (BHUP). Abel now lies within the corporate limits of Clemson.

Chapter 19. Anderson's Urban Community

1. There is no general history of Anderson city; Vandiver includes some material. David L. Carlton's *Mill and Town in South Carolina 1880–1920* refers frequently to Anderson; see esp. 30–31, 50–51; cf. *News and Courier* vignette on Anderson, reprinted in Moore, *South Carolina in the 1880s,* 15–19, and *AI* supplement (undated; filmed following Sept. 30, 1896). *Profiles of Black Folks* contains useful articles on people, churches, schools, and businesses, mostly from the 1900s; some articles are helpful for the 1865–1900 period also. Cf. Powers's *Black Charlestonians,* Moore's *Columbia,* Huff's *Greenville,* and Pruitt on Spartanburg (cited in "Introduction: A Piedmont Setting," note 9).

Much of this chapter derives from the same sources as Chapter 18; county tax records; business directories; Anderson County, Auditor's Tax Duplicate Book for 1885–1900; and *Walsh's Directory of the City and County of Anderson, S. C. For 1905–06* (Charleston: Walsh Directory Co., 1905); cited as 1905 City Directory.

Sanborn maps, referenced as "Sanborn Fire Insurance Company" maps, have borne various names; the 1884 usage was Sanborn Map & Publishing Co. Ltd. Colloquially they are termed simply Sanborn maps, as used below. Cf. J. H. von Hasseln's 1897 *Map of Anderson County, South Carolina* insert for the city of Anderson, which shows several black property owners, churches, and the Greeley Institute.

2. Published 1860 Census Bureau figures show 625 residents, which evidently applies only to free people, plus about 565 slaves in the Slave Schedule. The 1870 census (manuscript) does not distinguish town residents, divided between two townships that split the city, from rural population; but by 1880 the town was treated as its own township for census, tax, and school district purposes. The 1870 Census *Population* reports Anderson's population as 1432, divided as 673 "white" and 759 (53%) "colored." *AI,* May 10, 1877; Feb. 19, April 2, 1874. Payton, Anderson Town Council Minutes, Jan. 19, 1861 (SCDAH).

3. 1920 Census, *State Compendium: South Carolina,* 8; Dickson, 86; see "Schools, 1865–1900" in ch. 17.

4. Hunter, 29.

5. Also from Georgia: Henry Burch ("Racial Relations") and Seaborn McCurry, active in Reconstruction politics; *AI*, Feb. 7, 1884.

6. E. V. Gassaway, attending Union Theological Seminary (Richmond, Va.), married in 1891 a Virginia native. Mark Gassaway, who graduated from Claflin University in 1883, married Georgia native Carrie Walls, Spelman Seminary alumna and teacher in Belton, where he taught prior to Greeley; family sketches for Gassoways, McGowan, and Dooley in *Profiles of Black Folks*.

7. A brief description of Royal appears in an Oct. 21, 1938, clipping in WPA files. *AI*, Feb. 28, 1878; May 22, Nov. 27, 1884. Business development: *Historical and Descriptive Review* (New York: Empire Publishing, 1884), 3:244–54.

8. *AI*, June 8, 1880, May 22, 1884; *South Carolina Hand Book, 1895* (Charleston: Lucas & Richardson, 1895), cited as *South Carolina Hand Book, 1895;* 1905 City Directory; *AI*, March 6, 1895.

9. 1886 ME South Carolina Conference minutes and program. Policemen and fire brigade: *AI*, March 31, 1892, March 18, 1886; and 1901 Sanborn map; "fifteen people" from Anderson's 1885 tax rolls.

Guyton's wife Ruth (bought from Broyles, 1845; married Dec. 5, 1848) and their children (including Elbert) had belonged to J.P. Reed's family, as recorded in a Reed family notebook (copies at PDC); periodic comments about them appear in *Faithful Heart*. In 1866 Benjamin Guyton contracted with J. P. Reed for his son Elbert's services in a blacksmith shop ("Analysis of Labor Agreements, 1865–67" in ch. 12). These ties lingered. When Elbert Guyton died, evidently in Piedmont, on Christmas 1899, white C. A. Reed had Elbert Guyton's body shipped back to Anderson. The Jan. 10, 1900, *AI* reported that Guyton was "an old family servant and a worthy negro."

10. *AI*, July 1, 1875, Jan. 27, 1881; and *Pickens Sentinel*, May 13, 1886.

11. *South Carolina Hand Book, 1895*, 114–16; photographs of cotton sales day appear in local histories, e.g., Anderson and Seneca.

12. This number excludes cooks and servants living with white families. The basis for "84" comes from matching 1900 census notations of land ownership with tax rolls.

13. *Profiles of Black Folks*, 26.

14. Si Perrion, formerly on Anderson's police force, died Jan. 7, 1884; *AI*, Jan. 10, 1884. The telephone company also had a black lineman.

15. 1905 businesses could be found on North Main, South Main, and West Market streets; cf. Committee to Commemorate Black Businesses, comp., *The Legacy of Black Pioneers* ([Anderson, S.C.]: privately printed, 1982).

16. Some servants' houses shown on Sanborn maps likely survived from prewar years. Census sequences for 1870 and 1880 show clusters of blacks but not their specific location.

17. *AI*, Jan. 3, 1900. Photographs of Dooley's house in *Profiles of Black Folks*, 616–17.

18. *AI*, Sept. 5, 1894.

19. Eleven white people—including an extended Sullivan family—owned 81 houses; they had 5 to 22 each in 1900. Anderson Cotton Mills had 178 houses, a small number of them provided for black firemen, watchmen, and others who tended machinery.

20. *AI*, May 19, 1892, May 22, 1895; for less pleasant attitudes toward Gassaway, see ch. 23.

21. Leslie: *AI*, July 25, Aug. 1, 1900. Headline: *American Field* reprint, evidently *AI* title. *AI*, March 20, 1895; March 11, 1903.

Chapter 20. Divergent Views of Blacks

1. Anthropologists now do not give credence to "race" as an analytical concept. I am using the words "race" and "racism" in the late 1800s sense.

2. Additionally, about 775 names appear in RRBA and other church records and deeds plus teacher certifications. And, as shown in ch. 15, about 1225 AOP black men endorsed petitions between 1868 and 1877. These overlapping groups still provide at least one piece of information beyond the census for hundreds of blacks, mostly men.

3. Ordinarily newspapers reported only court of general sessions cases. Magistrates and justices of the peace heard lesser charges; virtually no such records or newspaper reports survive.

4. Other names appear in governors' correspondence, petitions, and *Reports and Resolutions*. Names of managers were listed primarily in legal notices in newspapers. *AI*, Feb. 28+, 1877; later published rosters of such taxpayers named 155 blacks; they are not included in this chapter's calculations.

5. A. P. Hubbard designed an advertisement of approximately 300 words, some set in large type. Those words, appearing at different parts of the notice, read: "A. P. HUBBARD . . . BOUGHT A NIGGER . . . IN NEW YORK CITY . . . FROM . . . HORACE GREELEY." Apparently Hubbard thought this was a cute way to entice buyers; but nothing comparable followed it, suggesting negative reaction.

6. *AI*, Aug. 30, 1877; see July 1879 for example of reprints.

7. *Pickens Sentinel* (cited as *PS*), May 24, 1888.

8. More on "Blind Tom" in "After Hampton" in ch. 21.

9. *PS*, March 24, 1887; *AI*, Nov. 14, 1894; Henry Burch's 1895 obituary, "Racial Relations in the City," ch. 19, p. 353; further examples in chs. 22 and 23, pp. 403 and 416–17.

10. *AI*, July 24, 1879.

11. Celebrations are treated in *Jubilation: African American Celebrations in the Southeast* (Columbia: [Univ. of South Carolina] McKissick Museum, 1993); also Tindall; and *PS*, July 14, 1910 (information supplied by Peggy Rich). Similar events happened elsewhere in the South: Williamson, *Crucible* (68).

12. Alec Dupree (Milly's son), who had recently graduated from Benedict, taught at Abel school around 1900 and may have been the source of information.

13. Other later ones included a Knights of Pythias newspaper in Anderson, the *Enterprise* in Greenville in 1908 (cf. below), *Friendship Banner* and *Messenger*, both in 1908 in Rock Hill, Jefferson's in Abbeville, and a much later one, *Anderson Herald* (ca. 1960). See *South Carolina Handbook*, 1908: 226. A brief account, "Can a Race Paper Survive in Greenville?" (Edgar Wallace Biggs Papers, SCL), refers to three evidently short-lived papers in the 1890s and early 1900s. Note Charles F. Behling, "South Carolina Negro Newspapers: Their History, Content, and Reception" (M.A. thesis, University of South Carolina School of Journalism, 1964).

14. John R. Wilson, *A Brief Sketch of the Life and Career of the Right Rev. William David Chappelle* (n.p.: n.p., [ca. 1913]), 23.

15. See sketches of Turner in AME, *Quarto-Centennial* and in *African Methodism in South Carolina: A Bicentennial Focus* ([Columbia, S.C.?]: AME Seventh District, 1987), 70–71; and Stephen Ward Angell, *Bishop Henry McNeal Turner and African American Religion in the South* (Knoxville: University of Tennessee Press, 1992).

16. Jefferson helped publish the *Palmetto Gleaner* in Columbia. *Recorder*: Strickland, July 11, 1878, May 20, 1880; Jefferson, April 26, 1887.

17. See "African American Families and Religion" (bibliography) for SCL holdings; unless otherwise noted, all references to RRBA, E&M, and ME(N) are to their minutes at SCL.

18. *KC*, March 18, Aug. 28, 1876; *AI*, July 13, Sept. 9, 1876, April, 1884; April 14, 1892; ME(N) South Carolina Conference, Minutes, 1881.

19. Cf. note 22, ch. 17; E&M, 1877: 7. The "Colored Methodist Episcopal Church" denomination, with several AOP congregations, may have been so labeled by white ME,

South leaders, who guided its formation. As a designation *colored* did not find favor in Charleston; *Negro* was the prevailing term there for postbellum organizations.

20. *AI*, Sept. 3, 1886.

21. To Liberia: *AI*, Jan. 30, 1879—specifically seven people from the community called Ninety Six. 1880 Pickens County, Easley Township, household 225; Williamson, 110.

22. *AI*, March 9, 1882; RRBA, 1884: 9, 10; E&M, 1877: vi; "sons": RRBA, 1890: 8; Semme: E&M, 1898; and RRBA, 1902. See ch. 2 for African-born residents and parents.

23. Vandiver, 61–62; *AI*, March 18, 1903, from *Savannah News*.

24. AME, *Minutes*, 1881: 54; *AI*, Sept. 3, 1886.

25. Yearly minutes list each student's aid and institution attended.

26. The *AI* reports "E.D.," for whom I find no plausible match; the man likely was G. D. Williams (b. 1850). Although the *AI* article suggests that S.C. alliances began in 1891, the May 4, 1889, *Appeal* (Chicago) reported "the organization in South Carolina of 'The Colored Farmers' National Alliance and Co-operative Union.'" Easley's early 1900s Grand Central Farmers' Aid Society evidently was never incorporated.

27. These include the National Afro-American League, organized in November 1889, but short-lived; its successor, the National Afro-American Council in 1898; and several newspapers, among them Baltimore's *Afro-American*, begun in 1892 and still published; the *Afro-American Beacon Light*, begun in 1896; and the *Afro-American Citizen* in Charleston, 1899–1900.

28. Further on "Prominent" in note 34, ch. 21; *PS*, May 25; it gave this meeting more coverage—extensive and unbiased—than to the incidents that precipitated it.

29. E&M, 1901, 35–36.

30. Colored Baptist State Convention, *Minutes*, 1906.

31. RRBA, 1906: 13; cf. 1904: 14, people should "remain on the farms instead of seeking the evils and pleasures of the cities, [and] to be industrious and economical, and to accumulate property"; *PS*, Feb. 27, 1879; Burton, 243–44.

32. Pink Holly (b. Anderson County) said that when he was "seven years old my papa pulled me off to Arkansas. We come on an immigration ticket" (ca. 1875); WPA, Arkansas, pt. 3, 306. *AI*, March 6, 13, and 20, June 19, 1884. In one instance, 75 whites left from Anderson and Oconee; *PS*, Nov. 24, 1887.

33. At least 11 young AOP men enlisted in the army in Ohio, 1913–16, and more did so during World War I when black volunteers were not being taken in South Carolina; two others enlisted during 1914 in Arizona and Hawaii. M. H. Gassaway moved to Ohio in 1918 (ch. 23). Some Sizemore families moved to Cleveland in the 1900s; *Sizemore*, 112–13. Tuskegee: *Legacy of Black Pioneers*. Philippines, 1898 and 1914: *AI*, July 10, 1901; Joseph Dendy in South Carolina Adjutant General, *The Official Roster of South Carolina Soldiers, Sailors and Marines in the World War, 1917–18* (Columbia: Joint Committee on Printing, General Assembly of South Carolina, 1929), vol. 2 ("Colored"). Cf. family accounts: Malone's *Sizemore* interviews; and Sheila Ferguson's *Soul Food*, which chronicles Oconee sharecroppers who never left, other relatives in the Charlotte area—some who stayed there and others who moved to Philadelphia, and still another ancestor who fled north and changed his name. Hunter, 92; Adrienne Cash Jones, *Jane Edna Hunter: A Case Study of Black Leadership, 1910–1950* (Brooklyn: Carlson Pub., 1990).

Chapter 21. Societal Attitudes and Oppression

1. AOP, as well as much of South Carolina, sustained a climate of violence throughout the 1800s; see note 2, ch. 11. Stephen West's dissertation has a valuable exploration of lynching, other violence, and liquor, as well as class relationships.

2. For post-1876 black voting, see text in ch. 16 as well as note 30 of that chapter. It is not easy to pinpoint the last black town or county officials. N. B. Gaillard was still serving as election commissioner in 1880. Nearby Spartanburg had a black council member in 1880, as did Greenwood in 1889; Moore, *South Carolina in the 1880s*, 151, 239. Beaufort continued to send black representatives to the state legislature until 1902. Williamson makes the same point about difficulty of defining when black politics ended. His *Crucible of Race*, insightful for this entire period, seems to concur on the amorphous character of the 1880s.

3. *AI*, Feb. 7, 1884; out-migration: *Pickens Sentinel* (cited as *PS*), Jan. 5, 1882; *PS*, Sept. 1, 1887; *Press and Banner*, reprinted in *AI*, May 15, 1884.

4. Isaac Wickliffe to State Supt. of Ed., May 17, 1874; Correspondence: General, SCDAH. *AI*, Jan. 28, 1886; [John Belton Townsend], "South Carolina Society," *Atlantic Monthly*, June 1877, 670–84; *PS*, Sept. 27, 1883; Oct. 8, Dec. 27, 1885.

5. Cf. Adger, *My Life and Times*, published in 1899; "Keowee Coon" in *PS*, July 18, 1889; later racial epithets: *Anderson Daily Intelligencer*, Dec. 27, 1914; and Vandiver's *Traditions . . . of Anderson County* (1928).

6. Lewis P. Jones, *South Carolina: A Synoptic History for Laymen* (Columbia, S.C.: Sandlapper Press, 1971), 194–98.

7. Tindall, 267–76; *PS*, Feb. 21, 1878; *AI*, May 1, 1877; April 10, 1884; cf. "Stockade Scandal" in ch. 22, on convict leasing and penitentiary staff corruption; *KC*, Oct. 6, 1887; *AI*, Jan. 1, 1896; *Reports and Resolutions, 1900*, 790.

8. Note a July 1868 day on which both Democratic clubs and Anderson Farmers' Associations met, one shortly after the other, "Spring to Fall 1868" in ch. 15; and a joint Grange-Democratic "united demonstration" in "The 1876 Campaign" in ch. 16.

9. C. Vann Woodward, *The Strange Career of Jim Crow* (1955; New York: Oxford University Press, 1974), 6; cited as Woodward; Francis Butler Simkins, *The Tillman Movement in South Carolina* (1926; Gloucester, Mass.: Peter Smith, 1964), 16–18, and chart, "Cotton Prices 1882–1896," opp. 18; cited as *Tillman Movement*.

10. White farmers were hard pressed by economic problems, which led to heavy mortgages. Between 1880 and 1889 mortgaged acreage in Anderson County increased by nearly two and a half time, more rapidly than the state as a whole or Oconee or Pickens. Census Office, *Report on Real Estate Mortgages in the United States at the Eleventh Census: 1890* (Washington: GPO, 1895), 620–24; cf. discussion below on rapid population change; *AI*, Feb. 4, 1884; *KC*, Jan. 6, 1887. Simkins's *Tillman Movement* should be consulted for all of this period. *PJ*, Nov. 1, 1894; March 14(?), 1895; *Tillman Movement*, 137. Earle to Tillman, Oct. 25, 1892; Jonas Armstrong to Tillman, Jan. 28, 1891 (SCDAH). "'Redneck' appeared as an epithet in the American South during the 1890s. . . . [and] one of the first appearances of the term in print came in 1893," West, "Yeoman to Redneck," i, 2, 592, and sources cited.

11. *AI*, Sept. 1894 through Feb. 5, 1895; Feb. 12 was the first subsequent issue without a Civil War–related article. Young black "Blind Tom, The Musical Phenomenon," in "Black Organizations and Festive Occasions" in ch. 18, note 27; *AI*, Nov. 5, 1891. Legislative *Reports and Resolutions*, which traditionally began with financial statements, started in 1900 with "Report of the Historian of the Confederate Records to the General Assembly of South Carolina." The same period saw romanticizing of slave life and of felicitous relations between masters and slaves; see 1908 Goober Jack and 1916 Essex accounts, "Runaways, 1820s–1865" in ch. 5. There was an early-1900s grand reunion of former Confederates and, ironically, reunions of former slaves, including one in Pickens.

12. Hunter, 32; she seems to place this episode around 1895.

13. Jane Hunter wrote about a young, high school "beautiful mulatto girl" lured into prostitution in Cleveland, Ohio; Hunter, 122. The 1906 event is recorded in a document held in private hands; my interview with Lucinda Reid Brown, Aug. 15, 1988.

14. There was also a dramatic increase in violence among whites, whose homicide rate tripled between the late 1880s and 1899; mill residents accounted for much violence, as did liquor, availability of guns, and probably rapid population increase (below). During the same time, there were forty-three lynchings throughout South Carolina. Cf. West, "Yeoman to Redneck," passim, esp. 400, 418, 429. *PS*, Sept. 13, 1883; *PJ*, May 2, 1901. See also Anderson County, Coroner's Inquisitions (SCDAH), for frequent descriptions of black on black violence that caused death, including Henry Yarborough (1901) and Tom Parks (1902). Black on black: *AI*, April 11, 25, Aug. 8, 1900.

15. There is extensive literature on lynching. Bruce E. Baker makes two Carolina contributions in volumes edited by W. Fitzhugh Brundage and published by University of North Carolina Press: "Under the Rope: Lynching and Memory in Laurens County, South Carolina" in *Where These Memories Grow: History, Memory, and Southern Identity* (2000), 219–45; and "North Carolina Lynching Ballads" in *Under Sentence of Death* (1997); see additional citations for reference note to my table 21.1 and citations of *Vogues in Villainy* and *Lynch-law* in ch. 11. Cf. Stewart E. Tolnay and E. M. Beck, *A Festival of Violence: An Analysis of Southern Lynchings, 1882–1930* (Urbana: University of Illinois Press, 1995).

Brundage and others have tried to assess regional differences, specific locations, alleged offenses by lynching victims, and composition of the mobs. Between 1895 and 1904 Anderson was one of only five S.C. counties to have three or more lynchings; the other four counties had black majorities. I find evidence for AOP too slender to venture observations beyond those contained in this section.

16. I have a forthcoming account of the 1914 Fair Play lynching in a publication based on the *Without Sanctuary* exhibit at Jackson State University in 2004. For Blease, see Bryant Simon, "The Appeal of Cole Blease of South Carolina: Race, Class, and Sex in the New South," *Journal of Southern History* 62: (Feb. 1996), no. 1:57 ff.; and Ronald Dantan Burnside, "The Governorship of Coleman Livingston Blease of South Carolina, 1911–1915" (Ph.D. diss., Indiana University, 1963). On upper-piedmont lynching, see West, "Yeoman to Redneck," esp. 363, 399 ff., 448, 451; and on Blease and lynching, 584–86. The Willie Earle lynching generated extensive contemporary material including NAACP research files and a 1987 thesis: David Redekp, "The Lynching of Willie Earle" (M.A. thesis, Clemson University, 1987); cf. Will Gravely, "Reliving South Carolina's Last Lynching: The Witness of Tessie Earle Robinson," *South Carolina Review* 29 (1997): 2, 4–23; Gravely deals especially with Earle's Pickens County roots.

17. "First" is a relative term. I am not counting the 1862 escaped slave Alfred (ch. 11). There was also an 1881 lynching that occurred just across the river in Greenville County. Both the victim and lynch mob ("two or three hundred people, white and colored") involved people from Williamston and perhaps elsewhere in Anderson County. Several lynchings or nonlynchings in Greenville County involved participants from Anderson; efforts to quantify by political boundaries can be misleading.

At least 272 AOP blacks joined petitions—either black or mixed—to pardon the convicted men. These include 24 black women in Anderson County, probably the first there to petition the governor; none did in the 1865–76 period. Governor Richardson's Papers, SCDAH.

18. Sources include *Pickens Sentinel* articles, Coroner's Inquests on Sherman and on Waldrop, and General Sessions trial records (source of quotations not otherwise cited). Cf. E. Don Herd, "Lynching in the Upcountry, 1784–1980," *The South Carolina Upcountry, 1540–1980* (Greenwood, S.C.: Attic Press, 1981–82), 2:510–21 (including "next morning"). Bruce E. Baker explores this lynching in more detail: "Lynch Law Reversed: The Rape of Lula Sherman, the Lynching of Manse Waldrop, and the Debate Over Lynching in the 1880s," *American Nineteenth Century History* 6 (September 2005): 273–93.

19. Solicitor Orr—interviewed earlier in 1887 by the Charleston *News and Courier* following lynchings in York County—blamed the legal process as well as influential citizens; as this interview was reprinted in the April 28, 1887, *KC*, surely the men who called on Orr to preside in the inquest knew of his views. Judge Norton presided over later trials; he and W. C. Keith, *KC* editor, had been partners in a law firm; *KC*, June 8, 1876. On Orr, see also West, "Yeoman to Redneck," 407–8.

Presumably some of the six had good relations with local whites, who supported them. Only Haywood and Williams appeared in the area's 1870 census; Bolton moved into town by 1880. Oral tradition holds that Haywood was very light, and his daughter Susan could pass when she went to other towns or cities.

20. Quoted by Herd, 520–21: *KC*, March 14, 1889; *PS*, date not given. *PS*, April 18, 1889; March 19, 1891; 1900 Census, Central Township, household 11; Petitions for Commutation of Sentence, Governor Richardson's Papers, SCDAH.

21. White men were arrested after 1914 and 1930 AOP lynchings, as well as the 1947 Willie Earle one. Most of these white defendants posted bail and did not have to stay in jail.

22. The *News and Courier* relied on local correspondents, at times AOP news writers, it seems, not wanting to print the incident in their own newspapers.

23. The *PS* reported on Jan. 7, 1886, a burning at the stake (and "shrieks of agony" as 500 watched) of a black victim in Clark County, Ala.; reportedly he killed a 17–year-old white female.

24. Confidential, sealed, oral interviews were conducted by another researcher with white descendants. I have neither heard the tapes nor know the interviewees' names. Cf. *KC*, Nov. 12, Dec. 10, 1902. This oral tradition perhaps appropriated the 1889 Central lynching, which may have been done in part by whites from Six Mile.

25. *AI*, Nov. 27; *PJ*, Nov. 28; *News and Courier*, Nov. 25; the *Laurens Advertiser* attacked this lynching, according to the *AI*.

26. *Anderson Daily Mail*, Sept. 21, 1905; *State*, Sept. 19, 20, 1905; cited by Mullins; Burton, 56, on peonage; Tillman quote from West, "Yeoman to Redneck," 27. By contrast, West says that the mayor of Anderson tried to deter the 1894 lynching of Ed Sullivan (451).

27. Printing is garbled; I've rearranged the article to make sense. *Greenville News*, as reprinted in *PJ*, July 18 and 25, 1895.

28. Three women gave testimony about the attack at the Coroner's Inquest, July 1, 1903, but offered no cause for the attack. One said that the white men seized a lamp from her hand, threw it at Elrod, and set him on fire. Anderson County, Coroner's Inquests, box 2; cf. *AI*, July 8; *News and Courier*, July 2, 1903.

29. Martin: as reprinted in the May 2, 1900 *AI*. Willis Jackson reportedly "brutally assaulted" an 11–year-old white girl. Anderson County, Coroner's Inquests, box 2. An earlier lynching in 1905 similarly involved an incident, victim, and mob connected with Honea Path, but the lynching occurred just a few miles away in Abbeville County. Reportedly Magistrate Ashley tried to prevent that lynching. *News and Courier*, Sept. 20, 1905.

30. *AI*, Jan. 31, 1884; *PS*, Sept. 1 and 8, 1887, and July 30, 1891.

31. April 14, 1887, p. 1 (top); 2 ¼ columns long.

32. According to the Greenville *Enterprise and Mountaineer* on July 9, 1879, Spartanburg grand jurors similarly said that "those citizens [lynchers] . . . merely anticipated the sentence of the law of the land." Quoted in West, "Yeoman to Redneck," 370. Tillman in 1893 attracted widespread criticism, including a *PS* editorial, for withdrawing guards who protected John Peterson at Denmark, after which Peterson was lynched. Later in May a group of "prominent negro leaders" (including E. V. Gassaway, E. A. Saxon, A. R. Bacote, and W. D. Chappelle) met in Columbia to protest the lynching. *PS*, May 4, 1893, and successive

issues; Jackson: *PS*, June 8, 1893; *AI*, July 10, 17, 1895; some of the lynchers came from Piedmont.

Chapter 22. Political and Economic Subjugation

1. Quotations below, not otherwise cited, come from the Constitution.
2. *The South Carolina Constitution of 1895*, 30, 35; cited as Wallace, *1895*.
3. Wallace, *1895*, 34. In 1914 10.8% of registered voters (i.e., white males) signed their names on Democratic primary rolls with an "x." The figures were higher in Anderson with 22% x's, and Pickens's 26.4% was the second highest in the state. No data was available for Oconee. *Annual Report, 1914*, 23–25. "Veterans": *PJ*, Nov. 1, 1894; *Civil Government of South Carolina* (Dallas: Southern Publishing, 1906), 153; State Superintendent of Education, *The School Law of South Carolina* (Columbia, S.C.: Bryan Printing, 1896); and *Statutes* 22: 31–57; the governor headed its board, which appointed county school commissioners. New voting regulations included proof of having paid poll taxes; restrictions against voting in any precinct other than the one designated on one's voting certificate (inconvenient for mobile sharecroppers); and compiling a separate list of men who voted. AOP's black voting that year dropped to less than 550 (based on Republican ballots cast; *Reports and Resolutions, 1896*).
4. Wallace, *1895*, 36; also Tindall, 297–300.
5. *News and Courier*, March 10, 1901; *AI*, May 8, 1915.
6. South Carolina in 1898 was the last southern state to prescribe segregated railroad seating, going beyond custom and harassment that usually imposed it. Segregation of residential areas is discussed in ch. 23; cf. Isaac DuBose Seabrook, *Before and After: The Relations of the Races of the South*, ed. John Hammond Moore (Baton Rouge: Louisiana State University Press, 1967), 30–33, and Moore, "Jim Crow in Georgia," *South Atlantic Quarterly* 66 (autumn 1967): 554–65.
7. Numbers of AOP blacks registered when new voter registration books were compiled in 1896; race is not indicated, but it is clear that perhaps hundreds of AOP black men did register. Mortuary owner E. W. Biggs, who lived in Greenville, had a 1932 "Voter Registration" certificate (Edgar Wallace Biggs Papers, SCL). In 1943 Calhoun's mayor wanted to allow blacks to vote in a town election but was overruled. S.C., Secretary of State, Corporate Charters, Town of Pendleton, 1898 (SCDAH).
8. *Annual Report* (1899), 104–6, 117 (Martin); McMahan in 1900 built upon antebellum plantation references in his 1899 report ("Schools, 1865–1900" in ch. 17).
9. *KC*, May 17, 1888; Woodward, 71–73.
10. Hunter, 35–36; cf. a similar episode that led to Berry Holland's death (Anderson County) in 1883, West, "Yeoman to Redneck," 357–58.
11. Glennon Graham, "From Slavery to Serfdom: Rural Black Agriculturalists in South Carolina, 1865–1900" (Ph.D. diss., Northwestern University, 1982), explores these issues elsewhere in the state.
12. A white Greenville doctor and farmer in 1887 complained of high debt incurred by tenants. *Pickens Sentinel* (cited as *PS*), April 25, 1889; *AI*, Feb. 12, 1874; West, "Yeoman to Redneck," 333; cf. *Statutes*, 17:560–65, 19:146.
13. Petition to Moses, 1874 (box 8, folder 32), refers to an appealed case but does not include the landlord's name. Anderson's General Sessions records are missing for a quarter of a century in the late 1800s—which may or may not be suspicious.
14. Some insights about white tenants come from Lawrence Edwin Lenhardt, "The Social-Economic-Composition of the Boards of Trustees of Anderson County, South Carolina" (M.A. thesis, University of South Carolina, 1931), 9, 26. Lenhardt's survey of 180 school trustees (all white) showed that 82 served no more than three years, possibly because "so

many of the [white] people throughout the county are of the nomadic element" and 64 trustees paid no real property taxes, thus "of the tenant class"; cf. Ballard (164) on oral contracts.

Using census figures, West shows that between 1860 and 1900 "landowners as a percentage of white farm operators" dropped sharply—by over 40%—in the upper piedmont. In Pickens the rate fell from 56.2% in 1880 to 42.5% in 1900; West, "Yeoman to Redneck," 303. West is referring only to "farm operators"; if all white families were the base, the percentage would be even lower. Nearly 90% of white Savannah Township households did not own land in 1900, a higher figure than for blacks! My interview (July 10, 1996) with M. O. Plyler (b. 1912) confirmed that many upstate farmers, white and black, had only oral contracts.

15. 1870 Honea Path Township (HPT; Anderson) Census (Population and Agriculture) checked against HPT tax records (1871, 1873, 1875); many men may have moved into nearby townships or to adjacent Laurens County; cf. William Pickens's descriptions in "1870 Overview" in ch. 14.

16. The categories are my conclusion based on the way black families were treated in various records and newspapers. Anecdotal information suggests that African Americans perceived these same categories, along with other community distinctions. Ballard (164–66) discussed three categories: "those who owned their own land . . . about ten percent," "the renters," and "sharecroppers, who made up close to half of the families." These categories could also apply, with different distributions, to whites. Anderson County, Auditor's Tax Duplicate Books, 1871–75 (Honea Path Township), 1900 (Savannah Township); compared with 1900 Census, Savannah Township, and 1899–1901 Anderson County, Index to Agricultural Liens (all SCDAH); "Anybody else": 1900 agricultural lien index.

17. *AI*, Jan. 2, 1895, Aug. 8, 1900; *PJ*, Oct. 11, 1900.

18. In 1870 only two black men—both carpenters—had employment other than as farmers, farm laborers, or laborers; both could read or write. Only one black family was shown as owning land—Elias Sherard; one woman and five men (including a house carpenter), two Cunninghams, and Jack Humphreys had personal property; cf. note 37, ch. 14, on literacy. About one in six white families had a domestic servant (assuming one each).

19. These 18 owners included 4 Sherards, 3 Keowns, and 2 McGees; 4 additional Sherard families owned land in adjacent Corner Township. Prue Wesley Sherard, son of an Savannah Township landowner, has a biographical sketch in Committee to Commemorate Black Businesses, comp., *The Legacy of Black Pioneers* ([Anderson, S.C.?]: privately printed, 1982), 49, as does Winston Sherard in *Profiles of Black Folks*, 320; Josephine S. Davis, "Origin and History of the Black Sherards in South Carolina" (typescript in Anderson County Library). Two Willifords appear in "Postbellum White Churches and Freed People" in ch. 17. Edmund Pickens, John Wesley Sherrard, Dump Sherrard, and James Williford testified on "November 1868 Elections" in ch. 15. Another judgment on long-term residency, and perhaps respectability, may be derived from the presence of specific sharecroppers' names (not identified as such or by race) and black landowners on von Hasseln's 1897 *Map of Anderson County*. It shows approximately 30 black residents; 14 of them match land ownership as indicated in the census.

20. Another 1868 family was the Neals; cf. W. A. Neal throughout "Stockade Scandal," pp. 401–2

21. Fair Play: my interviews on July 4, 1997, with several white and black families in Fair Play; Abbeville: private communication from the son of one of these families; Sherard: *AI*, July 10, 1901.

22. Quotation, referring to a later era, from *Sizemore*, 31.

23. *Profiles of Black Folks*, 754.

24. The sample consists of 100 people, mostly men, with liens in 1900, who were checked against 1899 and 1901 listings.

25. Hunter's lien arrangements appear in the Index, cited above. Additionally, I examined store's ledgers and miscellaneous correspondence for the 1890–1905 period; see note 1, ch. 23. Hunter Store Records, CU Special Collections.

26. Fertilizer, as an expensive item, was handled separately from ordinary purchases. Stores had to show documentation of these sales, as they provided the state large tax revenues. Hunter lent nearly $1000 in fertilizer money in 1900, and sold huge quantities of cotton to Pelzer mills. Cotton seed oil had become an important product.

27. Ballard says (164) that "Whites and Blacks needed each other, and economic necessity became a prime determinant of the relationship between them" and describes black dependency on whites.

28. Similarly, after December 1914 lynchings of three men at Fair Play—about ten miles northwest of Savannah Township—led to many families there leaving. Pickens, *Vengeance*, 12, 13; peonage charges against William McClure, 1915; U.S. District Court (National Archives and Records Admin.–Atlanta).

29. *PS*, June 11, July 2, 1891; *AI*, Sept. 30, 1896.

30. *Reports and Resolutions, 1900*, 794, 798; note E. P. Earle's hounds in "Complications," p. 403.

31. Cooley mistrial: *AI*, Jan. 28, 1892; deaths: *PJ*, Dec. 14, 1899. See Anderson County, Coroner's Inquests, box 2: Allen Giles, May 1, 1898; George Crayton, Sept. 5, 1898; Isaac Brown, Aug. 11, 1899; Reid Weir, Dec. 24, 1899; John Starks, July 4, 1900; and Wash Washington, July 5, 1900. During one week in late Dec. 1898, one of Ashley's tenants was "accidentally" shot and killed; also one of Watson's tenants was arrested; *AI*, Dec. 28, 1898. Elsewhere, "'Uncle Willis' [Davis] worked on the plantation of the late Judge Fowler. . . . [There] 'Uncle Willis' lost his right arm in a corn shredder"; *Profiles of Black Folks*, 86.

32. Neals, McGees, and Emersons were involved in 1868 voter intimidation; in 1901 J. A. Emerson was overseer for J. R. Miller; cf. "November 1868 Elections" in ch. 15. Judge Benet ordered magistrates to issue warrants that accused Fowler, two Hammonds, two McGees, Emerson, and five other men variously of false imprisonment, conspiracy, and assault and battery of a high and aggravated nature. After the court of general sessions returned true bills on these counts, all of the accused except Fowler pled guilty and paid fines of $50 each—in order to avoid attorneys' fees, they said. Fowler stood trial in June but was found not guilty after what seems to have been a pro forma jury deliberation. *AI*, June 12, 19, 26.

33. One of the earliest usages of courtesy titles appears in the *PS*, Sept. 15, 1881; Miller: *PJ*, June 11, 1896.

34. *AI*, Feb. 7, 1899; *PJ*, Feb. 1, June 15, 1899.

35. *AI*, April 3, July 3, 1895, May 30, 1900; Starks, 66–68.

36. *PS*, April 26, 1888; Goodman to Tillman, Feb. 7, 1892 (SCDAH); *AI*, Jan. 23, 1901.

Chapter 23. 1900: One Year in the Life of a Community

1. The 1900 census provides the first comprehensive data on African Americans in 20 years as the 1890 census accidentally burned. Somewhat like Milly Dupree's introductory vignette, part of this chapter is contrived. Its major component consists of actual general store transactions at Hunter Store in Pendleton from a CU collection by that name. Unfortunately it is missing records for black customers in 1900; I have drawn on entries from the 1894–96 and 1902–5 volumes. All charges were made by the person named in the same month indicated (except for two school purchases, shifted to the fall term), but for one of these proximate years. The Ashtabula records are from a 1900 surviving volume. Other information

comes primarily from the 1900 census and newspapers for the 1890s and early 1900s. Note additional references to Hunter's store in ch. 22, "Economic Subjugation, Sharecropping, and Crop Liens," pp. 399–400. Other events cited for 1900 happened in that year, except for Milly Dupree (see note 1 to "Prologue: Milly Dupree").

Most statistics on population, employment, and literacy come from the 1900 census, both manuscript schedules and printed reports; see table 19.2 for details of sample. Information about land ownership comes from census listings, tax records, and deeds. Emancipation: *AI*, Jan. 3, 1900; tenants: Wright's mortgage deed (1906) is in the author's possession.

Adapted from my "Pendleton's Black Community in 1900: A Portrait from Hunter's Store Accounts," Pendleton Foundation for Black History and Culture, October 13, 1996, and the Institute for Southern Studies, University of South Carolina, April 14, 1997.

2. Almost all town employers were white; half of Anderson's white families hired black maids; even some white tenants hired black farm laborers (chs. 18, 19).

3. Tax figures, readily identifiable for only Pickens and Oconee, show that 257 black people there owned property, one-third in towns, the remainder outside. Anderson tax records do not include the "c," "col," or "pc" used by Oconee and Pickens to designate "colored" or "person of color." It appears that 84 families in Anderson city owned land, although with only a total of 46 houses, typically valued at $100 each. Pendleton's black residents included 46 owners, 14 of whom had rural lands averaging $206 each; townspeople averaged $82. Town houses, averaging $35, ranged from $5 to $204 in value. As many as 500 black people may have owned land in Anderson County based on census reports.

4. Table 19.3.

5. *PJ*, Dec. 14, 1899; May 23, 1900.

6. Silver Spring: A. R. Robinson left the church in either 1899 or early 1900 to became minister at St. Paul, Anderson; a few years later he accepted an appointment in Philadelphia. In Aug. 1900 R. B. Bracey was the Silver Spring minister who headed RRBA's educational committee. A group began efforts in the 1990s to restore the Silver Spring building, damaged but still mostly intact; the congregation moved into a new brick building in the latter 1960s.

7. Hunter operations, "Economic Subjugation, Sharecropping, and Crop Liens" in ch. 22.

8. Beyond teachers' salaries, AOP spent a total of only $75 (including fuel and rent) for black schools that year. *Annual Report, 1900*; cf. my table 18.1.

9. One critic, complained that Starks later sold out to white Baptists and, in essence, betrayed his race. The Seneca community established a school before finding a president. None of the founding trustees had more than short-session grammar school education. It was one of a tiny number of black schools in the state under local black control. Initially offering only grammar school work, it added in stages a high school, training courses, and, in the 1920s junior college work. D. M. Minus, *The Struggling Boy* (Greenville, S.C.: privately printed, [1923]), 36; Lewis K. McMillan, *Negro Higher Education in the State of South Carolina*; Hunter, 95 ff.; Starks, *Lo These Many Years*, passim.

10. *AI*, Dec. 28, 1901.

11. *Pickens Sentinel*, Oct. 9, 1913; May 21, Sept. 17, 1914. When Mary Hallums (b. 1812) died in 1904, the *Pickens Sentinel* observed: "She leaves a good name, and her death is deplored by all the people of her community, white and colored, for she had the respect and confidence of them all."

12. *JCC* 16:415, 22:331–37, 23:338–40, 24:6–8; Burton, 151, 381 note 13; Edgefield DB GGG, 9, 170; Thomas Green Clemson to Patrick Calhoun, Aug. 6, 1850, Calhoun Papers, SCL;, and Floride C. Calhoun to Anna Clemson, Dec. 15, 1850, Clemson Papers, CU. Richardson's and Harlong's letters and Richardson's photograph belong to the Fort Hill Mansion collection, CU.

13. Loose paper in Pendleton town records; cf. Greenville's ordinances, 1912, ca. 1916, in Seabrook, *Before and After*, 32.

14. Contrasted to this story, see a favorable newspaper account in "Racial Relations in the City" in ch. 19; *Profiles of Black Folks*, 133. Descendants of Fanny Payton, who earlier moved to Abbeville, relocated as a group with other families to another Ohio town in the 1920s.

15. Viola Williams narrated her story following her BHUP oral history interview, June 19, 1990; I witnessed the 1998 exchange (note 17, ch. 18).

16. See, among others, Wyatt-Brown, *Southern Honor*, and applications by Burton (90–95) and S. West; *Those Who Remained* is a Smith Robertson Museum exhibit (Jackson, Miss.) that dealt with issues omitted from *Field to Factory*.

Selected Bibliography

An Essay

State and Local Documents
County-level public documents include deeds of real estate and of slaves, wills and estate papers, mortgages of real estate and of slaves, coroners' inquests, magistrates and freeholders' court records, sheriffs' sales, court of general sessions series, auditors' tax returns, voter registrations, and agricultural liens. These are held at the county courthouse or the SCDAH, in original and/or microfilm.

State records include governors' papers, which contain correspondence, petitions, and pardons; and records of the superintendents of education. *Annual Reports* and *Reports and Resolutions* of the Legislature and of the Superintendent of Education provide detailed reports and data. Department of Corrections records include the Central Register of Prisoners. The state conducted a census in 1869 and 1875. Petitions to the General Assembly are useful for the antebellum era. Death certificates begin in 1916.

Legal and judicial matters may be found in Thomas Cooper and David J. McCord, eds., *The Statutes at Large of South Carolina* (Columbia, S.C.: A. S. Johnston, 1836), and subsequent volumes; appellate cases in Helen H. Catterall, ed., *Judicial Cases concerning American Slavery and the Negro*, vol. 2 (Washington: Carnegie Institution of Washington, 1926); and a quasi-official account, John Belton O'Neall, *The Negro Law of South Carolina* (Columbia, S.C.: John G. Bowman, 1848).

There are several published compilations of abstracted documents for AOP: Betty Willie, *Pendleton District, S.C. Deeds, 1790–1806* (Easley, S.C.: Southern Historical Press, 1982); Pauline Young, *A Genealogical Collection of South Carolina Wills and Records* (1955; Easley: Southern Historical Press, 1984); James E. Wooley (ed.), *A Collection of Upper South Carolina Genealogical and Family Records* (Easley, S.C.: Southern Historical Press, 1983), 3 vols.; and Anne McCuen et al., comp., *Abstracts of General Sessions Court Case Rolls: Washington District, South Carolina, 1792–1799; Greenville County, South Carolina 1787–1799* (Greenville, S.C.: Greenville County Historic Preservation Commission, 1994).

Federal Censuses
Manuscript censuses (1790–1920), including Population, Agriculture, Industry, Mortality, and Slave schedules; published decennial reports (1790–1920) are available at SCDAH and in National Archives microcopy publications.

Compilations of census data and abstracts of local South Carolina data are found in James Dunworthy Brownson DeBow, *Statistical View of the United States . . .* (Washington: A. O. P. Nicholson, 1854); and U.S. Census Bureau, *Negroes in the United States* (Washington: GPO, 1904). Published AOP censuses include the following: William C. Stewart, comp., *1800 Census of Pendleton District, South Carolina* (Washington: National Genealogical Society, 1963); G. Anne Sheriff and Lavina Moore, comp., *Pendleton District South Carolina: 1810 Census* (Central, S.C.: privately printed, 1994); Anne Sheriff, Tom Wilkinson, Lavina Moore, and Jay Young, comp., *Pickens District, S.C. 1830 Census* (Central, S.C.: Faith Clayton Family Research Center, Central Wesleyan College, 1988); and Anne Sheriff, comp., *1850 Federal Slave Census of Pickens District, South Carolina, Eastern Division: Present-day Pickens County* and

1860 Federal Slave Census of Pickens District, South Carolina, 5th Regiment: Present-day Pickens County (Central, S.C.: privately printed, 1991 and 1989).

General South Carolina History
General South Carolina histories include Walter B. Edgar, *South Carolina: A History* (Columbia: University of South Carolina Press, 1998), the first comprehensive account to incorporate insights and research from recent decades of social history; and an earlier standard, David Duncan Wallace, *The History of South Carolina* (New York: American Historical Society, 1934), 3 vols. A briefer, useful guide is Lewis P. Jones's *South Carolina: A Synoptic History for Laymen* (Columbia, S.C.: Sandlapper Press, 1971).

Vital references works are *Mills' Atlas: Atlas of the State of South Carolina, 1825* (1825; Easley: Southern Historical Press, 1980); *Biographical Directory of the South Carolina State Senate, 1776–1985*, 3 vol.; and *Biographical Directory of the South Carolina House of Representatives*, 5 vols. (Columbia: University of South Carolina Press, 1974+).

The following are especially useful specialized studies: Norman Gasque Raiford, *South Carolina and the Issue of Internal Improvement, 1775–1860* (1974; Ann Arbor: University Microfilms, 1993); Thomas D. Russell, "The Antebellum Courthouse as Creditors' Domain," *American Journal of Legal History*, July 1996; John Barnwell, *Love of Order: South Carolina's First Secession Crisis* (Chapel Hill: University of North Carolina Press, 1982); William A. Schapter, *Sectionalism and Representation in South Carolina* (1901; New York: De Capo Press, 1968); and Stephanie McCurry *Masters of Small Worlds* (New York: Oxford University Press, 1995).

Upper Piedmont
Relatively few efforts deal with the upper piedmont as a whole, whether one refers to South Carolina only or to a broader swath. Among more recent studies are the following (in chronological order): Lacy K. Ford Jr., *Origins of Southern Radicalism: The South Carolina Upcountry, 1800–1860* (New York: Oxford University Press, 1988); John C. Inscoe, *Mountain Masters: Slavery and the Sectional Crisis in Western North Carolina* (Knoxville: University of Tennessee Press, 1989); Rachel Klein, *The Unification of a Slave State: The Rise of the Planter Class in the South Carolina Backcountry, 1760–1808* (Chapel Hill: University of North Carolina Press, 1990); John M. Coggeshall, *Carolina Piedmont Country* (Jackson: University Press of Mississippi, 1996); Wilma A. Dunaway, *The First American Frontier: Transition to Capitalism in Southern Appalachia* (Chapel Hill: University of North Carolina Press, 1996); David Colin Crass, ed., *The Southern Colonial Backcountry: Interdisciplinary Perspectives on Frontier Communities* (Knoxville: University of Tennessee Press, 1998); and Stephen West, "From Yeoman to Redneck in Upstate South Carolina, 1850–1915" (Ph.D. diss., Columbia University, 1998). The latter deals extensively with violence, a subtext throughout my work as well, as does Jack Kenny Williams, *Vogues in Villainy: Crime and Retribution in Ante-bellum South Carolina* (Columbia: University of South Carolina Press, 1959). Additionally, there is Washington Taylor, *A Diary of Transactions of Washington Taylor, 1835–1855, Greenville County, South Carolina* (Frederick, Md.: H. G. Taylor, 1988). West has a forthcoming book, tentatively titled "From Yeomen to Redneck in the South Carolina Upcountry, 1858–1915."

Separately, agricultural information may be found in John Durant Ashmore's "Book, 1853–59" (SHC), available on microfilm (Records of Ante-Bellum Southern Plantations, series F); an unpublished draft manuscript in William Hayne Mills Collection, CU; Joseph Davis Applewhite, "Some Aspects of Rural Society in South Carolina in 1850" (Ph.D. diss., Vanderbilt University, 1949); Donna Roper, "To Promote and Improve Agriculture: A Study of Four Antebellum South Carolina Farmers' Societies" (M.A. thesis, University of South Carolina, 1989); and throughout Calhoun letters, Ford, Racine, Taylor, and West.

Antebellum Anderson, Oconee, and Pickens Counties and Slaveowners
Contemporary accounts include both Robert Mills, *Statistics of South Carolina, Including a View of Its Natural, Civil, and Military History, General and Particular* (Charleston: Hurlbut & Loyd, 1826), and J. S. Buckingham, *The Slave States in America* (London: Fisher, Son, 1842). Mary Stevenson's two books draw heavily on diaries: *The Diary of Clarissa Adger Bowen, Ashtabula Plantation, 1865* and *The Recollection of a Happy Childhood by Mary Esther Huger* (Pendleton, S.C.: Foundation for Historic Restoration in Pendleton Area, 1973, 1976). See also "Summer Migrations of South Carolina Planters" in *Historical Papers* (1947; New York: AMS Press, 1970) and Sarah Edith Ann Smith Mills, *Reminiscences* (privately printed, 1935).

For an era before Pendleton District existed, see Anne Sheriff, ed., *Cherokee Villages in South Carolina* (Easley, S.C.: Forest Acres Elementary School, 1990). Craig Thompson Friend deals with the early period, "Frontier and Plantation, Pendleton, South Carolina, 1780–1830" (M.A. thesis, Clemson University, 1990).

Three books of varying quality deal with the area; those by Vandiver and Dickson lack documentation. Beth Ann Klosky, *The Pendleton Legacy* (Columbia, S.C.: Sandlapper Press, 1971); Louise Ayer Vandiver, *Traditions and History of Anderson County: History of Anderson County* (1928); and Frank A. Dickson, *Journeys into the Past: The Anderson Region's Heritage* (Anderson, S.C.: privately printed, 1975).

An account of one of the earliest wealthy slaveholding families is A. Charles Cannon, "The Maxwells, A Pioneer Greenville Family," *Proceedings and Papers of the Greenville County Historical Society* 8 (1984–90): 187–97. Genealogical information on many early families can be gleaned from R. W. Simpson, *History of Old Pendleton District: With a Genealogy of the Leading Families of the District* (Anderson, S.C.: Oulla Printing & Binding, 1913); published extracts from area newspapers including the *Pendleton Messenger;* and church records. Numerous slaveowners served in the state legislature and appear in its biographical directories.

The Calhoun-Colhoun families were among the most prominent locally. Among their treatments are: A. S. Salley Jr., *The Calhoun Family of South Carolina* ([Columbia, S.C.?]: n.p., [1906?]); Charles M. Wiltse, *John C. Calhoun*, 3 vols. (Indianapolis: Bobbs-Merrill, 1944–51); E. M. Lander, *The Calhoun Family and Thomas Green Clemson: Decline of a Southern Patriarchy* (Columbia: University of South Carolina Press, 1983); and Irving H. Bartlett's *John C. Calhoun: A Biography* (1993). Family papers are available at CU, SCL, SHC, and Duke University, as well as the 26-volume *The Papers of John C. Calhoun* (Columbia: University of South Carolina Press).

Other AOP accounts include Bert Reece, *History of Pumpkintown-Oolenoy* ([Pickens, S.C.?]: Miracle Hill Print Shop, 1970); W. J. Megginson, "1850 Pickens District Professions, Skilled Crafts, and Trades," *Pickens District . . . 1850 Census* (Central, S.C.: Old Pendleton Genealogical Society, 1995), 2 vols.; and, for an adjacent county, Lowry Ware, *Old Abbeville: Scenes of the Past of a Town Where Old Time Things Are Not Forgotten* (Columbia, S.C.: SCMAR, 1992).

Antebellum Religion
Thirty-five archived church records provide documentary information; they appear as table 6.2. Three church records have been published: Edwin H. Vedder, *Records of St. Pauls Episcopal Church of Pendleton, South Carolina* (Greenville, S.C.: A. Press, 1982); Richard Newman Brackett, *The Old Stone Church, Oconee County South Carolina* (1905; [Clemson, S.C.?]: The Old Stone Church and Cemetery Commission, 1972); and Franklin Albert Spearman, comp., *Visions and Victories: The Bi-centennial History of Big Creek Baptist Church, Williamston, South Carolina, Organized 1788: The Church Chronicles, 1788–1988* (n.p.: n.p., 1989). See also T. H. Garrett, *A History of the Saluda Baptist Association* (Richmond, Va.: F. B. Johnson Publishing, 1896). One biographical narrative deals with a local slave minister: James A. Tolbert, *Christ*

in Black; Or, The Life and Times of Rev. James R. Rosemond (Greenville, S.C.: Shannon & Co., 1902).

Numerous scholars have approached slave religious views by comparing them with African belief systems. Among these are Albert J. Raboteau, *Slave Religion: The "Invisible Institution" in the Antebellum South* (New York: Oxford University Press, 1978) and (as coeditor) *African American Religion: Interpretive Essays in History and Culture* (New York: Routledge, 1997); and Mechal Sobel, *Trabelin' On: The Slave Journey to an Afro-Baptist Faith* (Westport, Conn.: Greenwood Press, 1979).

Antebellum African American Life and Culture

Published primary and secondary literature on slavery, life, and culture is voluminous. George P. Rawick's *The American Slave: A Composite Autobiography* (Westport, Conn.: Greenwood Press, date varies) is based largely on the WPA "slave narratives"; his vol. 1, *Sunup to Sundown*, interprets their insights. Herbert G. Gutman's *The Black Family in Slavery and Freedom, 1750–1925* (New York: Vintage Books, 1976), Philip D. Morgan's *Slave Counterpoint: Black Culture in the Eighteenth-Century Chesapeake and Lowcountry* (Chapel Hill: University of North Carolina Press, 1998), and Ira Berlin's, *Many Thousands Gone* (Cambridge: Belknap Press of Harvard University Press, 1999) are important studies of local African American history and employ comparative approaches.

A diverse group of secondary South Carolina studies (listed chronologically) is helpful: H. M. Henry, *The Police Control of the Slave in South Carolina* (Emory, Va.: privately printed, 1914); Peter H. Wood, *Black Majority: Negroes in Colonial South Carolina from 1670 through the Stono Rebellion* (New York: Alfred A. Knopf, 1974); William Cinque Henderson, "Spartan Slaves: A Documentary Account of Blacks on Trial in Spartanburg, South Carolina, 1830 to 1865" (Ph.D. diss., Northwestern University, 1978); Orville Vernon Burton, *In My Father's House Are Many Mansions: Family and Community in Edgefield, South Carolina* (Chapel Hill: University of North Carolina Press, 1985); Charles Joyner, *Down by the Riverside: A South Carolina Slave Community* (Urbana: University of Illinois Press, 1985); David Golightly Harris, *Piedmont Farmer: The Journals of David Golightly Harris, 1855–1870* (Knoxville: Univ. of Tennessee Press, 1990), edited by Philip N. Racine; and Bernard E. Powers Jr., *Black Charlestonians: A Social History, 1822–1885* (Fayetteville: University of Arkansas Press, 1994).

Literature on free people of color is disproportionately small, and virtually none exists for the upper piedmont. One exception is Samuel Lorenzo Malone, *The Sizemore Family Tree: One Man's Search for His Roots* (n.p.: privately printed, 1980). Studies dealing with more generally with the state's FPC include Marina Wikramanayake's *World of Shadow* (Columbia: South Carolina Tricentennial Commission, 1973); Larry Koger, *Black Slaveowners: Free Black Slave Masters in South Carolina, 1790–1860* (Jefferson, N.C.: McFarland, 1985); and John Livingston Bradley, "Slave Manumission in South Carolina, 1820–1860" (M.A. thesis, University of South Carolina, 1964). Sources on laws and judicial interpretations also deal with FPC.

Civil War and Early Reconstruction

There is no good source for the war's impact on AOP, with virtually no diaries or newspaper holdings for 1862–64. Standard military accounts hardly touch the area; the account with most AOP relevance is Louise Matheson Bell, *Rebels in Grey: Soldiers from Pickens District, 1861–1865* (Seneca, S.C.: Greys of Oconee Chapter No. 1783, United Daughters of the Confederacy, 1984). The best and most recent account of the state's civilians is John Hammond Moore, *Southern Homefront, 1861–1865* (Columbia, S.C.: Summerhouse Press, 1998); it also sketches the major military actions in S.C. Several of his letters and references apply specifically to Greenville and Pendleton, as does *"Far, Far from Home": The Wartime Letters of Dick and Tally Simpson Third South Carolina Volunteers* (New York: Oxford University Press, 1994), edited by Edward W. Simpson and Guy R. Everson.

Four diaries by local young white women cover part of the Civil War and continue into Reconstruction: Floride Clemson, *A Rebel Came Home: The Diary and Letters of Floride Clemson, 1863–66* (Columbia: University of South Carolina Press, 1961), edited by E. M. Lander; *The Diary of Clarissa Adger Bowen, Ashtabula Plantation, 1865; The Life and Times of Ella Lorton, A Pendleton SC Confederate* (Clemson, S.C.: Clemson Printers, 1996), edited by Ernest McPherson Lander Jr.; and *A Faithful Heart: The Journals of Emmala Reed, 1865 and 1866* (Columbia: University of South Carolina Press, 2004), edited by Robert T. Oliver.

Chapters on the Civil War and Reconstruction depend heavily on federal sources at the National Archives. Most military papers are part of Record Group (RG) 393. The Department of the South, Department of the Carolinas, and 2nd Military District (titles varied over time) fall within RG 393, part 1; and Western South Carolina, in RG 393, part 3. Freedmen's Bureau records, including labor contracts, are in RG 105. Additionally, there are the Freedmen's Savings Banks records on microfilm for Atlanta, Ga., and Charleston, S.C.

Most serious issues relating to Reconstruction did not arise in AOP as early as 1865; an overview of major studies appears below. As on other issues, West's "Yeoman to Redneck" provides useful insights. The standard documentary account of the war is *A Compilation of the Official Records of the Union and Confederate Armies* (Washington: GPO, 1893).

Three AOP events generated several hundred pages of transcribed federal, county, and state proceedings: the trial of four white men charged with murdering U.S. soldiers in September 1865; the October 1867 account of a young white boy's murder by a black man, which formed part of the Secretary of War's 1868 *Annual Report*; and 1869 state legislative hearings on 1868 voter intimidation.

Biographical sketches for several people in the text can be found in *Dictionary of American Biography* (New York: Charles Scribner's Sons, 1927–); and photographs of some relevant Union officers appear in Robert McCaslin, Bobby Roberts, and Carl Moneyhon, *Portraits of Conflict: South Carolina* (Fayetteville: University of Arkansas Press, 1994).

Reconstruction Studies

Reconstruction literature on South Carolina is sparse but increasing. Early accounts, including those of James Pike's *The Prostrate State: South Carolina under Negro Government* (New York: D. Appleton & Co., 1874) and Henry T. Thompson's *Ousting the Carpetbagger from South Carolina* (Columbia, S.C.: R. L. Bryan Co., 1926), consist primarily of white Democratic attacks on Republican, black, and carpetbag-rule in the state. John Schreiner Reynolds's *Reconstruction in South Carolina* (Columbia, S.C.: State Co., 1905) shares the old Democratic bias but is useful as a compendium of political meetings (primarily white-controlled), delegates, and officials in state government. Hampton M. Jarrell's *Wade Hampton and the Negro* (Columbia: University of South Carolina Press, 1949) asserts that Hampton was sympathetic to, and beneficial for, South Carolina's black population. An early treatment sympathetic to African Americans is A. A. Taylor, "The Negro in South Carolina during the Reconstruction," *Journal of Negro History* 9 (1924).

A major advance in dispassionate, scholarly analysis for the state came with Francis Butler Simkins and Robert Hilliard Woody, *South Carolina during Reconstruction* (Chapel Hill: University of North Carolina Press, 1932). Efforts during the next decades to deal with Reconstruction on a national level and to incorporate serious analysis of the black role and of economic insights lacked parallels in South Carolina studies.

Reflecting post–World War II revisionism, Joel Williamson's *After Slavery: The Negro in South Carolina during Reconstruction, 1861–1877* (Chapel Hill: University of North Carolina

Press, 1965) is the first scholarly work after Simkins's study. Foner's *Reconstruction: America's Unfinished Revolution, 1863–1877* (New York: Harper & Row, 1988) offers primarily a national perspective. Two major additions after Williamson are Julie Saville, *The Work of Reconstruction: From Slave to Wage Laborer in South Carolina, 1860–1870* (New York: Cambridge University Press, 1994), and Richard Zuczek, *State of Rebellion: Reconstruction in South Carolina* (Columbia: University of South Carolina Press, 1996). There are hardly any substantial biographical studies, those of Orr and Perry being among the few that exist. Woefully lacking in studies of South Carolina from 1865 through 1877 is the role of the military. Thomas B. Keys, *The Army and Crawford Keys: Aftermath of the Brown's Ferry Outrage* (privately published, 1974) is a local account. Eric's Foner's "Forever Free: The Story of Emancipation and Reconstruction" (New York: Knopf, 2005) appeared while the present work was in production. Like Foner's other books, this one (coauthored with Joshua Brown) sheds much light and provides new interpretations and insights.

Some recent additions to S.C. Reconstruction studies include Lou Falkner Williams, *The Great South Carolina Ku Klux Klan Trials, 1871–1872* (Athens: University of Georgia Press, 1996) and Edmund L. Drago, *Hurrah for Hampton! Black Red Shirts in South Carolina during Reconstruction* (Fayetteville: University of Arkansas Press, 1998).

Postbellum Studies

A small sampling of important and relevant works on postbellum matters, largely race, follow (in chronological order): George W. Tindall, *South Carolina Negroes, 1877–1900* (Columbia: University of South Carolina Press, 1952); I. A. Newby, *Black Carolinians: A History of Blacks in South Carolina from 1895 to 1968* (Columbia: South Carolina Tricentennial Commission, 1973); Joel Williamson, *The Crucible of Race: Black-White Relations in the American South since Emancipation* (New York: Oxford University Press, 1984); Charles E. Orser, *The Material Basis of the Postbellum Tenant Plantation* (Athens: University of Georgia Press, 1988); Dwain Pruitt, *Things Hidden: An Introduction to the History of Blacks in Spartanburg* ([Spartanburg, S.C.]: City of Spartanburg Community Relations Office, [1995]); and Pat Pritchard, ed., *"If These Stones Could Talk," The Rediscovery of the Old Maxwell Cemetery* ([Westminster, S.C.]: Fair Play Camp School, 1997).

African American Families and Religion in Freedom

Despite a surprising array of information on AOP's black families, much of it is widely dispersed and little gathered into library and archival collections. Many church-based publications contain valuable church histories and family information and photographs, but have been distributed primarily to local constituencies; examples are *Seneca River Missionary Baptist Association, Centennial Yearbook, 1878–1978; Oolenoy River Education and Missionary Baptist Association of Pickens County, South Carolina, Centennial Celebration*, 1982; and *Rocky River Baptist Association, 100 Years*, 1968; all privately printed. Fortunately SCL has a rich collection of black Baptist association and state minutes (collected by John A. Middleton III), as well as microfilm of AME and black ME church materials. See also *Proceedings of the Quarto-Centennial Conference at Charleston, S.C., May 15, 16 and 17, 1889* (privately printed, 1890).

Among a few deposited family histories and genealogies are the following by Josephine Sherard Davis: "Origin and History of the Black Sherards in South Carolina" (typescript in Anderson County Library) and "Facts from the Family Tree of the Thompsons of Pendleton South Carolina," July 1977 (SCL); and "The Thompson Family Reunion, Pendleton, S.C., July 1–14 1985" (compiler not stated; SCL). Various materials also appear in newsletters of the Pendleton Foundation for Black History and Culture. Gwendolyn Anderson's *Profiles of Black Folks in Anderson County* (Spartanburg, S.C.: Reprint Co., 1993) is currently the most significant published collection of the area's black families and church and school histories.

Six accounts were written by or about local people: Jane Edna Hunter, *A Nickel and a Prayer* (n.p.: Elli Kani Publishing, 1940; D. M. Minus, *The Struggling Boy* (Greenville, S.C.: privately printed, [1923]); William Pickens, *Bursting Bonds* (Boston: Jordan & More, 1923), and *The Vengeance of the Gods* (1922; New York: AMS Press, 1975); J. J. Starks, *Lo These Many Years: An Autobiographical Sketch* (Columbia, S.C.: State Co., 1941); and James A. Tolbert, *Christ in Black, Or the Life and Times of Rev. James R. Rosemond* (Greenville, S.C.: Shannon & Co., 1902).

Towns

There are accounts, some published in the 1990s, of several AOP towns: George Benet Shealy, *Walhalla: A German Settlement in Upstate South Carolina, "The Garden of the Gods"* (Seneca, S.C.: Blue Ridge Arts Association, 1990); Frances Holleman, *Seneca, South Carolina Centennial 1873–1973* (Greenville, S.C.: Briggs & Associates, 1973); Joseph Gauzens, *Salem, Twice a Town* (Pickens, S.C.: Hiott Printing 1993); Mattie May Morgan Allen, *Central: Today and Yesterday* (Taylors, S.C.: Faith Publishing, 1973); Julia Jean Woodson and G. Anne Sheriff, *Liberty, South Carolina: One Hundred Years 1876–1976* (Central, S.C.: Faith Clayton Family Research Center, 1992); Jane Boroughs Morris, *Pickens: The Town and the First Baptist Church* (Pickens, S.C.: First Baptist Church, 1991); and *Honea Path Milestones* (Honea Path, S.C.: Seabury Press, 1976). A study of the town of Pendleton is conspicuously and sadly lacking. Relatively little information about black residents appears in most of the above. By contrast see two volumes of *Black History in Pickens District, South Carolina* (Easley, S.C.: Forest Acres Elementary School, 1991–98), edited by G. Anne Sheriff.

There are two accounts of Belton: Elmer Don Herd Jr., "Early History of Belton, South Carolina: 1700–1860" (typescript, CU), and Max Wilton Grubbs, "A History of the Social, Economic, and Political Development of Belton, South Carolina" (M.S. thesis, CU, 1960). See also *Down Home: Dacusville Yesterday, Today and Tomorrow* (Easley: Dacusville Community History Project, 1995), SCL.

For Anderson, see Gwendolyn Anderson, and *The Legacy of Black Pioneers* (privately printed, 1982), compiled by the Committee to Commemorate Black Businesses. Information on the city is found in David L. Carlton's *Mill and Town in South Carolina 1880–1920* (Baton Rouge: Louisiana State University Press, 1983) and John Hammond Moore, *South Carolina in the 1880s: A Gazetteer* (Orangeburg, S.C.: Sandlapper Publishers, 1989). An Anderson *Intelligencer* supplement (undated; filmed following September 30, 1896) has glowing articles on mills and various merchants. Hurley Badders, *Anderson County, A Pictorial History* (Norfolk, S.C.: Donning, 1983), deals mostly with the 1900s. Bernard Powers's *Black Charlestonians*, John Hammond Moore's *Columbia and Richland County: A South Carolina Community, 1740–1990* (Columbia: University of South Carolina Press, 1993), and Archie Vernon Huff Jr.'s *Greenville: The History of the City and County in the South Carolina Piedmont* (Columbia: University of South Carolina Press, 1995) provide useful gauges for the scale of Anderson's accomplishments, as well as of the Reconstruction era.

Business and city directories—beginning with *Smith's South Carolina Business Directory, 1876–77*, (Charleston: Lucas & Richardson, 1876) through *Walsh's Directory of the City and County of Anderson, S. C. For 1905–06* (Charleston: Walsh Directory, 1905)—include numerous AOP black businesses and, for 1905, Anderson's residents.

Manuscripts

CLEMSON UNIVERSITY
Dr. William Jenkins Day Book
Dr. William Robinson Papers
E. B. Benson & Sons Daybook, 1859
Hunter Store Records

John C. Calhoun Papers
"Overseer's Day Book of a Small Plantation, 1822–1917" [Abbeville County]
Pendleton Farmers' Society Records
"Pendleton Sunday School Society, Records, 1819–1824" (WPA typescript)
Ralph Beaumont Leonard, "The Graveyard of the Keowee Plantation"
T. J. Pickens Papers (Dr. Thomas J.)
William Hayne Mills Collection

SOUTH CAROLINIANA LIBRARY, UNIVERSITY OF SOUTH CAROLINA
Benjamin F. Perry Papers
Edgar Wallace Biggs Papers
Farmer Family Papers
Gen. Andrew Pickens Record, 1787–1858 (SCL photostats)
James Earle Hagood Papers
James Edward Calhoun Papers
James F. Sloan Papers
Joseph Jeptha Norton Papers
John Caldwell Calhoun Papers
John Ewing Colhoun [Sr.] Papers
John Ewing Colhoun [Jr.] (1791–1847) Papers
Louisa Rebecca Hayne McCord, "Recollections"
Papers of the Duncan, Kinard, Sanders, and Tucker Families
Papers of the Maverick and Van Wyck Families
Papers of the Norris and Thomson Families
Pickens Family Papers
Robert Fullerton Papers
Simpson Young Dean and Coleman Families Papers
Sitton Papers
Stribling Family Papers
Thomas Gilliland Boggs, Family Papers
Townes Family Papers
William Henry Trescott
William King Easley Papers

SOUTHERN HISTORICAL COLLECTION (SHC), UNIVERSITY OF NORTH CAROLINA AT CHAPEL HILL
Habersham Elliot Papers
John D. Ashmore, Plantation Journal
John Ewing Colhoun Papers
Templeman and Goodwin [Richmond firm], Account Book, 1849–51

SPECIAL COLLECTIONS LIBRARY, DUKE UNIVERSITY
Colhoun Papers
Josiah Edward Smith Papers
O. R. Broyles Papers

Newspapers
AME Christian Recorder (1865–1900)
Anderson Gazette (1843–54)
Anderson Intelligencer (1860–1915)
(Charleton) *News and Courier* (selected dates)

Greenville News (selected dates)
Pendleton Messenger (1806–48)
People's Journal (1893–1903)
Pickens Sentinel (1872–1915)
Walhalla Keowee Courier (Pickens, 1860–68, Walhalla, 1868–1915)

Index of People

Enslaved people's owners, where ascertained, are listed in parentheses. When an enslaved person's postbellum surname has been found, it is included in brackets.

Abram (James Wardlaw), 444n20
Acker families, 54
Acker, J. J., 50
Adams, Alf, 408
Adams, Clarissa, 186
Adams, Doc, 275
Adams, Mark, 225
Adams, Placidia, 135
Adams, Spencer, 244
Addison, Clarissa, 327
Addison, Richard, 327
Adeline (Jane Robinson), 172
Adger family, 292, 297
Adger, John B., 103, 138, 174, 206–7, 209
Adger, Robert, 197, 297
Agusta, Holly, 53
Aiken, Wyatt, 260
Aleck (John Warnock), 187
Alexander (Wash. Davenport), 448n44
Alfred (a runaway slave from Ga.), 95, 134, 187–88, 501n17
Alfred (a slave; husband), 142. *See also* Caroline (a slave; wife)
Alfred (George Mattison), 84–86
Alfred (J. B. Adger), 206, 209
Allen family, 236
Allen, Alfred (Forch). *See* Allen, Forch
Allen, Betsy, 64
Allen, Forch, 57, 64–65, 165, 329, 479n19
Allen, Frances, 64
Allen, Mary, 52, 64
Allen, P. B., 398–99, 409
Allen, Polly, 52, 56, 64
Allen, Richard, 64
Allen, Richard (AME), 488n8
Allen, Sarah, 64
Allums, Cato, 215. *See also* Hallum, Cato
Ames, Adelbert, 205, 207, 214
Amritta (Ashmore), 35, 49
Amy (Alfred Hester), 463n40
Amy (Colhoun Jr.), 155
Amy (E. Mills), 38
Anderson, Gwendolyn, 335, 427n12
Anderson, Jerry, 479n6
Anderson, Jim, 362

Anderson, Robert, 24, 35, 37, 54, 120, 174
Anderson, Will, 294
Andrew (a slave), 190
Andrew (Thomas Duckworth), 93, 159, 162
Andy (Calhoun), 165
Andy (J. B. Haddon), 99
Annie (Colhoun Jr.), 153
Anthony (Isaac Clement), 91
Anthony (Silas Holloway), 455n14
Armstrong, Jonas, 379
Arnold, Emery, 266
Arp, Bill, 379, 390, 402
Arter (surname), 239
Arter families, 55, 58, 65–66, 69, 236–37
Arter, Clint, 56, 68
Arter, Jackson, 56, 211
Arter, James, 94
Arter, Lemuel, 56
Arter, Martha, 65–66
Arter, Wesley, 56
Arthur families, 66
Asbury, Francis, 97
Ashley, Joshua, 388–89, 415, 417, 502n29
Ashmore, John D., 35, 47, 49, 86, 103, 128, 164, 185
Austin (James Bigby), 129
Austin (Mrs. Mattison), 167

Bacote, A. R., 365
Bailas (Esli Hunt), 93
Ball, Charles, 81, 135
Ballard, Allen, 426n9, 479n13, 482n2, 483nn17, 22, 488n9, 495n34, 504nn14, 16, 505n27
Ballard, William, 133
Banneker, Benjamin, 359–60
Barnes, Jane, 479n11
Barnett (Andrew Kennedy), 26
Barnett (Robert Maxwell), 78
Barnhill, David, 69
Barry (Julius NRoss), 82
Barton, Joseph. E., 351–52
Baskin, Davy, 61
Baskin, Ginney, 61
Baskin, J. H., 61

Baskin, Jack, 60–61
Baskin, Robert McKinley, 61
Bearden, J. P., 48
Bella (J. D. Ashmore), 49
Ben (Thomas K. Edwards), 68, 80, 91
Benjamin, "Brother" (a slave), 99
Bennett, Elisha, 141
Bennett, Polly, 451n12
Benson, Isaac, 238
Benson, J. B., 56
Benson, Warren, 243
Berry (Lemuel Hall), 109–10, 130
Beson, John W., 119
Bet (Sarah Cromer), 207
Betty Poll (a slave), 160
Bibbs, Winsome, 411
Bieman, D., 130
Billy (Col. Pickens), 104
Billy (Colhoun Jr.), 155
Bina (Mrs. Pickens), 104
Bird, Albert, 403
[Black], Sam, 193, 235
Blalock, J. S., 358, 486n59
Blassingame, Elijah, 342
Blease, Cole, 389
"Blind Tom" [Bethune, Thomas Green Wiggins], 358, 379
Bob (a slave), 160
Bob (Alexander Colhoun), 80
Bob (FPC), 29
Bob (Hugh Gantt), 84
Bob (John Fretwell), 131
Bob (Martin H. Smith), 131
Boggs, Aaron, 319, 332, 493n10
Boggs, Celia, 450n9
Boggs, Chesley, 187
Bolton, Henry, 382–84
Bonaparte, Yankee, 479n26
Bonneau family, 148
Bonneau, Floride, 30. *See also* Colhoun, Floride
Borin family, 58
Borin, Mary, 59
Borin, Mary Ann, 59
Bowen, Clarissa Adger, 197, 202, 204, 207
Bowen, O. A., 202
Bowen, R. E., 274
Bozeman, Charity, 31
Bracey, R. B., 506n6
Brackenridge, Bob, 225
Brackenridge, Thomas R., 47
Brawley, E. M., 361
Bray, Captain, 214, 215
Briant, John L., 187
Brock, J. H., 398
Brooks, Peter, 259
Brouster, Hugh, 69

Brown, A. J., 490n28
Brown, Calvin S., 201, 214, 215
Brown, Carl, 260
Brown, Daniel, 41, 95
Brown, E. R., 279
Brown, Jackson, 244
Brown, John, 47
Brown, Lucinda Reid, 143, 380
Brown, Simeon B., 198
Brown, Sue, 411
Brown, Tom, 412
Brown, William P., 204
Brownlee, George, 78
Broyles, Aaron, 114
Broyles, O. R., 84, 95, 217, 454n24
Brummer (Col. John McFall), 129
Bryce, Alexander, Jr., 225, 279, 284
Buck (a slave), 159
Buck (Leah Moore), 82
Buckingham, J. S., 46
Bugg, Samuel, 26
Burch, Henry, 353, 497n5
Burden, Olly, 56
Burdine families, 53, 55, 58, 69, 236
Burdine, Betsey, 56
Burdine, Daniel, 56
Burris families, 409
Burt, Sidney, 322, 405, 408
Burton, Vernon, 6, 9, 235, 239, 424n4, 426n11, 437n23, 457n1, 478n2, 479n12, 481n28
Butler (surname), 239
[Butler], Isaac (John C. Calhoun?), 155
Butler, M. C., 275–76
Buttle, Jacer, 279
Byna (Robert McCann), 117

Caesar (a preacher), 52, 56, 100–101, 128, 138, 287
Cain (1838), 160
Cain (John Robinson), 93
Caleb (Jacob Gueren), 92
Calhoun families, 45, 95, 115, 124, 148, 151, 159, 160, 163, 184, 187, 227
Calhoun, Ezekiel, 156
Calhoun, Floride, 94–95, 148, 159, 165, 183, 187, 206
Calhoun, James Edward, 81, 461n13
Calhoun, John, 62
Calhoun, John C., 1, 21, 26, 28, 30, 42, 48, 80, 94, 125, 130, 137, 147, 150, 161, 168, 170–71, 182, 226, 326, 332; sons of, 227
Calhoun, Sarah, 218, 228, 474n23
Calhoun, "Uncle" Jack, 326
Canby, E. R. S., 224, 226–27
Candas (Andrew Oliver), 129, 159, 162
Cannon (surname), 238

Cannon families, 55, 237
Cannon, Elijah, 66
Cannon, John, 407
Cannon, Simon, 56
Cannon, Sylvia, 128
Cannon, Thomas, 269, 455n8
Carlisle, Elijah, 268, 473n48
Carlisle, J. E., 339
Caroline (a slave; wife), 142. *See also* Alfred (a slave; husband)
Carroll, Richard, 361
Carter, Jack, 396
Cary, J. W. L., 63
Casey, J. R., 132
Casey, R. T., 132
Castleberry, Margaret, 120
Cato (Colhoun), 3
Cato (Dobson), 104
Cato, "old" (Robert Anderson), 116
Cato, "young" (Robert Anderson), 116
Celia (freed; Boggs), 32
Cella (Colhoun), 148
Chamberlain, Daniel H., 254, 266, 276, 278–81, 486n5
Chamblee, Moses, 262
Chappelle, Wm. David, 296, 360, 365
Charles (A. M. Smith), 50
Charles (J. B. Adger), 206, 209
Charles (Martha Bowen), 91
Cheatham, Henry, 217–18
Cherry, Andrew, 224, 234
Cherry, G. R., 473nn47, 48
Cherry, John C., 165
Cherry, Morris, 351, 353, 418
Chesnut, Mary, 37, 186, 193
Clara (R. F. Simpson), 192
Clark, Rena, 490n23
Clarke, Joseph, 69
Clayton, Narcissa, 189
Clemson, Anna, 332
Clemson, Floride, 184, 195, 197, 203, 205, 215
Clemson, Thomas G., 114, 158, 165, 171, 332, 379, 416, 493n10
Cleveland, Benjamin, 24, 29
Cleveland, Green, 477n47
Cleveland, Green, Jr., 225
Cleveland, John, 105
Clinkscales (baby), 144
Clinkscales, Bob, 259
Clinkscales, John George, 84
Coats, Anthony, 52, 56, 60–61
Coats, John, 60
Coats, Polly, 60
Cochran, Daniel H., 131, 483n14
Cochran, Grace, 257
Cochran, John R., 224, 257, 260, 262, 264–68, 270, 280, 303, 324, 351, 473n46, 484n29
Cochran, R. A., 319, 332
Colhoun families, 148, 153, 227
Colhoun, Floride, 156, 163. *See also* Bonneau, Floride
Colhoun, Henry D., 48, 107, 129, 164, 473n42
Colhoun, John Ewing, 21, 24–25, 46, 48, 136, 147, 148, 150, 153, 156
Colhoun, John Ewing (Jr.), 1, 3, 50, 107, 142, 150–51, 153, 416
Colhoun, Margaret, 151
Colhoun, W. R., 151, 439n39
Collins, B. C., 338–39
Conly family, 412
Cooley, D. H., 402
Cotrell, John, 189
Cox, Perry, 487n31
Craig, E. B., 296
Craig, Floyd, 218
Craig, Henry, 463n41
Crawford, James W., 45
Crawford, Samuel, 220
Crayton, Jake, 468n40
Cresia (a slave), 119
Crew, John P., 492n2
Crew, Rufus, 410, 417
Crew, Spencer, 417
Crews, Joe, 263
Cromer, Sarah Ann Atkins, 207
Crooks, Julia, 408, 412
Cudjo (Tucker May), 288
Cunningham families, 504n18
Cynthia (Clark), 104
Cyrus (a slave), 129
Cyrus (Joshua Stith), 444n20

Daphne (Calhoun), 416
Dave (John Burress), 80, 91
Dave (Jolly), 82
Dave T. (a former slave), 203
Dawdle, Hannah, 61
Dawdle, Harriet, 61
Dawdle, Morris, 61
Dawdle, William, 61
Day, Martha, 91
Dean, Captain, 225
Dean, Jack, 242
Dean, Thomas, 116
Dean, William, 242
Dearing, Alfred, 416
Dede, "Old" (Robert Anderson), 116
DeForest, William, 190, 217, 218, 224, 234, 242
Delight, John, 473n46
Dennis, Wade, 167

Di, Maum (McCord), 170
Dick (Clark), 104
Dick (William Harrison), 189
Dickson, Andrew Flynn, 103
Dickson, William, 63
Dinah (FPC), 69
Dinah (a slave), 104
Dobbins, J. E., 345
Doctor Tom (FPC). *See* Tom, "Doctor"
Dooley, David, 338–39, 345, 351, 497n6
Dooley, Joseph, 235
Dorsey, Edward, 316
Dot (Thomas Adams), 78
Douglass, Frederick, 360
Douthet families, 55, 441n11
Douthet, James, 117
Dowdle, Robert, 53, 61
Drayton (surname), 239
DuBois, W. E. B., 354
Duckworth families, 174
Duke families, 65–66
Duke, Rhoda, 65
Duke, William, 65
DuPree (surname), 239
Dupree, A. E. (Aleck), 1, 364, 414, 418, 461n39, 498n12
Dupree, Amelia, 418
Dupree, Edward, 461n39
Dupree, Frances, 3, 316, 334, 418
Dupree, Isaac, 461n39
Dupree, J., 345
Dupree, Milly, 1–3, 4, 155–56, 316, 334, 405, 418–19, 498n12
Dupree, Thomas (Tom), 4, 418
Durham, Allen, 215
Durham, Perry, 215

Earle family, 339
Earle, E. P., 401, 403
Earle, Elias, 27, 473n46
Earle, J. B., 129
Earle, Maj. J. T., 69
Earle, J. W., 379
Earle, John B., 69, 78
Earle, Samuel, 36, 42, 286; and his slaves, 42–43
Earle, Willie, 382
Easley, W. K., 63, 95, 426n11
Eaton, Gaylord, 382–83
Edmund (Ezekiel Murphy), 160, 167, 173
Edom (David G. Harris), 44, 165
Edward (Henry W. Ravenel), 470n8
Edwards, Lawrence, 345
Edwards, Lizette, 234
Edy, Elizabeth, 141
Elgins, Milton, 260
Eli (a slave), 100

Elifus (David G. Harris), 168
Ellen (Wm. Nevitt Jr.), 92
Elliott, Emily, 69
Elliott, Mary, 69
Elliott, Mary Jane, 69
Elrod, Reuben, 385, 389
Emerson, J. A., 505n27
Emerson, Samuel, 259
Emma (R. F. Simpson), 192
English, Dave, 412
Ephraim (Sherrill), 132
Essex (Clinkscales), 84
Esther (David G. Harris), 134
Esther (Martha Rankin), 188
Esther (Samuel Taylor), 116
Evans, Edward, 240
Evans, Jim, 407–8, 413
Evans, Kate, 240

Fair, Robert A., 103
Fair, Sam, 358
Fanny (Colhoun), 3
Farrar, Harry, 53
Farrar, Thomas, 53
Featherstonhaugh, G. W., 162
Ferguson, Amy, 479n6
Ferguson, Gabriel, 463n39
Ferguson, King, 330
Ferguson, Matthew, 331
Ferguson, Tony, 403
Fields, Emma Rebecca, 235
Fields, James Richard, 235
Finlay, D. B., 303
Flander, John (Colhoun), 155
Folger, Alonzo, 263, 269
Folger, O. A., 269
Folger, O. C., 255
Force, Alphon, 64
Fordin, James, 69
Foster, John Peter, 296, 345
Fowler, J. S., 401–2
Frazier, Nat, 225
Freeman, Harriet, 259
Freeman, Joseph, 483n17
Frierson, Tena, 496n49
Fruster, Frances, 243
Fruster, Thomas, 243
Fuller, William, 411
Furman, Lieutenant, 203

Gadsden, December, 225, 228
Gaillard (surname), 239
Gaillard, Napoleon, 224, 257, 265, 270, 338, 418, 489n13, 500n2
Gaillard, W. H. D., 114
Gailliard, William, 483n17
Gambrell families, 242

Gambrill, Charles, 440n44
Garrett, Fred, 225
Garrison, Peter, 80
Garvin, F. N., 182
Gary, George, 418–19
Gary, M. F., 265
Gassaway family, 329
Gassaway, Carrie Walls, 497n6
Gassaway, E. V., 338, 346, 361, 365–66, 417, 497n6
Gassaway, Larkin, 318, 329
Gassaway, Louisa, 37, 457n47
Gassaway, Mark H., 306, 338, 346, 351, 363, 417, 499n33
Geer, Samuel A., 217
George (a slave), 167
George (C. Irby), 173
George (Daniel Mattison), 130
Gibson, George, 386
Gibson, Green, 386
Gibson, Will, 387
Gilbert (Elizabeth Thomson), 82–83, 138
Gilliland, James, 25, 441n11
Gillmore, Q. A., 199, 200–201, 204
Golding, Reuben, 216–17
Goldman, James, 279
Goober Jack (John T. Sloan), 82–84, 118, 135
Goode, Robert, 275
Goodlett, York, 399
Goodman, J. S., 403
Gowans, Andy, 331
Grady, Henry, 378
Graham, Columbus, 138, 189–90
Graham, Salathia, 138
Graham, Washington, 189–90
Grant, Dinah, 445n28
Grant, Stafford, 227
Grant, Ulysses S., 265, 359
Green (Thomas Murphy), 94
Green, Al, 386
Green, John, 21, 28
Green, Lewis, 454n7
Green, Philip, 320, 410, 412
Green, Richard, 195
Green, Samuel, 260–61
Greene, John T., 266
Greenlee, Eli, 491n37
Greenlee, Hiram, 242, 266, 303, 491n37
Greenlee, Isaac, 303
Greer, Oliver, 385
Grief Presly (James Hembree), 117, 162
Grier, Daniel, 69
Griffin families (FPC), 59
[Griffin], Ben P. (Jacob Griffin), 193, 195, 319, 323, 468n40
Griffin, Elihu, 189
Grisham, Joseph, 138

Grisham, Joseph L., 103
Grisham, W. S., 255
Gutman, Herbert, 142, 239, 457n1, 458n14, 459nn21, 25
[Guyton], Ben (J. P. Reed), 161, 210, 339, 426n11, 459nn21, 25, 480n28, 489n13, 497n9
Guyton, Charity, 418
Guyton, Elbert, 210, 339, 405, 497n9
[Guyton], Eliza (J. P. Reed), 161
Guyton, Robert, 37–38, 48, 170
Guyton, Ruth, 418, 497n9
Gwinn families (FPC), 57

Hagar (a slave name), 110
Hagood, Amanda, 242
Hagood, Benjamin, 120, 481n31
Hagood, Dilsey, 240
Hagood, J. E., 184, 193, 223
Hagood, Queen, 330
Halbert families, 31
Halbert, Elizabeth, 141n1
Hall, Fenton (Jr.), 67
Hall, Johnson, 86
Hall, R. H., 67, 86
Hallum families, 59, 237, 362
Hallum families (FPC), 55, 59
Hallum (surname), 173
Hallum, Burris, 255
Hallum, Cato, 54, 59, 217. *See also* Allums, Cato
Hallum, William, 53, 59
Hallums, Mary, 506n11
Hamilton ("bound boy"), 61
Hamilton (surname), 239
Hamilton, Joe, 412
Hammond, B. F., 473n48
Hammond, Hall, 243
Hammond, J. S., 401–2, 410
Hammond, James Henry, 113, 158, 161
Hammond, W. Q., 401–2, 410
Hamp (a Spartanburg slave), 448n44
Hampton, Jim, 40, 468n38
Hampton, Wade, 2, 218; military concern about, 276–83; candidate, 374–75; governor, 484n33
Hampton, Wade (a black man), 353
Haner (a slave), 173
Hannah (FPC), 68, 80
Hannah (Elizabeth Stribling), 85
Hannah (Thornton Coleman), 105
Harbert (James C. Keys), 131
Harbin, Thomas W., 116
Harlin, Ellis, 53
Harlong, Myrtle, 416
Harriet (Ira Arnold), 85
Harriet (Pendleton Isbell), 116

Harriott (Colhoun), 3
Harris, David Golightly, 35, 43–44, 47, 120, 127, 160, 164, 170, 171, 182–83, 186–87, 199, 207, 209, 233
Harris, Ed, 231
Harris, Elbert, 385
Harris, Emily, 165, 182–83, 185–86, 191, 195
Harris, Henry, 468n40
Harris, Peter, 400, 410
Harrison families, 27
Harrison, J. W., 35
Harrison, Jack, 210
Harrison, James, 245
Harrison, Susie, 333
Harry (a slave), 102
Harry (Alfred Neal), 483n21
Harry (Joseph Taylor), 84
Harry (R. T. C. Foster), 93
Hawkins, Tom, 457n47
Hayes, Rutherford, 281
Haynie, Alfred, 245
Haywood, Ed, 410
Haywood, Harrison, 333, 382–84
Haywood, Susie, 490n27
Haywood, Washington, 333
Hazzard (Colhoun), 26, 148
Hembree, James, 162
Henderson, Jackson, 225
Henry (a slave), 126
Henry (a slave), 159
Henry (a slave), 448n44
Henry (Dr. Gibbes), 129
Henry (J. P. Reed), 469n5
Hester (R. F. Simpson), 36–37, 192
Hester, Alfred, 120, 173, 174
Hester, Bailus, 86
Highter (Billy Thompson), 78
Hill, D. C., 366
Hill, G. W., 346, 414
Hillhouse, W. C., 236
Hoge, Solomon, 257
Holdman, Henry, 57
Holland, Benjamin, 239, 270
Holland, Berry, 503n10
Holland, George, 239
Holland, Isac, 239
Holland, Jeremiah, 239
Holland, Simeon, 239
Holland, Thomas, 259
Holland, W. T., 239
Holland, William, 239
Holland, William W., 239
Hollingsworth, Malinda, 416
Holly, Lucinda, 56
Holly, Lydia, 56
Holly, Pink, 499n32
Holmes, Bill, 333

Horn, John J., 190
Horn, S. T., 57
Hortman, Henry, 189
Howard, P. L., 63
Hoyt, James, 200, 218, 221, 254–55, 257, 263, 266, 274–75, 277
Hudnal, Ezekiel, 52
Huger family, 158
Huger, Francis K., 137
Huger, Mary F., 163
Humphreys families, 409
Humphreys, Jackson, 245, 260, 504n18
Hunnicutt, Miles M., 222, 225–26
Hunt, Esli, 44, 93
Hunt, J. T., 56
Hunter, James, 219, 221, 396
Hunter, Jane Harris, 82, 169, 231, 252, 324, 328–29, 337, 367, 380, 394, 410, 413–14

Ingram, Jesse, 172
Isaac (Amy Borough), 93
Isaac (Robert Guyton), 38, 48
Izzy (John C. Calhoun), 94

Jack (Colhoun), 27
Jack (Samuel Blair), 120
Jack, "Old" (Samuel Taylor), 116
Jackson (Floride Calhoun), 187
Jackson, Ira, 385, 389
Jackson, Willis, 386, 390, 417
Jake (Samuel Johnston), 160
James (FPC), 53
James (a slave), 93
James (a slave), 192
James (Easley), 119
James (Hardin), 26
Jane (Martin Smith), 160
Jane Hurricane (a slave), 147
Jane, "Negro" (a slave), 99
Jefferson, Paul W., 490n23
Jefferson, Silas, 237, 296, 302, 303, 360
Jeffries, Mary, 53
Jemima. See [Pickens], Jemima
Jenkins family, 305, 345
Jenkins, Abram, 210
Jenkins, E. E., 358
Jenkins, Elias, 269–70, 275, 316
Jenkins, Green, 268
Jenkins, Major, 411
Jenkins, Warren D., 284, 303, 358, 362
Jenkins, William L., 1, 165
Jerry (a slave), 81
Jerry (a slave; Abbeville), 90
Jerry (a slave; Anderson), 91
Jerry (John Brown), 47, 132, 167
Jerry (Wm. NMartin), 88
Jillson, J. K., 301

Jim (Ashmore), 168
Jim (Earle), 69
Jim (John C. Calhoun), 130
Jim (Leah Moore), 82
Jim (R. F. Simpson), 171
Jim (Thomas Murphy), 94
Jinney (FPC), 26
Joe (Archibald Simpson), 131
Joe (James Burriss), 132
John (FPC), 221
John (Elizabeth Stribling), 85
John (Susan Lewis), 92
Johns, S. H., 64
Johnson, Andrew, 199, 200, 201, 215, 216, 222
Johnson, Daniel, 217
Johnson, H. A., 201
Johnson, Henry H., 305, 385
Johnson, Martha, 303
Johnson, Peter, 54, 62, 127, 479n12
Johnson, Samuel, 224, 229, 235, 261, 262, 264, 268, 270–71, 279, 281, 338, 340
Jolly, Manse, 203, 215, 222
Jones, Henry, 377
Jones, Rena, 418
Jones, S. J., 411
Jordan, Jack, 414
Joseph Africanus (a slave), 32
Joyner, Charles, 8, 146
Judy (Johnson), 105, 119
Judy, "Old" (Harris), 161
Julius (a slave), 172
Julius (David G. Harris), 164, 186

Kate ("Old Kate Maum"; Andrew P. Calhoun), 206
Kate (Samuel Taylor), 116
Katy (Brooks), 104
Katy (W. J. Jones), 129
Keaton, William, 141
Keels, Benjamin, 319
Keith, J. W. (James), 262, 269, 292, 477n47
Keith, John, 225
Keith, Peter, 86
Keith, W. C., 502n19
Keith, William, 264
Kennedy, Elias, 225, 228, 258, 260, 268, 477n55
Kennedy, Henry, 224, 228, 257, 261–62, 268, 361, 484n29, 489n13
Keown families, 397
Keys, Crawford, 162, 190, 204, 215, 216, 259
Kilpatrick, F. W., 193, 227
Kin (Jeremiah Looper), 93
Kirksey families, 55, 66
[Knight], L. K. (James Perry Knight), 192, 468n40
Knox, Foster, 382

Ladd families, 66, 237
Ladd, Amos, 29
Ladd, Stephen, 237
Ladison, John, 385, 388
Lancaster (Samuel Taylor), 116
Lathem, Mary, 190
Lawhen, Captain, 479n10
Lawhen, Rosa, 479n10
Lawrence family, 50
Lawrence, Bill, 416
Lay, Charles M., 37
Leah (J. Smith), 104
Leathers, Asa, 63
Lee families, 270
Lee, William C., 63
Lesley, W. A., 269
Leslie, Will, 351
Leverett, Quincy, 338–39, 345
Levi (Mrs. Groves), 455n14
Levrett, Stephen, 259
Lew (John B. Earle), 78, 90
Lew (Nathan Boon?), 81
Lewis (a slave), 171
Lewis (A. Thompson), 84
Lewis (Betsey Burris), 105
Lewis (John C. Calhoun), 135
Lewis (Joseph Whitefield), 131
Lewis (McAdams), 167
Lewis (R. F. Simpson), 36
Lewis, A. F., 473n48
[Lewis], Dick, 192
Lewis, John T., 69
Lewis, June, 319
Lewis, Susan, 92
Lige (Micajah Carter, Ga.), 47, 132, 167
Ligon families, 409
Lincoln, Abraham, 179, 196, 216, 222
Lindsey, Milton, 268
Little, P. S., 319, 322, 496n51
Livingston, J. W., 209, 227
Liza (a Greenville slave), 172
Long, Ezekiel, 290
Long, John, 183
Long, William, 483n19
Looper, J. Perry, 215
Looper, Jeremiah, 269
Lorton family, 198
Lorton, Ella F., 211, 214, 242, 473nn45, 48
Lorton, John S., 319, 453n12
Lorton, Mrs., 129
Lot (Asbury Taylor), 100
Louisa (McColister?), 172
Loveland family (FPC), 58
Lucinda ("faithful Servant"), 169
Lucinda (a slave), 102
Lucretia (FPC), 221
Lucretia (Colhoun Jr.), 155

Lucy (Elisha Bennett), 141
Lucy (Harris), 168
Lucy (R. F. Simpson), 192
Lucy and child (W. Simpson), 114

Mack (Jane Robinson?), 172
Mack (Taylor), 105
Major (David Sloan), 82
Major, S. A., 56
Mance, Jack, 270
Manerva (David G. Harris), 165
Manigault (surname), 239
Mansion, Aaron, 412
Manuel (Alex. Ramsey), 130
Manuel (J. P. Reed), 193, 469n5
Mariah (James C. Williams), 94
Mariah (John McPhail), 173
Marshall (Daniel Brown), 95
Martin, Jacob J., 305
Martin, James, 389
Mary (a slave), 100
Mary (Williams), 130
Mary Ann (Dr. O. R. Broyles), 84
Mary Ann (Micajah Williams), 160
Massey, Silas, 88, 91, 118
Masters, G. W., 132
Matilda (Colhoun Jr.), 155
Matilda (Joshua Mansell), 116
Mattison (John Brown Jr.), 85
Mattison, Marshall, 468n40
Mattison, Mary, 85, 174
Mattison, Olly, 94
Mattison, W. T., 353
Mauldin, Mulberry, 290–1
Maverick, Margaret, 291
Maverick, Samuel, 48–49, 69, 114, 452n4, 456–57n42
Maxwell, George, 296, 303, 336, 485n50
Maxwell, J. H., 271
Maxwell, Robert, 26, 35, 36, 56, 78, 100
Maxwell, S. E., 36, 44, 147, 161, 163, 174, 293, 331–32, 466n11
Maxwell, Tenus, 170, 174, 234, 265, 331–33
May (Dr. James Stuart), 93
Mazyck (surname), 239
McCord, Louisa, 170
McCully, Stacy, 259
McCurry, Seaborn, 497n5
McCury (surname), 239
McDougall, G. P., 217, 219
McDow (surname), 239
McDowell, Davison, 120
McElhenney, James, 103, 136
McElhenney, Susannah, 136
McGall, S. R., 115
McGee families, 397–98
McGee, Elias, 259, 402, 483n19

McGee, Jesse, 95, 483n19
McGowan, Ella, 490n27
McGowan, Henry, 338–39, 497n6
McKinney (surname), 239
McKinney, Frank, 259
McMahan, John J., 309, 365, 393, 413
McNeil, Charles, 235
McNeil, James, 235
McNeil, Sampson, 235
Means, Daniel, 69
Meser (Gantt), 105
Middleton (surname), 239
Miller, Anna, 402
Miller, Clark T. (C. T.), 284, 305, 307, 330, 358, 402
Miller, J. R., 402, 505n27
Miller, John I., 305, 366, 418
Milliner, Abe, 394, 413
Milliner, Caroline, 380, 394
Mills, Elizabeth, 38
Mills, Robert, 46, 137
Milly (Joseph Whitner), 455n14
Minus, D. M., 252, 300, 414
Mitchell, James W., 345
Moise, E. W., 282
Moll (Robert Anderson), 144
Monday (Robert Anderson), 116
Monemi (Colhoun), 31, 141, 457n3
Moore (child), 260
Moore, Alfred, 132
Moore, Henrietta, 279
Moore, Leah, 114
Moore, Prince, 233
Moore, Stewart, 259
Moore, Winnie, 259
Morris (FPC), 53, 61, 448n39
Morris families, 303
Morris, Frank, 260, 268, 292, 303, 330
Morris, "Mother," 298
Morris, Philip, 292, 361
Morris, Rosa, 418
Morris, Tabitha, 303
Morris, W. H., 489n13
Mose (R. F. Simpson), 192
Moses (Colhoun), 3; (Colhoun Jr.), 153
Moses, Franklin J., 254, 257, 263–65, 267, 486n1
Mulbery, "Brother" (a slave), 99
Murphy, John, 403
Murray, E. B., 271, 283, 485n50
Murray, J. Scott, 262

Nancy (Duckworth), 132
Nancy, "old" (Robert Anderson), 116
Nash, Prince, 315
Neal family, 504n20
Neal, Alfred, 259, 271, 486n59

Index of People / 527

Neal, W. A., 401–2
Ned (a slave), 190
Ned (John Brown), 88, 91
Nelly (Floride Calhoun), 145, 165
Nelson (John S. Allen), 82
Nero (Dr. William Anderson), 119, 132
Nevill, J. E., 279
Newell, W. S., 401–2
Niles, Charles G., 217
Nina (J. B. Adger), 206, 209
Niry, "Aunt" (a slave), 165
Noble, Ezekiel, 40
Norris family, 99, 466n17
Norris, A. O., 268, 485n48
Norris, Andrew, 475n29
Norris, J. W., 85, 174
Norris, John E., 84
North, John, 151
Norton, J. J., 208, 228, 383
Norwood, Williamson, 117

O'Dell, Perrin, 269
Oglesby families, 57, 61–65, 67, 236–37, 479n19
Oglesby, Betty, 52, 62
Oglesby, Dennis, 63
Oglesby, Elizabeth, 62, 64
Oglesby, Harrison (S. H.), 293–94, 334, 387
Oglesby, Jesse, 56, 62–63, 237
Oglesby, Joberry, 63
Oglesby, Martha, 64
Oglesby, Mary (FPC), 130
Oglesby, Milly, 63
Oglesby, Peg, 63
Oglesby, Priscilla, 62, 64
Oglesby, Rachel, 63–64
Oglesby, Richard, 62
Oglesby, Ruth, 54, 62–63, 127
Oglesby, Sam, 63–64, 88, 91, 182
Oglesby, Sarah, 63
Oglesby, Thomas, 62–63
Oliver, Henry, 410
Oliver, S., 411
O'Neal, Hill, 52
O'Neall, John Belton, 52, 103, 119, 182
Orr, James L., 41, 201, 205, 207, 214–15, 220, 223, 227, 255, 263–64, 267, 484n33
Orr, James L., Jr., 382
Osborn, Priest, 456n28
Owens, Christopher, 331
Owens, D. C., 269
Owens, General George Washington Independent Centennial, 330
Owens, Lee, 403
Owens, Lula McJunkin, 331
Owens, Mary, 316

Owens, Starling, 468n40
Owens, Willie, 330

Parker, Niles G., 254
Parker, W. R., 235, 261, 266, 268, 270–71, 281, 283–84, 292, 357, 361, 485nn54, 56
Parris (Thomas Alexander), 63, 130
Patsy (a slave), 49
Patsy (Joseph Rogers), 105
Patterson, Cyrus, 100
Payton families, 52, 55, 67–69, 86, 174, 236–37, 244, 303, 336, 507n14. *See also* Peyden, Polly
Payton, Amaziah, 56, 67–68, 217, 237
Payton, Eliza Jane, 67
Payton, Fanny, 57, 67, 86, 174, 237
Payton, Joberry, 271, 303
Payton, Joberry, Jr., 485n50
Payton, John, 418
Payton, Joseph (Sr.; Joberry), 67
Payton, Joseph, 237
Payton, Lucinda, 215, 237
Payton, Narcissa, 67
Payton (?), Rebecca, 67
Payton, Richmond, 56, 67–68, 224, 230, 237, 257, 262, 271, 303
Peek, Willis Ignatius, 366
Peggy (James Hembree), 117, 162
Peggy (John C. Calhoun), 38
Peggy (Kilpatrick), 158
Pelzer family, 412
Pendleton, Allen, 385
Perrion, Si, 497n14
Perry (J. J. Acker), 50
Perry (Joseph Thomson), 189
Perry, Benjamin, 173, 201, 277
Perry, Joseph, 479n12
Perry, Solomon, 440n44
Peter (FPC), 53, 59
Peter (a slave exhorter), 100
Peter (James Clinkscales), 189
Peter (Noah Richardson), 131
Peyden, Polly, 53
Phil (R. B. Hutchison), 91, 467n23
Philip (Colhoun), 25
Phillis (a slave), 85
Pickens families, 397
Pickens, Allen, 270
Pickens, Andrew, 20, 24, 54
Pickens, Carey, 59, 270, 395
Pickens, Edmund, 259
Pickens, Jacob, 316–17, 409
[Pickens], Jemima (Pickens), 59, 270, 286
Pickens, Mary, 59, 316–17, 320, 409
Pickens, William, 171, 231–32, 244, 252, 301, 306, 311, 316, 332, 367, 395, 400
Pickerell, Jesse, 258

528 / Index of People

Pillsbury, Gilbert, 223
Pinckney, Charles C., 103
Pinson, E. I., 256
Pinson, Maria, 408
Polydore (Colhoun), 31, 141n3, 150n28, 457n3
Pompey (J. D. Ashmore), 86
Poore, Annie, 120, 462n27
Potts, Jefferson, 94
Powell, Rachel, 385
Prince (Olly Mattison), 82
Priscilla ("black sister," a slave), 96
Purse, Frederick, 479n12

Rachel (J. P. ODell), 93
Rachel (John Chapman), 114
Randolph, B. F., 260
Ravenel, Caroline, 198
Redman families, 69
Redman, Moses, 69
Redman, William, 141
Redmond, W. R., 260
Reed families, 270
Reed, Becky, 175
Reed, Henry, 489n13
Reed, J. P., 40, 175, 198, 210–11, 257, 263–65, 286, 486n1, 497n9
Reed, John, 436n14
Reed, Sandy, 459n23
Reed, Sylvia, 479n11
Reese, John, 382–83, 418
Reeves, Georgia Ann, 298, 362
Reid families, 412
Reid, Butler, 410
Reid, Easter, 165, 173, 410
Reid, Peter, 56
Reid, Robert, 316
Rice, Elijah, 444n23
Rice, Eliza, 37
Rice, John, 485n50
Richard (a slave elder; Dr. Dart), 101
Richardson, Susan, 416
Richie, J. A., 413
Richmond (Fenton Hall [Jr.]), 67, 86
Rivers, Prince, 276
Roberts, Benjamin L., 56, 235, 237, 265, 271
Robertson, James, 283
Robin (Colhoun Jr.), 151
Robinson, A. R., 258, 367, 412, 414
Robinson, Aleck, 227
Robinson, Joseph, 485n50
Roper, Donna, 45
Rose (Colhoun), 148, 153
Rose, old (Robert Anderson), 37, 116, 174
Rosemon, Sam, 193, 468n38
Rosemond, James, 100–101, 175, 252, 255, 283, 295, 418

Rosemond, James, Jr., 418
Ross, Anthony, 103
Rutledge (surname), 239
Rutledge, Lawrence, 418–19

Sall (FPC; "yellow complexion"), 53
Sally (Kilpatrick), 206
Sally (Mrs. Pickens), 104
Sam (a slave elder; Charles Story), 101
Sam (Elisha Bennett), 141
Sam (J. W. Harrison), 454n7
Sam (John W. Beson), 119
Sam (Silas Massey), 88, 91
Sam (Widow Duckworth), 167
Sam, "Old" (a slave), 170
Sampson families, 270
Sampson, Samuel, 485n50
Samuel (a slave), 130
Sanders (C. Wakefield), 290
Sanders, Bob, 410
Sanders, David, 275
Sanders, Elias, 477n55
Sanders, J. H., 398
Sarah (a slave), 107
Sarah (Ira G. Gambrell), 85
Sarah (James Harkness), 99
Sarah (Mrs. Pickens), 104
Sargent, 203, 215
Sawney, "Old" (John C. Calhoun), 95, 152
Sawney, Young (Calhoun), 449n47
Saxon, E. A., 365
Scott, Dred, 88
Scott, George C., 238, 364
Scott, Jack, 257
Scott, Robert K., 205, 228–29, 254, 256–57, 262
Seab (Reid), 173, 174
Seaborn, George, 45, 129, 208
Shannon families, 62
Shannon, John, 29
Sharp, Mary A., 256
Sharpe, Elam, 138
Sherard families, 118, 397, 453n21
Sherard, Dave, 398
Sherard, Elias, 504n18
Sherard, Prue Wesley, 504n18
Sherard, Winston, 504n18
Sherman, Cato, 382–83, 493n15
Sherman, Lula, 382
Sherman, W. T., 182, 195, 199, 205, 359
Sherrard, Dump, 504n18
Sherrard, John Wesley, 259
Shumate, Gabriel, 56
Sickles, Daniel, 201, 203, 205, 207–8, 213, 215, 219, 222–24, 359
Simms households, 70
Simon (Colhoun Jr.), 151

Simon (Dr. O. R. Broyles), 131
Simon (John E. Norris), 84
Simon, "Old" (a slave preacher; Calhoun), 101
Simpson family, 36
Simpson, Dick (R. W.), 192–93, 379, 383, 412
Simpson, R. F., 474n9
Simpson, Rachel, 244
Simpson, Tally (Taliaferro), 37, 171, 192–93, 412
Singleton, David, 265, 269, 275, 361
Singleton, John, 333
Singleton, McDuffie, 489n13
Sitton, A. J., 272
Sitton, J. B., 50, 92, 210, 270–71, 302, 473nn45, 47
Sizemore (surname), 239
Sizemore families, 55, 59, 61, 65–67, 236–37, 242, 303, 314, 329, 499n33
Sizemore, Elias, 66
Sizemore, Elisha, 65
Sizemore, Fanny, 53, 65
Sizemore, Henry, 66
Sizemore, Isaac, 66
Sizemore, Joberry, 303
Sizemore, Julia Ann, 65
Sizemore, Levina, 53, 65
Sizemore, Martha, 66
Sizemore, Melinda, 65
Sizemore, Richard, 65
Sizemore, Sarah, 65–66
Sizemore, Simon, 66
Sizemore, Temperance, 66
Sizemore, Thomas, 66
Sizemore, William, 58, 65–67
Sloan, David, 81–82
Sloan, John B., 46
Sloan, John T., 82–83
Sloan, Lucy Crayton, 409–10
Small, Benjamin, 236
Smart, Data (?), 31
Smart, Lindsey, 31
Smith, Alfred T., 219, 225–26, 263
Smith, Anderson, 412
Smith, John R., 468n40
Smith, Martha, 397
Smith, Mary, 60
Smith, Robert, 225
Smith, Roseanah, 347
Smythe, Major, 394
Sobel, Mechal, 176
Solomon (Ira G. Campbell), 88, 91
Solomon (Robert Anderson), 116
Solomon (Violet Bowman), 168
Sophy (Sister McGregor), 105
Spearman, David, 358
Spight, Tom, 386
Squire (John Donald Jr.), 129

Stanton, Edwin, 215
Starks, John J., 252, 305, 329, 331, 367, 403, 414
Stephen (John Brown), 160
Stephen (John Brown Jr.), 85
Stephen (Thomas Williams), 82, 138
Stokes, John, 316, 418
Stone, William, 197, 211, 217, 220, 269
Stowers, Francis, 204
Stribling family, 184
Stribling, J. C., 83
Stribling, Warren, 192, 466n11
Strickland, G. T., 360
Strother families (FPC), 57
Stroudemire, J. L., 488n8
Sue (Colhoun), 3, 27
Suky (Colhoun), 26
Sullivan, Ed, 385
Susan (Calhoun), 460n34
Sylvia (Martha Williams), 84
Symmes, F. W., 129

Taliaferro, Zacharias, 35
Tate, Grief, 61
Taylor family, 323
Taylor, Joseph, 46
Taylor, Washington, 43–44, 47, 109
Teat, Amanda, 189
Terrell families, 55, 62
Terrell, Aaron, 443n6
Terrell, Elias, 339
Terrell, Joel, 29
Terrell, King, 330
Thomas family, 305, 339
Thomas, E. J., 366
Thomas, Julius, 489n13
Thomas, W. J., 364, 491n40
Thompson family, 33, 37–39, 329
Thompson, Julius, 268
Thompson, Lewis, 487n25
Thompson, R. A., 265, 274
Thompson, William, 303
Thornton (Silas Massey), 129
Tildy (Archibald Bowman), 80
Tillman, Benjamin, 378, 388
Timbers, Priscilla, 53
Toby (Mrs. Stone), 159
Tolbert, Ben, 324
Tom (David G. Harris), 25
Tom (Henry Adams), 86
Tom (Lemuel Hall), 173
Tom (Mary Keith), 86
Tom (W. L. Keith), 63
Tom (Wm. Sutherland), 168
Tom, "Doctor" (FPC), 62, 165
Tombo (a slave), 137
Tomlinson, Reuben, 264, 484n33

Toney (a slave), 25, 104, 199
Toney (Colhoun Jr.), 155
Toney (Easley), 119
Townes families, 35
Townes, H. H., 115
Townes, Samuel, 115
Trescot, William H., 191, 215, 219
Trowbridge, C. T., 200, 203
Truth, Sojourner, 360
Tudor, Frances, 221, 300–301
Turner, Henry M., 360
Turner, Nat, 9, 75
Turner, William, 277

Valentine families, 58
Van Wyck, William, 236
Vance, Augustus Thomas, 405
Vance, Martha Burt, 405
Vandiver, Louise, 198, 266
Venus (a slave), 104
Verner, Samuel J., 63–64
Vesey (a slave), 192
Vesey (Harris), 36
Vesey, Denmark, 54, 75, 79–80, 90, 97, 137
Vulcan (Colhoun Jr.), 151

Waddy (Thomas Blassingame), 463n37
Wadsworth, Levi, 60
Wadsworth, Robert, 60
Waites, Adam, 258
Wakefield families, 397
Wakefield, Henry, 29
Waldrop, Manzeo (Manse), 382, 385, 388, 390
Walker, A., 411
Walker, Andrew, 255
Walker, Dick, 165
Walker, Elbert, 316
Walker, Jack, 225, 477n55
Walker, P. L., 220, 221
Wallace, David Duncan, 392–93
Wallace, J. E., 306
[Warren], Taber, 43, 303, 485n50, 489n13
Wash (FPC), 69
Washington, Booker T., 354, 374, 404
Washington, F. J., 363
Washington, Frederick, 325
Washington, Mary J., 490n27
Waters, Bridget, 52
Watkins, Frank, 141
Watkins, Harrison, 311, 361, 491n39
Watkins, J. C., 293, 333
Watson, C. D., 398
Watson, Elias, 105
Watson, Jim, 398
Watson, Joe, 395
Watson, John, 215, 237
Webb, Elias, 265

Webb, Elijah, 41, 234
Webb, Lewis, 412
Webster, Shedrick, 324, 484n30
Welborn families, 409
Wells, Captain, 260
Welsby, Henry, 388
Wesley, John, 97
White, Anna Victoria, 479n12
White, James, 69
White, W. T., 169
Whitley, Moses, 69
Whitner, Anna (O. A. Bowen), 202
Whitner, Joseph N., 41, 99, 115, 117, 119
Whitner, Lucinda, 490n27
Whitner, Rex (O. A. Bowen), 202
Whitney, Eli, 45
[Wiggins], Betty (Colhoun Jr.), 153, 155, 156, 386, 418
[Wiggins], Ephraim (Colhoun Jr.), 153, 155, 461n39
[Wiggins], George (Colhoun Jr.), 153, 155–56, 286, 418
[Wiggins], Harrison (Colhoun Jr.), 153, 155, 194, 414, 461n39, 468n40
[Wiggins], Maria (Colhoun Jr.), 153, 155
[Wiggins], Thomas (Colhoun Jr.), 153, 155
[Wiggins], Turner (Colhoun Jr.), 153, 155
Wiley (James Anderson), 78
Will (Colhoun), 27, 78
Will (Simeon Smith), 202
Will, "Old" (David G. Harris), 171
William (Cokergee), 80–81, 90
William (Dr. Johnson), 92
William (John C. Calhoun), 95
Williams family, 303
Williams, Bob, 385
Williams, Campbell, 218
Williams, Cornelia, 303
Williams, Ellison, 138, 220
Williams, Green D., 264, 281, 324, 328, 363
Williams, Henrietta, 52
Williams, Joseph, 217
Williams, L. N., 411, 414
Williams, Leah, 114
Williams, Sarah Ann Broyles, 158
Williams, Sylvia, 347
Williams, Viola, 118, 417
Williams, William C., 382–84
Williamson, Joel, 6, 276, 285, 429n18, 463n48
Williamson, T. H., 399
Williford families, 397
Williford, James, 290–91, 411, 485n50
Williford, Jennie, 411
Williford, Major, 290
Williford, Samuel, 189
Willis (A. W. Ramsay), 189

Willis (J. W. Norris), 101
Willis (Martha Lawrence), 93
Willis (T. R. Brackenridge), 47
Wilson, Charlotte, 243
Wilson, James, 468n40
Wilson, Warren, 52
Wilson, William, 243
Winslow, Thomas, 52
Winston, Tenus, 412–13
Wright, Charles, 221
[Wright], Jackson, 193

Wright, Johnson, 265–70, 283, 468n40
Wright, Terrel, 406

Yankee (personal name), 239
York (David G. Harris), 44
Young, Della, 347
Young, Jack, 479n9
Young, James, 485n50
Young, Judy, 244

Zion (R. F. Simpson), 36–37, 171, 192

INDEX OF SUBJECTS

Abbeville, 80, 92, 275, 329, 398, 479n13, 483n22, 486n10
Abel (community), 1, 319, 332, 382, 407
abolitionists, activities, 139
acculturation, 18, 20, 30–33, 125, 137, 239; cultures, mingling, 145–47, 434n7. *See also* subculture
Adams Mortuary, 494n24
Affleck ledger, 3, 147, 149, 151–52, 439n41
Africa, 450n9; heritage, 6; birthplace, 6, 78, 146, 234, 245, 362, 433n4; ties to, 361–62
African continuities, 6, 24, 31–33; names, 32
African origins (specific), unknown, 31
African retentions, 135
Afro-American Real Estate Association, 363, 399, 415
age cohorts, 36, 433n13
aged, respect for, 142. *See also* elderly, faithful, respected, worthy black people
ages, estimated, rounded, exaggerated, 142
agricultural labor, percentages, 409; by women, 409–10; by whole family, 409. *See also* farm laborers
agriculture (antebellum), scale of operation, 8, 25, 44–46; red-dirt land, 17, 19; terrain, erosion, 17, 44; transportation, river access, 24, 40, 46; crops, 24–25, 40, 42–44; percentage, 31; local consumption, 40; dominance, 40–41; self-sufficiency, 40, 42–43, 437n23; cycle, 43, 44; improvements, machinery, 44; cotton gin, 44. *See also* corn; cotton; harvests; rice; sharecropping; tobacco
agriculture (postbellum). *See* cotton; crop liens; crops (and specific crops); farmers; farm laborers; labor agreements; sharecropping
Allen University, 296, 304, 306, 359
Amherst County (Va.), 35
Anderson (town), 40, 188, 492n3; city, 286, 312, 351, 496n1, 492n3
Anderson Building and Loan Association, 341, 345
Anderson County (founded), 22
Anderson County Colored Fair, 363
Anderson District (founded), 22
Anderson Farmers' Association, 500n8
Andersonville, 27

Arkansas, 289, 366, 415
army, joining, 398
arson, 64, 78, 282, 449n49
Ashtabula farm, 197, 408, 412–13; managers, 424
Atlanta, 415
attitudes toward blacks, conflicted, 374
Augusta, Ga., 40, 46, 132

bad harvests. *See* cotton prices, market; harvests
bands, 323–24, 326, 340, 352
banishment, 94, 467n23
Banneker Masonic Lodge, 334, 359
barbers, barbershops, 235, 237, 319, 338, 341, 345, 347, 493n15
bars, 317, 328; denounced, 328
baseball, 323, 340, 357
basket weavers, baskets, 32, 129, 130, 434n7
Beech Island Farmers' Society, 134
Belmina, 319, 325
Belton (founded), 314; 129, 138, 203, 220, 275–76, 279, 283, 286, 290, 292, 299, 300, 316–17, 320, 356, 363, 455n11, 497n6
Benedict Institute / College, 1, 304, 306, 359, 363, 413–14, 489n19, 498n12
Biddle University, 296
Bini, 449n47
biracial studies, 10
black barbershop, 347. *See also* barbers, barbershops
black businesses, 251, 413
black content, missing from textbooks, religious literature, 360
black crime, 354
black employers, 413
black landlords, 340–41, 413
black landowners. *See* property owners (postbellum)
"black majority," 17, 75
Black Names in America, 145
black newspapers, 498n13
black officials, 487n27, 500n2
black-white proximity. *See* races, proximity
blacks, elderly, 116–17, 331, 352–53
blacks, living in white households, 233, 239–42; with former owners, 233, 242

blacksmiths, 32, 41, 48, 57, 60, 114, 129, 163, 210, 224, 235–36, 244, 246, 268, 281, 297, 314, 316, 320, 338, 341–42, 405, 413, 418, 497n9; shop, 322; tools, 332
Bleeding Kansas, 88, 182
Blue Ridge Railroad, 129, 236, 314, 336, 443n13
boardinghouses, boarders, lodgers, 241, 347, 351–52, 418
bondage, economic, 400
books, owned by slaves, 138
brickmasons, bricklayers, 48, 57, 114, 244, 338, 347, 418. *See also* building trades; stonemasons
building trades, 319
burials, 12, 109, 155–56, 332; in white family plots, 331; preparation, 494n24
bushwhackers, 474n7
butchers, 319, 323, 338
buying freedom, 127

cabins, 232, 236; unrelated persons living in, 140–41; former slave dwellings, 232, 236; configuration, 232
Calhoun (town; a.k.a. Clemson), 1, 316, 317, 324, 352, 410, 415
Calhoun plantation (Floride and John C. Calhoun; Andrew Pickens Calhoun; Thomas G. Clemson), 44–48, 94–95, 102, 125, 128, 130, 135–36, 145–56, 159–63, 165, 167–68, 170–71, 184, 187, 206, 227, 279, 326, 332, 379, 417, 439nn35, 40, 41, 449n47, 453n10, 455n28, 456n36, 459–60n30, 460n31, 462n33, 463nn38, 42, 46. *See also* Fort Hill
camp meetings, 127, 134, 354, 357
Caribbean islands, 31
carpenters, 32, 41, 48, 57, 114, 129, 163, 224, 236, 244, 246, 257, 303, 319, 338, 340, 342, 504n18; tools, 332
Catechee, 312
cemetery, 333–34; restoration of, 332
census (1870), components, 230; reliability, 230
Central (founded), 314; 300, 316, 319–20, 326, 332, 363, 381–84, 388–90, 418
chain gangs, 376–77. *See also* convicts
Cherokee, 20
child labor, 342
Chiquola Hotel, 345
Christian Recorder, 360
Christmas, 466n19. *See also* year-end holidays
churches (antebellum): attendance, early, 12; churches, early, 25; joining, reasons for, and timing, 25, 86, 96, 108, 110; sanctions, expulsions, 25; percentages of blacks, 26; postbellum connections, 73; leaders, literacy of, 73; obedience to masters, 73; social contacts at, 73, 134; denominations newly organized, 96; split over slavery, 98; travel to churches, social opportunities, 96, 108; leadership developed, 96, 101–2, 112; denominations, numbers, and percentages of black members, 97, 106–7; allied with masters, 97; obedience, 96, 98, 102; camp meetings, 97, 108, 109; slave catechism, 97; Sunday schools, 97–98, 137; literacy, 98, 110; separate services, 98, 102; baptism of infants, of slaves, 99–100; seating arrangements, 99, 102; discipline and exclusion from, 99, 103–5; statements of faith, 99; singing, lined, 99; slaves joining different church from owners, 99, 107; slave complaints, testifying against whites, 99, 105; churches, controls by, 100, 102; slave elders, exhorters, preachers, 100–102, 450n10, and postbellum roles of, 101; slaves as monitors, 101–2; religion on plantations, 101–3, 109; ministers also slaveowners, 103; convergences with MFH, 105, and offenses near churches or on Sunday, 109; duration of membership, 107; subculture, network, and contacts, 108; root doctors, 110; names, religious, 110; spirituals, 110; foundation for postbellum churches, 112
churches (black, 1865–1870): contributions to community, 286, 300, 310; numbers, 287, 290, 297, 299, 400; property, 286, 300; members, numbers, and percentages, 287, 297, 299, 488n5; names of churches, meanings, 287, 293; church facilities for Republicans, benevolent societies, schools, 286, 300, 304; internal squabbles, 292; brush arbors, other temporary premises, 206, 293–94, 298; buildings, 294; limited finances, 294, 400; ministers, income, multiple assignments, distance traveled, 294; clergy, literacy of, training, 292, 297; RRBA, whites included, 293; Methodist denominations, rivalry, 294–95; northern support for, 295–96; "why join?" and numbers, 296; membership, 296–97; clergy, characteristics, 297; proximity to whites, 297; church music, 297; deeds, reversionary clause, 297–98; women's roles and organizations, 298, 490n27; baptisms, numbers, timing, 299; church sanctions, exclusions, attacks on pool, drinking, 300; RRBA, support for education, 304; town, 319, and rural, 331; Sunday school conventions, 323; white support, donations, 333; ministers, 338; religious censure of drinking, barrooms, hot suppers, pool rooms, gambling dens, 365–66; colored circuits, 488n8
churches (specific) and denominations: Abel Baptist, 294, 333, 384, 490n27; AME, 137,

295–96, 328, 351, 365, 411, 488nn8, 9; suppressed, 80, 137; ministers, 338; appointments, 356; AME churches, 289 (Pendleton), 324 (Anderson); AME, Zion, 295, 489n21; Anderson Presbyterian, 99, 102, 142, 185, 220, 290, 436n17, 475n29; Baptist, 25, 98; Barker's Creek Baptist, 104, 110, 186; Belton Baptist, 491n37; Belton Presbyterian, 290, 466n14; Bethesda Methodist, 472n37; Bethlehem Methodist, 169; Big Creek Baptist, 25, 100, 104–5, 119, 287–88, 290; Brown-Salem ME, 489n18; Carmel Presbyterian, 25, 99, 108; Cedar Grove Baptist, 304; Centennial ME, 292, 336, 346–48; Colored Baptist State Convention, 328; Colored Methodist Episcopal, 295, 400, 411, 498n19; Cross Roads Baptist, 65, 479n19; E&M. *See* S.C. Baptist Educational and Missionary Association; Ebenezer Baptist, 491n40; Ebenezer Methodist, 97; Edgefield Baptist Association, 288; Enoree Baptist Association, 292; Evergreen CME, 489n18; Fairfield CME, 489n10; Fire Baptized Holiness Church, 299, 411, 490n28; First Creek Baptist, 67, 85, 99, 102, 105, 107, 110, 287, 290; First Freedmen's Baptist, 207, 292. *See also* St. Paul Baptist; Flat Rock Baptist, 477n47; Freedmen's Church/New Hope Missionary Baptist, 292; Goldenview Baptist, 334; Griffin Ebenezer Baptist, 293, 311, 489n16; Holly Springs Baptist, 99, 298; Hopewell Presbyterian, 25–26, 54, 69, 99, 101–3, 108, 110, 137–38, 169, 289–91; Jefferson Chapel ME, 490n25; John Wesley ME, 271; Kings Chapel AME, 269, 295–96, 405, 410; Lebanon Baptist, 106; Liberty Baptist, 292–93, 299, 485n50; ME, North, 295–96, 411; appointments, 356; ME, S.C. Conference, 497n9; Methodist, 25, 97–98, 295, 429n1; churches, 287, 289; Mount Moriah Baptist, 490n28; Mount Nebo Baptist, 1, 461n39; Mt. Olive Baptist, 298; Mount Pisgah Baptist, 60, 202, 219, 287–88, 290; Mt. Sinai AME, 299; Mount Sinai campground, 328, 400; Mount Sinai ME, 293, 298, 400; Mount Zion Baptist, 299; Mt. Zion FBH, 490n28; Mountain Creek Baptist, 105, 110, 288–90, 294, 411; New Light Baptist, 292, 297–98; New Mount Pisgah Baptist, 290; New Olive Grove Baptist, 294, 357; New Prospect Baptist, 463n41; Oak View Baptist, 490n25; Old Liberty Baptist, 104, 105, 446n5, 452n28; Old Stone Church (*see* Hopewell Presbyterian); Old Westminster Baptist, 62–63, 218, 289; Oolenoy Baptist, 169, 330, 463n41; Oolenoy Baptist Association, 293, 489n16; Parker's Chapel (Baptist), 283, 297, 485n56; Pendleton AME, 289 (*see also* Kings Chapel AME); Pendleton Baptist, 289, 291; Pendleton ME (a.k.a. Bethel), 289; Pendleton Methodist, South, 289, 291; Pickens Circuit, Methodist, 106; Pleasant Grove Baptist, 270, 293, 299; Pleasant Hill Baptist, 489n20; Presbyterians, 25, 98; Quakers, 51, 429n1, 441n11; Roberts Presbyterian, 198, 291; Rock Springs Baptist, 293; Rocky River Baptist Association (RRBA), 255, 292–93, 296–97, 362–63, 365, 489nn17, 19, 490n27, 491n37, 498n2; number of members, 292; Royal Baptist, 339, 342, 497n7; St. Marks Baptist, 332; St. Paul Baptist, 286, 292, 336, 339, 346, 350, 491n30. *See also* First Freedmen's Baptist; St. Paul's Episcopal, 25, 69, 100, 107, 137, 143, 153–54, 159, 186, 238, 289, 291, 412, 463n41, 481n32; baptism, 107; marriage, 107; burials, 107; Salem Baptist, 26, 102, 105; Salem Presbyterian, 294, 296; Sandy Springs Camp Meeting, 159; S.C. Baptist Convention, 97, 110, 288, 293; S.C. Baptist Educational and Missionary Association (E&M), 362–63; S.C. Conference, Wesleyan Methodists, 299; S.C. Educational and Missionary Association, 98, 489n19; Secona Baptist, 25, 99, 104, 463nn41, 42; Seneca River Missionary Baptist Association, 292, 332, 414, 489nn16, 17, 495n47; Shady Grove Baptist, 102; Shiloh Baptist, 485n56; Shiloh Church, 475n29; Shiloh Methodist, 99; Shoal Creek Baptist, 25–26, 62, 82, 99, 102, 446n5; Silver Spring Baptist, 291, 306, 506n6; Snow Hill Baptist, 268, 485n56; Soap Stone Baptist, 330; Sweet Canaan Baptist, 293, 298; Union Campground, 326; Universal Pentecostal Holiness Church, 490n28; Varennes Presbyterian, 99, 101, 107, 289; Westminster Baptist, 63; Wilson's Creek Baptist, 297

churches (white; 1865–1900), racial attitudes of, restrictions on freed members, 287–92; black withdrawals, timing, 287–92, last, 290; church officials also landlords, 287; separate services for freed people, 287; dismissals and exclusions of freed people, 287; purged membership rolls, 287–91; departures, exodus, 287, 292; Sabbath schools, 288; white supervision of black ministers, 288, 297; "irregular" churches, ministers, 289; black members (1870s, 1880s), numbers, 289; "colored circuit," Methodist, 289; expulsions, political reasons, 290–91; "white" donations, 293, of pulpit, 287, of

churches (white; 1865–1900), (*continued*) land, 290, 297, and other assistance, 288, 291, 293; black burials, continued, 292
circuses, 134, 321, 323, 329, 494n19
Civil War, 37, 181–95; whites, joining Yankee army, 65, 190; AOP isolated, relatively calm, 181, 183–84; slaves, controls over and threats, 181, 187; stealing, 181, 188–89; freedom, expectation of, 181, 187 (in 1860), 191, 195; slaves, serving masters, 181; service and deaths, coast, balustrades, 181, 191–92, 193; lowcountry, interactions with slaves from, 181; contacts, expanded, 181; Va. service, 181, 184, 192–93; abolitionists, attacks on, 182; trafficking with Negroes, 182; FPC banished or sold, 182; vigilance committees, 182; John Brown's raid, 182; 1860 slave gathering, alarm about, 182, 187, and white fear of insurrection (1862), 187; religious fervor, 182; white females bearing mulatto children, 183, 186; secession, celebrations of, 183; Sherman's march, 183, 195; Unionists, 183, 190, 201, 217, 269, 466n13, 467nn29, 30, attacked, 190; women's roles, 183, 185; moods about the war, 183, 185–86, 191, 195; conscription of white males, 184; deaths of white males, 184; agricultural production, rationing, shortages, 184–85, 188, 195; overseers, 184; slaves hired, 184; communications disrupted, 185; deserters, 185; raids by deserters, 185, 189; church membership numbers, 185–86; church exclusions of whites, 186; slave "loyalty," contemporary statements, 186–87, 189, and later references, 187, 192; slave labor, slow-down, 187; battle news, slave awareness of, 187–88; executions, 187–89, and percentages, 189; hangings, in Greenville, 187, in Alfred, 188, in Oconee, 189; millennium of freedom, 187–88; MFH trials, percentages, convictions, heavier punishments, 188; MFH, trials of groups, 188–89, few trials of FPC, 189; slaves harboring runaways, 188; patrols and complaints about, 188; slaves stealing food, 188; whites selling to slaves, 189; stealing by whites, 189; slaves harboring Union soldiers, 83, 190–91; escapes by slaves, few, 191; subcultural communications, 191; Union soldiers escaping, local white assistance, fed by slaves, 190–91; Union soldiers captured by slaves, 191; relocations from lowcountry, 191; Zion, income, 192; slaves returning soldiers' bodies, 193; slaves escaping from Va., 193; owners refusing to send slaves to army, 193; owners compensated for slaves killed in service, 193; slave service, compensation for (1924), 193–95; USCT, 195; "negroes unmanageable," 195; slave aid to whites in Civil War, Reconstruction, 466n17

Civil War commemoration, 379–80. *See also* reminiscing, romanticizing about slavery, plantations, Civil War
Claflin University, 304, 306, 359, 414, 497n6
Clemson Agricultural College, 1, 316, 320, 379, 403, 410, 418; Clemson University, 150
clothes, stolen, 131
clothing, slave, 130–31
Cold Spring plantation, 1
Colhoun plantation, 1, 3, 4, 24–28, 30–31, 36, 43, 45–46, 48, 50, 53, 78, 107, 119, 124, 128, 135–36, 140, 142, 144, 146–56, 158, 163–64, 168, 208–9, 227, 234–35, 237, 332–33, 414, 416, 425n7, 427n11, 439n39, 440n45, 455n28, 457n3, 458n8, 459n22, 460nn32, 33, 34, 35, 36, 461nn37, 38, 39, 482n38
Colored [Farmers] Alliances, 363
Colored Farmers' National Alliance and Co-operative Union, 499n26
Colored Teachers Association, 346
communications network, slave contacts, 5, 10–11, 13, 95, 123–25, 132–33, 136, 139, 140, 156, 255, 449n1; groups, 95; laws to restrict, 126; separated family part of, 132; efforts to curtail contacts, information, 135–36
communities, community, 11, 29, 40, 85, 140, 156, 180, 243, 286, 300, 310, 336, 341, 354, 408, 411, 414, 419; community building, development, 13, 251–55, 285; expanded, 181, 191; plantation community fractured after emancipation, 233; strata, 236, 397; community leadership, literacy of, 267, 270, 286, 292, 296–97, 310, 319; local, 286, 297; town, 311, 335–36, 353, 354
community investment in property, educational, fraternal, religious, 286, 300, 303, 306, 332–33, 400, 499n26. *See also* Afro-American Real Estate Association
commutations, 228, 229, 403, 474n6, 477n55
constitution (1895), 391–93
continuities, 2, 4, 9, 11, 14, 31–33, 40, 50, 59, 65, 109, 129, 136, 138, 140, 144, 148, 155, 156, 167, 179, 180, 184, 196, 207, 210, 212, 231, 234, 242–44, 286, 297, 301, 304, 306, 317, 325–26, 329, 407–9, 416–18, 430n7, 449n1, 450n1, 497n16
convicts, 267, 282, 351, 355, 376, 377–78, 388, 395–96, 403, 486n59; escaped, 402; convict labor, camps, 399, 410–11, deaths, 411; labor, leased, 376–77, 401–2; public image, 376–77, 411. *See also* chain gangs; penitentiary

cooks, 1, 41, 43, 49, 114, 130, 134, 153, 163, 192, 195, 205, 210, 239, 243–44, 316–17, 320, 337, 341, 345–46, 351, 409, 434n7, 460nn31, 32, 468n40. *See also* domestic service
Cooperative Workers of America, 328
corn, 17, 24–25, 42
corn shuckings, 329
coroner's inquests, inquisitions, 61, 69, 119, 225–27, 281, 284, 349, 369, 381–82, 389, 454n7, 462n34, 474n12, 476n46, 487n31, 495nn36, 38, 501n14, 502n19, 502n28, 502n29, 505n31
cotton, 17, 40, 44–47, 128, 131, 312, 335, 373, 408, 412
cotton mills. *See* mills, cotton
cotton prices, market, 75, 80, 87–88
cotton sale days, 321, 323
county fairs, 323
couples (slave and FPC), 31, 36–37, 60, 64–67, 69, 116, 141, 143, 161, 167–68, 173, 189, 192, 206, 209, 221
Court of General Sessions, 131, 226
courtesy titles, 402
crafts, decline in black, 236
craftsmen, 41, 43, 48, 50, 114, 129, 153, 243–46, 268, 336, 409–10; slaves trained by white craftsmen, 50; white, 41; joint black-white, 57, 338. *See also* specific crafts
crime, "negro," 371, 375–76
crop liens, 13, 371; flight from, 398
cropping agreements, 312. *See also* sharecroppers
crops, 6, 8, 17, 23–25, 40–47, 128, 181, 184–85, 187, 195, 199, 204, 207, 209–11, 219, 221, 233, 282, 308, 317, 329, 356, 378, 395, 399, 400, 410, 412. *See also* corn; cotton; harvests; rice; sharecropping; tobacco
cross-racial circumstances, 9, 328, 426n11, 434n7, 479n6; whites, helped by, 5, 311; daily contacts, 8, 17, 73, 125, 133, 328; events, celebrations, 12, 81, 92, 134, 311, 323; housing, 23–24, 41; dances, 23, 214; work, 24, 28, 43–44, 47; relationships, 36; collaboration, 67, 293, 402, 416, in saving children from drowning, 174, in putting out fires, 272, 352, 402; diseases, 144–45; "economic necessity," enterprises, 312, 505n2; mixed neighborhoods, 317; gambling, 415. *See also* interracial sex; mulattos
crowds, sizes, 81, 321, 324; rowdy, 494n19
cruel owners, known, 118, 120; alleged abuse, 118–20
cultural transmission, 428n15, 434n7

Dacusville, 29, 269, 323, 328
daily contacts. *See* cross-racial

Dark Corner, 262
day laborers, 232, 243, 320, 338, 341–43, 351–52, 413, 415. *See also* labor, laborers
debts (owners'), separations by, 141, 150–51, 153, 155
departures westward, 234
dependency, 13, 236, 400, 409, 434n7
distillers, distilling, 42–43, 114, 167, 184, 210, 312, 430n7; liquor, 42, 55; whiskey, 47, 167, 324; whiskey wagons, 282–83; distillery, 438n26, 459n28, 492n2. *See also* liquor
domestic service, 40–41, 45, 170, 231, 243–44, 316, 320, 337–38, 341–42, 345, 349, 351, 394, 409, 412, 414, 418, 493n10, 481n29, 504n18. *See also* cooks; domestics living in white households; laundresses; seamstresses; work, women's
domestics living in white households, 337, 341, 349
Dooley's Hall, 339

Easley (founded), 314; 300, 305, 312, 317, 319, 324, 328, 381, 413
East Market Street businesses, 350
Eastatoe, 20, 256, 269, 476n34
Eastern Star, 324
economic liberation, none, 247
economic subjugation, 371–72
Edgefield, 10, 36, 113, 151, 235, 240, 275–76, 288, 442n24, 465n2, 478n2
education, better in towns, 316; financial support by Baptists, 363; handicaps, 375–76. *See also* literacy; Rosenwald schools; schools; teachers
education, state superintendent of, 393; gubernatorial control, 392
elderly, faithful, respected, worthy black people, 31, 36, 53, 116–17, 120, 142, 169–70, 174–75, 187, 192–93, 205, 227, 234, 236, 284, 331, 350–51, 353–54, 358, 389, 403, 411, 414, 416–17, 419, 458n8, 497n9
Emancipation Day observances, 323, 359, 405
Emancipation Proclamation, 181
emancipations, covert, 117, 453n17
employment. *See* work; specific skills and occupations
errands, 133, 135
escape to free state, 446n5, 447n17
European origins, 30
evictions, 394
excursion trips (train), 323, 326, 340, 357
executions, 355, 446nn4, 19, 448n38, 484n30; by burning, 502n23
exodus, Negro, 366
expelled from or forced to leave county, blacks, 371 376, 400

factories, antebellum, 41, 50, 150
Fair Play, 270, 381, 389, 398, 400, 493n13, 504n21, 505n28; lynching, 501n15
familiarity with slaves, 427n11
families (slave), 1, 11, 33–36, 132, 140–44, 153–55; mortality, life expectancy, 28–29, 140–42, 144–45; spouses, 33; interlocking slave families, 35; slave families divided among plantations, 115; slave families, specific, 116, 142–43, 153–55; disruptions of families, 116; in proximity, 117–18, 141–44, 144, 155–56; fictive families, 140; nuclear families, 140; orphans, fostering, 140, 142; infant deaths, 141, 144–45; separations, reasons for, 141, 142–43; wills, keeping families together, 142; marriages, 143, 153–55; postbellum, 144. *See also* couples (slave and FPC)
farm laborers, 57, 205, 233, 235, 237, 239, 242–46, 247–50, 297, 303, 316, 320, 397, 399, 409, 412–13, 415, 481n29, 482n35, 504n18, 506n2. *See also* farmers (postbellum)
Farmer and Planter, 44
farmers (postbellum), 232–33, 237, 243–44, 246, 269, 297, 303, 320–21, 328, 332–33, 338–39, 341, 373, 376, 378–79, 397–98, 409–10, 479n7, 504n18. *See also* agriculture; farm laborers
Farmers' Alliances, 328, 378
fears, 9, 12, 51, 53, 64, 68, 75–78, 80, 90, 92, 113, 138–39, 182–84, 188, 190–91, 196–97, 199, 203, 205, 211, 218, 224–25, 227–28, 257, 276, 279–80, 374, 380, 391–92, 426n9, 433n4, 445n2, 453n20, 487n25. *See also* arson; fires; insurrections; resistance; uprisings
fertilizer, 312, 371; loans, 395, 398–99
festive occasions, 130, 321, 323–26, 334, 410
feuds, whites, 94–95
fire brigades, 326, 340
firemen, black, 323, 342
fires (accidental), 92, 94, 134, 259–60, 271–72, 294, 333, 349, 352, 355–56, 358, 402–3, 427n12, 449n47, 502n28. *See also* arson; fears
forced off land, political threats, 236
Fort Hill, 140, 150, 156
"forty acres and a mule," 11, 136 179, 205
fostering, 242
fraternal organizations, 357
free people, identified by landowner's name, 231
free persons of color (FPC), 24, 51–68 passim; numbers and percentages, 19, 29, 30, 33, 58; in Va., 29, 52, 54, 62; disproportionately mulatto, 37, 58, 70; occupations, 41; documentary records, scanty, incomplete, 51; meanings of term, 51, 67; harassment and repression of, 51, 55; white households with FPC, 51, 55, 57, 59, 62, 69–70; numbers fluctuating, 51, 52, 54, 58, 442n24; harassment of, 51, 62, 63; geographic origins, 52; color, 52–53, 58, 62, 64, 65–66, 67; emancipations, Pendleton District, 52–54, by will, deed, or sale, 52–54, 59, for "faithful service," 53, 54, bequests to, 53–54, and by, 60; free pass, 53, 55; white mothers and affidavits, 53, 63, 67; Native Americans and, 53, 59, 61, 62, 64–66; possessions and property of, 53–54, 56–57, 59–61, 66, 68, 69; passes, 53; out-migration, 54; spouses of, 54, 68; humane treatment, 54; taxation of, 54–55, 69; MFH courts, 55–56, 63–54, 66, 67; harassment and punishments, 56; lawsuits by and against, 56, 68; patrol, 56; laws regarding, 54–55; guardians of, 55, 66; interactions with slaves, 55, 56; slave relatives, 56, 58, 61, 67, 145, 147; ownership of slaves by, 56; occupations and skilled crafts, 57, 68–69, 445n28; occupations, none stated, 57; relocations of, 58; household composition, 58, 60, 62–63, 64, 65–66, 69; passing by, 58; names, choices of, 59; postbellum roles, 61, 236, not dominant in Reconstruction, 236, land ownership, 236, 338; female-headed households, 62, 65–68; medicine, herbal, 65; literacy of, 66, 68, 457n45; Benson Hotel, 68; murder of, 69; executions, 69; church involvement, 69, disproportionately ousted, 109; timing, 73; families, 134, 137
Freedmen's Savings Banks, 141, 235
frolic, 67, 85
funeral homes, 324

gambling, 127
gas lighting, 336
Generostee River, 20, 40
geographic context, 2, 253, 424n2, 449n1, 482n2
Georgia, 21, 22, 27, 52, 55, 62, 64, 80, 81, 84–85, 93, 100, 132, 165, 187, 189, 198, 202, 204, 216, 231, 234–35, 245, 258, 260, 270, 326, 332, 336, 338, 346, 366, 414, 446n5
good owners, 118
Good Samaritans, 324, 339
Good Templars, 324, 339, 359
Grammar School No. 4, 345–46
Grand Central Farmers' Aid Society, 499n26
Grange, 265, 275, 378, 500n8
Greeley Institute, 270, 303, 306, 324, 336, 338, 340, 345, 346, 351, 362, 414, 496n1

Greenville-Columbia Railroad, 129
groceries, 339, 345
Gullah, 5, 31
guns, weapons, 13, 21, 76–77, 120, 129, 164, 191, 198, 215, 224, 226, 257–59, 262, 279, 335, 353, 382, 389, 424n2, 455n11, 501n14

hackmen, 342
Haiti, 77, 137
Hamburg, S.C., 40
Happy Kingdom, 495n41
harvests, 42, 44, 47–48, 50, 87–88, 165–67, 170, 184, 199, 204–5, 218–19, 221, 228, 233, 302, 304, 308, 371, 375, 378, 395, 399, 435n12
Hausa, 449n47
herb doctors, 329
hiring out slaves, earnings, 129, 143
holdings, size, 432n1
holidays, weekend. *See* weekends, time off
holidays, year-end. *See* year-end festivities
home ownership, 339–40, 341, 349, 350, 405, 407, 408, 415, 418
"home values," 365–66, 400–401
Honea Path (founded), 314; 133, 231, 269, 272, 277, 282, 286, 292, 299, 379, 381, 389–90, 413, 417, 502n29
Honea Path Township, 396, 504n15
honor, 417
hostilities, 312
hot suppers, 306, 329, 366
hotels, 57, 68, 127, 130, 316, 345, 380, 418, 454–55n7; contacts at, 127, 130
house servants, 37, 43, 49, 114, 153, 155, 159, 202–3
households, defined, 240; composition, 23–24, 29, 51, 55, 57–70 passim, 115, 134–37, 141–45, 147, 233, 239–43, 337–51 passim, 341–42, 350–52
housing (1865–1870), slave cabins still used, 236; limited stock, 236; new houses built by landlords, 236; living alone, 240; living with former owners, 496n49. *See also* blacks living in white households
housing, shortage (1865–1870), 236
housing, squalor, 329–30
Howard University, 296, 305, 366
Huguenot names, used by freed people, 137
Huguenots, 30, 239, 348
humane treatment, laws, 118–19
Hunnicutt murder crisis, 2, 225–28
Hunter's General Store, 399–400, 405, 493n10, 505n1; accounts and purchases, 407–14; seasonal variations, 408; employees, 410, 412–13

"If These Stones Could Talk," 332

illiteracy, white, 503n3
insurrection, 79–80, 88–89, 91, 139, 187, 205, 214, 222, 226, 278, 339, 446n9, 447n25, 467n29, 484n33. *See also* fears; resistance; uprisings
interlocking white families, 35
interpersonal relations, 12, 372
interracial sex, 373; couples, 375, 481n29; interracial marriage, outlawed, 375

janitors, 345, 491n32
Jenkins Brothers grocery, 345
"Jim Crow" constitution, 12

Keowee plantation.*See* Colhoun plantation
Kilpatrick estate, plantation, 48, 116, 129, 158–59, 161, 165, 227, 235, 239, 453n12, 456n36, 459n26, 482n38

labor, laborers, 5, 17, 19, 25, 27, 35, 40, 43–50 passim, 57, 60, 86, 91, 94, 114, 124, 129–30, 133, 153, 156, 181, 184, 191–91, 199, 202–214 passim, 232–33, 242–45, 252, 265, 272, 306–7, 314, 316, 320, 332, 337–38, 340–45, 351, 366, 379, 391, 401–3, 409, 414–15, 417. *See also* day laborers; farm laborers; convict laborers
land ownership, black. *See* property owners (postbellum)
landlords, black, 340–41, 408
lash, lashes, 27, 56, 53, 67–68, 84–86, 88, 91, 93–94, 1–5, 119–20, 168, 187, 190, 216, 259, 399, 448n44, 449n45, 452n33, 459n28, 464n58, 467n23. *See also* Magistrates and Freeholders Courts; whippings
latitude, 9–10, 17, 76, 124, 127, 166
laundresses, 1, 32, 57, 114, 320, 337, 341, 345, 351, 409, 412, 418. *See also* domestic service; work, women's
laundryman, 410
Laurens, 486n10
Lawrence Jones Masonic Lodge, 339
laws (antebellum), 27, 81; 1600s and 1700s, 75–76; 1800s; 1820 patrol law, 79; laws on passes, often ignored, 126
legislature, black members, 393
Leonard Medical College, 414
Liberia, 3, 32, 361, 479n9
Liberty (founded), 314; 169, 300, 317, 319–20, 328, 363, 494n33
liquor, 132, 499n1. *See also* distillers, distilling
literacy, 231, 236, 346; percentages, characteristics, 245–47, 308, 310, 371, 413; books owned, 245; antebellum, 300; towns, 317; Anderson, 346. *See also* schools; teachers
Little Africa, 495n41
Little Liberia (Beaufort), 495n41

Little Liberia (Pickens), 362, 415, 479n6
local study. *See* geographical context
lowcountry families, 1, 31
lowcountry influences, 136
lowcountry, relocations from, 31, 136
lowcountry, slaves from, 1, 31, 136–37, 148, 150, 156; numbers and percentages in Pendleton, 136
lowcountry, whites from, 136–38, 148
lower piedmont, 7, 438n31
Lunatic Asylum, 376, 380
lynchings, 81, 90–91, 188, 275, 312–14, 333 (1887), 358, 365, 371, 373–74, 376, 380–92, 394, 403, 410, 414, 415, 424n5, 429n19, 465n2, 467n23, 485–86nn56, 59, 499n1; crowds, 200, 312, 380, 388, 417, 499n1; in Abbeville, 275; threats, 312; press coverage, 358, 382–84, 388–90; "judge lynch," 365; mob activity, 380; classifications, 381; compilations, 381, 384–87; by mill workers, 381; official support for, 382, 388–90; justifications and rationalizations for, 382–84, 388–90, 502n32; by burning, 388; bloodhounds, 388; nonlynchings, 390; aborted, 394

Magistrates and Freeholders Courts, cases, trials, 26, 69, 119, 120, 127, 130–32, 134, 427n12, 438–67 passim; execution of slaves (legal), 26, 27, 78, 80, 88, 90–92, 135, by burning, 80–81, burning forbidden (1833), 81; punishments, 76, 80–85, 87–95; social events, 81; whippings, 88, 93; Spartanburg cases, 87; procedures, ad hoc, 88–89; wide discretion, 89; charges reduced, dismissed, 92–95; local impact on, 89; capital crimes, 90–92; noncapital crimes, punishments, 92–94; white owner's interventions, 92, 95; trials, multiple participants, 134. *See also* arson; fears; insurrection; resistance; revolts; uprisings; whippings
manufacturing, antebellum, 27, 41, 92; postbellum, 336, 338, 340–41. *See also* mills, cotton
maps, 6, 325, 430n8, 431–32n13; Pegg, 488n5; von Hasseln, 347–51, 488n5, 491n1, 492n1, 497n9, 504n19; Edgar, 492n4; Sanborn, 496n1
marriages, postbellum, 354, 358, 481nn28, 32
Masonic Hall (Anderson), 321
Masons, 265, 319, 335, 339
"maverick," 430n7
Maxwell plantation, 44, 147, 161, 163, 170, 174, 227, 234, 239, 293, 331–32, 417, 466n11, 482n38, 482n38
Maxwell vicinity, 479n6

McGowan's Hall, 339
mechanic, 57
medical care, 329
meeting facilities, 339
Meherey Medical College, 415
microeconomy, 5, 127–40
middle class, 251, 371–72, 415
midwives, 129
migration, rural into towns, 340
migration, white families, into Pendleton District, route, 19, 21, 52, 432n26; westward, 21, 31, 113, 234–35, 366, 430n7; in-migration, 414; out-migration, 366, 372, 374, 398, 415, 432n26
mills, cotton, textile, 41, 251, 299, 312, 335, 340, 378, 493n5; mill towns, 312, 378, 415 (white); company housing, 312; workers, 313–14; lintheads, 312; mill employment, 345. *See also* cotton; cotton sale days; sharecropping
ministers, 409–10, 414
ministers, rotating, disseminating information, 360
miscegenation laws, 105, 392
mobility, 398
money, held by slaves, 127–31
Morris College, 306
mortgaged cow, 396, 406
mortgaged land, 395
mortgages, white, 500n10
mulatto child, 444n20
mulattos, 37–39, 51–53, 56, 58, 61–70 passim, 81, 105, 145, 171–73, 183, 186, 218, 223, 236–37, 242, 245, 297, 302–3, 380, 444nn20, 26, 464n49, 479n6, 500n13
murder, black-on-black, 94
murders, 483n22, 492n2
music, resistance, 86; religious, 324
musicians, black, 324

names, African origins, 145–47, 153; European origins, 145; naming practices, 145–47, 156; choice, postbellum, 239, 359; political connotations, 330; shortened by whites, 375. *See also* surnames
Native Americans, 18, 20, 435n14, 463n49; treaties with, 20. *See also* Cherokee
Negro League, 323
New Pickens. *See* Pickens
"New South," 378–79
new towns, 251
Newry, 312
newspapers omitting black names, 397
nurses (child care), 244, 320

obituaries, black, 353, 506n11
Oconee County (created), 22, 317

Odd Fellows, 324, 335, 339
Ohio, 367, 417, 444n23, 499n33, 500n13, 507n14
old family servant, 497n9
Old Pickens. *See* Pickens
Oolenoy, Oolenoy Valley, 27, 28, 133, 169, 209, 293, 330, 432n23, 463n40, 495n41. *See also* Oolenoy Baptist Church

pay scale, 246, 316, 412–13, 491n36, 493n10
Pelzer, 251, 312, 351–52, 365, 381. *See also* Pelzer family (Index of People)
Pendleton (town), 21, 25, 40, 312, 316–17, 319
Pendleton District (established), 4, 8, 12, 20–23, 96, 430n8, 431n23; geographic setting, 6; size, 18, 20; frontier, 20–21, 23, 33, 97; population, 20; subdivided, 22–23. *See also* migration
Pendleton Farmers' Society, 44, 129
Pendleton Manufacturing Company, 50
Pendleton Messenger, 50
penitentiary, 376; black percentages, numbers, 376; officials, 401. *See also* convicts
peonage, federal laws and prosecution, 397, 400
perseverance and persistence, 4, 14, 17, 140, 156, 234, 416, 432n1
persistence, white, 398
personal property. *See* property, personal
petitions, 498n2; style, 485n48; 1887 lynching, 501n17; by women, 501n17. *See also* Reconstruction, political participation
Pickens (town), 492n3; old (founded 1828), 1, 40, 169, 182, 204, 223, 226–28, 231, 269, 312, 317; new (founded 1868), 25, 172, 231, 269, 284, 293, 306, 311, 312, 317, 319, 323–24, 326, 354, 366, 415
Pickens County (founded), 22
Pickens District (founded), 22
Pickensville, 269, 323
picnics, 326
Piedmont, 251, 299, 312–13, 351–52, 381, 389–90, 493n5, 503n32
Plantation Sermons, 103
plantations subdivided for tenants, 233
Plessy v. Ferguson, 375, 394
policemen, 497n9
political subjugation, 372, 374, 378–80, 391–95
poll, property taxes, 408
pool hall, 300, 323, 365–66
population changes, relocations (1860–70), 230, 235, 352
population, density, 7, 17, 19; rapid growth, 27, 251, 381; S.C.-born, 231
press, AOP, 354; complimentary, 340; attitudes, ridicule, 352–53; coverage, 354; fluctuating, 354; respected, aged, individuals, 354, 358; Reconstruction politics, elections, 354–58; accidents, victims, 355, 358; numbers (1870s), 355, 498n2; skewed toward men, 355; clergy, 355–56; "colored man," name omitted, 356; stereotypes, 358, 364. *See also* elderly, faithful, respected, worthy black people
primary elections, 487n29
primary, "white," 393
professional work, 316
professionals, 409–10
professionals, white, 41
Profiles of Black Folks in Anderson County, 335
"Prominent Negro Leaders," 365
property owners (postbellum), 236, 244, 251, 269, 270, 272, 319, 321, 330–33, 335, 338, 341, 349–50, 363, 377, 384, 395, 399, 405, 408, 496n1, 506n3; gifts to freed people (offspring?), 236; mortgaged, 317, 396–98; Little Liberia, 330; value, 331, 333; land ownership, white, declining, 397–98. *See also* community investment in property
property, personal, 231, 245–46
prostitution, 324, 380–81, 467n27, 500n13
Providence camp ground, 326, 378
Pumpkintown, 330

Quakers, 54
quilts, quiltings, 32, 124, 129, 159, 162, 167

race, pride, 367; race improvement, 13, 361, 365, 411–12; race consciousness, 252, 354, 365; "improvement of the race," 362; "race question," 363; racial consciousness, theories, 375; racial attitudes, worldwide, 394; concept discredited, 497n1
races, proximity, 297, 311, 326, 328, 337, 345–46, 351. *See also* cross-racial
racial stereotypes, terms, slurs: "wild and savage," 76; "nigger" (early usages), 86, 214, 473n1; "Run, nigger," 126; savages, 206; cannibals, 207; Caucasian (boasts), 265, 283; "nigger" in press, 282–83; "sensible darkies," 284; epithets, 349; "Nickel Row," 349; minstrel shows, 352; stereotypes, 352–53, 403; darkies, 353, 403; "Nigger," 353; "negro crime," 355; colored, black, Negro, 356, 361, 499n19, 506n11; "Bought a Nigger," 357; "blackness," 362; "negro," 362–63; Afro-American, 363; "Negro race," 365; stereotypes, loafing, 374; darkie, 375; son of Ham, 375; shortened names, 375; mongrelism, 379; "Nigger con.[stitution]," 379; "Negro" defined, 392; sharecroppers, "uppity," 394; "savage natures," 403;

racial stereotypes, terms, slurs (*continued*) "nigger hounds," 403; "clear blooded," "Yellow Sall," "Mulattoe slaves . . . born of a Negro woman," 464n49; "niggers," 473n48

racial relations, 352; good, 311–12

racism, 252, 371, 373–75; worldwide, 275

railroads, trains, 1, 203, 209, 311, 335; construction, 129; employment, 235, 243, 337–38, 409; companies, 282; labor on, 314, 317, 384; depots, labor at, 316, 374

Reconstruction (1865), 186–212; little change, orders to stay on same plantations, 196–99, 202, 208, 211–13, 219; freedom, perception by freed people, 196–97, 199, 202–7; Union troops, 196–97; Emancipation Proclamation, 196; Gillmore proclamation (May 14, 1865), 199, proclaimed on plantations (summer 1865), 202; diaries by white females, 197; raiders, deserters (Union, Confederate), 197; troops, May arrival, plunder by, 197–99; slave assistance to owners during federal occupation, 198; military, FMB views on AOP, 198–99, 202, 207; freed people leaving with troops, 198; white views (AOP) toward freed people, 198, 202–4, 207–8; crops and estimated harvests, top priority, 199, 202; army, ill-defined role, fears of large-scale relief needed, 199; life for whites, civil government, officials mostly unchanged, 199, 200, 202, 203, 219; communications and transportation problems, 200; army organization in S.C. and Department of S.C., 200, WSC district, 200, Anderson subdistrict, 200, posts, changing, 200, July 24 arrival of troops, 200, 202, USCT, 200–201; Freedmen's Bureau, 201–2, 207–8, 210; oaths of allegiance, 201; church exclusions, 202; army, attacks on, 203–4, Maine soldiers killed, 204; William P. Brown's ferry, 204; army orders to control freed people, 204; owners' control continued, 204; housing shortages, 204; food rations, 205; Field Order 15, 205; land, hopes for distribution, 205; farm laborers, 205; servants, 205; elderly free people, 205; care for ex-slaves, 206; Black Codes, 206; taxes on freed men, 206; relocations to Va., Columbia, Memphis, 206, to Ark., Fla., 209, from elsewhere to AOP, 206; reuniting families, 206, 209, 220; advertisements for labor, 206; churches largely unchanged, 206, 207, 219; livestock held by freed people, 206–7; 1865 constitutional convention, 206; year-end holidays, 207

Reconstruction (1865–1867), labor agreements, 199–200, 202, 205–6, 208–212; families, reuniting, 206, 209, 220; elderly, 210; former masters, 208, 210, and white control continued, 210–11; Keowee plantation, 208–9; "whipping," fear of, 208; patches, 209; specific work, 209; antebellum leaders, 209; divided tracts, 209; ownership of livestock, 209; women, household work, 209; blacksmith services, 210; obedience required, 210–11; penalties, 210–11, 213; children, 210; humane treatment, 211; ejected from land (1868), 211

Reconstruction (1866), 213–22 passim; military, FMB, views on AOP, 214, 217, 219; FMB, 142, 213–22 passim; staying on same plantations, orders by FMB, 213, 220; status quo, army support of, 213, 219; labor contracts, 214, 219–21; cross-racial events, dance, 214; circus, 214; white views (AOP) toward freed people, 214; freed people, mistreatment of, 214–15; FMB enforcement of contracts, 214, 220–22, social welfare, 221; Keys trial, 215–16, challenge to habeas corpus suspension, 216, verdicts, 222; whites sentenced to be hanged, 215; federal conflicts, 215; army, attacks on, 215, 222, verbal taunts, 218; troop numbers dwindling, 216; murders, 216–17; "Union men" protest, 217; deserters' mountain hideout, 217; agriculture, dire predictions, good autumn harvests, 217–18, 221; sexual mores changing, 218; veterans' groups, 218; white public meetings, 218, 223–24; Anderson Soldiers' Aid Association, 218, 221; white mothers, mulatto children, 218; infanticide, 218; picnic, freed people, 219; little change, 219, 223; local officials continued, 219; prohibitions against whipping, 219; relief, transfer to civil authorities, 219, 222; teachers, 220–21; opposition to northern teachers, 220; Sunday schools, by whites, 220; FMB enforcing contracts, 221–22; white, FMB distribution of rations, 222

Reconstruction (1867–spring 1868), 222–29 passim; Congressional Reconstruction, 213, 222–23; House Select Committee on the Murder of Union Soldiers, 222; federal conflicts, 222; Reconstruction Acts, 222, 2nd Military District, 223; white reactions to, 223; troop numbers declining further, 223; S.C. Republican Convention, 223; Union Leagues, political activity, AOP Republican leaders, 223–29 passim; registration and voting, 224, 228–29; Hunnicutt murder crisis, 225–29; military-gubernatorial cooperation, 225–28; Abbeville, fear of Union Leagues, 226;

insurrection, fear of, 226; petitions, 226; white protection, paternal, 227; "abundant" fall harvests, 229; constitutional convention, 229; white Republicans, 229; S.C. readmitted to Union, 229; end of military control, continued army presence, 229. *See also* Reconstruction, political participation

Reconstruction (1868), 254–60; intimidation, retaliation by whites, 253–55; constitution, 254–55; constitutional vote, 255; newspaper coverage, 255; Democratic clubs, black, 255; Farmers' Association, 255; county elections and elected officials, 255; local officials, refusal to protect blacks, 255; military protection, USCT, 255; voter registration, 255; voter intimidation, coercion, death threats, 256–61, 263; KKK, 256, 259–60, 263; murders of Union League officers, ministers, 256, 258; state hearings, Committee of Investigation, 256–60; church expulsions, political, 257; women beaten, 259; voters expelled from homes, 259; Union Leagues, renouncing, 290–91

Reconstruction (1870–1875), 261–73; militia, black, 254, 261–63, 269, 275; AOP county officials, legislators all white, 261; political thought, 261; United Workingmen of America, 261, 266; black county organizations, 261, 264; black candidates, 261–62, 265–66; Anderson town council seats, mayoral race, 261, 266; 1870 campaign, July 4 politicking, election, 261–63; Republican corruption, 261–62, 264–65, 274; arms, 262, 279; AOP important among white state political organizations, state Democrats, 263; voter intimidation, coercion (1870, 1873), 263; federal role, Enforcement Laws, 263; Congress, 263; troops, requests to retain, 263; Ulysses S. Grant, role of, 265; 1872 campaign, election, 264–65; Reform slates, 264; Republican splits, 264, 266; State Land Commission, 264, 272–73, Cochran/Scott collusion, 272; 1874 campaign, election, 266; minority status, limits by, 267; "Union men," 269; intimidation, 271, 273; harassment and criminal charges against Republican leaders, 271; arson, 271–72, leaders, AOP natives, few FPC, 272; "negro crime," 273; paternalism, 273. *See also* Reconstruction, political participation

Reconstruction (1876), campaign, election, 274–81; Redemption, 254, 275, 281; Democratic organization, 274; Democratic intimidation, 274–83; Democratic clubs, 274–75; Ulysses S. Grant, role of, 274, 278; federal troops withdrawn, 274; Reformers, 275; economic intimidation, 275–77; Hamburg riot, 275–76; Democratic platform, 276; Hampton, white support and AOP appearances, 276–77, 276–280, 283; Red Shirts, 277, 283; rifle clubs, 277; Democrats, mounted, 277–78, 283, numbers, 277–78, 283; Democratic clubs, black, 277; coercion, threats, 277–83; Democrats, taking over meeting, 278; Hampton, black support, 279, 281; Republicans, women's attitudes, 279–80; election results, 280, challenged, 281; Tilden-Hayes election, 281; (1876–1877) dual governments, 281; taxpayers to Hampton government, 281

Reconstruction, political participation, petitions to governors, 136, 226–27, 252–53, 261, 267–69; petitions, style, 267–69, subjects, 267–69, and types of petitioners, 270, teachers, 270, literate, 270; personal and community acts, 196, 213, 220–21, 253–64, 267, 269, 272; using FMB to challenge, 203, 214; signing contracts, 208–212; Union Leagues, 213, 224–26, 269–70; weapons, 224, 226; registering, voting, 213, 224, 228–29, 254–55, 279–80, 283–84; military protection, 214, 255; rallies, meetings, large gatherings, 219, 220, 262, 264, 269, 278–79, 283–84; delegates to S.C. Republican Convention, 223, 275; July 4 celebrations, 223, 262; jury pools, 223, 267, 284; securing aid from military, governor in Hunnicutt crisis, 228; U.S. census assistant marshal, 230, 257; legislative testimony, 252, 258–61; militia, 254, 262, 282; threats, intimidation, attacks, 255–63, 277–83; murders, 256, 258, 260, 284; voting for own race, 261; candidates, county offices, 261, 265–66, holding offices, 261–62, 283 (town council), and control of Anderson council, 266, 283; election managers, 261, 263, 266, 268–70, 332; election commissioners (appointed), 262, 266, 269–70; candidates, state representative, 265 (elected), 266; county organizations, 262, and chairman, 283; legislative candidates, 262, 265–66, 283, elected, 265; party factions, 263, and allies, 266; poll supervisors, 267–69, 283; letters to governors, 269, 279; participant roles, age variations, 269, and native leadership but few FPC, 272; county conventions, 275, 284; state convention delegates, 275; women's attitudes, 279–80; decline (1877–1900), 281–82; national guard members, officers, 284; federal jury pool and service, 284. *See also* voting

rednecks, 379

Reed Street School, 346

relocations of slaves. *See* slaves, relocated among extended white families
relocations (postbellum), local, frequent, 231–33, 472n34; to AOP, 234; to Charleston, Atlanta, Va., 235; skilled people, 237; to Ark., 353; westward, 374; frequent, 395; forced, 407, 411; 1865–1870, 472n34
reminiscing, romanticizing about slavery, plantations, Civil War, 83, 309, 379–80, 393, 503n8
resistance, 12, 17, 19, 26–27, 75–76, 78–88; testing boundaries, challenging system, 12, 73, 87, 125, 127; through poisoning, 26–27, 78; escape from owners, 78, 81, to free state, 78; arson, 78, 89–90, 92; minor, 85; confronting whites, defending themselves, 86; murder of owner, 80–81, 88, 92; passes, forged, 82–83, bought, 84; hiding in woods, 82, 84, 151; stealing, lack of food, 119; manipulating system, 428n17
resistance, revolts, 9, 27, 55, 73, 75–76, 78–80, 88, 90, 97, 137; 1816, 79. *See also* fears; insurrections; uprisings
restaurants, 347
Revolutionary War veterans, 20, 24, 35, 54, 95
rice, 24, 31, 40, 47, 128, 431n14
Richmond, 415
Rosenwald schools, 491n39
Rough and Ready fire brigade, 326, 340, 345, 497n9
running away, 26–27, 43, 78, 81–87, 120, 134–35, 467n32; escape to Cherokee, 26; escape to free state, 26; numbers unknown, 78–85; advertisements, 78–79, 81, 84; mostly local, 79, 82; from elsewhere, 80; visiting family, 82, 84, to own family, 115; whites harboring, 82; punishments, 82–85; pilfering food, 83; hiding, hideouts, 83; slave aid, 83–85; runaways, women's help, 84–85; female, 84, 85; long term, 84; Civil War, 95
rural areas, 231, 251; percentages, 267; lodging, 329; communities, numbers, 330
rural labor, 320. *See also* farm laborers; farmers; laborers; sharecropping

sale days, 115
Salem (Industrial) School, 296, 345
Sanborn Fire Insurance Company, maps, 347–51, 496n1
Savannah Township, 396, 399, 481n36, 504n14
Savannah Valley Railroad, 251, 313, 336, 352, 376, 415; black labor on, 376
saw mill, 320
schools (1865–1900), 286, 286–310 passim, 322; FMB schools, 239 (white landowner), 245–47, 286, 300–301; mulattos, 236–37, 242, 245; illiterate parents sending children to school, 245; local control, 286; education, desire for, 300; S.C. Department of Education, 300, superintendent, 413; large classes, short terms, agricultural cycle, 301, 304, 306; students, numbers and percentages, 301, 304, 307; terms, length, 304, 309; locally owned land, 303; Anderson school board, 303; Cedar Grove school, 304; black-white comparisons, numbers, class sizes, 304–5; rural, town, 305–6; buildings, 305; press support, 306; fund raising, 306; Vineland school, 307; exhibitions, 323, 330; segregated, 392. *See also* Greeley Institute; literacy; Rosenwald schools; Reed Street schools; teachers
Scots-Irish, 17, 30, 148
seamstresses, 114, 116, 243, 341–42. *See also* domestic service
segregation in towns, 351, 393, 415, 417
self-sufficiency. *See* agriculture (antebellum), self-sufficiency
Seneca (town; founded), 314; 138, 220, 277, 294, 299–300, 318, 320, 329, 359, 366, 384, 418
Seneca Institute, 1, 364, 403, 414, 418
Seneca River, 20, 24, 27, 40, 68, 84
Seneca Township, 239–40, 246, 418
servants (white), 463n41
sexual exploitation, 37, 371, 373, 380–81
sharecroppers, 13, 167, 179, 231, 233, 307, 312, 316, 329–30, 332, 337, 371, 378, 390–92, 394–403, 407–9, 415, 441n6, 479n7; housing, 330; surrounding white owners, 332, 397
Shaw University, 366
Shoal Creek area, 78
shoemakers, 41, 50, 57, 163, 210, 257, 303, 319, 338, 342, 353, 410; shoe shop, 319, 347
Sierra Leone, 6, 31, 298, 362, 434n5
singing schools, 323; convention, 494n19
Six Mile, 381, 400, 502n24
skilled labor, 316, 319
Slabtown String Band, 326
slave market, 24
slave overseers, 47–48
slaveowners, holdings, 7, 17, 23–24, 27–28, 33–35, 133, 141, 150–51; multiple, 35–36, large, 24; status, comforts, 36; planters, 41–42, wealthy, 73; importing slaves from other states, 77–78; indebtedness, 115, 140–42, 150–51, 154–55; tax obligations, 144; relocated among extended white families, 141, 148, 150–55; extended families,

142; purchases of slaves, 143–44, 148, 153; dispersals of slaves, 148, 150–51, 155–56; relocations of slaves, 151, 155
slavery, institution, brutality, 13, abolition, 19; slaves, gifts of, 27, 116, 141; property, slaves considered as, 37, 74, 113–18; hired, loaned out, 48, 114; importation into S.C., into U.S. forbidden, 77; legal protections, adequate food for, "natural rest" for, 75, 77; protection, 113; slaves, characteristics of, 113; sales of, 114; buyers' safeguards, 114; divided into lots, 113; as investments, 115; owners taxed on, 115; sheriff's sales, 115; dispersal of holdings, of families, 115; wills, dispersals of slaves, 116; estate inventories, 116; owners' wills, provisions for favored, elderly slaves, 116; slaves sold, 117; slaves to be kept together, 117; auctioned, 141; value of slaves, 151
slaves, as property, sold away by owner, rare, 37
slaves, life of, diseases, illnesses, 1, 144–45, 153, 155; numbers and percentages, 5, 7; housing, cabins, 25, unrelated inhabitants, 141; bequests to, 38; ownership of crops, patches, produce, 47, 128; money, selling, bartering by, 54, 62, 63, 128–30 (multiple transactions), 131 (permits); weapons, possession of, 76, 85; latitude, 76; music, 86; gifts to, 110, 117, 128; humanity of, 113; literacy, 125, 137–39; earning money, 127–30; tavern, slave, 132; weekends, 132–34, 140, 142–43; weekend visits, 142; feuds, slave, 167, 173–74; postbellum households, 141; slave ages estimated, rounded off, 142; mulattos, 145. *See also* slaves, travel
slaves, relocated among extended white families, 141, 148, 150; extended families, 142; purchases of slaves, 143–44, 148, 153, 416; dispersals of slaves, 148, 150–51, 155–56; relocations of slaves, 151, 155, 460n30
slaves, repression of, fluctuating, 5, 74, 75, 77–78, 95
slaves, travel, 9, 12–13, 19, 30, 37, 55, 58, 73, 76, 79, 91, 92, 95, 100–102, 107–9, 125–35 passim, 138, 140, 142–43, 148, 151, 160, 164, 166–68, 170, 174, 188–89, 191–93; long distance, 83–84
snakeroot, 452n33
societal changes, pressures, tensions, 9, 63–64, 66, 73, 76, 79–81, 87–88, 90, 93, 95, 105, 110, 179, 183, 218, 251, 312, 371, 374–78 passim, 381, 391, 417
songs, postbellum, 494n26
Sons and Daughters, 324
Southern Railroad (colloquial; formally, Southern Railway), 235, 251, 299, 312–14, 317, 367, 373, 384

space, shared, 17, 23–24, 41
Spelman Seminary, 414, 497n6
spouses, 17
stable home life, 365
Starr, 299, 415
State College (Colored, Normal, Industrial, Agricultural and Mechanical College), 303, 492n45
Sterling Institute, 414
stewardesses, 410
stockade scandal, 401–2, 415
stolen items, money, 127
stonemasons, 342
structural oppression, 13, 371, 374; patrol system, patrollers, searches, 76, 79, 126, 131; sold away, 83; hounds, 84; banishment, 94, 95; punishments, 117; by sale, 117; exceptionally cruel, 119. *See also* Magistrates and Freeholders Courts, cases, trials, and punishments
subculture, 4–6, 10–14, 18, 19, 24, 73–74, 108, 123–76 passim, 179, 191, 254, 255, 434n7. *See also* acculturation
subjugation, economic, 394–401
subjugation, political, 372, 374, 379–80, 391–93
Sunday contacts, 133
surnames, 237–39
surnames, choices: popular, unpopular, 237–39, 447nn24, 27, 451n21, 453n21, 486n59

tailor, 57
tanners, 129
tax rolls (1865–1868), 238
teachers, 220–21, 244, 270, 286, 346, 358, 413, former FPC, 301; gender proportions, 301; salary, 301, 309; other work, 302–3; certification, numbers, 303; county certifications, complicated, 305; state certifications, 305; length of service, 305; summer institutes, 306, 309; associations, 306, 346; licentiate certificates, degrees, 310, 414; racist views on education, 309; 409–10; certifications, 414; pay, 491n36. *See also* Greeley Institute; literacy; schools
technical work, 419
technological change, 252, 311–12
temperance movement, 339; societies, 182
temporary workers, 335
tenants, white, 24, 25, 28, 41–42, 45–46, 394, 396, 407, 437n23, 503n14, 506n2
terrain, poor land, 328, 331
themes, 11–14
tinsmith, 210, 319, 338, 342
tobacco, 17, 24–25, 40, 47
tombstones, 332–33

town council members, 336
town incorporations, 319; incorporated (few), 40
town populations, numbers and percentages, 231, 319, 352. See also Anderson; specific towns
town schools, terms, 317
town stores, 319
town-rural links, 326, 338, 346
towns. See specific listings
Townville, 283, 319–20; incident, 355
Toxaway plantation See Maxwell plantation
trading with slaves, 467n27
travels, slaves'. See slaves, travels
trickster, 84
Turner's Hill Farmers' Aid Society, 363, 494n33
Tuskegee Institute, 366

Union supporters, Unionists. See Civil War
upper piedmont, defined, 1, 4, 6–8, 4–14, 17, 424–25n5
uprisings, 68, 75, 80, 136, 205. See also fears; insurrections; revolts
USCT, 486n5

Varennes, 27, 85, 94, 102, 107, 242, 344, 350, 431n23, 440n42
vegetables, 24
violence, national, 182, 373–75, climate of, 373, 380, 383, 465n2, 499n1; white-on-white, 182, 190, 375, 501n14; black-on-black, 381, 501n14; local, 470n8. See also murder, black-on-black
violists, 494n27
Virginia, 36, 52, 56, 62, 78, 135, 146, 148, 181, 192–93, 234, 245, 337, 346, 347, 412, 491n37
voting, 213, 224, 228–29, 254–55, 279–80, 283–84; registration, black (1896), 393, 503n7; restrictions, 503n3

wage pay. See pay scale
Walhalla (founded, 1850; courthouse, 1868), 492n3; 57, 94, 130, 133, 188–91, 198, 200–201, 203, 216, 218, 221, 224, 226, 231, 235, 245–46, 254–56, 262, 265–66, 269, 272, 277, 281, 293, 300, 307, 314, 316–17, 319–20, 320, 322–23, 354, 358
Washington, D.C., 415
WCTU, 335, 339
weapons, slave possession of, 76, 85
weekends, time off, 12–13, 50, 108, 124, 133, 138, 140, 142, 161, 166, 168, 170, 210, 346

well-digging, 345; well-cleaning, 410
Westminster (founded), 314; 300, 314, 316, 319–20
whipping, 56, 68, 76–77, 82, 86, 88, 91, 93–94, 105, 119–20, 124, 219, 259, 274, 366, 371, 376, 379, 389, 391, 400, 402, 411, 417, 487n25; whipping post, 208, 379. See also lashes; Magistrates and Freeholders Courts
white employers, 286; numbers, percentages, 403
white families' control, extended, 409
white fathers, 242; oral tradition, 37; on census, 37
white landlords, 349, 351–52
white relatives, 242
white support for blacks, 340, 384, 477n55; contributions, 352
white supremacy, 371
white views, convoluted, 73–74
white women, sex with blacks, 91–92
whites, collusion in crime, 132
whites, illegal trading with slaves, 127, 130–32
whites, teaching slaves to read, 138
will, separations by, 141
Williamston (founded), 314; 188, 262, 269, 301, 317–20, 492n3, 493n13
wills, court battles, 118
women, white, few legal rights, 118
work, 19, 24, 40–50, 56–58, 157–59, 184, 206, 243–45, 320–21, 337–39, 341–47. See also day laborers; farmers; farm laborers; laborers; craftsmen; specific crafts; work, women's
work, child, 341
work, women's, 43, 49, 57, 243–44, 316, 341–45, 351, 409–10, 412–14. See also cooks; domestic service; domestics living in white households; laundresses; nurses; seamstresses
WPA interviews, 9, 109, 120, 126–28, 132, 135, 163–64, 166, 172, 203, 205, 328, 424n2, 447n19, 448n30, 451n19, 453n20, 454n6, 455nn9, 11, 456nn30, 31, 39; photographs, 329; Inventory of Church Records, 289, 292–93

year-end festivities, 13, 50, 105, 126, 130, 132, 167–68, 170, 187, 189, 204–8 passim, 414, 457n48, 466n19, 495n35, 497n9. See also Christmas

About the Author

A native of upstate South Carolina, W. J. MEGGINSON has devoted much of his professional life to the study of the African American experience in the state's piedmont region. Currently working as an independent scholar, Megginson has lectured at Arkansas State University, Hendrix College in Arkansas, Drexel University, and La Salle University. Chief curator of the "Black Heritage in the Upper Piedmont" exhibit funded by a Humanities Council South Carolina grant, Megginson is the author of *Tracing Your Family Roots, before Slavery and Shortly Thereafter* and *Black Soldiers in World War I: Anderson, Pickens, and Oconee Counties, South Carolina*.

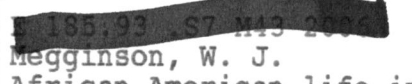
Megginson, W. J.
African American life in
South Carolina's Upper

DEC 19 2007